Lincoln's Cavalrymen

A History of the Mounted Forces
of The Army of the Potomac, 1861–1865

Edward G. Longacre

STACKPOLE
BOOKS

Published by
STACKPOLE BOOKS
5067 Ritter Road
Mechanicsburg, PA 17055
www.stackpolebooks.com

Printed in the United States of America

10 9 8 7 6 5 4 3 2 1

FIRST EDITION

Library of Congress Cataloging-in-Publication Data

Longacre, Edward G., 1946-
    Lincoln's cavalrymen : a history of the mounted forces of The Army of the
    Potomac, 1861-1865 / Edward G. Longacre.—1st ed.
        p. cm.
    Includes bibliographical references (p.) and index.
    ISBN 0-8117-1049-1
    1. United States—History—Civil War, 1861-1865—Cavalry operations. 2.
    United States. Army—Cavalry—History—Civil War, 1861-1865. 3. United
    States. Army of the Potomac. Cavalry Corps. I. Title.

    E470 .L818 2000
    973.7'4—dc21
                                                                99-086635

In Memory of My Father,
Edgar Thorp Longacre
(1913–1998)

CONTENTS

ACKNOWLEDGMENTS

Since the spring of 1975, when I began to research this study, I have incurred debts to numerous individuals who assisted me in one way or another. Those most deserving of recognition include Leona T. Alig and Tom Rumer, Indiana Historical Society, Indianapolis; Gary P. Arnold and Charles A. Isetts, Ohio Historical Society, Columbus; Joseph G. Bilby, Wall Township, New Jersey; Marilyn Blackwell, Vermont Historical Society, Montpelier; Ruth M. Blair and Eunice Gillman DiBella, Connecticut Historical Society, Hartford; De Anne Blanton, National Archives, Washington, D.C.; Carey S. Bliss, Harriet McLoone, and Virginia Rust, the Huntington Library, San Marino, California; Barbara Adams Blundell, James Duncan Phillips Library, Essex Institute, Salem, Massachusetts; John C. Broderick, Library of Congress, Washington, D.C.; William G. Burnett, Rocky River, Ohio; Phyllis Burnham, University Archives and Regional History Collections, Western Michigan University, Kalamazoo; Marie T. Capps, U.S. Military Academy Library, West Point, New York; Howson W. Cole, Virginia Historical Society, Richmond; William H. Combs and Frederick L. Honhart, Michigan State University, East Lansing; Judy Cross, Indiana State Library, Indianapolis; Alice C. Dalligan, Detroit Public Library; John C. Dann, William L. Clements Library, University of Michigan, Ann Arbor; Christopher Densmore, Getzville, New York; Ronald L. Filippelli, Fred Lewis Pattee Library, Pennsylvania State University, University Park; Connell Gallagher, Guy W. Bailey Library, University of Vermont, Burlington; John Hinz and Paul G. Smithson, Kalamazoo College Library, Kalamazoo, Michigan; Elliott W. Hoffman, Newmarket, New Hampshire; Harold Iden, Culver City, California; Mary Jacobs, John E. Shelly, and David W. Shoff, Pennsylvania State Archives, Harrisburg; Perry D. Jamieson, Crofton, Maryland; Mary Jean MacEwen, Rochester Public Library, Rochester, New York; Bettina Manzo and Don Welsh, Earl Gregg Swem Library, College of William and Mary, Williamsburg, Virginia; David J. Martz, Jr., Stuart C. Sherman, and John H. Stanley, John Hay Library, Brown University, Providence, Rhode Island; Paul McCarthy, Elmer E. Rasmuson Library,

University of Alaska, Fairbanks; Walter L. McMahon, U.S. Army Center of
Military History, Washington, D.C.; Allan Melia, Rahway, New Jersey;
William Miles, Clarke Historical Library, Central Michigan University, Mount
Pleasant; Archie Motley and Larry A. Viskochil, Chicago Historical Society;
David J. Olson, Michigan Department of State, Lansing; Robert F. O'Neill, Jr.,
Stafford, Virginia; Mary Jo Pugh, Bentley Historical Library, University of
Michigan, Ann Arbor; Rodney A. Pyles, West Virginia University Library,
Morgantown; Michael A. Riley, Mountville, Pa.; Richard A. Sauers, Soldiers
and Sailors Memorial Hall, Pittsburgh; Judith A. Schiff, Sterling Memorial
Library, Yale University, New Haven, Connecticut; Nathaniel H. Shipton,
Rhode Island Historical Society, Providence; Donald A. Sinclair, Alexander
Library, Rutgers University, New Brunswick, New Jersey; Donald C. Skemer,
New Jersey Historical Society, Newark; Thomas A. Smith, Rutherford B.
Hayes Presidential Center, Fremont, Ohio; Richard J. Sommers, U.S. Army
Military History Institute, Carlisle Barracks, Pennsylvania; Paul Spence, Illi-
nois State Historical Library, Springfield; Bryce Suderow, Washington, D.C.;
Jamie Suits, New York State Library, Albany; Karl E. Sundstrom, Chicago;
Alva B. Van Dyke, Nappanee, Indiana; Henri Veit, Brooklyn Public Library,
New York; Valerie Wingfield, New York Public Library, New York; Eric J.
Wittenberg, Columbus, Ohio.

   Also deserving of thanks are William C. Davis, Michelle Simmons, and
Leigh Ann Berry of Stackpole Books; Paul Dangel of Philadelphia, who
designed the maps for this book; Combined Publishing, Inc., of Conshohocken, Pennsylvania, for permission to reprint four maps from my book
Custer and His Wolverines; and my wife, Melody Ann Longacre, who helped
greatly with research and editing.

PREFACE

This book has no predecessor, although two works—one published a century ago, the other, eighty years later—more or less come close. Like Charles D. Rhodes's *History of the Cavalry of the Army of the Potomac* (Kansas City, Mo., 1900), the present volume describes the organizational, administrative, and operational history of the mounted arm of "Mr. Lincoln's Army." Unlike Rhodes's slim volume, however, this book treats in detail all aspects of the cavalry's service—its life in camp, on the march, in battle, and on expedition. It covers the gamut of cavalry life—not only field operations, but also the recruiting, organizing, mounting, remounting, equipping, training, tactical instruction of, and war-long support of this critical branch of the nineteenth-century army. Furthermore, the book highlights the cavalry's more influential commanders and examines the depth and quality of their leadership. It also seeks to place the mounted arm in the context of its army and the war effort as a whole.

Like major portions of the first two volumes of Stephen Z. Starr's *The Union Cavalry in the Civil War* (3 vols., Baton Rouge, La., 1979–84), the book attempts to portray "the cavalry's role in the war as realistically as the mass of surviving records, official and personal, will allow." Unlike Starr's weighty tome, *Lincoln's Cavalrymen* concentrates on the horsemen of the Army of the Potomac, characterizing them not only through printed works and government documents, including regimental, brigade, division, and corps headquarters records, but also through a mass of hitherto-unpublished first-person material—more than 400 collections of letters, diaries, and memoirs written by the officers and men who fought from Yorktown and Williamsburg to Petersburg, the Shenandoah Valley, and Appomattox. These documents provide a rich portrait of the cavalry's rank and file, representing as they do nearly every mounted unit in the main Union army in the East. Also unlike Starr's work, this book gives adequate coverage to the horse artillerymen and the Regular cavalrymen that were as much a part of the Army of the Potomac's mobile arm as the volunteer horsemen who provided the majority of its manpower.

Occasionally I scrutinize Starr's observations and question his analyses, and I make bold to offer a few theories of my own.

Given the preponderance of soldiers' accounts that went into this book, the story is told largely in the words of the troopers and horse artillerists themselves. For the most part, the focus is on the division or brigade level, although a small-unit perspective is frequently provided. And though the book concentrates on the Army of the Potomac, the operations of other mounted units that became part of this army—including those who garrisoned the defenses of Washington, D.C., until mid-1863, and who closed in on Richmond and Petersburg in 1864–65 as parts of Benjamin F. Butler's Army of the James—receive such coverage as is necessary to present a coherent, overall picture of the war in the East.

The operations of the forces under Sheridan in the Valley in 1864 are given wider coverage. Although officially members of the Army of the Shenandoah, Sheridan's troopers remained, for all intents and purposes, members of the 1st and 3rd Divisions, Cavalry Corps, Army of the Potomac; in the Valley they retained not only their divisional identities, but also their leaders at all levels of command. By April 1865, when these units returned to the Army of the Potomac's front to take part in the Appomattox campaign, the semantical distinctions had become virtually obliterated. The great majority of these troops considered themselves, first and always, Lincoln's cavalrymen.

The Civil War cavalry has received intermittent, uneven, and romanticized coverage since Appomattox. A part of the story may be said to have been recently told. But the story deserves a new telling, if only because the subject is large enough and complex enough to accommodate new themes, to admit of new interpretations and the rejection of untenable judgments, and to incorporate new research.

An editorial note: Unless otherwise indicated, all regimental references are to cavalry outfits.

The story of war has no more thrilling periods than those which tell of the achievements, in all ages, of warriors on horseback.

—Lt. Richard S. Tuthill, U.S.A., 1883

Chapter One

An Uncertain Heritage

Carl Schurz—German émigré, Republican Party activist, and U.S. minister designate to Spain—was a frequent visitor to the White House. As leader and spokesman of the politically powerful German-American bloc whose support had helped elect Abraham Lincoln, Schurz had discovered that he need only state his desires and the president would do his utmost to grant them. Thus on the present occasion, two months after the formation of the Confederate States of America and less than two weeks after South Carolinians had shelled Fort Sumter in Charleston Harbor, Schurz foresaw no difficulty in gaining approval of his latest project: the raising of a regiment of troops in New York City for service in defense of the Union, with himself in command.[1]

Lincoln appeared sympathetic to his visitor's request, but he was unusually noncommittal. Recruiting matters, he explained, had to be referred to General in Chief Winfield Scott and Secretary of War Simon Cameron. Those officials had the final word; the president would not overrule them except in unusual circumstances.

After some small talk, an unfazed Schurz bade his party's leader farewell and strolled down Pennsylvania Avenue to the War Department, where he arranged an interview with the stoop-shouldered, portly, seventy-four-year-old Scott. Afterward, his aplomb rather shaken, Schurz secured an audience with the leonine war secretary—an audience that further discomfited him. To the surprise and chagrin of the distinguished visitor, neither of his hosts seemed disposed to grant his request.

Schurz thought their rejection absurd, and he told Scott and Cameron so. In the two weeks since Sumter's surrender, prominent men from all corners of the North, whether possessing military experience or—as was far more often the case—wholly lacking it, had secured not only authority to raise regiments of volunteers, but also commissions as colonels, lieutenant colonels, and majors. A few well-known civilians had even been promised appointments as general officers. Why should a Republican stalwart, a confidant of the president's, be denied an opportunity extended to such men, many of them critics of the administration?

1

The aged general and his civilian superior patiently explained that the authority to recruit had gone to those desiring to raise regiments of infantry. Schurz, on the other hand, wished to create something the fledgling Union Army in the East conspicuously lacked—a regiment of volunteer cavalry. Schurz politely interrupted. He was certain that cavalry material abounded among the German communities of New York and Philadelphia, which included veterans of mounted service in Prussia, Hesse-Cassel, and other militaristic states. And cavalry, a combat arm equal in value to foot soldiers and artillerymen, would be a boon to any army that invaded the South, would it not?

Schurz's hosts were unmoved by his arguments. They agreed that cavalry, as an abstract principle, was a good thing to have. But the war that was taking form as they spoke would necessarily be brief—a few weeks, a month or two at the most. Infantry and perhaps artillery could contribute to the Union's military fortunes during that period, but a well-mounted, well-armed, and well-equipped regiment of cavalry would take many months to assemble. Moreover, it was an accepted fact that due to the complexities of mounted service, two or three years were needed to properly train a horse soldier. And that timetable applied to the spit-and-polish troopers of the regular establishment, where training was rugged and discipline severe. How much longer might it take to make cavalrymen of civilians?

Scott and Cameron shuddered at the thought of volunteers on horseback. Short-term citizen-soldiers would neglect and abuse horseflesh and fail to maintain the weapons and tack entrusted to them. Moreover, volunteers would absorb the tactical lessons of their arm so slowly and imperfectly as to turn a regiment of cavalry—whose annual upkeep cost ninety thousand dollars—into a gaggle of joyriders. And even should volunteer cavalry become available through the largess of private benefactors, the anticipated battleground of the war—Virginia, which had just passed an ordinance of secession—was too densely wooded, too riven by watercourses, too lacking in cleared ground to admit the employment of horse soldiers on the scale common to the wars of Europe. No, volunteer cavalry, in any strength, was impractical.

Scott and Cameron agreed that whatever duties short of combat horsemen might perform—reconnaissance, guard duty, intelligence gathering, provost and courier service—could easily be handled by the five mounted units of the Regular Army. Therefore, the government would not supply the horses and accoutrements Schurz's troopers would need. Would he care to raise an infantry regiment instead?[2]

Perhaps, thought a weary Schurz. Upon concluding his interviews, enlightened in the obtuse ways of the War Department, he left Washington for Philadelphia and then New York, where he sought to recruit units of all arms. The success of his efforts is instructive. The four regiments of foot soldiers in whose organization he played a role, however minor—the 7th, 8th, 11th, and 20th New York Infantries—were mustered into Federal service in the last days of April and the first week in May. They went off to war without Schurz, who, after much deliberation, accepted an appointment to Madrid. He did not return to America to accept a field command in the Army of the Potomac until February 1862. The regiment of horse that Schurz never stopped dreaming of, which later became known as the 1st New York (Lincoln) Cavalry, was not accepted by the War Department until late that summer, after the first land actions of the war had ended in Union defeat. No other regiment of volunteer cavalry had received government sanction, either. The 1st New York therefore ranked as the first volunteer cavalry regiment of the war.[3]

><!·◄►·•·O·•·◄►·!·<

If the secretary of war and the commanding general of the Army truly believed that the regular service would carry cavalry's burden in the coming war, they were either ignorant or deluded. In fact, the five mounted units available to the nation in April 1861, the youngest of which had been in existence for only six years, were too few to meet the needs of a single army in wartime, let alone the several field commands the Union would establish before year's end in various theaters of operations. Moreover, years of lax recruiting, heavy detachments to staff duty, and the resignations of dozens of officers and men of Southern birth or inclination, a trend that increased as more states joined the Confederacy, had depleted the strength and compromised the readiness of every regiment.[4]

With the exception of European immigrants in the ranks, many of whom were educated members of the middle class, some with prior military experience, the Regulars were notorious for the poor quality of their recruits. Many troopers had enlisted to gain a livelihood they lacked the brains or talent to forge in the outside world. Only through liberal application of discipline and punishment could commissioned and noncommissioned officers hope to turn such unworthy material into professional soldiers. The Regulars were beset by other evils as well. Military appropriations sometimes fell so low that entire regiments of cavalry had been dismounted for years at a stretch.[5]

Another handicap was the inferior quality and unreliability of the troopers' weapons and equipment. Beginning in 1833, the armywide emphasis on retrenchment had resulted in the formation of hybrid units whose soldiers were expected to serve as infantry as often as they performed cavalry functions. These "dragoons," first organized in 1832, were the direct descendants of European horsemen of the same name, a cross between the heavy and light cavalries of the Napoleonic army. Operational versatility was achieved by arming the American dragoon with weapons common to both foot soldiers and troopers: a shoulder arm (later rifled), a sword, and a pistol.

By the mid-1840s, when the dragoons saw extensive service in and outside this country, the shoulder arm was apt to be a North-Hall breechloading carbine, whose light weight enabled it to be wielded either on foot or in the saddle but whose barrel, which was shorter than that of a typical infantryman's musket, limited its accuracy at long range. Moreover, gases that escaped from the carbine's powder chamber upon firing posed a safety hazard to every shooter. The dragoon's blade was likely to be an unwieldy European-style saber, and his fragile handgun was either a single-shot percussion pistol or a 44-caliber Colt "Hartford Dragoon" revolver.[6]

Well armed or not, the horsemen were a valuable commodity in the pre-war army. By 1836 the 1st Dragoons had proved their worth to such an extent that a second hybrid outfit was organized. From its early days, the 1st had patrolled the frontier, guarding the routes of migration as far south as the Red River and as far west as the Rocky Mountains. The newly formed 2nd Dragoons saw their first service during the Seminole Wars of the late 1830s and early 1840s. Both outfits were sent below the Rio Grande to oppose the Mexican army in 1846–47; seven regiments of mounted volunteers also participated in that war.[7]

After the United States conquered a peace in Mexico, the 1st Dragoons returned to the frontier, where the 2nd soon joined it. Both regiments saw extensive service along the trails of western settlement, battling Comanches and Apaches in Texas and the New Mexico Territory, confronting the Sioux and Cheyennes on the Central Plains and in the Dakotas, and seeking to contain the Snakes, Spokanes, Yakima, and other tribes in the Pacific Northwest. On the frontier, however, the dragoons did not serve at regimental strength, as they had in Mexico, but in widely scattered detachments. When the Civil War began, one or two companies of each regiment continued to garrison distant outposts, sometimes hundreds of miles from regimental headquarters.

The constabulary duties the dragoons performed on the frontier were not limited to Indian campaigns. In the late 1850s, as sectional discord began to divide the nation, elements of several Regular regiments, including the main body of the 2nd Dragoons under Lt. Col. Philip St. George Cooke, were sent to keep the peace in "Bleeding Kansas." The dragoons did their job well, keeping free-state and pro-slavery settlers as far apart as possible, disarming and arresting lawless bands on both sides, and refraining from shows of favoritism toward either. It was grueling, dangerous work, with the horsemen liable at any time to become caught in a crossfire, but the troopers persevered. Perhaps their greatest asset was the familiarity they had gained with irregular warfare in their encounters with the Indians.

Keeping white men from each others' throats occupied the army for only a few months; Indian fighting was always its primary mission on the frontier. The government recognized that only horse soldiers could pursue, overtake, and fight the American Indian, the apotheosis of the light cavalryman. By 1846 territorial expansion had so increased as to require the formation of a third mounted regiment. Like its predecessors, this unit promoted mission flexibility. The so-called Regiment of Mounted Riflemen was, in effect, mounted infantry—soldiers who rode only to reach the scene of action.[8]

Not until 1855 did the army form regiments designated as cavalry, and then it created two. Like their predecessors among the dragoons and mounted riflemen, the new outfits were composed of ten eighty-seven-man companies;

unlike the older units, the 1st and 2nd United States Cavalry were armed with rifled carbines as well as with sabers and Navy Colt 36-caliber revolvers.

The newcomers, who until the Fort Sumter crisis battled American Indians from Oregon to Texas, proved popular enough to attract unusually promising young officers. As one historian has pointed out, the roster of the new outfits read "like a Civil War roll of honor," including Colonels Robert E. Lee, Albert Sidney Johnston, and John Sedgwick; Majors George H. Thomas and George Stoneman; and Captains and Lieutenants George B. McClellan, J. E. B. Stuart, William J. Hardee, Earl Van Dorn, John Bell Hood, Fitzhugh Lee, George D. Bayard, and David S. Stanley.[9]

But such celebrities remained the exception rather than the rule in the mounted arm. Like their comrades in the several infantry outfits and artillery companies that constituted the antebellum army, the various regiments of horse continued to face the problem of poor-quality personnel. Whether on or off duty, most of these recruits could be counted on for rowdy, unruly behavior, including an inclination to loot and carouse. The 2nd Dragoons acquired an especially widespread reputation for indiscipline and unmilitary behavior. During their service in Mexico, the dragoons were responsible for what one staff officer called "disgraceful brawls and quarrels, to say nothing of drunken frolics. The dragoons have made themselves a public scandal." One of their commanders, Bvt. Maj. Gen. William J. Worth, made a disconcerting discovery during one of the battles outside Mexico City: "On my left are the Second Dragoons, an Augean stable, but I fear [with] no Hercules to cleanse it."[10]

The cavalry was also saddled with officers of questionable ability, many of them political appointees of superannuated status whose only claim to high rank was seniority. Many of those in shoulder straps, who had begun their service as bright-eyed, energetic subalterns, had fallen victim to an institutionalized form of fossilization. One postwar military critic, formerly a Confederate general, blamed the situation on a narrowly focused education and the stultifying influence of garrison service: "Take a boy of sixteen from his mother's apron strings, shut him up under constant surveillance for four years at West Point, send him out to a two-company post upon the frontier where he does little but play seven-up and drink whiskey at the sutler's, and by the time he is forty-five . . . he will furnish the most complete illustration of suppressed mental development of which nature is capable." This same observer quoted a colleague, Richard Stoddard Ewell, a prewar mounted officer and after 1861 a Confederate general, to the effect that frontier service taught him nothing of the art and science of war except how to command a single company of dragoons. The cavalry contained numerous such examples.[11]

>-+◇-·O-·◇+-<

As Ewell's comment suggests, prewar mounted officers were handicapped by the small scale and narrow focus of their responsibilities. The scope and pace of their frontier constabulary mission did not prepare them for service in a nationwide war involving armies of 150,000 men, as would come into being between 1861 and 1865. Then, too, the tactics that small-unit commanders had absorbed on garrison duty were not able to sustain them during the hostilities that lay ahead.

The army of the 1840s and 1850s was hampered by an absence of tactical doctrine. For instruction, horse soldiers relied on drill manuals and a handful of tactics books whose information and advice confused as much as they enlightened. Guidance varied from text to text, and few tactical questions were answered decisively. There was not even a consensus on the basic issue of when and how a horseman should fight in the saddle and when and how he should fight on foot.[12]

Recent history provided few unambiguous clues. In Indian fighting, the brand of warfare with which the prewar army was most familiar, tactics were largely determined by the size and intentions of the enemy. Dismounted fighting against the Indian was always a chancy undertaking, useless when on the offensive and risky on the defensive. Once troopers surrendered the advantage of mobility, they placed themselves at the mercy of the foe and often were surrounded and entrapped. On the other hand, the classic saber charge seemed out of place in the Badlands of the Dakotas and the canyons of the Southwest. Hostile bands of Indians rarely maneuvered so as to receive a mounted attack, and they rarely struck in that fashion if able to dispatch their quarry at long range with bows and arrows or captured rifles.

And yet the saber was used against hostiles just often enough to make those occasions a memorable feature of Indian campaigning. One of the most notable examples occurred in July 1857 along the Smoky Hill River in the Kansas Territory, in which 600 Cheyennes were pitted against six companies of the 1st Cavalry. In the forefront of the charge, which scattered the Indians and precipitated a several-mile pursuit, was Lieutenant Stuart of the 1st, who never forgot the success his outfit's attack achieved. He also remembered the pursuit, in which he received a wound from a pistol ball—the only battle injury he suffered until May 1864. What he seems to have forgotten was the reason for the wound: He had challenged the revolver-wielding Indian with his saber and had lost the duel.

Attacks at the gallop were uncommon on the Plains, but fast-paced pursuits such as the 1st Cavalry's were frequent, as the superior firepower of the cavalry at long range often caused its enemy to flee. Sometimes the saber could be used effectively in pursuit, such as in the rout of Chief Little Thunder's band of Sioux at Ash Hollow, Nebraska Territory, in September 1855. Springing from ambush along Blue Water Creek, Lt. Col. Philip St. George Cooke, Lt. John Buford, and other members of the 2nd Dragoons fell upon the tribesmen, who had been chased in the horsemen's direction by an accompanying infantry force. Buford and many of his comrades were cited for their participation in the ensuing close action, which resulted in the death by saber blows of numerous Indians, at least a few of whom suffered amputations. The large number of women and children among the casualties gave Ash Hollow the appearance of a massacre, further sullying the already tarnished image of the 2d Dragoons.

Despite the effectiveness of cold steel in certain situations, pistols were the preferred weapons of pursuers, as they were more easily wielded than the heavy saber. But because many revolvers were unreliable, the troopers sometimes had to resort to other forms of combat. During a September 1858 engagement against the Pelouse Indians in the Washington Territory, Lt. William Dorsey Pender of the 1st Dragoons overtook an Indian brave. Lacking time to draw his saber, Pender reached for his pistol, only to have it jam. When the Indian turned to challenge him, Pender grabbed his opponent and hurled him onto the ground, "when a soldier behind dispatched him."[13]

If Indian fighting taught the horse soldier to fight as best he could, using whatever maneuver and weapon suited his taste, the Mexican War gave him the impression that there was only one way for cavalry to fight. American horsemen became enamored of the mounted charge as a result of a few small but highly publicized successes on the road to Mexico City. Units of the 1st Dragoons under Capt. Philip Kearny delivered a highly effective saber charge while pursuing Mexicans fleeing from the battlefield of Churubusco. And at Resaca de la Palma, Capt. Charles A. May led a body of the 2nd Dragoons in a charge that overran a battery supported by infantry. May's men not only made the enemy's position untenable, but also captured a Mexican general and, according to some observers, helped turn the tide of battle.[14]

Understandably, the victorious forces congratulated themselves on the spirit and boldness of their effort. In so doing, they overlooked an inconvenient truism: Retreating infantry, especially if too demoralized to rally, makes an easy target for mounted attackers. May's troopers also disregarded the fact that their charge—poorly executed and disorderly—succeeded because artillery had suppressed the Mexican battery's fire prior to the dragoons' appearance on the field.[15]

The manner in which May's charge ended—with horsemen strung out all over the field, out of supporting range of one another and vulnerable to counterattack had the enemy been capable of mounting one—illustrates the potential hazard of a mounted attack. When horses gallop en masse, they generate a momentum that is often uncontrollable. The power they wield is capable, if the conditions are right, of surmounting every obstacle. But pounding steeds can just as easily run away with their riders. They can diverge wildly from the path of advance or turn and rush to the rear with as much speed as they had shown minutes before in the opposite direction. Many Civil War cavalrymen would become all too familiar with the disruptive effects of out-of-control horses. The historian of the 1st New Jersey Cavalry, who observed his regiment's rout by Confederate riflemen near Harrisonburg, Virginia, in June 1862, gave a graphic account of a saber charge gone awry:

Pressing upon one another, strained to the utmost of their speed, the horses catch an infection of fear which rouses them to frenzy. The men, losing their places in the ranks, and all power of formation or hope of combined resistance, rush madly for some point of safety upon which it may be possible to rally. Each check in front makes the mass behind more dense and desperate, until horses and men are overthrown and ridden over, trampled on by others as helpless as themselves to rescue or to spare. The speed grows momentarily greater. Splashing through the pools of mire, breaking down fences, darting under trees, with clang of sabres and din of hoofs, officers wild with shame and rage, shouting themselves hoarse with unavailing curses, and the bullets of the enemy whistling shrilly overhead, the mingled mass sweeps on, until utter exhaustion stops them.[16]

Largely due to this inherent wildness, a mounted charge was rarely decisive when directed at infantry, cannon, or fieldworks. Unless braced with infantry or artillery support, attacking troopers generated precious little staying power. New momentum almost invariably defeated old momentum, attack falling victim to counterattack. Victory usually went to the force that at battle's end retained uncommitted reserves.

>—⊷—○—⊶—⊰

On-scene observation should have made the prewar army conversant with the drawbacks and limitations of saber attacks. And yet most cavalrymen continued to ignore the facts, as did their instructors. By the early 1860s tacticians were still promoting the speed and power of the saber charge, some even declaring that under certain conditions foot soldiers and cannoneers as well as other horsemen were appropriate targets.[17]

The tactics books of the time were virtually unanimous in their belief that cavalry was basically an offensive weapon, most effectively utilized in the mounted charge. This lesson hearkened back to Napoleon's campaigns of the late eighteenth and early nineteenth centuries. The celebrated maxims of the Corsican's staff officer, Baron Antoine Henri Jomini, published in 1838 under the title *Summary of the Art of War,* could ignore the power the long-range rifle exerted on charging horsemen, for in that day such weapons were imperfectly made and in short supply. But the omission of this subject from the pages of later works by American tacticians was indefensible, for growing numbers of rifles were made available to the army in the 1840s and 1850s, and in the mid-1850s the American army adopted as its standard infantry round the cylindro-conoidal minié ball, which enabled riflemen to fire accurately up to a thousand yards from their target and to do so three times or more per minute.[18]

Cavalry tacticians, however, seemed blithely ignorant of technological progress. In his influential treatise, *Advanced-Guard, Out Post and Detachment, Service of Troops . . .,* first published in 1847, Dennis Hart Mahan, the nation's most original military theorist, agreed with Jomini that the finest "qualities of cavalry lie in the offensive." Both experts believed that cavalry could successfully strike not only cavalry but infantry as well, especially if friendly infantry or artillery had softened up the target. In that situation, hard-riding horsemen brandishing edged weapons might have a decisive, lasting effect. At the least, attacking horsemen would force the enemy to prepare to receive their attack, perhaps by forming human squares as some textbooks taught, thus bringing the infantry's advance to a standstill.[19]

For twenty years before the Civil War, mounted units were instructed according to a three-volume manual commissioned by Secretary of War Joel Poinsett, which went through four editions between 1841 and 1861. Poinsett's text, an adaptation of a French dragoon manual, shared Jomini's and Mahan's faith in the efficacy of a well-timed, properly executed charge. So too did a competing two-volume manual, also commissioned by the War Department, written in 1858 but not published until 1861–62. The author of the new *Cavalry Tactics,* now-Colonel Cooke of the 2nd Dragoons, canonized the mounted attack as "the decisive action of cavalry." Cooke devoted much detail to the manner in which a charge should be mounted, even recommending the most desirable gaits for horses to maintain: the trot as far as 200 paces from the enemy's line, the gallop "with increasing speed" until within fifty or sixty yards of the objective, the extended gallop the rest of the way.[20]

In Cooke's view, if a saber charge could be coordinated with other elements of the army, if it was led by a commander with "a *cavalry eye*" for terrain and enemy dispositions, and especially if it was launched against an unsuspecting and incoherent force, it could overawe units of any arm. A mounted charge was the inevitable result of the close support cavalry should extend to infantry and artillery comrades.[21]

This supporting mission was always dear to Cooke's heart—perhaps too much so. At the battle of Gaines's Mill in June 1862, he carried out this mission with unforeseen and tragic results. His failure on that occasion, however, largely resulted from his disregard of one of his own rubrics: A cavalry leader must strike the enemy at precisely the right time, for tactical opportunity is fleeting. Cooke's experience on that warm summer day would reveal that he lacked that all-important "cavalry eye."[22]

Other texts that appeared on the eve of the Civil War, some of them mere syntheses of earlier works such as William Gilham's *Authorized Cavalry Tactics, U.S.A.* (1861) and George Patten's *Cavalry Drill and Sabre Exercise* (1862), more or less upheld the emphasis on offensive warfare as embodied in the charge. These manuals also ordained the saber rather than the pistol as the proper weapon in the attack and emphasized the need to maintain close-order formation that nevertheless left space in the charging column to permit horsemen to wheel to either side as conditions dictated.[23]

About the only matter of dispute involving the charge was the number of ranks, or lines of troopers, the attack column should consist of. Older texts such as Jomini's, Poinsett's, and the European-influenced *Elements of Military Art and Science,* first published in 1846 by Henry Wager Halleck, a future commanding general of the U.S. Army, preferred the double-rank formation that was also prescribed for an infantry attack. These tacticians believed that the second rank increased the shock effect of the charge, while helping to close gaps that opened when the first line made contact with the enemy. Two ranks also increased the number of swordsmen involved in the melee that followed such contact.[24]

Other theorists agreed, some heartily, others half-heartedly. George B. McClellan, another future commanding general, numbered among the latter. McClellan, who in the late 1850s studied the cavalries of Europe at the behest of the War Department and who published his findings in 1861 under the cumbersome title *Regulations and Instructions for the Field Service of the U.S. Cavalry in Time of War,* called for would-be troopers to be instructed in double-rank tactics. But he hedged his bet by giving conditional approval to Colonel Cooke's preference for a single-rank formation. Cooke's innovation had been prompted by his concern that a double-rank offensive promoted disorder in the ranks, horses in the rear crowding and scattering those in front. A single-rank assault would also be easier to conduct, having no need to coordinate movements between widely spaced forces.[25]

In the double-rank formation, a regiment would deploy in lines of five companies each. Under Cooke's system, four companies, known collectively as a battalion, would form the single line. One squadron—the tactical unit for maneuver, two companies grouped under the senior captain—would cover each flank. The third battalion would be placed in a reserve position 300 to 400 paces in rear of the line. Held so far from the front and withheld from an initial attack, the rear squadrons would be shielded from the enemy's fire and thus kept intact. Nor would they be affected should the charging rank be forced to retreat or surrender.[26]

Although Cooke's system seemed to promise obvious benefits, the War Department considered his tactics too new and their utility insufficiently proven to be taught to the cavalrymen called to duty in the Civil War. As a result, all but a few regiments serving in the eastern theater from 1861 to 1865, as well as most of those in the West, were required to adopt the double-rank formation and use it in battle.

A notable exception was the "Wolverine Brigade," four regiments of Michigan volunteers in the Army of the Potomac commanded for most of its existence by Brig. Gen. George Armstrong Custer. For several months after its formation in June 1863, the Wolverines hurled themselves against the enemy—often with much success—in the manner prescribed by Cooke. Early in 1864, however, the hard hand and inflexible policies of the War Office descended on the brigade, which for the remainder of the conflict used the double-rank formation. The change was made without a great deal of negative comment, although as Col. James Harvey Kidd of the 6th Michigan noted,

"The utility of the change was, to say the least, an open question, and it necessitated many weeks of hard and unremitting toil on the part of both officers and men."[27]

>─┤─◆>─●─<◆─┤─<

Discussions about how cavalry should form for a charge and what weaponry it should use were well and good, but their practical utility was a matter of debate. High-ranking leaders might be inclined to scrutinize Jomini and argue the value of Poinsett's tactics over those of Cooke, but the regimental officers and enlisted men who made up the Civil War cavalry had limited opportunity—and most of them a limited desire—to absorb the contents of tactics manuals; they barely had time to assimilate the most basic elements of drill. Early in the war Congress appropriated funds for the publication of tactics books for the volunteer army, but few were read by those who might have profited from them, and fewer still were adequately digested.[28]

But even if they had memorized the contents of these texts, it seems unlikely that the average volunteer would have been prepared for what lay ahead. Dangerously outmoded, overtaken by technological progress, unable to keep pace with man's genius for finding better ways to kill one another, the manuals promoted a brand of warfare that bordered on mass suicide.

Chapter Two

The Right Hand of Active Warfare

Understrength and underfunded, scattered to the corners of the nation, indifferently equipped and armed, overburdened with frontier duties, their fighting ability compromised by government neglect and lax recruiting, the mounted regiments of the U.S. Army awaited a new call to arms. That call was slow in coming. By the time word of the Fort Sumter crisis reached the garrisons along the outer rim of civilization, young men with dreams of martial glory were flocking to recruiting offices from Maine to Minnesota, from the Carolinas to Florida and Louisiana.

When the Regulars began to mobilize for the coming fight, it was too late to protect facilities, arms, and supplies in the seceding states. In South Carolina, Georgia, and elsewhere in the Deep South, forts, arsenals, and depots were taken over by forces loyal to the infant Confederacy. In Texas the departmental commander, Maj. Gen. David E. Twiggs, a native Georgian, handed over his installations to state troops. Detachments of the 2nd Cavalry serving along the Rio Grande found themselves surrounded and disarmed by Texas Rangers. Forced to take ship in the Gulf of Mexico, the horseless, weaponless troopers sailed north to refit at the cavalry depot and school of instruction at Carlisle Barracks, Pennsylvania.[1]

Emboldened by success, the Rangers forged westward to attack isolated parties of Mounted Riflemen in the New Mexico Territory, confiscating their horses, arms, and equipment. These assaults so decimated and disorganized the regiment that it did not return to the field until the third year of the war. Elsewhere in the suddenly divided Union, Regulars scampered out of harm's way. Two weeks after Fort Sumter was shelled, Lt. Col. William H. Emory led most of the 1st Cavalry out of the Indian Territory and into Unionist enclaves in Kansas. His ability to keep a few steps ahead of red and white Confederates owed largely to the long, risky journey that Lt. William W. Averell of the Mounted Riflemen had made from Washington through "a savage country infested with wild beasts and wilder humanity" to bring Emory word of his regiment's call to the capital.[2]

The physical and emotional blows dealt the cavalry by their newly proclaimed enemy were exacerbated by the hasty resignations of four of the five regimental commanders, including Albert Sidney Johnston of the 2nd Cavalry, who cast their lots with the Confederacy. Because enlisted men were not permitted to resign, a belief sprang up, given credence for decades afterward, that no trooper shifted his allegiance during the war. In fact, dozens of Southern-born privates and noncommissioned officers deserted their units at the first opportunity, then headed south to enlist in the provisional Confederate army. As one historian notes, the vacancies they left were eventually filled by recruits and transferees but not by trained cavalrymen.[3]

Regardless of the gaps in their ranks, most of the Regulars were, like the 1st Cavalry, ordered to Washington City, doubtless in preparation for invading the South. As Capt. Theophilus F. Rodenbough of the 2nd Dragoons noted years later, when summoned east, "but few of the regular cavalry regiments were able to proceed *en masse*. Scattered throughout the Western plains or among the foot-hills of the Rocky Mountains, in the more congenial duties of frontier service, they turned by detachments—with some reluctance, perhaps—towards the heart of civilization, wondering if the great questions of which they in their simplicity and exile knew but little, must only be settled by blows and blood—a brother's blood!" Once the march began, however, the gravity of the national crisis so impressed itself on the troopers that most left their misgivings behind and vowed to defend their government "against all her enemies and opposers *whomsoever.*"[4]

It took time for the far-flung detachments to reach the seat of war. Colonel Cooke's 2nd Dragoons, for example, dribbled into Washington over a several-month period. The first squadron—Companies D and H, under Capt. Innis N. Palmer—arrived on April 14, the day Sumter surrendered; the tag end of the regiment, Companies C, G, and I, did not report until early the following year.[5]

Those units near Washington when the shooting started arrived in time to see early service. On April 19 the first combat casualties of the war occurred in the streets of Baltimore when a Massachusetts militia outfit en route to the capital fired on a mob of angry secessionists, killing nine civilians and losing four of its own men in return. In the aftermath of the bloodletting, Southern-sympathizing Marylanders boasted that they would permanently close the northern approaches to Washington. The following day General in Chief Scott ordered Major Thomas of the 2nd Cavalry, then at Carlisle Barracks with four companies of the regiment following their eviction from the South, to proceed to Harrisburg, Pennsylvania. From there the troopers would accompany 4,000 infantry volunteers bound for Washington.[6]

At this point, the military unpreparedness of the North became painfully apparent. Maj. Fitz John Porter, adjutant to Maj. Gen. Robert Patterson, commander of the Department of Pennsylvania, lamented that the volunteers "had no arms whatever or equipments even for cooking purposes, and the troops at Carlisle were as deficient." No means existed to furnish the supplies Thomas's battalion required on its journey: 400 Sharps carbines, 300 Colt revolvers, 300 sabers, and 32,000 rounds of ammunition. Also in short supply were training and experience; as the post commander at Carlisle Barracks informed Major Porter, Thomas's troopers, who included numerous raw recruits, "are by no means well instructed. They have been too short a time at the depot for them to be well drilled."[7]

Given the magnitude of the logistical problem, it is not surprising that by late in the month Thomas's battalion was still refitting in Carlisle. Then, on the twenty-eighth, it was ordered not to Washington but to Chambersburg, Pennsylvania, to join Patterson's main force. Reportedly, Patterson was about to launch a campaign against Confederate forces in Virginia's Shenandoah Valley. When finally supplied sufficiently to wage a field campaign, the men of the 2nd Cavalry headed westward toward the enemy's country and toward war.[8]

>─┤─◆>─·O─·◆─┤─<

As soon as their many detachments grouped at Washington, the Regulars were assigned a multitude of responsibilities. In the main, they rode picket duty around the ever-increasing camps of the volunteer infantry. Those camps sprawled outward in all directions, from the upper reaches of Rock Creek east to Anacostia, Maryland, south to Arlington and Alexandria, Virginia, and west toward the suburbs beyond Chain Bridge on the Potomac. The cavalry also helped guard the innumerable forts that ringed the district. Parties of each regiment performed scouting duty south of the river, reconnoitering toward Upton's and Munson's Hills, Bailey's Cross Roads, and Falls Church, where advance units of the enemy were believed to lurk. Sergeants and corporals were tapped to instruct the volunteers in the rudimentary duties of soldiering, which applied equally to foot soldiers and horsemen.

Meanwhile, junior officers were detached from their units and sent by train to all points of the North, there to muster into Federal service those volunteer regiments completing their formation. In a matter of days many of those outfits reached Washington, further crowding the already congested "seat of war." By the end of May Lieutenant Averell of the Mounted Riflemen, who was preparing to leave the district on mustering duty, calculated that almost 100,000 volunteers and militiamen were encamped north of the Potomac, with more than 20,000 others on the other shore guarding the southern approaches to the capital. Averell realized that even in this early morning of the war, the blue cordon stretched for hundreds of miles to the north and west: "Troops, in separate departments, occupied the frontier of Union sentiment from the mouth of the Potomac to the mouth of the Ohio and reserves were assembled to cover Baltimore, Philadelphia, and Cincinnati."[9]

That long blue line was composed of infantry, bolstered by batteries of Regular and some volunteer artillery. Only one company of volunteer horsemen had thus far gained government approval, and only because its commander, Capt. Samuel W. Owens, had bankrolled the unit's formation. The enlistment term of the company, composed of Unionists from the District of Columbia and mustered into service on April 26, was three months, too short a period to have a lasting effect on military affairs. Brig. Gen. Charles P. Stone of the 14th U.S. Infantry, inspector general of militia and volunteers for the District of Columbia, called for volunteer cavalry to augment Owens's company, the only mounted force available to patrol Washington's streets and suburbs. Stone's cry went unheeded by a War Department that determinedly maintained its stand against would-be soldiers on horseback.[10]

By this time cavalry proponents in virtually every state had sought authority to raise companies or regiments, only to be refused government assistance. A typical letter of rejection went from Secretary Cameron to Gov. Richard Yates of Illinois early in May: "I am again obliged, at the solicitation of General Scott, to decline acceptance of cavalry. Adjutant-General [Lorenzo] Thomas is clear in his opinion that they cannot be of service adequate to the expense incurred in accepting them."[11]

By the time he sent this latest refusal, however, Cameron was showing signs of yielding to pressure from Yates, other state officials, and also the president to accept cavalry recruits. The enemy was already doing so. In the states that had left the Union, mounted militia units with colorful uniforms and equally colorful names, such as the Charleston Roughriders and the Yell County Dragoons, were flocking to the colors of the fledgling Confederacy. In Virginia, which awaited the results of a statewide ratification vote on its ordinance of secession, preparations to form a mobile defense force were well under way. On May 1 Maj. Gen. Robert E. Lee, the newly appointed commander of Virginia's troops, began to concentrate forces including cavalry at Harpers Ferry in the lower Shenandoah Valley. There the troopers came under the authority first of Col. Thomas Jonathan Jackson and later Gen. Joseph Eggleston Johnston.[12]

The day that Lee acted, Secretary Cameron began to respond to what appeared to be the public will. In a letter to the governors of the loyal states, he called for volunteers with cavalry experience to fill a single mounted regiment. The government would furnish the outfit with weaponry, but its members would have to procure their own mounts and equipment; they would be reimbursed at the rate of fifty (later forty) cents per day. Though this action cannot be called a watershed event in cavalry history, it marked the beginning of a slow, gradual shift in the government's attitude toward its mounted defense.[13]

The spirit of change was furthered two days later, when Lincoln himself announced the need for an across-the-board expansion of the Regular army, the additions to include nine regiments of infantry, one twelve-battery regiment of artillery, and one regiment of cavalry. Lincoln's call caught the ear of Congress, which passed the enabling legislation on July 29. The statute not only formed a sixth mounted regiment, but also mandated that the new outfit should consist of twelve companies, subdivided into three battalions of two squadrons (four companies) each. Each battalion was to be commanded by one major—two majors per regiment had long been the norm—while, as before, a colonel and lieutenant colonel rounded out the regimental field staff.[14]

The legislation recognized a long-standing need for larger mounted regiments. Because of the space occupied by a trooper's horse, a cavalry outfit could not place as many men in battle line as an infantry regiment; the addition of 174 troopers per regiment would help compensate for this imbalance. On August 3 Congress completed the cavalry's reorganization by mandating that all existing Regular regiments be recruited up to the same strength as the new outfit. The legislation also had an effect, however delayed, on volunteer regiments. Most of those accepted during the first year and a half of the war mounted only ten companies. But by early or mid-1863 the majority of these were recruited up to the new twelve-company, three-battalion standard.[15]

Much of what went into the August legislation found widespread satisfaction in the ranks of the Regulars. The new regiment, which became known as the 6th United States Cavalry and was temporarily entrusted to Lieutenant Colonel Emory, became a haven for officers of promise who transferred from the dragoons, mounted riflemen, and older cavalry regiments. Many of these later distinguished themselves in the mounted forces of the volunteer army. Among the future brigadier generals and brevet brigadiers of cavalry, in addition to Emory, were Captains David McMurtrie Gregg, his cousin John Irvin Gregg, Charles Russell Lowell, and August V. Kautz. Recruited principally in Ohio, Pennsylvania, and western New York, under Emory's supervision, the regiment was ready to take the field, although only 984 strong, by year's end.[16]

One provision of the law provoked bitter complaint, however. For the sake of consistency (perhaps also, in the case of the dragoons, to delete any vestige of foreign influence), Congress renumbered and redesignated the five earlier regiments of horsemen. All mounted units were now known as cavalry. To honor seniority, the 1st Dragoons were transformed into the 1st Cavalry, the 2nd Dragoons into the 2nd Cavalry, and the Regiment of Mounted Riflemen into the 3rd Cavalry. The old 1st Cavalry became the 4th Cavalry, and the former 2nd Cavalry the 5th Cavalry.

The action shocked, saddened, and outraged many veterans, who considered their heritage defiled by Washington bureaucrats. Writing long after the war, Lieutenant Averell, the erstwhile Mounted Rifleman, still bristled at the memory of the "ill-advised act" that "wiped out the time-honored regimental names with the romantic and heroic history which had distinguished them— the glory and inspiration of the oldest mounted regiments—forever." The name change was a major mistake, he said, because "war, even with its best justification . . . needs to cloak itself with all the glamour that . . . prancing squadrons and thundering cannon can lend to hide its essential and hideous brutality; and above its most murderous vortices of death and destruction must be spread the alluring bewitchment of glory. Regiments lose a great inspiration when they lose names that have been glorified."[17]

>─┤─◆>─○─<◆>─┤─<

The nucleus of what would become the Army of the Potomac entered upon its first field campaign in the darkness of morning on May 24, 1861. Just past midnight, hours after the results of Virginia's ratification of secession had become known, General Scott ordered Brig. Gen. Joseph K. F. Mansfield, commander of the Department of Washington, to wrest Alexandria from the enemy and occupy that important Potomac River port. The two-pronged invasion force—one column crossing Long Bridge, the other sailing south aboard river steamers—was composed overwhelmingly of infantry, although it did include two companies of horsemen. Captain Owens's District of Columbia volunteers led the advance of a body under Brig. Gen. Samuel P. Heintzelman, escorting inexperienced foot soldiers through the inky darkness. Meanwhile, a company of the 2nd United States Cavalry, under Capt. Albert G. Brackett, supported the main body of the invasion force, that accompanied by the expeditionary commander, Maj. Gen. Charles W. Sandford of the New York State Militia. Once the town had been secured, both units patrolled the roads to ensure that no Rebels advanced from the south to evict the invaders.[18]

Alexandria had been ripe for the taking since the fifth of the month, when the local commander, fearful that a horde of Yankees might descend on him without warning, had evacuated the area. The only casualty resulting from the occupation occurred when one of Sandford's regimental commanders, Col. Elmer Ephraim Ellsworth of the 11th New York Zouaves, struck a blow at the enemy's symbol of nationhood. Ellsworth, a law student, prewar drill-team organizer from Chicago, and close friend of Abraham Lincoln, hauled a secession banner down from the roof of the Marshall House hotel, only to receive a shotgun blast at point-blank range from the proprietor of the establishment. The Zouave leader was at once avenged by one of his men, who bayoneted his assailant. A few days later, cavalry officers joined representatives of the other branches as well as a throng of civilians, including the inconsolable Lincoln, in paying their respects to Ellsworth's remains, which lay in state in the East Room of the White House.[19]

From Alexandria the occupation forces, screened by the few cavalrymen among them, pushed steadily southward and westward. They found that Virginians, as well as troops from South Carolina and other seceded states, occupied outposts only a few miles off, near Fairfax Court House and Centreville. These positions masked a much larger force—some seven thousand strong, including a battalion of cavalry—that since early May had been gathering near the rail station known as Manassas Junction, ten miles farther south. At that strategic depot, the key to the defense of northern Virginia, the southward-running Orange & Alexandria met the westward-leading Manassas Gap Railroad, which cut through the Bull Run and Blue Ridge Mountains into the

Shenandoah Valley. The latter road linked the forces at the depot, initially under Brig. Gen. Philip Cocke, then Brig. Gen. Milledge Bonham, with Valley points within marching distance of Johnston's bailiwick at Harpers Ferry.[20]

By the last day of May the horsemen around Alexandria had been augmented, at General Sandford's order, by a second company of Regulars, led by Lt. Charles H. Tompkins, 2nd United States Cavalry. That day Tompkins was given an assignment by his local superior, Virginia-born David Hunter, the recently appointed colonel of the 6th Cavalry as well as a brigadier general of volunteers whose New York infantry brigade occupied Camp Union, outside Alexandria. Hunter wished Tompkins to scout toward and, if possible, beyond Fairfax Court House, eight miles from the enemy rendezvous at Manassas. Although the courthouse was considered off-limits to Union troops at this stage of the conflict, the lieutenant was advised (not ordered, it would seem) to ascertain the numbers and positions of any local Confederates. "If you can manage to get into the place," Hunter told Tompkins, "it will be a feather in your cap." His subordinate saluted and rounded up his company.[21]

Tompkins and his seventy-five troopers left recently occupied Falls Church at 11:30 P.M. on the thirty-first and reached Fairfax Court House at three o'clock the next morning. They found the place occupied by two cavalry companies, as well as by Capt. John Quincy Marr's Warrenton Rifles, later a part of the 17th Virginia Infantry. The entire force was under the command of Lt. Col. Richard S. Ewell of the provisional Confederate army. The old Regular was about to learn something more than how to command 100 dragoons.[22]

Although Ewell had been enjoined to be vigilant for signs of the enemy, Tompkins's arrival found the colonel asleep in his room in the village's only hotel. Ewell's forward pickets were likewise taken by surprise, and a few of them were captured. Those troops in the town were no less surprised when Tompkins's men came charging in on the Falls Church Road, shouting and shooting. The Rebel horsemen scattered, sleep-clouded troopers running for their lives. Civilian residents, however, joined the nightshirt-clad Ewell in the streets to fire on the invaders; other citizens wielded rifles and shotguns from windows and rooftops. Then Marr's riflemen rushed up to form in a clover field just off the Little River Turnpike, which ran east to west through the town, and treated the Federals to a volley that caused them to veer westward. His road south blocked, Tompkins led his troopers, who had suffered no casualties except to several of their horses, along the turnpike toward Germantown and Chantilly.[23]

Although twice unhorsed, injuring a foot in the process, Tompkins rallied his men in the streets of Chantilly. Turning them about, he prepared for a second go at Ewell's men, only to be fired on yet again by civilians. Judith McGuire, a refugee from a Yankee-infested corner of the Shenandoah Valley, peered out a window of the house in which she was staying and "saw by the moonlight a body of cavalry moving up the street, and as they passed below our window . . . we distinctly heard the commander's order, 'Halt.' They again proceeded a few paces, turned and approached slowly. . . . In a few moments there was another volley, the firing rapid, and to my unpractised ear there seemed a discharge of a thousand muskets. Then came the same body of cavalry rushing by in wild disorder. Oaths loud and deep were heard from the commander."[24]

Back up the turnpike raced the troopers, aiming to visit revenge on their military and civilian assailants. By now a half hour had passed since their hasty departure and in the interim reinforcements had reached Fairfax Court House, some led by another future general and a once and future governor of Virginia, William "Extra Billy" Smith. Aided by the newcomers, Marr's company again sprayed rifle balls down the length of the speeding column. His men hemmed in by roadside fences, his horses verging on panic, Tompkins gave the order to retreat. Tearing down the obstacles, his troopers galloped cross-country toward the north. Regaining the Falls Church Road, they raced east, pursued by two just-arrived companies of Virginia cavalry.[25]

The results of this small but spirited encounter on the doorstep of Washington were many. Tompkins's ranking superior, Brig. Gen. Irvin McDowell, commander of the newly formed Department of Northeastern Virginia, praised the lieutenant's dash and gallantry. Somehow McDowell concluded that the skirmish "has given considerable prestige to our regular cavalry in the eyes of our people and of the volunteer regiments." In the same dispatch, however, McDowell took Tompkins to task for ranging so far from Alexandria. (General Hunter's involvement in the affair was not mentioned.) McDowell also chastised the lieutenant for frustrating "unintentionally, for the time, a more important movement." On this subject he provided no details. Finally, he decried Tompkins's newspaper connections: The lieutenant's report of the skirmish had appeared in the *New York Tribune* before it reached departmental headquarters.[26]

Such criticism did no lasting harm to Tompkins's career; some months later he became colonel of volunteers and commander of the 1st Vermont Cavalry, and he ended the war as a brevet brigadier general. In 1893 he was awarded, a trifle belatedly, a Medal of Honor for his dash into Fairfax. Meanwhile, the exploit drew the attention of Tompkins's army to the enemy's southern outposts and increased its desire to move against Manassas Junction, where one of the Confederate's most celebrated warriors, Brig. Gen. Pierre T. G. Beauregard of Louisiana, had just taken command.[27]

The fight of June 1 also had major effects on Tompkins's opponents. For overseeing the effort that repulsed the Yankees, Dick Ewell won the acclaim of his superiors and, soon afterward, promotion to brigadier general. Billy Smith's role in the affair brought him the offer of a brigadier generalship of state troops from Virginia governor John Letcher. Captain Marr, whose riflemen played the critical role in Tompkins's repulse, received no promotion, although Letcher had recently approved his elevation to lieutenant colonel of Virginia forces. Marr was dead, a stray bullet from one of the retreating Federals having struck the honors graduate of the V.M.I. in the heart. He thus became the first in a long line of soldiers to fall in the cause of Southern independence.[28]

>─┼─◆>─○─<◆─┼─<

The dash on Fairfax may have sparked interest in a forward movement, but just where that movement would take place, and under whose direction, were matters of debate. The pacification of Virginia was a four-pronged effort, and by early June each pincer was moving without an overall attempt at strategic coordination. It did not help the Union cause that at least three of the four leaders involved appeared to lack the personal and professional qualifications to ensure success, or at least make success possible. Nor did it help that none of the four had an abiding appreciation of the value of cavalry and, consequently, lacked an adequate mounted force.

The best of the lot appeared to be George B. McClellan. Having resigned from the army in 1857 to pursue a career in transportation, McClellan was living in Cincinnati, where he was serving as president of the Ohio & Mississippi Railroad, when the war began. Gov. William Dennison considered him the man to lead Ohio to triumph and gave him command of troops invading the western reaches of Virginia, with the rank of major general of Ohio volunteers. McClellan was reputed to be a military genius—since West Point he had exibited high competence, if not downright brilliance—but he tended to irresolution and vacillation when things did not go according to his plans, which was fairly often. In his favor was the fact that in the Virginia mountains, he was facing something less than the Confederate first team. Then, too, he was served by able and less volatile subordinates, including Brig. Gen. William S. Rosecrans, on whom he could rely in a crisis. "Little Mac" soon proved adept at taking the credit for any success these lieutenants achieved.[29]

Seemingly at the other end of the scale of professionalism was Maj. Gen. Benjamin F. Butler of the United States Volunteers, soon to make his mark as the most notorious politician-general in American history. The former Massachusetts legislator and militia commander, whose Democratic affiliation and war fervor had prompted Abraham Lincoln to overlook his lack of soldierly experience, had been given command of thousands of volunteers in Hampton Roads. Butler oversaw not only a formidable command, but also a strategic theater from his headquarters at Fort Monroe, at the tip of the Virginia Peninsula—one of only two garrisons in Southern territory to remain in Union hands.

For all his amateurism, it was Butler rather than some ex-Regular who made initial inroads into enemy-held portions of the Old Dominion. Because he did so blindly, however, he precipitated the first large land battle of the conflict, which took place on June 10 at Big Bethel Church, seven miles above Hampton, Virginia. It was perhaps due to Butler's lack of mounted reconnaissance—certainly due to the greenness of his troops, two columns of which had made a night march to their common objective only to collide and fire on each other, thus alerting the enemy—that Big Bethel ended in Union defeat.[30]

Butler should have heeded an editorial that the *New York Times* had run nine days before his lumbering, blundering advance. A lack of cavalry forces in the field, the *Times* believed, constituted "an element of weakness in the Northern army to which adequate attention has not yet been drawn." The editorial continued: "Cavalry is the right hand of active, open warfare. Without cavalry the great army of the Union, now upon the march to crush rebellion, is crippled and imperfect."[31]

The other principal commanders in Virginia, Irvin McDowell and Robert Patterson, were just as ill disposed to heed this warning. Neither had an adequate mounted force to support his mission—McDowell was to neutralize Beauregard's troops near Manassas, while Patterson was to invade the Shenandoah and confront Joe Johnston near Harpers Ferry—and neither seemed overly concerned about the situation. It was true that when McDowell submitted a plan of advance against Manassas early in June, he asked for, among other troops, a regiment of Regular horsemen—but he should have demanded more cavalry than that.[32]

Although Scott, Cameron, and Lincoln approved McDowell's strategy, they did not fully grant his manpower request. When in midmonth McDowell began to develop a plan to best Beauregard, he commanded only seven companies of horse soldiers, four from the 2nd Cavalry, two from the 1st Cavalry, and one from the 2nd Dragoons. Grouped under their senior officer, now-Major Palmer, the troopers were assigned to one of the five divisions McDowell had formed on July 8, led by the steadily rising David Hunter, who had absorbed no blame for Tompkins's repulse at Fairfax. As a cavalry veteran, Hunter might have been supposed to know how to use Palmer's companies to good effect, but his direct connection with the horsemen ended when he further assigned them to the brigade of Andrew Porter. Like his superior, Porter had recently become a brigadier general of volunteers, but his Regular rank was colonel of the 16th Regular Infantry. How effectively he could be expected to use the cavalry was yet to be determined.[33]

>–◆–○–◆–◄

McDowell's ignorance of the value of cavalry is understandable; at forty-two years old, and despite more than twenty years in the service, he had almost no experience in field command. Until May he had been a senior member of General Scott's staff, on which he had served since the Mexican War. It would appear that his qualifications for departmental command were his staunch Unionist sentiments, his willingness to lead raw recruits, his eagerness to please his military and civilian superiors, and the support given him by Sen. Salmon P. Chase and Governor Dennison, as he was an Ohio native.[34]

Patterson's story differed from McDowell's in many ways, but its underlying theme was similar. A contemporary of General Scott's, Patterson was pushing seventy and was physically frail. A veteran of not only the Mexican campaigns but also the War of 1812, he was suited neither by experience nor by temperament for an operational command, especially one that carried such heavy responsibilities. Like McDowell's, Patterson's 18,000-man army contained a mere sprinkling of horsemen: Major Thomas and three of the 2nd Cavalry companies that had been refitting at Carlisle Barracks plus a mounted militia unit, the 1st Troop, Philadelphia City Cavalry, whose history dated to the Revolutionary War.[35]

Slowed not only by age, but also by a cautiousness bordering on sloth, Patterson was no match for his opponent, Johnston, an energetic, astute, and crafty officer. In mid-June, while McDowell continued to assimilate his raw levies around Washington, and only after much prodding by General Scott, Patterson's command marched from Chambersburg into western Virginia. Conscious of being outgunned, Johnston headed south with his 12,000 men, enabling Patterson to occupy Harpers Ferry and seize its venerable armory and arsenal.

Only three days later, however, Patterson reacted to exaggerated rumors of Johnston's strength by returning to the north side of the Potomac, where he appeared content to stay. The War Department erred by calling some of the general's troops, including all of the Regular cavalry, to Washington. The loss made Patterson suddenly aware of his lack of reconnaissance units. This concern became an excuse to remain in Maryland for more than two weeks, ignoring Scott's entreaties to retake Harpers Ferry.[36]

While Patterson dawdled, McDowell tried to gauge the capabilities of his volunteers. Uncertain of their ability to mount an effective offensive, he feared the order to march on Manassas, even though his 35,000 troops outnumbered Beauregard's almost two to one. "I wanted very much a little time" to train, he lamented, "all of us wanted it. We did not have a bit of it. The answer was: 'You are green, it is true; but they are green, also; you are all green alike.'"[37]

Initial tests did not look promising. Outpost skirmishes usually went to the enemy, and on June 17 McDowell's 1st Ohio Volunteer Infantry suffered a well-publicized setback. Sent by train along the Loudoun & Hampshire Railroad to scout enemy positions, the Ohioans, who lacked cavalry support, rode into the hands of the troops they were seeking. At a bend in the track near the hamlet of Vienna, fifteen miles west of Alexandria, their train came under a shelling by two pieces of Rebel artillery. Alerted to the Federals' coming by some of his 140 cavalry, Col. Maxcy Gregg of the 1st South Carolina Infantry had set a trap for the invaders. His guns derailed two passenger cars, and his foot soldiers killed or wounded a dozen passengers. Instead of returning fire, the bruised survivors dashed into trackside woods and scattered like sheep.[38]

By July 2 McDowell, reacting to Union-wide pressure to march on to Richmond via Manassas, made ready to lead his citizen-soldiers out of Washington. By now Patterson had recovered his composure sufficiently to recross the Potomac and reoccupy Harpers Ferry, which Johnston had not visited in his absence. That day part of Patterson's advance tangled near Falling Waters, Virginia, with Johnston's advance element under Thomas Jackson. At first held at bay by Jackson's foot soldiers and Col. J. E. B. Stuart's 1st Virginia Cavalry,

the Federals regained momentum and thrust their opponents south. At a critical point in the action, George Thomas, recently promoted to colonel of the
2nd Cavalry and even more recently named commander of one of Patterson's
brigades, maneuvered so adroitly as to turn Jackson's right flank. With that, the
Confederates retreated in haste and with some confusion. Patterson, fearful of
being drawn into a trap, mounted a four-mile pursuit that failed to overtake
Jackson, then halted.[39]

With Stuart ably covering his withdrawal, Jackson fell back to Martinsburg, five miles below Harpers Ferry, then to Darkesville, not far above strategic Winchester. Johnston joined him there and appeared ready to fight, but on
the seventh the Confederate leader—over the protests of officials in Richmond—withdrew from the enemy yet again, this time as far as Winchester.

Still within reach of Martinsburg, Johnston's army seemed in the grasp of
Patterson's larger force. If so, the Union leader failed to press his advantage,
remaining on the defensive, hesitating to commit himself to an advance.
Enjoined by the War Department to keep a close eye on Johnston lest he slip
away to reinforce Beauregard at Manassas, Patterson did little more than probe
clumsily toward Winchester with his cavalry-poor vanguard. Infantry scouts sent
back erroneous reports that made Patterson fear he was up against far more
troops than Johnston commanded. The renewed prospect that he was being led
into a trap by a more formidable army held Patterson hostage to his own fears.

On the eighth he renewed his advance, only to allow his subordinates to
talk him into halting until reinforcements could reach him from Washington.
The delay proved critical, as did another that soon followed. On the fifteenth,
as marching orders circulated through McDowell's camps at Washington, Patterson finally stirred himself, this time moving to within five miles of Winchester before going into camp. The next day he advanced further, but bereft as
he was of mounted scouts, he feared running into the enemy. Instead of moving south, he sidled eastward to Charles Town, where he waited for Johnston
to make the next move.[40]

That move, made on the eighteenth, was aimed at neither giving battle nor
retreating. Unimpeded by the enemy, Johnston turned east and started his army
toward Piedmont Station, six miles from Winchester. Late that day he placed
regiments and cannon aboard flatcars on the Manassas Gap Railroad and sent
them through the mountains to join Beauregard before McDowell could strike
from the north. The withdrawal from Winchester was masterfully covered by
Stuart's horsemen, whose movements above the town in plain view of the Federals convinced Patterson that his opponent remained in force not far away.

Despite overage engines, overloaded cars, and poorly maintained tracks,
the advance elements of Johnston's army arrived at Manassas late in the afternoon of the nineteenth, eight hours out of Piedmont Station. Beauregard was
so happy to see them that when Johnston himself arrived late that day to super-
sede him in overall command, the Louisianan took his demotion with good
grace. Already the Yankees had probed the Confederate lines around Manassas

Junction and along the south bank of a meandering stream known as Bull Run. There was no telling when they would strike in force—but if they held off for just a few more hours, by the time the battle began, Beauregard's line would be more than half again as strong as it had been just days before.[41]

>-+-◆>-O-<◆-+-<

With his meager cavalry force leading the way, McDowell marched out of Washington on the morning of the sixteenth. The general was in anything but a buoyant mood, even though his spirits and those of his volunteers had risen with the recent news that McClellan had won a smashing victory at Rich Mountain on the eleventh. Credit for the outcome was due to General Rose-crans, but it was his boss, the "Young Napoleon," whom reporters showered with praise. Two days later came word of another success by McClellan's Ohioans, this at Corrick's Ford on the Cheat River, where an enemy force had been obliterated. Suddenly Little Mac was all the rage, although Irvin McDow-ell would supplant him in the North's consciousness should the Ohioan truly sweep on to Richmond.[42]

McDowell would not get that far—not by a long shot—but he would fail through no lack of effort or nerve. By the seventeenth his advance guard was evicting sharpshooters from Fairfax Court House (Dick Ewell and Billy Smith had cleared out long ago) and Centreville, almost within sight of Beauregard's main line. That line appeared formidable—according to a recent article in the *Times,* it included a great deal of cavalry—and McDowell's recruits were in no shape to attack. Thus the commander withheld a blow that, had it fallen that day, before Johnston's troops came in, might have stopped the campaign—and perhaps the war—in its tracks.[43]

The eighteenth saw a fierce little skirmish at Blackburn's Ford on Bull Run, in which one of McDowell's divisions, on an errant reconnaissance, was roughly handled by equally green troops with the advantage of prepared works. The Federals did, however, uncover some of Beauregard's positions, largely due to the shelling of two cannon that drew the Confederates' fire. For much of the day the guns were supported by one of Palmer's squadrons, under Captain Brackett, which served largely dismounted. Otherwise, the cavalry saw no action at Blackburn's Ford.[44]

It sat just as idle three days later, when McDowell at last put his plan of attack in motion. The early action at Blackburn's and elsewhere along the Con-federate right and center so alerted Beauregard's men that McDowell tabled his original plan to strike again in those areas. Instead, on the morning of the twenty-first, he launched a limited attack against Beauregard's (now John-ston's) center before sending a strike column, composed of the divisions of Generals Hunter and Heintzelman, against the weakly guarded left. The recruits made a long, slow march of it, but shortly before 9:00 A.M., they splashed across Bull Run at Sudley Springs Ford, turning the enemy flank.

The game appeared to be in the attackers' hands until Johnston and Beauregard rushed up troops from the other end of their line to slow the advance. The increasing weight of the Federal drive forced the Rebels onto high ground along the Warrenton Turnpike known as Henry House Hill. On that field, Jackson's brigade, having prayed for a chance to influence the fighting, formed a new defensive line. Through their steadfastness under pressure, the men won their commander the enduring nickname of "Stonewall" Jackson.[45]

While the battle pivoted precariously on Jackson's men and their supports, McDowell fed units into his main assault force as well as into a secondary attack column opposite the Rebel center. Despite the whirl of activity, Palmer's cavalry idled in the rear. Three days before, some of its men had experienced what one recruit referred to as "the first time I was ever under fire—the real article." Many of the troopers wanted to go in again, but for several hours General Porter could find no place for them south of Bull Run. As the afternoon wore on, and the sound of firing below the stream rose and fell in an incomprehensible pattern, the troopers stood to horse, waiting, wondering, and in the case of one lieutenant of the 1st (soon to become the 4th) Cavalry, reciting poetry aloud to while away the time. Major Palmer did not stand the wait well; one of his men described him as "in a woeful state of mortification." Palmer's embarrassment deepened when he failed to interest General Heintzelman in a mounted attack against Henry House Hill.[46]

Equally downcast—"anything but jubilant," as one observer described him—was Lt. George Armstrong Custer of the 2nd (soon the 5th) Cavalry, who had been looking forward to his first battle since leaving West Point in June for the scene of action. No action came Custer's way all afternoon. In his postwar memoirs, the subaltern recalled a charge made early in the fight by a squadron under Capt. Albert V. Colburn of the 1st Cavalry, but official accounts fail to corroborate this.[47]

Late in the day, with the tide of battle turning against the attackers, Palmer's troopers were finally ushered across Bull Run. Near the scene of action on Henry House Hill, they were placed in position to support a battery, as some of them had four days earlier. As on the seventeenth, supporting a battery was about all they were called on to do. At one point, a small detachment was sent to reconnoiter on the far left, but if a weakness was discovered in that sector, it was never exploited.

If the troopers bristled at being underemployed, they must have burned with shame when, in late afternoon, McDowell's offensive collapsed under the weight of more Confederates than he should have been fighting. Thanks to Patterson's timidity and vacillation, Johnston's main force had arrived just in time to tip the balance of battle in favor of the defense.[48]

Defeat was bad enough, but the ensuing retreat was ugly. Confederate infantry and artillery fired into the rear of McDowell's beaten troops, and then the cavalry was let loose. Stuart, with most of the 1st Virginia, attacked along the left flank of Jackson's staunchly held position. Striking the main retreat column, Stuart's men shot and sabered their way through the confused mass of blue, taking numerous prisoners. Meanwhile, on Jackson's right, the 30th Virginia Cavalry, under Col. R. C. W. Radford and Lt. Col. Thomas T. Munford, overtook several infantry regiments in midflight, laying several of their men low with saber strokes and capturing Col. Michael Corcoran of the 69th New York.

One of Munford's companies, a famous militia unit known to friend and foe alike as the "Black Horse Cavalry," solidified its reputation by riding down the 11th New York Infantry, taking a fearful toll of the "Fire Zouaves" and stampeding their survivors. When broken-down wagons snarled traffic on a bridge across a Bull Run tributary known as Cub Run, the fugitives became chaotically intermingled with sightseers from Washington who had come out to watch the battle, toting a picnic lunch. As the screams of Rebel troopers echoed in the rear, it suddenly became every man for himself. Wagons and cannon were left behind in the mad rush to safety. Radford's men exploited the confusion; the next morning, as Lieutenant Colonel Munford observed in his after-action report, "I had the honor of delivering to his excellency the President of the Confederate States, ten rifled guns, their caissons, and forty-six horses."[49]

The ferocity of the cavalry's pursuit would become one of the great legends of the battle. For its part, Palmer's battalion, which guarded the flanks and rear of the retreat column, did a fine job in the only active service assigned it this day. Eventually the Regulars chased off the Rebel troopers and even took a few prisoners. Even so, the Union cavalry's role in the fight would inspire no tales of martial glory.

Late that day, from a White House window, Abraham Lincoln watched McDowell's dispirited remnants stream over the Potomac bridges in abject defeat. The situation seemed gloomy, the cause in peril, but the president realized that all was not lost. He considered it unlikely, as did General Scott, that the enemy would follow up its triumph by attacking the capital. The formidable ring of forts around the city would turn back all but the largest, most experienced assault force. As it happened, Lincoln was correct. The troops under Johnston and Beauregard had been as disorganized by victory as their opponents had been by defeat. They were capable only of a limited pursuit—little more than a harassing action on the roads to Centreville and Fairfax Court House. In time, Johnston did place outposts within sight of the Capitol dome, but these were far enough away and so lightly manned that the enemy's term for the operation—the "siege of Washington"—was a patent misnomer.

Still, the first major clash of arms had ended in disgraceful defeat for the government, and Lincoln needed to take steps to ensure that there would be no recurrence. He called George McClellan to Washington and offered him command of this beaten but still potent command, which McClellan later christened the Army of the Potomac and armed, equipped, and instructed until it was on a par with the finest armies in the world.

Lincoln also redoubled recruiting and opened it to all arms of the service. The wisdom of this policy had already become clear to many lawmakers. The day after the debacle along Bull Run, Congress enacted legislation giving the president power to call into the army up to 50,000 more volunteers for terms ranging from six months to three years. This quota, unlike the earlier call to arms, included cavalry regiments—as many as the government could mount and train for a return encounter with the forces of secession, disunion, and ruin.[50]

Chapter Three

No Work in The Trenches!

Few of the young men who joined the cavalry in 1861–62 knew what they were getting into. Looking back years later, they realized how naive they had been to think that they were joining an exalted and privileged branch of the service. Fighting on horseback might have seemed like a genteel way of serving one's country, but the realities were harsher, the service more difficult and burdensome than most would-be cavaliers could have imagined.

The problem was that thanks to his mount, a cavalryman was so mobile and versatile he could perform a wide variety of functions. While infantry, the "Queen of Battles," remained the dominant force in combat, its lack of mobility restricted it to fairly simple forms of offensive and defensive warfare. That same limitation meant that during lulls between battles, periods that might last for months, the foot soldiers remained in camp, leisurely readying themselves for the next go at the enemy. In contrast, the cavalry was capable of a lot of work both in and out of combat. In addition to adding weight to offensives by the main army, horsemen reconnoitered the enemy's positions to discover his strength and determine his intentions; performed counterreconnaissance by foiling the intelligence-gathering abilities of opposing cavalry; guarded the head, flanks, and rear of their army on the march; rode in advance to gain a foothold on the battlefield that slower comrades might exploit; took the advance during pursuit, prodding the enemy into flight and preventing him from regrouping and counterattacking; bought time for their own army's retreat, falling back from point to point and offering resistance whenever conditions permitted; and raided communication facilities, supply depots, and other strategic targets behind enemy lines.

When away from the battlefield, the typical trooper was not permitted to lie idle; he served on a daily basis as a vedette (mounted sentry), a courier, a member of an escort unit, a provost guard, a forager. The cavalryman was on duty virtually every waking minute and often grew sore, tired, dirty, hot or cold, and hungry—a far cry from the knight-errant that many a young recruit fancied he would be.[1]

Cavalry recruits may have been overly romantic at the outset, but they learned quickly. "This branch of the service," wrote a lieutenant in the 3rd Pennsylvania in October 1861, "is as severe as it is important, and but few can stand the duties of this life." Looking back on his service after the war, a New York trooper agreed: "The cavalry is the hardest branch there is in the service. . . . A cavalryman is kept busy all day long." As well as being hectic and severe, a trooper's job was dauntingly complicated, especially as he and his mount had to learn by intricate and intensive training how to act as one. An officer from Michigan noted that "the duties of cavalry are as arduous, complex and diversified as it is possible for any branch of the military service to be."[2]

One reason for this was that the trooper had to learn other soldiers' duties as well as his own. According to an early twentieth-century cavalry historian, "a trooper must perforce learn much of what his comrade in the infantry knows, and in addition must be taught all that pertains to horses and horsemanship. Those who had been fascinated by the glamour and dash of the cavalry life doubtless wished many times, during those laborious days, that they had the more frequent hours of recreation granted their neighbors of the infantry."[3]

It took a special breed to embrace a life filled with so many burdens and complexities. Capt. Charles F. Adams Jr., of the 1st Massachusetts, summed up the requirements succinctly: "Alertness, individuality, reliability, and self-reliance." A fellow subaltern from Pennsylvania believed that only "powerful and well-built men" need apply to the cavalry. The historian of the 1st Maine recalled that cavalry recruiters sought "a better class" of recruit than the norm, "as the grade was higher, and only men of superior intelligence were wanted."

According to oft-stated qualifications, the ideal cavalryman was in his late teens or early twenties. He was unmarried, stood no more than five feet, seven inches, and weighed 125 to 140 pounds. Some regiments set other standards, or at least professed to. During recruiting the 1st Maine sought "none but sound, able-bodied men in all respects . . . of correct morals and temperate habits, active, intelligent, vigorous and hardy." Such qualifications were trumpeted in recruiting propaganda, although it seems unlikely that they were applied strictly. Thus, the reality of its service notwithstanding, recruiters pitched the cavalry as an elite arm to which only the best physical and mental specimens could aspire. These supposed standards flattered the recruit into thinking highly of himself and his branch, an attitude that served to heighten morale.

It would seem that experience in equestrianism should have been a prerequisite for cavalry service, as also a general knowledge of things military. Such traits, however, were in short supply among those who joined the mounted ranks of the Army of the Potomac in the aftermath of Bull Run. The majority of those youngsters, the median age of whom was about twenty-three, had little or no experience on horseback. The typical recruit from New England and the Middle Atlantic states, the main population base from which "Mr. Lincoln's Army" drew, knew a horse only as a farm animal or as the motive power for a streetcar.[4]

While Southerners, whose native region lacked good roads and transit facilities, habitually rode wherever they must go, urban Yankees made as much use as possible of public transportation. Moreover, Southerners were considered to have been bred on the martial spirit, imbued with the military ethic, and conversant since birth with firearms and fighting. Northerners, while not quite viewed as pacifists, were never accorded such fierce characteristics. In fact, the typical Northerner appears to have joined the cavalry not because he liked horses or was conversant with weapons, but because he regretted having lacked the opportunity to ride, shoot, and fight. The enlistees' ignorance of equine use and care prompted one critic to conclude that "each recruit for the cavalry thought the especial requirements for that branch of the service was that he could neither ride, saddle, nor groom a horse."[5]

They also joined because they had been captivated by visions both romantic and sanguinary. Boys who had grown up on Thomas Mallory and Sir Walter Scott saw the cavalry as the last bastion of chivalry in the modern world. Other youngsters viewed the trooper as the ultimate warrior, one who visited terror, death, and chaos on the foe—a childhood fantasy never outgrown. George Custer was one: "From my earliest notions of the true cavalryman I had always pictured him in the charge bearing aloft his curved sabre, and cleaving the skulls of all with whom he came in contact." For another lad, who in 1861 rushed from the farm to the cavalry recruiter, the typical horse soldier was "a swashbuckler, who rode terrifically with his sabre gripped by his teeth, a revolver in each hand and his breath almost aflame as it spurted from his nostrils."[6]

Youths such as these needed few inducements to sign up. If they were not already disposed to cavalry service, they were put in that frame of mind by the eloquence of the recruiter. In 1861 a farmer's son from Ohio, Adna R. Chaffee, was about to enlist in a local infantry regiment when he conversed with an officer recruiting for the new 6th United States Cavalry, one of the five Regular regiments that were later assigned to the Army of the Potomac. The teenager found himself spellbound by tales of mounted glory described "in such fascinating terms" that he joined up on the spot. He remained in the service for fifty years, rising to the rank of major general and seeing Fort Chaffee, Arkansas, named in his honor.[7]

Some who turned a willing ear to the recruiter were not, like Adna Chaffee, seeking to escape the drudgery of farm work but hoping to flee the boredom and sterility of business life. "God! What an escape!" Charles Francis Adams, Jr., of Boston recalled of his enlistment in the 1st Massachusetts. "I was swept off my feet, out of my office and into the army. Educationally and every other way, it was the most fortunate event in my life." Another recruit easily persuaded was the infantry veteran. Hampton S. Thomas of Philadelphia, who had served in a three months' unit at war's outbreak, spoke with an acquaintance in the cavalry and suddenly "discovered that I was more fitted for riding a horse than for trudging through the slush and mud with a heavy 'Harpers Ferry' musket on my shoulder."[8]

Recruiters, however, could not count on romantic dreamers, weary farm lads, bored businessmen, or footsore veterans to supply the manpower they needed. They worked hard to sell the service to an often disinterested, sometimes doubtful public. They set up shop in every major city, and many small towns, between Baltimore and Boston. The dedicated ones scoured every hamlet and farming village that boasted a facility that could be used for recruiting: a town hall, a schoolhouse, a church. In such places, they beat the drum—sometimes literally—to attract potential troopers.

Recruiters also advertised in the local newspapers and littered the towns with placards touting the benefits of joining a particular regiment. These notices also emphasized any bounties—enlistment bonuses—that the state, county, or locality might offer. America's advertising industry may have been in its infancy in 1861, but recruiters waxed creative in announcing their blandishments and inducements. A typical poster, seeking recruits for the 10th New York, stressed the unique virtues of the arm:

Cavalry to the Front!
The Best Paid Arm of the Service!
NO WORK IN THE TRENCHES!
Three Complete Uniforms!
LESS FATIGUE! LESS MORTALITY!
A Chance is still open for a few more able bodied men of good character in Company H, Colonel Lemmon's Cavalry Regiment.[9]

The advertisement implies limited space in the local unit. If the posters were to be believed, nearly every regiment had only a little room to fill, enough to accommodate just "a few more men." Virtually everyone who wanted to enlist got the opportunity, however. The 1st Maine's call for recruits of robust physique and sound morals was nothing but a ploy, for in few regiments were enlistment standards high. Except for the obvious boy, the infirm graybeard, and the midget, the service accepted everyone fit enough to walk to the recruiting office.

One notable exception was the "Anderson Cavalry," later the 15th Pennsylvania, a detachment of which served briefly in the Army of the Potomac. When this regiment was organized in the summer and fall of 1862, potential recruits had to obtain letters of recommendation from men of social, political, and military standing in their region and also pass a stringent physical examination. Every recruit—even obvious officer material—had to enlist as a private and prove himself worthy of rank. Had such standards been the norm, few regiments of cavalry would have completed formation in time to fight.[10]

Occasionally a regiment filled up so quickly that would-be troopers were left out. In many recruiting offices, some who missed the cut gave way to tears or curses, as though they had lost the chance of a lifetime. Yet most of these unfortunates were quickly assimilated into other outfits whose quota was not yet full. In many instances, this happened after the recruit had been sworn in to what he supposed was his regiment, only to find himself shuttled into a less desirable unit against his will but beyond his ability to do anything about it. Excess enlistees in the 5th Michigan, organizing in Detroit, were sent by train to Grand Rapids, where they became members of the 6th Michigan. The 6th's overage was sent to another part of Grand Rapids and dumped in the half-filled training camp of the 7th Michigan. Without intending to, some recruits went to war from a state other than their own because of arrangements between regiments. Many youngsters who desired to join the 1st New Jersey found themselves, instead, members of the 5th Pennsylvania. Numerous regiments contained companies or battalions raised in neighboring states.[11]

Officers gained their commissions through many channels—ability, favoritism, local prominence, political clout—but rank was often payment for their effectiveness as recruiters. Governors whose states were compelled to meet a recruitment quota or—beginning in 1863—face that dreaded alternative, the draft, thought highly of those who could persuade other civilians to enter the ranks alongside them. In many states, a man who could guarantee a platoon of relatives, friends, colleagues, or students was likely to win a lieutenant's rank. One who furnished upward of a hundred recruits would become a captain in the regiment he helped build. Sometimes a governor would create incentive as well as competition by promising a major's or captain's rank to the first man who enlisted the requisite number to support a battalion or company. This ploy sometimes caused trouble when resentful losers were forced to serve under those who had beaten them.[12]

The greater the influence and drawing power of those who raised units, the greater the rewards. This policy tended to make officers of the politically connected but militarily inept. Yet a political reputation was not an absolute necessity. Some men received colonel's eagles by paying the cost of recruiting, clothing, mounting, arming, and equipping a body of troopers and, in some cases, furnishing their training camp as well.

A few such patriots, including James H. Van Alen of the 3rd New York and John F. Farnsworth of the 8th Illinois, parlayed their wealth into a brigadier's star. Money seemed to count more than talent. Though Farnsworth possessed some ability as a cavalryman, even Van Alen's closest friends admitted that he had no military qualifications whatsoever. One observer called him "radically incapable of commanding his regiment, much less of leading it into battle." Still, this friend of the Astors and the Vanderbilts retained his appointment for two years before finally facing his shortcomings and resigning from the service.[13]

><-<>-O-<>-><

After enough men had been gathered to form the nucleus of a cavalry regiment, they were collected and placed in a camp or rendezvous. A regiment ordinarily went into one training camp and then to another, the first in its recruiting region, the second in Washington, D.C., or northern Virginia. Both sites were spacious enough to accommodate the men, usually in barracks but often in tents, and horses, most often in stables but sometimes hobbled or tied to picket ropes. Typically the camp was situated away from populated areas, occupied elevated ground, was adjacent to fresh water, and had enough cleared ground to permit the training of men and mounts. Some existing facilities offered perfect accommodations: The 1st Michigan trained at the old Hamtramck Racetrack, three miles above Detroit. Other, less appropriate sites were converted into training grounds, such as the lager beer garden, dubbed "Camp Parker," where the 3rd Pennsylvania camped outside Washington. Even less appropriate—despite its powerful symbolism—was the abandoned cemetery in which the 1st Vermont encamped soon after reaching the capital.[14]

An experienced quartermaster with an eye for good ground was supposed to have laid out the training camp. This was not true in every case; recruits in numerous regiments complained about their accommodations, or the lack of them. Farnsworth's 8th Illinois, which arrived in Washington in October 1861, was at first quartered in a well-situated camp amid healthy, pleasant surroundings, only to be relocated a few weeks later to low ground at the base of Meridian Hill, the only water source a polluted stream. According to the medical director of the Army of the Potomac, the new camp "became intolerably muddy in the course of the winter. The part occupied by the horses was a perfect quagmire, never policed at all. The men became discouraged and careless, and in January, 1862, there were 207 cases of typhoid fever among them."[15]

Cavalry camps were such breeding grounds of disease that each regiment suffered a dozen or more fatalities before it ever saw combat. Too often whole regiments were laid low by illness. The same surgeon who reported the epidemic in the 8th Illinois found that eighty members of the 5th New York, also camped near Washington, had debilitating maladies, including epilepsy. Late in 1861 a surgeon inspecting Camp Scott, Staten Island, New York, found that conditions were so unsanitary that more than a hundred members of the 6th New York had come down with fever and the measles. The victims included the regiment's assistant surgeon and its hospital steward.[16]

Some forms of illness were preventable but through ignorance and neglect ran rampant. A lack of cold-weather clothing and firewood left the men of the 1st Massachusetts, in the words of Lt. Col. Horace B. Sargent, "shivering, & suffering . . . in danger of disease." Inadequate clothing was one of the causes of the 8th Illinois's long sick list below Meridian Hill. By the last days of 1861 the men's trousers had worn through but had not been replaced. "Many of them," said the medical director, "were reduced to their drawers."[17]

In warm weather, men in training camp slept outdoors or, more often, in tents. Often four to six comrades "spooned" together under canvas, sharing body warmth to ward off the chill. When regiments went into winter quarters, the men stockaded their tents by laying a corduroyed floor of wood to keep bodies off the frozen earth. Ideally, a camp would be adjacent to woods extensive enough to provide timber for log cabins, many of which were heated by rude fireplaces with hollowed-out barrels that served as chimneys.

Not every camp featured well-insulated dwellings. A lack of adequate shelter was another cause of poor health in many regiments. In the winter of 1861–62 Lt. Joseph D. Galloway of the 3rd Pennsylvania complained that when winds whipped through Camp Parker, the lack of cabins and winterized tents forced troopers to spend "horrible night[s] . . . near freezing to death." On a rainy day, Galloway noted in his diary that "all hands are nearly drowned, and our tents leak dreadfully."[18]

That same winter Lt. William H. Mallory of the 2nd New York, the "Harris Light Cavalry," one of three mounted regiments named for Sen. Ira Harris, wrote from Washington to let his family know how "it makes my heart ache to see my strong & brave boys falling prey to the diseases, instead of dying on the battlefield with less of suffering and more of glory." Part of the blame for this high incidence of sickness can be laid at the feet of lax and neglectful commanders; the rest owed to the unhealthy habits of the troopers themselves. "We were all so inexperienced," recalled Charles Adams. "We knew nothing of the laws of health and self-preservation, and we thought those laws not worth knowing. Why any of us survived, I cannot now see."[19]

Another reason for widespread disease was the poor-quality rations distributed in training camp. Officers were paid well enough to purchase bountiful meals from sutlers and farmers, but their men were less fortunate. Capt. William Wells of the 1st Vermont advised his parents to discourage his younger brother from enlisting, warning that "the rations that the privates have he could not stand, at least I should hate [for him] to." Those rations—which usually included salted beef and pork, a few vegetables, and that staple of the soldier's diet, the crackerlike hardtack—were lacking in taste, bereft of nutrients, and liable to be in short supply. Encamped regiments were often at the mercy of food service vendors whose government contracts were so ironclad that they could with impunity foist on the troops spoiled meat, moldy bread, and weevil-infested flour. "We would go without eating," a New York enlisted man informed his parents, "rather than to take such stuff into our stomachs."[20]

The conditions under which some regiments were fed seem hardly conducive to good digestion. On Staten Island each company of the 6th New York "was marched three times a day to the cook house for meals, which were eaten standing at a long board table in a rough shed, open at one side. The fare was very plain." Two weeks before Christmas 1861 the men staged a protest, demanding better food and more comfortable dining. When their demands went unanswered, the troopers tore down the cookhouse and vandalized the commissary, manhandling any officer who tried to stop them. Their rampage continued until Lt. Col. Duncan McVicar advanced on them waving a pair of Colt pistols.[21]

Another drain on regimental health, as well as on morale, was the sometimes hectic, sometimes monotonous routine that ruled most training camps. A typical schedule was posted by Lieutenant Colonel Sargent of the 1st

Massachusetts. His regiment's day began with buglers blowing reveille before sunrise. Regulations called for cavalry regiments to include trumpeters, whose instruments produced a deeper and more melodious call than infantry bugles, but in practice buglers were always more numerous. Stable call was blown every morning at 6:30, accompanied by sick call, followed by orderly call at 7:15 and breakfast at 7:30. Water call was sounded and guard mounting commenced at 8:30.

The first drill of the day began at 9:30, with recall an hour later. A second drill session began at 11:00. Recall was again blown at noon, and the men broke for dinner at 12:30. Drill resumed at 2:00 P.M., with recall and stable call at 3:00. Supper was eaten at 5:00. Officers received tactical instruction and the men tended to their mounts and a myriad of other chores until a quarter hour before sunset, when the regiment held retreat and dress parade. Tattoo, a lights-out call, sounded at 9:00 P.M., ended the trooper's day. After July 1862 the haunting refrain known as Taps, composed by Maj. Gen. Daniel Butterfield, gradually replaced the tattoo throughout the Army of the Potomac.[22]

Every moment that the trooper was not eating, sleeping, using the latrine, doing guard duty, or exercising on the drill plain, he was attending to some other chore, usually an onerous and boring one. The maintenance and upkeep of his horse, which included a one-hour grooming session twice daily, consumed the greater part of his "free" time. And if he had nothing to keep him busy in his own camp, he was often posted to guard the infantry camps.

Most citizen-soldiers were not accustomed to such unceasing labor. Those who were, the erstwhile farmboys, had joined the army in hopes of leaving such a life behind. "Our life is a monotonous but busy round of drill, stable duty, dress parade &c," wrote a member of the 1st New England (later the 1st Rhode Island). A colleague in the 1st Maine put his feelings about work into a little ditty that soon circulated through his regiment's camp:

> Six days shalt thou labor and do all thou art able,
> And the seventh attend inspection and corduroy the stable.[23]

To break the boredom of camp routine and maintain morale, during the few off-duty hours granted them the troopers created their own amusements, dealing cards, forming glee clubs and theatrical troupes, playing baseball, tossing horseshoes, staging horse races. The more religious members of the regiment organized Bible study groups and sang hymns. When recreation was lacking, the men filled the time with roughhousing, which could lead to injury and the destruction of camp property. A member of the 8th Pennsylvania wrote to his sister from Camp Leslie, outside Washington, "We were playing the fool around the camp fire and I accidentally got stuck in the knee with a large fork which did not feel good I can tell you."[24]

When liquor was involved, roughhousing could escalate into violence. Lieutenant Galloway of the 3rd Pennsylvania reported drunken sprees and brawls in the regimental camp throughout the first winter of the war. On Christmas Eve holiday cheer overflowed the camp, and an unusual amount of violence erupted. The tent of a company commander disliked by some men was knocked down and set afire, the skull of one trooper was cut open by a sword, and another man was stabbed in the back. Although the officers put down the outbreak, it resumed the next morning and ended with more troopers cut, bruised, and bleeding.[25]

Drunken fights continued to plague the regiment through the winter and into the spring. In March 1862 Galloway reported a shocking number of regimental personnel "drunk all the time while the officers are about the same." A few days later he observed that "the morning dawned upon a wretched looking party of drunken soldiers, they managed to keep in the same condition all day." When the regiment was sent to Virginia later that month, several troopers managed to become inebriated aboard the transport carrying them up the Potomac; more than one fell overboard and drowned.[26]

Enlisted men were not the only ones to drink and run wild in camp. Theoretically, they were barred from purchasing alcoholic beverages. To evade that prohibition, a sergeant in the 6th Pennsylvania asked his brother to send him whiskey, saying, "You can tell the folks that I want it for medical purposes." Officers, on the other hand, usually had greater access to liquor, which was the most sought-after of the sutlers' wares, as well as more funds with which to buy it. Some drank surreptitiously while off duty; a few imbibed in public, which usually led to their dismissal from the service. A Rhode Island lieutenant wrote to a friend from Washington on a drizzly afternoon, "Still it rains but my bowels are lined with ale, and I defy the elements, [e]specially water." When unable to purchase liquor, this officer had a hard time of it. "There is nary whisky nary claret within these barracks," he lamented, adding that by necessity, "I have been beastly sober for many a day."[27]

Too frequently, alcoholic officers made spectacles of themselves in camp. A captain in the 1st Massachusetts complained that his colonel, rumored to be a tippler, made himself a "laughing stock on the drill field by blunders which ought to disgrace a corporal." Apparently insobriety ran in the family; it was said of the colonel's younger brother that "Capt. [Lucius] Sargent is a crazy man & that too brought on by *intemperance.*" For an officer, the only crime worse than drinking on duty was selling whiskey to enlisted men. One lieutenant caught doing so in the camp of the 5th Pennsylvania outside Washington turned out to be a relative of the state's governor, Andrew G. Curtin. This man was cashiered, but abuse of alcohol could result in a harsher fate. A trooper in the 5th New York reported that his company commander had died in camp, "the doctor said of brain fever but others say of delirium tremens."[28]

Some regiments were saddled with more alcoholics than others. It would appear, however, that every cavalry regiment in the Army of the Potomac—in fact, every regiment in every arm of the service—had its share of habitual drunkards, to the continuous detriment of unit morale and effectiveness.

Throughout the war soldiers drank in camp, in the field, even on the march, but because training camp provided a regiment with easier access to alcohol and more time to consume it, the incidence of alcoholism in an outfit was probably greatest during its first months in the service.

>—+—◆>—O—<+—+—<

The average recruit did not feel like a soldier—and could not think of himself as one—until issued his uniform. During training some regiments remained in mufti or a combination of civilian and military dress for the first several weeks of their service. Finally, state or federal quartermasters would dole out the attire the trooper would wear throughout his enlistment. In most cases, the uniform included a dark blue forage cap, a derivative of the French army's kepi, and a short-waisted jacket, also of dark blue, with collar, cuffs, and seams trimmed in yellow, the traditional color of cavalry (in the old dragoon regiments the trim had been orange; in the Regiment of Mounted Riflemen, green).

Many soldiers, both officers and men, procured sack coats or blouses, which they wore in place of jackets. Every trooper wore a woolen overcoat during cold-weather operations. The cavalryman's trousers, light blue with a yellow stripe down the legs, were made of kersey or other woolen material and featured a padded seat to withstand the wear of long hours in the saddle. The trooper's wardrobe was topped off by thigh- or knee-high black boots fitted with spurs of "old army" pattern. The only insignia most cavalrymen carried on their uniforms was a set of crossed sabers in brass fastened to the crown of the cap. Often a brass letter above the sabers identified the man's company and a numeral below, his regiment.[29]

The average trooper was proud of his appearance and took pains to look good in uniform. As befit his elite image, a cavalryman was prone to swagger, but swaggering was difficult if the uniform was askew. When those men of good character in the 15th Pennsylvania were issued oversize uniforms, an enlisted man recalled that "to those of us who were wont to be well dressed and who now expected lady friends to visit us in camp, it was a mortal struggle with pride to swath our forms in this huge toggery." Some recruits, however, were so enamored of their flashy attire that they tolerated a poor fit. When the 3rd Pennsylvania was clothed in camp, "some of the boys received men's pantaloons, and proud of the blue, would roll up the superfluous cloth around their ankles, and strut about oblivious to the fact that a bale of hay could be stowed away in the seat of their breeches."[30]

But the standard attire was not flashy enough for some. Maj. Gen. George Stoneman, a former Regular who in May 1862 was appointed chief of cavalry of the Army of the Potomac, envisioned a more distinctive and impressive uniform for his command. According to one of his staff officers, the general wanted his troopers clad in scarlet jackets and caps and pea green trousers.[31]

Someone with better fashion sense dissuaded him, but after Stoneman had passed from the scene a few regiments did take to the field in gaudy clothes.

Company A of the 2nd Massachusetts was composed not of Bay Staters but of native Californians who, wishing to fight and make money at the same time, had offered themselves to the state paying the highest bounty. When they reached Boston, the men of Company A wore green and gold uniforms and carried a silken flag emblazoned with their state's symbol, a grizzly bear. Apparently the outlandish garb was retired at an early date, for there are no later references to it.[32]

The 3rd New Jersey wore uniforms just as outlandish throughout its year of service in the Army of the Potomac. Organized in the spring of 1864 and grandly styled the "First Regiment, United States Hussars," the outfit wore European-style uniforms complete with pillbox hats and jackets fairly smothered in gilt. The spangled attire gave the Jerseymen such a picture-pretty appearance that less colorful regiments dubbed them "the Butterflies." Endless jokes were directed at the Hussars; comrades never tired of advising them to see the surgeon, for it was possible to cure "the yallers" if treated early.[33]

Once active service began, new uniforms became old very quickly. Many were made of shoddy material by unscrupulous contractors and did not last. Others were discarded in favor of something more comfortable or durable, or perhaps for clothing less likely to make the wearer a target. Then there were troopers who simply preferred nonissue attire. The predilection of enlisted members of the 1st Vermont for broad-brimmed felt or straw hats in place of their forage caps was a contant source of annoyance to their officers.[34]

Within a few months after entering the field, most commanders discarded the early emphasis they had placed on official attire. In February 1862, having just left training camp for the field, several members of the 1st New York—the "Lincoln Cavalry" that Carl Schurz had helped raise—were taken prisoner while on a scouting mission. Their captors could not identify the Yankees' unit or even tell that they were cavalry for, as one of the New Yorkers admitted, "none of us had on our uniform jackets." An officer in the same outfit, a contributor to the *Army and Navy Journal,* observed midway through the war that he could not recall "ever having seen a single squad or a set of fours [riders four abreast, the standard front of a marching column] who were uniform in uniform. . . . Individual fancies and peculiarities more than the much abused regulations govern our equipment."[35]

Beyond matters of taste and comfort, there was another reason for soldiers to don items of civilian dress: When they did, they could pocket the $49.57 the government paid each trooper as an annual clothing allowance. The variegated attire of these men gave their outfits the look of irregulars, vandals, or worse, hobos. More than a year after the 1st Massachusetts began campaigning in Virginia, Charles Adams noted that "we have few rules of dress, simply enforcing dark hats or caps and dark blue blouses, with light blue trousers; but, I am sorry to say that in all these respects our regiment is far ahead of the average of our cavalry, which, while it straggles through a country like a cloud of locusts, looks like a mob of ruffians, and fights and forages like a horde of Cossacks."[36]

Clothing made the man, but not necessarily the soldier. On the heels of being issued his uniform, the cavalry recruit usually received the tools of his new trade—his weapons and equipment—and began to receive instruction in their maintenance and use. Usually only then was he introduced to the beast of burden that gave him his unique identity and permitted him to ride to war while the less fortunate, or less deserving, walked.

Chapter Four

All Sorts of Ways Except the Right Way

S ome regiments did not receive their full complement of arms until they had been in the field for some time—in one case, for three-quarters of its service term. The 1st Maine was not outfitted with sabers until March 1862. The 3rd Indiana went without carbines until August 1862, the 8th New York until early 1863, and the 1st Vermont until early 1864, almost three years after breaking camp in Burlington. Most troopers, however, received their weapons during their first, home-state encampment—or at the latest, soon after arriving in Washington.[1]

The carbine was the cavalryman's principal armament, permitting him to make a stand against an enemy at short or medium range. Numerous models and brands of carbines were made available to the cavalry of the Army of the Potomac. All were breechloaders, able to be loaded through the rear of the barrel. This feature enabled the trooper to reload with some ease on horseback and more rapidly than a foot soldier could reload his rifle. The breechloading carbine was also lighter in weight and, with its shorter barrel, less unwieldy, permitting it to be fired from the saddle as well as from the ground. The trade-off was that the carbine had a shorter potential effective range—roughly 500 yards as compared with 900 yards for the English-made Enfield rifle, an arm used principally by Confederate troops but by many Union infantrymen as well.[2]

Breechloaders were of two types: repeating and single-shot. The best-known and most reliable repeating carbine, the seven-shot Spencer, did not come into general use until the autumn of 1863, although its rifle version had become available ten months earlier. A handful of regiments in the Army of the Potomac, including half of the "Wolverine Brigade," received the Spencer rifle in time for the Gettysburg campaign of that June and July. An earlier repeater, the Colt's revolving rifle, which made use of a six-shot cylinder and was reputed to be capable of hitting a target 400 yards away, was issued in late 1861 and early in 1862 to a few regiments, which reported much success with it. But the revolving rifle was expensive to produce and therefore in short supply. It also had operating drawbacks. It took longer to reload than a single-shot carbine, and critics claimed that when it was fired, more than one chamber was likely to go off, endangering the shooter; it would appear, however, that such a possibility was quite remote. Another potential hazard was the gas leakage that occurred during firing as well as the flash of burning powder visible at the juncture of the cylinder face and forcing cone. For these and other reasons, the revolving rifle declined sharply in popularity once magazine-loaded repeaters such as the Spencer came into use.[3]

The Spencer eventually gained a reputation as the most effective carbine of the war. Even the enemy is supposed to have paid tribute to this weapon, calling it "the rifle that can be loaded on Sunday and fired all week." Many Federals swore by its durability and prized its volume of fire, which paid especial dividends during encounters with infantry. This arm was most effective when used with the Blakeslee Quickloader, a case fitted with preloaded tubes of seven cartridges, fed into the butt stock during reloading. Quickloaders, however, saw limited use, most having been produced in the last months of the war.

The Spencer was heavier and more unwieldy than single-shot weapons, and the powder charge fixed to its specially made "56-56" cartridge (the bullet itself being only 52 caliber) was considered too light to ensure accuracy beyond 200 yards. Ironically, the greatest attribute of the Spencer was also its principal drawback. The speed with which it could be worked—nine to ten shots per minute compared with six or fewer of other firearms—proved a detriment to fire discipline. Too often a carbineer quickly expended the forty rounds he usually carried and had to quit a fight in midcourse. Proponents of the carbine nevertheless stressed its critical advantage, the ability to throw a lot of lead at the enemy. As Brig. Gen. James Harrison Wilson, in 1864 commander of the 3rd Cavalry Division, Army of the Potomac, put it, "that is what tells in a fight."[4]

A more effective repeater, but available only as a rifle, was the Henry, which did not make its appearance in large numbers until mid-1864. Basically an infantry weapon during the war, it saw its most extensive usage as a civilian arm in the postwar era. A few cavalry units, however, used the Henry with much success in 1864–65.

Repeaters facilitated firepower by extracting the spent cartridge and chambering the next round by means of a lever that was integral with the trigger guard and operated a movable breechblock or bolt. Initially, officials including Brig. Gen. James W. Ripley, the War Department's chief of ordnance, were prejudiced against repeaters, considering them profligate of ammunition. When the government finally sanctioned their purchase in quantity, it did so on the basis of the weapons' durability and power, not their rate of fire.[5]

The small arms that saw the most extensive service in the Army of the Potomac's cavalry were not repeaters but single-shot carbines, with the Sharps and the Burnside ranked first and second in numbers produced and used. Both were potentially accurate up to 400 yards or farther from the target, and both facilitated reloading. The Burnside's innovations included a metallic, paper-wrapped cartridge and an ejector that, upon firing, bumped the used casing into position for easy removal. Other models, such as the Ballard carbine, also had an ejector, but none worked as well as the Burnside's. The Sharps had no ejector but needed none; its paper and linen cartridge casing was totally consumed when the powder charge ignited. The cartridge that fit the less used but still reliable Starr carbine had this same feature but did not perform as effectively as the Sharps.[6]

The Sharps had another feature that incorporated the latest technology: a pellet primer contained in a magazine alongside the breech that spring-shot a wafer of priming compound into the breechblock during the firing process, thereby obviating use of a priming cap, as required by every other carbine. Thus the Sharps easily outperformed not only the Burnside and Smith, but every other carbine available to the Union cavalryman, including the Merrill, the Gallager, the Maynard, the Ballard, the Joslyn, the Gibbs, and the Cosmopolitan, also known as the Gwyn & Campbell.[7]

Most models of carbines did not reach the Army of the Potomac until mid- and late 1862. All carbines except the Sharps lacked manufacturing facilities capable of mass production. Then, too, gun manufacturers found that it took much time, even in the midst of war, to win War Department approval and gain enough contracts to make large-scale production feasible. Ammunition for various carbines was also in short supply during the war's first year and well into its second. Furthermore, demands by high-visibility sharpshooter units such as Hiram Berdan's two regiments kept the Sharps Manufacturing Company making rifles rather than carbines. The time the firm took in 1862 to manufacture 2,000 rifles for Berdan could have been used to produce more than 6,000 carbines for the cavalry.[8]

Thus, for many months after entering service, numerous regiments were armed with antiquated and even obsolete firearms such as the Hall carbine, which the 8th New York originally toted. A few regiments—mostly in the western theater, far from the principal sources of arms production—even went to war toting rifles or, worse, muskets, as did many of their Confederate counterparts. In almost every case, however, these regiments were more properly armed within a few weeks or months of entering service.

>—+◦→—◦—◦←+—◦

In addition to carbines, the average trooper in the Army of the Potomac carried one or two pistols. Those most often supplied to the cavalry were the Model 1860 Colt 44-caliber Army and the less popular 36-caliber Navy revolvers. Earlier models of both revolvers had been used with confidence since the Mexican War, and by 1861 Colt had become the preeminent weapons contractor to the army. The firm's reputation appeared to be justified by the preference soldiers gave its revolvers. Numerous troopers went on record as praising the Colt's superior handling and sighting capabilities.[9]

Other pistols furnished to the cavalry—all of them, like the Colt, loaded with combustible cartridges that contained ball and powder, ignited by percussion caps—included the Remington, which the army did not receive in quantity until 1864 but which by war's end was the dominant pistol in service, thanks to a fire which destroyed the factory of its main competitor, Colt. Like the Colt, the Remington was a single-action revolver, meaning that the user had to cock the hammer once to rotate the cylinder into firing position and a second time to fire. The 36-caliber Savage revolver, which General Stoneman favored for his cavalry in 1862 but which ended up going to relatively few regiments in the East, sought to speed the firing process by providing a cocking ring as well as a trigger, sparing the user from thumbing the hammer twice.[10]

The Starr revolver, introduced in 1862, was the first double-action handgun to see service in the eastern theater. Later-war issues, however, were for single-action revolvers only. Like the Savage, the Starr had deficiencies that, when fired, sometimes imperiled its user. Other, outdated pistols could also be difficult and dangerous to operate. At war's outset some regiments, such as the 3rd Indiana, were armed with a foot-long pistol reminiscent of the old dragoon model, probably Model 1836s or 1842s converted to percussion. As one Indianan related (doubtless with some hyperbole), when fired, the sidearm "kicked about as hard as it would shoot, and the man behind it was in more danger than the man in front."[11]

>—◇—◎—◇—<

The pistol might have been the weapon of choice for close-quarters fighting, but for the cavalry, the saber ranked close behind. Civil War swords were generally of two types. The straight-bladed Model 1840 "heavy" cavalry saber, copied from Prussian and French patterns, was known widely and justifiably as "the Wrist-breaker." Just before war broke out, a lighter, more easily wielded saber entered the army's inventory; it became prominent in the ranks by late 1863 or early 1864 despite the early use of inferior metal. Those furnished in 1861 to the 1st Vermont, for example, bent or broke with only moderate use. Later-war issues proved more durable, and their owners consequently placed growing confidence in their offensive and defensive capabilities.[12]

Over the past century and a quarter, historians have cast doubt on the Union cavalryman's faith in, and regular use of, his saber. According to this school of thought, few troopers called on their sabers in battle when a pistol was handy and loaded. This theory is open to question. Civil War cavalrymen and the tacticians who instructed them had been bred on the saber charge, that dramatic and memorable, if perhaps anachronistic, feature of the Mexican War and even of Indian fighting. George B. McClellan, the Europhile who exerted such a strong influence on the Army of the Potomac during its formative months, believed that "the strength of cavalry is in the spurs and sabre," and he filled his mounted ranks with like-minded officers.[13]

Saber exercise was a ritual of Union cavalry training, one to which drillmasters devoted much time and energy. The preponderance of European immigrants residing in the North in 1861–62 probably ensured that more Federals than Confederates were trained by Prussian, French, and English veterans. Looking to their own experience, these instructors would have favored the use of the saber in various tactical situations and would have inculcated that attitude in their students.

Even though they engaged in considerable swordplay, Union troopers were wont to downplay the use of edged weapons, which in some quarters carried a connotation as primitive, terror weapons. Many Southerners appear to have felt the same; as a whole, the Confederate cavalry in the East was said to lack confidence in the saber. In fact, in several encounters with their Union counterparts, Stuart's horsemen were heard to cry, "Put up your sabers and fight like gentlemen!"[14]

It would appear that many, perhaps most, Federals failed to comply. Neither arms manufacturers nor the troopers themselves may have kept their sabers razor-sharp, but grindstones were a mainstay of cavalry camps, and most troopers used them on a weekly basis. A typical comment on the subject comes from an officer in the 1st New England, who informed a friend in Rhode Island that "I turned [the] grindstone today while the old meat axe was sharpened up for service."[15]

Troopers not only honed their blades regularly, but they used them regularly. In almost every cavalry encounter for which a written record survives, references to the use of the saber abound, along with testimonials to its effectiveness—often in sharp contrast to that of the pistol, the reloading of which while in the saddle was a nigh impossible process. One influential postwar theorist, formerly an officer in the 6th New York, claimed that in every mounted engagement between 1862 and 1865 in which he took part, saber-wielding Federals routed pistol-carrying Confederates.[16]

Another bladed weapon received much publicity, if not much usage, in the cavalry of the Army of the Potomac. Displaying his European influences, in November 1861 McClellan suggested that a regiment of horsemen be armed with lances. When that regiment, the 6th Pennsylvania, went to war a month later, each of its enlisted men brandished a lance made of Norwegian fir, weighing 8 pounds, and composed of an 8 $\frac{1}{2}$-foot-long shaft, a 5$\frac{1}{2}$-inch-long butt, and a blade measuring nearly 11$\frac{1}{2}$ inches, with a scarlet pennant fastened near the tip of the shaft. Neither McClellan nor the commander of the 6th, Col. Richard H. Rush, seemed to realize that such an unwieldy weapon, no matter how fierce it might make its bearer appear, would prove unsuitable for warfare in America, where the lack of cleared ground would prevent the extended charge necessary for lancer tactics.[17]

Those who carried the weapon found it an awkward burden and of doubtful utility. "The officers like it," one Lancer informed the readers of the *Army and Navy Journal,* "but the men do not, and the officers wouldn't if they had to use them." The method of employing such a weapon baffled many civilians; members of the regiment had to deny rumors that they tossed the lances through the air like spears, attempting to impale their enemy.[18]

Most of those who carried the lance never expected to use it in battle. A detachment of the 6th Pennsylvania did conduct a lance attack at one point in the Peninsula Campaign of spring 1862 but achieved nothing decisive. Increasingly, the arms became the butt of jokes throughout the army and a source of embarrassment to "Rush's Lancers." Even General Stoneman, during an inspection of the regiment, referred to its arms as "those damned poles." By May 1863 the lances were retired as being of little tactical use and replaced by carbines, although at first each company received only twelve of these "for picket and scouting duty." The experiment with the weapon of antiquity was over, but it took months before the entire regiment was equipped with firearms.[19]

Carbineers and even lancers toted about a variety of other equipment, much of it of dubious value. The typical horseman carried a square of canvas that, added to those owned by his tentmates, would form a shelter tent. Slung over his saddle were a blanket, an overcoat, extra shirts and socks, and perhaps drawers as well. Kitchen utensils, including a skillet, cup, knife, fork, and spoon, hung from the saddle skirt. Many riders discarded most of their kitchen gear in order to save weight, keeping only a tin cup and perhaps a spoon. In his saddlebags, the horseman carried a haversack filled with three to five days' prepared rations. Attached to the belt around his waist were a canteen, cartridge box, cap box, sword, and pistol. A carbine, usually positioned just in front of the right knee, hung from a saddle ring.

The saddlebags also accommodated horse-grooming articles: currycomb, brush, hoof pick, and often a lariat rope and lariat pin. The last two items, according to a member of the 11th Pennsylvania, seemed "all right, perhaps, out on the Western plains, but rather out of place in a Cavalry regiment." In addition to this paraphernalia, the rider lugged his horse's forage, nosebag, and extra tack, plus his own "odds and ends of luxuries, which the recruit is wont to stow away surreptitiously." The accumulated baggage seemed to take up every square inch of the horse's back. The historians of the 1st Massachusetts claimed that "the most difficult thing a recruit had to do when ready for the march was to get in and out of the saddle, and a derrick, sometimes, would not have been a bad thing."[20]

It should have been obvious that the more the horse had to carry, the more it suffered. Many troopers loaded fifty pounds or more onto their mounts, in addition to the rider's own weight. Not surprisingly, by late 1861 sore backs had become epidemic among the horses of the Army of the Potomac. Heavy loads could sometimes have other effects on the animals that carried them. A captain in the 10th New York observed that during his regiment's first long march, many recruits buried their mounts beneath pounds and pounds of superfluous equipment. The rattling and clanking that resulted so unnerved the horses that they bucked, reared, swerved from side to side, and disarranged the entire marching column.[21]

>–⊹⊶⊙⊷⊹–◅

Before he placed himself, by whatever means, in the saddle, a trooper had to become acquainted with the animal beneath. Since so few recruits had an equestrian background, this often proved the most frightening experience of the cavalryman's life in camp. At the outset of the war, however, that experience was deferred for many enlistees. The postponement was inevitable; although the typical Southern trooper furnished his own mount, Union cavalrymen were supplied with horses by a government procurement and distribution system that for several months after its establishment remained unproductive and inefficient.

The problem was not a shortage of horseflesh. In 1860 the horse population of the United States was the world's largest. Furthermore, the majority of these animals—according to the 1860 census, a grand total of 4,504,852—were concentrated in the states and territories that remained in the Union. Nor did the North want for forage; by 1861 hay had become enough of a money crop that it was grown extensively throughout the North. In that year, three-fourths to four-fifths of the cultivated land in New England and northern New York grew hay. By mid-1861, however, the War Department owned such a small percentage of available horses and so little forage that a major supply system had to be established and made to function smoothly in as short a time as possible.[22]

Late in 1861 a network of depots and corrals was set up in many corners of the Union. There officers and civilian employees inspected and purchased horses, in lots large and small, from brokers, farmers, and private citizens, and arranged their shipment to every war zone. After the fall of 1863 the U.S. Cavalry Bureau, a War Department office that focused special attention on the mounted arm, oversaw this prodigious operation, one of the most complex and difficult logistical undertakings up to that time.[23]

The government's efforts proved successful enough that during the first two years of the conflict, 284,000 cavalry mounts were furnished to approximately 60,000 troopers in all theaters of operations. Yet the supply system took months to gear up and overcome its growing pains. In the war's early period, a host of dishonest contractors, sometimes in collusion with inspectors and purchasing agents, foisted on the army horses well under or far over the six-year age standard, below the desired height of fifteen hands, and under the minimum weight of 950 pounds. In one lot of 400 horses sold to the quartermaster at St. Louis in late 1861 for more than the going price of $150 a head (this later fluctuated between $161 and $185), five animals were found dead hours after the army took custody, and three hundred others proved to be undersize, under- or overage, blind, or ill.[24]

It was not only contractors who defrauded the government's purchasing agents. In late September 1861 the commander of the quartermaster depot at Washington, the main supply hub of the Army of the Potomac, discharged every horse inspector on the payroll; each had been found guilty of extorting bribes from contractors. As a veteran of the 1st New York observed in 1864, "in no other branch of the service has there been so much fraud, so much corruption, so much utter worthlessness."[25]

Those regiments fortunate enough to be mounted in late 1861 soon faced new problems. A majority of government-purchased horses were shipped from the West in carload lots; few of them had been broken for riding. Moreover, many of the new arrivals were found to be suffering from or susceptible to a variety of equine diseases such as glanders, spavins, grease-heel, tetter (or "hoof-rot"), and a form of heart disease known as "the thumps." Few regiments had veterinary surgeons. Semitrained farriers and blacksmiths substituted for the missing horse doctors, rarely with happy results. Nor could the army fill the void, for it maintained neither a veterinary board nor a single equine hospital.[26]

Mounts found to be sound of limb still had to be broken for service, especially if they had just come from the cart or plow. This proved an ordeal for boys unused to horses. Many who tried to mount, quickly found themselves on their backs on the ground. They would have to summon enough courage for a second attempt, an especially frightening prospect if the horse, like one young Regular's, kicked its heels "in such a lively way that one had to beat a hasty retreat . . . and then, made angry by this mishap, [the horse] would reach around and nip with strong fore teeth, some individual close at hand, who was stooping over in a state of blissful ignorance as to the fate that lay in store for him." Those recruits who avoided being bitten often got kicked. The surgeon of the 8th Illinois recalled that during the early months of his regiment's service, dozens of men suffered kicks to their legs, "frequently laying bare the bone."[27]

Recruits thus injured could develop a permanent dread of their mounts. An experienced rider in the 3rd Pennsylvania recalled of the urban-born recruits in his outfit: "Many of them showed much more fear of their horses than they ever did afterward of the enemy. The wild fumbling after mane or saddle-straps, the terror depicted on some faces . . . are a lasting source of amusement." In contrast, the youngsters of the 1st Pennsylvania, who hailed not from the streets of Philadelphia but from the farms outside the city, showed little fear of their mounts and quickly proved themselves "at least good, if not properly trained riders."[28]

By trial and error, outfits learned horse-taming techniques. One of the most effective methods, practiced by the Harris Light Cavalry, among others, was to run the most fractious animals up a steep hill again and again, to the accompaniment of kicks from spurred boots, until "the evil has been sweated out of them." Other recalcitrant mounts were eventually tamed by curb bits that cut into the soft tissue of the mouth when they moved abruptly or otherwise acted up. At first, however, those bits produced "a most rebellious temper, causing many of them to rear up in the air as though they had suddenly been transformed into monstrous kangaroos."[29]

When first introduced, a trooper and his mount usually eyed each other warily, with suspicion and distrust. But once horse and rider had trained together long enough to become a team, they might come to regard each other with respect and even affection. Men remarked about the finely tuned instincts of their animals and sometimes attributed to them human characteristics. A veteran of the 1st District of Columbia, whose regiment never served in the Army of the Potomac, nevertheless expressed the feelings of horse lovers in every fighting force when he recalled that over time, "horse and rider grew to know each other's needs and to strengthen each other's work. The pricking of his ears was a sure sign of sound or alarm, and he never failed to hear the clink of the sabre of the coming relief before his rider." This man added that throughout the war, "I never knew a man trampled upon by his horse, and why? There is a higher instinct, a sense of danger and of sympathy for friends, in the lower animals than we understand. The nobility and fine instinct of the horse, his sensing of danger by sound, smell, and even touch, is marvellous."[30]

But not all cavalrymen came to regard their mounts as friends or cared for them as a friend would. Many resented the feeling that, as Charles Adams put it, "you are a slave to your horses." Given most troopers' unfamiliarity with the needs of horses, during the first winter of the war the army's animals were, on the whole, poorly treated. Especially in regiments run by inexperienced or lax officers, horses went unattended and were rarely exercised or groomed. Some outfits stationed around Washington did not bother to erect stables, leaving their mounts vulnerable to rain, wind, snow, and freezing temperatures. Others threw together shelters that collapsed in the first wind, leaving the horses adrift in mud and slush, then complained when disease began to ravage the animals.

The Regulars were stricter in their care of mounts, ensuring that they received food and water before their riders did, were properly stabled or otherwise shielded from the elements, were groomed at least one hour daily, and were carefully inspected for illnesses. Some volunteer regiments also exhibited a strong interest in the welfare of their animals—notably the 3rd Indiana, the only Union cavalry in the East to furnish its own horses throughout the war—but diligent care was the exception, not the rule. When newly commissioned Lt. Walter Raleigh Robbins joined the 1st New Jersey, he was appalled by the lack of consideration given the regiment's horses. When the men of his company did a particularly shoddy job of grooming, he called them to order and had them repeat the chore, slowly and carefully. To potential protesters he explained, "It is my duty not only to look after your welfare, but that of the horses." The men "looked surprised, but were not sullen, and there were no murmurs audible." Thereafter, Robbins's unit devoted noticeably more attention to their mounts. Other companies followed suit, and the change soon improved the fighting condition of the entire regiment.[31]

Lieutenant Robbins and the few other humane officers notwithstanding, during the winter of 1861–62 the Army of the Potomac as a whole treated its horses with contempt, if not downright cruelty. The situation only worsened after regiments left training camp for the field of action. Too many troopers saw their mounts as expendable commodities, to be replaced, as soon as ill or worn out by service, by the North's increasingly efficient remount process.

A few soldiers, shocked by the wide-scale neglect and abuse of horses, decried the government's policy of working a mount to death and then discarding it. In October 1863 Alonzo D. Still, a semiliterate member of the 2nd Massachusetts, wrote from Washington to inform President Lincoln that "the horse is of all anamels the most useful and at the same time the moste abused of any." Trooper Still, whose regiment joined the Army of the Potomac later in the war, was concerned that too often "the noble anamel" went without forage, was improperly shod if at all, suffered abuse at the hands of troopers and teamsters, and was left to die without so much as a word of thanks for its faithful service. Through such treatment, "hundreds of horses are ruined and distroyed every week."[32]

A more polished assessment of the army horse's plight was furnished earlier the same year by Captain Adams of the 1st Massachusetts in a letter to his family:

> The horse is, in active campaign, saddled on an average about fifteen hours out of the twenty four. His feed is nominally ten pounds of grain a day and, in reality, he averages about eight pounds. He has no hay and only such other feed as he can pick up during halts. The usual water he drinks is brook water, so muddy by the passage of the column as to be of the color of chocolate. Of course, sore backs are our greatest trouble. Backs soon get feverish under the saddle and the first day's march swells them; after that day by day the trouble grows. No care can stop it. . . . Imagine a horse with his withers swollen to three times the natural size, and with a volcanic, running sore pouring matter down each side, and you have a case with which every cavalry officer is daily called upon to deal, and you imagine a horse which has still to be ridden until he lays down in sheer suffering under the saddle. Then we seize the first horse we come to and put the dismounted man on his back. . . . Poor brutes! How it would astonish and terrify you and all others at home with your sleek, well-fed animals, to see the weak, gaunt, rough animals, with each rib visible and the hip-bones starting through the flesh. . . . It would knock the romance out of you.[33]

Once the trooper was able to stay on his horse long enough to entertain the hope, however faint, that he might accomplish something of military value, he led his mount to the field of instruction. There man and beast came face-to-face with the exacting requirements and contorted evolutions of cavalry drill.

Because few recruits had riding experience, the lessons they had to absorb came especially hard and fast. It did not help that the movements and formations required of the arm were so many and so complex. "Cavalry tactics are ten-times more difficult to learn than those of the infantry," wrote a New York recruit who, although he lacked the infantry experience to support his contention, spoke the truth. Looking back after the war, an officer in the 5th Michigan observed that callow troopers had to endure "a long course of drill training, both mounted and dismounted; and if any one imagines that even a hard and thorough course of drill training entirely fits a trooper for active campaign service, he will find himself much mistaken."[34]

At the outset, even basic instruction was difficult to digest. A typical recruit found that staying in the saddle during maneuvers was sometimes a Herculean task. "The first mounted drills," wrote a Pennsylvanian, "were a mixture of comedy and tragedy. . . . There was kicking and rearing, running and jumping, lying down and falling down on the part of the horses. . . . There was crowding in the ranks, and striving to get back into place, pushing forward and hanging back, going backwards and sideways, and all sorts of ways except the right way."[35]

Such chaos could sometimes be blamed on untrained horses, which were spooked by any sight or sound out of the ordinary, including the collective rasp of metal. "When we draw sabres," an 8th Illinois trooper noted, "the horses run away and the Col. swears harder than ever." The 11th Pennsylvania had a similar experience; when the men unsheathed their "meat axes" for the first time in unison, their animals "went forward, and some backward in utter confusion." The regiment's commander "had to flee for his life."[36]

Such a performance, regardless of where the fault lay, could arouse the ire of a drillmaster, many of whom were quick to anger and just as quick to chastise. Some reacted only verbally. "Oh, stupid! stupid!" one Michigan instructor wailed whenever his students wheeled the wrong way. "Even an ox may be taught to know right from left, but ye will never learn!" A few instructors inflicted physical punishment, using a whip, meant for ornery horses, on their clumsy riders. One lieutenant in the 7th Michigan kept a collection of rocks in his pocket, one of which he hurled at every trooper who broke formation, adding for good measure "a volley of blood-curdling oaths." At least one instructor took out his disgust and frustration on himself. Col. Jonas P. Holliday, an old Regular who preceded Charles Tompkins as commander of the 1st Vermont, became so distraught over his recruits' inability to master the simplest of maneuvers that he walked off by himself, unholstered his Colt .44 and blew his brains out.[37]

The first maneuvers required of man and horse were fairly basic ones. In the camp of the 1st Michigan, a veteran recalled, "a pole was placed on two crotches and we practiced our horses at leaping the pole. Some would make a good leap to the height of five feet but few would take the six foot pole," especially since at that time the 1st lacked saddles, its men being forced to ride bareback. This jumping exercise, however, was not without incident. A Pennsylvania captain reported the result when some riders reached the bar: "As the horses are all green . . . some [men] fell, the horses rolling over them. . . . Other[s] were thrown onto the necks of horses, &c."[38]

When the recruits were required to perform maneuvers more intricate than clearing a bar or crossing a drill field—especially when forced to practice the lesson over and over again—displeasure could spread through the ranks. A veteran of the 3rd Pennsylvania recalled: "Our drills, mounted and dismounted, were incessant. Mutterings of dissatisfaction because of these were loud and unceasing. We could not then understand why we should be compelled to jump our horses over ditches and fences, especially so if we were awkward, and both riders and horses together fell into the ditches instead of jumping over them. Nor could we see the necessity of our being required to mount with stirrups crossed, nor why we should ride in a circle, and cut bags off poles with quick strokes of the sabre. These exercises were irksome, and were not relished by the officers any more than by the men." And yet such lessons, as disagreeable as forced repetition made them, helped the trooper polish his skills, improve his self-image, and look to the future with growing confidence.[39]

Sometimes the men did poorly at drill because those assigned to instruct them were just as inexperienced or inept. It was not unusual for officers fresh from civilian life to keep barely a lesson or two ahead of the men in tactical instruction. But no officer wished to demonstrate his ignorance in front of his unit. Just before Christmas 1862 a Pennsylvania captain informed a friend of something "which made me very happy to-day. . . . I drilled my company for the first time alone, and did not make a single mistake."[40]

Many officers who had received their commissions through political connections had no inkling of how to drill their troopers and could not or would not learn. A captain in the 6th Pennsylvania so frequently erred in maneuvering his company that he drew guffaws and catcalls whenever he rode through camp; his ability to lead having been destroyed, he was forced to resign his commission.

Some instructors possessed ability but lacked knowledge. One such officer, a captain in the 1st Maine, had no experience as a cavalryman but much as a seaman. When one of his men broke formation during drill, the officer bellowed, "What in hell are you falling astern for?" The culprit, also a seafarer, replied in a voice just as loud, "I can't get the damn thing in stays!" Replied the captain with impeccable logic, "Well, give her more headway, then!" Even experienced instructors were sometimes guilty of lapses in judgment or attention. A sergeant instructing a platoon of the 10th New York in trotting and galloping became distracted just long enough for several troopers and horses to tumble into a canal basin along the edge of their camp. Had the basin's water not been shallow, men or mounts might have drowned.[41]

Some would-be tacticians were so inept as to be beyond hope of improvement; still, they would not admit their incapacity. One such officer was Col. Robert B. Lawton of the 1st New England, who made so many ludicrous mistakes while drilling his regiment that several of his subordinates signed a petition seeking his resignation and threatening to submit their own if he refused to go. As one of their number put it, "Col. Lawton is a God damned fussy old pisspot utterly incompetent for the position he holds. . . . Things may come out all straight . . . but that damned Col will be hung I fear like a mill stone about our necks." Eventually the colonel, realizing that he had lost the confidence of his officers, left the service.[42]

Drill could be a frightening experience, especially when a leader like Robert Lawton was in charge. A jaunt through the countryside abroad green mounts could be even more terrifying, but also oddly exhilarating. A young officer in the 5th New York reported that his company's instructor "drilled us in the [riding] school about 5 minutes and then says he you can never learn to ride by riding around here. Form fours, march, trot, gallop and away he took us across the country through mud up to the horses knees across fields full of stumps. O I tell you it is fun but sure death if you fall off. That is the way we drill, dead gallop for about $1^{1}/_{2}$ miles."[43]

One would think that a mainstay of drill would have been practice in the mounted charge, given the storied history of that maneuver, the intricacies of which every trooper would have mastered even if he neglected every other tactic. In reality, by 1861 the charge was already a lost art; few outfits attempted it in training camp, and those that did were chagrined by the results. In an oft-repeated passage, a veteran of the 1st New York Dragoons (also known as the 19th New York Cavalry) described how difficult it was for his regiment, "one of the best drilled and most efficient bodies of mounted men in the service," to maintain even a modicum of cohesion at the extended gallop: "At our best, to have turned us off the road (taking the going as it came), and set us across country at any such a gait as is understood by a cavalry charge, and out of our whole ten troops there would not have been so much as a corporal's guard left at the end of six hundred yards."[44]

>-I-◆>-O-◆-I-◄

Nevertheless, despite the lack of cohesion, poise, and professionalism that characterized the volunteers of Lincoln's Army through their first several months in service, time, training, experience, and trial and error served to cure most woes and banish most vices. By mid-1862 most of the regiments in the Army of the Potomac were much improved not only at drill, but also in the myriad functions and duties of mounted service. They had learned from, and risen above, their early mistakes. Their horses had begun to respond to the nuances of their riders' body language, to intuited wants as well as to spoken commands. And many of the incompetent officers who had held back their regiments' progress were gone, having been persuaded to resign, dismissed from the service, or weeded out by the officers' examining boards that sprang up throughout the army in late 1861 and early 1862. The result was a cavalry force increasingly confident of its abilities and ready—even eager—to meet in battle the vaunted cavaliers of J. E. B. Stuart.

Chapter Five

False Start

Although pundits had already christened it "Mr. Lincoln's Army," General McClellan came to regard the Army of the Potomac as his personal possession. He frequented its camps around Washington, seeing and being seen throughout the ranks. Sometimes he galloped through on a coal black charger, with staff officers, orderlies, and escort troops trailing behind. Despite his slight stature, he looked the part of the great warrior: ramrod straight, immaculately groomed, handsomely tailored, lavishly accoutered. He took every opportunity to converse with officers and men, addressing them on the parade ground, during inspections, and sometimes in private sessions. His evident interest in the army and his desire to improve its well-being paid dividends. In time McClellan won the respect of virtually everyone under him and the affection of many, perhaps most.

The bond that linked McClellan and his troops entrapped the army leader. He took such pride in his command, and invested so much time and care in its training, arming, and equipping, that he could not bear to think of sacrificing it in battle. Thus, for eight months after the disaster at Bull Run, the main army remained in camp, where it continued to drill as if repetition ensured perfection. Perhaps, thought some observers, McClellan believed that displays of energy and dedication would persuade the Rebels to lay down their arms.[1]

Never privy to his general's aspirations or, for that matter, his intentions, President Lincoln began to wonder if Little Mac would ever nerve himself to leave the capital's defenses. McClellan did not even stir himself to oppose the batteries that Joe Johnston had placed on the lower Potomac. To the chagrin of Lincoln and other government officials, those lightly manned guns had imposed a partial shipping blockade on Washington.[2]

To be fair, McClellan never locked the entire army inside the capital's fortifications. While his main body drilled under the summer sun and in the autumn chill, scattered segments of the army, mainly outposts, made intermittent contact with the enemy. Most of these outposts were manned by infantry, but mounted pickets also patrolled the no-man's land between the armies. In almost every instance these "videttes" were fragments of regiments—companies, squadrons, and battalions that, having been declared combat-ready, had taken the field in advance of the rest of their outfits, which remained encamped in or just outside the Capital.

A few camp-bound troopers had yet to reach Washington. At least two regiments, mounted and equipped but not yet ready for active service, had been sent to train near the cavalry depot at Carlisle Barracks, whose drillmasters assisted in their instruction. Other outfits were dispatched to railheads well north of Washington. Shortly before Christmas 1861, the 6th New York (the 2nd Ira Harris Guard) entrained for York, Pennsylvania. At about the same time, the 10th New York pitched camp twenty miles to the east, in a county seat named Gettysburg. Both regiments spent months far from the seat of war; even so, they took casualties. Two days before the year ended, Trooper John W. Congdon of the 10th, who had died from a fall while riding atop a troop train, became the first of many thousands of Federal soldiers to be interred in a Gettysburg cemetery.[3]

The first volunteer cavalry to embark on active campaigning in regimental strength, twelve companies strong in contrast to the prevailing ten-company standard, was the 3rd Pennsylvania, also known as Young's Kentucky Light Cavalry after its organizer, Col. William H. Young, a native Kentuckian. Under Young's recently appointed successor, William Averell, the 3rd Pennsylvania proudly took the field on September 11, 1861. It beat into service even the 1st New York, which, despite a head start on recruiting, did not begin operating at full strength until mid-November.[4]

By the time the 3rd Pennsylvania started campaigning, however, the 1st New York had already achieved a distinction in the field. On August 18, one company of the "Lincoln Cavalry," under Capt. William H. Boyd, became the first volunteer horsemen to smite the foe with a saber charge. The target was a body of Confederate horsemen loitering near Pohick Church, a dozen miles southwest of Alexandria. When Boyd reconnoitered the church grounds (site of George Washington's 1759 wedding), he discovered that most of the enemy had fled. At once he attacked the few that remained, who fired upon his unit with musket balls, conferring on Pvt. Jacob Erwen the unenviable title of first volunteer cavalryman to die in action. The regiment gained another unwanted honor six months later, when one of its subalterns was shot dead while charging Rebel pickets near Sangster's Station, Virginia. Lt. Henry B. Hidden became the first officer of Union volunteer cavalry killed in action.

The 1st New York had no monopoly on casualties. A second enlisted man fell eight days after Trooper Erwen: Peter Brennan of Colonel Averell's regiment was killed while helping escort an infantry force on patrol near Munson's Hill. Just as Erwen's death had shocked the men of his regiment, the death of

Trooper Brennan brought his comrades in the 3rd Pennsylvania, as one of them noted, "face to face with the stern realities of war."[5]

>⊶⊷⊙⊷⊶<

Although he seemed to have a difficult time deciding when and where to move against the Rebels, McClellan had clear and definite ideas of the size and shape his mounted arm should assume. As early as August 2, 1861, he sent a memorandum to President Lincoln calling for a mounted force of twenty-eight regiments—by his count, 25,500 officers and men. The proposal was highly ambitious; at the time he wrote, his army included fewer than 3,000 trained, armed, and equipped troopers. Furthermore, Little Mac's arithmetic was suspect; twenty-eight twelve-company regiments should have provided nearly 33,600 men.[6]

McClellan did not share the belief of General Scott, whom he succeeded as general in chief on November 1, that volunteer cavalry was too expensive to maintain in force equal to the needs of a field army. Military theorists of the time believed that cavalry should make up ten to fourteen percent of an army's total strength. Given the steady influx of newly organized regiments, the Army of the Potomac should have consisted of more than 100,000 soldiers when it began active operations. Thus McClellan's calculations would result in a mounted force equal to one-quarter of his army. As it turned out, his cavalry never approached such proportions. At no point in McClellan's initial field campaign on the Virginia Peninsula (March–August 1862) were more than 6,000 troopers available to him.[7]

If the commanding general was a poor arithmetician, he knew whom he wanted to lead his horsemen. In mid-August he announced newly promoted Brig. Gen. George Stoneman as chief of cavalry. The choice appeared a logical one. Stoneman, a thirty-nine-year-old New Yorker, had been an officer of dragoons and later of cavalry after graduating from West Point in 1846. He had gained national attention when, stationed in Texas as a captain in the 2nd Cavalry, he refused to be included among the forces that General Twiggs surrendered to state authorities. After escorting his company inside Union lines, Stoneman had commanded the cavalry school at Carlisle Barracks, a plum assignment. Later, as a major, he had been a faithful member of McClellan's staff during the western Virginia campaign. Along with a few other trusted aides, he had accompanied his superior east following Bull Run.[8]

Few soldiers knew more about the tactics of his arm, or could more effectively inculcate them into raw recruits, than Stoneman. A conservative, careful, sometimes plodding soldier, he could be a stickler about drill and deportment but was unfailingly considerate of his men and their animals. An enlisted man in the 8th Illinois called him, with a touch of pride, "a very strict disciplinarian." Captain Adams of the 1st Massachusetts declared: "Stoneman we believe

in. We believe in his judgment, his courage and determination. We know he is
ready to shoulder responsibility, that he will take good care of us and won't get
us into places from which he can't get us out."[9]

Stoneman's ability to withstand hard campaigning was a matter of some
concern within McClellan's military circle. The new brigadier suffered greatly
from what one surgeon euphemistically termed "polypal tumors of the rectal
area." Hemorrhoids had plagued him for at least eight years; before the war he
had submitted to a surgical procedure that appeared to have aggravated rather
than ameliorated his condition. Whenever it flared up, he was unable to remain
in the saddle for extended periods.

This drawback, however, did not greatly concern his superior. Like many
"old army" veterans, McClellan considered Stoneman's greatest qualification
to be his organizational and administrative talent. In truth, Little Mac regarded
him as a staff officer rather than a combat leader. He made an unambiguous
statement on Stoneman's status, as well as that of the army's artillery commander, Brig. Gen. William F. Barry, when, late in March 1862, he decreed
that "the duties of the chiefs of artillery and cavalry are exclusively administrative. . . . They will not exercise command of the troops of their units unless
specially ordered by the commanding general, but they will, when practicable,
be selected to communicate the orders of the general to their respective corps."
Despite its wording, this decree rarely prevented Stoneman and Barry from
exercising command of field forces as they saw fit. It was more in the order of
a reminder that they were, in effect, staff officers to the commanding general
and thus should be highly responsive to his desires.[10]

When Stoneman assumed command, the army had few mounted units.
Nor could it boast many cavalry officers whose qualifications recommended
them for any post above regimental command. Rather than grouping regiments
into brigades and creating additional general officers, McClellan opted to
break the cavalry into small detachments assigned to the army's brigades and
divisions (the army was not yet divided into corps when Stoneman took over).
This practice, which endured to some degree for the next seventeen months,
ensured that the cavalry would be used, as McClellan desired, in close cooperation with the main army. Yet it also prevented the arm from serving as a large,
cohesive body; it denied its soldiers a strategic role in combat; and it ensured
that their destiny would be controlled by infantry officers ignorant of their mission, requirements, and tactical value.

The first recorded assignment of cavalry to the components of the army
predated Stoneman's appointment by almost two weeks. The order that brought
this about linked the four infantry brigades that made up McClellan's "Division
of the Potomac" with four cavalry companies, three of Regulars and one of volunteers. On August 4 McClellan attached Company G of the 2nd United States
Cavalry to the brigade of Brig. Gen. Philip Kearny; Company H of the 2nd Cavalry to Brig. Gen. William Farrar ("Baldy") Smith's brigade; Company I of the
same regiment to the brigade of Brig. Gen. William Tecumseh Sherman, who

had fought as a colonel of Regulars at Bull Run and was about to be transferred to the western theater; and Captain Boyd's company of the 1st New
York to Brig. Gen. William B. Franklin's brigade.[11]

As regiments such as the 3rd Pennsylvania entered the field, the cavalry
reorganized to accommodate them. By mid-October McClellan had carved out
a brigade that answered directly to Stoneman; it consisted of one Regular regiment, two regiments of volunteers, and two volunteer companies. Additionally, nine regiments of volunteers and part of a tenth were attached to the
various divisions of the army, while two companies of Regulars were assigned
to the Washington-based City Guard of Andrew Porter. A few months later
McClellan relieved some of these troopers from the burden of supporting
infantry. Stoneman then grouped them into an independent brigade commanded by the ranking horseman at Bull Run, Innis Palmer, now also a
brigadier general of volunteers. When these regiments were returned to the
control of infantry generals early in 1862, the versatile Palmer transferred to
the infantry as well.[12]

Stoneman was anxious to give his embryonic command the support and
leadership it deserved. He painstakingly inspected its camps, outposts, and
picket lines. He ensured that rations were plentiful, if not especially nutritious,
and that medical facilities were up to Army standards, such as they were. He
strove to correct deficiencies in arms, ammunition, and equipment, including a
shortage of saber belts, cartridge boxes, and saddles. He scrutinized the behavior of regimental commanders, disciplining those he considered inefficient or
unmilitary. He came down especially hard on officers who neglected their
duties while enlisted men languished and regimental morale plummeted. One
target of Stoneman's wrath had gone on furlough while leaving his troopers
"poorly cared for, badly instructed, and a good deal dissatisfied." Stoneman
saw to it that the mistake was not repeated.[13]

Many officers wanted to do their duty but did not know how. In mid-September Stoneman bewailed the "almost total want of knowledge on the part of
both officers and men, of what constitutes a cavalry soldier." He urged McClellan to assign a competent instructor, one with substantial experience, to each
volunteer regiment. He also recommended that the War Department establish
review boards to weed out unfit officers and that it lift the ban on Regular officers transferring to volunteer regiments, where their leadership and instruction
were sorely needed.[14]

Stoneman viewed with disdain, if not outright contempt, those politically
connected, militarily inept officers he found everywhere he looked. The power
that governors conferred on those who organized regiments wrought havoc
with the brigadier's plan to instill discipline and order throughout the ranks.
But slowly the situation improved. Stoneman's emphasis on discipline and rig-
orous drill resulted in the resignation or discharge of many men who had no
business in the army—some of whom had leaves or eagles on their shoulders.
Although inept colonels such as Van Alen and Lawton stayed on, Col. William

Halsted of the 1st New Jersey submitted his resignation that winter, as did Col. Max Friedman of the 5th Pennsylvania. Other less-than-competent regimental leaders exited the army later in the year or in 1862, including Lawton, Christian F. Dickel of the 4th New York, Samuel J. Crooks of the 8th New York, and James T. Lemmon of the 10th New York.[15]

The housecleaning, combined with Stoneman's emphasis on instruction and discipline, yielded benefits. Before October ended General Palmer was reporting from his headquarters at Ball's Crossroads, Virginia, that his troops, though still green, were progressing at drill and that the command as a whole was displaying signs of efficiency. But while some men began to act like soldiers, others began to look like felons. A week after Palmer praised his men, Stoneman scolded Col. David Campbell, whose 4th Pennsylvania had looted citizens' homes near Alexandria.[16]

It is uncertain whether Stoneman's admonition against looting had an effect, for the mobility their mounts provided cavalrymen made plunder not only possible but simple. Moreover, in every Union regiment there were dozens of men who considered it acceptable, even patriotic, to confiscate secessionists' crops, horses, and valuables and burn or vandalize what they could not carry off. Some officers condoned the practice; a few promoted it. The sergeant major of the 6th New York informed his family that his commander "has given a few of us permission to forage all we liked if we did not say anything to him about it. . . . Since then we have lived high, go out in the morning, come back about noon with Green peas—Radishes—Salad—Asparagus—Hams—Chickens—Ducks—Milk and in fact everything that farmers raise."[17]

A few commanders not only permitted stealing but joined in it. In the fall of 1861 Lt. Col. H. Judson Kilpatrick of the 2nd New York, an opportunistic officer with a rather unsavory reputation, encouraged his troopers to loot and burn as they wished. Kilpatrick himself stood accused of confiscating horses from pro-Confederate Virginians and, instead of turning them over to the quartermaster, selling them for profit to government brokers and even to his own enlisted men. Kilpatrick's little scheme, if indeed it was such, must have taken place behind the back of his superior, for Col. J. Mansfield Davies was, by all accounts, a model of rectitude. Thus it is not surprising that the lieutenant colonel figured in a little anecdote, circa 1862. Supposedly a Virginia farmer complained to Kilpatrick that freebooters from the 2nd New York had cleaned him out: "Everything that I have they have taken, everything except my hope in the hereafter, but that they can't take." A nonchalant Kilpatrick is said to have replied: "Don't be too sure, the Tenth New York is coming right behind you."[18]

>−·+>−·O−·<+·−·<

Fully trained or not, well or poorly disciplined, the army had to move before spring came in; if it did not, the Union effort in the East would be seen as a sham. As January 1862 neared an end with no sign of an impending movement, and with a mildly ill McClellan inaccessible to his civilian superiors, Lincoln decided that he must act. The only plan of campaign McClellan had broached to him, a vague and open-ended one at that, called for the army to be transported down the Chesapeake Bay and up the Rappahannock River to Urbanna, a nondescript hamlet on the northern shore of Virginia's Middle Peninsula. From Urbanna, McClellan could cross the York River to the lower Peninsula, thus turning Johnston's Manassas-Centreville line and rendering useless his batteries on the Potomac. Once on the Peninsula, the army could march on Richmond, fifty miles to the north, via the city's unguarded rear.[19]

Because the plan would take a long time to execute, Lincoln and his closest advisors, including Secretary of War Edwin McMasters Stanton, Cameron's successor, doubted it would achieve the element of surprise McClellan claimed for its greatest asset. Thus, late in January, Lincoln roused the fever-stricken McClellan from his sickbed and ordered him to implement a plan devised by the president himself. Lincoln's strategy involved a turning movement, not by the Chesapeake but via the Occoquan River, only two days' march from the Washington defenses.[20]

Little Mac saw the plan as badly flawed, although its primary defect appears to be that it had originated with someone other than him. A now-healthy McClellan, at Lincoln's urging, convened a council of war on March 7 at army headquarters in Washington, at which twelve of his subordinates voted the two plans up or down. The general in chief desired a unanimous endorsement of the Urbanna movement, but the three senior attendees, McDowell, Edwin V. Sumner, and Samuel P. Heintzelman (each of whom became, the following day, corps commanders in the army), opposed any move so far afield of Washington and so logistically complicated and strategically risky. So too did the army's chief engineer, Brig. Gen. John G. Barnard, whose professional opinion ought to have carried weight.

The others in attendance—Fitz John Porter (the former adjutant general of Patterson's Department of Pennsylvania), Louis Blenker, William B. Franklin, Erasmus D. Keyes, George A. McCall, Henry M. Naglee, Andrew Porter, and Baldy Smith—supported the strategy of the general who had secured their appointments. The majority having ruled, Lincoln was presented with a plan he had not favored. He consoled himself that at least the army had a blueprint for action—one it should carry out within the next few weeks.[21]

But it was not to be. For weeks after the conference, McClellan continued to tarry, not only because the Urbanna plan presented risks, but also because he feared the enemy he would encounter in acting upon it. By spring 1862 the Army of the Potomac consisted of more than 100,000 effectives. Yet McClellan believed its fighting strength to be much less, given the detachments he had made to secure Washington against attack, thus easing the minds of those bureaucrats whose hides he was getting tired of protecting.

Joe Johnston, on the other hand, could pit a little more than 40,000 men against McClellan, augmented by fewer than 20,000 others on the Virginia

Peninsula under Maj. Gen. John B. Magruder. Thanks partly to his own self-doubt and partly to the exaggerated reports of his "intelligence" operatives, most of whom were inexperienced civilians under the supervision of the nationally known detective Allan Pinkerton, McClellan believed, or professed to believe, that the number of gray-clad troops between Centreville and the tip of the Peninsula approached 150,000. Under this circumstance, extreme caution must rule any offensive. Already McClellan was chafing under Lincoln's stipulation that the movement commence no later than March 18.[22]

Not even the prospect of forfeiting his role as savior of the Union could goad McClellan into what he considered precipitate action. For one thing, he doubted that he would ever lose his hold on the Northern public. In early and mid-February Maj. Gen. Ulysses S. Grant had captured Confederate forts and large numbers of prisoners along the Tennessee and Cumberland Rivers. In February and mid-March, Maj. Gen. Ambrose E. Burnside attacked the North Carolina coast, snatching up the garrisons of Roanoke Island and New Berne. These exploits had attracted a great deal of publicity, but McClellan consoled himself that no one had ever described the countrified Grant or the portly, balding Burnside as a young Napoleon.[23]

>──┤◆>──O──<◆┤──<

McClellan need not have fretted about being rushed into combat, for he never had to put his Urbanna strategy to the test. In late February Joe Johnston, who was just as concerned about his opponent's strength as was McClellan, determined that his army must fall back toward Richmond to avoid being cut off and destroyed. On March 7 and 8, with the grudging approval of Confederate president Jefferson Davis, Johnston began to evacuate his lines around Manassas. As his troops marched south, the batteries that commanded the Potomac were disassembled and carted off, while millions of rations stored inside their lines were put to the torch to prevent their confiscation by the enemy.

Johnston's maneuver should not have taken McClellan by surprise, but it did. Little Mac's logical reaction was to send a body of cavalry to scout the nearest Rebel position, just outside Fairfax Court House. According to one account, only the 2nd New York, encamped on Arlington Heights, was immediately available for this assignment. At daylight on the eighth, the main body of the regiment, under Judson Kilpatrick, set out for the abandoned lines. Passing through now-deserted Fairfax Court House, the New Yorkers spurred into equally quiet Centreville. Continuing beyond the town, they encountered Johnston's rear guard and evicted it from the "burning ruins of Manassas."[24]

That evening the New Yorkers supposedly encamped twelve miles in advance of the rest of the army. The next day, the enterprising Kilpatrick led the way down the Orange & Alexandria toward Johnston's abandoned supply depot at Catlett's Station. Meanwhile, Washington came alive with movement and excitement as the main body of McClellan's expeditionary force took shape under Stoneman's supervision. That effort took a day and a half, which suggested that readiness was not a top priority of the army's cavalry.[25]

After a series of false starts, a column of some half dozen regiments, spearheaded by Averell's 3rd Pennsylvania and the 8th Pennsylvania of Col. David McMurtrie Gregg, left the Falls Church vicinity on the morning of the ninth, Stoneman riding in the vanguard. In apparent contrast to the 2nd New York, the troopers moved with great caution. After retracing Kilpatrick's path to Fairfax Court House, which they reached late in the afternoon, they remained in that area for the rest of the day.

The timid pursuers did not reach the abandoned works at Centreville until early on the tenth. Several Pennsylvanians clambered over the nearest defenses to find, rather than cannons and soldiers, logs painted black and six-foot-tall sticks planted in the ground, which from a distance resembled people. Examining the "Quaker guns," the troopers realized that for weeks their army had been duped into believing these lines held in heavy force.[26]

From Centreville, Stoneman's column plodded south to Manassas, arriving after nightfall. Averell found the local defenses to be "as extensive as ours and much more commodious and comfortable." Capt. Walter S. Newhall of Averell's regiment agreed. Just "to have something to talk about," Newhall violated Stoneman's order against entering the enemy camps. After inspecting one campsite, the captain dismounted, stretched out, and "passed a very comfortable night in a Secesh tent."[27]

The next morning other troops—mostly Regulars—joined the Pennsylvanians at Manassas, after which the column proceeded south in a stop-and-start fashion that tried the endurance of both men and animals. The troopers encountered rows of abandoned cabins near Bull Run and, beyond them, the still-burning supply depot along the O & A. "The confederate commissary buildings were still burning," recalled Pvt. Sidney Davis of the 6th United States Cavalry, "and flour, rice, sugar, broken muskets, bayonets, shot [and] shell, bullets—all the paraphernalia of war without its pomp—were scattered along the railroad and among the fortifications."[28]

Stoneman's continually augmented force marked time near Manassas for the next three days, as patrols probed the positions of the nearest Rebels. On the morning of the fourteenth, Stoneman culled out the 5th and 6th United States, the 3rd Pennsylvania, and a battalion of Illinois cavalry known as the McClellan Dragoons, and in tandem with Col. Samuel Zook's 57th New York Infantry, they set off down the O & A to study Johnston's relocated position. By midafternoon the advance regiment, the 5th Cavalry, had passed Kettle Run and Bristoe Station to draw within view of the Confederate rear guard, about a mile and a half shy of Catlett's Station. By now the enemy's main body was beyond capture; still, Stoneman wished to demonstrate the fighting spirit of his troopers. Hoping to draw blood, he ordered the officer in command of the 5th, Capt. Charles Jarvis Whiting, to drive in the Rebel rear guard, a body of cavalry of indeterminate size.

An embarrassing moment ensued when Whiting asked for volunteers and none of his company commanders responded. Disgusted by their silence, twenty-two-year-old 2nd Lt. George Armstrong Custer "stepped up and volunteered to drive in the enemy's pickets if [he] was given enough men." Fifty men were immediately placed at his disposal, while a second company, under Lt. John Baille McIntosh, who, like Custer, was destined to gain a general's star in the volunteer service, was positioned to protect the rear.

Hesitating not a moment, Custer led his detachment at a trot toward the enemy, now estimated to number 300. When halfway to his target, the subaltern had his men draw pistols, "I taking my place on the right and to the front of my company in order to be out of the way of their shots. We then took the gallop and charged the rebels but before we reached them they broke and ran. We [went] after them as hard as we could go chasing them a mile or two."[29]

The pursuit ended when the Confederates crossed a wooden bridge over a ravine. They unplanked the span under a covering fire from troops in impregnable positions. "The bullets rattled like hail," wrote Custer, adding that "several whizzed close to my head." Other missiles struck three of his men before he saw the futility of further opposition. Under cover of McIntosh's company, Custer disengaged and withdrew in orderly fashion. Rejoining his regiment, the lieutenant found himself interrogated by Stoneman, who "seemed well pleased with the manner in what [which] I performed my duty." Even more pleasing to the ambitious Custer was that, although Stoneman failed to cite his exploits in an after-action report, they received coverage in several newspapers, including the influential *New York Tribune*.[30]

After bivouacking along Cedar Run for the evening, Stoneman sent a detachment of Zook's regiment to try to drive the enemy from their woods across the stream. When this effort failed, the expeditionary leader turned his force about and led it northward in a drenching rain. The return trip was slow and uncomfortable, thanks especially to mud-clogged roads. By the time they reached Centreville at midday on the sixteenth, Trooper Davis and his comrades were "very sore, hungry, and tired, and thoroughly disgusted with the cavalry service."[31]

Although the mission left his men in a foul mood, Stoneman returned in high spirits. The reconnaissance, the first he had undertaken in brigade strength, gave him grounds for optimism about his troopers' growing maturity. By ascertaining that Johnston had fallen back behind the Rappahannock River near Fredericksburg, the expeditionary force had achieved its primary goal. It had also noted the whereabouts of enemy cavalry, infantry, and artillery in advance of the Rebel line. The intelligence would prove of much value to McClellan. Especially as exemplified by Lieutenant Custer, the cavalry had shown dash and valor and had cooperated well with the foot soldiers assigned to it.

Stoneman's optimism was somewhat tempered by the knowledge that his men, as well as their counterparts in the infantry, still had much to learn. Although the scouting force had suffered no fatalities, during skirmishing en route to Cedar Run, two Pennsylvania troopers had shot themselves through the foot and one of Zook's men managed to stab himself with his own bayonet.[32]

>‑‑‑O‑‑‑<

Johnston's escape from his lines below Washington prompted muttering and grumbling from some of his opponents, who feared that through timidity and lack of vigilance, an opportunity to overwhelm the Confederate army had slipped their grasp. This same sentiment was expressed in the White House as well as in some of the more critical journals throughout the North. It seemed obvious to McClellan's critics that though he had taught his army how to fight, he had not prepared it to the point that it could fight on short notice.

For his part, the general betrayed no hint of disappointment or regret over the enemy's unchallenged departure; he professed to be preoccupied with more critical concerns. The foremost of these—one that had already driven some government officials into a panic—was the damage done to the Union flotilla in Hampton Roads by the Confederacy's iron-plated behemoth, *Virginia,* on the morning of the ninth. The reincarnation of the sunken Union warship *Merrimac,* the ironclad not only sank or ran aground wooden warships off Fort Monroe, but also threatened to exert the same effect on McClellan's plans.

If Hampton Roads and the line of the York and James Rivers could not be made safe from the *Virginia,* McClellan could see no point in transporting his army by water into the Confederate rear. As it happened, however, neither McClellan nor his civilian superiors had grounds for alarm. Having anticipated this trend in naval warfare, the Union navy had recently commissioned an ironclad of its own, the *Monitor.* The unprepossessing "cheesebox on a raft" made her appearance in Hampton Roads one day after the *Virginia*'s debut, seeking a fight. Throughout the tenth, the ungainly looking vessels pounded each other to a draw, cannonballs bouncing harmlessly off their sides. The *Monitor* might not be superior to her Confederate adversary, but she proved herself mighty enough to neutralize the *Virginia* and keep Hampton Roads safe for Union shipping.[33]

By the eleventh McClellan, who this day was relieved of responsibility for armies operating elsewhere in the Union that he might concentrate on running the command he considered his own, was at last ready to implement his strategy of advancing on Richmond from below. But now he had a new plan. Johnston's fallback to the Rappahannock suggested that the Urbanna project had been compromised. Even if it had not, it had been stripped of the all-important element of surprise. Forced to strategize anew, McClellan had activated a contingency provision of his original plan, which called for the army to take ship to Fort Monroe, at the base of the Virginia Peninsula, there to embark for an overland trek to Richmond.

Fort Monroe, on Old Point Comfort, would remain in Union hands throughout the war, along with Fort Pickens in Pensacola Bay. With its commodious wharves and ample loading facilities, the Virginia garrison was a natural staging point for any offensive in the enemy's rear.

One of the contingency plan's few drawbacks was that unlike Urbanna, Fort Monroe might appear a logical destination for an invasion of Virginia, again costing the Federals any chance to surprise the enemy. Another liability was that when the army disembarked at the fort, it would be seventy-five miles from its objective, which was reachable by a limited number of roads. Although McClellan's topographical engineers assured him that the byways of the Peninsula were numerous, commodious, and durable, they were in fact few, narrow, and when inundated by rain, the consistency of soup.[34]

Ignorant of this potential difficulty, a suddenly energized McClellan went ahead with the preliminary phase of the new plan. During the last half of March dozens of transports and cargo ships materialized off Alexandria, upon whose wharves an immense array of supplies—rations, heavy ordnance, ammunition, wagons, caissons, ambulances, and more—had been piled. By the seventeenth, troops were marching to the river from various points around Washington.

One after another, infantry units—their men ignorant of the route ahead but hopeful it would carry them to Richmond—crowded onto the decks of the transports, waved farewell to comrades onshore, and were carried down the brackish Potomac to its confluence with the Chesapeake Bay. As the Alexandria flotilla put to sea, smaller numbers of troops were boarding Potomac River steamers at Washington and Annapolis, Maryland.[35]

Whatever lay ahead, the campaign to take the war to the enemy's country had gotten under way. After too many missteps and false starts, the Army of the Potomac had left the snug confines of its defenses and gone on the offensive.

McClellan watched proudly as the first ships steamed out of Alexandria; he would join them at Fort Monroe once the expedition was judged to be well under way. As he had recently informed one of his supporters in the Democratic Party, "I shall soon leave here on the wing for Richmond—which you may be sure I will take."[36]

Such confidence—and the progress on which it was based—would have pleased not only McClellan's backers but many Republicans as well. One of these—the man who occupied the White House—must have heaved a sigh of relief as the ships put to sea.

Chapter Six

First Blood

The embarkation process was more complex and time-consuming for the cavalry than for their comrades in the other arms. Most of the mounted regiments did not board their transports until several days after the first ships had departed Alexandria. Once aboard, the cavalry did not go anywhere quickly. Much time was spent in hoisting their horses into the holds via hand-operated winches and steam-powered derricks. It took more than one day for some regiments to be fully loaded and for their ships to put out into the Potomac. Already used to the waiting game, most troopers passed the time without a murmur. To a man, they would gladly trade boredom and discomfort for the opportunity to confront the army that had throttled theirs at Bull Run.

The cavalry boarded not only by regiments but by larger organizations, for many transports could accommodate more than a single outfit. These organizations were the product of an order issued by army headquarters on March 24. The order assigned cavalry units not only to the divisions of the army but also to the newly created corps of Generals McDowell, Sumner, Heintzelman, Keyes, and Nathaniel Prentiss Banks, who was a former congressman and speaker of the House of Representatives. Col. Andrew T. McReynolds's 1st New York and Colonel Davies's 2nd New York were assigned to McDowell's I Army Corps. The regiments' grouping created the first cavalry brigade in the Army of the Potomac, whether or not it was yet called by that name. To command it, McClellan initially made an odd selection: Brig. Gen. John Porter Hatch, a New York-born West Pointer whose prewar experience had been with the infantry, having transferred to the 3rd Cavalry only in August 1861. In a matter of days, however, Hatch was reassigned to the cavalry of Banks's V Corps. No other corps received a chief of cavalry, even temporarily, at this time.[1]

The horsemen attached to Sumner's II Corps included Van Alen's 3rd New York and Farnsworth's 8th Illinois, as well as Companies D and K of Col. Thomas C. Devin's 6th New York Cavalry. Colonel Averell's 3rd Pennsylvania, plus the 1st New Jersey, now commanded by Col. Sir Percy Wyndham, a British soldier of fortune, were assigned to Heintzelman's III Corps. General

Keyes's IV Corps received Col. George D. Bayard's 1st Pennsylvania, the 5th
Pennsylvania of Col. David Campbell (recently transferred from the plunder-
ing 4th Pennsylvania), Dickel's 4th New York, and Companies F and H of the
6th New York.[2]

Banks's corps was assigned by far the most mounted regiments, as well as
some of the finest ever to serve in the eastern theater: Col. Samuel H. Allen's
1st Maine, the 1st Vermont of Colonel Holliday (after his death led by the Fairfax Court House raider Charles Tompkins), Col. Thornton F. Brodhead's 1st
Michigan, the 1st Rhode Island (whose inept Colonel Lawton retained his
position well into the year), and the 5th New York of Col. Othneil De Forest.
In later weeks, Crooks's 8th New York would be attached to the corps. As if
not already well supplied with horsemen, Banks's corps also included three
mounted units below regimental strength: a battalion of Pennsylvanians under
Capt. John Keys, eighteen companies of Marylanders, and a squadron of loyalist Virginians.[3]

Taking a page from Napoleonic organization, McClellan created a separate
mounted command known as the Cavalry Reserve. This force, which had a coun-
terpart in the artillery, whose reserve batteries were commanded by Col. Henry
Jackson Hunt, stood ready for use with whatever corps, division, or brigade
needed it on a given occasion. To make the Cavalry Reserve a nucleus of professionalism, McClellan packed its two brigades with Regular regiments, although
two volunteer outfits also served in it. The Reserve was entrusted to that well-
known tactician, Philip St. George Cooke of the 2nd Cavalry, who the previous
November had been appointed a brigadier general in the regular service.[4]

Cooke assigned command of his first brigade to now–Brigadier General
Emory; it consisted of Emory's 6th United States in its entirety, plus five companies of the 5th United States Cavalry and the lancers of the 6th Pennsylvania.
Another old Regular, Col. George A. H. Blake of the 1st Cavalry, took charge
of Cooke's second brigade, which consisted of a battalion from Blake's regiment, Gregg's 8th Pennsylvania, the McClellan Dragoons (later a component
of the 12th Illinois Cavalry) under Capt. Charles W. Barker, and the Oneida
Cavalry, a New York company led by Capt. Daniel P. Mann. The last two units
were later assigned to the headquarters of the army, where they joined seven
companies of the 2nd United States Cavalry and a squadron of the 4th United
States in handling escort, courier, and orderly duties.[5]

The assignments announced on March 24 proved to be anything but permanent. Over the next week or so, several regiments nominally a part of
McClellan's army were reassigned to the defenses of Washington. These
included the 3rd New York (perhaps because its commander was deemed too
incompetent to take the field), the 1st New Jersey, the 1st Pennsylvania, and
the 4th New York. Early in April, however, the last three regiments were
removed from the capital and assigned to McDowell's corps.[6]

Other cavalry outfits then or soon afterward assigned to duty in Washington included Col. R. Butler Price's 2nd Pennsylvania, Col. James T. Childs's
4th Pennsylvania, the remaining eight companies of Devin's 6th New York,

plus the 7th, 9th, 10th, and 11th New York. For a brief period, Washington was also protected by Companies A through F of the 3rd Indiana Cavalry. The three squadrons were all there was of the 3rd Indiana in Virginia. Through a unique arrangement, the other six companies of the regiment—its "left wing"—served throughout the war in the western theater.[7]

Except for the 3rd, 7th, and 11th New York, every cavalry regiment that defended Washington in late 1861 and early 1862 later joined the Army of the Potomac. Of those that did, Lemmon's 10th New York and Maj. George H. Chapman's battalion and a half of the 3rd Indiana were initially assigned to the Middle Department, comprising several states along the eastern seaboard, with headquarters in Baltimore. Thanks to this intermediate assignment, neither Lemmon nor Chapman reached McClellan in time to aid him on the Peninsula.

Regiments that did not go from Washington to McClellan's army until the Peninsula campaign ended included the 2nd Pennsylvania and the main body of the 6th New York. Only the 4th Pennsylvania and Col. John Beardsley's 9th New York left Washington in time to serve on the Peninsula. While Colonel Childs's men fought as cavalry, two-thirds of Beardsley's regiment was forced to perform guard and fatigue duty as members of Hunt's Artillery Reserve and as wagon train guards.[8]

When the embarkation for Fort Monroe began, McClellan realized that several units of cavalry, infantry, and artillery assigned to his army would be withheld from him, some temporarily, others for an indefinite period. Early in March Banks's corps had been removed from McClellan's jurisdiction and ordered to the Shenandoah Valley to oppose "Stonewall" Jackson, whose small but fast-moving army had been harassing outposts throughout western Virginia. By late March, his mission presumably accomplished, Banks had begun to send his troops eastward with the intention of rejoining the Army of the Potomac. However, one day before McClellan issued his order assigning cavalry regiments to the V Corps, Jackson attacked and threatened to overwhelm one of Banks's divisions, stationed at strategic Kernstown. Although Jackson was forced to withdraw, his aggressiveness made government officials uneasy, for they feared the Rebels might range eastward to strike the capital. Lincoln responded, as Stonewall and his superiors hoped he would, by directing Banks to remain in the Valley.[9]

McClellan was not dismayed by Banks's detaching; he had expected to leave most of the V Corps behind to guard Washington, a mission McClellan believed Banks could accomplish from the Valley. But Lincoln and Stanton considered Banks too far from the capital to stop any movement in that direction by the Confederates under Johnston. Their fear led them to make a move that McClellan had not anticipated and that caused him great consternation. On April 4, two days after Little Mac reached Fort Monroe, Lincoln ordered McDowell's corps, the rear of the embarkation force, to remain within protective range of Washington until further notice.

McClellan regarded Lincoln's action as evidence of the administration's perfidy. The event became the first in a series of strategic disputes that drove an ever-widening wedge between army headquarters and the White House.

The conflict need not have been long-lasting, for McDowell's detaching was not. In late April Franklin's division of the I Corps (and with it, the 1st New York Cavalry) was returned to the Army of the Potomac. Two months later Lincoln also released McCall's division (and the 4th Pennsylvania) to McClellan. Still, during the critical period of his first field campaign, McClellan went without the services of thousands of detached troops. Adding up the loss of Banks plus Lincoln's subsequent decision to transfer Blenker's division (and the 4th New York) from McClellan's army to a newly created command in western Virginia, Little Mac calculated that he was short 55,000 men earmarked for his command.[10]

He was somewhat compensated for his loss in cavalry. Soon after reaching Fort Monroe, he assimilated into his field force two squadrons of Col. Josiah Harlan's 11th Pennsylvania, which had been stationed at the fortress since the previous November. Six companies of the regiment were, or soon would be, serving on the south side of Hampton Roads; another squadron was posted to Newport News, a fortified landing at the southwestern tip of the Peninsula. The uneven trade did nothing to ease McClellan's peace of mind or to lessen his anger over Lincoln's unilateral manpower decisions.[11]

>-+‹›-•-O-•-‹›+-‹

One of the main waterways that washed the Peninsula, the James River, had been closed to Union shipping by the enemy's shoreline batteries and by local warships including the *Virginia*. McClellan therefore decided to make the York River his base of operations and supply. To do this, he believed he must capture the Rebel stronghold at Yorktown, whose guns commanded shipping in the river. Overwhelming Yorktown's garrison became his initial objective.

Yorktown posed formidable obstacles. Early the previous year John Magruder had occupied the port village with 15,000 troops. They not only held the town but also a seven-mile line of breastworks that stretched all the way to the James. Some of these works had been superimposed upon battlements that Continentals under Washington and redcoats under Cornwallis had constructed eighty years earlier.[12]

The road to Yorktown ran through Hampton, the oldest English-speaking municipality in the nation, then through Big Bethel, scene of Ben Butler's debacle of the previous June. Hampton posed no threat to McClellan's advance, for Rebel cavalry had torched most of its dwellings the previous August after learning that the town might become a resettlement community for slaves who had escaped to Fort Monroe. Big Bethel, whose breastworks were manned by an enemy force of unknown size, was a different matter. An infantry column must approach it carefully, with horsemen in front and on the flanks. Thus McClellan's cavalry became a prized commodity as soon as it reached Fort Monroe.

The first mounted unit to complete the sea voyage, debarking on March 27, was the 3rd Pennsylvania. By midafternoon, as William Averell reported, the

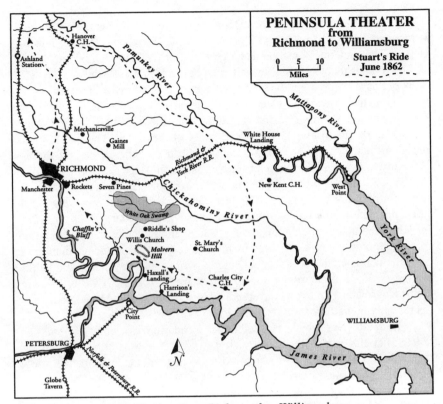

Map of the Peninsula Theater from Richmond to Williamsburg

regiment had assembled outside Hampton, "ready for the strife." The next day, one of the colonel's squadrons took the lead as an 8,000-man column of infantry and artillery under Fitz John Porter marched to Big Bethel as part of a reconnaissance in force. Short of their objective, the Federals encountered what the visiting assistant secretary of war, P. H. Watson, estimated as 1,500 Rebels and what Gen. John E. Wool, the new commander of Fort Monroe, called "nothing but a picket," mostly cavalry. Whatever their number, the enemy fled upon the approach of Averell's squadron—first into their works, and then toward Yorktown.[13]

It is possible that the Pennsylvanians gouged the enemy from their defenses through dismounted fighting. They would have known how to do this for, like all volunteer cavalrymen, they had been trained in the basics of infantry drill before learning mounted tactics. It seems more likely, however, that the squadron remained mounted throughout the action, brief as it was, as the unit reported only two casualties in the fight, both of them captured. Averell, like Stoneman, was a traditionalist who preferred his troops to fight in the saddle even when facing breastworks, especially when infantry was available to handle any footwork that was called for.

Following a brief pursuit, the reconnaissance force returned to Fort Monroe. It reported the road to Yorktown open as far as Harwood's Bridge, north of Bethel. That landmark anchored the eastern flank of the lowermost of three defensive lines that General Magruder had built across the Peninsula. The west flank of this six-mile-long line ended at Young's Mill, a heavily entrenched position on the road to Warwick Court House. Magruder's middle line of defense lay about eight miles farther north, stretching from the outskirts of Yorktown to Lee's Mill on the Warwick River, a tributary of the James. The northernmost line, constructed where the Peninsula was less than five miles across, ran through Williamsburg, Virginia's colonial capital, a half- hour stage ride from Yorktown.

McClellan was unwilling to march on Yorktown in a single column via the main road north. To protect his left flank and rear, a second wing would move north along the banks of the James via Warwick Court House. McClellan supposed that both columns would be near enough to each other to permit mutual support, but he was fooled by his lack of good maps and his inability to gain an understanding of the local geography from runaway slaves and helpful Unionists. The only maps available made it appear that the roads to Warwick Court House and Yorktown converged. In fact, they remained miles apart, connected only by narrow forest trails.[14]

The roads over which McClellan advanced were not only few and constricted but also soggy. Early on April 4, when Little Mac assembled enough troops at Fort Monroe to fuel a forward movement, a cloudburst pelted troops, cannon, wagon trains, and the loamy soil of the Peninsula. At 6:00 A.M. two thoroughly soaked divisions under Fitz John Porter retraced the army's path to Big Bethel, followed by a III Corps division under Brig. Gen. Charles S. Hamilton and the II Corps division of Brig. Gen. John Sedgwick. Reserve infantry, artillery, and cavalry followed Sedgwick's command. The going was difficult, and the column maintained a glacial pace. Even before clearing Bethel, batteries and wagons had sunk to their axles in the mud, creating a traffic snarl that took hours to clear.

Progress was only slightly less difficult for the troops in the advance, Averell's Pennsylvanians. The colonel had anticipated his position in the line of march, predicting to his sister in New York, "I shall have the honor of leading the advance." The honor, such as it was, was muted by the elements as well as by the lack of opposition on the route to Harwood's Bridge. Not until late afternoon did the column reach Magruder's lowermost line. Just before arriving, Averell's men had to help the infantry repair a dismantled bridge and remove a timber-laced abatis from the road. Fatigue duty did not befit the exalted status to which most horsemen thought themselves entitled; the 3rd Pennsylvania performed the work grudgingly.[15]

While Porter's column slowed to a halt, the troops under Keyes were moving slowly but surely up the road from Newport News to Warwick Court House. Keyes had marched with two divisions of his own IV Corps, those of "Baldy" Smith and Brig. Gen. Darius N. Couch. Their advance was covered by the 5th United States Cavalry of Whiting, McIntosh, and Custer. The cavalry

negotiated the marshy road with minimal trouble, and the foot soldiers in their
rear managed to keep moving although they were continually splattered with mud
kicked up by the horses' hooves. Still, as Keyes complained in his after-action
report of the day's operations, it was all but impossible for cannon, caissons, and
limbers to keep pace with the rest of the column. The expeditionary leader feared
that if he encountered a heavy enemy force at or before Warwick Court House, he
would have to send well to the rear for the bulk of his firepower.[16]

Both columns halted far short of their objectives. Porter's wing stopped
opposite Harwood's Bridge, where it was opposed briefly by an estimated 400
infantry, a few dozen cavalry, and two artillery pieces. Meanwhile, Keyes's
advance—part of Smith's division—chased pickets from the banks of Water's
Creek before halting within sight of the trenches at Young's Mill, which were
found to be occupied by two regiments of foot soldiers. Both sets of defenders
fled with little or no provocation, but neither column advanced far beyond
the point of first contact. Miles apart, at Harwood's Bridge and Young's Mill,
the advance echelon of the Army of the Potomac passed a wet and chilly night
in bivouac.

The rain continued into the fifth, as stiffening resistance slowed Porter's
advance near the Yorktown suburb of Cockletown and Keyes's about midway
between Warwick Court House and Lee's Mill. From Cockletown, Porter sent
one of his brigades, under Brig. Gen. George W. Morell, augmented by one of
Averell's squadrons and some artillery, to probe the outer works of Yorktown.
The previous day, Averell had led the balance of his outfit eastward to Ship Point,
a fortified peninsula formed by a tributary of the Chesapeake Bay. As he had a
month earlier at Manassas, Averell found the position, whose water battery had
been cut off from the rear by Porter's advance, abandoned. Unlike their base at
Manassas, the Confederates had evacuated Ship Point too hastily to put anything
to the torch, "the barracks, &c., for 3,000 men being in excellent condition."[17]

On the fifth, Averell's men moved up in rear of the works astride the Yorktown Road and took position there. Like the rest of McClellan's cavalry, the
3rd Pennsylvania saw no action for the next several weeks. The regiment
merely picketed the enemy's positions, scouted the countryside, and marveled
at the operations of McClellan's aeronaut, Professor Thaddeus S. C. Lowe,
who observed daily activities inside Yorktown from balloons based near Warwick Court House. Army officers, including the thrill-seeking George Custer,
often accompanied Lowe during his ascents. On April 11 one of the professor's balloons came loose from its moorings before Lowe could board it,
carrying its single occupant, General Porter, on an unplanned flight. "He cried
lustily for help," Walter Newhall observed, "as he passed our camp at the rate of
six miles an hour. He fortunately came down in a Federal camp, badly scared,
and a little lame."

This diversion aside, the 3rd Pennsylvania had little to occupy its time. As
Newhall reported on the twentieth, "we still keep up our masterly inactivity,
drilling twice a day in a broiling sun, and those nearest the enemy dodging the

shells." The regiment came increasingly within range of enemy guns; by the twenty-first its forwardmost pickets were only 300 yards from Magruder's lines.[18]

While McClellan's easterly column confronted the Rebels in Yorktown, Keyes's troops advanced gingerly toward the right flank of the enemy's defense perimeter. As Keyes's skirmishers approached the works near Lee's Mill on the Warwick River, their defenders suddenly moved in such a way as to threaten the Union left. At once Keyes ordered up a brigade of foot soldiers, covered by the 5th Cavalry; later he dispatched two batteries and three more infantry regiments in that same direction. Their advance halted the enemy's maneuver and permitted Keyes to take at good look at the works confronting him. He did not like what he saw: The enemy "is in a strongly-fortified position behind Warwick River, the fords in which have been destroyed by dams, and the approaches to which are through dense forests, swamps, and marshes. No part of his line as far as discovered can be taken by assault without an enormous waste of life."[19]

Throughout that day and well into the next, Keyes sparred with the Rebels at long range, while the 5th Cavalry moved up in an effort to locate weak points in the line. Instead, the Regulars encountered what appeared to be an ever-lengthening line of Confederates moving inside their works. Neither the 5th nor anyone else in Keyes's column suspected that Magruder had ordered the few units holding Lee's Mill to march across their enemy's line of vision and, when out of sight, to sneak back to their starting point and repeat the movement. Equally clever comrades inside the works at Yorktown were giving Porter's troops the same carefully orchestrated impression—that several times as many troops as Magruder had were confronting the invaders of the Peninsula.[20]

Magruder's ruse convinced Keyes that nothing could be gained by attacking in his sector. He was wrong. On the sixth some of Smith's troops under an aggressive brigadier, Winfield Scott Hancock, and supported by cavalry, broke through a section of the Lee's Mill defenses. Unwilling to exploit the success in the face of what he supposed were 10,000 Confederates, Keyes recalled Hancock's men. His action was immediately approved by McClellan, who was reluctant to become heavily engaged before he had studied his enemy's di ,positions and weighed every strategic option.[21]

Keyes's gloomy assessment of affairs, combined with sharp but inconsequential skirmishing between Porter's advance and infantry and artillery along the Yorktown Road, made McClellan believe that any offensive would prove futile. His opinion hardened after he accompanied his engineer officers on a reconnaissance of the nearest works.

He was immediately impressed by the depth and complexity of the defenses just south of town, the main section of which crossed the field where Cornwallis had surrendered to American and French troops in October 1781. Those works appeared to have been so carefully constructed that relatively few troops could hold them indefinitely. McClellan was also aware that even as his army closed up on Yorktown, troops under Joe Johnston, having abandoned the Rappahannock line, were heading for the stronghold from the opposite direction. Within days the works that stretched from the York to the James would be held by 40,000 troops, perhaps many more—enough to make an attack on even mediocre defenses a costly mistake.

In the end—inevitably, given his cautious nature—McClellan decided that he must besiege Yorktown. He sent to the rear for the siege train that had been outfitted at Alexandria. In a matter of days, 100 big guns were en route to Fort Monroe: 4.5-inch ordnance rifles, 30-pounder Parrotts, 8-inch howitzers, and coehorn mortars. To these instruments of long-range destruction, he later added several 13-inch seacoast mortars. Fatigue parties supplied with sling carriages manhandled these behemoths into position at several points outside the city. By mid-April fifteen heavy batteries had been emplaced along a semi-circular line running from the banks of the York southeast of the town nearly as far as the line of works to the west.[22]

A year and a half later, one of McClellan's erstwhile subordinates examined at close range the defenses that had stymied his commander. The officer doubted that the works, which he considered "by no means formidable in themselves," should have blocked any army worth its pay. Looking back, he lamented that McClellan, "cautious, doubting, timid, fearful, sat down for a siege, toiling week after week in building roads & trenches, when he might in three days have marched his whole army from Fortress Monroe to Yorktown, keeping entirely protected from the guns of the fort in the many deep & capacious ravines that run from miles out in the country up to within 300 or 400 yds of the fort, and then, debouching suddenly, might have swept the place from the face of the earth."[23]

This man may not have taken into account every obstacle the Army of the Potomac faced in early April 1862, but his suggestion that McClellan might have used the local terrain to better advantage is well taken. Unfortunately, no one in the general's inner circle was willing to offer such advice. Even if someone had, it seems doubtful Little Mac would have heard him out. Already he was ignoring similar advice from his civilian superiors. On April 6 Abraham Lincoln warned him by telegraph that "you [had] better break the enemies' line from Yorktown to [the] Warwick River, at once. They will probably use time, as advantageously as you can." In later days, Lincoln and his secretary of war repeated this advice. How McClellan operated against Johnston and Magruder was his own business, "but you must act." The unheeding commander merely continued his battery building, confident that he could take Yorktown by a bloodless investment. So much greater was the reputation of the general who prevailed without sacrificing his army in needless assaults.[24]

>─+─◆─+─○─+◆─+─<

The investment of Yorktown dragged on for four weeks; so too did the trials and dangers of trench warfare. McClellan's troops, especially those setting up his siege batteries, suffered not only from baking heat, clouds of dust, seas of torrential rain, and mud, but also from near-constant sniper and artillery fire. The firepower of the enemy's long-range guns was frighteningly impressive. Sgt. Maj. David C. Ashley of the 6th New York, an avid baseball player, informed his parents that "the game they have been playing here I have not learned yet. They throw such big balls and throw them swifter than we used to."[25]

Bored and irritated by their stationary existence within marching distance, if not sight, of the Confederate capital, the army began to grumble and curse. Cavalrymen joined in the discontent. Maj. Alfred Pleasonton of the 2nd United States Cavalry, one of the few field-rank Regular cavalry officers in McClellan's army, grumbled that McClellan's "first great mistake" had been shifting over to siege operations before Johnston joined Magruder to make Yorktown impregnable, a process completed before the middle of April. By then, McClellan's siege batteries looked ready to go to work, but most of them remained silent, as though Little Mac lacked the will to use them. On April 13 Trooper Charles Bates of the 4th United States Cavalry, McClellan's escort unit, complained that although "everything is ready for the ball to be opened," no one seemed willing to dance. On the sixteenth, Baldy Smith made a brief lodgment in the center of the Confederate line, but the thrust across the Warwick River was beaten back, and no further efforts were made to cross.[26]

The inactivity rankled Trooper William Band of the 3rd Pennsylvania, who had recently learned of Ulysses S. Grant's dramatic victory near Pittsburg Landing, Tennessee, a battle later known as Shiloh. Previously Grant's army had captured strategic garrisons on the Tennessee and Cumberland Rivers. To Band, "It looks too bad that we the armey of the potomack should be kept idle wile the [troops in the] grate wester[n theater] do all the fighting." The Philadelphian informed his wife that the army's inaction "is not the mens falt I ashure you." Only the sloth or the faintheartedness of the high command allowed Yorktown to remain standing.[27]

The pace of the siege especially bothered those cavalrymen who had been forced to shoulder unauthorized burdens. Late in April many of those 9th New Yorkers attached to the Artillery Reserve or assigned to shoulder infantry arms and guard the army's supply trains began expressing themselves as "humiliated and resentful." Several refused to do duty with their new units and demanded the return of their horses and carbines. The regiment's grievances were not unheard of; at about the same time, the 8th New York, then garrisoning Harpers Ferry, Virginia, and later a member of the Army of the Potomac, was reported in a "disorganized and mutinous condition" after being forced to serve temporarily as infantry.

For a time it looked as though the 9th New York had committed military suicide. An angry McClellan charged the most vocal protesters with "displaying a spirit of cowardice" and recommended the entire regiment be returned to New York State for discharge. Only the intervention of Secretary of War Stanton saved the regiment from ruin. In mid-May Stanton ordered its men to Washington for muster out. The following month he changed his mind and remounted and reequipped the regiment as cavalry. The opportunity was thus granted the 9th to regain its good name, and it went on to become one of the finest mounted units in Mr. Lincoln's Army.[28]

The grousing and complaining ended on the evening of May 3, two days before McClellan planned to open with his siege batteries, pounding Yorktown to rubble and forcing Johnston to give up. After sundown the Rebel artillery unleashed its heaviest salvos of the twenty-nine-day siege, filling the night with what David Ashley called "one continuous roar of artillery. . . . The ground fairly shook and I anticipated a great fight." His expectations went unfulfilled. Not long after it began, the shelling tapered off, then ceased, and an eerie silence enveloped the Confederate line. Troops across the way looked at one another in wonder. Had Johnston, cowed by the guns rising all around, decided to surrender before those monsters opened on him?[29]

Not until daylight did McClellan and his men understand what had happened. When General Heintzelman went aloft in Professor Lowe's balloon, he observed unmanned defenses and empty campsites; Yorktown, he reported, was as "quiet as the grave." Within minutes of the ascent, McClellan realized that the enemy had evacuated in the direction of Williamsburg, doubtless bound for Richmond. His heavy cannons and mortars, so painstakingly erected, would not be needed.[30]

A frustrated McClellan would have been forgiven had he lashed out at his opponent. Yet not until afternoon did he take steps to pursue Johnston and Magruder. In the interim, he sent a part of his army to occupy the town and its defenses. Only after subordinates, including Stoneman, importuned him to act did he permit elements of cavalry and infantry to start off after the evacuees. The horsemen, who would take the lead in any pursuit, were assigned directly to Stoneman.

By then, several cavalry units had already entered Yorktown. The 3rd Pennsylvania, followed by a phalanx of foot soldiers, trotted inside the abandoned works at 10:30 A.M. On all sides, they noted the refuse of their retreating enemy: spiked and silent cannons, broken rifles, empty hardtack boxes, overturned wagons, splintered caissons. The scene exerted a powerful effect. A Michigan infantry officer observed that "it was no small gratification to enter those works which had held us in check for a month." Others expressed disgust that the enemy had evaded the trap carefully set for them. Major Pleasonton ascribed Johnston's escape to "a decided want of vigor" on the part of McClellan and his ranking subordinates.[31]

Still others were more charitable toward their leader. Examining the empty, silent works south of town, Sergeant Major Ashley shook his head, saying: "Nothing could have made our men feel worse. . . . To have them slip the halter and leave us in the lurch has brought on a feeling of disappointment that can be imagined better than described." But while many of Ashley's comrades believed that "McClellan's fame is all blown away with this evacuation," some thought "he deserves praise for scaring them if not whipping them as he certainly would [have] if they had remained here a day or two more."[32]

Four mounted units were told off for the pursuit, initially under the command of General Cooke. Ready to move by early afternoon, the force consisted of the 3rd Pennsylvania, the McClellan Dragoons, and two Regular regiments grouped under General Emory: the 1st United States, led by Lt. Col. William N. "Old Billy" Grier, one of the most popular Regular officers in the army; and Emory's former outfit, the 6th United States, under Maj. Lawrence Williams. Well in rear of the horse soldiers came the infantry portion of the pursuit column, the divisions of Baldy Smith and Brig. Gen. Joseph Hooker. Several batteries of field artillery completed this so-called advance guard of the army.[33]

The artillery included four batteries of light (or horse) artillery, attached directly to the cavalry. Three were units of the 2nd United States Artillery Regiment: Battery A, the army's most celebrated light battery, famous for its Mexican War record, under Capt. John A. Tidball; combined Batteries B and L, under Capt. James Madison Robertson; and Battery M, under Capt. Henry Benson. The fourth was Capt. Horatio G. Gibson's Battery C, 3rd United States.

This day marked the first recorded instance that McClellan's cavalry served in the field alongside artillery units capable of keeping up with them. Their mobility owed to two factors. One was their relatively lightweight cannons, mainly 3-inch ordnance rifles. These wrought-iron guns weighed a little over 1,000 pounds, and they could throw solid shot, explosive shell, or shotgunlike charges of canister up to 1,850 yards at 5 degrees' elevation. A few horse artillery units mounted other maneuverable cannons, including 10-pounder Parrott rifles and 12-pounder smoothbore "Napoleons." The second facilitator of mobility was the manner in which the members of the batteries were mounted. Whereas artillerymen attached to the army's infantry sat atop limber and caisson chests when their units were in motion, each flying artilleryman rode his own horse.[34]

At the start of the pursuit, the cavalry experienced command and organization problems, the result of McClellan's decree that only in special cases would Stoneman exercise tactical leadership. When Stoneman took charge of the advance guard, he ruffled the feathers of his senior lieutenants. Finding himself reduced to the command of the two Regular outfits in the column, a disgruntled General Cooke in turn displaced General Emory. The equally unhappy Emory was thus relegated—temporarily, as it turned out—to the command of his old regiment.[35]

In contrast to McClellan's attitude toward pursuit, Stoneman's cavalry and artillery rode long and hard, in the process leaving their infantry supports far behind. As they must have suspected, their principal opponents were the cavaliers of J. E. B. Stuart, the rear guard of Johnston's army. This day, the "Beau Sabreur of the Confederacy" led the 1st, 3rd, and 4th Virginia regiments, as well as the mounted portions of the Wise, Hampton, and Jeff Davis Legions.

Other cavalry officers took seriously their duty to pursue the enemy. Even before Stoneman started out, a squadron of the 5th United States under Capt. William P. Chambliss had crossed the Warwick River to monitor Stuart's movements. Near Lee Hall, General Magruder's former headquarters,

Chambliss encountered a Rebel delaying force but flanked it into retreat. From Lee Hall, the 5th Cavalry's detachment, which also included the ubiquitous Lieutenant Custer, marched to Skiff's Creek, a James River tributary, which one of Stuart's units had recently crossed before setting the bridge on fire. While comrades exchanged long-range fire with the Jeff Davis Legion, Custer helped put out the fire, thus saving the bridge. Chambliss's squadron crossed the blackened span until Baldy Smith, whose advance echelon had come up in the cavalry's rear, ordered it to halt. Smith hoped that by permitting Stuart to move unmolested along the Williamsburg Road, he might stumble upon Stoneman's larger force, to his regret.[36]

In point of fact, in late afternoon Stoneman's column overtook the better part of Stuart's force near the Half-Way House, perhaps eight miles south of Williamsburg and not far from the point at which the main road to the village joined the more westerly road from Lee's Mill. Near the hostelry, a squadron of Grier's regiment under Capt. William T. Magruder (no kin to the Confederate general) absorbed a destructive picket fire. At once, Stoneman sent to Magruder's assistance Capt. John Savage's squadron of the 6th Cavalry, as well as Captain Benson's battery. Emplacing his guns to sweep the main road, Benson cleared it sufficiently to allow the cavalry to resume its advance.

As the Regular regiments continued up the road under General Cooke, Stoneman sent Emory, with the 3rd Pennsylvania, the McClellan Dragoons, and Benson's battery, cross-country to gain the Lee's Mill Road and cut off an infantry column that had been observed there. The tactic was a good idea, but Stuart ambushed Emory's column with a large portion of the 3rd Virginia, sending the first unit it struck, the McClellan Dragoons, to the rear in panic and confusion. To salvage the situation, Emory sent the 3rd Pennsylvania to confront Stuart. Discovering that most of the Rebels had taken position in a woods, Averell repressed his desire to fight in the saddle. He dismounted two squadrons, placed one on each side of the road, and sent them forward. Working their carbines furiously, the Pennsylvanians rejoiced to see their enemy remount and scramble to the rear. Capt. William Miller always remembered "the impetuosity with which the enemy were driven over fields, through swamps and underbrush."[37]

While Averell pressed ahead, Stoneman attempted to do the same. He found himself facing not only Stuart's horsemen, mounted and on foot, but also a force of infantry that had retraced its path down the road from Williamsburg after hearing the opening shots of the cavalry fight. The newcomers took cover behind a ready-made line of defense, the uppermost of the three lines Magruder had constructed from the James to the York. Infantry and gunners took advantage of the dozen redoubts that studded the seven-mile line, especially its centerpiece, Fort Magruder, whose six-foot-tall parapets commanded the convergence of the Williamsburg and Lee's Mill Roads.

The hastily assembled garrison plied Stoneman and Cooke with steady rifle and cannon fire. The Federal leaders responded by dismounting their

Regulars behind whatever cover the terrain afforded and sending Captain Gibson's battery to shell the Rebel works from as many angles as possible. Supported by Grier's 1st Cavalry, Gibson slowly moved his guns 400 yards up the road into a position from which to return the enemy's fire. Meanwhile, Stoneman ordered Major Williams to mount four squadrons of the 6th Cavalry and strike the rear of Fort Magruder via a long, deep ravine that would shelter his riders from their opponents' view.

Williams advanced as ordered, entered and cleared the ditch, and poised to attack the fort from its blind side. As he did, Stuart, with the 4th Virginia and the Wise and Hampton Legions, moved so as to threaten his flank. Fearing for the safety of his regiment, the major cut short his mission, turned about, and returned to the ravine, only to be overtaken short of it by Stuart. Williams's rear guard, commanded by Capt. William Sanders, wheeled about and met their attackers with sabers and pistols. Aided by the next squadron in line, led by Capt. John Irvin Gregg, whose savvy and combativeness soon won him higher rank in the volunteer cavalry, Sanders's men fought off their assailants long enough to clear a swamp that led back to the starting point of their advance.[38]

At the height of the melee near Fort Magruder, Cooke sought a decision from Stoneman, who had moved his field headquarters farther to the west, whether to fight on or to retreat. The officer who carried the inquiry was Capt. Wesley Merritt of the 2nd Cavalry, Cooke's old regiment. Braving a gauntlet of fire with such élan that Stoneman soon added the captain to his own staff, Merritt found Stoneman in a gloomy mood. The cavalry chief had learned that Hooker's infantry, having had been delayed on its march, would not reach Williamsburg in time to support the horse soldiers. After a few minutes' hesitation, as Emory later related, Stoneman decided it was "worse than useless to try to hold our position . . . and therefore gave directions to withdraw and take up a defensive position."[39]

Receiving the order, Cooke obeyed it reluctantly but resignedly. He found, however, that to withdraw was not a simple maneuver. His Regulars covered Benson's battery as it limbered up under fire. Despite Cooke's best efforts, the enemy pressed the battery so closely that one of its guns and four of its caissons, all of which had bogged down in the rain-sodden road, could not be extricated in time to prevent capture.

Cooke's loss might have been worse. When the 6th Cavalry brought up the rear of the retreat column, foot soldiers and horsemen pressed it so closely that the regiment avoided being cut off only through the stubborn resistance of Billy Grier's regiment, the colonel taking a wound in the melee and having his horse shot from under him. Once darkness came on and Hooker came up, Stuart and his supports drew off, ending a day of frenetic skirmishing.[40]

Although they had been forced to withdraw, Stoneman, Cooke, and Emory viewed the fight just ended as a partial victory. Their men had fought well all over the field; on Emory's front, they had even driven some of Stuart's people into panic-stricken flight. Cavalry and horse artillery had cooperated effectively in this, their first pairing on a battlefield. The Federals had suffered thirty-five casualties, but they had inflicted nearly as many losses on the enemy. And by undertaking the pursuit in the first place, despite McClellan's lethargy and Stuart's six-hour head start, the advance guard had shown dash, aggressiveness, and initiative.

In his report, Cooke stated, "My command generally gave me high satisfaction." Stoneman went further, praising the conduct of every element of his force and asserting that only the infantry's tardiness had prevented a lopsided victory: "Had Hooker not been delayed we could have taken possession of the empty earthworks before the enemy could have reoccupied them, and Stuart's cavalry [would] have been cut off and captured."[41]

The implication was clear. The enemy may have made good their escape beyond Williamsburg, but the fault lay with neither the cavalry nor the flying artillery of the Army of the Potomac.

Chapter Seven

Advance and Retreat

Rain fell shortly after midnight, leaving Stoneman's troopers, in their makeshift bivouacs south of Williamsburg, wet, cold, and miserable. Morning of May 5 brought little improvement in the weather. Although the conditions seemed hardly conducive to battle, soon after dawn the recently arrived infantry of Smith and Hooker began to square off with the Rebels who continued to hold the Fort Magruder line. Later they were joined by the III Corps division of Philip Kearny.

McClellan, who continued to appear anything but eager to engage the enemy, remained in Yorktown through most of the fifth, having dispatched his senior corps commander, Edwin Sumner, to oversee the fighting. When Joe Johnston countered by sending Maj. Gen. James Longstreet to Fort Magruder with several infantry brigades and Stuart's cavalry, combat intensified along the roads into Williamsburg. Despite the downpour, the fighting continued through the day, accounting for nearly 1,000 Federal and more than 1,250 Confederate casualties. Despite the disparity in losses, the battle of Williamsburg ended as a tactical draw. It might have been a decisive victory for the Army of the Potomac had not Hancock's brigade, for the second time in a month, been recalled by overly cautious superiors after breaching a portion of the enemy's line.[1]

For most of the fight, the cavalry played a spectator's role. Most of the horsemen congregated on Sumner's left flank, where they safeguarded Hooker's position, exchanged shots with Stuart's cavaliers, and awaited a call to advance that never came. The most active of Stoneman's regiments was the 3rd Pennsylvania, whose men reconnoitered the Confederate left, although they kept beyond range of the enemy's rifles. Averell's outfit suffered no casualties, but the 8th Illinois, which had been ordered to join the advance guard on the fourth but had failed to reach Williamsburg until evening, lost two men killed and one wounded. A member of the McClellan Dragoons wandered too close to the enemy's lines and ended up missing.[2]

By day's end, Longstreet had accomplished the mission assigned him, having held his adversary at arm's length until Johnston's main body cleared the

Williamsburg area. Feeling cheated of a victory, but inspired by McClellan's tardy arrival on the field, Sumner's command rested on its arms through the night. The rest of the army, minus Franklin's division of the I Corps, which McClellan had sent by transport up the York and Pamunkey Rivers to ambush Johnston and cut his line of retreat, had accompanied their leader from Yorktown. By the morning of May 6 they stood ready to pursue Johnston up the northwestward-leading peninsula toward Richmond, perhaps catching him between pincers en route.[3]

Advancing to Williamsburg, the main army found the going rough, and not only because of the weather. Besides being rain-soaked, many of the roads, especially in the vicinity of Fort Magruder, were infested with land mines called torpedoes. These were rigged to explode on contact, but the weight of a horse and rider was necessary to detonate most of them; thus the cavalry had an especially hard time of it. As he neared the battlefield, Pvt. Christian Geisel of the 6th Pennsylvania managed to avoid the mines but saw two of his comrades "blown up by shells which the rebels have buried all around their works." Riding in the Pennsylvanians' rear, David Ashley turned a jaundiced eye on these terror weapons, which seemed at odds with the professed chivalry of the Southern army. He decided that his enemy was "the most cowardly set of people I ever saw. There is nothing to[o] mean for them to do."[4]

Torpedoes were not the only hazard the cavalry encountered in Williamsburg. On May 10, as McClellan's rear guard left the vicinity for points north, six companies of the 5th Pennsylvania arrived from farther down the Peninsula to occupy the town, which McClellan wished held as an outpost on the road between Yorktown and Richmond. Its strategic location made Williamsburg a center of communications, intelligence-gathering, and espionage for the rest of the war.[5]

Upon arriving, Colonel Campbell of the 5th placed Williamsburg under martial law in hopes of curbing the activities of its Confederate sympathizers. Even so, two days later two members of his regiment fell victim to bushwhackers in the local countryside. Christian Geisel heard that the troopers "were found . . . tied to a tree and their brains blowed out." This action set the tone for the regiment's service in Williamsburg, which lasted for a year and a half, ending with the reunited outfit's transfer to the south side of Hampton Roads.

The uneasy truce that prevailed between occupiers and occupied was broken several times by townspeople who desired to evict the Yankees at all costs. On at least two occasions, residents aided Confederate troops in surprising the 5th's camp at Fort Magruder. One of these attacks resulted in the regiment's rout and the capture of more than 100 of its members, including Colonel Campbell. When the second attack ended, surviving Pennsylvanians retaliated by torching several buildings on the campus of Thomas Jefferson's alma mater, the College of William and Mary.[6]

>─I─◆>─○─<◆─I─<

Despite Franklin's best efforts, the Confederates resisted being brought to bay along the Pamunkey. Debarking on the seventh at Eltham's Landing,

Franklin's troops pushed inland, determined to snare the rear guard and the supply trains of the retreat column. To their surprise, they met an even more resolute enemy, whose offensive-defensive tactics kept the Federals off-balance and at bay, just as Longstreet had fended off Sumner's divisions on the fifth. Like many another commander, Franklin was not particularly adept at employing cavalry; this day he failed to use the 1st New York in the fighting, holding the regiment well in rear of the firing lines.[7]

Stoneman's cavalry could not overcome the head start Johnston's main body had gotten at Williamsburg. Thus, when they left Franklin behind, the Confederates were home free on the road to Richmond. By midmonth most had put the Chickahominy River between themselves and their pursuers and had filed inside prepared defenses five or six miles east of their capital.[8]

As the disappointed pursuers lumbered along the north bank of the Chickahominy, McClellan told off Stoneman's troopers for a variety of assignments, not merely to harass Johnston. Some scoured the Peninsula for guerrillas and bushwhackers like those who had struck the 5th Pennsylvania. Meanwhile, detachments of the 6th Pennsylvania and other regiments reconnoitered the communication lines recently abandoned by Johnston; still other units made contact with Union gunboats in the James.[9]

Stoneman's main force set a strong pace as it led the army toward Richmond. His force now embraced Emory's 1st and 6th United States, the main body of the 6th Pennsylvania, the 8th Illinois, a detachment of the 3rd Pennsylvania, Robertson's battery, and more than a dozen miles farther back, two infantry regiments. By May 8 Stoneman's vanguard had reached New Kent Court House, less than thirty miles from Richmond. At their leader's order, a party of the 6th United States charged into the lightly guarded village, securing it and rounding up several prisoners.[10]

Stoneman's command amounted to less than half the horsemen available to the army; the others McClellan had parceled out to his corps. When the Regulars left New Kent, one of those regiments, David Gregg's 8th Pennsylvania, backed by a small force of infantry, came up to occupy the village. The 8th Pennsylvania was picketing near the courthouse when, on the afternoon of the thirteenth, Stuart's troopers surprised the regiment and scattered it across the countryside.

The Pennsylvanians' retreat was bad enough in itself, but in their haste they burst through the ranks of the infantry, forcing it to flee as well. Other regiments, including the 1st Massachusetts, hustled up to chase Stuart away and restore order. By then, according to Charles F. Adams, the 8th Pennsylvania "had gained an unenviable reputation for the speed it made in getting away from the enemy," one that other outfits did not let it live down. Gregg's people regained at least some of their honor the following week, when on successive days they drove toward Richmond bodies of infantry and horsemen.[11]

From New Kent Court House, Stoneman's column turned north and east, a portion of it taking possession of White House Landing on the Pamunkey, the terminus of the Richmond & York River Railroad, as well as Cumberland Landing, farther down the same stream. At Cumberland, Tidball's Battery A, 2nd United States, arrived to join the advance guard. His firepower thus augmented, Stoneman pushed toward the banks of the Chickahominy, the gateway to Richmond. By the seventeenth the cavalry had drawn to within three miles of Bottom's Bridge on the Chickahominy; there Stoneman halted to await the rest of the army.[12]

The stopover did not mean the troopers sat idle on a riverbank. Detachments, some trailed by infantry, ranged well to the north and west. On the nineteenth a portion of the 6th United States crossed the Richmond & York River Railroad, heading for the Pamunkey River. A few miles shy of the stream, the Regulars took possession of Old Church, where they confiscated horses, mules, and commissary items earmarked for shipment to Richmond.

The next day, Stoneman personally led the 6th United States and 8th Illinois up the Chickahominy to New Bridge, eight miles above Bottom's Bridge. Northeast of their objective, near Gaines's Mill, the horsemen skirmished with a party of Stuart's men, which they pushed steadily before them. Despite their momentum, Stoneman's people suffered several casualties. This outcome the Illinois troopers, who considered themselves veterans, blamed on the relatively new and inexperienced Regulars with whom they were teamed—and from whom they were supposed to learn the cavalryman's art.[13]

When McClellan's vanguard reached the Chickahominy on the twentieth, so did Professor Lowe and his balloons. The following morning Stoneman joined the aeronaut in ascending 500 feet above the river. From that lofty perch, the cavalry leader saw a column of Rebels that filled the highway from Bottom's Bridge to Richmond; other troops were partially hidden in woodlots on both sides of the road. Clearly visible in the distance were the spires of the enemy capital.[14]

Apparently Stoneman also spied gray troops on the upper reaches of his side of the river. Two days later infantry from the newly created V Provisional Army Corps of Fitz John Porter were dispatched to Old Church to aid Rush's Lancers in guarding against any flanking movement from that direction. That same day, Stoneman placed Robertson's and Tidball's batteries at New Bridge to dispute any attack across the river. The batteries fired on infantry and cannons across the stream, forcing their retirement. Then they limbered up, turned north, and fell in with a mounted force under Stoneman, heading for the Richmond suburb of Mechanicsville.

Despite opposition from infantry and artillery, which tried to block its path, Stoneman's column held the Mechanicsville area until relieved that evening by infantry. The next morning, the twenty-fourth, the foot soldiers pushed their enemy back across the river; to keep them there, a company of the 8th Illinois braved a storm of rifle and cannon fire to destroy the bridge that carried the Mechanicsville Turnpike across the river. While their comrades completed this chore, the better part of the 8th trotted upstream to wreck a Virginia Central Railroad span and to lever up sections of track on the north side of the river.[15]

Though most of the Federals seemed content to keep the Rebels on the far side of the Chickahominy, some wanted to drive the enemy from the far shore. On the twenty-fourth Lieutenant Custer talked an infantry colonel into letting him lead four companies of Michigan soldiers across the Chickahominy above New Bridge. On the far shore the attackers poured volley after volley into the Confederates, gouging them out of their rifle pits and forcing them to retreat so hastily that fifty fell into Custer's hands. When he learned of the successful dash, McClellan termed it a "very gallant" affair and personally congratulated Custer on the outcome. Soon afterward, Little Mac added the daring young officer to his staff.[16]

The pleasure Custer's success brought his commander was short-lived. McClellan was concerned about the difficulties that would beset his army while crossing the Chickahominy. He feared he lacked the manpower to surmount without heavy loss that last major natural barrier to Richmond. For a week he had been buoyed by Lincoln's promise to release the bulk of McDowell's corps, then stationed at Fredericksburg, to the Army of the Potomac. By an overland march, McDowell was to descend on Richmond along the line of the Virginia Central Railroad until his left flank connected with McClellan's right. "I now felt confident," Little Mac had written in reply to this news, "that we would on his [McDowell's] arrival be sufficiently strong to overpower the large army confronting us." In fact, the army across the river was little more than half the size of McClellan's, but as at Yorktown, the general was convinced that he was outgunned and outpositioned. Thus his new confidence was dashed by the news he received by telegraph late on the twenty-fourth. A renewed offensive by Stonewall Jackson against Harpers Ferry had forced Lincoln to suspend McDowell's movement south. Within a few days, McClellan learned that the I Army Corps was going to the Shenandoah instead of to Richmond.[17]

Having counted on the I Corps' assistance, McClellan had taken steps to facilitate its march from Fredericksburg. When he heard on the twenty-third that an enemy force had crossed the river to Hanover Court House, sixteen miles north of Richmond and just east of the Virginia Central, Little Mac twice sought to determine the size of that force. On the twenty-fourth Colonel Rush and 125 of his lancers scouted the vicinity. Two days later Rush supported a larger force—the 1st United States, the McClellan Dragoons, and a New York infantry regiment—that scoured the same area.

The only action on either mission took place on the twenty-sixth, when the 6th Pennsylvania and its supports engaged a large picket post on the Pamunkey. On this occasion, Company C of the 6th used its lances to drive off enemy cavalry—one of the few times this weapon was used in combat. The lance may have been unwieldy and unsuited to heavily wooded Virginia, but its power as a terror weapon was undeniable. A few days later, some POWs were taunted by the men of a Union regiment who believed the Rebels had fled from them. "O it wasent you we run from," a prisoner was recorded as replying, "it was the Fellows with them long Poles."[18]

McClellan learned that from 3,000 to 6,000 Confederates and at least six cannons held the courthouse and points nearby. He was troubled by so many secessionists on his far right. On the twenty-seventh he sent Porter with 12,000 troops, including Emory's 5th and 6th United States and Benson's battery, to Hanover Court House. The same troops that had supported the second expedition, including Rush's Lancers, accompanied Porter.

The cavalry that composed Porter's advance guard encountered waves of Rebel pickets well in advance of their objective. Then, near Slash Church, two and a half miles southwest of the courthouse, the advance absorbed rifle fire. The cavalry managed to hold its ground until Porter's foot soldiers came up to spell them. At once the Rebels fell back, whereupon Emory's Regulars pursued for almost five miles, taking many prisoners.[19]

While the fighting raged at and beyond Slash Church, one of Emory's squadrons, at Porter's directive, trotted westward to wreck more trackage on the Virginia Central. Short of its objective, this force, a portion of the 5th Cavalry, traded carbine fire with Stuart's ubiquitous troopers. When the Regulars discovered that their opponents were screening a much larger force, one that appeared to be readying an assault on Porter's main body, they disengaged, returned to Slash Church, and warned Porter. His infantry turned about and parried the enemy's blow, after which the Confederates drew off dejectedly. Rush's Pennsylvanians followed for three miles, snatching up Rebels who surrendered at the sight of the "long poles."[20]

The cavalry that Porter had detached to the Virginia Central mangled track, then captured and destroyed a mail train. They then loped west to the Richmond, Fredericksburg & Potomac, where, after chasing off a large but irresolute defense force, the 8th Illinois dismantled a bridge near Ashland Station. Not content with this damage, the next day Porter sent General Emory with the 5th and 6th Cavalry, supported by infantry, to both railroads. Wielding axes and crowbars, the cavalrymen destroyed a long section of track on the Virginia Central before moving against those R, F & P bridges that crossed the Pamunkey and South Anna Rivers.

The Regulars proved to be demolition experts. Before the day was out, they had burned or dismantled two long bridges while capturing prisoners, a field hospital, and a cache of commissary stores near Ashland. Thus the cavalry had made Porter's mission far more than a sweep of Hanover Court House. They had displayed a talent for hurting their enemy in his most sensitive area—his lines of communication and supply. As one historian has asserted, "At no other time in the [Peninsula] campaign was the cavalry used more effectively or to better purpose."[21]

>–•›–O–‹•–‹

Porter's expedition, which McClellan described as disastrous for the enemy— "not a defeat, but a complete rout," and "one of the handsomest things in the war"—relieved the army leader's concern that he must close in on Richmond with his upper flank under threat. Already he had pushed Keyes's corps over the Chickahominy, advancing it as far as a landmark known as Seven Pines and Fair Oaks Station on the Richmond & York River railroad, eight miles from the enemy capital. In Keyes's rear Heintzelman's III Corps held a less advanced position two miles west of Bottom's Bridge. Sumner's II Corps, Porter's V, and the new VI Corps of General Franklin—like the V, a provisional command whose organization was later confirmed by the War Department—remained on the north side of the rain-swollen stream.[22]

Keyes's exposed position invited attack. Just past noon on the last day of May, Joe Johnston, hoping to preempt a siege such as McClellan had imposed on Yorktown, launched an assault that should not have come as a surprise, but did. For a time, Johnston had Keyes's troops, especially his westernmost regiments, on the ropes. Some brigades broke on contact, including one commanded by the former cavalryman Innis Palmer. Heintzelman rushed up supports but failed to stem the gray tide. Only after McClellan hurried Sumner's corps across the river via Grapevine Bridge were the Rebels slowly and gradually contained. As it was, fighting continued into the afternoon of June 1, by which time Johnston had been disabled by a wound and his successor, Robert E. Lee, lately the military advisor to Confederate president Jefferson Davis, withdrew the troops he would soon christen the Army of Northern Virginia.[23]

Two days of combat took a heavy toll of both armies: More than 5,000 Federals and almost 6,200 Confederates had become casualties. No cavalrymen were included among McClellan's losses, for no role had been found for them during the fight except as orderlies and couriers. This situation was not unique; it cropped up again and again in later months. Neither Little Mac nor his several successors understood how horsemen might contribute to the army's fortunes in combat. Troopers could be valuable in support of a relatively small expeditionary force, but there seemed to be no room or job for them on a battlefield.

One of the few duties the cavalry was assigned on May 31-June 1 was to picket ground north and east of Seven Pines. One unit so involved comprised two squadrons of the 5th United States under Capt. William L. Royall. The Regulars were sent to Old Church to guard the rear of the army and its communications on the Pamunkey. Other rear-echelon assignments moved lancers as well as conventionally armed troopers to Wormley's Ferry on the Pamunkey, where roving bands of cavalry were harassing McClellan's supply trains. By the first week of June mounted units including the 11th Pennsylvania were patrolling south of White House Landing as well as along the York River Railroad. Along the far borders of the army, the 8th Illinois picketed the right flank, while the 3rd Pennsylvania and other outfits guarded the left, from the Chickahominy to the James.[24]

Since McClellan believed the cavalry's forte was guard duty, not battle, he expected much of the horsemen who patrolled his flanks. The demands he placed on his relatively small mounted arm stretched it across so many miles of disputed ground that gaps were bound to open in its lines.

One such gap appeared in the second week of June near Old Church. Through it, on the morning of the thirteenth, rode 1,200 troopers and two batteries under J. E. B. Stuart and his ranking subordinates, Brig. Gen. Wade Hampton; Col. Fitzhugh Lee, nephew of the commander of the Army of Northern Virginia; and Col. W. H. F. "Rooney" Lee, Robert E. Lee's second son. The Rebels were reconnoitering McClellan's right flank, whose exact location and approximate strength would be critical to the offensive Robert E. Lee was planning to launch before McClellan could invest Richmond.

Before reaching Old Church, the raiders had surprised a detachment of the 6th United States Cavalry, which they failed to capture but drove west of Hanover Court House. At Haw's Shop near Totopotomoy Creek (future site of one of the war's fiercest cavalry clashes), the Confederates had scattered another small mounted force before entering the Union rear at Old Church. By now, Stuart had gathered the intelligence he had sought. The ease with which he had come this far, and the lack of infantry in the area he had traversed, told him that McClellan's upper flank was unanchored and thus susceptible to being turned.[25]

A mile from Old Church, Captain Royall's squadron of the 5th Cavalry came up to join the fugitives from Hanover Court House in opposing Stuart. The Confederates swarmed over Royall's position atop a hill, where a savage saber-and-pistol melee broke out. They surrounded Royall himself, who took a half dozen saber slashes, four about the head and face. Three of his men fell dead or mortally wounded, and a dozen others were wounded and most of them captured. Only one attacker fell: Capt. William Latane of the 9th Virginia, whose burial at the hands of female residents of the area inspired a now-famous painting.

Bleeding from his many wounds, Royall galloped to safety, along with other members of the defeated force; they carried word of Stuart's raid to the main army, but they did not tell their comrades—they could not have known—that Stuart planned to pass around their rear and lower flank instead of returning home the way he had come.[26]

The first commander to learn of Stuart's presence near Old Church was his father-in-law, Philip St. George Cooke. Most of Cooke's Cavalry Reserve was encamped only a few miles from Hanover Court House but had not received timely word of the enemy's coming. Cooke relayed the news to Stoneman, who assigned the loyalist Virginian to lead the pursuit. That assignment was, or at least could be, a stepping-stone to promotion—in fact, lifelong honor awaited the man who overtook and bested the "Beau Sabreur of the Confederacy."

For reasons of his own, Cooke shied from the responsibility conferred on him. Although he later reported mounting a pursuit as soon as he learned of the raiders' presence at Old Church, in truth he did not start out for several hours, having delayed to supply himself and his men with rations. Then he picked up an erroneous report that Stuart had infantry support, which led him to dither over the effectiveness of any pursuit. At least one of Cooke's troopers surmised that the general purposely delayed for fear of overtaking his son-in-law and being captured by him, a humiliation the old Regular could not have borne.[27]

Whatever the reason, Cooke did not break camp until 8:00 on the thirteenth. By that time his relative was well along the trail to Tunstall's Station on the Richmond & York River Railroad, about twenty miles south of Old Church. And it was to Old Church, long free of raiders, that Cooke led his Regulars and lancers.

If the white-bearded general wished to avoid catching Stuart, he must have been relieved by an order from Fitz John Porter, to whose command the Cavalry Reserve had recently been attached. Porter directed Cooke to remain for a time at Old Church and to refrain from attacking a superior force. Not till 4:00 A.M. on the fourteenth did Cooke depart Old Church in pursuit of his presumed quarry.[28]

Parrying the efforts of mounted parties along his route to slow or stop him, Stuart led his men into Tunstall's Station, where they overawed its small guard and shot up an approaching troop train. By now the raiders were home free, especially after they cut telegraph lines that might have brought accurate information on their progress and location to General Cooke.

After midnight on June 14–15 Cooke's advance, the 6th Pennsylvania, General Emory at its head, finally reached Tunstall's. The men and their mounts were weary after a long ride under a hot sun; Emory decided to rest them instead of pushing his pursuit. They did not pick up Stuart's trail until 8:00 A.M. By then it was too late: A few hours before, Stuart's hard-riding troopers, despite being loaded down with plunder, including many horses and mules, had crossed the raging Chickahominy on the ruins of a bridge that fatigue parties had temporarily replanked. The lancers watched as the rear of Stuart's column disappeared over a rise south of the again inoperable bridge.[29]

Although the importance of the raiders' accomplishments remained unknown for almost two weeks, for months after Stuart's escape critics blasted the slow pace and ineffectiveness of Cooke's pursuit. One of them was Stoneman, who blamed Cooke for failing to place elements of his force where he had been told. In so claiming, Stoneman may have been covering himself, but censure of Cooke and his senior lieutenant, Emory, was prevalent throughout the army. Representative of the feelings of the troops involved, however peripherally, in the pursuit was the comment of Lieutenant McIntosh of the 5th Cavalry: "If the Cav'y had been properly handled, the whole force could have been cut off & captured. . . . As long as our Cavalry is managed in that way, we will never succeed." Looking to the long-term repercussions, he added, "We must expect to have some broken heads."[30]

Events met McIntosh's expectations. Even as he tried to downplay the extent of the enemy's success, McClellan launched an investigation into how the raiders had ranged so freely behind Union lines and returned home safely. Not surprisingly, Cooke and Emory were the focus of the inquiry and not surprisingly, both labored hard to explain why they should not be blamed. Emory thought the controversy overblown: "The damage done by the enemy is not commensurate with the bold spirit with which the raid was dictated." Stuart's father-in-law declared, with some heat, that "whenever a thousand or two of cavalry under a bold leader has it in its power to get in rear of the army, to make a dash on its communications and depots, [and] if it follow on the heels of the pickets into a camp of equal force . . . it may chance to destroy it."

In defending himself, Cooke ignored his role in the pursuit, choosing to emphasize the obvious: McClellan's mounted arm was not sufficient to cover by itself the army's flanks and rear. Thus it was wrong to blame it and its leaders for an outcome that only battalions of infantry could have prevented.[31]

If Stuart's father-in-law feared that his career had been jeopardized by recent events, he need not have fretted. Thanks to a second event hard on the heels of the first, that career was almost over.

For days following Stuart's raid, his adversaries sought to recoup lost pride. On the fifteenth troopers revisited Ashland Station, where they surprised and captured a small guard. McClellan chose to believe that this success had "repaid the enemy for his raid of Friday night." That same day, on a reconnaissance to the far left of the army near White Oak Swamp, a detachment of the 8th Pennsylvania drove in Rebel pickets, capturing their camp. Aware that stealth was a quality not often ascribed to the Union cavalry, Pvt. Robert Cummings boasted that "we came on them so quick that they had not time to fire at us but left everything and run." By everything, he meant "one horse, some clothing, pistols, swords, and muskets."[32]

Three days later Cummings's regiment made, in McClellan's words, "a handsome reconnaissance to Charles City Court-House [along the north bank of the James River] and recovered some of the mules driven off by Stuart." As though to convince himself, the army commander concluded, "We are about even with Stuart now." Still, he could not persuade his subordinates that Stuart's expedition was behind them. On June 22 he received a report from General Porter who, upon inspecting Cooke's command, had found that the Regulars expressed "little confidence in their ability to defend themselves" against a repetition of Stuart's ride. Nor did the troopers express confidence in "their commander."[33]

Three days later the beginning of a chain of events, later known as the Seven Days' Battles, gave General Cooke an opportunity to restore the luster his reputation had lost at his relative's hands. By the twenty-fifth McClellan had moved each of his corps except Porter's below the Chickahominy and was ready—as ready as he would ever be—to move against Richmond. That morning elements of the III Corps advanced beyond the Fair Oaks-Seven Pines vicinity to drive in the outposts opposite them, near Oak Grove and King's School House. Unexpectedly, they met heavy opposition. For hours the fighting seesawed back and forth, guttering out after darkness fell. The only action seen by Stoneman's troopers was a mild skirmish near Ashland Station between the 8th Illinois and a party of Stuart's people. Colonel Farnsworth's men also reported the advance of Stonewall Jackson's command. Jackson was en route from the Valley, where he had flummoxed McDowell and other Yankees through a combination of surprise, stealth, hard marching, and harder fighting.[34]

Although McClellan's army remained nominally on the offensive following Oak Grove, June 25 marked the last time it would assume that posture during its time on the Peninsula. The next morning various Confederate
forces—but not Jackson's, thanks to a series of miscues and misunderstand-
ings—struck all sectors of McClellan's line.

Lee landed his heaviest blow on Porter's isolated corps near Mechanicsville. Initially the Federals were sent reeling, although tactical errors and an
inability to coordinate prevented Lee from routing Porter. Day's end found
more holes in the attackers' lines than in the defenders'. And yet McClellan
was so shocked by his opponent's aggressiveness—Lee lashing out with his
back to the wall—that by midafternoon on the twenty-sixth he was planning to
retreat all the way to the James River.[35]

During the fighting at Mechanicsville, Stoneman's troopers—especially
Cooke's Reserve, and particularly Emory's portion of it—had given a strong
account of themselves, maintaining the integrity of their picket line along the
exposed flank and in the vulnerable rear of the V Corps. Emory's men might
have done more but did not. Lt. George B. Sanford was on duty with his company of the 1st Cavalry near Old Church when Lee's infantry drove toward it.
Sanford's squadron commander, Captain Magruder, "was apparently in considerable doubt as to what course to pursue, and for that day and the next he
solved the question by not doing anything at all. Why we were not gathered in
by the enemy is more than I could understand . . . except that they were not
bothering their heads much about stray cavalry squadrons."[36]

General Stoneman, with the main body of his cavalry as well as two
infantry regiments, had begun the day well in the rear, guarding the region
from Meadow Bridge on the Chickahominy to the Pamunkey River. When the
Rebels struck Porter's corps, to which most of Stoneman's command, including the now-detached Cavalry Reserve, had been reattached on June 16, they
interposed between the cavalry and the rest of the V Corps. Unable to fight his
way through to Porter, Stoneman fell back below a Pamunkey River tributary,
putting the obstacle between himself and the attackers. On the afternoon of the
twenty-seventh he was called to McClellan's supply base at White House.
There some of his horsemen guarded their army's property until able to
reestablish contact with Porter.[37]

Cooke's Reserve did not accompany Stoneman to White House but
remained intermittently in touch with Porter and attempted to conform its
movements to his. Early that evening, when the fighting at Mechanicsville
tapered off, McClellan ordered Porter, as part of an armywide withdrawal, to
fall back to Gaines's Mill, a little more than four miles to the southeast. As
everyone in the high command must have anticipated, Lee followed, and on
the morning of the twenty-seventh he attacked the V Corps in its new semicircular position behind Boatswain's Creek. Doubtful that he could flank the Yankees out of their hastily constructed but serviceable breastworks, Lee decided
to smash head-on into them. Porter's line broken, Lee could sweep down along
McClellan's line, rolling it up like a thick blue carpet.[38]

When Lee's assault began, Cooke had massed what remained of his casualty- and detachment-depleted Reserve—fewer than 650 officers and men—behind Porter's extreme left. On Cooke's right were a pair of Stoneman's outfits, the 8th Illinois and the untried and therefore sizable 4th Pennsylvania. In that sector, bordering the Chickahominy lowlands, Cooke was expected to guard the flank, seal off access to the rear, and shield several batteries positioned nearby, including Robertson's horse artillery. Initially, most of Cooke's troopers and many of the guns were hidden from sight behind a plateau atop which Porter had constructed the greater part of his line.[39]

Assailed by 60,000 attackers, Porter's 35,000 men were hard pressed all day on all parts of their line. At several points, his left appeared to waver. Each time, the artillery shored up the flank by advancing against Longstreet's division and holding it back by sheer firepower.

As the only general officer on that part of the field, Cooke had—or at least believed he had—the power to position guns and gunners as he thought best. For most of the battle, he kept the batteries well forward, firing into the teeth of the oncoming Rebels. Late in the afternoon, however, with darkness approaching and ammunition running low, he ordered most of the guns behind the ridge. This decision displeased General Porter, who believed that only the artillery's advanced position had kept the flank intact.

Porter's displeasure increased geometrically when, just shy of 7:00 P.M., Confederates broke through on the left, not far above Cooke's position. Suddenly Union soldiers were running to the rear, creating a gaping hole where General Morell's division had once been. Soon batteries began to limber up and pound to the rear as well. Then Brig. Gen. George E. Pickett's brigade of Longstreet's command swept to within 100 yards of the guns Cooke was supervising. Only the shelling of those cannons kept the dike from breaking south of the point at which the first breach had occurred.[40]

Cooke—who had received no orders from Porter—considered it his duty to protect those batteries at all costs. All Porter had told him was to refrain from moving his horsemen from behind their ridge and onto the plateau in front. That ground was so flat and so devoid of cover that if they crossed it, they would become easy targets. Yet Cooke believed he had to risk a forward movement. As he later tried to explain, only an offensive by the cavalry could save the guns from being overrun, and on the guns' safety the life of Porter's corps depended. Therefore the old Regular ordered the 250 men of Whiting's 5th United States to charge the nearest Rebels.[41]

Whiting's men were asked to gallop perhaps 300 yards across the plateau and somehow retain enough momentum to drive the enemy on the other end. Minimal preparations would be taken to support them; on their flanks, the 1st Cavalry and the 6th Pennsylvania would provide a covering fire. To Whiting, this seemed precious little assistance, but there was no help for it. The captain may have doubted the practicality of a mounted assault against a solid line of infantry, but he saluted and gave the order to draw sabers. Backed by his senior subordinate, Captain Chambliss, he led the truncated regiment, in two columns, across the plain in a style reminiscent of the Light Brigade at Balaklava.

A sobering parallel with the earlier charge was the futility of Whiting's effort. Well short of its objective, nearly half of his outfit, including every officer but one, fell from the saddle, victims of massed musketry. Whiting himself was wounded, and Chambliss took seven wounds. Somehow both survived the day, Chambliss in enemy hands.

Most of the attackers never reached Pickett's line. Once they appreciated the doomed nature of the effort, they wheeled about and returned to their point of origin. Some who raced to the rear fell prey to ungovernable momentum and charged into the batteries they had been trying to save, scattering men and caissons. A few fortunate souls made their way, unhurt, across the plain and crashed into the enemy's ranks; in the process, however, at least two received bayonet wounds. All told, the 5th Cavalry lost one officer and three troopers killed, five officers and twenty-five men wounded, and twenty-four men and an equal number of horses captured.[42]

It should be stressed that the charge exerted no influence, for good or ill, on the battle, which had already been lost by the time Whiting's stalwarts unsheathed their swords. By nightfall Porter's corps was in flight across four bridges over the Chickahominy, straining to join comrades on the south bank, its retreat covered by the rest of the Regular Cavalry.

Even so, Porter held Whiting's charge responsible for everything bad that had happened to his corps this day. To a large extent he was trying to shift the blame from his infantry, but his shock at Cooke's fatal disregard of orders had been genuine. When he caught up with his subordinate after the battle, his first words were: "My God, Genl. Cooke[,] your cavalry have ruined the army!"[43]

Others' observations on the outcome and effect of the charge were less sweeping but just as damning. Some of those who observed it, and a few who had taken part in it, considered it a good idea resorted to at the wrong time or one not pushed far enough; one cavalry officer even predicted that a second attack by the remainder of Cooke's force would have blunted the Rebel drive. The majority of those who witnessed and commented on the charge, however, condemned it as poor decision-making and a tragic waste of limited resources based not only on faulty tactics—specifically, on Cooke's preference for a mounted attack against all odds—but also on a fundamental disregard for the lives of men and animals.

Cooke might have lived down his inability to catch his son-in-law, but he never rose above the notoriety of his actions at Gaines's Mill. On July 5 the renowned theorist asked to be relieved pending the outcome of another inquiry into his generalship. Sent to Washington soon afterward, he never again served in the field. He closed out his war career as commander of the army's recruiting service.[44]

Chapter Eight

On the Heels of the Invader

For several days after Gaines's Mill, the Army of the Potomac took the express route to the James, triumphant Confederates in pursuit. The southward race was punctuated by daily fighting—at Garnett's and Golding's Farms on the twenty-eighth; at Savage's Station and Allen's Farm on the twenty-ninth; and at White Oak Swamp and Frayser's Farm on the thirtieth. Each bore the earmarks of a Union victory, Lee suffering heavier losses in failing to drive his enemy from well-defended positions. Nevertheless, at the close of each day, McClellan only redoubled the pace of his retreat. His single-minded goal was to reach the river and the sanctuary of the gunboat fleet anchored in it.[1]

Those cavalry units attached to the main army helped smooth McClellan's path by keeping the enemy at a sufficient distance, reconnoitering the country that lay ahead, and guarding strategic crossroads and bridges that had to be kept open to their comrades and blocked to their opponents. Meanwhile, the regiments under Emory moved to White House Landing, where, on the twenty-eighth, they joined Stoneman in facilitating the transfer of the army's base from the York and Pamunkey to the James. Troopers became longshoremen, loading transports with everything from cracker barrels to artillery caissons. Once full, the ships cast off for Fort Monroe, from there to steam up the James to the army's new home near Harrison's Landing.[2]

What could not be carted off, including warehouses crammed with rations, equipment, even medical stores, was torched to deny it to the approaching enemy. Then, as Lieutenant Sanford recalled, "in the blaze of the burning buildings, with Stuart's artillery thundering in our rear, we began our night march down the Peninsula." A forced movement over roads choked with artillery units, supply vehicles, and sutlers' wagons brought Stoneman's and Emory's tired, dusty horsemen to Yorktown late the following day.[3]

Though Stuart failed to overtake Stoneman's people at White House, he did encounter mounted regiments covering McClellan's withdrawal. On the last day of June three companies of the 3rd Pennsylvania, supported by a small contingent of infantry and artillery, were patrolling near Jones's Bridge over the Chickahominy when they observed the approach of Stuart's 1st North Carolina and 3rd Virginia. Colonel Averell and his comrades baited a trap into which their opponents were kind enough to fall. Chasing a small party of Federals around a bend in the road, Stuart's troopers received fire from hidden artillery. Propelled into flight, the Confederates were pursued by a squadron of Pennsylvanians, who took prisoners and otherwise finished off the rout.[4]

Averell's troopers then moved south, reuniting with their army at Malvern Hill, thirteen miles from Richmond and eight miles northwest of Harrison's Landing. Atop that lofty eminence, McClellan had posted a rear guard consisting of thousands of well-dug-in foot troops and battery after battery from Colonel Hunt's Artillery Reserve (a trooper called it "the most artillery I have ever seen . . . in one field"). Hunt had stacked more than 100 pieces hub-to-hub on the crest. They commanded every approach Lee might take to reach his enemy. The position was so secure it assured McClellan's ability to reach Harrison's Landing with his main army intact.[5]

Studying the impregnable works atop the hill, Averell doubted that Lee would be foolish enough to press his pursuit that far. He was wrong. On the morning of July 1 the Army of Northern Virginia hurled itself at the northeast face of the hill in wave after wave of attack. Each was broken up far from its objective by the rear guard, especially Hunt's artillery.

Lee refused to admit defeat until nightfall; by then the foot of the hill was a scene of carnage that defied comprehension. It remained so the next morning, when Averell, whom McClellan had placed in charge of a new, mobile rear echelon, heard "shrieks, and groans, and the murmur of a multitude." Peering down from the summit, he beheld a sight he would never forget: "Over five thousand dead and wounded men were on the ground, in every attitude of distress. A third of them were dead or dying, but enough were alive and moving to give the field a singular crawling effect."[6]

>-+-‹›-•-O-‹›-+-‹

While the Army of Northern Virginia labored under a truce flag to succor its wounded and inter its dead, the Army of the Potomac fortified its base on the James. The work meant a new round of picket and scouting duty for the already overworked cavalry. Like the majority of the other services, Stoneman's horsemen were not only dispirited by their flight from the gates of Richmond, but also bone-weary from weeks of near-constant duty and weakened by lowland-inspired illnesses and poor and irregularly issued rations. Trooper Silas Wesson of the 8th Illinois barely had the strength to scrawl a diary entry for July 1: "No sign of rest, no let up in the fighting. I am so sleepy I cannot eat and so hungry I cannot sleep. My horse has worn his saddle for a week. He is tired and sleepy too." Lieutenant McIntosh informed his wife that after weeks of eating on the run, "I do not believe I will weigh over 130 lbs. My ribs fairly stick out."[7]

As soon as camp was pitched, dozens of troopers in every regiment turned out for sick call, and hundreds of overworked and broken-down mounts were

declared unfit for future service. Most of the disabled horses were shot and
their carcasses tossed into the James. A Pennsylvanian observed that "on the
surface of the river was a scum of refuse hay and oily fragments of decomposing animal matters."[8]

Not only the common soldiers were unwell. General Stoneman was nearly
prostrated by a flare-up of his piles, which had been aggravated by his recent,
nearly incessant service in the saddle. For the time being unable to ride, he petitioned McClellan to let him go to his home in Washington on sick leave. Apparently his request did not sit well with his commander, for on July 5, as Stoneman
prepared to accompany the unfortunate General Cooke to the capital, Little Mac
issued an order replacing Stoneman with Averell. Perhaps the order had a ring of
permanence; Stoneman canceled his leave at once. After a hasty meeting with
Little Mac, the following day he was reinstated as chief of cavalry.[9]

In his order of July 6, McClellan reminded Stoneman—rather unnecessar-
ily, one would think—to "report direct to, and receive his orders from, the general commanding the army." The tone of the edict suggests a coolness between
the army leader and his number-one cavalryman, as if Little Mac held Stoneman responsible for Stuart's escape and Gaines's Mill. McClellan neither then
nor afterward recognized or applauded the unstinting service Stoneman's
horsemen had rendered the army, often under difficult conditions, from Yorktown to Harrison's Landing.[10]

Friction also appears to have developed at this time between Stoneman and
Averell, although the official record yields few clues to the cause. It may have
been nothing more than a conflict of personalities. Stoneman was a quiet sort,
soft-spoken, self-effacing, and a bit dour—by no means a politician. A conservative old Regular, he favored substance over style and evaluated subordinates on
the basis of performance, not reputation. On the other hand, some observers,
Stoneman perhaps among them, considered Averell a fop as well as a glad-han-
der, self-promoter, and devotee of army politics. Averell was a well-known volunteer, and his regiment, the first of its kind in the field, never wanted for
newspaper publicity. Stoneman may also have resented Averell's close association with McClellan—he was ever a favorite of the army's inner circle—while
he himself could not seek medical treatment without incurring penalties.

McClellan's regard for Averell showed clearly in the order by which he
reinstated Stoneman. Little Mac directed his cavalry chieftain to consolidate
his force into two brigades, one led by the colonel of the 3rd Pennsylvania.
The dutiful Stoneman did as he was told.[11]

The reorganization promoted not only Averell but also David Gregg, who,
perhaps more than any other field-grade officer of volunteer cavalry, had
emerged from the campaign just ended with the loftiest reputation, his regiment's flight from New Kent Court House notwithstanding. As commander of
the 1st Cavalry Brigade, Averell was assigned his own regiment, plus
McReynolds's 1st New York and Childs's 4th Pennsylvania. Gregg was given
his own 8th Pennsylvania, Lt. Col. William Gamble's 8th Illinois (Colonel

Farnsworth was on leave), and a squadron of the 6th New York under Lieutenant Colonel McVicar, the officer who, on Staten Island, had overawed rioting enlisted men with firepower and a fierce stare. As a part of other, miscellaneous assignments, the McClellan Dragoons and detachments of the 5th Pennsylvania, 1st New York, and 8th Illinois were attached to the various corps. Averell's brigade was assigned to cover the front and right wing of the army, Gregg's to patrol the left. Each commander was ordered to report daily to army headquarters on his operations.

Stoneman's approach to reorganizing the former Cavalry Reserve appears tentative and uncertain, perhaps because its regiments—now the 1st, 5th, and 6th United States—had been whittled down so low that he lacked a firm idea of their numbers. His decree noted only that "the whole regular cavalry will be consolidated into as many complete squadrons as the numbers present will allow, and the officers will be assigned to each as the interests of the service may demand." No one replaced Cooke in overall command; until further notice, that role would be filled by the senior Regular. As for the volunteer component of the Reserve, Stoneman attached the 6th Pennsylvania to his own headquarters, while directing that twenty-man detachments of lancers report daily to each army corps for service as scouts and guides.[12]

The order that saved Stoneman's job cost Emory his. Without fanfare, the brigadier was transferred to the infantry. A few days later he assumed command of one of the IV Corps brigades that had been demoralized at Seven Pines. Later Emory was sent to the western theater, where he moved up to divisional command and managed to repair the reputation that had been damaged in pursuit of Stuart's raiders.[13]

The vacancy created by Emory's departure suggested that the cavalry was owed a new general officer. Averell, Gregg, or Farnsworth would have been an ideal choice, but for a number of reasons, none won a star for some time— Averell not until late September, Gregg and Farnsworth two months later. When it was announced, the new appointment must have surprised Stoneman, for it is unlikely he would have recommended the recipient. Doubtless with McClellan's endorsement, on July 18 Major Pleasonton of the Regular Army was named a brigadier general of volunteers. Given Pleasonton's new rank, Stoneman had to put him in the place of the less senior of his brigade leaders, Gregg.[14]

Pleasonton's promotion was surely a reward for his quietly competent service throughout the campaign just ended, which included a daring mission at the outset of McClellan's withdrawal to the James. On June 29 the major had led his 2nd Cavalry, along with the McClellan Dragoons, from White Oak Swamp to the river. There he opened communication with the gunboats supporting the army and sized up Harrison's Landing as a base of operations and supply. McClellan came to appreciate not only Pleasonton's dash but also his eye for terrain.[15]

His elevation to brigadier was the last promotion Pleasonton won solely on merit. Thereafter he played every military and political connection he could establish to advance his standing in the cavalry. Even more than Averell, he was flamboyant and flashy, craved publicity, and made good copy. He seemed to spend the greater part of his time polishing his image instead of validating it. Also like Averell, Pleasonton had a penchant for rubbing his less ostentatious, more circumspect superior the wrong way. In time Stoneman came to share two well-publicized opinions about the man, the first, voiced by one of Pleasonton's subordinates, that "he does nothing save with a view to a newspaper paragraph," and the other, offered by a fellow general, that "his vanity is over-weening."[16]

Pleasonton enjoyed an early opportunity to shake hands with someone who could advance his career. On July 25, two weeks after President Lincoln paid a call at Harrison's Landing, the new general in chief of the Army, Maj. Gen. Henry W. Halleck, came down from Washington to confer with the man whose job he had taken. Halleck was on a fact-finding mission, and what he found along the James was not much to his liking. Like Lincoln before him, Halleck was disappointed to find McClellan, in his current position, unable or unwilling to undertake anything resembling an offensive.[17]

In fact, McClellan seemed able to do nothing that would promote the war effort in the East—an effort whose strategic importance had been underscored by two recent decisions by Lincoln. One called for 300,000 additional three-year volunteers to save the Union; the other created an army in middle Virginia under Maj. Gen. John Pope, like Halleck a supposedly brilliant transferee from the western theater. Pope's department embraced three predecessors that covered both the Rappahannock River basin and the Shenandoah Valley. Pope's stated objective was to consolidate all forces in Virginia except McClellan's, then move against Lee's communications along the Virginia Central Railroad, thus taking the pressure off the Army of the Potomac.

Pope's reputation and brand of politics ensured that McClellan was not his friend. Halleck realized this; for that reason, nothing gave him a clearer picture of McClellan's frame of mind than his response to a question the general in chief put to him. When asked to choose between renewing his movement on Richmond with 20,000 reinforcements or quitting the Peninsula and sending some troops to Pope, McClellan selected option two. He wanted to remain on the James, but taking the offensive required far more supports than Washington could afford to send him.[18]

Although Halleck's decision to haul the army northward was soon a foregone conclusion, not for three weeks after he returned to Washington did McClellan pack up and depart Harrison's Landing for the wharves of Fort Monroe. In the interim, Stoneman's horsemen saw much service along and above the river. Many of their accomplishments during this period were never recorded. As one cavalry historian put it, "Daily patrols often led to brief skirmishes where men whose names are lost to history died in small numbers on back trails and roads on the outskirts of the army."[19]

A few deeds would prove worthy of note, either for their strategic importance or for their uniqueness. On the last day of July, acting rather on a whim, J. E. B. Stuart showered McClellan's forces with shells from batteries he had positioned on the south bank directly opposite Harrison's Landing. Stoneman's camps appear to have been his primary target; the barrage killed eight troopers in three Pennsylvania outfits. The gunboats in the James returned fire, chasing off the attackers, but not before they created some impressive pyrotechnics. To Robert Cummings, "the flashing of the cannons" appeared to set the "river . . . ablaze." Christian Geisel noted that "the balls and shells whistled pretty sharp over our camp . . . like sky rockets going through the air."[20]

The next day McClellan, fearing a renewal of Stuart's assault, sent Averell, with 300 3rd Pennsylvanians and 5th Regulars, plus infantry and artillery, over the James at Coggins Point. The hunters swept the south bank clear of Rebel troops, of which they found few. They should have known that Stuart would not have tarried long enough to risk being gobbled up.[21]

Taking a page from Stuart, McClellan gave the impression of wanting to retake the offensive. On August 3 he sent Averell to the bridge over White Oak Swamp, there to guard the northern approaches to Malvern Hill. Supposedly, McClellan wished the eminence, which he had relinquished to the enemy, held as a possible stepping-stone to a new movement against Richmond. Averell's force moved stealthily enough to interpose between a squadron of Stuart's 10th Virginia and the bridge in question, which the Confederates were guarding from too great a distance. Forced into a quick retreat through the swamp, the Virginians lost almost thirty men to Averell's pursuit.[22]

Early that same day, the newly minted General Pleasonton also led his brigade, plus some horse artillery, toward Malvern Hill. Over the next two days his command engaged and bested North Carolina cavalry, held infantry and artillery at bay till a portion of the main army came up to secure Malvern Hill, pursued retreating cavalry, and brazenly, though unsuccessfully, charged a Georgia infantry regiment. Lieutenant Colonel Gamble, whose 8th Illinois made the ill-fated attack, took a severe wound as the enemy sped away. The dogged Pleasonton pursued, taking prisoners, then capped his assignment by reconnoitering up the New Market Road toward Richmond. By the time he returned to camp, the "nice little dandy," as he was known in some parts of the army, had demonstrated enough competence to silence his critics—at least for a time.[23]

McClellan's flirtation with the offensive did not endure. By August 7 the cavalry was helping secure his departure from the James prior to embarking for Washington and Pope's headquarters. The army would have to catch Pope on the run. Two days later the new commander was clashing with Stonewall Jackson at Cedar Mountain, seventy-five miles northwest of Harrison's Landing. Robert E. Lee, secure in the belief that McClellan no longer posed a threat to Richmond, had dispatched a portion his army to confront Pope near Gordonsville. As soon as McClellan gave signs of debarking for the North, Lee planned to lead the rest to Jackson's support. After whipping Pope's so-called Army of Virginia, Lee could return his attention to McClellan, wherever he turned up.[24]

By the fourteenth McClellan had started Heintzelman's and Porter's corps for the Peninsula. Two days later the evacuation of Harrison's Landing was completed, as the balance of the Army of the Potomac, its march covered by Stoneman's troopers, started for Alexandria via Fort Monroe and Yorktown.[25]

>─┼─◄▷─•─○─•─◁▷─┼─◄

John Pope had inherited the troops formerly assigned to Irvin McDowell and Nathaniel Banks, among other commanders. Thus, simply by assuming command of the Army of Virginia, he acquired some of the finest cavalry regiments to serve the Union cause. He also gained the services of two of the finest general officers of cavalry. One had come to him from McDowell's corps: George D. Bayard, a brigadier since April 28. A New York native and New Jersey resident, Bayard had amassed an active record in the prewar 1st Cavalry. He carried on his left cheek a livid scar from a poisoned arrow with which a Kiowa warrior had nearly killed him. A rigid disciplinarian but even-tempered and fair-minded, Bayard had turned his initial command, the 1st Pennsylvania, into a model regiment, and later, when assigned to catch Jackson's "foot cavalry" in the Shenandoah, he had succeeded as well as anyone involved in that hopeless task, and better than most.[26]

Bayard was especially adept at reconnaissance and intelligence gathering, a strength shared by his colleague John Buford. This stocky, mustachioed, tawny-skinned Kentuckian was likewise a well-known veteran of the old army, having risen to captain in the 2nd Dragoons on the strength of tactical acumen and faultless leadership. When war came, however, Buford rose no higher in his arm; he was forced to join the inspector general's office to win promotion. Pope, whose family and Buford's shared some roots, suspected that the major's Southern birth had prejudiced him in the eyes of the War Department. Rumor said that Buford had been offered a commission in the Confederacy, one he scornfully rejected. To Pope's credit, on August 3 he gave Buford his first field command, one that would catapult him into national prominence.[27]

Blessed as it was with talented lieutenants, Pope's army was no match for Lee's, principally because Pope was not one-tenth the soldier his opponent was. Three weeks after Cedar Mountain, Lee's soon-to-be-reunited army followed Pope's to the edge of the old Bull Run battlefield. Implementing a simple but inspired plan, Lee had Jackson hold Pope in place on August 29, while the peripatetic Longstreet took position the next morning opposite the left flank of their unsuspecting foe. On the thirtieth Longstreet overwhelmed and crushed that flank, sending survivors flying—most of them as far as the defenses of Washington. The troops McClellan sent Pope had availed him nothing; in fact, in Pope's mind, they had cost him a victory. Afterward an irate Pope charged Fitz John Porter with willful disobedience of some orders and unconscionably poor execution of others. Although many in Porter's corps considered the charges politically motivated, the following January a military court convicted Porter on several counts and ordered him cashiered.[28]

By the time the balance of McClellan's army made it to Washington, it was too late to do anything but back up Pope's demoralized survivors and vow revenge on Lee. This resolve stiffened when, on September 4, advance elements of the Army of Northern Virginia crossed the Potomac into border state Maryland. Lee's intention seemed clear: to carry the war, for the first time, into his enemy's country. A major victory on what the North regarded as its soil might bring intervention on behalf of the Confederacy from the European powers. A campaign above the Potomac would also relieve war-torn Virginia, at least temporarily, of her unwanted guests in blue.[29]

At first Lee moved as if to attack Washington. This was, of course, the most frightful prospect the Lincoln administration could entertain. The capital's fears quieted only after it was learned that the Confederates were heading for western Maryland. Reports of Confederate progress threw both the White House and the War Department into a panic. On September 2, the day McClellan returned to the capital, Lincoln and Stanton called at his home and asked the Young Napoleon—as a personal favor to the president—to retake the field, this time at the head of not only his own army but also what remained of Pope's. The Army of the Potomac would be further enlarged by the addition of Maj. Gen. Ambrose E. Burnside's IX Corps, which had recently departed Hampton Roads after ending its coastal campaign in North Carolina. Enjoying his visitors' predicament, and especially the pleading tone of their request, McClellan agreed. Not till the seventh, however, did he leave the capital for Rockville, Maryland, where the advance of his enlarged command had moved.[30]

One of McClellan's first duties after reaching the front was to reorganize in order to manage the consolidation of the armies. Thanks to Pope, Little Mac now led, in addition to the II, III, IV, V, VI, and IX Corps, the I Army Corps, to the command of which he assigned Joe Hooker (McDowell had been relieved, along with Pope, for alleged misconduct at Second Bull Run); the XI Corps, under Maj. Gen. Franz Sigel; and the smallest component of the new army, the XII Corps of Maj. Gen. Henry W. Slocum.

McClellan enjoyed such a reserve of manpower that he could afford to leave behind three corps—the III, V, and XI—to man the defenses of the capital, thus easing the government's invasion fears. He entrusted the defense force, some 73,000 strong, to Nathaniel Banks. Even with these subtractions, the Army of the Potomac numbered more than 87,000 officers and men. Whether or not McClellan realized it (and if he did, he would not have announced it), his opponent in Maryland mustered about half as many troops.[31]

The most sweeping changes McClellan made upon retaking the field affected the cavalry. Two of his early decisions seemed to demonstrate that, whether or not he was a better soldier than John Pope, McClellan was a less astute judge of talent. On September 10 he permanently removed Stoneman as chief of cavalry and in his place instated John Buford. At least McClellan provided Stoneman a command commensurate with the one he had left; on the thirteenth Stoneman took charge of the 1st Division, III Army Corps.[32]

Buford's new position entailed tremendous administrative burdens but did not grant him tactical command of the army's horsemen. Originally,

McClellan had conceived of Stoneman's post as strictly administrative; yet on most occasions he permitted his subordinate to command in the field. Based on the results, he may have regretted his decision, for now he made the position strictly a desk job.

McClellan may have given Buford the assignment because he feared the old dragoon was not physically capable of taking the field. It was true that Buford had received a wound in the ankle at Second Bull Run, but the injury had been painful rather than disabling; in the week since, he had healed and gone back to duty. McClellan should have understood that Buford's tactical gifts would have made him an asset to the army even if he was less than 100 percent fit. The officer had demonstrated his fighting and intelligence-gathering abilities time after time in the recent campaigning. On one reconnaissance, he had captured some of J. E. B. Stuart's staff, Stuart's plumed hat, and very nearly Stuart himself. Then, too, had Pope heeded the timely information that Buford sent him late in the recent campaign, Second Bull Run might not have ended as a Union disaster.[33]

McClellan compounded his mishandling of Buford when he ordered the Kentuckian's brigade, along with Bayard's, to remain in the rear of the army as it moved to Maryland. Both commands were relegated to picketing near the Washington fortifications and reconnoitering between Falls Church and Alexandria. Neither would contribute to Federal fortunes during the coming campaign. And yet, perhaps this was for the best. Over the past six months, Buford's and Bayard's men had seen even longer and harder service than their counterparts in the Army of the Potomac, and their lack of battlefield success had demoralized many of them. As an officer in Bayard's 1st New Jersey put it, the "two days at Bulls Run were hard fought battles where shot and shell fell fast enough to satisfy the most ardent" of cavalrymen.[34]

To handle the tactical responsibilities denied to Buford, McClellan tabbed a soldier in whom he had confidence. Command of the army's mounted division, including the erstwhile Reserve, passed to Buford's long-time colleague in the 2nd Dragoons, Alfred Pleasonton. The horsemen assigned him were grouped into brigades under now-Major Whiting (consisting of the 5th and 6th United States), Colonel Farnsworth (the 1st Massachusetts, 3rd Indiana, 8th Illinois, and 8th Pennsylvania), Colonel Rush (the 4th and 6th Pennsylvania), and Colonel McReynolds (the 1st New York and the recently acquired 12th Pennsylvania).[35]

When Pleasonton took over, William Averell was on sick leave, suffering from a strain of malaria known as "Chickahominy fever." Had he been with the army at the time, he would have received command of the 1st Brigade. In later days, Averell's 3rd Pennsylvania would be grouped with another newcomer, the 8th New York, in a provisional brigade commanded by the 8th's colonel, Benjamin F. "Grimes" Davis. A hard-bitten West Pointer from Mississippi, Davis was stationed at Harpers Ferry in mid-September when Stonewall Jackson's Confederates surrounded the outpost and demanded its surrender. With his commander's permission, Davis led his own regiment, along with the 12th

Illinois, 1st Maryland, and 1st Rhode Island Cavalries, 1,300 men in all, on a daring journey by night through the enemy's lines. Davis not only made good his escape, but he also captured a ninety-seven-wagon train that held Confederate ammunition.[36]

In addition to the five brigades Pleasonton directly commanded, miscellaneous mounted units were attached to and scattered about the main army. The 1st Maine and a detachment of the 15th Pennsylvania remained unbrigaded, while the Oneida Cavalry and detachments of the 1st, 2nd, and 4th United States, 1st Maine, 1st Michigan, 2nd and 6th New York, 6th Pennsylvania, and 1st Ohio performed escort duty at corps and division headquarters.[37]

Early in September, Pleasonton's men moved out of Washington with speed fueled by an urgency to overtake the enemy short of the Mason-Dixon Line and as if to make amends for a recent spate of inactivity. Due to a temporary dearth of shipping in Hampton Roads, most of the troopers had not reached Alexandria until September 1. Over the next three days many were put to work picketing old haunts such as Falls Church and Fairfax Court House; other returnees lolled about Fort Albany, inside the capital defenses. On the fourth, with Pope's fugitives assembling not far away, they were relieved on patrol by Bayard's brigade. That day, as McClellan's new and improved army started for Maryland, the cavalry was ordered to Tennalytown, northwest of Washington. Pleasonton led them fourteen miles northward; they bivouacked at Darnestown on the night of the sixth. Meanwhile, sixteen miles to the west, Lee's army continued to ford the Potomac at and near Leesburg, Virginia. Its advance element pushed north in the direction of Frederick, Maryland.[38]

It was on the fifth that Pleasonton began to perform one of the most important duties of a cavalry leader, sending army headquarters word of the enemy's heading and progress. From scouts and local Unionists, he was able to inform McClellan that Lee was heading for Frederick with as many as 45,000 troops. This information was accurate and worth knowing. Soon after he sent it in, however, Pleasonton began to exaggerate the strength of Lee's detached forces, including Jackson's Harpers Ferry column. He also relayed incredible rumors about the enemy's whereabouts and cockeyed assessments of Lee's intentions. For instance, a day after accurately reporting Lee's strength, Pleasonton reduced it by 15,000, then passed along a report that Jackson with 60,000 more was heading for Baltimore, which he planned to capture and occupy. The following day 40,000 troops, including 5,000 cavalry were heading for Baltimore under an unknown commander. By the evening of September 8 the invaders had grown to 100,000; they were still making for Baltimore but now via the resource-abundant country around York and Gettysburg, Pennsylvania.

Not knowing what to believe, McClellan accepted some of Pleasonton's least believable assessments of events. In response to the report about Gettysburg, he had the cavalry leader send the 1st New York in that direction, though the outfit soon returned empty-handed. Undaunted, Pleasonton kept upping

McClellan's opposition. By the ninth Lee's army had expanded to 118,000, including a huge corps of artillery.[39]

Even McClellan, who made a career of exaggerating his enemy's size, suspected that some of Pleasonton's estimates were "not fully reliable." He must have shaken his head over the "intelligence" Pleasonton sent him on the thirteenth: Joseph E. Johnston and a force of 150,000 were at Poolesville, poised to cut off McClellan's northward march. Meanwhile, Lee, from some unspecified point and with an unknown number of additional troops, was cooperating with Johnston to lure the Army of the Potomac into a trap. Little wonder that one postwar Confederate writer, upon reviewing Pleasonton's 1862 dispatches, dubbed him the "Knight of Romance."[40]

Along with exaggerations and improbabilities, Pleasonton treated army headquarters to a litany of complaints. He was painfully aware that he had left the District of Columbia with less than his entire command. For most of his westward jaunt, he was accompanied by the 6th United States, four companies of the 1st Cavalry, the 8th Illinois, the 1st Massachusetts, the 1st New York, the 8th and 12th Pennsylvania, and what there was of the 3rd Indiana. For artillery support, he could call on Robertson's and Benson's batteries. Other horsemen had been left with the main army to guard its flanks and rear on its outing in Maryland. Thus on the fifth Pleasonton wired McClellan's chief of staff and father-in-law, Brig. Gen. Randolph B. Marcy, that "I want more cavalry . . . also Tidball's Battery." On the tenth, during a stopover at Barnesville, he complained that his horses were short of forage and shoes and that his men lacked Sharps carbines (apparently only that brand would do on the present occasion). Later he importuned Marcy for permission to shift his headquarters from a site McClellan had favored to some "more central" locale. With a sigh, one imagines, the chief of staff gave in.[41]

Pleasonton's ability to gather intelligence may have been impaired, but he did keep headquarters informed of his whereabouts on a daily—in fact, an hourly—basis. On September 6 he wired McClellan fourteen times, the following day eleven times more. Between the eighth and the fourteenth he sent in at least fifty-five dispatches, some with the most trivial information imaginable. Incredibly, on the ninth McClellan reprimanded him for failing to keep headquarters "fully and frequently" informed on enemy movements. Perhaps the word Little Mac was searching for was "accurately."[42]

By September 10 Pleasonton's headquarters was still at Barnesville, although detachments of his command stretched as far east as Hyattstown and as far north as Monocacy Ferry on the river of the same name. Two days earlier his men had engaged a few Rebels near Poolesville, and the next day near Monocacy Church, but it was on the tenth that real fighting began. That morning horsemen north of Barnesville opened fire on Pleasonton's lines with three horse artillery pieces emplaced atop Sugar Loaf Mountain. Once McClellan informed him that the position "must be carried" if the march was to continue, Pleasonton attacked it three times but failed to neutralize it. The following day a portion of the just-arrived VI Corps, backed by Farnsworth's Illinoisans (who, Pleasonton informed Marcy, "behaved with their accustomed gallantry"), carried the position, and the army moved on to Frederick.

By the time they reached the city, the Rebels were long gone, yet they had left behind a gift to their enemy. Through a grievous error, a copy of Lee's orders for the campaign, which outlined the exact position of his army, had been lost, and Union soldiers found it. Through this incredible stroke of luck, McClellan learned that Lee had split his forces. Jackson was moving on Harpers Ferry, Longstreet was heading northwestward toward Hagerstown, and Stuart's cavalry and some infantry were lingering about South Mountain.[43]

But because the ever-deliberate McClellan failed to act upon it at once, the lost orders had no major effect on his showdown with the Army of Northern Virginia. Still, they enabled him to direct his westward-marching army through two defiles of South Mountain: Crampton's Gap and, seven miles to the north, Turner's Gap. On the fourteenth he sent Franklin's corps through Crampton's Gap in an effort to reach Harpers Ferry in time to lift Jackson's investment. Meanwhile, he sent through the upper defile the IX and I Corps, with Pleasonton's horsemen in front and on the flanks of the column.[44]

Approaching the summit of the mountain via the historic National Road, that morning Pleasonton rode proudly in advance of Burnside's IX Corps. Almost immediately upon reaching the gap, he encountered the rear guard Lee had placed in its mouth, part of Maj. Gen. D. H. Hill's infantry, as well as Stuart's horsemen. Pleasonton sent back for, and was supplied with, an infantry brigade, which he led up to the gap. Sharp skirmishes broke out in and just short of the gorge, and continued for hours.

When the IX Corps division of Brig. Gen. Jacob D. Cox came up at about 9:00 A.M., its men gradually relieved the cavalry, who fell back on the foot soldiers' flanks. The fighting grew hotter as other divisions joined in, but it no longer involved Pleasonton's main body. The only action the troopers saw during the balance of the day came when Pleasonton, acting upon a request, lent the 1st Massachusetts and 3rd Indiana to the vanguard of Joe Hooker's corps, coming up to the rear of Burnside. Through someone's oversight, both outfits were placed uncomfortably close to the flight path of Union artillery shells. "Here we sat on our horses for two hours," wrote Captain Adams of the 1st, "doing no good and unpleasantly exposed," until late in the afternoon, when they were led to the rear.[45]

When the attackers finally dislodged Hill and Stuart and debouched from the gap, it was past 10:00 P.M. Soon afterward, the Confederates quit the field. While Pleasonton allowed most of his troopers some rest, he led the 8th Illinois in pursuit of Stuart through Boonsboro. Later he reported clashing with Stuart's rear guard in the streets of the mountain village. His troopers charged the enemy "repeatedly, and drove them some 2 miles beyond the town."[46]

The following day, the sixteenth, as the army pushed west toward Sharpsburg, where Lee was massing along the banks of Antietam Creek, Pleasonton's men occupied their time "in reconnaissances, escorts, and supports to batteries." Their leader may have considered these activities a menial prelude to the coming battle, but when that battle began early on the seventeenth outside Sharpsburg, it was something of an anticlimax for the cavalry. Just as he had during the several battles on the Peninsula, McClellan intended that his horsemen remain well behind the firing lines on this, the bloodiest single day in American history.[47]

During the morning, Pleasonton found himself supporting Sumner's corps along the right center of the line, some 500 feet from the waters of the Antietam. He spent hours seeking an opportunity for more important activity. Finally, at midday, he was able to advance a large body of skirmishers, as well as Tidball's battery, across Middle Bridge on the Boonsboro Pike. Despite being subjected to a massive barrage that killed, among other troopers, Colonel Childs of the 4th Pennsylvania, Pleasonton held the position he carved out for himself. He strengthened his grasp on it by hauling up four other batteries, those of Gibson and Robertson as well as Capt. Alanson M. Randol's E/G, 1st Artillery, and Lt. Peter C. Hains's M, 2nd Artillery.

The combined fire of these units not only kept their position secure, but also eased the pressure that Sumner's corps had been experiencing at the hands of infantry and artillery along Lee's right. At one point, the batteries swiveled south to cover the IX Corps on the far Union left. Pleasonton's greatest accomplishment this day, as he explained in his report, was to pour shot and shell into a column of Rebel infantry concentrating behind Sharpsburg Ridge with the intention of turning Sumner's left. At 7:00 P.M., after seven hours or more under fire, the horse artillery was withdrawn and placed in bivouac outside the village of Keedysville.[48]

The guns under Pleasonton had performed ably this day, but the cavalry had hardly been involved. A few troopers in close proximity to the guns had suffered substantially from counterbattery fire. A few others had made what Capt. Robert Milligan of the 6th Pennsylvania called "a handsome charge" over Middle Bridge. Most of the cavalry, however, had not truly been committed to the battle. Pleasonton could boast to McClellan that he had "saved the left of Sumner from being crushed. . . . My artillery fire broke the rebel line & threw them back." But he could not trumpet his horsemen's performance on the offensive. The fault lay not so much with him as with an army leader who knew precisely how to employ foot troops and cannoneers in battle but whose mind went blank whenever horse soldiers entered the equation.[49]

Chapter Nine

Cold, Idle and Anxious

Neither side could boast of a victory along Antietam Creek; the primary outcome of the fighting was the extraordinary carnage, a combined total of more than 26,000 dead, wounded, and missing. Because of its limited exposure, Pleasonton's command had suffered only thirty casualties, one-third of them in the ranks of the horse artillery. At this price, the combatants had purchased a tactical draw. McClellan, however, reaped the strategic benefits, for the following evening Lee, believing his losses too steep to permit a continued sojourn in his enemy's country, recrossed the Potomac to Virginia. His retreat meant only a respite for the Army of the Potomac, but because it had failed to land a fatal blow, it would have to confront Lee again, this time on his own soil. As Capt. Charles Russell Lowell of the 6th United States Cavalry put it, "our victory was a complete one, but only decisive in so far as it clears Maryland."[1]

Decisive or not, the victory had to be followed up, and that was the job of the cavalry. At 6:00 A.M. on the eighteenth McClellan directed Pleasonton to push reconnaissance parties "to the right, left, and front of the position occupied by this army," gathering information on Lee's strength, opposition, and movements. The assignment made for arduous, time-consuming duty—but the cavalry's work was only beginning. Early on the nineteenth, scouts having brought McClellan word of Lee's withdrawal, Pleasonton moved to pursue. Moving forward, his men got their first close-up look at the battlefield, rife with bloated, blackened corpses, the carcasses of battery horses, and all manner of refuse. Pvt. Daniel Pulis of the 8th New York told his brother in Rochester of seeing "men with one leg[,] one arm[,] bodies without heads or with only part of a head. I saw one man . . . with the back part of his head cut entirely off. He was still alive." Passing a field hospital, Pulis spied "a stack of arms and legs 4 feet high." Reliving the scene as he wrote about it, the trooper shuddered involuntarily.[2]

The sight of commingled warriors in blue and gray, their enmity spent, brought home to a Union trooper from Virginia, a member of the Kanawah Division of the IX Corps, the horrors of civil war. "This," he wrote, "is an unnatural war. . . . As I rode over the bloody fields . . . and saw men of the same blood, of the same dialect, of the same country lying side by side[,] their bodies mangled and chilled in death—to what other conclusion could I come[?]"[3]

Once the shock of these horrors wore off, the troopers moved toward Lee's rear. As he led on, Pleasonton grew increasingly upset that McClellan had held back the cavalry until the enemy had virtually left the state. But he vowed to overtake the Rebels, and he envisioned an end to the fighting when he did. As he later recalled, "I was convinced a rapid and energetic pursuit would have routed them, if it had not caused Lee himself to surrender."[4]

While this statement smacks of self-serving exaggeration, the mounted leader was truly shocked when he learned, in later days, that the main army would remain in Maryland indefinitely. As when Johnston had slipped away at Yorktown, Little Mac saw little to gain, and possibly much to lose, by a "rapid and energetic" pursuit. He sent large detachments over the water more than once during this period, but he refused to lead the entire army across the Potomac until the last days of October, six weeks after Lee left his front.[5]

Obsessed as he was with his own reputation, Pleasonton could not afford to emulate his commander's laziness. On the nineteenth he met and struck the shank of a Rebel column near Shepherdstown Ford, capturing 167 stragglers, along with an abandoned cannon and a Confederate banner. Once at the river, however, the rear guard, which included artillery pieces, stymied Pleasonton, keeping his command on the north shore.[6]

Later that day, and again on the twentieth, McClellan moved Porter's corps to the far side of the river to probe the rear guard's strength. The first effort was largely successful, as infantry and cavalry drove their enemy well to the south. The second mission, however, ended prematurely when the reinforced Confederates thrust the V Corps back with loss. With that, the opposing infantries broke contact for a lengthy period. Lieutenant Sanford, whose 1st Cavalry had been in the advance on the nineteenth, recalled that "for nearly two months after this action, the two armies lay opposite each other with the river between them, recuperating their strength for another trial."[7]

The cavalry refused to sit idle. On the twenty-first Pleasonton, with his cavalry and artillery units attached to the II and V Corps, launched small-scale reconnaissances south of the river. On the twenty-third two regiments and some horse artillery under his command marched to Harpers Ferry and from there scouted toward Martinsburg and Charles Town. In so doing, Pleasonton scotched rumors that Lee had sent troops to attack outposts in the lower Shenandoah.[8]

On the twenty-eighth a similar rumor—that outlying detachments of Lee's command were operating north of Winchester—prompted Pleasonton, with 1,500 troopers and two batteries, to begin a several-day sweep of the Shepherdstown-Martinsburg region. Near Shepherdstown, the reconnaissance force drove cavalry pickets in on their infantry, from whose path Pleasonton withdrew without loss. In and around Shepherdstown, his men found virtually every home transformed into a hospital for the treatment of the wounded of Antietam. About 600 of these he captured and paroled. Theoretically, his act removed a Confederate regiment from the war, at least for a time: A paroled prisoner was not supposed to take up arms until receiving notice that he had been exchanged for a designated enemy POW.[9]

Pleasonton was still in Shepherdstown on October 1. That morning he led the 8th Illinois, three squadrons from the 8th Pennsylvania, an equal number of the 3rd Indiana, and Battery M, 2nd U.S. Artillery (now commanded by Lt. Alexander Cummings McWhorter Pennington, a mouthful of a name, with an excellent reputation behind it), and drove Stuart's 9th Virginia Cavalry along the westward-leading road to Martinsburg. Halfway there, the Federals were fired on at long range by a Rebel battery on the opposite bank of Opequon Creek. "I paid no attention to this," Pleasonton reported bravely, "and the rebels themselves saw their absurdity, and stopped firing." Continuing into Martinsburg, he shoved a large detachment of Hampton's command out of town, and kept it out.[10]

After gaining intelligence on local Confederates from loyalist residents of Martinsburg, Pleasonton led his troops out of town at a leisurely pace. Crossing the Opequon, he scattered would-be pursuers with "six or eight well-directed shells" from Pennington's battery. Thereafter, he returned to Shepherdstown and thence to the main army. In his after-action report, Pleasonton exaggerated the accomplishments of the mission, but it did demonstrate that the horsemen of the Army of the Potomac were not afraid to reconnoiter deep into enemy territory, even with the most celebrated cavalry of the war lurking in the area.[11]

⊱⊹⊶⊙⊷⊹⊰

On October 2 President Lincoln again visited army headquarters in the field. As on previous occasions, he inspected the troops—including the 194 officers and 4,349 enlisted men of the army's cavalry—and they, in turn, inspected him. Most decided they liked what they saw. "He is a good man," Surgeon Elias Beck of the 3rd Indiana decided, but he would be better "if he had only more back-bone." Doctor Beck hoped that Lincoln would use his visit to persuade McClellan to get off his behind and follow the enemy into Virginia: "Our Army is in good spirits and we are sure of a victory—the enemy is in bad spirits & short of ammunition." To let such an opportunity slip away would be criminal.[12]

Beck was hopeful but also realistic; he expected that nothing but reviews and inspections would come of Lincoln's visit. He was essentially correct, at least in the short term. McClellan frustrated Lincoln's every attempt to commit the army to an early resumption of the offensive. When he left for Washington on the fifth, the disappointed president was mulling over his options, which included firing his commander, regardless of how popular he remained with his troops. In the end he came to the regrettable but inescapable conclusion that Little Mac must go.

McClellan furnished most of the nails for his own coffin, but one was added, a few days after Lincoln returned home, by J. E. B. Stuart, with help from McClellan's own cavalry. Stuart had come to feel that one raid around the Army of the Potomac was not enough. It failed to satisfy his urge to tweak, taunt, and embarrass his enemy. Besides, only a dramatic feat such as a raid would repay McClellan for the thrusts his cavalry had been making into hitherto inviolate Confederate territory. His thinking meshed with the strategy of his commander, for Lee hungered for intelligence on McClellan's dispositions and intentions. From the meeting of their minds came a plan under which Stuart, with 1,800 officers and men, would penetrate far into McClellan's lines, scrutinizing his communications and, if possible, reaching north into Pennsylvania. Lee mentioned that outside the town of Chambersburg, 35 miles above McClellan's present position, the railroad that connected the Federals to their supply base at Hagerstown crossed a vulnerable bridge. Burning that trestle would perhaps be a crippling blow, forcing McClellan to rely for his supplies on the overtaxed and less accessible Baltimore & Ohio. Stuart nodded in agreement and made the necessary preparations.[13]

From the first, the Union response to the expedition was slow and erratic. When the head of Stuart's raiding column—five brigades plus the Stuart House Artillery, under Maj. John Pelham—splashed across the Potomac near McCoy's Ferry on the foggy morning of October 10, it swatted aside pickets of the 12th Illinois and headed for the Pennsylvania line. Patrols along that stretch of the river quickly sent in word of the raiders' movements. McClellan must have received the news by midday, but he made no response for several hours.

The two elements of his army in the best position to overtake the Confederates were Pleasonton's main body, stationed near Berlin, Maryland, twenty-two miles southeast of McCoy's Ferry, and a half dozen regiments led by now–Brigadier General Averell, his bout with malaria behind him, along the B & O at the mouth of the south branch of the Potomac. By the afternoon of the tenth both forces had learned of Stuart's coming, but because McClellan was ignorant of the size and heading of the enemy, he did not release the pursuit forces until, in Averell's case, late that evening and, in Pleasonton's, early on the eleventh. By then it was too late to stop the raiders short of their immediate objective. Rebels were already galloping through the Pennsylvania countryside, seizing horses, rations, and other resources of which the Army of Northern Virginia lacked an adequate supply. They were also destroying government and public property, while panicking citizens, politicians, and home guards.[14]

Stuart's opponents pinned their hopes on overtaking him before he returned to Virginia. That is, Pleasonton did—General Averell made sure he came nowhere near the raiders. For eight hours after learning Stuart had crossed into Maryland, Averell remained in place, and when he finally set out, instead of turning northeastward, he led his command directly north for more than fifty miles. He ended up in McConnellsburg, Pennsylvania, so far from Chambersburg that, for all it contributed to the pursuit, his brigade might have been on the moon.[15]

Alfred Pleasonton did not shy from catching Stuart—not at first, at any rate. On the morning of the eleventh he rushed north to Hagerstown, then, for unknown reasons, he turned west toward Clear Spring, all the while promising McClellan that he would "keep moving till I hear of the rebels." He would hear nothing in that direction, but it took a few hours before he discovered (or at least admitted) he had made a mistake.

After countermarching to Hagerstown via the National Road, Pleasonton decided to continue east in hopes of intercepting Stuart near Mechanicstown, atop the Catoctin Mountain range. But now, if he found the raiders, he was unsure he could put up much of a fight. By late afternoon his men had marched seventy miles since departing Berlin, leaving men and horses, as Pleasonton said, "pretty well used up." If this sounded like a ready-made excuse, it may have been. In his dispatches to McClellan, he also gave the impression that he led fewer men than Stuart was suspected of having. In reality, Pleasonton commanded more than 2,000 troopers. Some of these he had detached to scout on the fringes of the main column and thus were not immediately available to him. Even at that, Pleasonton's force at least equaled, and probably exceeded, Stuart's.[16]

By design or happenstance, Pleasonton timed his arrival near Mechanicstown almost perfectly. Just south of the village, at about 9:00 P.M., his advance encountered a segment of Stuart's column. Instead of forcing a confrontation, however, Pleasonton pulled his troopers southward, paralleling the enemy's line of march. He later claimed that he failed to learn of Stuart's proximity for several hours after his scouts discovered it, but this assertion strains credulity. By turning south, Pleasonton was merely acting in character. Like the army leader whose timidity he sometimes derided, he feared to engage any force, especially a sizable one led by enterprising and combative officers, unless his force was much larger than the enemy's or he enjoyed infantry support.[17]

Pleasonton knew that McClellan had sprinkled pickets, including foot soldiers from the division of George Stoneman, along that stretch of the Potomac toward which the raiders appeared to be heading. One of the points thus covered was the mouth of the Monocacy River, where Pleasonton believed Stuart would recross to Virginia. If so, he would not have to challenge Stuart all by himself. Thus he guided his column in that direction.

He should have closed with Stuart when he had the chance, for his latest decision was a near-fatal error. Instead of recrossing near the Monocacy, Stuart guided his column almost three miles farther south, to little-used White's Ford. In so doing, he interposed between Pleasonton, who by then had reached the Monocacy via Frederick, and the main body of Stoneman's command, three miles to the southeast, near Poolesville.[18]

When Pleasonton became aware of enemy movements south of his new position, he still had time to cut Stuart off from the river, especially since he now enjoyed the infantry support he craved. But instead of heading at once and in strength to White's Ford, he tentatively advanced a few companies of the 8th Illinois, followed by perhaps twice as many foot soldiers. These were too few to overwhelm Stuart's advance guard—600 members of Rooney Lee's brigade.

Furthermore, many of the Rebels wore U.S. Army greatcoats, which they had taken from warehouses in the Chambersburg area. Pleasonton's men at first took the raiders for members of the 1st Rhode Island Cavalry, which was known to be attached to Stoneman's division. The flat-footed Yankees made a target Stuart could not resist; at his order, Lee's advance charged them, forcing them to flee across the Little Monocacy River. Before Pleasonton's main force could react, Stuart had established a bulwark of sharpshooters and cannons to hold back intruders while the rest of his force forded the Potomac.[19]

Pleasonton elected not to challenge Stuart's guard except in long-range skirmishing. Evidently he hoped that Stoneman's main body would come up from Poolesville to form a pincers with the cavalry. But when the head of Stoneman's column, under Brig. Gen. W. H. H. Ward, finally appeared east of the ford, the same troopers who had mistaken Stuart's people for Federals now wondered if Ward's men were Rebels attached to Stuart's column. The outcome of this comedy of errors was that cavalry and infantry remained stationary and largely inactive as the rear of Stuart's column crossed the river. By the time General Ward reached Pleasonton and suggested a cooperative pursuit on the other shore, the cavalryman declined, pleading fagged-out horses and declaring that in any case, it was too late: "You should have been here three hours ago!" Had Ward asked Pleasonton what the cavalry had done during that time, it is doubtful he would have received a truthful reply.[20]

Stuart's expedition had not attained its every goal—the iron bridge near Chambersburg had proven too sturdy to destroy—but he had reconnoitered McClellan's positions while destroying all manner of property and gathering an immense cache of spoils in Pennsylvania that would feed, clothe, and equip his command for months to come. As the Beau Sabreur himself put it, "the results of this expedition, in a moral and political point of view, can hardly be estimated, and the consternation among property holders in Pennsylvania beggars description."[21]

His most noteworthy accomplishment had been to circumnavigate his enemy for the second time in four months, prompting Northern editors and politicians to ask if anyone guarded the flanks and rear of the Army of the Potomac. The boiling controversy embarrassed the army and threatened its commander's career. McClellan, who did not feel comfortable on the defensive, except in battle, blamed "our deficiency in the cavalry arm," which apparently took in its leadership. His subordinates reacted predictably. Averell's performance had been indefensible, so the brigadier wisely kept his mouth shut. Pleasonton, on the other hand, loudly sought to indict Stoneman for the raiders' escape. His old superior would have none of it, however. Stoneman insisted that the cavalry's effort at cutting off Stuart had been so feeble that it had no grounds for criticizing anyone else.[22]

The rest of the army was outraged at Stuart's escape. A typical reaction was that of an artilleryman who called the outcome "a very shameful, humiliating thing indeed." McClellan's provost marshal, Brig. Gen. Marsena R. Patrick, agreed that the episode was "a burning disgrace" to all involved.

Patrick added an opinion shared by hundreds of soldiers in the other branches of the service, one strengthened to the point of immutability by the recent events: "With the exception of a few regulars and two or three other regiments, I fear our cavalry is an awful botch."[23]

><+>•O•<+>—<

After October 12 the army's horsemen had something to prove, quickly and convincingly. Heads had rolled, although not far. Buford was retained as chief of cavalry, but his duties remained almost exclusively administrative. Although Averell kept his brigade, his survival appears to have owed to his friendship with McClellan. Still, the cavalry was reorganized, and on October 21 Pleasonton, the commander on the scene when the raiders escaped, was demoted to the command of a brigade consisting of the 6th United States, the 8th Pennsylvania, the 8th Illinois, the 3rd Indiana, and the 8th New York. Thus put on probation, Pleasonton realized that to keep his star, he must succeed in the field and sustain that success.[24]

It would not be easy. He had blamed his inability to bag Stuart not only on his infantry supports, but also on the cavalry's weakness in horseflesh. In response, Secretary of War Stanton yelled at Quartermaster General Montgomery Meigs, who defended himself by explaining that over the six-week period beginning September 1, he had shipped the Army of the Potomac an ample supply of remounts—no fewer than 10,254 of them—at a cost of $1.2 million. He blamed the cavalry's sorry performance not on its lack of animals, but on its abuse and neglect of those it had. Some observers believed the cavalry had no complaint on any score. When he learned of McClellan's concern over his "fatiegued horses," Abraham Lincoln returned a memorable retort: "Will you pardon me for asking what the horses of your army have done since the battle of Antietam that fatigue anything?"[25]

The president's jab targeted the general inactivity of the army, not merely the cavalry, and few troopers took offense. However, Meigs's criticism, being sharper and more focused, appears to have stung Pleasonton—perhaps because he saw the truth in it. In any case, no shortage of horseflesh, real or imagined, would protect the cavalry from the consequences of its future mistakes.

On the other hand, the cavalry's troubles were not always of its own making. Riders and horses were always overtaxed and often misused. Each day the army spent in Maryland, the infantry and the artillery cleaned their shirts and wrote letters home. Horsemen, meanwhile, were picketing, scouting, reconnoitering, carrying messages, and engaging the enemy well in advance of the main army. Moreover, cavalry's oldest bugaboo—its misappropriation by infantry generals to whom it was attached—was becoming a graver problem every day. On October 23, as elements of the army probed westward in preparation for quitting the Sharpsburg region, Walter Newhall of the 3rd Pennsylvania complained that Brig. Gen. John Newton, commanding the 3rd Division, VI Corps, "is awfully afraid that we don't get enough to do, and so in spite of our crippled condition, keeps sending scouting parties along the main road to Hagerstown daily."[26]

If the cavalry was overburdened while most of the army idled away the fall, its plate became fuller—mainly thanks to combat assignments—once McClellan finally stirred himself to return to Virginia, an operation that lasted from October 26 to November 1. On the first day out, Pleasonton's brigade led the way over the Potomac and into the Catoctin Valley; on the final day of the move, Averell's brigade brought up and guarded the army's rear.

Pleasonton not only facilitated his own army's movements, he searched for Lee's. The Army of Northern Virginia was known to be heading south through the Shenandoah Valley. Thus Pleasonton's horsemen veered toward the gaps in the Blue Ridge to keep tabs on the enemy's dispositions. In the rear of the army, Averell reconnoitered in the same direction.[27]

The cavalry's advance produced opposition from scattered elements of Stuart's cavalry. On the twenty-seventh Pleasonton moved south and west, chasing mounted pickets out of Purcellville, Snickersville, and Snicker's Gap. The next day he mixed with Stuart's riders at Philomont, along the Snicker's Gap Turnpike. At the same time, he dispatched scouting parties as far south as Middleburg, on the pike from Ashby's Gap. In that vicinity he was assisted by the recently arrived brigade of General Bayard, which had been sent up the Little River Turnpike from Chantilly to cooperate with the Army of the Potomac. On the last day of the month Bayard added his command to McClellan's field force, an occasion that must have cheered the overextended troopers under Pleasonton and Averell. Thereafter, Bayard cooperated closely with the other commands in clearing Rebels from Aldie, White Plains, and various other Loudoun Valley points.[28]

When November arrived, it brought, along with snow flurries, stiffening resistance from Stuart as the Yankees drew closer to the mountain gaps Lee's army wished to take to its destination, the Rappahannock River basin. On November 1, spirited clashes broke out between the cavalries at Philomont and Aldie. They reprised their roles at Union on the second and at Upperville on the third. Most of these clashes ended with Pleasonton, Averell, and Bayard driving the enemy from the field—but only, it seems, when Stuart wished to take up a blocking position somewhere else.[29]

Throughout, Stuart performed his counterreconnaissance duties extremely well, ensuring that the Yankees never laid a hand—or hardly an eye—on Lee's main body. Thus protected, the Army of Northern Virginia made a successful crossing of the mountains. By the third Jackson was on the east side of the Blue Ridge and Longstreet had pushed through to Culpeper. This meant that Lee had beaten McClellan to ground with which he was familiar and which he could readily defend.[30]

This proved the final straw for Lincoln. On November 5 he drew up an order relieving Little Mac from command and replacing him with Ambrose Burnside, the stocky, balding, bewhiskered Hoosier–turned–Rhode Islander who had become one of the Union's earliest heroes. McClellan received the order two days later at his headquarters at Rectortown. On the tenth he left the army on a special train mobbed by soldiers who continued to idolize him despite his shortcomings as a strategist and tactician.

Relatively few of those Little Mac left behind refused to share in the gloom his leave-taking cast over the army. Of these, however, more than one was a cavalryman. Wesley Merritt spoke for many in this group when he later observed that throughout his tenure, McClellan had demonstrated "ignorance of the proper use of cavalry" and had failed to provide "a fit management of this important arm of the service."[31]

When Burnside took over, he made the capture and occupation of Richmond his initial priority. He would feint against Lee's army at Culpeper, or perhaps farther south against his communications near Gordonsville. As soon as Lee shifted to meet this movement, Burnside would hasten east to Fredericksburg. With Lee out of position, the drive to Richmond would be an almost leisurely affair. By the time Lee reached the scene, his capital would already be lost; to guard his supply lines, he would have to give battle on open ground, where the superior strength of the Army of the Potomac would surely prevail. On November 14 a hopeful but perhaps doubtful Lincoln approved Burnside's strategy.[32]

Like every newly appointed army commander, the thirty-eight-year-old Burnside, a prewar arms manufacturer (inventor of the carbine that bore his name) and a railroad executive to boot, quickly stamped his imprint on the army by reorganizing it. He gathered in one of the three corps (the III) that had remained near Washington following the Peninsula Campaign, and grouped it and the corps that had fought at Antietam into Grand Divisions. The Right Grand Division, comprising the II and IX Corps, he assigned to Sumner. The III and V Corps he combined into the Center Grand Division under Hooker. He formed the Left Grand Division, commanded by Franklin, by grouping the I and VI Corps. Later, Burnside also created a Reserve Grand Division, assigned to protect the capital, under General Sigel; it consisted of the XI and XII Corps.[33]

The reorganization had a major impact on the cavalry. Burnside opted to keep Buford, an "old army" friend, at the top, but he continued to restrict the man to paperwork. Pleasonton he returned to division command, while keeping Averell and Bayard at the brigade level. Pleasonton was assigned the brigades of Farnsworth (the 8th Illinois, 3rd Indiana, and 8th New York) and Gregg (the 6th United States, 6th New York, and 8th Pennsylvania). Burnside attached the division to Sumner's command. Averell's 5th United States, 1st Massachusetts, and 3rd and 4th Pennsylvania he assigned to Hooker, while Franklin received Bayard's brigade, composed of the 1st Pennsylvania, 1st Maine, 1st New Jersey, 2nd and 10th New York, and an independent company of District of Columbia troopers. Burnside divvied up the horse artillery this way: Pennington's battery to Pleasonton, Robertson's to Averell, and Gibson's to Bayard. Other batteries that had formerly served with the cavalry, including Tidball's, were placed in the Artillery Reserve.[34]

The reorganization caused a minimum of shifting about; thus the cavalry hardly missed a step as it went about its duties under the new regime. Even as Burnside took the reins, the horsemen under Pleasonton, Averell, and Bayard guided the army to its concentration point at Warrenton, eighteen miles north of, and across the Rappahannock from, Culpeper.

The cavalry's role expanded beginning on the fifteenth, when Pleasonton escorted Sumner's grand division down the Warrenton Turnpike toward the army's next objective, Falmouth, across the Rappahannock from Fredericksburg. To cover the movement, the rest of Pleasonton's command feinted southward, a show of force designed to give the enemy the impression that Burnside was heading elsewhere. The deception worked brilliantly, for the first Federals reached Falmouth two days later—twenty-four hours before Lee realized Sumner had left Warrenton.[35]

By the twentieth, when the rest of the army moved into the Falmouth area, Pleasonton's men were picketing the river as far upstream as the road to Kelly's Ford, eighteen miles from the town. Other troopers guarded the army's rear supply base at desolate Belle Plain on Potomac Creek, north of Falmouth (Major Chapman of the 3rd Indiana called the site "a place, but no town or village"). Since the riverbank teemed with Confederate regulars and partisans, everyone had a dangerous job.[36]

The weather did not make things easier, having turned cold enough for the first true snowfall of the season. When sent along the river, Trooper Davis of the 6th Regulars regretted that his regiment still wore their summer uniforms: "I grew so cold during that ride that my hands became numb and helpless, and my body shivered as with an ague fit." When a Rebel picket on the shore fired a ball in Davis's direction, "what a change seemed to take place. . . . That single shot raised my blood from forty degrees fahrenheit to about two hundred, and sent it rushing through my veins like hot steam." His fingers no longer dead, Davis worked his carbine so rapidly that the enemy seemed to melt away in retreat.[37]

The country along the Rappahannock was so barren and forbidding that everyone hoped he would not remain there long. The prospect of staying through the cold weather season, rumors of which grew ever more credible the longer the army sat on the riverbank, gave many soldiers pause. Captain Adams, for one, doubted that the army would retain its strength if it tried to winter at Falmouth: "Winter hardships are severe enough in the most comfortable of camps. Winter campaigns may be possible in Europe, a thickly peopled country of fine roads, but in this region of mud, desolation and immense distances, it is another matter." Many feared that the continued inactivity meant that Burnside's strategy had run aground. Major Chapman noted "no movement of troops" and asked desperately, "For what do we wait?"[38]

Burnside himself had no wish to remain along this frigid river. He had intended to stay only long enough to bridge and cross the water. For one thing, the enemy would not remain ignorant of his whereabouts indefinitely. But then unforeseen problems, mainly logistical in nature, conspired to frustrate and delay. Burnside had known that the foot and railroad bridges opposite Falmouth had been destroyed; for this reason, he had ordered up a pontoon train that had been assembled at Washington. Through miscommunication, however, the boats did not arrive until a full week after the army's advance reached Falmouth. By then, Burnside's surprise offensive had gone the way of every plan unraveled by unanticipated complications. Lee had arrived and was digging in along a six-mile line on high ground southwest of Fredericksburg. The road to Richmond was effectively closed.[39]

For the next two weeks, Burnside stared across the water and tried to think of what to do, then stared some more. In the interval, his cavalry kept busy fighting, and fighting off, the enemy. On the morning of December 1 Burnside ordered Averell, with two of his regiments, to disperse Confederate horsemen near Barnett's Ford. That same day, a rash of bushwhacker attacks on the army's picket lines—some the work of Union deserters, others of Confederate guerrillas—led General Sumner to send Pleasonton to "scour that whole country" along the north bank and "shoot down anyone found committing these depredations."[40]

Over the next week, cavalry units served in diverse areas on a variety of missions. While Averell reconnoitered along the upper Rappahannock and Pleasonton hunted up marauders, Colonel David Gregg's 8th Pennsylvania—later joined by the 3rd Indiana—patrolled more than fifty miles farther east along the same river, studying Rebel artillery emplacements near Port Conway. On the ninth, however, orders went out for the cavalry to concentrate near Falmouth within two days. It appeared that Burnside had finally made up his mind to act.[41]

>─┼─◆>─○─<◆─┼─<

Burnside was stubborn—one of the least attractive attributes in an otherwise honest, likable man, and often ruinous in a general. For weeks he had planned to cross the river at Falmouth, and cross it he would, even with Lee awaiting him. On December 10 he called in outlying troopers and put his army in motion. The next day he led his advance down to the water, its march covered by 147 cannons placed atop adjacent heights by now–Brigadier General Hunt, William Barry's successor as chief of artillery. In front of the troops, engineers attempted to place four pontoon spans atop the water, only to be halted by Confederate sharpshooters in Fredericksburg. Only after an hours-long cannonade, followed by infantrymen paddling across the stream in pontoon boats, were the marksmen silenced and the bridges laid.

At last the army could cross to the Fredericksburg side. The operation consumed the rest of that day and much of the twelfth. Then, on the thirteenth, Burnside gave the orders that sent his army into the teeth of the most deadly infantry and artillery fire of the war.[42]

Burnside's ranks advanced along a several-mile line stretching well south of Fredericksburg. Franklin's grand division went in first, achieved limited success, and fell back, bleeding. Then Sumner's command tried the Confederate center. To reach their objective, the old man's troops had to cross a long, open plain, then ascend a slope to the top of Marye's Heights. It was—as Burnside ought to have foreseen—a march to the slaughter. Not even reinforcements hastily provided from Hooker's grand division could stiffen the assault or halt the bloodletting. In a matter of hours, it was all over. By dusk a high percentage of the nearly 13,000 casualties the Army of the Potomac suffered this day lay strewn across the plain below Lee's impregnable defenses.

To what extent did the cavalry participate in this exercise in futility? As Sumner advanced, a small body of Pleasonton's horsemen preceded his infantry in the time-honored role of skirmishers. Another equally small force crossed above Sumner's right flank and tried unsuccessfully to curl around the enemy's left. Other troopers supported the batteries in rear of the Right Grand Division.[43]

On the left, Bayard's 3,500-man brigade led Franklin's advance and skirmished at long range with Stonewall Jackson's infantry. Taking up an exposed position on the far flank, the brigade came under a barrage that made one trooper feel he was "living an age in an hour." But then the cavalry was permitted to retire; Franklin did not use it to anchor his flank or to neutralize Stuart's horse artillery, which helped turn back the Left Grand Division at the height of the battle.[44]

To some extent, the ineffectiveness of Bayard's horsemen can be attributed to their commander's mortal wounding, which occurred at about 2:00 P.M. Bayard had been taking part in an outdoor war council with Franklin and other generals when the party attracted artillery fire. While senior officers scattered for safety, Bayard, whose back was to a tree, took his time getting to his feet. As soon as he stood up a shell screamed overhead, and one of its fragments shattered his right thigh. He died twenty-four hours later, four days shy of his twenty-seventh birthday. The tragedy of his loss was deepened by his forthcoming wedding. He had canceled the leave he was to take in New Jersey when Burnside began to advance on Falmouth.[45]

This, then, was the extent of the role Burnside's cavalry played in the deadly battle. Although only a small part of Pleasonton's division was engaged, and Bayard's brigade was under fire for only an hour, at least they took part. Averell's brigade saw no action at all. Most of its men had not even crossed the river with the rest of the army. Their inactivity was the result of Burnside's acutely limited imagination with regard to using cavalry in battle—a malady he may have caught from his predecessor.

The recollections of Averell's troopers indicate how far most of them were placed from the scene of action. The 3rd Pennsylvania was sheltered in woods so distant from the field that its men could not learn anything about the course of the battle. "But little news reaches us," noted Lieutenant Galloway. John McIntosh, who had recently transferred to the volunteers and had risen to colonel of the 3rd Pennsylvania, moved close enough late in the fight to hear musketry and artillery fire but could not see much of the fight.

The impressions of Captain Adams, whose Massachusetts regiment was in camp a short distance from McIntosh's, spoke for Averell's entire command when he wrote later that day: "Evidently a terrible battle was going on, but with what result we could only guess, for we could only hear, and . . . did not see an enemy or hear the whir-r-r of a single shot. There we lay, cold, idle and anxious, aware only of the severity of the contest, expecting soon to take part in it and knowing nothing of the result. The day past slowly away, ending in the heaviest musketry fire by all odds that I ever heard, and again we passed a moonlight evening over our camp-fires."[46]

Chapter Ten

Winter of Gloom, Springtime of Hope

As if stunned into immobility, the Army of the Potomac remained on the Confederate side of the river throughout the fourteenth. Still believing that Marye's Heights and adjacent positions could be taken, Burnside wished to renew the effort all along the line; he gave up the idea only after his subordinates argued vehemently against it. Not until darkness fell on the fifteenth, after the army had buried as many of its dead as it could reach, did Burnside recross the Rappahannock to Falmouth. The few troopers who remained on the south bank covered the movement. At first it appeared to be a dangerous assignment for the cavalry, but after an hour or so it became clear that Lee had decided not to contest the pullout. He allowed his adversary to draw off, slowly and painfully, like a wounded animal dragging its legs behind it.

Although many Northern newspapers called Burnside's failure a limited setback or even, by some convoluted logic, a victory, the rank and file were not fooled. "Our men have been sloutered like hogs," wrote Pvt. Ashley Alexander of the 12th Illinois, ". . . and we did not kill hardly anny of the Rebils." A trooper attached to Sigel's XI Corps believed his army "pretty well whipped" and noted that "some say we have lost ten to the Rebs [one] & some put it as high as twenty." Once he learned that the army had recrossed the river, Charles F. Adams, Jr., still encamped well to the rear, decided that "the campaign was a terrible failure—in a word, all our cake was dough."[1]

Those who had been led to the "slouter" were quick to blame the man at the top. Some had heard that Burnside tried to beg off when Lincoln had offered him command of the army, believing himself unequal to the position. Now his men could see all too clearly that he had been correct. John McIntosh asked himself: "Beyond what Burnside did in North Carolina with a force of 10 or 12 thousand men, when did he show the ability to command a force of 100,000 men[?] On what grounds did the powers that be place him in command?"[2]

A majority of the army wanted no part of a commander whose incapacity had been demonstrated at such terrible cost. Looking back years later, Sidney Davis recalled that well before the attack on the thirteenth, he and his comrades had anticipated failure: "The Army of the Potomac fought that battle with the belief that it would be repulsed—a belief that of itself was sufficient to insure defeat in any other than an American army. It struggled against fate from a sheer sense of duty to the country—as a forlorn hope that goes to its death for the cause it represents." Lacking confidence in the man who had realized its worst fears, the army began to yearn for a commander it could trust and even love, regardless of his shortcomings. "There was much yearning after McClellan," Davis remembered, "which was expressed in murmurs at times. . . . It seemed to be felt that, although he would not effect more, he would risk less, than General Burnside."[3]

As the army straggled back to its cheerless camps, the cavalry resumed the endless task of picket duty amid the desolate country that lined the river. It had snowed shortly before the army had crossed to Fredericksburg, and it did so again soon after it returned to Falmouth. The late December weather was bitterly cold, even deadly; on some mornings, one or two of the troopers who had escaped the carnage on the thirteenth were found dead around their inadequate campfires, their bodies frozen to the earth. Comrades who had feared the prospect of spending the winter in such a forbidding environment now found the idea unbearable.

Of necessity, the army tried to put its fears behind it and go on. "Tuesday the 16th," wrote Captain Adams, "they actually took us out to drill, to exercise the horses and occupy the time." Other regiments were placed on active service. On December 17 Wade Hampton began a raid into the army's rear near Occoquan, capturing pickets as well as army and sutlers' wagons. Hampton's troopers easily eluded their pursuers, including members of the cavalry attached to Sigel's corps: the 4th and 9th New York, the 6th Ohio, the 17th Pennsylvania, and detachments of the 12th Illinois, 1st Maine, 1st Michigan, 1st Indiana, 3rd Virginia, and what would become the 1st Connecticut. By late on the eighteenth Hampton had returned to his lines, toting everything from 300 pairs of boots to baskets of champagne and claret.[4]

Although the raid hardly touched the Army of the Potomac, it was regarded as another embarrassment to every Federal in eastern Virginia. By the twenty-first erroneous rumors had the raiders lingering in a section of the country they had crossed en route to Occoquan. That evening Burnside ordered Averell's brigade on a reconnaissance of the area, including Warrenton, Elk Run, White Ridge, Greenwich, Brentsville, and Catlett's Station on the Orange & Alexandria Railroad.

The sweep came up dry. Averell encountered no one except some nondescript pickets, which he chased for two miles but failed to overtake. Returning to home base, he turned in a report that must have disappointed both Burnside and Sigel. As for Hampton's men and other "small parties of the enemy who are roaming about the country," he wrote, "I do not believe they can be captured" except by large bodies of pursuers stationed well in the army's rear. He considered Sigel's troopers unequal to the task. On his journey Averell had found at least 200 of them (he did not specify their regiment or regiments) in "very insecure positions, wandering about. I cannot imagine why the enemy does not capture them."[5]

The holiday season found the Federals on the Rappahannock enjoying little in the way of good cheer. On the twenty-fifth Silas Wesson reported sharing "mud and rain for Christmas." The birthday of the Prince of Peace and the approaching end of another year prompted Wesson and his comrades to ruminate grimly on their army's position and prospects. "Christmas has again rolled around," noted Joseph Galloway, "and still finds us as far from Richmond as we were this day 12 months ago."[6]

The enemy wished to make the season even bleaker and less joyous. Two days after Christmas came news of another raid into the area north of Falmouth, this also aimed at severing Burnside's communications with Washington—and led by J. E. B. Stuart himself. This time, no troopers from the Army of the Potomac were sent in pursuit, even belatedly. Instead, Stuart was followed by some of the cavalry assigned to the defenses of Washington, including the 5th New York, and a few of Sigel's regiments, including the 17th Pennsylvania.

None of them could prevent Stuart from capturing wagons and guards near Dumfries and Occoquan, nor could they stand up to the raiders when Stuart turned on them. Screaming Confederates overran the bivouacs of the 17th Pennsylvania, then led the 5th New York on a merry chase. As one New Yorker admitted, "we left camp to follow them up and we followed them right around in a circle and came up with their rear guard the next day right in our own camps." After that, Stuart faced no pursuit worthy of the name. His column returned to its lines below the Rappahannock on New Year's Day 1863, an immense cache of booty—even greater than Hampton's—in tow.[7]

Once again Stuart had ridden successfully through and behind his enemy's lines—this time, however, refraining from circling the Army of the Potomac. Although it had not tried to stop the raid, the Army of the Potomac was embarrassed and disgusted by this latest headline-grabbing exploit in its rear. "We are fiddling around the country as usual," wrote Maj. Henry Lee Higginson of the 1st Massachusetts, "this day after Stuart, the next after Hampton, all in vain." Most of the criticism for Stuart's latest escape fell—as it should have—upon the 17th Pennsylvania and 5th New York. Since both regiments joined the Army of the Potomac during the next six months, their faulty performance would appear to call into question their value to their new command.[8]

>—+—<+>—+—O—+—<+>—+—<

As on the twenty-first, Averell's brigade had been in the best position of any of Burnside's mounted units to counter this latest raid. It could not do so until too late because Burnside had recently given it a major assignment, one it was on the verge of carrying out when Stuart came calling. Ironically, the raid was at least partly to blame for the assignment's being scrapped.

Averell's mission dated to a December 9 strategy session at Burnside's headquarters that involved the army's senior leadership. When the conference broke up, Burnside called Averell aside to suggest that during the coming movement his brigade cross the Rappahannock in rear of Hooker's grand division. Averell disliked that idea, fearing—and rightly so—that he would not get across until the battle was nearly over. Whereupon Burnside, who admitted that he had no real plan for using cavalry in the campaign, asked Averell if he had a better idea. At once the cavalryman proposed a grandiose project that he had been developing since the latter stages of the Peninsula campaign. Under this plan, his brigade would cross the Rappahannock not at Falmouth, but twenty miles upstream at Kelly's Ford. Then it would ford, in succession, the Rapidan, the James, and the Appomattox, before passing south of Petersburg to link with Union forces in Hampton Roads, near Suffolk. Averell would not simply ride south; en route he would strike Lee's communications with Richmond as well as his supply lines to the Deep South. Averell's efforts would be directed against the James River Canal, via which Richmond gained much of its sustenance, as well as against railroads, bridges, and telegraph lines above and below Petersburg. Moreover, he would time his attack to coincide with the main army's movement against Fredericksburg.[9]

The plan was ambitious, even sweeping in its objectives and imaginative in its proposed route of march. This was to the good, for ambition and energy sometimes seemed rare commodities among Union cavalry leaders, and it was about time that the Army of the Potomac did some long-distance raiding of its own. Still, the plan had flaws. Averell underestimated the obstacles and resistance he would encounter around Richmond and Petersburg, including the forces that guarded the bridges and railroads that Jefferson Davis's government could not afford to have put out of commission. Averell would not be permitted to ride south without being trailed by at least a portion of Stuart's cavalry. Then, too, at such a distance from his army as he proposed to travel, he could not have guaranteed his ability to strike just as Burnside moved against Lee. The plan's greatest potential drawback was that its leader was no Stuart; he was not even Wade Hampton. Through more than a year of campaigning, Averell had never demonstrated the capacity to mount such a complex and dangerous exercise in independent command.

Averell never learned why Burnside, on or about December 12, deferred the project, but perhaps the army leader had more sense than is generally attributed to him. By late December, however, Burnside was desperately seeking some stratagem by which to reassume the offensive and achieve enough success, if not to make amends for the debacle of the thirteenth, at least to distract the nation's attention from it. The day Stuart set out on his most recent raid, Burnside was toying with the notion of a limited offensive against Lee's army. He remembered Averell's plan and decided that, if successful, it would provide an effective diversion for the larger operation. Thus he recalled

Averell, promised him 1,000 men "from all the cavalry in the army," and gave him the go-ahead.[10]

An overjoyed Averell quickly selected his force, which included detachments of every Regular regiment with the army as well as of the 3rd and 4th Pennsylvania, the 8th New York, the 1st Massachusetts, and the 1st Rhode Island. He also chose two sections of Pennington's battery, which had provided such effective support during Pleasonton's post-Antietam operations. A supply train was loaded with three days' rations per rider and twelve pounds of forage per mount.[11]

Everything ready, on the morning of the last day of the year Averell led his column up the river from Falmouth. The first set of fours was about to cross at Kelly's Ford when a courier arrived with news that the expedition had been canceled. Instead, Averell was to turn about, head north to Warrenton, and there or thereabouts, nab Stuart's raiders. By then, based on what he knew of the Rebels' progress, Averell realized that it was too late to accomplish anything. But "the order was imperative," and so, with a sigh, he started off as directed. When he reached Warrenton, "I found that Stuart had passed through there about five hours before" and was now beyond range of any of Averell's men. Therefore, Averell took his dispirited troopers to Hartwood Church, not far from the river, to await further orders. The only order that reached him, a week later, scuttled the expedition.[12]

Averell never knew for certain who or what lay behind Burnside's final decision, but he suspected it was the mean-spirited opposition of his immediate superior. In putting together the expeditionary force, Averell had made the mistake of selecting some regiments and colonels assigned to Pleasonton's division—which, under Burnside's orders, he had a right to do. Averell later learned that Pleasonton, in a formal communiqué to Burnside's headquarters, not only protested the details made upon his command, but also objected to the expedition itself.

Pleasonton may have been responsible for the ultimate demise of Averell's raid, but its initial suspension was the work of Abraham Lincoln. The night before Averell's force started for Kelly's Ford, Burnside received a telegram from the president calling off any movements by the army until further notice. Whatever the factors involved, Averell's relationship with Pleasonton was never the same afterward. Averell held the division leader responsible for destroying not only a cherished project, but a mission that, once begun, could not have failed: "With a thousand picked men I could have gone anywhere, and come back again."[13]

>––◦––<

The new year found Burnside alternately weighed down with gloom and hopeful of overwhelming Lee's army in open combat. On January 5, four days after unsuccessfully petitioning Lincoln to let him "retire to private life" and on the same day that he sent the president his resignation, to be acted on at any time

Lincoln desired, Burnside confided to General Halleck his plan to recross the Rappahannock and renew battle. Burnside knew that most of his generals were opposed to the plan, and he suspected that several—Hooker, Franklin, Smith, perhaps others—were working behind his back to secure his relief from command. But on the seventh Halleck, with Lincoln's endorsement, approved an early crossing of the river so as to place the army "in a position where we can meet the enemy on favorable or even equal terms."[14]

Burnside waited for the elements to favor his offensive. When the bitter weather appeared to abate in the third week of the month, he hauled his army out of camp and on the nineteenth placed it on the road to Banks's Ford, about six miles above Fredericksburg. At that point Burnside planned to cross a large portion of the army, via a pontoon bridge, into Lee's rear, there to strike an unexpected blow. Although the plan provoked strenuous objections from those generals Burnside feared were after his job, it had some merit. At the outset, at least, it appears to have taken his enemy by surprise, and surprise was one of two factors on which the success of the operation hinged.

Unfortunately, Burnside could not control the other factor. On the evening of the twentieth, as Hooker's grand division poised to cross just above Banks's Ford, Franklin's a short distance below it, an icy rain began to fall. The rain continued, more or less at full force, for the next thirty-six hours, after which sleet and snow set in.[15]

The rain and snow turned the roads into frigid muck in which pontoon trains, artillery batteries, and supply wagons sank, some nearly out of sight. Trotting along with the main column, Allen Bevan of the 1st Pennsylvania reported passing sunken "Caissons or Army Wagons nearly every one hundred yards." Having to avoid these obstacles only worsened the plight of those who marched up the riverbank. The chaplain of the 6th Pennsylvania noted that "horses, wagons, and troops, wear one universal coat of mud. Men march in it to their knees, and are splashed with it to their heads." Slow progress was bad enough, but even worse, as Trooper Bevan observed, was Burnside's inability to lay his pontoons near the ford "on account of the high water or the mud, I don't know which." One member of the 4th United States Cavalry found humor in the army's predicament, suggesting that if the river continued to rise, Burnside could float down to Richmond aboard his pontoons.[16]

Even a man as stubborn as Ambrose Burnside realized he could not campaign actively in rain and snow. By the twenty-first he had turned his cold and wet troops about and was leading them back to their starting point. The few mounted units that had started out—mostly members of Averell's brigade—were told to return to their camps near Potomac Run and White Oak Church and stay there. The following day the rest of the troops who had hit the roads on the nineteenth and twentieth were back at Falmouth.[17]

By then the army's morale had registered new lows. It plummeted even further when it was learned that the weather would prevent commissary trains from reaching Falmouth for an indefinite period. That part of the army that had not yet taken up the march when Burnside called it off joined in the general despair. Sidney Davis found that even soldiers who had not succumbed to the prevailing gloom after Fredericksburg now "seemed to develop a bitter feeling" toward the army's command section.[18]

As had Pope after Second Bull Run, Burnside chose to blame his failures on the subordinates who had argued against his December 13 attack as well as against what had already become known as the "Mud March." He was not alone in believing these generals responsible for at least some of the army's woes. Lt. George N. Bliss of the 1st Rhode Island declared that "some of our leading generals appear to be determined to ruin Genl B. at any cost." Such obstructionism Bliss considered unconscionable, even if understandable.[19]

Burnside tried to turn the tables on his adversaries. On the twenty-third he drew up General Order No. 8, which indicted eight general officers and, rather curiously, one lieutenant colonel for "unjust and unnecessary criticisms" of the policies and decisions of the army's commander. The order dismissed from the service Joe Hooker and two other generals, while relieving from duty Franklin, Smith, and the other culprits.[20]

It is doubtful whether Burnside expected Lincoln to sustain his action. Earlier, Lincoln had publicly deplored the high-level intriguing he knew to be going on behind Burnside's back. Now, however, the prospect of losing so many of the army's senior leaders gave the president pause, as did the obvious fact that Burnside had lost the confidence of virtually everyone under him. In the end, Lincoln refused to approve the order, which was never issued. Instead, on the twenty-fifth he relieved Burnside from command "at his own request" and named General Hooker to take his place.

Lincoln informed Hooker that he had been appointed in spite of, not because of, the unethical meddling he had engaged in throughout Burnside's tenure. But Lincoln stopped short of condemning Hooker for past indiscretions. For one thing, he could not afford to get off on the wrong foot with his new commander. Hooker gave the impression of an able strategist and tactician, and he had a wealth of ideas aimed at improving the army's spirit and efficiency. Lincoln was desperate enough to believe he needed such a man.[21]

>-+-<>-O-<>-+-<

It may have been that the army also needed Joe Hooker. While any fresh face would have seemed an improvement just now, the new leader sounded truly able to restore the self-confidence the Army of the Potomac had once carried into battle.

The command Hooker inherited was in need of both a physical and psychological revival. For months—perhaps ever since McClellan had left it—the army had been irregularly supplied with rations and equipment, and perhaps as a result, its sick list had grown to alarming length. Moreover, it continued to be handicapped by incompetent officers, while its organization—especially Burnside's unwieldy grand division system—cried out for streamlining.

The cavalry shared these problems but also suffered from others unique to itself. Its most pressing deficiency was in horseflesh. In the wake of the recent campaigning, hundreds if not thousands of remounts were needed, and those horses considered serviceable required improved care and more and better forage. In some respects, this was the fault of the quartermaster general. His claims to the contrary notwithstanding, General Meigs had failed to keep the army supplied with quality animals on a regular basis. Even the resourceful Brig. Gen. Rufus Ingalls, chief quartermaster of the Army of the Potomac, could do only so much to rectify the deficiency. On January 15 Ingalls informed his superior in Washington that "the cavalry and artillery horses are in fair condition, considering that the quality of the animals never was first-rate. First-class horses have never yet found their way into this army." He might have added that so many underage, overage, and chronically ill horses had been foisted on the army that the shortage of horseflesh had reached epidemic proportions. It had been a major concern at least since the previous September, when Pleasonton, during his pursuit of Lee's army in Maryland, brought it to McClellan's attention. Pleasonton's complaint had given credence to his attempt, the following month, to explain away the escape of Stuart's Chambersburg raiders.[22]

Those horses not already unwell or infirm when distributed to the cavalry had become susceptible to a variety of diseases that hard campaigning and a general lack of veterinary attention only aggravated. Late in October an outbreak of "scratches" had plagued the cavalry, and "grease-heel" also made an unwanted appearance. The following month an artillery colonel found "a terrible disease breaking out among the battery horses, which seems to be spreading very fast. . . . The hoof cracks right around the crown, in some cases so badly that you can put your finger between it and the crown. Should it spread much more we shall be helpless." This malady, known as "hoof-rot," did not spread far, but it did not go away either. And by early 1863 a virulent form of distemper had broken out among the army's horse herds, hitting the battery teams especially hard.[23]

Some observers attributed the poor condition of the army's horses to the unnaturally severe burdens that had been placed on the cavalry over the past three months. To Lincoln's October jest about his horses having done little or nothing since Antietam, McClellan had replied that during the period in question, the cavalry had been "constantly employed in making reconnaissances, scouting, and picketing" 150 miles of riverfront, and that at least six regiments had logged 200 miles while chasing those Chambersburg raiders. Little Mac added: "I beg that you will also consider that this same cavalry was brought from the Peninsula, where it encountered most laborious service, and was, at the commencement of this campaign, in low condition, and from that time to the present has had no time to recruit."[24]

McClellan's reply conveyed sympathy for his overworked troopers, but their horses suffered at least as much, and perhaps more, from the cavalry's ever-increasing workload, especially when not properly cared for. In November Daniel Pulis of the 8th New York had described his regiment's camp west of Warrenton as "an awful place . . . to kill horses, where they are rode sometimes 24 hours without a mouthful to eat." In the camp of the recently remounted 9th New York, horses sometimes went two or even three days without being fed. As one New Yorker put it, "it seems hard to ride a horse with nothing to feed him but we have to do it."

Sometimes riders, deliberately or unconsciously, added to their animals' ordeal. In the same letter in which he deplored his mount's irregular feeding, Trooper Pulis admitted that on several occasions "I have kept my horse on a dead run for 2 hours at a time." Through this combination of overwork, disease, inadequate forage, and abuse, horses went lame or died in such numbers that half the men in regiments such as the 1st Massachusetts were, at any given time, dismounted.[25]

Although he could not eliminate the cavalry's problems overnight, Hooker promised to reform, rectify, and redress. To the surprise of many and the gratification of all, he made good on his pledge. Within weeks of his taking over, every trooper under his command was better fed than before, as was his steed. The army's supply depots began to provide better-quality rations and forage, and the flow never ceased.

To better the cavalry's lot, Hooker saw to it that qualified veterinary surgeons were detailed to the army and that every mounted regiment was assigned a blacksmith and a farrier. He stressed that cavalry officers should promote better care of their regiments' mounts. He also ensured that the remount system operated at peak efficiency. As a result, friction between the army and the Quartermaster's Department began to subside.

Hooker's reforms went beyond more and healthier horses. Under his regime, troopers were better clothed and accoutered than before, enjoyed better medical care, and wielded most dependable weaponry, including increasing numbers of those Sharps carbines that Pleasonton favored. Hooker tightened up the cavalry inspection system to certify that deficiencies in horseflesh and arms were quickly rectified. He promoted an increase in drills and reviews, to keep units in fighting trim and high spirits. He reopened those schools of instruction for both commissioned and noncommissioned officers that had lapsed under McClellan and Burnside. And he breathed new life into the officers' examining boards, which had exerted so much influence over army personnel in the earliest days of the war. These review panels, which convened both in Washington and in the field, were soon recommending the dismissal of incompetent and untutored officers, while calling for promotions for deserving ones. The new commander also instituted a system under which the best-disciplined soldiers in each regiment were granted furloughs.[26]

The effects of Hooker's reforms were felt almost immediately. In mid-March, Maj. William H. Medill of the 8th Illinois spoke for less articulate comrades when he wrote that "Gen. Hooker took this army in its gloomiest moment, when discouragement prevailed, when demoralization was apparent to any one, when no one thought it could be rescued from being disbanded . . . and by unceasing toil, by severity and kindness, he has rebuilt its foundation, extracted the rotten beams and replaced them by sound ones." Even outsiders were impressed by what they heard of Hooker's revival efforts. At about the time Medill wrote, Maj. James H. Kidd of the 6th Michigan, a regiment then attached to the Defenses of Washington but later a member of Hooker's army, observed that the general "seems to be bringing order out of chaos," something the horsemen of the Army of the Potomac sorely needed.[27]

Of all the improvements Hooker instituted, none had a greater impact or a more lasting benefit on the cavalry than his organizational reforms. When he dismantled Burnside's grand divisions and returned the army to the corps system, he created a corps composed entirely of mounted units. This act, which went into effect on February 5, grouped almost 9,000 officers and men under a single commander drawn from their ranks. In addition to giving it a cohesive organization, Hooker's decree placed the cavalry on an equal footing with the army's largest infantry component. The stature it thereby assumed gave the cavalry an increased sense of identity and a large helping of esprit de corps.[28]

The identity of the soldier who first suggested a corps organization for cavalry is unknown. When implementing the concept, Hooker had been influenced by the views of many officers. Several, including Bayard and Pleasonton, had agitated for a corps organization since the close of the Peninsula campaign. According to at least one account, Burnside took steps to form a cavalry corps but lost his job before he could complete the process. Reviewing the success of the idea after the war, several officers claimed credit for suggesting it.

Pleasonton had a legitimate claim to the honor. In December he had written a memorandum in which he argued that to realize its full potential as an intelligence-gathering apparatus and a force in combat, the cavalry should be grouped into a corps under a single commander. While it may seem ironic that a general who excelled neither in intelligence work nor in battle should advance such views, Pleasonton's argument was well reasoned and well presented. Showing great restraint, he remained silent on the one reform he sought above all else—that he command the new organization.[29]

In selecting the man for that job, Hooker surprised not only Pleasonton but other senior officers as well by returning George Stoneman to command of the army's horsemen. Since being shelved by McClellan five months earlier, Stoneman had lost some of his identity as a horseman. During that period, he had risen to command the III Corps—but not to the rank of major general. According to Hooker, Stoneman had led his command satisfactorily, if not with distinction, at Fredericksburg. Apparently, Stoneman desired a return to the cavalry and although Hooker never considered him highly talented in any arm, he respected his seniority. Not only did he grant his subordinate's wish, but he also eventually gained a second star for him. The assignment pleased both men. For one thing, it permitted Hooker to place a friend and fellow Republican, Maj. Gen. Daniel E. Sickles of New York, in the position Stoneman vacated.[30]

Seniority also appears to have ruled Hooker's selection of the cavalry's division and brigade commanders, which he announced on February 12. Probably against Stoneman's wishes, if not against his protests, Pleasonton took the 1st Division, which pretty much mirrored the organization he had commanded during Burnside's regime. One change was that his 1st Brigade was now led by Grimes Davis instead of John Farnsworth, who in the fall had regained his seat in Congress. Under Davis the brigade received a fourth regiment, the once-unhappy 9th New York of Col. William Sackett. Pleasonton's 2nd Brigade, formerly led by David Gregg, was now commanded by Tom Devin; its only addition was a single company of the 1st Michigan.

Hooker also toed the seniority line when he named Averell to command the 2nd Division of the Cavalry Corps. Averell's 1st Brigade originally consisted of the 1st Rhode Island and the 1st Massachusetts and was commanded by Horace B. Sargent of the latter regiment. By late February the command—now in the hands of a native Frenchman, Col. Alfred N. Duffié of the 1st Rhode Island—had added the 4th New York and the 6th Ohio. Averell's 2nd Brigade comprised the 3rd, 4th, and 16th Pennsylvania; its leader was Averell's successor as commander of the 3rd, James McIntosh.

Stoneman's 3rd Division was placed under David Gregg, whose most recent command had been the brigade originally led by George Bayard. On December 13 the dying Bayard had requested that his friend and fellow Democrat Gregg succeed him, and the appointment was made before the day ended. The original brigade had been large enough to be broken into two, and Stoneman did so upon assuming overall command. Three of its original regiments, the 1st Maine and the 2nd and 10th New York, now made up Gregg's 1st Brigade, under the recently promoted Col. Judson Kilpatrick. Two other regiments of Bayard's command, the 1st New Jersey and 1st Pennsylvania, made up half of Gregg's 2nd Brigade, which had been fleshed out with the addition of the 12th Illinois and the 1st Maryland; Col. John P. Taylor of the Pennsylvania regiment originally commanded the whole.

Hooker and Stoneman decided to attach a single horse battery to the 1st and 2nd Divisions: Lt. Joseph W. Martin's 6th New York Independent Battery went to Pleasonton, and Pennington's Battery M, 2nd United States Artillery, was assigned to Averell. Why no artillery went to Gregg's division remains unknown, although Stoneman created an artillery reserve consisting of three Regular batteries, one of them an amalgam of two undermanned units.[31]

If any subordinate had a right to feel slighted by these personnel decisions, it was John Buford. During the army's two most recent campaigns, he had been its titular chief of cavalry. Now he was relegated to command the so-called "Reserve Cavalry Brigade," consisting of the army's four understrength Regular regiments. Although originally designated a "special detachment," evidently because of its unique weaponry, the 6th Pennsylvania was later added to the brigade.

Buford was in Washington—testifying at Fitz John Porter's court-martial, then appearing before McDowell's court of inquiry—when the selections were made and thus was not on hand to state his case for higher command. The seniority issue appears to have hurt him more than any other factor, although his service under the discredited John Pope may have played a part in his failure to gain a division.[32]

Buford seems to have anticipated being passed over for a division; therefore, in early February he asked Stoneman for command of all the Regular regiments serving with the army. It was the least Stoneman could have done for him. Of those units that had served with the Army of the Potomac since the war's start, Buford gained command of all but the single squadron of the 4th Cavalry, which was transferred to the western theater about the time he took over. Theoretically, the Reserve Brigade was attached to no division, but in practice it served with the 1st Division.

Now and again, Buford must have reflected that had his commission as a brigadier general of volunteers been issued twelve days sooner, he would have ranked, and thus commanded, Alfred Pleasonton.[33]

Chapter Eleven

Good for the First Lick

Having lavished so much care and consideration on his horse soldiers, Hooker wanted a quick return on his investment. Instead, his cavalry suffered another surprise at the hands of one of Stuart's subordinates that embarrassed every member of the new corps and led Hooker to wonder if his efforts to revive the arm had been in vain.

While Averell's pickets invited the attack, they were not to blame for it—Hooker was, on two counts. The army leader believed his troopers' primary mission was counterreconnaissance. He expected them to perform this function twenty-four hours a day, seven days a week. Not only was this expectation unrealistic, so too was Hooker's belief that his cavalry could totally prevent intrusion. As long as Hooker remained at Falmouth, the Cavalry Corps maintained a picket line that virtually encircled the main army. That line covered nearly 100 miles of snow-caked earth—far too much ground to be properly held at every point.[1]

Stuart and his lieutenants realized this fact, as they had when confronting McClellan's pickets the previous June. They also realized that one of the weakest links in the line lay opposite Kelly's Ford, one of the most accessible crossing points on the Upper Rappahannock. Above the ford and extending southeastward to Hartwood Church, eight miles from Falmouth, Averell's picket posts—most of them located too far apart to make mutual support possible—tried to guard Hooker's far right flank. It was anything but an easy task, and late in February Fitzhugh Lee, now a brigadier general, determined to make it more difficult still.

With Stuart's blessing, a "reconnaissance in force" commenced on the morning of the twenty-fourth. With characteristic stealth, Lee, a West Point comrade of Averell's, slipped across the ford with 400 picked men of the 1st, 2nd, and 3rd Virginia and headed for Hartwood Church. The next morning his men attacked and broke a long section of the picket line. Lee claimed that before the day was over, he had captured about half of Averell's picket reserve, five officers and 145 men, "with all their horses, arms, and equipments." Those Federals not immediately captured—some 300 of them—were put to ignominious flight.[2]

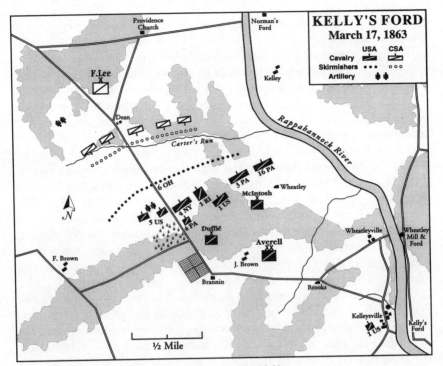

Map of the Battle of Kelly's Ford, March 17, 1863

Lee's claims were not farfetched; George Bliss, whose squadron of the 1st Rhode Island patrolled an eight-mile line around Hartwood Church, claimed that his regiment alone lost 100 men captured or missing. Bliss was not surprised by the scope of the enemy's success, but he was angry about it: "Such an event has been predicted by many pickets among us, and unless our Genls improve this lesson and make better arrangements on this flank of our army the rebels will do the same thing again."[3]

The panic that Lee caused along Averell's picket line, especially that section held by the 16th Pennsylvania, was terrible to behold. When officers of the 3rd Pennsylvania and 1st Massachusetts rushed up to stem the rout, they found the job all but impossible. Dismounted fugitives raced past Charles F. Adams, Jr., deaf to his orders to rally and re-form. "Then wrath seized my soul," the righteous Bostonian recalled, "and I uttered a yell and chased them. I caught a hapless cuss and cut him over the head with my sabre. It only lent a new horror and fresh speed to his flight. I whanged another over the face and he tarried for a while. Into a third I drove my horse and gave him pause, and then I swore and cursed them. I called them 'curs,' 'dogs,' and 'cowards,' a disgrace to the 16th Pennsylvania, as the 16th was a disgrace to the service, and so I finally prevailed on about half of my line to stop for this time."[4]

Spreading consternation as they rode, the Confederates moved north to bivouack for the night at Morrisville, nine miles northwest of Hartwood. The next morning they nonchalantly returned to the river, crossing without incident at Kelly's Ford, their mortified prisoners in tow. As if the loss of so many men was an insufficient blow to Averell's pride, Lee left him a note in which he ridiculed the fleeing pickets and beseeched his old friend to "put up your sword, leave my state and go home. . . . If you won't go home, return my visit and bring me a sack of coffee."[5]

As on too many past occasions, the Federal cavalry's pursuit degenerated into a comedy of errors. Alerted to Lee's foray on the afternoon of the twenty-fifth, Stoneman, then at Falmouth, ordered both Averell and Pleasonton to chase down the raiders. Averell was to move directly to Hartwood, while Pleasonton took the road north toward Stafford Court House, Aquia Church, and Dumfries, where he might nab the Rebels if they continued north. Before riding off to take command of the operation, Stoneman directed the Reserve Brigade, under Capt. George C. Cram of the 6th Cavalry (Buford was still in Washington) to head for Hartwood Church as well.

Averell did not have to be told to pursue. Even before Stoneman wired him, the New Yorker started for Hartwood with the better part of his division. Pleasonton, on the other hand, failed to respond to a second order Stoneman sent him by telegraph at midnight. Pleasonton was to quit the northern route, turn west, and make with all speed to Morrisville, Lee's last-known whereabouts.[6]

The new assignment must have brought Pleasonton up short. At or near Morrisville, he stood to meet a Rebel force that, according to rumors Pleasonton had no way of knowing were exaggerated, amounted to some 2,000 riders. This prospect did not activate any combative spirit in the division commander. Four months after shying away from Stuart's raiders, he did so again. Instead of hastening west, he marked time at Aquia Church, between Stafford Court House and Dumfries. When army headquarters learned of his presence there on the morning of the twenty-sixth, Hooker's chief of staff, Maj. Gen. Daniel Butterfield, scolded him: "I don't know what you are doing there. Orders were sent you . . . to push for the enemy without delay."[7]

Pleasonton later defended himself by denying he ever received the telegram directing him to Morrisville. Thus, when he finally reached his new objective, the Rebels were long gone. Averell, however, was in the area; the two divisions joined in a fruitless attempt to overtake Lee's compact, fast-moving column before it hit Kelly's Ford. In his after-action report, Stoneman hinted that he disbelieved Pleasonton's claim about an errant dispatch, but he stopped short of calling his subordinate a liar.[8]

Even after learning that Lee had recrossed the river, Stoneman was not at once permitted to return to Falmouth. On the morning of the twenty-sixth he received a rather preposterous dispatch from Hooker ordering him, if unable to stop the Rebels short of their lines, to "follow them to their camp, and destroy them." Hooker was on another flight of fancy. As he saw it—as he several times explained to Stoneman—the army's horsemen had been armed, equipped, trained, fed, and mounted to the point of invincibility. In open battle they should never fail to annihilate their opponents. Hooker gave the impression that anything less was wholly unacceptable.

On the present occasion, at least, the army commander eventually came to his senses. For six hours he permitted Stoneman to contemplate crossing the river and, without prior reconnaissance, taking on Stuart's entire command ("a prospect anything but cheering," as Stoneman himself put it). Finally, just after noon on the twenty-sixth, Hooker countermanded the order and recalled Stoneman, Pleasonton, Averell, and Cram to their camps near Falmouth.[9]

Hooker's change of mind proved to be temporary. For three weeks after Lee's reconnaissance, Fighting Joe wailed and gnashed his teeth over his cavalry's inability to stand up to its adversary. Hooker's biographer claims that he treated Stoneman and his subordinates to a daily dose of vituperation, on one occasion exclaiming: "You have got to stop these disgraceful cavalry 'surprises.' I'll have no more of them. I give you full power over your officers, to arrest, cashier, shoot—whatever you will—only you must stop these surprises. And by God, sir, if you don't do it, I give you fair notice, I will relieve the whole [lot] of you and take command of the cavalry myself."[10]

Averell, whose lax picketing appeared to have been responsible for the disaster of the twenty-fifth and who had been the object of Confederate taunts, realized that the burden of avenging Hartwood Church was his alone. Hooker kept jabbing the point home through almost daily lectures to his subordinate and appeals to his thirst for revenge.

For a time, Averell simply took his punishment. He had already done what he could to make amends. Little more than a week after Hartwood Church, Stoneman and he had revamped the army's picket lines so as to make better use of infantry support and thus decrease the possibility of another debacle at Stuart's hands. Officers who had been captured by Lee's men had been recommended for dismissal, while noncommissioned prisoners had been reduced to the ranks. Beyond this, Averell could do little until the weather cleared. He could not operate south of the river with any confidence on half-frozen, half-thawed roads. The end of February found snow still covering much of the Rappahannock shore. In places where it had responded to sunlight, Silas Wesson found the mud "getting deeper every day."[11]

March brought the promise of moderate weather but not much activity along the army's front. Farther north, it was a different story. From February 27 to March 3 troopers of Col. Sir Percy Wyndham's cavalry of the Defenses of Washington, including the 5th and 6th Michigan, marched to and from Falmouth on a Rebel hunting operation. And on March 9 the "Gray Ghost," Capt. John Singleton Mosby, led his partisan raiders behind Union lines for perhaps the hundredth time, occupying Fairfax Court House and kidnapping the local commander, Brig. Gen. Edwin H. Stoughton. Mosby's true target on this occasion, Percy Wyndham, escaped capture but soon afterward lost his command, which was expanded to division size and assigned to the Hungarian-born Maj. Gen. Julius Stahel. Meanwhile, Sir Percy, who had been serving apart from his regiment, the 1st New Jersey, for some months, rejoined it and by virtue of seniority assumed command of David Gregg's 2nd Brigade.[12]

By midmonth, weather conditions along the Rappahannock had improved so much that Hooker could plan a retaliatory strike against Stuart. On the twelfth he had Stoneman reconnoiter every crossing between Falmouth and Kelly's Ford. The scouting mission turned up no Rebels along that stretch of river but confirmed that the camp of Lee's brigade remained twelve miles west of Kelly's Ford, near Culpeper Court House. Wade Hampton's brigade was thought to be encamped in the same area. Lee, at least, appeared to have copied his enemy's mistake by setting up a loose picket line between his camps and the river.[13]

This was all the information Hooker needed. At 8:00 on the morning of the sixteenth, he sent Averell forth at the head of Duffié's and McIntosh's brigades, plus 800 members of the Reserve Brigade under Capt. Marcus Reno of the 1st Cavalry, and Martin's New York battery, this day commanded by Lt. George Browne, Jr.—almost 4,000 officers and men and six guns. The column was directed to Morrisville. From there it was to cross at Kelly's Ford, and "attack and break up" as many of Stuart's regiments as possible. His ears ringing with three weeks' worth of condemnation, Averell must have been happy to comply.[14]

Yet he could not bring his total force to bear on the enemy. On the way to the river on the evening of the sixteenth, he detached Sargent's 1st Massachusetts and most of Col. William E. Doster's 4th Pennsylvania with orders to guard the Brentsville area, which, according to some reports, teemed with enemy horsemen. The precaution proved unnecessary, and the loss of Sargent and Doster—who found only a handful of scouts near Brentsville—cost Averell nearly a third of his force. The brigadier claimed it left him with only 2,100 men. It would appear, however, that he still led five regiments and parts of three others, in addition to his artillery. A force of that size must have totaled at least 3,000—more than enough to handle Lee's brigade and perhaps Hampton's as well.[15]

Soon after 6:00 A.M. on the seventeenth, Averell's advance guard encountered detachments of Fitz Lee's 2nd and 4th Virginia, guarding both sides of Kelly's Ford. Thrusting aside the small force on the upper shore, the Federals plunged into the swift-moving, ice-cold stream, which ran four feet deep at the ford. Before midway across, they attracted a fusillade of carbine fire. Averell's advance echelon—about sixty men of the 4th New York and 1st Rhode Island of Duffié's brigade—made three unsuccessful attempts to gouge the Virginians on the far bank from rifle pits protected by fallen-tree abatis and wire entanglements. A party of troopers wielding axes joined in the attacks; to one onlooker, their involvement "suggested thoughts of the ancient Roman and his battle-ax."[16]

When Averell came up with the vanguard of his column, he was livid that such a small force should block his crossing. He also feared that so much firing would alert Lee and Hampton to his coming. As it turned out, however, Lee had not yet learned of Averell's advance, and Hampton never did. At Averell's sharply delivered order, his chief of staff, Maj. Samuel E. Chamberlain of the 1st Massachusetts, led perhaps thirty New Yorkers and Rhode Islanders in another charge, whose only result was Chamberlain's severe wounding. A small party of the 1st Rhode Island did make its way across the stream, only to be surrounded and taken prisoner.

The ford was cleared and the captives were liberated only after Colonel Duffié sent the rest of the Rhode Island regiment, under Maj. Preston Farrington, through the stream in a body, sabers swinging and pistols cracking. Incredibly, Major Chamberlain, blood streaming down his face, rode at the head of the column. In the charge he took a second wound and was finally put out of action. Through such determination as Chamberlain had demonstrated, Farrington's men pried the defenders loose from their works, killing several and taking twenty-five prisoners. By day's end Averell's column had captured more than sixty Confederates.[17]

Not until after 10:00 was the entire Union force on the enemy's side of the Rappahannock. Then its commander delayed to water his horses and carry artillery ammunition across the stream, which had risen so high that Browne's caissons could not cross for fear of being swamped. By noon, the Federals were finally riding inland, seeking Fitz Lee's main body. By now Averell had lost the advantage of time as well as of surprise; still, he remained determined to whip his West Point comrade in an open fight.

If Averell expected that fight to take place in daylight, he should have marched swiftly on Culpeper. Instead, he moved slowly, warily, as though suddenly aware of the dangers of Confederate territory. His apprehension peaked when, less than a mile beyond Kelly's Ford, a long column of horsemen in gray and butternut brown came into view inside a tree-bordered field on property owned by a farmer named Brannin. Within minutes, opposing skirmishers were trading shots at long range and Browne's guns were going into battery. Averell deployed his main body in a line of battle 2,000 yards long, Duffié's brigade on the left, McIntosh's to the right, with some of Reno's Regulars on Duffié's flank and in the rear, taking on the reserve mission that had given their brigade its name.[18]

Initially only Lee's 3rd Virginia was on the scene in full strength. The brigade leader's other four regiments had been picketing well in the rear when the shooting started and were now racing to the front. But if he lacked manpower, Lee did not want for leadership. J. E. B. Stuart was on the scene, fresh from court-martial duty in Culpeper; so was Stuart's young and highly talented artillery chief, Maj. John Pelham, who had been on leave, visiting friends in the vicinity.[19]

Now began five hours of charging and countercharging. In almost every case, Lee attacked while Averell met and absorbed the blow, and occasionally struck back. The offensive was a role with which Stuart was intimately familiar, one he had never failed to handle successfully. Today, however, he got off to a poor start. When the 3rd Virginia, backed by the newly arrived 2nd Virginia, moved forward as though to charge Browne's battery, portions of Duffié's and McIntosh's brigades treated the Rebels to a converging fire that drew much blood.

Unwilling to remain on the defensive, the sometimes impetuous Colonel Duffié—an honors graduate of the French military academy at St. Cyr and a veteran of European cavalry actions but a novice in brigade command in America—took it upon himself to advance his main body. The movement triggered the first mounted attack of the day, launched by the 2nd Virginia. "They came on boldly," recalled a Federal officer, "yelling like demons, and apparently confident of victory."[20]

When the Rebels were only 100 yards off, Duffié ordered Farrington's regiment to meet them head-on. The columns collided with a resounding crash, men and horses going down all across the farm field. Survivors locked in hand-to-hand combat until Farrington's men cut a path through their enemy with their sabers. It was here, for the first time, that the Federals' opponents entreated them to sheath their swords, take up their pistols, and "fight like gentlemen."[21]

Refusing to comply, Farrington's troopers forced their adversaries to turn about and ride off. Looking on from the rear, Stuart and Lee could hardly believe their eyes. For the first time in recorded history, a regiment of Virginians had fled from an encounter with a Yankee force of equal size. The only onlooker not impressed by the maneuver was Averell, who was determined that his entire force remain on the defensive indefinitely. He castigated Duffié for acting without orders and took steps to ensure that no other attack was launched.

For the Confederate hierarchy, things seemed to be getting out of hand. After the 2nd Virginia rode off, the 3rd attacked Averell's right flank near the Wheatly Farm, only to be bounced backward by canister from Browne's cannon and carbine balls from sharpshooters in McIntosh's brigade, who had taken cover behind a stone wall. A nonplussed Stuart now placed himself at the head of the 1st and 4th Virginia, both of which had come up during the repulse of the 3rd, and led them toward Duffié's position, the re-formed 2nd Virginia in the rear. The heftiness of this column availed Stuart not at all, for once again Browne's shelling and the fire of dismounted Federals turned back the charging troops. Stuart rallied his broken ranks and hurled them at Averell's line two more times. According to one Pennsylvanian, each effort enjoyed "worse success than the first, becoming more easily . . . demoralized each time."[22]

Upon the third repulse, the Virginians retreated a half mile before Stuart could rally them. Discouraged but not defeated, he built a new line and awaited another opportunity to attack. Averell had the chance to press Stuart as he retired but elected not to do so. After tending to his relatively few casualties and his many prisoners, he led his victorious troopers and horse artillerymen slowly and deliberately toward the new position. Short of it he again deployed, Duffié's and Reno's men on the left in columns of four, McIntosh and other

Regular units on the right, many of them afoot, others mounted as if ready to deliver a saber charge.

Apparently thinking his enemy's position weak, Stuart ordered another charge, this time by all five of Lee's regiments simultaneously. At his word, the 2nd and 4th Virginia raced down the west side of the road to Kelly's Ford, aiming at Duffié's brigade, while the 1st, 3rd, and 5th Virginia charged east of the road, toward McIntosh's position. The Federals met both assaults coolly and intelligently. Browne's gunners—not yet tied down by Stuart's horse artillery, which was just now reaching the field—thinned out the attacking columns before they could close with their opponents. Then, as soon as the Rebels came within carbine range, dismounted marksmen blew them apart.[23]

On Duffié's front, the Virginians broke and fled before able to saber or shoot any Yankees. On the right, the larger column bore down on McIntosh's brigade, whose men stood their ground with extraordinary equanimity. "We held our carbine-fire," recalled Captain Newhall of the 3rd Pennsylvania, "till we could almost see the whites of their eyes." The attackers' momentum carried them through McIntosh's first line, but defenders farther to the rear contained and then dispersed the attackers. Apparently with Averell's approval, that portion of McIntosh's brigade that had remained mounted launched a counterattack that quickly cleared the field. Those involved included members of the 16th Pennsylvania, thereby making amends for their regiment's execrable conduct at Hartwood Church.[24]

Stuart's latest repulse occurred sometime after 5:00 P.M. The short winter's afternoon drew to a close before he could undertake another offensive. Darkness ended a day that had seen five of his regiments broken apart and forced to withdraw at least twice, and one, the 2nd Virginia, three times. This was unheard of, a cataclysmic flouting of the established order. Stuart must have expected the sun to set in the east.

His victor might have punctuated his triumph by pressing Stuart into headlong retreat, or at least remaining on the hard-won field throughout the night. Averell did neither. His horses and men appeared exhausted, and he did not like the look of those earthworks behind which many of Lee's troopers had retreated. Then, too, he thought he heard the sound of trains arriving at nearby Brandy Station; perhaps they were carrying Rebel infantry out to cut the Federal line of withdrawal. Finally, the coming of night made Averell even more insecure and homesick. For all these reasons, and apparently over the objections of some of his officers, at twilight Averell led his men across the river and back to camp.[25]

Despite his slowness to advance and his reluctance to take the offensive, Averell had accomplished a great deal on this St. Patrick's Day. For one thing, he had exposed the fallacy behind the term "Stuart's Invincibles." Thanks to a shell from Browne's artillery, he had mortally wounded John Pelham, robbing Stuart's horse artillery, at least temporarily, of its effectiveness. He had answered the taunts of an old friend, having left on the battlefield a sack of coffee beans, with a note attached: "Dear Fitz: Here's your coffee. Here's your visit. How do you like it?"

Above all else, he had removed a huge burden from his shoulders, thereby pleasing not only Joe Hooker but also Edwin Stanton, who soon afterward congratulated the army leader "upon the success of General Averell's expedition. It is good for the first lick . . . and I hope now soon to see the boys up and at them.'"[26]

As they departed Kelly's Ford, Averell's "boys" were in high spirits, and for good reason. They had won, in convincing fashion, what the *New York Times* called "The First Real Cavalry Fight of the War." As an officer in the 1st Massachusetts observed, the battle had been fought "for the purpose of adding prestige, if possible, to our troopers, before the spring campaign," and it had achieved its purpose. No longer would the Federals feel inferior, overmatched, on the defensive when they engaged their enemy. As Walter Newhall wrote one day after the fight, "We are more than ever sure that on a fair field the Rebel Cavalry can't stand [up to] us." Colonel Doster observed that "the spirits of our men never were as good as they are now."[27]

Not only the participants felt heartened by Averell's success. Although little more than a third of the command had been engaged, the morale of the entire Cavalry Corps soared as a result of Kelly's Ford. At least one historian has derided the notion that every trooper in Hooker's army benefited in mind and spirit from Averell's accomplishments, but he fails to appreciate the psychological concept known as identification. This concept holds that every member of a close-knit organization—which Hooker's cavalry had become by early 1863—receives a boost in self-esteem from the achievements of a few.[28]

Before March 17 the Federal horseman were desperately seeking evidence that their faith in themselves—so sorely tried on so many occasions—had not been misplaced. After Kelly's Ford, they stopped questioning their ability to achieve and succeed. In this sense, the St. Patrick's Day victory, incomplete and imperfect as it was, exerted a more powerful and longer-lasting impact on the cavalry of the Army of the Potomac than any later victory.

>─⋅◆⟩⋅─O─⟨◆⋅⊣─<

Early in April good weather returned to eastern Virginia, apparently to stay; with it came President Lincoln, who on the sixth was the guest of honor at a gala review of the Cavalry Corps, held on farmland north of Falmouth. By all accounts, both reviewer and reviewed liked what they saw during the two-hour spectacle. Dan Pulis of the 8th New York reported that "Gens Hooker & Stoneman was present as well as Old Uncle Abe. We had a grand time." When the president inspected Pleasonton's division, "he took off his hat and rode the whole length of our line with his hat in his hand," a display of respect that gratified every trooper.[29]

The president was not a handsome man, and he looked ungainly in the saddle; still, he made a strong impression on the soldiers around him. "As he rode past us," recalled a trooper in the 9th New York, "we could see how kind his face is and how sad his eyes [are] and you forget how funny and awkward he looks on horseback." One of Private Pulis's comrades was concerned to find the president looking "extremely thin and careworn, as if his strength would scarcely carry him to the end of his term."[30]

More than one trooper believed, as William Doster put it, that Lincoln's presence "forebodes a great battle." In fact, with winter over and the roads drying, General Hooker was readying his well-fed, well-armed, and well-equipped army, now 122,000 strong, for its first general offensive under his command. He had determined to succeed where his predecessor had failed, turning Lee's left flank upstream from Falmouth. While the main force sneaked into the Confederates' rear, other troops would move up in front, holding the enemy in place until a stunning blow could be struck from the blind side.[31]

Hooker's plan for his turning movement included a major role for his rejuvenated cavalry. Six days after its review by Lincoln, Hooker ordered Stoneman to take most of the Cavalry Corps up the north fork of the Rappahannock. Once beyond the line of the Orange & Alexandria, they were to cross the river and head into the heart of the enemy's country, smashing the communication lines—especially the Virginia Central and the Richmond, Fredericksburg & Potomac Railroads—that linked Lee to his capital. By inflicting as much damage as possible on these and other supply conduits, Stoneman would distract Lee's attention at a critical time, perhaps causing him to fall back on Richmond even before Hooker enveloped his left. If, on the other hand, Lee held on near Fredericksburg, Stoneman would be in position to strike him when he fell back under the weight of the infantry's attack. Either way, the cavalry would make an important contribution to Fighting Joe's strategic masterpiece.[32]

Stoneman may have had misgivings about trying to exploit an envelopment days before it occurred, but if so, he told no one. On the twelfth he called in outlying detachments, grouped everyone near Falmouth, and outfitted them for the march. The next morning all 8,000 marched up the river—mounted men followed by horse artillery pieces, caissons, and limbers, pack mules, led horses, ambulances, and a small line of supply wagons. Never before had so many riders moved as one body; Stoneman's column must have impressed even the infantrymen who watched it break winter camp at Falmouth.

For this undertaking—the first raid the cavalry of the Army of the Potomac had attempted since war's outbreak—Stoneman had selected the divisions of Averell and Gregg. To Averell's force he had added Grimes Davis's brigade, while the Reserve Brigade, with John Buford at last at its head, had been attached to Gregg's command. Pennington's battery also rode with Averell; four other horse artillery units trundled along behind the troopers of Gregg and Buford.[33]

The inclusion of Davis's and Buford's commands meant that a single brigade of cavalry had been left with the main army: the 6th New York, the 8th and 17th Pennsylvania, and the single company of Michiganders—ordinarily led by Tom Devin but on this occasion commanded by Alfred Pleasonton.

Stoneman's failure to include the division leader in his raiding force may have been a matter of happenstance. More likely, it was the result of the argument the two had engaged in following the escape of the Chambersburg raiders. By leaving his most senior but least favorite subordinate behind, Stoneman was denying him a role in an operation that would surely add to the honors the cavalry had won on March 17.

Stoneman's expedition got off to a flying start, but things quickly turned sour. After making more than twenty miles upriver on the first day out, the main column poised to cross at Beverly Ford, eight miles upstream from now-celebrated Kelly's Ford. Buford, meanwhile, was supposed to ford at a point two miles downstream. The two wings would remain miles apart as they headed south, Buford's guarding against interference from Stuart's cavalry, most of which was encamped between Kelly's Ford and Fredericksburg.

Even so, enough gray-clad cavalrymen were stationed south of both fords that Stoneman spent all day on the fourteenth sparring with them across the water. The lost day became a major blunder when a hard rain fell throughout the night, not only spreading discomfort through Stoneman's bivouacs, but also raising the river to the point that it could not be crossed safely. Daniel Pulis called it "the most dreadful storm I ever saw. The creek which comonly was about 18 inches high swelled up to the horses' sides. It carried one man down the stream and to cap all when the storm was at its highth it began to haile like great guns."[34]

When, after dawn on the fifteenth, Stoneman changed his mind and directed Buford to ford at Beverly, the Kentuckian could not obey. The ford, Buford reported, was "swimming" and the road to it had become "a sea" of rain and mud. It was Burnside's Mud March all over again.[35]

Except for brief respites, the downpour continued for almost two weeks, and the river remained dangerously high. Long before that period was up, Hooker was sending Stoneman impatient orders to cross as soon as possible. The cavalry, he declared, was holding up the army; with each passing day, an immobile Stoneman harmed the turning movement's chances for success. Abraham Lincoln, who was closely monitoring the raid from the White House, was also worried about the delay. Late on the fifteenth he wired Hooker: "General S. is not moving rapidly enough to make the expedition come to anything. . . . I do not know that any better can be done, but I greatly fear it is another failure already."[36]

Stoneman was as concerned about the delay as anyone else but was powerless against the elements. Until April 29 he kept his troopers and horse artillerymen on the north bank, engaged in drilling, local reconnaissances, and other exercises calculated to keep their minds off their predicament and their morale high. His efforts appear to have failed. One of his officers recalled that "the whole force changed camp frequently, grew weary with marching and countermarching, used up its supplies, and became always less confident and able."[37]

The delay prompted Hooker to alter his strategy. He had become convinced that the advantage of surprise had been irretrievably lost, and he doubted that the cavalry would reach the Confederate rear in time to distract Lee from the infantry's movements. Now the main army would take Lee in rear and the cavalry would operate on its own against the rail lines near Richmond. No longer would the movements of two forces be closely coordinated.

Stoneman's revised instructions called for him to ride, via Culpeper and Gordonsville, to the junction of the Virginia Central and the R, F & P. He was to travel in two columns: One, which he would entrust to Averell, would go down the line of the O & A, en route besting Confederate horsemen, under now Brig. Gen. Rooney Lee, thought to be near Rapidan Station. The other, under Gregg and Buford, would move to the Rapidan River, crossing that stream at Raccoon Ford and making for Louisa Court House on the Virginia Central, before pouncing on the railroad to Fredericksburg. Hooker expected the wings to meet somewhere along the Pamunkey River, where they might yet harass Lee's retreat.[38]

The Rappahannock receded to the point that Stoneman could cross on the morning of the twenty-ninth. By then he had had plenty of time to prepare for the march. Yet he was still calling in detachments and issuing rations at 8:00 A.M., when the head of Hooker's turning column appeared at the ford. Thousands of infantrymen crossed the river on a pontoon bridge recently laid near Kelly's Ford, while red-faced cavalrymen milled about in their rear. By the time Stoneman's main body was over the river, it was 5:00 P.M. Then, instead of moving south without further delay, Stoneman called his ranking subordinates to a war council. Darkness was approaching when the two columns finally began their excursion into Rebeldom.[39]

The eleventh-hour conference had been designed to familiarize Averell, Gregg, and Buford with the job and the territory ahead. It failed to do so. Unaware that he was to coordinate his operations with, and eventually rejoin, his associates, Averell took off down the Orange & Alexandria, believing he was on an independent mission. About a half hour after leaving the river, with the other column lost to sight, he encountered about 700 troopers of Rooney Lee's brigade. Though he outnumbered this force perhaps five to one, Averell allowed his adversaries—members of the 13th Virginia, later reinforced by a portion of the 9th Virginia—to dog his heels for several hours. Sometime after dark, resistance began to fade, but then Averell heard what turned out to be an erroneous rumor that Stuart himself, with four brigades and a large complement of artillery, was sitting astride the raiders' route near Brandy Station. The following morning Averell advanced on the depot with as much caution as he had displayed when searching for Fitz Lee on St. Patrick's Day. Greatly relieved to find no Confederates at Brandy, Averell moved on to Culpeper Court House, his advance guard sweeping through the village at an extended gallop.[40]

Although his orders called for a swift advance on Rapidan Station, Averell lingered near Culpeper for several hours, destroying Confederate supplies and reading captured enemy dispatches. Finally, about sundown—and only after a courier brought him a sharp reminder from Stoneman—he left Culpeper for the Rapidan.

At the depot named for the river, Averell was greeted by shells from the single artillery piece that Rooney Lee, who had looped around the raiders' rear, had at his disposal this day. Stymied not only by the shelling, but also by approaching darkness, Averell remained on the north bank throughout May 1, at one point attempting to burn the O & A bridge there, as though his mission were not to attack Lee but to keep Lee from attacking him. When the enemy did the job for him, torching the bridge, then riding off to confront the larger raiding column, Averell whiled away another twenty-four hours along the now-unfordable stream, contenting himself with the knowledge that parties from his command were wrecking bridges farther up the river and downing the telegraph to Rapidan Station.[41]

Averell was still staring across the river, trying to locate Rooney Lee when, at midmorning on May 2, he received a dispatch from Joe Hooker, asking him what he was doing on the Rapidan when he should have been much farther south. Hooker was especially perturbed when he learned that Averell had remained immobile long after Lee had given him the slip.

For the army commander, the final straw was Averell's slow, roundabout trip to the army's new headquarters on the Rappahannock. When the cavalryman finally reported to him, Hooker gave him a dressing-down, relieved him of command, and ordered him to Washington to await further orders from the War Department. His travel north was preceded by an angry telegram in which Hooker informed Secretary Stanton that Averell "seems to have contented himself between April 29 and May 4 with having marched . . . 28 miles, meeting no enemy deserving of the name, and from that point reporting to me for instructions." Determined to polish off the object of his ire, Hooker added, "This army will never be able to accomplish its mission under commanders who not only disregard their instructions, but at the same time display so little zeal and devotion in the performance of their duties."[42]

By the time Hooker wrote, the grand strategy by which he had planned to crush Robert E. Lee had come unraveled. Thus, in flaying Averell, he may have been sacrificing a convenient scapegoat. Yet regardless of what had provoked it, Hooker's diatribe to Stanton had an immediate and powerful effect. Barely six weeks after Averell had won a landmark battle, his career in the Army of the Potomac was over. Colonel Doster's last glimpse of his division commander was of Averell sitting in his headquarters tent on the day before he started for Washington. He was "quite alone," Doster recalled, "with his head resting on his hand . . . dejected." Averell, he thought, looked "much like a condemned cavalry horse."[43]

>–⊷–○–⊷–<

Thanks to Stoneman's dilatory habits and imperfect understanding of his mission, the raid would furnish more than one scapegoat. Incredibly, he tarried on the south bank of the Rappahannock for nearly twenty-four hours after Averell set off on his ill-starred mission. He spent the time on chores he should have attended to long before, including culling unfit horses from Gregg's and Buford's commands and returning his pack animals to the main army, supposedly to speed his marching pace. Late on the thirtieth—nearly two weeks after he had left Falmouth on an expedition heavily dependent on a prompt start—Stoneman headed south through the pinelands below the Rappahannock.[44]

Early that evening, Buford, who led the march, reached Raccoon Ford, where his Regulars flanked and captured some of Rooney Lee's men who had been guarding the site. Some of the prisoners brought Stoneman welcome news: Stuart, with the brigades of Hampton and Fitzhugh Lee, had passed through the area hours earlier, en route to Fredericksburg in response to Hooker's advance. As the next day, May 1, proved, the raiders' path to and across the Rapidan was free of enemy resistance except that provided by those pesky outriders under Rooney Lee.

Thus unimpeded, the Federals turned to their work. On the first, Gregg's advance guard overwhelmed a picket at Orange Springs, a dozen miles north of Louisa Court House. There Gregg also wrecked military stores and pursued, but failed to overtake, a supply train that had left the town hours before. Then Stoneman led the main column into the seat of Louisa County, which he reached at 2:00 on the morning of the second. There and elsewhere along the Virginia Central, the raiders ripped up track and tore down telegraph cable, while keeping Lee's people at arm's length. When its labors were done, the column followed Stoneman to the South Anna River, bivouacking for the night at Thompson's Crossroads.[45]

Soon after reaching the South Anna, Stoneman revised his plans and revamped his itinerary. Recently Hooker had called on him to "dash off to the right and left," doing "a vast deal of mischief." Originally Stoneman had intended to create that mischief by keeping Gregg's column intact, to be used as one mighty instrument of destruction. Now he decided to fragment his force, sending parties in many directions to accomplish a variety of deeds. Assembling his subordinates for an evening conference, Stoneman (as he later recalled) "gave them to understand that we had dropped in that region of country like a shell, and that I intended to burst it in every direction . . . and thus magnify our small force into overwhelming numbers."[46]

In the abstract, the idea had merit; certainly it seemed to respond to Hooker's wishes. As it turned out, however, Stoneman would have been better served by keeping Gregg's and Buford's people a cohesive, coordinated force. That, after all, had been the philosophy that underlay the corps organization for cavalry. By breaking up his force, by preventing it from bringing its full weight to bear on any single objective, Stoneman ensured that his troopers would inflict isolated, small-scale destruction that would appear random rather than patterned, spur-of-the moment instead of part of a carefully designed strategy.

Four major detachments of Gregg's division rode off on the morning of the third to implement the "bursting shell" strategy, while a portion of Buford's brigade operated against targets not far from Thompson's Crossroads. Sir

Percy Wyndham, with his 1st New Jersey and the better part of the 1st Maryland Cavalry, moved southwestward, crossing the Chickahominy River and reining in at the confluence of the James and Rivanna Rivers, near the town of Columbia. There the Briton tried but failed to destroy the stone aqueduct that spanned the nearby James River Canal. Wyndham did, however, destroy large quantities of quartermaster's, commissary, and medical supplies found in Columbia, as well as canal locks and gates, before rejoining Stoneman that evening, just ahead of Rooney Lee's pursuers.[47]

Soon after Wyndham had ridden out, Colonel Kilpatrick moved eastward at the head of his 2nd New York, striking the R, F & P at Hungary Station. After wrecking tracks and depot buildings, Kilpatrick turned toward Richmond and made as if to assault its outer works—a maneuver he repeated, under much different circumstances, ten months later. This time, he was bluffing; after capturing some officers on the capital's outskirts, he bypassed Richmond to the north, heading for the Chickahominy River. There he destroyed supplies and torched strategic Meadow Bridge. Meanwhile, some of his men, experienced engineers, ran a captured locomotive off another span and into the river. Still other raiders captured wagon trains hauling goods into the capital. Kilpatrick capped his operation by eluding various pursuit forces, attacking and routing one of them, before making for the Peninsula in line with contingency orders from Stoneman. On May 7 the colonel led his plucky New Yorkers inside the Union lines at Gloucester Point, then crossed the river to equally well-defended Yorktown.[48]

At Yorktown Kilpatrick was greeted by Lt. Col. Hasbrouck Davis and his 12th Illinois, which had left Thompson's Crossroads on the third. During a three-day spree that rivaled Kilpatrick's in terms of resources demolished, Davis's troopers had mangled track and burned two bridges on the Virginia Central and the R, F & P, while also destroying depot buildings, telegraph cable, culverts, turnarounds, a train loaded with supplies, and warehouses along both lines. Moving to Tunstall's Station on the York River Railroad— one of J. E. B. Stuart's ports of call during his raid the previous June and now in Confederate hands—Davis attacked a fully loaded troop train and nearly captured it. Only when persuaded he could not overcome the hundreds of infantrymen aboard the cars did he lead his Illinoisans toward the Peninsula.[49]

The fourth major raiding party was led by General Gregg himself. At the head of the 1st Maine and 10th New York, the division commander ranged north of Thompson's Crossroads, destroying several bridges on the road between Louisa Court House and Richmond. In his work Gregg was aided by Captain Merritt of Stoneman's staff, who had been sent at the head of a detachment of the 1st Maryland to perform a similar mission in the same general vicinity. By midafternoon on the third Gregg and Merritt had joined forces to level five spans. Only late on the fourth, when the countryside began to swarm with pursuers who prevented the raiders from torching yet another bridge, did the united command return to Stoneman's side.[50]

While the several detachments were revamping the transportation system of middle Virginia, Stoneman had remained on the South Anna with Buford's brigade as his escort. On May 3 and again the next day, detachments of Reserves burned two bridges, secured others in case they were needed during a retreat, and reconnoitered possible routes of withdrawal. On a couple occasions, the Regulars tangled with Rooney Lee's diehards; on one, the Rebels trapped and thrashed a party of the 5th Cavalry near Yanceyville, northwest of Thompson's Crossroads. When the Regulars beat a retreat, the Confederates, who had marched more than seventy miles since chasing Percy Wyndham out of Columbia, found themselves too tired to pursue.[51]

By May 4, when all detachments except Kilpatrick's and Davis's had rejoined Stoneman, the raiders had engineered a vast amount of destruction west, north, and southeast of the Confederate capital. If coordinated with a successful turning movement by the main army, those accomplishments would attain strategic significance. Unfortunately, not long after Stoneman led his reassembled column northward on the evening of the fifth, he picked up reports—at first unsubstantiated, later confirmed—that Hooker had met with a major reverse in the dark and clotted woodland known as the Virginia Wilderness. Even before the raiders rejoined the army west of Falmouth on the afternoon of the eighth, they knew some details of Hooker's May 2–3 defeat at the hands of Stonewall Jackson, whose 26,000-man corps had enveloped the Federal right flank in the Wilderness—the same tactic Fighting Joe had planned to use against his enemy. Perhaps the greatest stroke of irony in Hooker's defeat was that Stuart's main body, which had ignored Stoneman in order to join its army in time for the battle, had located Hooker's vulnerable flank and had sent word of it to Robert E. Lee. By electing not to pursue what he correctly judged to be an isolated movement uncoordinated with the Union infantry, Stuart had made a major contribution to the defeat of Hooker's turning movement and the success of Jackson's.[52]

By the time Stoneman reported to Hooker, the army commander was in almost as foul a mood as when Averell had loped in to report his mission unaccomplished. This day, as on that prior occasion, Fighting Joe declared the cavalry's accomplishment barren of lasting effect. This view was correct: The majority of the damage done to Lee's communications was repaired by work gangs less than two weeks after Stoneman returned to the army. Calculating that two scapegoats were better than one, Hooker blasted Stoneman's performance—which he declared to have "amounted to nothing at all"—to his subordinate's face. Later he repeated his harsh assessment in dispatches to his civilian superiors and in conversation with newspaper reporters. Having thus greased the skids, two weeks after Stoneman's return, Hooker sent him to join Averell in Washington—ostensibly to seek medical treatment for his piles.

Thus, ten months after sick leave nearly cost Stoneman his job under McClellan, it cost him his job under Hooker.[53]

Chapter Twelve

Epic Encounter

Coming hard on the heels of Kelly's Ford, Stoneman's raid gave another shot of pride and confidence to Hooker's cavalry. Troopers who had not contributed to the earlier victory could boast that they had taken part in the first large-scale raid by Federal horsemen in the East. They could also revel in the destruction they had inflicted on a wide expanse of enemy territory that included the environs of Richmond. McDowell, McClellan, and Burnside had not reached Richmond, but, by God, the cavalry had—and it could have taken that cockpit of rebellion, had it wished to.

Initially, those involved gave themselves rave reviews. One of Hasbrouck Davis's sergeants, writing from Gloucester Point, called the journey just ended "one of the greatest <u>Raids</u> of the war. . . . It will surprise the whole nation when the news of these [past] two weeks comes to light." Allen Bevan believed that the expedition's success was changing opinions throughout the army: "The Infantry for the present think the Cavalry can do something towards helping to whip the enemy. In fact, the Cavalry are the Lions for the time [being]." Even nonparticipants hailed the raid as a major feat of arms. Captain Custer, just back with the army after a period of detached duty, believed it "surpass[es] any that Stuart ever made. . . . Stoneman has excelled Stuart."[1]

Within a week of the raiders' return, however, revisionist thinking set in. In the absence of strategic significance, the operation appeared to have cost far more than it achieved. "We did not accomplish anything," admitted Henry Frost of the 8th New York, "only we lost nearly a thousand horses." That figure covered only those animals that had broken down and been abandoned during the trip; hundreds of others returned to the army unfit for further service. The value of the lost and disabled mounts was later assessed at $400,000. For this reason and others, Capt. Charles B. Coxe of the 6th Pennsylvania (whose outfit was only days away from losing its lances along with what Coxe called its "individuality as a regt.") observed that "raids are grand humbugs." They made inhuman demands on riders and horses and yielded meager returns.[2]

146

As Coxe realized, any raid not coordinated with the movements of the main army was virtually worthless. To be sure, there was some truth in the postwar claim of the chaplain of the 1st New Jersey, that this first large-scale operation of the Cavalry Corps raised the morale of everyone involved. Essentially, however, the raid was a demolition project of fleeting value to its army and temporary inconvenience to its foe. In the long view, Stoneman's extended absence from the front hurt Joe Hooker far more than it did Bobby Lee.[3]

Not surprisingly, one of the most vocal critics of the raid was Alfred Pleasonton. Months later, when testifying before the congressional watchdog panel known as the Joint Committee on the Conduct of the War, the division leader implied that Hooker and Stoneman were equally to blame for "the sending off of large detachments near the day of battle." Such a tactic, in Pleasonton's opinion, invited too much risk, especially when it left a single brigade of horsemen to serve the main army. One suspects, however, that had Pleasonton led the expedition, he would have viewed it as a risk any army leader had to take.[4]

In leaving Pleasonton behind, Stoneman may have intended that his subordinate stew in the juices of frustration and regret. But rather than being hurt professionally, Pleasonton was rewarded for remaining with the army. As soon as he jettisoned Averell, Hooker put Pleasonton in his place, while keeping Pleasonton in command of the 1st Division. Now in charge of two-thirds of the corps, Pleasonton took all of it on May 22, when Stoneman entrained for Washington. Given the magnitude of Pleasonton's ambition, this sudden elevation surely ranks as the most glorious hour of his military career.[5]

Pleasonton won promotion because he had done a competent job of screening the army's advance south of the Rappahannock, and convinced Hooker that he had done an absolutely brilliant job. At the head of Devin's brigade, Pleasonton had preceded the infantry as it passed over the Rappahannock and the Rapidan, while also guarding Hooker's flanks and rear. It was a major task that properly called for more resources than Pleasonton had at his disposal. He got a great deal of support, however, from Colonel Devin and his regimental commanders, especially Lieutenant Colonel McVicar of the 6th New York. On April 30, two days after Hooker's turning movement got under way, some of Stuart's cavalry, en route to join Lee's army, attempted to hinder an infantry column moving eastward through the Wilderness. Pleasonton sent McVicar's New Yorkers to drive them off, and they did a fine job, forcing one of Stuart's regiments into retreat near Wilderness Tavern, near the intersection of two woodland byways, the Orange Turnpike and the Germanna Plank Road.

McVicar was not done. That night he was reconnoitering off the lower flank of the army, about six miles southeast of Wilderness Tavern, when he again encountered Stuart, this time backed by three regiments. Scattering two of the outfits with well-directed carbine fire, McVicar ordered his men to charge the third; in the process, he was shot through the heart. Although most of his men escaped north to a Union-held crossroads known as Chancellorsville, Pleasonton and Devin considered McVicar's loss an irrecoverable blow.[6]

The cavalry saw sporadic action over the next three days as it accompanied the infantry ever closer to Lee's position and moved to protect it once Lee took the offensive. The most serious threat to the army's well-being occurred late in the afternoon of May 2, when Stonewall Jackson struck its unguarded right, held by the XI Corps of Maj. Gen. O. O. Howard. The flank collapsed, and much of the corps fled in panic. As fugitives headed toward Chancellorsville, fleet-footed Confederates right behind, one of Pleasonton's regiments, the 8th Pennsylvania of Maj. Pennock Huey, was called on, either by Pleasonton or Devin, to restore order. At the time they received their orders, Huey's men were idling in a farm clearing known as Hazel Grove, southwest of the strategic crossroads. In that same stretch of open ground, the rear-guard elements of Hooker's army—reserve artillery, supply wagons, infantry stragglers—had congregated.[7]

Huey's orders sent him and his outfit, in gathering darkness, up a narrow woods trail toward Chancellorsville. Before they could reach their destination, however, shadowy figures came out of the trees to the left of the road, and others crossed the regiment's path. At first Huey and his second in command, Maj. Peter Keenan, took these troops to be Federals—the 8th had yet to hear of Howard's rout and Jackson's pursuit. Too late, they discovered that the newcomers were Confederates, cutting them off from Chancellorsville. Knowing no other course, Huey ordered his men to draw sabers and charge.

At an extended gallop, the Pennsylvanians burst through the enemy line under a smattering of musketry and gained the Orange Plank Road. Turning east toward Chancellorsville, they found their path again blocked, this time by a much larger force of infantry. Huey, hoping somehow to circle through the woods to safety, ordered everyone to turn about and head west. As the column countermarched, Keenan now at its head, more shadows loomed up on all sides. The regiment had gained only 100 yards in the new direction before a volley of rifle fire tore out of the trees and into the column. The 8th Pennsylvania came to an abrupt halt, accordioning in on itself as rear ranks slammed into those in front. Horses neighed in panic and men shouted warnings to their comrades; some of them tumbled from their saddles, to be trampled by riders in the rear. At the height of the melee, Major Keenan, two other officers, and thirty men fell dead or mortally wounded; another seventy were taken prisoner. Slashing right and left, Huey led the rest to safety inside a fortified clearing southwest of Chancellorsville.[8]

By this point, out of Pleasonton's command, only McVicar and Huey and their men had been committed to the fighting. Their superior hungered for the same opportunity, although he desired it to end more agreeably. Pleasonton found—or contrived to find—his chance a short time after the 8th Pennsylvania was ambushed, when perhaps 200 members of Jackson's corps, a party from the Georgia brigade of Brig. Gen. George Doles, penetrated to Hazel Grove, taking prisoners and creating bedlam among Hooker's rear echelon. Panic-stricken teamsters, certain that Lee's entire army was after them, drove forage wagons and ambulances through the clearing, breaking up the formation of four artillery units—three attached to the III Corps, the fourth being Martin's horse artillery—striving to meet Doles's advance.[9]

Those batteries, along with nearby elements of the III and XII Corps, repulsed the attack quickly. In fact, Doles's superiors, concerned that he had advanced too far and that further maneuvering should wait till morning, had recalled his men to their position; that was why the Confederates fell back so rapidly. But Pleasonton, who also got involved in the repulse, claimed primary credit for parrying a heavy blow. According to the account he later gave to Hooker, to the Committee on the Conduct of the War, and to anyone who would listen, Pleasonton took charge of every battery at Hazel Grove, directed their fire where it would do the most good, and managed through outstanding leadership "to stop a stampede & check Jackson," meaning Jackson's corps in its entirety—a total, Pleasonton said, of 35,000 men. In written and spoken testimony, he also took credit for sending the 8th Pennsylvania to Chancellorsville, and even for ordering it to charge the enemy in its way. The facts are these: The attack on Hazel Grove was made in less than regimental strength; the Confederates themselves halted it; and Pleasonton directed the fire of only one battery, Martin's. Any connection he had with the 8th Pennsylvania occurred after its bloodletting in the woods.[10]

Although some of the artillery officers at Hazel Grove later tried "to refute the fictions that General Pleasonton attempts [to] palm off as history," the influential people he most wanted to impress appeared to accept his version of events. Dan Sickels, whose III Corps helped fight off Doles's brigade, upheld his claim; so did Sickles's friend, Joe Hooker. In fact, during a May 6–7 visit to the army by Abraham Lincoln, a bystander overheard Hooker say, "Mr. President, this is General Pleasonton, who saved the Army of the Potomac the other night."[11]

Nothing was too good for such a hero. Tendering him command of every horseman in the army was the least Hooker could do.

>─◄▸─○─◄▸─►◄

Soon after returning from their outing under Stoneman, the raiders heard what Charles Adams called the "gross results" of Hooker's attempt to outfox and outmaneuver Lee. When word leaked out that Fighting Joe had halted his turning movement at the point that success seemed in his hands, they readily believed what Hooker himself later confessed, that he had lost his nerve at the eleventh hour, leaving his army vulnerable to attack and overthrow.[12]

Thereafter, especially after he tried to blame Stoneman and Averell for his failure, Hooker retained the confidence of few members of the Cavalry Corps. Writing after the war, a member of the 1st Maine recalled, with a dash of sarcasm: "It was said at that time that Hooker had a poor opinion of the Cavalry. Whether he was dissatisfied or not with our raid . . . I think we accomplished as much as he did." Of those who continued to believe in their commander, many no longer believed in themselves. "I think that Hooker will cross [the

Rappahannock] again in a short time," wrote Sgt. Thomas W. Smith of the 6th Pennsylvania. "And if he does this Army will get whipped so damn bad that they won't know themselves. I never seen the Army so much demoralised as it is at the Pressent time."[13]

Few troopers appeared buoyed up by the recent command changes. When Pleasonton's ascension to corps command was announced, some of his new troops were plainly bemused. According to William Doster, "'Who is Pleasanton [sic]?' is the general inquiry." Other officers knew enough of Pleasonton's reputation to react negatively to his promotion. Colonel McIntosh, who, upon Pleasonton's rise, fell from brigade to regimental command, declared, "I never had such a disgust in me before"—not over his demotion, but over Pleasonton's promotion. Several times in later weeks, McIntosh—who also blamed Hooker for incompetence at Chancellorsville as well as for firing McIntosh's friend and mentor, Averell—threatened to resign his volunteer commission, but each time his staunchly Unionist wife talked him out of it.[14]

McIntosh's subordinate in the 3rd Pennsylvania, Walter Newhall, had no intention of quitting: "This being under Pleasanton [sic] is very demoralizing, though, and we sincerely trust the Government will . . . promote him to a Maj General of New York Home Guards, or something in the sinecure way that we may be rid of him." Another who both misspelled and condemned the new commander was Surgeon Beck of the 3rd Indiana, who opined that "poor little pusillanimous Pleasanton . . . is about as fit for [corps command] as any 2d Lieutenant in the command."[15]

Less controversy appears to have surrounded the promotions that occurred as a result of Pleasonton's elevation and Averell's demise. Two took place almost immediately. The appointment of Colonel Duffié to take over the 2nd Division appears to have been made strictly on the basis of seniority and without input from Pleasonton. It seems unlikely that the new corps leader would have approved such a lofty position for a Frenchman, for Pleasonton, like many another native-born American, was prejudiced against general officers born abroad. A month after taking over the corps, he declared in a letter to his former subordinate, Congressman Farnsworth: "I have no faith in foreigners saving our Government. . . . I conscientiously believe that Americans only should rule in this matter & settle this rebellion—& that in every instance foreigners have injured our cause."[16]

Pleasonton probably had no objection to another promotion made at the same time and ruled by seniority: John Irvin Gregg's replacement of McIntosh as commander of Duffié's 2nd Brigade. As McIntosh himself noted in a May 13 letter to his wife, "Col Gregg only found out yesterday that he ranked me by 7 days. I have been commanding the brigade all winter & [I am] the youngest Col in it."[17]

A third promotion occurred as a direct result of Pleasonton's rise to the top. Curiously, it did not take effect until the first days of June, weeks after Duffié and Gregg moved up. This was the long-overdue assignment of John

Buford to lead the 1st Cavalry Division. As Pleasonton's senior lieutenant, Buford should have been an easy, early choice to take the higher position. He surely had the credentials for the job, as well as the confidence of almost the entire corps. Though he had taken a field command in the army only two months ago, during that time the gruff but fair-minded brigadier had become known throughout the ranks as an able tactician with an eye for terrain and a nose for enemy intelligence. Perhaps Buford's Kentucky roots had hurt him again; he never seemed to have the full confidence of the War Department. Whatever the reason, those who welcomed Pleasonton's departure from the 1st Division were elated by Buford's coming.

>—+—◆>—O—<◆>—+—<

Whether in good spirits or poor, within a day of returning to the north bank of the river, the cavalry resumed the routine it had left off late in April. Portions of Gregg's and Buford's commands took station on the Orange & Alexandria, patrolling it from the river at Rappahannock Station to as far north as Cedar Run. Meanwhile, many other troopers, including those under Duffié, went to the rear to secure remounts at Belle Plain.[18]

Remounting may have been a dire necessity, but officials far from the scene had other priorities. When the War Department learned of these dispositions—Stoneman's last as cavalry commander—General in Chief Halleck took alarm. It was more important, he believed, that the cavalry guard the railroad—the army's main line of supply—and the river crossings that gave access to it. Halleck won Secretary Stanton over to his view, and Stanton persuaded Lincoln.[19]

The result was that by the twenty-fourth, David Gregg, temporarily in command of Duffié's division as well as his own, was ordered to march from Belle Plain to the railroad and the river. At least as it affected his own division, Gregg protested the assignment. He informed Pleasonton what the latter must already have known, that due to its exertions during Stoneman's raid, and with Kilpatrick's and Davis's regiments still on the Peninsula, the 3rd Division now consisted of fewer than 2,000 effectives and even fewer serviceable horses. As a result of its new responsibilities, "this force is drawn out like a thread over a line of about 40 miles."[20]

Pleasonton collected statistics on the strength of the other divisions, and on May 27 he passed them along to army headquarters. He gave 4,677 as the grand total of troops ready for duty in the corps, noting that approximately 2,000 others were serving on detached duty or were temporarily assigned to duty at Yorktown. Pleasonton took a parting shot at his deposed predecessor when he added that though he would strive to make the force at his disposal as effective as possible, "the responsibility of its present state, it is proper the major-general commanding should know, does not belong to me."[21]

David Gregg may have appreciated Pleasonton's effort in his behalf. By the twenty-seventh, when the 3rd Division was in position along the railroad and on the riverbank from the O & A bridge to the far right flank of the infantry line outside Falmouth, Gregg was in a less agitated mood. He assured corps headquarters that he and Duffié would do all that was required of them. He asked only that the wagons and supplies left at the divisional camp on Potomac Creek be sent to his present position, a favor that Pleasonton readily granted. Presumably Gregg was further mollified when, on the twenty-eighth, Hooker ordered Judson Kilpatrick, with the 2nd New York and four companies of the 12th Illinois, to return to the army by an overland march across Virginia. The rest of the Illinois outfit remained at Yorktown for months.[22]

While Gregg and Duffié covered the far flank and supply line of the army, Buford—still commanding only the Reserve Brigade—guarded the army's rear near Dumfries. He had been sent there to hunt bushwhackers and guerrillas, a difficult, thankless task that had been performed by Duffié's division before its recall to picket duty alongside Gregg. Either Buford made a quick job of it or no irregulars turned up, for on the twenty-eighth Pleasonton sent the Reserve Brigade, along with Lt. Samuel S. Elder's Battery E, 4th Artillery, to the O & A depot of Bealton Station, there to "drive the rebel scouts and parties in the neighborhood of Warrenton and Sulphur Springs across the Rappahannock River."[23]

The Confederates Buford was to disperse had been found that day in the Warrenton-Sulphur Springs area by scouts of Gregg's division. They were feared to be the advance contingent of an expeditionary force bound for Union territory to the north or west. When ordering Gregg's division to the railroad, Halleck had been acting on a rumor that "Stuart and Lee are collecting a cavalry force at Culpeper. If so, it is probably for a raid upon Alexandria or into the Valley of the Shenandoah, which the cavalry of the Army of the Potomac should be prepared to prevent." A second dispatch from Pleasonton to Buford on May 28 directed him to drive the Rebels across not only the river, but to their rendezvous at Culpeper, and from there to the south side of the Rapidan. This would have been a daunting task for any brigade leader, but the laconic Buford replied, "I'll do my best."[24]

He spent the next three days scouring the area in question as far south as Waterloo, as far west as Orleans, and as far north as Gainesville, without finding any Rebels "save those who have been here all winter." The report appears not to have calmed any fears over a raid, for on June 2 Hooker's headquarters relayed to Buford, still at Bealton, a report that three brigades of Rebel horsemen had passed into the Shenandoah, perhaps in prelude to a raid somewhere. Buford was asked to check out the information. He did so, informing Pleasonton on the fifth that based on a thorough reconnaissance of the area, the report had been groundless.[25]

Yet the Army of Northern Virginia was far from idle. On June 3 elements of Lee's infantry had begun to move west and north of Fredericksburg. Their advance ended six months of occupation duty across from Falmouth and ushered in a new invasion of Northern territory. That advance would carry Lee's veterans into south-central Pennsylvania on a tide of victory that had begun on the Virginia Peninsula and had surged through the Wilderness.

Cavalry—not members of Stuart's division, but horsemen brought in from points west for the invasion—screened the infantry's movement from Fredericksburg, but the movement created so much activity that horsemen across the river took notice. That day Duffié reported a "considerable force" of the enemy crossing the Rappahannock at Sulphur Springs. As a result of this report and others right behind it, two days later part of Hooker's army made a reconnaissance in force in front of some pontoon bridges that had been laid south of Fredericksburg. When the probe encountered the corps of Lt. Gen. A. P. Hill, which Lee had left at Fredericksburg until the rest of his army could depart the area, Hooker surmised that his enemy remained across from him in force.[26]

When checking the rumor about Rebel cavalry in the Valley, Buford confirmed other reports recently brought to his attention. The most significant of these was that Stuart had grouped his cavalry division, plus some new additions—perhaps as many as 20,000 troopers, all told—near Culpeper Court House. Buford did not speculate on the reason, but when he sent in the report, both Pleasonton and Hooker immediately visualized a raid into the North.

Hooker spent two days digesting the information and by the afternoon of the seventh was planning a counterstroke. He ordered Pleasonton to lead his entire corps, with the support of 3,000 infantrymen from George Gordon Meade's V Corps, across the river to Culpeper via Brandy Station. Pleasonton was instructed to "disperse and destroy" Stuart's force. Later, however, the cavalry leader claimed he had been sent on a mere reconnaissance aimed at gathering information on Stuart's dispositions and, if possible, his plans.[27]

Pleasonton called up his men early on the eighth. That afternoon and evening he moved his troopers and horse artillerymen to the river in two columns. Buford, finally in command of Pleasonton's old division, would cross at Beverly Ford at dawn on the ninth. To the south, on the other side of the O & A, Duffié's division, followed by Gregg's, would ford the stream at Kelly's. The wings would move inland with the intention of reuniting at Brandy Station on the railroad, Buford from the northeast, Gregg from the southeast. Duffié would meet them at Brandy only after occupying Stevensburg, three miles directly south of the depot, thus covering the lower flank and rear of the expeditionary force.[28]

On the eve of his first major operation in corps command, Pleasonton should have taken every precaution to ensure success. He failed to do so. During the two weeks he had been in charge of the cavalry, the Knight of Romance had failed to gather accurate information on Stuart's whereabouts. He knew that on the fifth the Rebel leader had been at Culpeper, treating an audience of onlookers—some from as far away as Richmond—to a grand review of his cavalry and horse artillery. Subsequently, however, Stuart had moved his soldiers into bivouac in the Brandy Station area; they were to remain there until the morning of the tenth, when they would escort Lee's infantry over the river.

Therefore, Pleasonton planned to unite his wings in the midst of an enemy encampment.[29]

Nor did he realize that he had barely enough troopers to meet Stuart on even terms. In response to Pleasonton's complaints about how puny his command was, Hooker had ordered his infantry commanders to return mounted units that had been attached to their brigades and divisions. Then, on or about June 4, Kilpatrick's New Yorkers rejoined the army. The additions brought Pleasonton's strength up to almost 10,000.

With so many men, plus the infantry support assigned him, Pleasonton calculated that his attack column outweighed Stuart's division. Neither he nor Hooker realized that Stuart's recent additions—a brigade from the Valley and another from the Carolinas—gave him nearly as many troopers as his antagonists had; additionally, Stuart enjoyed more horse artillery. Then, too, Pleasonton's attack plan was based on the blithe assumption that no Confederate infantry was within supporting reach of Stuart. In fact, members of Lt. Gen. Richard S. Ewell's infantry corps (formerly the command of Stonewall Jackson, who had been mortally wounded at Chancellorsville) had already reached Culpeper Court House, although they were too far from Brandy Station to aid Stuart come morning. Pleasonton may not have been advancing blindly into battle, but he had at least one eye closed.[30]

Yet his opponent was just as unprepared for a fight. Because Stuart elected to cover ten miles of Rappahannock shoreline with a thin line of pickets from the brigades of Hampton and Brig. Gen. Beverly H. Robertson, Pleasonton and Buford, riding together in the upper column, had little trouble capturing and crossing Beverly Ford just before 4:30 A.M. on the ninth. Then the vanguard of Buford's division—the 8th New York, followed by the 8th Illinois and the truncated 3rd Indiana—hit the heavily timbered shore. Next came Captain Robertson's battery of horse artillery, followed by the New Yorkers and Pennsylvanians of Tom Devin and the Reserve Brigade under the newly promoted Major Whiting, now of the 2nd Cavalry. Behind the mounted column trudged the infantry brigade of Brig. Gen. Adelbert Ames.

Not far along the southwestward-running road to St. James Church, where most of Stuart's horse artillery lay in park, the Federals were met by elements of two Virginia regiments from the "Laurel Brigade" of Brig. Gen. William E. Jones. Before Jones's men could strike, Colonel Davis lunged toward Stuart's batteries, most of them unlimbered in a woodland clearing and thus quite vulnerable. A lieutenant in the 6th Virginia singled Davis out for personal combat. Ducking a saber stroke from the Mississippian, the Confederate stood up in his stirrups and fired a pistol ball into his antagonist's skull. "He died in the front," Buford later wrote of Davis, "giving examples of heroism and courage to all who were to follow."[31]

Upon Davis's fall, his somewhat demoralized brigade fell back a short distance, then withdrew further under the massed carbine and rifle fire of Jones's troopers. Then the advance element of Devin's command came upon the field,

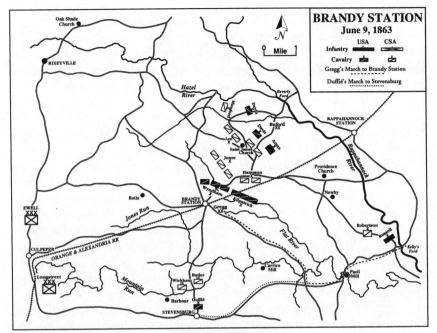

Map of the Battle of Brandy Station, June 9, 1863

and the combined force gathered enough momentum to thrust the Confederates back.

Again Buford's column surged ahead in the direction of St. James Church, only to be slowed, then stopped, by the arrival of "Grumble" Jones and the balance of his brigade. Before Jones could reach the scene in full force, however, a portion of Devin's command, on Buford's right, overran the hastily formed defensive line and made for a pair of Confederate howitzers in their exposed position. Suddenly those cannon unleashed the first enemy barrage of the day, and both brigades staggered backward. As they reeled, another of Jones's regiments rushed forward and swarmed over them. A Confederate artilleryman described the scene as "a mingled mass, fighting and struggling with pistol and saber like maddened savages." Eventually the outnumbered Virginians were forced backward, but not before they enabled the artillery to escape the Yankees' clutches.[32]

Buford's men started forward yet again and this time encountered the last elements of Jones's large brigade, one regiment and one separate battalion. Knocked off-balance by the Confederates' surge, the brigade formerly led by Davis fell back to the river, temporarily blocking their comrades' path to the front. One of those who rushed to the rear—without intending to—was George Custer, who had accompanied Grimes Davis's brigade, ostensibly in the role of a staff officer, and whose horse had run away with him, spooked by cannon fire.[33]

After Davis's men withdrew, Devin's—as soon as the road could be cleared—attacked, shoving the better part of Jones's brigade back through the clearing near the church. For a time, the road to St. James Church again appeared open. When the Reserve Brigade—only three regiments today, the fourth left behind on picket duty—came up in Devin's rear, Buford and Pleasonton led the re-formed column toward Brandy Station. They never reached their objective. Finally alerted to the attack across Beverly Ford, J. E. B. Stuart rushed up from Brandy with most of Hampton's brigade and all of Rooney Lee's. (Through miscommunication, Fitz Lee's brigade never reached the field of battle.) Hampton formed on Jones's embattled right, while Lee created a bulwark on the left. Abruptly, Buford's advance halted.[34]

At this point a lull ensued, as each side launched sporadic, small-scale assaults, both mounted and afoot. With Pleasonton's approval, Buford brought up Whiting's Regulars and the rest of his artillery and positioned Ames's foot soldiers on his flanks. As he deployed, Buford tried to establish communication with Duffié and Gregg, but without success. Then, when Hampton's brigade pressed and threatened to dislodge his left flank, the Kentuckian redeployed to meet the advance. He took the drastic step of ordering the newly arrived 6th Pennsylvania, supported by skirmishers from the 2nd Cavalry and flankers from the 6th Cavalry, to charge Hampton's position.

The erstwhile lancers responded with a shout, galloping across 800 yards of broken ground. Their momentum initially forced Hampton's troopers to withdraw, but in the process the attackers took heavy losses from dismounted carbineers and mounted men brandishing revolvers. Maj. Henry C. Whelan of the 6th recalled that "as we flew along—our men yelling like demons—grape and cannister were poured into our left flank. . . . We had to leap three wide, deep ditches, and many of our horses and men piled up in a writhing mass in those ditches and were ridden over." Finally the lancers gave way, falling back with speed born of desperation. Although badly cut up, they had done their job. "This attack relieved my left," Buford observed, "which was sorely pressed, and drew the enemy to my extreme right." After he moved Devin's brigade to counter this concentration, another lull settled over the field.[35]

By now it was noontime, fighting having swirled across the clearings northeast of Brandy Station for almost seven hours. Suddenly the battle shifted south as Stuart learned that Duffié's and Gregg's column had pushed across at Kelly's Ford and was coming at him from the south. With most of Hampton's brigade and some of Jones's, the Beau Sabreur pulled out of the St. James Church area and hustled to Brandy to counter this new intrusion.[36]

At about 2:00 P.M., Buford attempted to regain the advantage, turning sharply south and launching a series of attacks in that direction, aiming at that point on the enemy line where Rooney Lee's brigade joined the portion of Jones's brigade that Stuart had left behind. "Out flew the sabers," Buford observed, "and most handsomely were they used." Yet the relatively few remaining Confederates managed to check his progress. Possibly because Pleasonton failed to give him a free hand, and despite his infantry support, Buford made inroads toward Brandy but never reached the depot. Especially when Rooney Lee moved a segment of his command as if to threaten the Federals' route to the river—a prospect that greatly concerned Pleasonton—Buford's column was stymied.

Either Buford or his superior tried to regain momentum by sending the battered 6th Pennsylvania on a second charge, this time backed by dismounted sharpshooters as well as by horsemen from the 2nd United States. The Philadelphia bluebloods gave another solid account of themselves, but to little avail. In the hand-to-hand fighting that ensued, Wesley Merritt of the 2nd Regulars lost his hat to a saber slash from Rooney Lee himself. Two regiments of Lee's brigade sent both Pennsylvanians and Regulars whirling backward. Following up their success, they struck Buford's main line and for a time caused it to waver.[37]

By the time the weary Federals forced their equally tired enemy to draw off, the fighting on Buford's front was over. For the rest of the afternoon, the opposing artilleries carried on the action, while Alfred Pleasonton turned toward home. By 5:00 he was ushering Buford's scarred but jubilant brigades over the river, their crossing covered not only by Ames's foot soldiers but by Brig. Gen. David A. Russell's infantry brigade, which had lumbered north from Kelly's Ford. Russell reported that the fighting on the lower flank had ended, but he did not know the result.[38]

>—1—◇—O—◇—1—<

If Buford was having a rough time north of Brandy Station, Duffié and Gregg were experiencing a worse one below the depot. Duffié's command, leading the column, had taken a wrong road to Kelly's Ford and been forced to make a time-consuming countermarch. The error was the fault of a civilian guide, who had either lied about his knowledge of the countryside or deliberately led the Frenchman astray. The delay meant that the lower wing did not begin crossing at Kelly's until almost 6:00 A.M., ninety minutes after Buford forded upstream.

This was bad enough, but it took almost an hour for Duffié's troopers to navigate the cold waters of the Rappahannock. All the while, Gregg's people waited in the rear, disgusted at getting off to such a late start. They could hear the sounds of gunfire to the north and west, indicating that Buford was heavily engaged and suggesting that the Rebels were much closer to the river than anyone had supposed. That being the case, Gregg's route to Brandy might enable him to catch Stuart in a pincers. If so, however, Duffié's tardiness ensured that any trap would be late in closing.[39]

When his entire force reached dry ground, Duffié tried to make amends for his errant movement. As Gregg's division began to cross, the colonel led his command southwestward, past Paoli Mill and along the curving trail to Stevensburg. Along the way, he passed the trail that led directly to Brandy Station. In his rear, the vanguard of Gregg's command veered in that direction, leaving Duffié to continue on alone.

Given what he knew of Stuart's dispositions, Duffié doubted that he would encounter a large force in the Stevensburg vicinity—a few pickets, perhaps, but that prospect did not trouble him. Before anyone crossed at Kelly's, an advance party of Gregg's division had snatched up a long line of Rebel pickets, quickly and easily. Other pickets, members of Robertson's brigade, had remained well back from the ford as the Federals crossed, as though conceding them the road, and the advantage. There was nothing to suggest that Duffié would meet more resolute defenders.[40]

The colonel did not realize how wrong he was until around 10:00, when his advance guard, the 6th Ohio, ranged beyond Stevensburg on a scout, then fell back to the village. Before Duffié's main body could join them, the Ohioans came under fire from a body of South Carolina horsemen. The Rebels had ridden south from Brandy Station, led by Wade Hampton's younger brother, Col. Frank Hampton. The small band succeeded in shoving the 6th Ohio through the streets of Stevensburg. Then the elder Hampton's senior subordinate, Col. M. Calbraith Butler, arrived at the head of a larger group of South Carolinians, perhaps 200 of them, with a Virginia regiment not far behind him.

By the time Duffié and his main force, including Pennington's battery and a long queue of supply wagons and ambulances, came up from the east, dismounted Confederates were popping away at the 6th Ohio from hiding places south of Stevensburg, including the ruins of an old seminary. Soon after arriving, Duffié's 1st Brigade, this day led by the Italian-born Col. Luigi diCesnola of the 4th New York, came under this same fire. Unwilling to sit their horses and take a pounding, a good portion of diCesnola's 1st Massachusetts charged the hiding places of Butler and Hampton, their advance covered by the rest of the brigade as well as by Irvin Gregg's just-arriving command. Several Confederates hastily mounted and hurled themselves at the galloping Federals; the ensuing collision unhorsed riders on both sides. Outmanned and outpositioned, Frank Hampton took a mortal wound, and his little band melted away in retreat.[41]

Following the fracas, Butler's main body withdrew up the road to Brandy Station, followed at a rapid gait by the 1st Massachusetts, much of the rest of diCesnola's brigade, and a part of Gregg's. The pursuers not only overtook the Carolinians as they crossed Mountain Run, they also broke the formation of the 4th Virginia as it came up in Butler's rear. To avoid annihilation, both units turned and raced north. "It was a regular steeple chase," observed one of Gregg's troopers, "through ditches, over fences, through underbrush."[42]

As many Virginians as their commander could rally opened a skirmish fire at long range. Even so, the road to Brandy Station was essentially clear; it should have taken Duffié no more than a half hour to reach the depot, there to link with David Gregg. But the colonel hesitated, fearing that other Confederates were lurking just ahead, where the sounds of battle were getting louder. Instead of resuming the advance, he recalled diCesnola and Gregg, moved Pennington's guns closer to Butler's new position, and established a defensive line just below Mountain Run.

Not until the middle of the afternoon did the colonel nerve himself to push on to Brandy. By then it was a little too late. As he started off, a courier from

David Gregg reached him with word that Duffié must join Gregg's division at Brandy. Duffié's inflexible European mind would not permit him to chance a push toward the depot from his present position. The only road he knew to be open led back the way he had come. After further delay, he turned his column about and countermarched. As he should have realized, the roundabout route ensured his inability to reach Gregg until the battle was over. Duffié should also have realized that recriminations would follow.[43]

>─◄►─○─◄►─►─◄

At noon the head of David Gregg's column finally came within sight of Brandy Station. The delay caused by Duffié's belated crossing had slowed the division, but enemy opposition had not. Robertson's pickets had been both invigilant and unassertive, and Gregg had easily bypassed them. Just to make sure they did not menace his rear, he had left Russell's infantry at the river to keep open the road home. This proved to be a mistake, for Gregg could have used infantry support up ahead. Another possible error was his choice of routes to the depot. He might have taken a more direct path to Brandy than the road on the south that he chose. On the other hand, by the time he crossed the river, Gregg knew that a large force was opposing Buford; the southward route might enable him to hit Stuart when his back was turned.

The trouble with the road Gregg took was that it cost him additional time. Compounding the problem was the decision by Colonel Wyndham, at the head of the column, to halt short of the depot, just below the line of the O & A. Through his field glasses, Wyndham had spied a cannon atop a long ridge known as Fleetwood Heights, north and west of Brandy. Fearing that a substantial force confronted him, the Britisher threw out skirmishers and brought up a two-gun section of Martin's battery under Lt. M. P. Clark.[44]

Unknown to Wyndham, the 6-pounder howitzer staring him in the face was alone and out of ammunition, having retired from the fighting at St. James Church. It had been trundled to the summit of the ridge by order of Maj. Henry B. McClellan, Stuart's adjutant general and a cousin of Little Mac. McClellan believed, correctly, that the sight of artillery would cause the oncoming Yankees to delay long enough for him to rush word of their approach to Stuart, two miles to the north.

The staff officer had done better than he knew. Although counterbattery fire from Clark's section eventually put the howitzer out of commission, it had retained its threatening posture long enough. Before the Federals saw through McClellan's ruse, Stuart was galloping to the threatened site at the head of two regiments and a battalion of Jones's brigade, a pair of horse batteries rocking and bouncing behind. At a greater distance came Hampton's brigade, which had just disengaged from St. James Church, ready for the fray.[45]

Minutes before Stuart arrived—perhaps 1:00, perhaps a bit later—Gregg ordered Wyndham's brigade to advance. The main column pounded straight ahead, aiming for Fleetwood Heights, while a smaller force, mainly composed of Wyndham's lead regiment, the 1st New Jersey, angled to the left and made for a spur known as Barbour House Hill. Gregg himself led the larger force up the heights. A member of his staff recalled that his usually dignified superior "showed an enthusiasm that I had never noticed before. He started his horse on a gallop . . . swinging his gauntlets over his head and hurrahing."[46]

As the blue column pounded up the slopes, the first regiment that Stuart had led down from Buford's front slammed into it. Horses and riders were bowled over by the force of the collision, but more Rebels than Yankees went down. Lacking the time to switch from marching order to battle formation, Stuart's outfit was ripped apart by the flashing sabers of the 1st New Jersey. Again the cry went up from the Confederates: "Put up your sabres; draw your pistols!" It was too late: The swordsmen sliced their way through not only the 12th Virginia but, in its rear, the 35th Virginia Battalion.

The Federals fell back upon the arrival of the third enemy outfit. Its advance covered by Stuart's batteries, the 6th Virginia evicted the Jerseymen from both Fleetwood Heights and Barbour House Hill. In turn, the Virginians were uprooted by the balance of Wyndham's command, the 1st Pennsylvania and the 1st Maryland. But the Southerners did not go quietly; a Pennsylvanian recalled "the cutting and slashing, the firing from pistols, carbines, and cannon, the neighing of horses, the yelling of men. . . . Men and horses fell in every direction, some forward, some backward, others sideways. Some horses reared and fell, others plunged forward and rolled over, carrying their riders with them."[47]

With the 6th Virginia's retreat, Gregg's column had undisputed possession of the high ground around Brandy Station—for a few minutes. Then Hampton's vanguard reached the summit, cannoned into Wyndham's brigade, and chased its people down the hill in full retreat, casualties from both sides littering the slope. At the base of the heights, the Confederates shot and slashed their way through Martin's battery, which had lost too many horses to make an escape. Eighty percent of the battery personnel fell dead or wounded. Survivors staggered off, abandoning their guns, but only after spiking them to prevent their immediate use by Hampton.[48]

The frenetic succession of charge and countercharge neared a close when Gregg's 2nd Brigade, under Judson Kilpatrick, crossed the railroad and galloped toward Wyndham's embattled right. Fresh from his return to the army following his successful part in Stoneman's raid, the bewhiskered colonel may not have felt he had something to prove this day. Perhaps, however, he needed to clear his name, which had suffered under a new series of criminal charges.

"Kill-cavalry," as his overworked troopers sometimes called him, had recently been accused of fraudulently appropriating forage and other supplies from the quartermaster of his 2nd New York—and not for the first time. He may have done so for personal use or he may have intended to resell the items for profit. As if this were not bad enough, early in January, while on duty in Washington, Kilpatrick had been brought up on charges for insulting and obstructing Lafayette C. Baker, chief of War Department detectives and the capital's provost marshal. For either or both offenses, the accused had been thrown into Old Capitol Prison. There he spent a couple weeks, until freed by order of Edwin Stanton. Whatever the degree of truth behind the allegations, Kilpatrick's unsavory conduct off the battlefield continued to overshadow his accomplishments in combat.[49]

Nothing changed on this particular occasion. True to form, in advancing toward Fleetwood Heights, Kilpatrick ignored the pleas of one of Gregg's staff officers, who begged the colonel to save Martin's battery from being overrun. Kilpatrick wasted no time on lost causes; the only cause that mattered to him was glory and fame, and he would achieve them only by taking Fleetwood Heights.

This he failed to do. As his men reached the heights, Wade Hampton's still-feisty troopers rammed into the lead regiment, the 10th New York, and sent it flying in all directions. Seething with rage, Kilpatrick abandoned the scattered 10th, rode to the head of his former regiment, and led the Harris Light into the fray—only to be flanked and battered by other just-committed outfits under Hampton. When the 2nd New York fled in the same state of disorder as the 10th, Kilpatrick rushed back to the base of the hill and led forward his last regiment, the 1st Maine, under Col. Calvin S. Douty, a bluff, burly ex-seaman. This third charge was the charm. The men of Maine swept Hampton's now-weary troopers from the crest and sent them racing toward their battlefield of the morning.[50]

Douty's charge should have won the day, but it did not. To his and Kilpatrick's angry disbelief, Hampton and Stuart rallied the retreating Confederates and led them back, at an extended gallop, to the heights. Rushing up the slope, they put the 1st Maine and the remnants of Kilpatrick's other regiments to final flight. At the same time, one of Grumble Jones's regiments, till now lightly engaged, broke up pockets of Union resistance around Brandy Station and maneuvered as if to threaten Gregg's route of withdrawal.[51]

With his division fought out and evening coming fast, Gregg decided to pull out. He had just reached this decision when a messenger from Pleasonton notified him that Buford was withdrawing and ordered Gregg to do the same. The wing commander disengaged and headed back to the river without major opposition, a fact that relieved his mind. Gregg's mood changed, however, when Duffié joined him in midretreat, too late to influence the course of the fighting at Brandy Station. Gregg could only imagine how events might have gone differently had Duffié joined him an hour or two earlier. Somehow, it seemed a fitting end to a day of opportunities overlooked, ignored, and squandered.[52]

Chapter Thirteen

Advancing to Armageddon

As the Union troopers crossed the river and trotted along the railroad to their new camps at Catlett's Station and Warrenton Junction, a sense of pride and accomplishment began to sweep through the ranks. Although forced to withdraw, they had not been overmatched on any part of the field. If the Rebels had forced them off Fleetwood Heights and Barbour House Hill, they had done the same to Stuart, more than once. Had their leaders been less concerned with retreating in one piece and more interested in maintaining the offensive, they might still be matching the riders of Hampton, Jones, and Lee saber stroke for saber stroke, pistol ball for pistol ball.

To be sure, they had retreated, and statistics made the battle look like a Rebel victory. Stuart had suffered approximately 500 casualties, almost 400 fewer than his opponents initially reported—this despite lacking their infantry support. Still, the Beau Sabreur had been fought to a standstill; moreover, he had been taken by surprise—not once, but by both Buford and Gregg. That had never happened before. Added to Averell's smashing success at Kelly's Ford, Brandy Station told the average Union cavalryman that he was equal to, and potentially better than, his more celebrated opponent. Even the enemy gave the Federals credit for a moral, if not an actual, victory at Brandy Station. In assessing the results of March 17, the fear-minded Major McClellan wrote after the war that Brandy Station "*made* the Federal cavalry" in that it gave Pleasonton's troopers the self-confidence they had never before enjoyed but would never again lack.[1]

By itself, self-confidence was a good thing, but the cavalry of Hooker's army realized they must apply that attitude to the unfinished work ahead. That meant reacting precisely and decisively to Robert E. Lee's next moves. Euphoric over the success he had gained at Stuart's expense, on June 10 Pleasonton assured Hooker that he had destroyed any plans Lee might have had for a raid into, or an invasion of, Union territory. His superior was not so sure. Convinced that Lee was planning a run around his right flank, Hooker ordered

Pleasonton to stretch his picket line farther up the Rappahannock than ever before.

The cavalryman complied, but only to an extent. Concerned that his battle-weary troopers needed rest, and unwilling to move far from Stuart's encampment, Pleasonton moved his pickets only as far west as ten miles above Beverly Ford, while telling Hooker they extended all the way to the Blue Ridge Mountains. Had this been the truth, Pleasonton would have learned that on the twelfth Confederate infantry was marching through the gaps in that mountain range.[2]

As was his wont, Pleasonton paid more attention to administrative responsibilities than to tactical duties. On June 11 he reorganized the Cavalry Corps by merging Duffié's division, the smallest in the command, with Gregg's. As senior officer, Gregg took command of a new 2nd Division. Ostensibly Pleasonton acted to streamline and simplify. To some extent, however, he was punishing Duffié for his admittedly poor performance on the ninth. Four days later, when he completed his report on Brandy Station, Pleasonton conspicuously omitted the Frenchman from honorable mention. Yet he did not neglect to cite the conduct of dozens of other officers, including Buford, Gregg, several brigade and regimental leaders, and current or future staff officers, including Captains Custer, Merritt, and Elon J. Farnsworth, John Farnsworth's nephew and his temporary successor as commander of the 8th Illinois.[3]

Duffié, who was reduced to brigade command during the reorganization, was not the only foreigner harmed by Pleasonton's changes. On the eleventh Colonel diCesnola's brigade was broken up, and its units were assigned to other brigades. Its commander reverted to the command of Pleasonton's least favorite regiment, the 4th New York, a truly cosmopolitan outfit whose ranks teemed with Germans, Frenchmen, Italians, and Hungarians, and whose officers, it was said, had to issue orders in six or seven languages. Pleasonton did not have to demote a third foreigner, for Percy Wyndham had been wounded in the leg on Fleetwood Heights and had gone to Washington to recuperate. In the Briton's place, Pleasonton installed a true American, John McIntosh.[4]

Other personnel changes made at this time replaced the late, lamented Grimes Davis with Colonel Gamble of the 8th Illinois, who had held brigade command intermittently since recovering from the wound he had taken the previous August at Malvern Hill. Gamble joined Devin as two of John Buford's three ranking subordinates, the third being Maj. Samuel H. Starr of the 6th United States Cavalry, who, shortly after Brandy Station, replaced Major Whiting, his junior, as commander of the Reserve Brigade. At this same time, the Reserves were made an organic part of the 1st Division. A final organizational change sent all the batteries in Robertson's battle-scarred artillery brigade, including Martin's cannonless unit, to the Artillery Reserve for a needed overhaul. In Robertson's absence, the four batteries of John Tidball's brigade were transferred from the Reserve to the Cavalry Corps; they remained with it after Robertson rejoined the corps late in the month.[5]

>─┤◆➤─O─◆┤─◄

The Knight of Romance kept what he believed was a close watch over his foe south of the river. For this reason he could scarcely believe reports, received on June 13, that the bulk of Lee's army had passed around his flank in the vicinity of Sperryville, apparently heading for the Shenandoah. Disbelief led to inactivity, even after Hooker heard the story and ordered his cavalry to determine its validity. Before Pleasonton could do so, Hooker learned that the outpost at Winchester was under attack by Ewell's corps, Army of Northern Virginia. The surprise assault was successful, and the garrison surrendered on the fifteenth.[6]

Upon receiving the news, a disgruntled Hooker ordered the right wing of the army—its I, III, and XI Corps, under Maj. Gen. John F. Reynolds—northward, in a hurry. Then he laid plans that eventually lifted his entire command out of the winter camp it had pitched last November. Hooker's initial destination was Fairfax Station, along the upper reaches of the O & A, and he wanted his cavalry to range even farther to the north, as well as a considerable distance to the west. It had become obvious that at least a large portion of the Army of Northern Virginia—and probably all of it—was on an invasion course. Timely and accurate intelligence of its movements was a dire necessity.[7]

Pleasonton responded by sending Buford's division from Catlett's Station toward Thoroughfare Gap in the Bull Run Mountains. Soon afterward, Gregg's horsemen were also moving north, crossing the still-littered battlefields of Bull Run on the fifteenth. Troopers inured to death played catch with skulls and bones that protruded from too-shallow graves. Over the next forty-eight hours, as supply trains rolled down from Alexandria, Pleasonton distributed to his troopers rations, forage, and a variety of materiel, including hundreds of carbines, pistols, and sabers, and thousands of rounds of ammunition. They would need these resources in the days ahead, for almost everyone had a sense that a major confrontation was shaping up either in Virginia or farther north. As Pvt. Charles M. Smith of the 1st Maine put it, "We all think here that we are on the eve of a great battle. It will be one of the most severe the country ever witnessed."[8]

Resupplied and refreshed, the horsemen under Buford and Gregg ranged westward, seeking signs of Confederate infantry. These they did not find, but they did encounter small, outlying detachments of Stuart's cavalry, up from Brandy Station to screen the right flank of the invasion column. Minor skirmishes broke out near the mountains, but a major clash did not materialize until the afternoon of the seventeenth.

Late the previous day, with most of his army at and near Fairfax Station, Hooker ordered Pleasonton to take Gregg's men, followed by Buford's, to

Aldie Gap, thirty miles to the northwest. That Bull Run Mountain pass gave entrance to the Loudoun Valley, a corridor to the Shenandoah. From Aldie, the cavalry was to fan out toward Winchester, where they would surely find elements of Ewell's corps.[9]

Pleasonton did not suppose that entering Loudoun Valley would involve his men in a fight; he believed that only scouting parties would be located east of the Blue Ridge. Just in case, when on the road to Aldie he sent Duffié, whom he temporarily reduced to command of his old 1st Rhode Island, through Thoroughfare Gap, twelve miles south of Aldie. From there he was to head north to Middleburg, scouting the Loudoun Valley as he went and spending the night in the town. The next day, Duffié was to continue north, rejoining the rest of the corps along the Potomac River, which Pleasonton expected to reach on the eighteenth.[10]

On the march to Aldie, the advance was led by newly appointed Brigadier General Kilpatrick, to whom Pleasonton had assigned most of diCesnola's old brigade. "Kill-cavalry" might not have made a triumphal showing at Brandy Station, except briefly, but he had exhibited enough dash and determination to warrant promotion, one that Pleasonton—who appears to have perceived a kindred spirit in the little Irishman—had actively supported.[11]

Kilpatrick had an early chance to prove such support well founded. Nearing Aldie Gap at about 4:30 P.M. on the seventeenth, his advance guard spied troopers from Fitz Lee's brigade (today under Col. Thomas T. Munford) marching toward them, about a mile away. At once Kilpatrick charged them, sending the Rebels speeding through the gap and out the Little River Turnpike. Just before Kilpatrick's 2nd New York reached the pass, however, it was set upon by a full regiment of Stuart's cavalry. Once again, counterattack repulsed attack; within minutes the New Yorkers were rushing back upon their main body, minus several casualties.[12]

Kilpatrick sent for Captain Randol's Battery E/G, 1st Artillery, and supported its guns with diCesnola's 4th New York. One of the gunners later recalled: "The rebels had six pieces firing on our two. The solid shot fell thick around us and the shells burst above and before us. Nothing daunted we kept up our fire making almost every shot tell and one shell we fired exploded and emptied sixteen saddles of rebel cavalry."[13]

Under such an effective shelling, Kilpatrick sent elements of the 1st Massachusetts out the Snickersville Road, which branched northwestward from the turnpike. Unable to see far ahead due to the sloping nature of the road, part of Horace Sargent's regiment was suddenly charged by hitherto-unseen assailants. The Rebels had their way with the invaders, cutting through their ranks with an unusual show of swordplay that left Major Higginson and several other Federals with painful, and in some cases deadly, scars. As many of Sargent's men as could break free of the deadly embrace galloped to the rear. Many failed to escape. As Charles Adams recalled: "My poor men were just slaughtered and all we could do was to stand and be shot down. . . . The men fell right and left and the horses were shot through and through." Adams's squadron alone lost 40 men out of fewer than 100 engaged.[14]

At last the Virginians broke off the fight, permitting the remnants of the 1st Massachusetts to depart. Kilpatrick responded by shifting his attention to the turnpike. Along it he sent a detachment of the 2nd New York, then watched in horror as his old soldiers were decimated by horse artillery and dismounted marksmen of Munford's 1st Virginia. A new effort by other elements of the 2nd New York, backed by the 6th Ohio, ended Confederate resistance along the turnpike, but by then great harm had been done to Kilpatrick's left flank.

Turning again to the upper byway, Kilpatrick sent along the Snickersville Road previously uncommitted elements of the 1st Massachusetts, backed by the 4th New York. This advance fared no better than the last. Before they got close to their objective, the attackers were met by the better part of Munford's brigade and severely handled. Battered detachments of the 1st Massachusetts soon were withdrawing once again, this time followed by the less heavily engaged New Yorkers.[15]

With evening approaching and enemy resistance near Aldie apparently as strong as ever, Kilpatrick made a final effort to gain and hold the advantage, this time sending the entire 4th New York out the Snickersville Road. Confirming the worst suspicions of a nativist like Alfred Pleasonton, the polyglot outfit broke apart under sharpshooter fire, turned, and retreated before making hard contact with the enemy. A few of their number, however, kept riding until they struck the enemy; one of these was Colonel diCesnola, who was surrounded, captured, and sent to Richmond's Libby Prison, where he spent the next ten months.[16]

The conduct of diCesnola's regiment distressed Kilpatrick, but he felt worse when he saw portions of the 1st, 2nd, and 5th Virginia heading his way through the shadows of dusk, threatening to unhinge this upper flank. In an act of desperation, Kilpatrick called up his last regiment, Douty's 1st Maine, and prepared to throw it at the charging troops. Appreciating the importance of the movement, he placed himself beside Douty at the head of the regiment—whatever else might be said of him, Kilpatrick was not afraid to risk his own life along with those of his men. Another rider always willing to charge was the ubiquitous glory hunter George Custer. In the ensuing attack, the lieutenant cut down so many antagonists with his long Toledo blade that he gained another round of the newspaper publicity he cherished.

The performance of Douty's men fulfilled Kilpatrick's every wish. With the assistance of the 1st Massachusetts and the 2nd New York, the men of Maine charged up the Snickersville Road, spraying dismounted Confederates with pistol balls and prying them loose from a line of stone walls adjacent to the road. They also drove all three Virginia regiments from the road itself, easing Kilpatrick's concern about his flank and filling him with the degree of exhilaration that only a mounted attack—especially a successful one—can provide.

The Mainers took as heavy a toll on their enemy as cavalry weapons could produce. Trooper William Howe noted: "The column plunged on through . . . a dugout road in the side of the hill and elevated on the right by a heavy stone wall. The dugout was litterally filled with dead and dyeing men and horses."[17]

Douty's charge ended the day in such a fashion as to make Kilpatrick appear the victor. If victory it was, it had been won at a bitter price: more than 300 casualties, including the death of a senior officer. In the midst of the fighting, Private Howe had found himself charging alongside his regimental commander: "Here it was . . . as the Colonel was turning to the right to go into the open field beyond, with his sword hand raised that I last saw him alive. Just then a vol[le]y came from behind the stone walls and the Colonel fell." Douty's troopers recovered his body and gave him a proper burial.[18]

The victory for which the colonel had sacrificed himself might have been more decisive. Throughout the afternoon, Kilpatrick had committed his units piecemeal. Had he attacked in powerful combinations, he might have destroyed rather than damaged Munford's command. Kilpatrick could have employed the balance of Gregg's division, which had come up in rear of his brigade early in the fight and whose men had remained there as onlookers. Perhaps he feared that calling for help in his first battle as a brigadier would somehow be seen as a sign of weakness.[19]

Kilpatrick's tactics demonstrated that the cavalry had not learned to flex its might and cohesiveness. Kelly's Ford had been almost entirely a defensive fight; the few attacks Averell launched had been sporadic and small-scale. Stoneman had split his raiding column into tiny components, when keeping it intact would have served him better. Some day perhaps the cavalry would remember why it had been formed into a corps, 10,000 strong.

>—⊢⟨⟩—O—⟨⟩⊢—⟨

Kilpatrick's inability to damage Munford seriously had been as much Pleasonton's fault as his; supposedly the corps commander had exercised overall command of the fighting. The same day, Pleasonton committed a more serious mistake—perhaps deliberately—when he sent Colonel Duffié and his 275 Rhode Islanders on what amounted to a suicide mission, then abandoned them to their fate.

When Duffié passed through Thoroughfare Gap into the Loudoun Valley at 9:30 that morning, he ran into unexpected trouble from Stuart. Near the mountain village of Salem, he discovered the presence of a number of North Carolinians from the brigade of Rooney Lee, now under Col. John R. Chambliss, Jr., Lee having been severely wounded at Brandy Station. Pleasonton had led Duffié to believe he would encounter no opposition on his reconnaissance. Now, suddenly, all bets were off.[20]

Perhaps demonstrating the European military mind, Duffié refused to alter his timetable to meet the changing situation. He had been instructed to bivouac that night in Middleburg, and he would do so regardless of how many Rebels crossed his path. Leaving a small dismounted force to hold off Chambliss, he turned north toward his objective.

Duffié was surprised to leave the North Carolinians behind. By the time his regiment closed up on Middleburg, he began to breathe a bit more easily, supposing he was a short jaunt from rejoining Pleasonton's main body. He was wrong. J. E. B. Stuart himself was in Middleburg, accompanied by a small escort, and the majority of his command was within twelve miles of the town. Still, the Rhode Islanders' entrance, charging through the village streets, shouting a facsimile of the Rebel yell, forced the Beau Sabreur into hectic retreat, the second time in a little over a week that he had been taken by surprise.[21]

Stuart avenged his indecorous flight by returning at about 7:00 P.M. at the head of a large body of Robertson's command—perhaps three times as many men as Duffié had—just up from Rector's Crossroads, eight miles to the southwest. Long before their arrival, many of Duffié's men had experienced what one called "a sense of impending disaster." Acting on their premonition, they had erected barricades made of whatever material looked like it would stop a ball. These proved of little value, however, for when Stuart attacked, his men evaded or surmounted every obstacle, flailing away with carbines, rifles, shotguns, pistols, and in a few cases, sabers.[22]

Many Federals immediately took to their horses and raced out the Aldie Road. In midflight they were overtaken by the main body of Chambliss's brigade, which had reached the scene just in time to capture dozens of fugitives. Those Federals still in town managed to fight on, despite being surrounded, till the wee hours of the eighteenth, when Stuart, Robertson, and Chambliss rounded up the last of them. When the shooting ceased, 100 Rhode Islanders were dead or wounded, and more than that number had been captured. By hard riding, hedge and fence jumping, and good fortune, Duffié, with fewer than 100 others, escaped, eventually reaching the army and safety.

Just before Stuart attacked, Duffié had sent a courier to Pleasonton's field headquarters with word of the regiment's plight. Pleasonton responded by sending troops toward Thoroughfare Gap—the following day, far too late to do Duffié any good. Later, when the extent of the debacle at Middleburg became known, Pleasonton criticized Duffié for "not fighting his men properly," implying that he had gone to Middleburg against, rather than according to, orders. In September, when Pleasonton finally penned his report of the fighting in Loudoun Valley, he noted that the 1st Rhode Island was still in process of reconstruction and that "Colonel [then Brigadier General] Duffié, himself, has never joined this command since, and his conduct on that occasion, as testified by the men of his command, shows that he is totally unfitted to command a regiment."[23]

><+>-O-<+>-<

On the eighteenth Pleasonton, from Aldie, launched several reconnaissance and rescue missions. He sent toward Middleburg two of Gregg's brigades, that led by his cousin John, the other normally commanded by McIntosh and today by Colonel Taylor of the 1st Pennsylvania, McIntosh having gone to

Washington to secure remounts for his command. Taylor's force was sent to
Thoroughfare Gap to search for Duffié and his antagonists, while Colonel
Gregg's had orders to scout as far as Ashby's Gap in the Blue Ridge. Two of
Buford's brigades were also put in motion, Devin's toward the Bull Run
Mountains to search for Stuart's main body, and Gamble's (backed by Battery
A, 2nd Artillery, formerly Tidball's, now commanded by Lt. John Calef) to
another Blue Ridge gap, ten miles north of Ashby's.

No expedition was entirely successful. Taylor did not find Rhode Islanders,
Virginians, or North Carolinians near Thoroughfare. Gregg stumbled into a
fight with elements of Stuart's division outside Middleburg and never reached
Ashby's Gap. Devin tried to blanket the Bull Run range with scouts but failed
to detect the passage of Grumble Jones's brigade through the area on its way to
rejoin Stuart. And Gamble was stopped at Philomont, short of Snicker's Gap,
by Munford's brigade, whose interposition persuaded the former sergeant major
of the 1st United States Dragoons to return his brigade to Aldie.[24]

Pleasonton begged off on a fifth scouting mission. Hooker desired the cavalry to retrace its steps south and determine if any Confederate infantry
remained on the Rappahannock. At Pleasonton's suggestion, Hooker borrowed
for the job Stahel's 3,000-man cavalry division of the recently constituted XXII
Corps, Defenses of Washington. When he ran the errand, Stahel discovered
Hampton's brigade still in place south of the river—it would not join Stuart for
another two days—but he saw no infantry for miles in any direction. The intelligence eased Hooker's concern over a strike from the rear, but he may have
been left wondering why outside help had been necessary to gather it.[25]

Perhaps realizing he had let his commander down, Pleasonton pledged to
serve him more responsively. When, on the evening of the eighteenth, Hooker
reminded him that the Shenandoah Valley should be thoroughly searched,
Pleasonton saluted. He was aware that the main army, now grouped around
Fairfax Court House, would not move until it received definite word of Lee's
dispositions.

On the morning of the nineteenth, Pleasonton sent David Gregg to Middleburg at the head of Irvin Gregg's brigade, followed by Kilpatrick's and
Gamble's (the latter on loan from Buford). The entire force was to continue as
far west as the Blue Ridge, but it never got that far. About 7:00 A.M. Gregg's
column was brought up short of Middleburg by Stuart's pickets. When
Doster's 4th Pennsylvania charged them, the Rebels took to their heels. By the
time Doster reached the town, he found it empty except for a few stragglers.
Then his scouts wandered west and discovered Stuart, with Robertson, Chambliss, and several horse artillery batteries, dug in a mile west of the village,
blocking the direct route to the Valley.[26]

Gregg had enough men to keep Stuart busy while flanking his position
and reaching the Blue Ridge. Instead, he chose to take on the Confederates, as
if his mission were combat, not intelligence gathering. Although subjected
to a shelling from Stuart's artillery, Gregg spent most of the day slowly and

carefully deploying for battle. He positioned skirmishers from Irvin Gregg's and Kilpatrick's brigades on the outskirts of town, then brought up and precisely emplaced his own guns, including the ordnance rifles of Lt. William D. Fuller's Battery C, 3rd Artillery. Finally, near 6:00 P.M., he sent his cousin's troopers in a charge along the road that Stuart blocked. The main attack was made not on horseback, but on foot, by the 4th and 16th Pennsylvania, while Kilpatrick's 1st Maine, now led by Lt. Col. Charles H. Smith, galloped up the road in a diversionary effort.[27]

At first the attack seemed doomed to failure. Chambliss's and Robertson's men held their ground along the crest of a tall ridge and unleashed a blistering fire that threatened to blow Gregg's formation apart. Then Fuller's gunners found the enemy's range, clearing a path for their mounted and dismounted comrades. The combined effort broke Stuart's outer line on the ridge, but reserves rushed up on horseback as if to overwhelm the attackers. Irvin Gregg, the on-scene commander, threw in part of a second regiment lent him by Kilpatrick, the 10th New York, but the New Yorkers were raked by the fire of Chambliss's sharpshooters and forced to retire.

Shouting in triumph, Stuart's reserves charged up the pike, scattering Gregg's assault force. A sudden narrowing of the road siphoned off much of the Confederates' momentum, however, as did the spirited resistance of New Yorkers and Mainers who held their positions, refusing to be driven into retreat. Even so, many Rebels made it as far as the streets of Middleburg, only to be driven out by the rest of the 10th New York and all of the 2nd, led personally in a charge by Judson Kilpatrick. This latest drive cleared not only the town but the country to the west. Stuart's people withdrew toward Ashby's Gap, defiantly forming a new line in front of Upperville.[28]

Though the Yankees had gained ground westward, they had far to go to reach the Blue Ridge, and Stuart was still barring their way. Pleasonton attempted to make up the difference on the twenty-first, following a rainy day that featured little contact between the cavalries other than long-range skirmishing. Troubled by Stuart's recent reliance on dismounted skirmishers, and recalling how well the infantry had supported Buford at Brandy Station, Pleasonton secured the assistance of a full division of the V Corps in ripping apart Stuart's counterreconnaissance screen. At about 7:00 A.M. on Sunday, the twenty-first, he led both his fast-moving troopers and the slow-footed infantry—a combined force of more than 12,000—toward Upperville.[29]

His strategy was to send Buford out the Upperville Pike against Stuart's left flank, threatening his rear. To hold the enemy in place while Buford maneuvered, David Gregg, backed by the infantry brigade of Col. Strong Vincent, would demonstrate against the Rebel center. The rest of the foot soldiers, from Brig. Gen. James Barnes's command, would remain outside Middleburg, covering the cavalry's rear.

The plan was simple yet ambitious, but like Pleasonton's of June 8, it was based on faulty reconnaissance. Because Devin had failed to detect Jones's arrival in the area three days ago, Pleasonton did not know that Jones had extended Stuart's left to a point above Goose Creek. Consequently, when Buford moved into position below the rain-swollen stream that morning, his men quickly bogged down on muddy roads in front of Jones's skirmish line. Buford found the unexpected roadblock so formidable he believed it could be turned only from across the river. He was compelled to countermarch to a point where the stream could be forded, all the while cursing the effect his delay would have on the day's strategy.[30]

Initially unaware of Buford's problems, Pleasonton went ahead with Gregg's and Vincent's attack, which showed early success. Gregg's horse artillery, planted along the Upperville Road, held off Stuart's skirmishers long enough for the foot soldiers to gain a position on their right, into which they poured a devastating enfilading fire. Their path suddenly clear, Judson Kilpatrick's horsemen rushed up the road and, aided by the infantry on their flank and the batteries in their rear, forced Stuart to pull back closer to Upperville.

In their new position, the Confederates kept Kilpatrick immobile for perhaps ninety minutes. Then Stuart moved his line well to the west of Upperville. The Confederates' backs were now to the Blue Ridge; a little more progress and the Federals would be inside the passes that gave entrance to the Shenandoah and uncovered the camps of Lee's army.

Kilpatrick, unwilling to put off the moment of triumph, led his riders through town, where they rammed into Stuart's rear guard—elements of Robertson's command and the newly arrived brigade of Hampton. For several minutes, saber and pistol duels swirled through the streets of Upperville. Pleasonton's generals involved themselves in the fray. David Gregg's horse was shot from under him and for a brief time, until released by his own men, Judson Kilpatrick was a prisoner of war.[31]

The battle appeared to turn when a body of the 6th United States Cavalry, sent down from the north by Buford, readied a charge against Hampton's and Robertson's strung-out lines. Cram's small regiment started for the town at a gallop, but farm fields and fences intervened, slowing its advance to a crawl and enabling a mounted force under Hampton to frighten it into flight. The Regulars' brigade commander, Major Starr, was so incensed by Cram's faulty advance that he gave the officers and men of the 6th a violent tongue-lashing while still on the field of battle.[32]

Cram's repulse essentially brought Pleasonton's offensive to a close, although the troopers of Gregg and Kilpatrick continued to duel with remnants of Robertson's and Hampton's brigades until nearly dark. In one of these clashes, the 4th New York made a small but successful charge that helped cleanse the reputation the regiment had sullied at Aldie.[33]

The day ended as a tactical setback for Pleasonton, mainly because of what had happened along his right. For all of Buford's marching and countermarching, he never located the end of the flank above Goose Creek. Realizing that he would contribute little or nothing to the day's fortunes, he sent Cram's regiment to David Gregg with the suggestion that his command make the main assault, without reference to the 1st Division.

Late in the day, Buford encountered Jones's troopers, batteries, and supply trains as they fell back toward the Blue Ridge in response to Stuart's order. At once Buford attacked with Gamble, hoping to gain some tangible success, but his subordinate never touched the retreat column, thanks to the rapid and accurate fire of Jones's carbineers and artillerists. When Tom Devin failed to come up in support at a critical hour, Gamble broke off the fight. Still, Devin had arrived in time to foil a counterattack by two of Jones's regiments.[34]

While Buford's day had been marked by a conspicuous lack of progress, he capped it by gaining a major piece of intelligence. When Jones retired, Buford followed him all the way to the Blue Ridge. At sundown, his skirmishers climbed ridges adjacent to Ashby's Gap and from their summit spied hundreds of tents just inside the Valley, which they identified as the camps of James Longstreet's corps, Army of Northern Virginia. When apprised of the discovery, Pleasonton knew that at least two-thirds of Lee's army was in the Shenandoah. In fact, Ewell's corps had been in Maryland since the fifteenth; the day after the fight at Upperville. it crossed the Mason-Dixon Line.[35]

The only drawback to Buford's sighting of Lee's infantry was its timing. With Ewell poised to enter lower Pennsylvania and Hill's corps moving up in Longstreet's rear, the Army of Northern Virginia could not be prevented from striking a blow in the North. Stuart's reconnaissance barrier had been penetrated, but too late to stop the invasion from reaching high tide.

><-+-<>-<->-O-<->-+-><

By the twenty-second Pleasonton considered his job in the Loudoun Valley well done. Reviewing the events of the past week, he took satisfaction in what his corps had accomplished. It had been involved in some of the heaviest mounted and dismounted fighting of the war, as its casualty count indicated: Since the seventeenth, the Federals had lost almost 900 officers and men, the Confederates almost 500. Adding in the figures from Brandy Station, since early June Pleasonton had suffered 1,700 casualties to more than 1,000 for Stuart. The toll underscored the fact that since the start of Lee's invasion, the fighting had been carried on almost exclusively by the armies' horsemen.[36]

Although Stuart had left his front by the twenty-second, Pleasonton remained at Aldie for four more days. He spent the time plugging manpower gaps, while seeking promotion and an enlarged command. He had recently added to his staff twenty-five-year-old Elon Farnsworth, whose bravery and leadership at Brandy Station had caught his eye. Apparently, more than the captain's combat credentials had recommended him for the position. On the twenty-third Pleasonton induced his newest aide to write his congressman uncle—Lincoln's fellow Illinoisan and personal friend—in hopes of securing the second star that should have accompanied Pleasonton's rise to corps command but had not. "The Genl. speaks of recommending me for Brig[adier

General]," the youngster explained. "I do not know that I ought to mention it for fear that you will call me an aspiring youth. I am satisfied to serve through this war in the line. . . . But if I can do any good anywhere else of course `small favors &c.' Now try and talk this into the President and you can do an immense good."[37]

Along with his own letter, Farnsworth sent his uncle a missive from Pleasonton that spelled out the quid pro quo the captain had alluded to, while asking the congressman's help in adding to the Cavalry Corps the large but—according to Pleasonton—underused division of Julius Stahel, another foreigner whose lethargy and incompetence had "injured our cause."[38]

Regardless of what John Farnsworth could do for him, Pleasonton was aided by the commander of Hooker's forward wing, General Reynolds, whose infantry Stahel accompanied as part of a northward movement that began on the twenty-fifth. That day the Hungarian's horsemen followed Reynolds's foot soldiers to the Potomac. Reynolds crossed the river via a pontoon span at Edwards's Ferry, Stahel by way of a nearby ford. Once in Maryland, Stahel sent large parties toward South Mountain, beyond which Longstreet and Hill were believed to be moving. On the twenty-eighth one of these parties, two Michigan regiments under Brig. Gen. Joseph T. Copeland, ranged into Pennsylvania and entered Gettysburg, seat of Adams County, which had been visited briefly by Rebel infantry two days before.[39]

Copeland's men sent back word that Confederates lingered above Gettysburg, near Carlisle, while others were moving eastward toward York, and that Lee had recently established his headquarters at Chambersburg, twenty-three miles west of Gettysburg. The intelligence was valuable—it was worth more than any Pleasonton would have come up with in a similar situation—but Reynolds disliked the fact that Stahel had not accompanied any of his detachments. He sent Hooker exaggerated claims of Stahel's inefficiency, claims that helped hasten the foreigner's demise.[40]

On the twenty-seventh, one day after ending his stay at Fairfax Court House, Hooker led the vanguard of his main body into Maryland, crossing at Edwards's Ferry and adjacent points, and joining John Reynolds outside the city of Frederick. There Hooker planned to remain until he had a still better picture of Lee's progress and heading, and until the rest of the infantry joined him via the line of the O & A.[41]

By now the cavalry was active again, as well as fragmented. When Reynolds bridged the Potomac on the twenty-fifth and twenty-sixth, Buford's horsemen had guarded his front, flanks, and rear. Gregg performed the same service for the rest of the army, including its long and ponderous supply train. Gregg's riders, the last to tread the pontoons, crossed at Edwards's Ferry on the evening of the twenty-seventh, to the accompaniment of a band on the northern shore playing "Maryland, My Maryland." Despite the almost palpable danger that lay ahead, virtually every trooper expressed pleasure and relief upon entering a state with a largely loyalist population. "Getting out of old

Virginia," wrote one of Gregg's men, "was like getting out of a graveyard and into Paradise."[42]

While the army lolled near Frederick, its high command, and the future of the conflict, changed overnight. Ever since Chancellorsville, Joe Hooker had been on a slippery footing with the White House and the War Department. The occupants of both had long asked themselves the same question many of Hooker's own soldiers were mulling over: Could Fighting Joe halt Robert E. Lee short of Baltimore, Philadelphia, or Washington, D.C.? Finding no answer, on the twenty-eighth Lincoln fired Hooker and named George Meade, commander of the V Corps and a resident of Pennsylvania, as his successor. Reynolds, another Pennsylvanian and Meade's senior, had been sounded out for the job, but fearing political interference in any strategy he might devise, he had turned Lincoln down.[43]

At least at first, Meade's succession was a boon to Alfred Pleasonton, who had already received several gifts. On the twenty-second, evidently without the aid of John Farnsworth, he had received his commission as major general of volunteers. Six days later, perhaps at the congressman's urging, the War Office relieved Stahel from command of his division and packed him off to a minor post in Harrisburg, Pennsylvania. Stahel's troopers—who turned out to number about 3,500—were assigned to Pleasonton. The additions raised the strength of the Cavalry Corps to 12,700 officers and men—a far larger force than Stuart could pit against it, even when his organic command was augmented, as on the present occasion.[44]

The realization that he commanded more horsemen than any general who had served in the East warmed Pleasonton's heart. He was doubly grateful when his new superior granted him the authority to designate additional general officers for his expanded command. Keeping his bargain with Captain Farnsworth, Pleasonton jumped the youngster to star rank along with two other staff officers who had long impressed him, Custer and Merritt. While his selections generated much comment in the officer corps, especially among the dozens over whose heads they had been promoted, in the main they were well received, based largely on the trio's conspicuous service to date. And because the reinforcements enabled Pleasonton to re-create the 3rd Cavalry Division, he was able to reward another subordinate by tendering Judson Kilpatrick its command.[45]

To lead Kilpatrick's brigades, Pleasonton assigned him Farnsworth and Custer. Farnsworth assumed command of the 5th New York, the 2nd and 18th Pennsylvania, the 1st Vermont, and a squadron of the 1st Ohio. Soon after the newly minted general took over, however, he lost the 2nd Pennsylvania to provost service and the Ohio squadron to escort duty at division headquarters. Custer replaced Copeland at the head of the "Wolverine Brigade," the 1st, 5th, 6th, and 7th Michigan. Meanwhile Merritt, although junior to most of the officers placed under him, was assigned command of the Reserve Brigade. Buford, who doubtless had some say in the personnel decisions, was highly gratified by his old subordinate's appointment.[46]

Pleasonton took the opportunity to make other organizational changes. He added Robertson's horse artillery brigade, just back from its refit in Washington, to Tidball's, giving the cavalry corps the finest one-two horse artillery combination ever seen in the eastern theater. Three other units were grouped into a reserve force, while the other six batteries were attached to the cavalry divisions: Calef's, along with Capt. William Graham's K, 1st Artillery, to Buford; Randol's and Fuller's to Gregg; Elder's and Pennington's to Kilpatrick. To round out the organizational and personnel changes, while the army was still at Frederick, McIntosh returned to it, reassuming command of the 1st Brigade, 2nd Division, while Pennock Huey's 8th Pennsylvania, formerly attached to Buford's command, transferred to Gregg's division, whereupon Huey took charge of its 2nd Brigade, formerly Kilpatrick's.[47]

At least occasionally, Pleasonton tore himself from administrative matters to make field assignments. As Meade prepared to lead the army into his home state, Buford was assigned to cover its left, or forward wing, Kilpatrick its center, and Gregg its right. As the mounted commander closest to the enemy's assumed position, Buford had an especially important job to perform. On the twenty-seventh Pleasonton sent him through Turner's Gap in South Mountain to Boonsboro and points north in the direction of Fairfield, Pennsylvania. Two days later Buford was directed to retrace Copeland's path through Adams County. The following evening he was to lead the 1st Cavalry Division into Gettysburg.[48]

Chapter Fourteen

Much Service at Gettysburg

As the Army of the Potomac learned on June 28, Stuart was raiding again. In the small hours of the twenty-fifth, the Confederate leader had left Salem, Virginia, about twenty miles southwest of Aldie, with almost 6,000 men—the brigades of Hampton, Chambliss, and Munford (with an ill Fitz Lee accompanying the column aboard an ambulance)—heading southeastward. At Stuart's urging, Robert E. Lee had assigned his cavalry the mission of riding around or through the Federal army, gaining information on its movements and intentions and destroying its communications. Stuart was also to scour Maryland for all manner of supplies before making for Pennsylvania and linking with the army's advance echelon, Ewell's corps. Stuart had left with the main army the brigades of Robertson and Jones, while a third brigade, Brig. Gen. Albert G. Jenkins's, guided Ewell into Pennsylvania. If used properly, these horsemen would provide ample support to the invasion force.[1]

After riding through a portion of Hooker's army, Stuart's column crossed the Potomac River at Rowser's Ford, north of Dranesville, Virginia, early on the twenty-eighth. The raiders' route placed them in territory David Gregg had been assigned to patrol. Some hours after the fording, Alfred Pleasonton—as befit his intelligence-collecting skills—informed Gregg that a single brigade of Confederate horsemen was north of the river, apparently bent on destroying the Baltimore & Ohio Railroad. Pleasonton's subordinate was directed to have two-thirds of his division, supported by a battery, reconnoiter the rail line as far east as Ellicott's Mills. Late that afternoon Gregg sent McIntosh's brigade to Ridgeville, where elements of it inspected towns south of the B & O, including Cooksville, Lisbon, and Poplar Springs. The following day McIntosh sent parties farther east. Meanwhile, portions of Huey's brigade scouted farther north and west, near the depot of Mount Airy.

The scouting parties came up dry. Although McIntosh heard, early on the twenty-ninth, that many of Stuart's men were dislodging railroad track near Hood's Mill, the colonel considered the force too large to take on without reinforcements. By the time he reunited with Gregg at Mount Airy, the Confederates had left the railroad, heading north. That being the case, Gregg saw no point in returning to Hood's Mill.[2]

Already Stuart's raid appeared to have produced success. On the twenty-eighth the Confederate leader had fulfilled one of his mission requirements by overtaking and capturing more than 100 supply wagons at Rockville, eight miles northwest of Washington. The proximity of Rebel cavalry had thrown the capital into a panic. City streets had been barricaded, home guards and hastily armed government employees had turned out to man the barriers, and Percy Wyndham, temporarily in command of the cavalry depot outside the capital, was trying to form a mounted defense force even as he recuperated from his Brandy Station wound.[3]

But Stuart had no intention of striking Washington; he was intent on keeping his rendezvous with Ewell in the vicinity of York, Pennsylvania. He could not foresee how badly his newly acquired impedimenta would compromise his progress. Nor could he know that Union cavalry would slow him down at Westminster, Maryland, and Hanover, Pennsylvania, making him unable to meet Ewell on schedule.

Neither of those forces was led by Gregg. Soon after McIntosh and Huey rejoined him late on the twenty-ninth, the division leader started north at a rapid pace that never flagged. Although his troopers' ordeal was lightened somewhat by good wishes and gifts of food and drink from the Unionist residents of upper Maryland, the rigors and discomforts of the march were severe. Believing that Stuart's men were just ahead of him, Gregg kept the march going throughout the night. When the 2nd Cavalry Division reached Westminster, seat of Carroll County, Maryland, at daybreak on June 30, troopers and horse artillerymen were dead tired. To remain awake, some resorted to pricking themselves with pins and slapping each other's faces.[4]

The previous afternoon, ninety-four plucky or foolhardy troopers of the 1st Delaware Cavalry, an element of the Baltimore-based VIII Corps, had attacked the head of Stuart's column as it neared the town. Although quickly decimated, the Federals had taken enough of a toll that Stuart remained in and near Westminster for a part of the evening. He was gone, however, by the time Gregg arrived. He had left behind only a few stragglers and looters; these Gregg's advance snatched up via a mounted charge through the streets of town.[5]

Gregg tarried in Westminster for only a couple of hours, but long enough to give his men the rest they desperately needed. By late morning, bleary-eyed troopers were again in motion, heading for the Mason-Dixon Line. As the tag end of the column wended its way through the town, the men's attention was drawn to a woman and her two young daughters, standing in front of their house, each silently holding the Stars and Stripes in salute to the passing soldiers, a "pitying benevolent expression" on their faces. Years later a veteran of Randol's battery recalled that the patriotic tableau "nerved many a man for encounter, and inspired them . . . to stand manfully by the old flag and fight valiantly for it."[6]

>─┤─◆>─◦─<◆>─┤─◄

Pleasonton wished to accompany his corps in the field as it moved toward a confrontation with Lee in Pennsylvania. Given his druthers, he probably would have joined Buford's column as it approached Gettysburg, via Emmitsburg, Maryland, on the last day of June. Buford, his old colleague in the 2nd Dragoons, was Pleasonton's favorite subordinate; he had accompanied Buford at Brandy Station, the Kentuckian's first fight in divisional command, and Pleasonton surmised that Buford would make first contact with the Rebel army. On Buford's front the glory—the military and the political awards of active service—would be won, and Pleasonton pursued glory like a knight seeking the Holy Grail.

Unfortunately, his new commander had other ideas as to where Pleasonton could do the army the most good. Meade had a decidedly low opinion of cavalry's value as an independent force; he prized it only as an auxiliary of the main army—a tactical, not a strategic, asset. Present conditions dictated that most of the horsemen should serve apart from their comrades in the infantry, but that did not mean Pleasonton had to. Following the thinking of McClellan, Burnside, and to a certain extent, Hooker, Meade considered his cavalry commander principally a staff officer. Pleasonton's years of pre-war experience as an adjutant appeared to fit him perfectly for this role. In fact, before the campaign was over, Meade would appoint him acting co-chief of staff of the army. Under certain conditions, Meade would consider assigning Pleasonton duties in the field—but not while the campaign in Pennsylvania was shaping up. Until the Confederates were brought to bay, Pleasonton would be on a short leash. Whenever the army camped, Meade saw to it that Pleasonton's tent was pitched only a few yards from his own.[7]

No doubt Pleasonton was frustrated, and probably angry as well, over what he considered his second-class status. His attitude may have prevented him from doing his duty at a critical stage of the campaign. If unable to be at the front, a dedicated commander would have made the most of his rear-guard position by supplying his forces with up-to-date information on enemy movements. Instead, on the thirtieth, when Stuart's path took him into the sector patrolled by the new 3rd Cavalry Division, the Knight of Romance provided Kilpatrick (as well as his other division commanders) not with helpful information but with bombast calculated to nerve the men for the task ahead. In orders issued that day, to be read to every regiment in the corps, Pleasonton alerted everyone to "the immense issues involved in the result of the engagement that may soon be expected with the enemy. Our own soil has been invaded; houses, firesides, and all domestic relations are being rudely trampled on by a mercenary foe. To the cavalry arm of this army, it is only necessary to mention these facts to fire them [presumably, the troopers] with the determination of victory so distinguished at

Beverly Ford, Brandy Station, Aldie, Middleburg, and Upperville." He closed
by authorizing his subordinates to order "the instant death of any soldier who
fails in his duty at this hour."[8]

The day before Pleasonton composed his address, Kilpatrick's column—
Farnsworth's brigade, plus half of Custer's—moved northeastward from Frederick, and crossed the Pennsylvania line. They spent the night in the appropriately
named hamlet of Littlestown. The next morning, perhaps fortified by their corps
commander's call to arms, they pushed on to Hanover under a light rain. After
passing through the town, the Wolverine Brigade, the vanguard of the column,
was strengthened by the arrival of the 5th and 6th Michigan, just back from their
trip to Gettysburg under Custer's predecessor, General Copeland.[9]

Kilpatrick would need all the men he could gather, for just after noon the
rear of Farnsworth's brigade was attacked by hordes of Rebel cavalry. Too
late, Kilpatrick realized that the force he should have been seeking had
instead found him. Now he could do nothing except fight for the life of his
new command.

Stuart's assault shoved Farnsworth's rear regiment through the streets of
Hanover. In their haste to escape capture, troopers of the division's greenest regiment, the 18th Pennsylvania, littered the road to town with discarded carbines,
pistols, and sabers, all of which their pursuers appropriated. Reaching the center
of town, the rookies collided with Kilpatrick's supply train; for several minutes
confusion reigned, as men tried to separate themselves from neighing horses
and runaway wagons and build a semblance of a defensive line.[10]

Trying to recover from his command's inauspicious start, young
Farnsworth rallied his men, sorted them out, and slowly established an effective perimeter. When Stuart's leading brigade, Chambliss's, struck that line, it
was tossed back and shoved out of town. Meanwhile, Kilpatrick rushed back
from north of Hanover to supervise Farnsworth's dispositions and to deploy
Custer's Michiganders west of town, along the railroad from Littlestown.

In their new position, the 5th and 6th Michigan met their boyish brigade
commander for the first time. They found him sitting on his horse along the
railroad, his yellow hair curling down over the shoulders of an outlandish uniform of his own creation, one awash in gilt and silver trim. Custer had created
it as a means of announcing his position in battle to everyone in his command.
Capt. James H. Kidd of the 6th stared at the gaudy officer, "whose appearance
amazed if it did not for the moment amuse me . . . [and] who sat his charger as
if to the manner born. Tall, lithe, active, muscular, straight as an Indian and as
quick in his movements, he had the fair complexion of a school girl."[11]

Farnsworth's men—the 5th New York up front, the 1st Vermont and 1st
West Virginia on the flanks, the fugitive Pennsylvanians huddling in the rear—
held Chambliss on the outskirts of Hanover for much of the afternoon. The
fighting kept Stuart—who desired to disengage as soon as possible and continue on to York—glued to Hanover. Otherwise the combat availed the Federals
little. Several times Kilpatrick tried to mount an offensive, advancing elements

of Farnsworth's brigade toward Chambliss's position, but any advantage he gained was short-lived.[12]

Late in the afternoon the division leader shifted his attention to Custer's front, where the Michigan Brigade confronted the Virginians of Fitzhugh Lee, now in position on Chambliss's left. Already Custer had placed some of his troops inside the town, where they helped Farnsworth's brigade man the barricades. He had also sent dismounted skirmishers of the 7th Michigan to hold in place the Rebels in their front, which included a battery of horse artillery. Now the twenty-three-year-old general dismounted the 6th Michigan and led more than 500 of its men, each wielding a Spencer repeating rifle, across the railroad tracks. As they neared Lee's line, which stretched across a tall ridge, several Wolverines dropped to their hands and knees to evade enemy detection.

When within 300 yards of the ridge, the attackers responded to a signal from Custer by leaping to their feet and spraying the Rebels with volley after volley. The gray line wavered, many of its men rushing to the rear to escape the hail of balls, several others falling dead or wounded or being taken prisoner. The men of Michigan felled so many artillerists that for a time the guns on the ridge fell silent. Reinforcements from Lee's main body rushed up to stabilize the line and save the cannons, but they failed to dislodge dozens of Federals whom Custer held in a position from which to threaten the stability of the Rebel left.[13]

Stuart's concern for that sector influenced the balance of the fight. He made no further attempt at an offensive; as soon as darkness fell, he cleared the Hanover vicinity. First, Lee's brigade disengaged to cover the captured wagons. Then Hampton's fresh brigade went into position alongside Chambliss until able to bring up the rear of the raiding column.[14]

It appeared that the fighting had ended in success for Judson Kilpatrick, whose men held the battle-torn streets of Hanover. The victors, however, had suffered nearly 200 casualties—most of them early in the fight, when Farnsworth was nearly routed—to fewer than 150 for Stuart. Perhaps influenced by his losses, rather than pursue Stuart in force, Kilpatrick remained on the field through the night, tending to his casualties, interrogating his captives, and scouting the immediate vicinity. He did not leave town until daylight, when he headed north and east.

By then Kill-cavalry had lost sight of Stuart. Still, he believed he knew where the rest of Lee's army could be found. Displaying an eye and ear for intelligence that rivaled his superior's, early that evening he informed Pleasonton at Taneytown, Maryland, that, based on the reports of local people, the main body of the Army of Northern Virginia lay only ten miles northeast of Hanover, around East Berlin. By then the Army of Northern Virginia was concentrating at Gettysburg; thus Kilpatrick's assessment was fifteen miles off the mark. But the Knight of Romance not only accepted Kilpatrick's assessment of events, he relayed it to army headquarters along with his endorsement that both in battle and reconnaissance, "Kilpatrick has done very well."[15]

To be fair, Kilpatrick was not the only cavalry commander conveying the impression of a Rebel movement toward Berlin. This was the deduction that General Reynolds made that evening when a dispatch from Buford reached the wing commander's headquarters south of Gettysburg. Reynolds may have misinterpreted a report from Buford—now in the Adams County seat—that a division of Lt. Gen. A. P. Hill's corps had been sighted marching east of Chambersburg, toward Berlin and York. Even so, Reynolds was sharp enough to know what Kilpatrick did not: The idea that any Rebels were in the Berlin area was a fantasy.

Whether or not Buford was right about Hill's heading, he had sent other information that not only made sense to Reynolds but concerned him. Upon entering Gettysburg that morning, the 1st Division had found a regiment or more of Confederate infantry advancing toward the town from the west. Other infantry, identity and size unknown, appeared to be hovering on the northern outskirts of Gettysburg. The report told Reynolds that trouble lay just up the road from his present position—and in the very midst of Buford's.[16]

>─┤◆≻─O─◁◆├─┤◄

En route to Gettysburg, Buford expected to run into the invaders of Pennsylvania. He was not disappointed. On June 29 the better part of his division—Gamble's and Devin's brigades, plus Calef's battery—ranged close to the Pennsylvania line, while Merritt's Reserves and Graham's battery accompanied Buford's supply train, as Pleasonton had ordered, to Mechanicstown, Maryland. Shortly after entering Pennsylvania on the morning of the thirtieth, the head of the larger column bumped into a Rebel outpost outside Fairfield, manned by two foot regiments and some artillery from the division of Maj. Gen. Henry Heth, part of Hill's corps. A firefight broke out, but it did not last long. Buford's orders were explicit: He was to reach Gettysburg without delay. Holding the Confederates in place with Devin's skirmishers, the brigadier led the balance of his command back into Maryland. As soon as he could, Devin disengaged and followed.[17]

Buford later ascertained that his opponents, once the fight had ended, decamped for Cashtown, seven miles west of Gettysburg. At about 9:30 A.M., he relayed the intelligence—possibly in person—to John Reynolds, at that time stationed at Emmitsburg. Then Buford looped back into Pennsylvania and headed for his next port of call.[18]

Gamble's brigade, followed by Devin and the artillery, covered the ten miles to Gettysburg in about two hours. Under a misty drizzle, the advance guard, a party of skirmishers from Chapman's 3rd Indiana, entered the town shortly before 11:30. The local people, who had felt abandoned since Copeland's regiments departed, gave the troopers a rousing welcome, treating them to food, drink, flowers, and song.[19]

While Buford conferred with residents who claimed to have information about the enemy, scouting parties trotted out the northwestward-running Chambersburg Pike toward South Mountain. From that direction, a brigade of Ewell's corps had come to Gettysburg on the twenty-sixth, foraging, looting, and scaring the wits out of the locals. Now elements of Hill's corps lingered along the pike, as though prepared to emulate Ewell's behavior.[20]

Moving behind the scouts, Buford's main body passed through the streets of Gettysburg to bivouac on high ground known as McPherson's Ridge, a mile and a half northwest of town. Directly in their rear was Seminary Ridge, on which sat a Lutheran theological academy. Buford's signal officer sized up the cupola of the seminary building as an observation perch. From that vantage point, he and Buford enjoyed a long, unobstructed view in every direction.

Their attention was most often directed to the geography west of the village. About 1,300 yards to the cavalry's front, beyond Willoughby Run and mostly south of the Chambersburg Pike, ran Herr Ridge. A little more than half a mile farther out loomed another stretch of high ground, Belmont Schoolhouse Ridge. Buford saw at once that he could use each of these ridges as defensive positions if Hill returned to town the next day, as seemed likely.

Before the afternoon was done, Buford's scouts—some of whom had been sent above the town, as well as toward the mountains—reported that Hill was only part of Buford's problem. Elements of Ewell's command were moving their way from the north and northeast; they would probably be on the scene come morning. Their marching columns appeared to include few or no cavalry, but thousands of muskets and dozens of cannons.

Buford realized all too well what was happening. Lee was concentrating his far-flung army for a showdown with Meade, a feat facilitated by the plethora of roads that radiated from Gettysburg like spokes on a wheel. Buford could get nothing close to a head count, but he suspected that within a few hours as many as 40,000 Confederates would be sweeping in from three or more directions to oppose his 3,000 troopers and six guns. Subtracting the one man in every four who, when the fighting started, went to the rear with his own horse and the mounts of three comrades, by morning the 1st Cavalry Division would find itself outnumbered seventeen to one.[21]

One might think only a fool capable of viewing such a situation as a challenge. But John Buford was no fool—he was a realist, with a fighter's spirit, a cavalryman's eye for terrain, and a touch of the gambler. As the afternoon wore on, he became increasingly intrigued by the vision of his savvy, tenacious troopers using defensible terrain to hold back hordes of infantry, leapfrogging from one position to another until the advance of the Army of the Potomac came up to relieve them. Before nightfall he had decided that he would hold Gettysburg until forced to give it up. He sent couriers with that message to John Reynolds, now five miles to the south. Reynolds promised to come to Buford's assistance at an early hour in the morning.

By evening Buford had placed his main body between the two crests of McPherson's Ridge. Gamble's brigade held a line that ran from below the Chambersburg Pike to the grading of an unfinished railroad, parallel to and perhaps 150 yards north of the road. From the grading, Devin's line stretched as far north as the road to Mummasburg. Reserves from both brigades had taken position on Seminary Ridge, while Calef had unlimbered in the midst of Gamble's bivouac, his ordnance rifles commanding both sides of the turnpike.[22]

Well in advance of Buford's main position, along a several-mile-long line stretching from the Fairfield Road to the Carlisle Pike, vidette posts had been established. These four- and five-man units of mounted pickets would sound the alarm when the enemy approached. In response to Buford's belief that first contact would occur along the road from Chambersburg, the videttes in that sector had been instructed to be especially vigilant.

Around the headquarters campfire that night, Tom Devin supposedly predicted that his men would easily hold back any Rebels who came their way. A boast of this sort seems out of character for the quietly capable colonel, but if he said it, Buford had the perfect rejoinder: "No you won't," he is quoted as replying. "They will attack you in the morning and they will come booming—skirmishers three deep. You will have to fight like the devil to hold your own until supports arrive. The enemy must know the importance of this position, and will strain every nerve to secure it, and if we are able to hold it, we will do well."[23]

The morning of July 1 confirmed Buford's words. North of town shots were exchanged shortly after dawn between Devin's videttes on the road from Carlisle and scouts from Ewell's corps. But the day's first sustained combat occurred on Gamble's front about three hours later. Sometime after 7:00 A.M., Heth's main body came trudging along the Chambersburg Pike behind three lines of skirmishers. Members of a vidette post near Marsh Creek, about three miles from the center of Gettysburg, watched the Rebels emerge from the morning mist. A lieutenant of the 8th Illinois opened the contest in that sector with a shot from a borrowed carbine. As the fighting quickly expanded, couriers from the front galloped to Buford's headquarters to apprise him of the situation.[24]

According to a prearranged plan, the cavalry commander sent forward reinforcements from the vidette reserve. They offered so much resistance that Heth halted and sent back for his artillery. Once these guns were up and exchanging shells with Calef's rifles, two infantry brigades resumed the advance, one above the turnpike, the other below it.

Their movement was clearly seen by Buford's signal officer in the seminary tower. In response, Buford sent perhaps 500 dismounted skirmishers across Willoughby Run and onto Herr Ridge. They formed a line in rear of the videttes, many of whom had been driven from Belmont Schoolhouse Ridge and points west. Spacing themselves at thirty-foot intervals, the skirmishers formed a wall behind which the pickets could rally. As they did, shells from Calef's battery screamed over their heads to burst in the Rebels' midst.

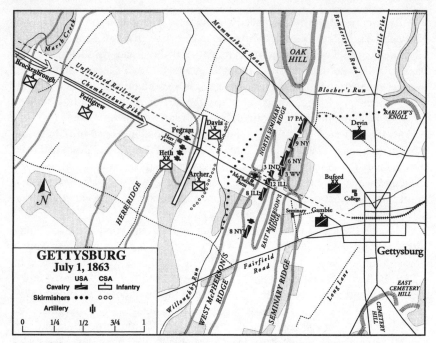

Map of the First Day of the Battle of Gettysburg, July 1, 1863

The combined opposition of skirmishers, videttes, and cannoneers slowed Heth's advance to a shuffle. Stunned by the volume of fire created by Buford's breechloaders, the division commander began to wonder if he were facing infantry rather than dismounted horsemen. In the continued absence of Stuart, Lee's infantry had been wandering all but blindly through Pennsylvania. Now Heth was forced to make sense of the expanding fight without the luxury of mounted reconnaissance.

His eventual response was just what Buford had hoped for. Heth halted once again, about a half mile from Herr Ridge, this time to form his brigades into lines of battle, a cumbersome and complicated process. At least half an hour, perhaps ninety minutes, elapsed before the gray line surged forward, and by then, Buford, from his cupola, had spied the headquarters flag of the I Army Corps approaching from the south.[25]

Accounts conflict over the location of Buford's reunion with Reynolds. Some sources have them meeting in the belfry, others at Buford's headquarters in Gettysburg. The traditional venue is the seminary grounds, where, upon arriving, Reynolds shouted up to the cavalryman: "What's the matter, John?" and Buford replied, "The devil's to pay!" According to this version of events, Reynolds asked whether Buford's troopers could hold until Maj. Gen. Abner Doubleday's advance echelon arrived, and the laconic cavalryman replied, "I reckon I can."[26]

Descending from the cupola, Buford mounted and accompanied Reynolds out the Chambersburg Pike, along which many troopers were now retreating, having been driven from Herr Ridge. Shouting to make himself heard above the roar of battle, the cavalry leader pointed out his dispositions, and Reynolds nodded in approval. As they rode along, Colonel Gamble is supposed to have rushed up to Reynolds, shouting: "Hurry up, General, hurry up! They are breaking our line!"[27]

At once Reynolds wheeled about and rode off to meet the head of the I Corps as it arrived. En route, he sent a courier to urge another component of his wing, the XI Corps, to hasten up from Emmitsburg. He sent a second galloper to Taneytown, alerting Meade that at least two of his corps would soon be engaged in southern Pennsylvania. The news killed Meade's plan to fight Lee on the hills of northern Maryland. As soon as he learned of Buford's fight, the army commander hastened north, while sending on ahead to Gettysburg General Hancock, one of his most trusted subordinates. Hancock, leader of the II Army Corps, was empowered to assume overall command until army headquarters could reach the scene of action.[28]

Some time after 10:30 A.M.—minutes before Gamble's main body could be uprooted from McPherson's Ridge—Reynolds returned to the seminary at the head of Doubleday's column. The infantry hustled into position behind their grimy, sweat-stained friends in yellow-trimmed jackets, who rallied in the rear and on the flanks of their reinforcements. Many troopers fought alongside the foot soldiers for hours, some remaining in position long after being ordered to fall back.

When Heth's troops collided with Doubleday's atop McPherson's Ridge, a segment of the hastily constructed infantry line began to waver, and Reynolds rushed up on horseback to try to steady it. Moments later he toppled from the saddle, a sharpshooter's ball in his neck. Following his mortal wounding, elements of Doubleday's command blunted the enemy's drive on both sides of the turnpike, forcing Heth to call up his last two brigades. One withdrew, however, for fear of being outflanked and cut off; the other, led by a more combative officer, Brig. Gen. J. Johnston Pettigrew, did not become heavily engaged until about 2:30. By then, not only had the remainder of Doubleday's command reached the field, so had the advance of Howard's corps. Just shy of noon, with Lee on the field and the division of Maj. Gen. William Dorsey Pender poised atop Herr Ridge, a lull settled over the field, in some sectors lasting two hours.[29]

With his men no longer hard-pressed, Buford seized the opportunity to recall Gamble to a relatively quiet sector closer to Gettysburg. Only Maj. John Beveridge's 8th Illinois remained in close contact with the enemy on and east of Herr Ridge. From their position on that portion of McPherson's Ridge crossed by the Fairfield Road, the Illinoisans not only observed Heth and Pender resume their advance late in the afternoon; but they raked Heth's right flank with a galling fire.

Most of the firepower was delivered on foot, but enough of Beveridge's men remained mounted to make General Pettigrew suspect that a saber charge was coming his way. Quickly he formed some of his men into hollow squares, a Napoleonic tactic designed to shield foot soldiers from a mounted attack. The formation may have done its job, but it also rendered Heth's flank immobile for an extended period. As the Confederates stood about, awaiting attack, Beveridge remounted every trooper and withdrew to Gamble's new position.[30]

Buford had a tough enough job holding back Hill's corps, which, despite some setbacks, was moving on Gettysburg with the confidence of veteran troops accustomed to success. Soon, however, Buford's men were fighting in a second—and then a third—direction at the same time. The result was the sternest test ever faced by Union cavalry in the eastern theater.

At about 11:00 A.M., while Gamble's men helped the I Corps defend McPherson's Ridge, Devin's troopers spied the advance element of Maj. General Robert E. Rodes's division of Ewell's corps passing down the road from Carlisle. The head of Rodes's column—three regiments of skirmishers—ran into Devin's videttes near Keckler's Hill, five miles north of Gettysburg. A few hundred yards farther south, Devin's skirmishers emulated Gamble's by forming a discontinuous but formidable line behind which the pickets might rally. Though hard-pressed from the start, Devin had been anticipating Rodes's entrance. He had shifted his brigade to block Ewell's path the moment the I Corps had released him from his westward-facing position above the Chambersburg Pike.[31]

Although Rodes swept the videttes from his path with little trouble, his advance slowed appreciably once he hit Devin's skirmish line. For more than an hour, the 2nd Brigade stymied its opponents by letting loose with carbines and pistols, then falling back, digging in, and firing again. They offered opposition until the last minute; when the infantry finally closed in, they mounted and galloped out of harm's reach, answering the Rebel yell with one what trooper called "a ringing loyal cheer."[32]

Pressure on Devin's position began to abate at about 12:30, when the head of Maj. Gen. Carl Schurz's XI Corps (with Howard having replaced the fallen Reynolds in wing command) reached the front and formed on Doubleday's right. Schurz's line stretched well to the northeast of Gettysburg, although it did not extend far enough to cover the York Turnpike. As this road was a likely avenue of Confederate advance, Devin took pains to bring the position to Schurz's attention. Even so, no infantry was moved into that sector, a failing that especially bothered Devin when, just short of 1:00 P.M., he heard reports of enemy movements farther up the road.

The colonel's concern was well founded. Just after 1:00, by which time his brigade had fallen back to form a line from the Carlisle Road east to Rock Creek, the skirmishers of Maj. Gen. Jubal A. Early's division of Ewell's corps appeared in the road. Since Early's heading placed him in a perfect position to flank Schurz's line, Devin fought long and hard to hold the Rebels back. Col.

William Sackett of the 9th New York, in immediate command of the brigade skirmish line, held the constantly increasing enemy in check until the gray tide had
swollen to mammoth proportions. Seeing his men outpositioned as well as outnumbered, Sackett hauled them to the rear. By 2:00 P.M. Devin had massed the
entire brigade just off the York Pike, beyond range of most of Early's riflemen.[33]

In his new position, Devin might still shield Schurz's flank while the latter opposed Rodes to the north and Pender to the west. But the troopers could
not remain there long enough to do any good. Soon after massing below the
road to York, they attracted shells from an XI Corps battery that had mistaken
them for Rebel horsemen. The artillery had unlimbered on top of Cemetery
Hill, the northern spur of another of those long, wooded ridges characteristic
of the local topography: Cemetery Ridge, a mile east of, and parallel to, Seminary Ridge. When the friendly fire persisted, Devin shepherded his people into
the streets of town. The fallback, while inevitable, uncovered Schurz's flank to
Early's still-arriving infantry, making its collapse a matter of time.[34]

Even if Devin had held his ground, it is unlikely he could have prevented
the Confederates' superior strength from deciding the afternoon's fighting. At
2:30 or a little later, Lee launched a new series of attacks, spearheaded by Heth
and later by Pender. This offensive broke the Federal left on McPherson's
Ridge and sent Doubleday's foot soldiers into headlong flight to the ridge that
held the seminary. Then, about an hour after Heth went forward, Rodes overran Doubleday's right and Early smashed all segments of Schurz's line. Within
minutes of the breakthroughs, blue-clad fugitives were streaming through the
streets of Gettysburg. Those not captured by their pursuers rallied on and near
Cemetery Hill, where General Hancock found them upon his arrival.[35]

Thanks to Buford's foresight, the left flank of the new line on Seminary
Ridge was anchored by the men of Gamble and Calef. Since early afternoon,
when they broke their bivouac on the edge of town, many of these troops had
hungered to return to the fight. They got their chance when Pender's division,
advancing past Heth's on its way to Seminary Ridge, neared their line of fire.
The majority of Gamble's men waited, dismounted, behind a tree-shaded stone
wall that fronted the path of Col. Abner Perrin's South Carolina brigade. Farther to the west and south, Beveridge's 8th Illinois had deployed in an orchard
at right angles to another element of Pender's division, the North Carolinian
brigade of Brig. Gen. James H. Lane.

From their respective positions, Buford's men let loose with their carbines, doing damage out of proportion to their relatively small numbers. As
Perrin's southernmost regiments, the 12th and 13th South Carolina, drew near
Seminary Ridge, they came under a shower of carbine balls. "We went to popping at them," wrote a member of Gamble's 8th New York. "They fell like
rain. The ground soon got covered with them. The front column broke and
started to run, but their rear column pressed on."[36]

Turning to confront their tormentors, Perrin's second rank unleashed a
volley that eventually cleared the stone wall. Some troopers did not ride off,

however, until the South Carolinians were within ten paces of their position. Meanwhile, the 400 members of Beveridge's regiment produced even greater carnage when Lane's right flank came within carbine range. Their firepower so disordered Lane's advance that his flank regiments veered south of the Fairfield Road until about three-quarters of a mile below the seminary.

When Lane finally faced about, he spied a mounted reserve waiting in rear of Beveridge's line, pistols and swords in hand. Again, the cavalry's opponents formed hollow squares in anticipation of a saber charge. For several minutes the North Carolinians remained stationary, unable to assist Perrin in clearing Seminary Ridge. Only when Lane organized a flanking column and placed it to threaten Beveridge's position did the colonel pull out and lead his men, by a roundabout route, to Buford's main body.[37]

Even without Lane's full participation, Pender's division and the remainder of Heth's managed to wrest the high ground from their adversaries. Imperiled by the retreat of Schurz's corps through Gettysburg, by 4:30 Doubleday's troops were in full retreat to Cemetery Ridge, a position Buford had sized up before the battle as a last-ditch rallying point. His foresight was rewarded when Hancock and Howard began to build a defensive line along the ridge.[38]

Although the position was naturally strong, the Union leaders needed time to make it unassailable. To buy that time, Buford's nearly exhausted men were pressed into service. Sometime after 5:00 P.M., Doubleday sent a staff officer to Buford's new position at the base of Cemetery Hill. A large portion of the I Corps had yet to reach the ridge, and Pender's troops appeared on the verge of pursuing and attacking them in midflight. Could Buford do something—anything—to foil that pursuit?

The cavalryman met the request with incredulity. Jabbing a finger at Seminary Ridge, he thundered at Doubleday's aide, "What in hell and damnation does he think I can do against those long lines of the enemy?" Then, reining in his temper, Buford wheeled his gray charger about, rode to Gamble's bivouac (most of Devin's men, now grouped east of the town, had yet to rejoin Buford), and led a large part of the 1st Brigade slowly and deliberately toward the high ground to the west. Just beyond rifle range of the enemy position, Buford halted and ordered everyone to draw sabers. The action had the desired effect. Fearing a charge, Confederates at the base of Seminary Ridge quickly assumed defensive positions. According to one account, for the *third* time this day Southern infantry formed hollow squares.[39]

Like Beveridge before him, Buford was merely feinting. As soon as Doubleday's fugitives reached safety, Buford countermarched Gamble's men back to Cemetery Hill. The troopers had displayed just enough might and menace to make Cemetery Ridge secure. Hancock, looking on from the rear, pronounced Buford's maneuver one of the most effective shows of force ever made by the Federal cavalry.

After Buford withdrew, the sun dropped so low that Lee had no time in which to launch a new offensive. By then, too, reinforcements were pouring into Gettysburg; soon after nightfall, Sickles's III Corps and the XII Corps of Maj. Gen. Henry W. Slocum were within supporting distance of the Union line, and Meade had arrived to assume overall command. The rest of the army would be on the field by noon of the second, ensuring that the antagonists would fight the balance of the battle at full strength.[40]

The crisis past, a good day's work behind him, Buford led the men of Gamble and Calef—to whom he eventually added Devin's prodigals—to the far left of the army. They bivouacked for the night just off the Emmitsburg Road, near a peach orchard that became a landmark of the next day's fighting. There Buford made the rounds of his campfires, receiving reports from his subordinates, interrogating prisoners, and congratulating officers and men on the service they had rendered on so many parts of the field.

Each and every encomium was justified. The troopers and horse artillery-men of the 1st Cavalry Division had convincingly demonstrated their tactical versatility, their ability to fight effectively on foot and in the saddle as appropriate, and the staying power that favorable terrain and quality leadership could generate. By stubbornly defending the high ground west and north of Gettysburg, they had held back several times as many foot soldiers, forced them into time-consuming deployments, and when they did advance, slowed and stymied them time after time. In so doing, Buford's men had given their own army time to reach the field. Through the rest of the day, they had covered the army's flanks and rear, facilitated its withdrawal to more defensible ground, and made possible its ability to rally and hold on to the field. Cavalry was not expected to do as much as Buford's men had accomplished on July 1, especially in such rapid succession—that made their success all the sweeter.

The 1st Division had paid for its success with 130 casualties, a relatively high total for horsemen, who rarely dug in and held positions for as long as Buford's men had done throughout the day. Even so, the losses represented less than 5 percent of the effective strength of the command. Thus the men would have been pardoned had they expressed surprise when, sometime before 9:00 A.M. on July 2, they were ordered to pack their gear and prepare to depart the field. Until then, as Lieutenant Calef reported, "every one [had] showed himself ready for a continuation" of the fight.[41]

Buford did not leave because cavalry's job was over on that part of the field. Well before he departed, fighting had resumed, heating up first along the Union right, then shifting toward Buford's sector. Dan Sickles, whose III Corps held the nearest stretch of Cemetery Ridge, lacked intelligence on the Confederate positions across from him on Seminary Ridge, something he believed Buford's men could bring him. Thus Sickles was dismayed when, with the exception of a single squadron of the 9th New York that Buford left behind, Gamble's brigade, between 9:00 and noon, left the field for the rear, Devin's men following two hours later. All headed for Taneytown, and from there for the army's railhead at Westminster. At Westminster, well beyond the range of Confederate guns, Buford's command would rest and refit until the evening of the fourth.[42]

The division's withdrawal was the work of Alfred Pleasonton, who, after accompanying Meade to Gettysburg, sought out Buford and scrutinized his casualty list. Meade agreed with his cavalry commander that the 1st Division deserved a rest and approved its departure from the field. Buford must have agreed, although, in common with his superiors, he could not have named the force that would take his place in a sector where mobile reconnaissance was a necessity. Along with Pleasonton and Meade, Buford ought to have foreseen that his departure would have consequences. In fact, not long after the cavalry moved off, Sickles used its absence as an excuse to move his corps halfway toward the Rebel line. That controversial decision precipitated hours of desperate fighting by other elements of the army to close the gap that Sickles's rashness had created.[43]

Whatever the propriety of his leaving, there is no denying that Buford and his men had earned a rest. On this field they had done everything cavalry was trained and equipped to do in battle, and more. Buford acknowledged the fact in his after-action report, when he noted that on July 1 "a heavy task was before us; we were equal to it, and shall all remember with pride that at Gettysburg we did our country much service."[44]

>––◊>––O––<◊>––<

As if on cue, within two hours of the start of Buford's pullout, David Gregg's troopers neared the battlefield from the southeast. This day the 2nd Division was at two-thirds of its normal strength, Gregg having detached Huey's brigade, as per orders, to guard the supply base at Manchester, Maryland. With the brigades of McIntosh and Irvin Gregg and Randol's battery, Gregg had pushed on from Hanover, alert to indications that Stuart's cavalry had passed through the area the previous day. When signs suggested that Stuart had veered toward York, however, Gregg gave up any hope of overtaking the Confederates and turned westward at McSherrystown, heading toward the distant sound of cannons. In the short term, at least, his division was needed at Gettysburg.

The shelling had grown louder by 10:00 A.M., when Gregg halted his column five miles east of the town. After a few minutes' deliberation, he rode off to obtain orders from army headquarters. In his absence, McIntosh led the shortened division a mile and a half closer to the battlefield. Near the intersection of the road from Hanover and the Low Dutch (or Salem Church) Road, McIntosh halted in response to an order carried by a courier from Pleasonton. At the colonel's signal, both brigades dismounted and fell out, worn-out men sprawling in the fields that fringed the intersection, their horses nibbling on the abundant grass. McIntosh's brigade bivouacked north of the Hanover Road, Gregg's south of it.[45]

Not everyone caught up on sleep. To secure his position, McIntosh sent a few hundred of Gregg's men more than a mile to the west. There they connected with a skirmish line maintained by two XI Corps regiments. As soon as Gregg's men made contact, the infantry pulled back closer to its original position at the base of Cemetery Hill. Its skirmishers were replaced along a strategic stretch of elevated ground, Brinkerhoff's Ridge, by pickets of the 10th New York. McIntosh then advanced the division's artillery along the Hanover Road until within supporting distance of the New Yorkers.[46]

Not only did Randol's battery move up, so did a recent addition to Gregg's command, a section of Company H, 3rd Pennsylvania Heavy Artillery, this day serving as light artillery. A member of the Baltimore defense forces, this two-gun unit, under Capt. William D. Rank, had been cut off from its command by the invasion of Maryland, falling in with the 2nd Cavalry Division as it passed through Carroll County. So, too, had a company of horsemen from the Purnell Legion, another Baltimore-based unit, led by Capt. Robert E. Duvall. While survival instincts had motivated Rank and Duvall to join the Army of the Potomac, Gregg had been glad to add them to his command.[47]

Late that afternoon—soon after McIntosh, at Pleasonton's order, had detached the 4th Pennsylvania from Gregg's brigade to hold the position Buford had vacated on the far left—David Gregg returned from cavalry head-quarters. Having previously lost one regiment, the 1st Massachusetts, to detached duty, he was concerned about the Pennsylvanians' detaching. He believed, correctly, that he would need all the strength he could muster this afternoon. Pleasonton had informed him that his division constituted the rear guard of its army. Thus it must fend off any attempt by Lee or Stuart to penetrate as far as the line on Cemetery Ridge. The danger seemed quite real; soon the New Yorkers on Brinkerhoff's Ridge were trading shots with Rebel infantry massing in the woods about a mile northwest of the cavalry's position. This opposition suggested that a major attack was coming in that sector.

By 6:00 P.M., with darkness fast descending, Gregg discovered that his opponents had been reinforced, as if ready to strike. To preempt the blow, the division commander sent a squadron-size detachment of the 10th New York toward the timber, only to see it halt in front of a line of gray infantry that had left the trees and was advancing toward Gregg's position. The oncomers were members of the 2nd Virginia Infantry, part of the famed "Stonewall Brigade." The regiment formed the left flank of an assault force Ewell was readying against Culp's Hill, a XII Corps position perhaps a mile and a half southwest of Brinkerhoff's Ridge.[48]

Gregg realized he would have to stop the Virginians before they and their comrades could threaten Cemetery Ridge. His first move was to order the gunners under Randol and Rank to shell the infantry into retreat, a result quickly, if temporarily, achieved. Then he sent Lt. Col. Edward S. Jones's 3rd Pennsylvania up the Hanover Road, then northward into Cress's Woods. After leaving the trees, Jones dismounted two squadrons and sent them at the double-quick toward a low stone fence, roughly equidistant between Brinkerhoff's Ridge and Gregg's bivouac. Already the Confederates had begun to advance on the fence from the opposite direction. The Pennsylvanians won the footrace, reaching the fence twenty paces in advance of the Virginians. The winners squeezed off round after round from their Sharps carbines. Gregg's artillery covered the troopers in the rear, as did mounted and dismounted skirmishers of the 1st New Jersey and Duvall's company of Marylanders.[49]

The combined might of carbineers and gunners kept the enemy well back from the fence for the next hour, and longer. During that time, the Virginians made unsuccessful efforts to wrest the position from their adversaries. The frequency of these attempts suggested to Gregg that the Rebels were desperate to gain a lodgment in Meade's rear. In actuality, the infantry hoped to neutralize Gregg's men and then join Ewell's offensive on Culp's Hill. Once passing time killed that prospect, the Virginians switched tactics, hoping to prevent the cavalry from interfering with the offensive. That hope, too, went by the boards. Not only did Gregg pin down the 2nd Virginia, he prevented the entire Stonewall Brigade from participating in Ewell's assault. As it happened, the Confederates failed to seize and hold Culp's Hill by a narrow margin. Their repulse had been a near thing. The loss of a brigade of Virginians that ranked among the best in Lee's army might have made the difference.[50]

After darkness had settled, the 2nd Virginia finally pried the cavalry from its fenceline by overlapping its right flank and striking its rear. This success, however, proved short-lived; reinforcements from the rear regained the position, this time for good. Ewell's assault having spent itself, the 2nd drew off into the shadows from which it had come. By 10:00, Gregg felt sufficiently confident of his staying power to put most of his men to bed; a thin line of pickets held the embattled ridge.

Though the fighting had died out on his front, Gregg suspected his sector would come under a new attack by morning. For this reason, he planned to remain near the strategic road junction throughout the night, ready for action if the enemy disrupted his sleep. Instead, at midnight he received an order to move his command into bivouac along the Baltimore Turnpike. Gregg obeyed, but with severe misgivings. Taking a diagonal road to the southwest, he led his men across White Run to the designated position, which lay near the park of the army's Artillery Reserve. There the division leader bedded down for the rest of the night. Increasingly concerned about the ground he had been forced to vacate, he got precious little sleep.[51]

Chapter Fifteen

Thrust and Parry

At first it appeared that David Gregg's concern for the safety of the army's right rear would go unheeded. Shortly after 6:00 A.M. on July 3, Pleasonton sent him an order to move to the north and west to guard the Baltimore Pike bridge across Rock Creek. In that position, Gregg could support the XII Corps as it held Culp's Hill against renewed Confederate attacks. When Gregg argued against the shift of position, Pleasonton agreed to send a brigade from Kilpatrick's division, which had just reached Gettysburg from the north, to take up the post Gregg had held the previous day.[1]

Gregg, whom Pleasonton assigned to relay the order to Kilpatrick, sent a courier to the latter's last-known position, Two Taverns, five miles down the Baltimore Pike. When the messenger arrived, he found that Kilpatrick, in response to another order from Pleasonton, had mounted up and ridden toward the far left. Farnsworth's brigade had accompanied Kilpatrick; Custer's was preparing to follow. As soon as he learned of Gregg's concern, however, Custer marched his troopers and Pennington's battery to the Hanover and Low Dutch Roads. Apparently he did not inform Kilpatrick of his move—apparently, too, Kilpatrick did not miss him for five hours or more; not until noon did he send back for the Michigan Brigade, which had been detached, he supposed, through "some mistake."[2]

Even when assured that Custer would hold the right rear, Gregg was unwilling that his division abandon that sector a second time. He believed that a single brigade—especially a brigade that had served in the Army of the Potomac for less than a week, whose steadfastness had yet to be proven—was insufficient to hold such an important position. Thus Gregg refused to obey Pleasonton's order to move closer to Culp's Hill. At about 10:00 he placed McIntosh's brigade in bivouac roughly between the Baltimore Pike and the Hanover Road. There it was within supporting distance of Custer's new line, which had been set up inside the northwestern angle of the crossroads.

At this point, McIntosh's command was the only force available to Gregg. Through some harebrained planning, Gregg's cousin's brigade had been

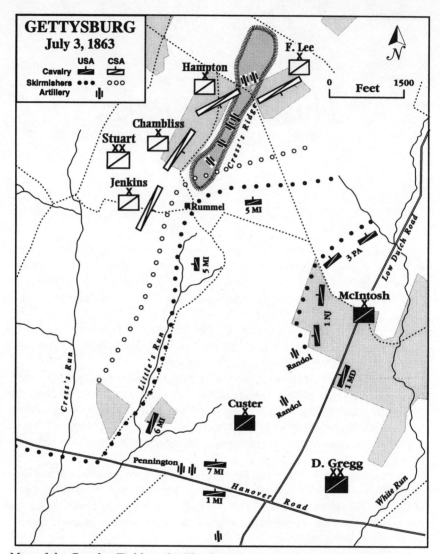

Map of the Cavalry Field on the Third Day of the Battle of Gettysburg.

detached from the division and ordered to proceed up the Taneytown Road to report on Rebel dispositions inside Gettysburg. Fortunately, before Irvin Gregg could take up the risky assignment, the order was countermanded. Sometime after noon, Pleasonton returned the brigade to David Gregg's headquarters.[3]

At this same time, Pleasonton indicated that David Gregg's concern for the right rear had been well founded. Pleasonton's subordinate was informed that pickets of the XI Corps stationed near Cemetery Hill had observed a long column of horsemen trotting out the York Turnpike as though aiming for the

Federal right flank. This force turned out to be Stuart's. It consisted of the brigades of Hampton, Fitz Lee, Chambliss, and Jenkins (led this day by Col. Milton Ferguson), as well as three batteries (five others had been detached from Stuart's command or were temporarily unserviceable due to a lack of ammunition).

The raiding leader had only recently rejoined his army following a critical eight-day absence. After failing to locate Ewell near York, Stuart had moved north to attack Union-held Carlisle, where a courier from Lee had located him. Stuart had reached the battlefield via Hunterstown, five miles northeast of Gettysburg. At Hunterstown late on July 2, his rear echelon, Hampton's brigade, had clashed with a part of Kilpatrick's division as it, too, headed to the field of combat.[4]

When Gregg's advance arrived near Custer's position at the road intersection, Colonel McIntosh had a long confab with the newly minted commander of the 2nd Brigade, 3rd Division, Cavalry Corps. The "Boy General of the Golden Locks," as his half-amused but wholly admiring troopers called him, gave McIntosh details of his most recent action—that sharp little clash with Hampton the previous day.

The fight had shown Custer at his most energetic and daring, but it had brought no accolades to him or his opponent. At midafternoon on the second, Kilpatrick's advance had charged through the streets of Hunterstown, chasing out the tag end of Hampton's brigade, which stretched almost to Gettysburg. An angry Hampton turned his main force about and led it at the gallop toward the town.[5]

Too late, Kilpatrick realized he had provoked a fight before he was able to place artillery in position to support his horsemen. To buy the necessary time, he had Custer deploy sharpshooters along the narrow, fence-lined road to Gettysburg. That done, Custer placed himself at the head of the 6th Michigan and hurled it at Hampton's oncoming column. Custer's combativeness was proverbial—that quality, after all, had won him a star—but he was inexperienced at defensive dispositions. His faulty placement of the sharpshooters resulted in a crossfire that felled several Wolverines including a few comrades at the fenceline. The fire also emptied many saddles in Hampton's lead unit, Cobb's (Georgia) Legion. Custer may also have fallen victim to friendly fire; he found himself soaring through the air when his horse was shot from beneath him. He escaped death or capture only because a young trooper as impetuous as he galloped through a fusillade of musketry to haul the dazed brigadier onto his horse, then carried him to safety.[6]

After the initial charge, which proved inconclusive, Custer and Hampton went on the defensive. Sobered by their flawed tactics (Hampton had erred by sending in the Cobb Legion minus close support), as well as by the heavy losses that had been their penalty, both commanders allowed riflemen and cannoneers to finish the fight. When darkness approached, Custer disengaged and rejoined Kilpatrick, who had guided Farnsworth's brigade into bivouac near Two Taverns.[7]

Despite the 6th Michigan's battering, Custer's brigade remained relatively fresh, almost three-fourths of it having seen little or no action at Hunterstown.

Thus its commander was in a fighting mood when McIntosh met him near the intersection at about 10:30 on the morning of the third. By then, pickets from Custer's 5th and 6th Michigan had been probing Stuart's lines for three hours. Only a few Confederates had shown themselves, most of them from vantage points on and near John Rummel's farm, which sprawled about a mile northwest of the intersection.

Custer's men had come under a brief shelling, though apparently it had not been directed at them. Soon after Stuart reached the Rummel farm, one of his batteries had unlimbered atop Cress's Ridge, a long, steep elevation dotted by groves of trees that ran southwestward from the York Pike, past Rummel's, toward the Hanover Road. From the ridge, a Parrott rifle had fired four rounds from as many directions, perhaps as a signal to Lee that the cavalry was in position to strike Meade's right and rear. Later, when Lee launched an assault against the Union center with 12,500 infantry, including the division of Maj. Gen. George E. Pickett, many Federals suspected that Stuart intended to strike in conjunction with that attack, hoping to catch the Army of the Potomac between pincers.[8]

The activity north and west of his skirmish line told Custer that a fight was shaping up in his front. He told McIntosh as much, pointing out Cress's Ridge as an assembly point for Rebel troopers and remarking, "I think you will find the woods out there . . . full of them." Custer, however, doubted that he would have the chance to find out, for McIntosh informed him that Pleasonton had ordered Gregg to replace Custer's command with his own. Once relieved, the Wolverines were to proceed to the other end of the line, where Kilpatrick and Farnsworth were operating.[9]

Doubtless with some reluctance, Custer made ready to depart. He withdrew all but his forwardmost pickets; he ordered Pennington, who had unlimbered south of the Hanover Road, to prepare to get under way; and he started his advance guard on the journey south. The troopers withdrew to the accompaniment of a furious cannonade. Although it originated three miles away, this din—the product of 150 guns attempting to soften up Cemetery Ridge in prelude to what would become known as Pickett's Charge—was so clearly audible on the cavalry's front that one of Irvin Gregg's troopers hoped never again to hear such a terrible sound.[10]

Unsurprisingly, the barrage sent Stuart into action. Shortly after 1:00, as McIntosh's pickets began to relieve Custer's, the Confederate leader advanced Ferguson's skirmishers from the Rummel farm toward the crossroads. To support them, the battery that had fired the quartet of salvos began to target the nearest Federals. Custer, still on the field, saw that because of the shelling, those pickets closest to the enemy would be unable to disengage. Since the majority of his brigade had not yet left the field, he tabbed it to bolster his flanks, while directing Pennington to return Stuart's fire. Two of Battery M's sections responded with such accuracy that the guns on Cress's Ridge quickly fell silent.[11]

No longer subjected to shot and shell, Custer's pickets could now remount and fall back. To replace them, McIntosh sent most of the 1st New Jersey, under Maj. Hugh H. Janeway, on foot across Little's Run toward the Rummel farm. The rest of the regiment, some of its men mounted, others afoot, took position astride the Low Dutch Road, many of them sheltered by the trees of the Lott Woods. As the Jerseymen advanced, Ferguson's recently reinforced Virginians did the same, meeting them on the opposite side of a long fence.

Before the Federals could secure their position, Ferguson flanked it on the left and threatened its rear. Realizing that he alone was near enough to assist the skirmishers, Custer sent a portion of the 5th Michigan, under Maj. Noah H. Ferry, toward the fence—only to see the reinforcements menaced by Ferguson's ever-growing skirmish line. Under a barrage of carbine and rifle fire, several members of the 5th fell dead or wounded; others broke for the rear. When Ferry attempted to rally them, a rifle ball penetrated his skull.[12]

With Janeway's men and their would-be rescuers trapped at and near the fence, McIntosh sent in the Purnell Troop and two squadrons of the 3rd Pennsylvania. He placed the balance of the 3rd above the Lott Woods, where it joined the 1st New Jersey in giving their embattled comrades a covering fire.

As Duvall and the Pennsylvanians advanced, Ferguson's men, who were running low on ammunition, began to withdraw across the Rummel property. Other elements of the brigade, however, came down from Cress's Ridge to spell them, bolstered by elements of the recently arrived brigades of Chambliss and Hampton. The newcomers tipped the balance to such an extent that the Federal line began to bend backward.[13]

At this critical juncture, General Gregg reached the front. Until now he had remained near his bivouac, perhaps being treated for the intestinal illness he had contracted on the march to Gettysburg. Now recovered, he took charge of the fighting. Accompanying him were two sections of Randol's battery. Unlimbering northwest of the road junction, the four guns began to shell the Rebel buildup while also exchanging rounds with Stuart's batteries. Randol's cannonade, added to the accurate fire of Pennington's battery, proved devastating. Within minutes, Ferguson's men and their supports were withdrawing, and the men of Janeway, Jones, and Duvall were staging a limited pursuit. General Gregg later observed that "never was there more accurate and effective fire delivered by Artillery than by the guns of Randol and Pennington."[14]

The enemy's pullback led to a brief lull in the fighting. Gregg took the opportunity to ask Custer to remain on the field until the fight was decided, and the boy general readily agreed. As couriers rode off to order the Michigan units that had withdrawn to countermarch, the fighting resumed. Major components of Fitz Lee's brigade twice left the upper reaches of Cress's Ridge, heading for the position shared by the 1st New Jersey, 3rd Pennsylvania, and Purnell Legion. The first advance was turned back by Randol and Pennington, but the second, which occurred at about 2:30, shoved back many of the Union skirmishers, themselves now low on cartridges. Custer sent dismounted detachments of the 5th Michigan to drive Lee away, but they could advance no farther than the precarious position occupied by McIntosh's people. Men of the 5th huddled behind a post-and-rail fence parallel to that held by the skirmishers they had sought to relieve. There the Michiganders sought shelter not only from Lee's carbineers, but from the shelling of two recently arrived units of the Stuart Horse Artillery.[15]

Then occurred the first significant mounted action of the day, as Lee's 1st Virginia formed for a charge in front of the trees atop Cress's Ridge. To counter the expected advance, McIntosh had no uncommitted troops, for his remaining regiment, the 1st Maryland, had been moved, without his knowledge, well to the east of the Low Dutch Road. Again Custer came to the rescue, this time at the head of his largest but least experienced regiment, the 7th Michigan. This outfit, led by Col. William D. Mann, had returned to the field after starting off in search of Kilpatrick and Farnsworth.

The 7th's effort was timely and well intentioned, but flawed. Even as the 1st Virginia spurred into a charge, Custer led Mann's troopers toward it, shouting, "Come on, you Wolverines!" The 7th broke into a gallop with the enthusiasm and awkwardness of rookies, rumbling northwestward, dismounted comrades fleeing from its path. At first Custer seemed assured of turning the tide of battle, but when halfway to their objective, many of Mann's troopers slammed into the fence behind which the 5th Michigan had rallied, men and horses going down as though struck by brickbats. Those who regained their footing, as well as comrades who had managed to halt short of the fence, jammed their pistols through the rails and fired at the 1st Virginia, obeying officers' orders to "kill all you can & do your best each for himself!"[16]

A portion of the regiment, Custer still in the lead, evaded the barrier and charged onward, only to become strung out, momentum lost, a few hundred yards short of the target. Seeing no profit in continuing the attack, Custer turned the survivors around and guided them homeward, pursued by portions of the 1st Virginia as well as by two regiments sent down from Cress's Ridge by Wade Hampton. When dismounted members of Chambliss's brigade fired into their flanks, the Michiganders accelerated their retreat, prompting observers, including Gregg and McIntosh, to fear that the day had been lost.[17]

But Custer was not through. As soon as he returned from the failed attack, he rode to the front of the veteran 1st Michigan, which, under Col. Charles H. Town, had formed a column just south of the Hanover Road. The brigadier realized that with this, his last remaining regiment—composed as it was of savvy veterans—he must deliver a charge that would sweep the enemy from the field.

By now it was past 3:00, and Pickett's Charge was at its height, with the outcome of three days of fighting hanging in the balance. Stuart's role in the battle may have been overdue, but he was prepared to make amends by shattering the barrier formed by the Federal cavalry. Even before Custer placed himself at Town's side, Hampton's brigade had emerged from the trees near the Daniel Stallsmith Farm, about half a mile north of the fence that had ambushed the 7th Michigan. The South Carolinian's men were moving forward at a trot, their obvious intent being to break Gregg's and Custer's lines by brute force.[18]

Hampton's advance was a sight to behold. Watching from the Lott Woods, William Miller of the 3rd Pennsylvania noted that the Confederates "marched with well-aligned fronts and steady reins. Their polished saber-blades dazzled in the sun. All eyes turned upon them." They clearly had the attention of the 1st Michigan, which started off with Custer, swords raised, heading for the point of Hampton's column. Once again, dismounted men on both sides scattered for cover as the Wolverines came on, their speed increasing and their momentum growing. As they charged, Irvin Gregg's troopers south of the Hanover Road, along with the gunners of Randol and Pennington, gave them a covering fire. The artillerymen kept up their shelling until the charging troops entered their field of fire, whereupon they fell silent.[19]

Anxious to meet and parry Custer's thrust, Hampton's men moved from the canter to the gallop as they rushed south, keening the Rebel yell. Midway between Cress's Ridge and the Hanover Road, the columns collided with a resounding crunch, men and mounts fusing together in a giant ball. Captain Miller likened the impact to "the falling of timber" and described the collision as "so sudden and violent . . . that many of the horses were turned end over end and crushed their riders beneath them. . . . The clashing of sabers, the firing of pistols, the demands for surrender and cries of the combatants now filled the air."[20]

Hampton's men had prepared themselves for a blow in front, but they had not counted on being struck simultaneously on both flanks. Detachments of the 3rd Pennsylvania and members of McIntosh's headquarters unit, including the brigade commander himself, charged against the Confederate right flank, slicing through it for a considerable distance and inflicting many casualties. Noting these effects, portions of the 5th and 7th Michigan also struck the right side of Hampton's column, staggering it. Meanwhile, a squadron of the 1st New Jersey stationed near the Lott Woods threw itself at the Rebel left. Members of this band penetrated as far as Wade Hampton's position. The Carolina grandee, who had absorbed a saber slash at Hunterstown, received new gashes to his skull that forced him to the rear for medical attention.

Not wanting to miss the climactic action, Captain Miller disregarded orders to remain in position by the Low Dutch Road and led his squadron in on the heels of the Jerseymen. Charging northwestward, his unit cut its way almost to the rear of the Confederate column, killing, wounding, or capturing almost every Rebel that crossed its path. After breaking through to the enemy's rear, Miller looped around to the east and south to sever Hampton's retreat route. This effort proved tough going. Reeling from the numerous blows directed at it from all sides, the Confederates began heading north in such numbers that Miller and his men had to race homeward to avoid annihilation. By a roundabout route, the captain and what remained of his squadron reached the starting point of their wild but highly effective ride. By then Miller had earned a Congressional Medal of Honor—one that took thirty-four years to reach him.[21]

The 1st Michigan and its supports continued to hack away at its opponents until few remained. Within a half hour of the start of Custer's attack, the field was clear of Rebels except for the dead and wounded. Not only had the Yankees held their ground, they had decisively parried Stuart's blow, whether or not it had been delivered in coordination with Pickett's Charge. Casualties had run high on both sides—254 for Custer and Gregg, fifty fewer for Stuart—but though the fight had been close to a tactical draw, the defenders of the Union right and rear had won a strategic victory on July 3. Their success marked the culmination of the steady, albeit not uninterrupted, success the cavalry of the Army of the Potomac had enjoyed since Kelly's Ford.[22]

>-+-+>-+-O-+<+-+-<

Not all of Meade's horsemen on the field could claim results comparable to Gregg's and Custer's. While the fighting raged three miles east of Gettysburg, other mounted units—members of the 1st and 3rd Divisions—saw action both apart from, and in close cooperation with, the main army. For the most part, their efforts fell short of the success that two years of training and field experience ought to have assured them.

Late in the morning, Merritt's brigade of Buford's division marched toward Gettysburg from Emmitsburg, where it had arrived the previous day after leaving Mechanicstown. Merritt's Regulars and lancers carried orders from Pleasonton to strike the Rebel right on Cemetery Ridge in cooperation with an advance toward the same point by Kilpatrick. En route to his objective, however, Merritt took on a second, unauthorized, mission. Apparently on a whim, he detached Major Starr, with eight companies of the 6th United States, and pointed him toward Fairfield, Pennsylvania, about eight miles north of their present position. Starr's target was a Confederate wagon train that a keen-eyed citizen had found bulging with foodstuffs and valuables confiscated from Pennsylvania farms. By depleting his force for this purpose, Merritt was making a grave mistake. No amount of spoils would compensate him for even the temporary loss of so many veteran troops.[23]

Major Starr, still fuming over his regiment's performance at Upperville, headed north well in advance of Merritt's main force until reaching the hamlet of Millerstown. There he divided his force to move against the train from two directions. Starr continued toward Gettysburg with three of his squadrons, while the fourth turned west and headed toward the mountains. Splitting the force was an unwise move; as Starr discovered only minutes later, he could have used every trooper at his disposal.

Closing up on Fairfield, where at least some wagons lingered, Starr's leading squadron, under Lt. Christian Balder, spied the 7th Virginia of Jones's brigade heading toward it from the direction of Gettysburg. No one in Starr's regiment had an inkling that a sizable body of horsemen was operating in this area. In fact, Jones had been here for only a few hours, having recently been recalled to Lee's army in company with Robertson's brigade. Both commands, which Stuart had left behind when starting on his expedition to Pennsylvania, had been expected to guide Lee's steps through Pennsylvania. Instead, through misinformation and a lack of communication, Jones and Robertson had idled among the passes of the Blue Ridge, sixty miles from Lee's side, until the Confederate commander belatedly noticed their absence.[24]

Jones was determined to make amends for the foul-up he had helped create. Without hesitating, he charged Starr's detachment with the 7th Virginia. The Confederates had a large numerical advantage, but Balder's men, with the help of a second Federal squadron, held the Virginians off until Starr could dismount the rest of his men inside an orchard and behind roadside fences. At first the position appeared quite strong; from there the Regulars unleashed volleys that made the 7th Virginia fall back in confusion. When the squadrons Starr had sent west of Millerstown unexpectedly struck the 7th's exposed right flank, the Rebels fled north in full-fledged panic.[25]

A mortified Jones quickly committed his 6th Virginia, the unusually large regiment that had held Stuart's upper flank so steadfastly at Brandy Station. To meet the threat, Starr guided most of his men from behind their cover, remounted them, and led them in a countercharge. This proved to be yet another error; the Regulars bounced off the Virginians, who swarmed over them and cut them to pieces. Those who escaped wounds made ineffectual efforts to flee; Jones's men chased them down, felling most of them with pistols and sabers. In the lopsided melee, Lieutenant Balder was mortally wounded, Starr was severely wounded (he would lose an arm) and captured, and 240 other Federals were rendered *hors de combat*. A handful of survivors rejoined Merritt through desperate riding and circuitous routes; dozens of others trickled back to the regiment in later days.[26]

While Starr's outfit was suffering its most grievous loss of the war, the balance of the Reserve Brigade continued on to Gettysburg, its march slowed by the divisional wagons it continued to escort. By early afternoon, as it neared the Rebel right, Kilpatrick saw it and, as per Pleasonton's orders, added it to his command—just compensation, he must have figured, for the unexplained loss of Custer's Wolverines. He placed the Reserve Brigade about 300 yards to the west of Farnsworth's position, just east of the road it had taken from Emmitsburg.[27]

It is not known how much supervision Kilpatrick exercised over the brigade's subsequent operations, but it is possible he directed it more or less closely, which would answer questions that continue to surround its actions on this field. For over the next two or three hours, Merritt's men operated on foot when terrain and enemy dispositions appeared to call for mounted action. At about the same time, Farnsworth's brigade made a mounted advance over ground so rough and broken that only foot troops could have accomplished anything there. Given Kilpatrick's shaky grasp of tactics and his demonstrated incapacity for directing two or more forces simultaneously, his handiwork was visible on both ends of his sector.

At first Merritt made good use of the terrain he occupied. At about 4:30, following some hours of long-range skirmishing, he advanced the mounted 6th Pennsylvania toward the position held by enemy infantry along Lee's far right. As it cantered forward, nearing a skirmish line maintained by the Georgia brigade of Brig. Gen. George T. Anderson, the regiment was covered in rear by Graham's battery and on the flanks by detachments of every other outfit in the brigade, including what remained of the 6th Regulars. The Pennsylvanians were especially aided by Capt. Julius W. Mason's 5th United States Cavalry, which made a mounted charge that broke through a line of defenders west of the Emmitsburg Road.[28]

As they neared Anderson's skirmish line, the 6th Pennsylvania drove forward-posted adversaries from strategic points including the Kern homestead, a snipers' nest just off the road. Then, suddenly, the Union advance slowed as a large number of foot soldiers came down from Seminary Ridge to oppose them. The ranking defender in the area, Brig. Gen. E. M. Law, commanding the division formerly led by Maj. Gen. John Bell Hood, had given little thought to holding the ground west of the road, having anticipated no trouble in that direction. Now he rushed the bulk of Anderson's brigade to the threatened sector, preventing Merritt from gaining a foothold there.[29]

Merritt responded to the buildup in curious fashion. He dismounted most of the 6th Pennsylvania and sent its men, minus their horse holders, forward afoot. The attackers soon found themselves facing not only additional foot soldiers but, farther to the rear, at least ten cannons. When the cannons opened, the troopers scattered behind trees, ridges, and a stone wall that ran perpendicular to the road. After the war, Capt. Frederick C. Newhall of the 6th Pennsylvania recalled that the opposition "had that confident look of being there to stay, which soldiers appreciate, and either Merritt called a halt, or Law brought him to a stand, just as you may happen to fancy from the report of one or the other."[30]

Despite intermittent shelling, the 6th Pennsylvania maintained its position, threatening the enemy flank. A frustrated Law then led two of Anderson's regiments against the Pennsylvanians' left. The effort was so threatening that many troopers hustled to the rear, along with the majority of their supports. By 5:30, a sudden shower had burst over the battlefield, preventing Law from staging a close pursuit but ensuring Merritt's inability to launch additional advances during the hour or so of daylight that remained.

The outcome should have come as no surprise. As Captain Newhall observed, "A brigade of infantry backed by an army in position will stop, if it wishes to, a brigade of cavalry outside the lines of its own army, devoid of support." Merritt had made things easier for his enemy by dismounting the 6th Pennsylvania, thereby forfeiting the advantage in numbers he had originally enjoyed.[31]

While the Reserve Brigade had given the occupants of the Confederate right cause for concern, its operations had not resulted in troops being withheld from Pickett's Charge, as some Federals later claimed. As an independent operation, Merritt's effort was a failure, one that gained no discernible advantage and cost him some fifty casualties. Yet it is impossible to determine how much of the blame was Merritt's and how much rightfully belonged to Kilpatrick, who claimed to have supervised the Reserve Brigade's operations at long distance.[32]

>-!-◆)-◆-O-◆-!-◄

Despite its failure to seriously threaten the enemy flank, Merritt's involvement in the battle of July 3 had value as a cooperative venture. About a half hour before the Pennsylvanians and Regulars broke contact with Law, Kilpatrick sent Farnsworth's brigade on a desperate errand that effectively closed out the cavalry's participation at Gettysburg. The Reserve Brigade supported this operation by holding the attention of troops that might have confronted Farnsworth. Merritt also added the long-range firepower of Graham's battery to the more immediate support Farnsworth received from Elder's Battery E, 4th United States.[33]

Although Merritt failed to save Farnsworth's attack from failure and loss, the outcome was solely the fault of Farnsworth's superior. This day, as on many past occasions, Judson Kilpatrick acted on his firm belief that a well-led mounted force could operate successfully in any combat environment—"everywhere but at sea," as one of his officers quoted him. He also believed that only an active commander reaped career rewards—recognition, promotion, glory. Prior to 4:00 on July 3, Kilpatrick had been mostly inactive, seeking but failing to find an opportunity to strike decisively at the Confederate right. Still, he was determined to find that opportunity; if he had to, he would manufacture one.[34]

Since late in the morning, Kilpatrick had been maneuvering Farnsworth's brigade toward the nearest Confederates, probing for an opening. At first Farnsworth skirmished with infantry along the rear slope of Round Top, principally the Texas and Arkansas troops of Brig. Gen. Jerome B. Robertson. Just north of this point the previous afternoon, Kilpatrick's comrades in the V and II Corps had won imperishable fame by shoring up the Union left after Sickles's imprudent advance uncovered it. Kilpatrick hoped to emulate their success, but his dreams of glory seemed dashed when, at about 11:00 A.M., two of Law's batteries shelled Farnsworth's approaching brigade, forcing it to take shelter in a patch of woods southwest of Round Top.

To test the strength of the Rebel position, Kilpatrick sent two squadrons of the 1st Vermont, under Capt. Henry C. Parsons, up a country road toward the batteries. After cutting through a cordon of skirmishers, Parsons's men took up a position about 800 feet to the east of the Emmitsburg Road. Kilpatrick hoped that this lodgement would force the enemy's hand; a movement against Parsons might open a gap through which Farnsworth's main body could charge, threatening the entire flank. But when Robertson merely dosed Parsons's men with shot and shell, Kilpatrick had to pull them out of harm's reach.[35]

A disappointed Kill-cavalry soon learned that troopers he had sent west of Round Top toward the position later occupied by Merritt's brigade had found no room to attack in that direction, either. His frustration peaked a few hours later, when Pickett's Charge was blasted to pieces short of its objective, Meade's center. Close to 5:00, a courier from the main army galloped across Kilpatrick's rear, shouting, "We turned the charge, nine acres of prisoners!" Pickett's repulse suggested that the battle was winding down; so did the waning daylight. Kilpatrick's chance to win renown at Gettysburg appeared to have died.[36]

Or had it? Farnsworth's Vermonters had shown themselves to be ready and willing to engage the enemy who remained in position at the base of Round Top—a position that suddenly appeared vulnerable to assault. With the day ending, Law and Robertson would hardly expect a mounted attack. By now, too, Merritt was actively engaged against Law's far flank; his attention thus diverted, the Rebel commander would be unprepared for a strike from the other direction. An hour or so earlier, Farnsworth's 1st West Virginia had made an unsuccessful strike against that sector, but its effort appeared to have failed due to rough terrain and natural and man-made barriers rather than because of enemy resistance. After considering these facts, he ordered Farnsworth to attack the rear of Round Top at the head of one or two regiments. Years later Captain Parsons claimed that the order to attack came not from Kilpatrick but from Meade, who afterward covered up his action, but no evidence sustains the captain's contention.

Farnsworth may have been a callow youth, but he was wise enough to doubt that a second attack over much the same ground as the first would fare any better. Captain Parsons, who overheard Kilpatrick give the brigade commander his orders, wrote a postwar memoir that remains a principal source on the event. In his original account (before it was edited heavily for publication), Parsons recalled that Farnsworth protested the assignment, declaring that a handful of men would accomplish nothing of lasting value while suffering grievous losses. The reply nettled Kilpatrick, who explained that while one regiment should make the principal effort, it would be closely supported by the rest of Farnsworth's brigade: "You have the four best regiments in the army!"[37]

Farnsworth reminded his superior that the division not only lacked Custer's command but also the 18th Pennsylvania, which lay well to the west, forming a junction with Merritt's brigade. Furthermore, the 5th New York "you have sent beyond call; and I have nothing left but the 1st Vermont and the 1st West Virginia, regiments fought half to pieces. They are too good men to kill!"[38]

The implication that Kilpatrick did not know his business rankled Farnsworth's superior, who, within earshot of numerous officers and men, replied that if Farnsworth was "afraid to lead the charge," he would. Stung by the implication of cowardice, the brigade leader demanded its retraction—he would make the attack without further discussion. Apparently, Kilpatrick withdrew the insinuation, whereupon his subordinate rode to the head of Parsons's regiment, drew his saber, and ordered it forward. It was a few minutes after 5:00.[39]

The 1st Vermont moved out in two battalions, one led by Maj. William Wells, which Farnsworth accompanied, the other by Captain Parsons. The remainder of the regiment, under Lt. Col. Addison Preston, initially remained behind, covering the movements of both units, but later joined Farnsworth's column. Preston might have stayed home, for all the good he could do; the addition of his battalion made no difference in the outcome of the charge, which was doomed to bloody defeat.

Farnsworth probably realized as much from the start. The opposition was so formidable that it had turned back not only the 1st West Virginia but a second, limited attack by the 18th Pennsylvania. Since charging horsemen were never a match for well-fortified infantry and artillery, Farnsworth must have known this was one assignment from which he would not return.[40]

While it enjoyed no more success than Farnsworth's column, Parsons's battalion, given its route of advance, encountered fewer Confederates and suffered less heavily. Initially riding in tandem with Farnsworth's and Wells's detachment, Parsons's men rushed north to break through the long, thin skirmish line of Robertson's 1st Texas, which stretched from beyond the Emmitsburg Road to the rear of Round Top. While Farnsworth and Wells quickly curved to the east, however, Parsons kept heading north. He and his unit did not cut eastward until they had turned down the lane leading past the Slyder homestead.

Parsons's battalion had managed to get this far in one piece because it rode so close to the batteries east of the Emmitsburg Road that the guns fired too high, missing their target. But when Parsons veered southeastward from the Slyder property, he came near enough to Round Top to draw the fire of Law's nearest regiment, the 4th Alabama. The Alabamians' first volley was also pitched too high, but a second fusillade caused the troopers to turn south, hurdling a pair of stone walls in a frantic race to the starting point of their journey. En route, Parsons spied Farnsworth and Wells heading north along the base of Round Top, but a plethora of obstacles, both natural and man-made, prevented the captain from aiding his comrades. Parsons's unit continued south down an incline that gave it the momentum it needed to break through the Texan's skirmish line a second time.[41]

Parsons had lost several men during his gyrations behind enemy lines, but these paled in comparison to the casualties suffered by the other column, which now included Preston's battalion. After crossing Parsons's path, Farnsworth, Wells, and the others hurtled toward Round Top as though intent on sweeping Law's well-entrenched infantry from that vital position. But then the defenders, beginning with the 15th Alabama, came down from the high ground and poured volleys into the horsemen as they passed. Because the first infantry to reach the scene had arrived on the run, lacking time to form properly, its fusillade also passed over the Federals' heads. At this point, if not before, Farnsworth should have seen the futility of it all and started for home. Instead, he led his column along the rear of the Confederate position, absorbing successive blasts from the 4th, 44th, 47th, and 48th Alabama.

Not until well above the Slyder homestead did Farnsworth lead his riders westward. Soon he and his men were staring into the muzzles of Confederate cannons and the barrels of rifles wielded by the 9th Georgia. The Georgians had rushed up from west of the Emmitsburg Road, where they had helped Law stymie Merritt. Predictably, they sliced up Farnsworth's column, which, under pressure, broke into three groups, many of its men falling dead or wounded, others being unhorsed, including Farnsworth himself.

While the majority of his detachment turned south and raced for safety, every man for himself, Farnsworth borrowed a trooper's horse and, along with a few followers, turned back toward Round Top. Why he chose to challenge opponents who had already taken a toll of his column is unknown—perhaps he preferred riding a gauntlet of infantry to challenging heavy ordnance. Again he rode past the defenders of Round Top, who by now had come down in force to oppose him. Members of the 15th Alabama were close enough to call on Farnsworth to surrender; when he refused, they shot him off his borrowed horse. Cautiously, the assailants approached the fallen rider, who had been wounded in several places but briefly clung to life. After the war some witnesses claimed the brigadier had shot himself in the head to end his agony, but their accounts are inauthentic or implausible; most historians believe Farnsworth died of his wounds, several of which would have been fatal.[42]

Thus ended an exercise in folly, one that forever stained the record of the man who had ordered it, especially in the eyes of Farnsworth's troopers. The ill-conceived charge had taken almost seventy lives, while leaving dozens of other participants wounded or in enemy hands. At such cost the operation had gained not a particle of tactical or strategic success—nor could it have. The attack had not only been pointless, but to judge from the movements of the riders involved, it was also aimless. The best description of the assault—one that even Judson Kilpatrick might have endorsed—came from one of Farnsworth's opponents, for whom the operation was nothing less than "wholesale slaughter."[43]

Chapter Sixteen

The Race to the Potomac

Farnsworth's charge ended the cavalry's service at Gettysburg on a foul note, but the Union troopers had the satisfaction of knowing they had contributed to their army's overall success in what already appeared a pivotal engagement. Yet the troopers realized that the war was far from over. When, on the evening of the fourth, following an Independence Day free of sustained combat, Lee prepared to leave Gettysburg for home, the cavalry hoped to stop him short of Virginia and complete the destruction of his army.

It was not to be. Instead of keeping his command a large, cohesive force, Pleasonton saw it fragmented and sent in many directions at the same time. The lack of an overall directing hand prevented the horsemen from bringing their full weight to bear at any time against any portion of the Army of Northern Virginia. When the rain-swollen Potomac forced Lee to remain on the Maryland side for several days, giving Meade a chance to cut him off from his home base and defeat him in detail, the cavalry made fitful, uncoordinated efforts to burst Stuart's protective screen and smite the army huddling behind it.[1]

The timing of the cavalry's pursuit depended on the timing of Lee's retreat. By the afternoon of July 4, Lee's hope that Meade would counterattack against Seminary Ridge had died, and he resigned himself to heading south in defeat. At about 4:00 P.M. he started hundreds of ambulances and supply wagons through the mountains west of Gettysburg, then south toward Williamsport, Maryland, where the Potomac might be crossed. Lee would lead his main army, accompanied by a second, smaller supply column, to the same destination via Fairfield Gap in Jack Mountain, a defile that had been held by the troopers of Grumble Jones since their defeat of the 6th United States Cavalry on the third. Elements of Robertson's brigade were within supporting distance of Jones, guarding other passes in the same mountain range.[2]

Lee entrusted the larger train to Brig. Gen. John D. Imboden, whose roving brigade of cavalry, mounted infantry, partisan rangers, and horse artillery had reached Chambersburg on July 1 to serve as the army's rear guard. Lee considered Imboden's mission a critical one: He could not afford to lose the rations and forage the supply vehicles carried, nor the hundreds of wounded men in the ambulances that also made up the train. Therefore, he augmented the escort force with several artillery units, including some of the finest ever to serve in the Army of Northern Virginia, as well as with the brigades of Fitz Lee and Col. Laurence Baker, successor to the wounded Wade Hampton.[3]

Lee's intent to depart Gettysburg did not become clear to his enemy until well after dark. Not until early on the fifth did the Army of the Potomac leave its positions outside Gettysburg and head south in Lee's wake. By then, however, various units of horsemen were hot on the Confederates' trail. Curiously enough, the first command to move out in anticipation of Lee's withdrawal was Judson Kilpatrick's. By 3:00 P.M. on the fourth, thanks to a characteristic burst of hard riding, Kill-cavalry had reached Emmitsburg with the brigades of Custer and Col. Nathaniel P. Richmond, who had replaced the lamented Farnsworth. There the 3rd Division linked with Huey's brigade, which remained afield of David Gregg, and added it to its ranks. At least temporarily, Kilpatrick's was no longer the smallest component of the Cavalry Corps.[4]

At Emmitsburg, Kilpatrick learned that a wagon train, which he supposed to be Lee's main supply column but in fact was the smaller of the two trains, was heading toward Fairfield Gap. Like Merritt on July 3, Kilpatrick set out to capture a prize of war on wheels. Arriving near Fairfield late in the day, he sent Colonel Town and his 1st Michigan against the rear of the train, which was already trundling through the gap. With the bulk of his enlarged command, Kilpatrick headed southwestward to Monterey Pass. If he could gain the far side of Jack Mountain in advance of the train, wagons and ambulances would be his for the taking.

Once inside Fairfield Gap, Town's Wolverines laid waste to a few of the slower vehicles but were repulsed by a sizable body of Jones's troopers before they could inflict critical damage. Meanwhile, Kilpatrick met lighter opposition inside Monterey Gap—at first, only a platoon-size force of Maryland cavalry—but achieved mixed results. Well before it could reach the head of the Rebel column, Kilpatrick's main body was slowed, then virtually halted, by a twenty-man detachment of the 1st Maryland Cavalry Battalion, under Capt. G. M. Emack. Through some error left to guard Monterey Pass by itself, the tiny band should have quickly gone under. Instead, thanks partly to a mountain thunderstorm that prevented their enemy from glimpsing their size, the Marylanders copied Buford's July 1 tactics by fighting, retreating when about to be overwhelmed, redeploying, and fighting some more. For five hours Custer's brigade, leading the Union column, chased Emack's people across the grounds of Monterey Springs, a mineral-bath resort, without quelling their resistance.[5]

About 3:00 A.M. on the fifth Custer finally flanked the Marylanders, forced them to flee, then swarmed over the wagons they had protected for so long. Until portions of Jones's and Robertson's brigades arrived, in response to Emack's call, to chase them off, the Federals had their way with the train. When Kilpatrick drew off some time after sunrise, his men had overturned, torched, or otherwise destroyed dozens of wagons—Union estimates ran as high as 140—while making prisoners of nearly 1,400 wounded Confederates. An unknown number of other wagons fell prey to local citizens, embattled farmer types who emerged from the shadows carrying axes and hatchets. Although as much as half the train survived Kilpatrick's attack, his foray contributed a good start to the pursuit of Lee.[6]

The larger Confederate train, which was escorted by Imboden, for a time also appeared in danger of destruction short of the Potomac. Its initial assailants were members of Gregg's division, although eventually other cavalry units converged against it. Despite the heavy opposition—including John Buford's best efforts to ensure the train's destruction—Imboden did a masterful job of guiding Lee's principal supply column to its assigned destination. In so doing, the Virginia brigadier, who until recently had been involved only peripherally in Lee's invasion, ensured the continued existence of the Army of Northern Virginia.

For reasons that remain obscure today, at the outset of the pursuit, the 2nd Cavalry Division was fragmented and most of it removed from David Gregg's supervision. Already Kilpatrick had appropriated Huey's brigade. Late on the fourth, the men under Irvin Gregg were sent north to Hunterstown, then south and west along the Chambersburg Pike, in pursuit of Imboden. It appears that the division leader accompanied his cousin for only one leg of the journey; thereafter, at least until the twelfth, David Gregg's movements and whereabouts are unknown. Finally, on the fifth, McIntosh's brigade was detached from the division and sent to Emmitsburg. There the colonel learned he had missed Stuart's main body, which had passed through en route to Frederick. The following day McIntosh moved even farther from Gregg's side when he fell in with a division of VI Corps infantry—the advance echelon of Meade's main pursuit force—and was placed under the division's commander, Brig. Gen. Thomas H. Neill.[7]

Irvin Gregg's and McIntosh's contributions to the pursuit of Lee's army varied considerably. Throughout the fifth Gregg's brigade moved west at what one trooper called a "rather tame" pace, causing him and his comrades to wonder if their commander feared to overtake his quarry. Not till midday of the sixth, when near Greenwood, Pennsylvania, did the Federals strike Imboden's caravan, which had turned southward toward Williamsport. A desultory and inconclusive fight broke out between the head of Gregg's column and Imboden's troops, while at nearby Marion a heavier skirmish ensued when Fitz Lee came up to challenge Gregg's main body. The Confederates resisted only until the wagons were beyond enemy reach, whereupon they broke contact and galloped south. The uncombative Gregg let them go. Over the next two days, he compounded his listless performance by making tentative advances toward Boonsboro, Maryland, where Lee's army had begun to congregate. As if a show of force were sufficient to quell the enemy, Gregg lingered near Boonsboro through the remainder of Lee's sojourn north of the Potomac.[8]

McIntosh and Neill made more strenuous efforts to keep the Confederates in Maryland. On the seventh the combined force, which included two batteries, pursued Ewell's corps as it moved through Fairfield Gap toward Waynesboro. Neill's infantry marched too slowly to overtake the Rebel column, and so McIntosh, accompanied by four guns, ranged on ahead. Near Hagerstown, Maryland, within striking distance of the Potomac, the cavalry found itself confronting Ewell's left flank. McIntosh did not hesitate to engage his more heavily armed opponents; in brisk skirmishing, his dismounted troopers pushed the nearest continent of Rebels across Antietam Creek.[9]

Looking on approvingly from the rear was General Neill, one of a limited number of infantry commanders who appreciated the tactical value of cavalry (another was his VI Corps colleague, Brig. Gen. Alfred T. A. Torbert; still another, their common superior, Maj. Gen. John Sedgwick, formerly colonel of the 1st United States Cavalry). Neill noted that McIntosh's movement was made in "gallant style" and concluded that it prevented Ewell from gaining a dangerous foothold on the east side of the stream. In his after-action report, Neill went out of his way to "bear tribute to the gallantry and good judgment" of McIntosh and the skill with which his men fought afoot. Over the next five days, until reunited with David Gregg, McIntosh enhanced his reputation by keeping at bay not only Ewell's people, but also detachments of Stuart's cavalry.[10]

Impressive as McIntosh's services had been, they had not been directed against the cavalry's primary targets, Stuart's main body and Imboden's supply train. Kilpatrick attempted to accomplish the first mission by confronting the Beau Sabreur outside Smithsburg, Maryland, a dozen miles east of Hagerstown, while Buford moved against Imboden at Williamsport. The combined results, however, were meager.

On the afternoon of the fifth Stuart passed through the mountains southeast of Smithsburg in two columns, entering narrow defiles that converged in the direction of Hagerstown. Kilpatrick, fresh from his qualified triumph at Monterey, lay in wait atop nearby hills as if relishing a fight. Admittedly, he had made skillful dispositions. Huey's brigade and Fuller's battery, backed by Custer and Pennington, blocked Chambliss's path, while Richmond's brigade and Elder's battery barred Ferguson's way.[11]

Kilpatrick's advantage of position ought to have decided the outcome of his encounter with Stuart, but it did not. From the moment shooting broke out, Chambliss was in a tight corner. Huey's dismounted skirmishers and their artillery support wrought havoc on the brigade formerly led by Rooney Lee. Appreciating his subordinate's predicament, Stuart ordered Ferguson, who had entered the adjacent pass, to countermarch and join Chambliss in opposing Huey. The movement paid an unexpected dividend. As soon as he saw Ferguson's men turn about, Kilpatrick broke off the fight and decamped for Boonsboro, twenty miles to the south. Later he claimed to have withdrawn because by recalling Ferguson, Stuart also appeared to be pulling out. In his report of the affair, however, Kilpatrick admitted that he, not his opponent, wished to retreat, "to save my prisoners, animals, and wagons."[12]

When he reached Boonsboro, Kilpatrick was not only beyond Stuart's reach, but in a position to aid Buford in attacking Imboden's train. The wagons and ambulances had reached Williamsport at midday on July 5, where the steadily rising Potomac had trapped them. Aware that Lee's main army was still well to the north, and that Fitz Lee and Baker were also a good distance from the river, Imboden dug in to defend the train. He posted his troops across every road into town, paying special attention to those leading northeastward to Hagerstown and southeastward to Boonsboro. His men were augmented by numerous artillery pieces emplaced to sweep the most likely avenues of approach.[13]

Imboden's wealth of firepower served him well when, about 1:30 P.M. on the sixth, Buford approached the river from the direction of Boonsboro. The previous day Buford had joined Kilpatrick for a hasty conference to determine how each might assist the other. It had been decided that Buford would assault Imboden, while Kill-cavalry rode to Hagerstown, Stuart's most recent known whereabouts, renewing battle with the cavalry from whom he had fled at Smithsburg. The Kentuckian must have believed he had drawn the easier assignment: In contrast to Stuart's cavaliers, the western Virginians under Imboden were a ragtag, undisciplined bunch, while their tactical ability, to say nothing of their steadfastness, was a matter of doubt.

For this reason, Buford must have been surprised and possibly shocked when Imboden's horsemen and cannoneers put up a stiff fight from behind well-constructed breastworks. The Confederates dosed their enemy with so many carbine, rifle, shotgun, and artillery rounds that Buford found himself unable to threaten Imboden's position, except briefly. When cannons laced his right flank with uncanny accuracy, the division commander pulled back and re-formed. He brought up his own guns, but Calef and his supports drew such a destructive barrage that Battery A proved ineffective throughout the fight.[14]

When sundown approached, all that Buford could show for several hours of fighting was the capture of a handful of wagons that had been left in a vulnerable position on the road to Downsville. Sometime before 4:00, the frustrated brigadier sent a distress call to Boonsboro, where Kilpatrick had been battling Stuart for much of the afternoon with fluctuating results. This outcome should have come as no surprise to Buford. At Smithsburg, Kilpatrick had failed to stand up to two brigades; this day, he was opposed by Jones and Robertson in addition to Chambliss and Ferguson.[15]

Even so, Kilpatrick and his troopers had given a much stronger account of themselves this day, beginning with a headlong charge that had swept Hagerstown clear of Rebels. The attack had been led by an officer who, while not a member of the 3rd Cavalry Division, carried credentials that would have impressed Kill-cavalry: Ulric Dahlgren of the army headquarters staff, a steel-nerved adventurer known and admired throughout the ranks. A member of a prominent military family—son of Adm. John A. B. Dahlgren, inventor of naval ordnance and commander of the North Atlantic Blockading Squadron, stationed off Charleston—the twenty-one-year-old captain had already taken a dramatic part in the Gettysburg Campaign. He had accompanied Buford's column at Brandy Station, had struck Lee's far rear on July 2 while leading a small cavalry force, and two days later had gained command of a 100-man detachment of the 6th Pennsylvania, which he hurled against Imboden's train as it rolled through Pennsylvania, wrecking several wagons.[16]

Today, however, Dahlgren's glory-hunting days appeared to come to an end. Riding at the head of two squadrons of the 18th Pennsylvania assigned him for this purpose, with the bulk of the regiment not far behind, the captain toppled from the saddle, his right leg shattered by a carbine ball. Still, the youngster was not done with the war. He would live to serve alongside Kilpatrick on a mission seven months hence, one fraught with the danger and strategic importance that gave his life meaning.[17]

When Dahlgren fell, the 18th Pennsylvania emulated its behavior at Hanover, careening through the streets of Hagerstown in disorganized flight. The rest of Richmond's brigade, however, came up in time to repulse a counterattack by part of Chambliss's brigade. This thrust cleared the town for some time, but when the balance of Stuart's command came on the scene, with Lee's infantry not far behind, Richmond was abruptly forced out of town.

His retreat may have been precipitated by Kilpatrick's decision to send Custer's brigade, which had been supporting Richmond, to aid Buford at Williamsport. Because Custer responded too late to turn the tide against Imboden, the day ended badly for both Federal divisions, which disengaged from their respective fights and went into bivouac southeast of Hagerstown. Throughout the night, their men relived the day's events and winced at the memory of lost opportunities.[18]

>-+-<>-+-O-+-<>-+-<

Over the next week, the cavalry attempted not only to battle Stuart's riders but also to harass their main army as it moved to the Potomac. Despite engaging both foot soldiers and horsemen several times during that period, often within striking distance of Lee's defenses and trains, the Federals achieved scant success. Not even the arrival of Meade and the infantry, which debouched from the mountains outside Boonsboro on July 9, improved the situation. The foot troops provided little immediate help beyond relaying the recently received news of the fall of Vicksburg, which boosted cavalry's morale. For the past seven weeks, that major Confederate stronghold on the Mississippi River had resisted the efforts of Ulysses Grant to besiege it into submission. The garrison's surrender on Independence Day not only split the Southern nation down the middle but elevated Grant (if his previous victories had not already done so) to the status of national hero.[19]

By the time Meade emerged from the mountains, limited time remained to strike Lee with any hope of crushing him against the Potomac. The Army of Northern Virginia may have been cornered, but only as one corners a wild animal; the Rebels had dug in behind an ever-strengthening line of defense stretching from Williamsport to and beyond Downsville, ten miles to the southeast. The cordon of earthworks, redans, and redoubts enclosed Falling Waters, where a raiding party from the Union garrison at Harpers Ferry had destroyed a pontoon bridge erected by Lee's engineers. By now a new bridge, a makeshift but serviceable affair, was taking shape in approximately the same location. Meanwhile, rafts and ferryboats were crossing the turgid river at regular intervals, depositing soldiers, prisoners, wounded men, and supplies on the Virginia shore. The river having crested, most of Lee's army would be back in its namesake state within a few days. From Washington, President Lincoln and other government officials were urging Meade to act before time ran out.[20]

The cavalry did its best to provide the opportunity to land a decisive blow. Between the seventh and the thirteenth, it clashed daily with Stuart and the growing number of foot soldiers available to support him. Not every day brought success. On the seventh, for instance, fighting raged at Funkstown, southeast of Hagerstown. There what remained of the 6th United States Cavalry chanced to meet the 7th Virginia, the regiment it had dispersed on July 3. The Virginians got their revenge this day, routing the outnumbered Regulars with a saber charge and chasing those they did not disable or capture for up to four miles. Observing the result, Grumble Jones crowed that "the day at Fairfield is nobly and fully avenged."[21]

That same day, Buford tangled with another portion of Stuart's command, plus infantry, which pressed him as he moved from near the river toward Boonsboro via Beaver Creek. Turning about, Buford positioned skirmishers of Devin's brigade to hold off the Rebels with delaying tactics, enabling the balance of the command to cross the creek in safety. The following morning Buford again engaged Stuart, now screening the transfer of Lee's rear echelon from Hagerstown to the Potomac. Through most of the day the 1st Division was kept on the defensive, its lines enfiladed by carbineers and horse artillerymen. Then the unusually timely arrival of Kilpatrick changed the complexion of battle, enabling Buford to force Stuart back to Funkstown. Through hard fighting, the united Federal force held its adversaries at arm's length for the next two days.[22]

On the tenth Buford again engaged a mixed force of horse and foot units, this time along Antietam Creek. By means of what one of his men called "a rapid walk," the division leader shoved his enemy well north of the stream. When infantry resistance stiffened, Buford found himself pushed back in turn. Again comrades came to his aid—this time a division of Sedgwick's VI Corps. Once relieved, Buford fell back to a more defensible position, where he kept his men well in hand, ready for further action. That posture was also assumed by Kilpatrick's command, as well as by the now-intact division of David Gregg.[23]

Prodded by his civilian superiors, Meade finally moved against Lee on the eleventh, hoping to force him to contract his lines. In support of the operation, the cavalry moved out in advance, while also guarding Meade's flanks. Buford struck that part of the enemy position near Bakersville, on the river southeast of Williamsport, while Huey's brigade of Gregg's division, on a reconnaissance in company with a portion of Slocum's XII Corps, opposed Confederates of all arms closer to Williamsport. At the same time, Kilpatrick's division,

Custer's Wolverines in the lead, chased some Rebels out of Funkstown and toward the river. The next day Kilpatrick's men charged into nearby Hagerstown, now empty of Confederates, and pursued stragglers toward Williamsport. Lee's lines had indeed tightened, but they remained intact and formidable.[24]

With the Potomac falling and the new bridge complete, Meade determined to attack all along the line on the morning of the thirteenth. At a council of war that evening, however, he deferred to several subordinates who wished to withhold an assault until headquarters made a thorough examination of the enemy defenses. By the time the reconnaissance had been completed, Lee had begun to cross his main body to the Virginia shore, a portion of it fording at Williamsport, the majority trodding the pontoons at Falling Waters. Meade's last chance for a climactic encounter above the Potomac was guttering out.[25]

Before dawn on the fourteenth the cavalry detected Lee's pullout. As soon as it was light, Kilpatrick began a pursuit from Hagerstown to Falling Waters, Buford from Downsville to the same destination. Cooperation might have ensured the capture or dispersal of the rear guard, under General Pettigrew, that Lee had placed at the bridgehead. En route to the river, Buford informed Kilpatrick that if the 3rd Division held the rear guard's attention at long range, the 1st would interpose between Pettigrew and the bridge, cutting off much of the rear guard, including several cannons. Supposedly, Kilpatrick promised to act according to his colleague's plan.

Instead, when he encountered the advance of Pettigrew's force two miles from Falling Waters, Kilpatrick attacked, shoving its members to the entrenchments at the bridge. At about 7:30 A.M. he approached the bridgehead and, before Buford could arrive from the east, attacked again. Elements of Custer's brigade inflicted casualties, including the mortal wounding of Pettigrew, but lost heavily in return when the occupants of the trenches opened on them with rifles and cannons. Kilpatrick's precipitate advance persuaded the greater part of the rear guard to race for the bridge, which most of them crossed before their pursuers could overtake them. Just as Buford's advance reached the scene, Confederates on the Virginia shore cut the pontoons loose from their moorings, foiling pursuit.[26]

A disappointed and frustrated Buford realized at once what had happened. The race to the Potomac was over, the Army of the Potomac had lost, and the war would go on.

>−+−+>−○−<+−+−<

Lee's escape left the horsemen who had worked hard to keep him in Maryland with mixed emotions. Obviously, they had failed in their task, not from lack of effort but through the absence of an overall strategy and a dearth of coordination among widely dispersed forces. Due as much to those failures as to Stuart's opposition, the Federals had suffered heavily not only in killed and wounded, but also in exhausted men and broken-down mounts. Upon returning to Virginia, Lt. William Rawle Brooke of the 3rd Pennsylvania informed his uncle in Philadelphia that "nearly all the officers are home sick, from the effects of our hard work" above the Potomac.[27]

Yet the troopers had much to show for their exertions and losses. They had helped their army deal Lee his most decisive defeat of the war, while accelerating and harassing his flight from Pennsylvania. The past six weeks had witnessed a remarkable series of triumphs by Meade's troopers; only occasionally had Stuart's men gotten the best of his feisty, tenacious opponents. Clearly, the balance of power had begun to tilt in an unexpected direction.

The Federals felt the change and were proud of it. During the race to the Potomac, one of Custer's troopers informed his family that "our cavalry is doing mighty things whereof we are glad." An officer in this man's regiment bragged in a letter to the editor of his hometown newspaper that "the world has never seen such Cavalry fighting as we have done." Meanwhile, an Ilinoisan under Buford boasted that not even the general himself could stop his troopers "when we once get the Rebbs to running," a feat they had achieved several times during the recent campaigning. Not even in the aftermath of Kelly's Ford had the morale of the Cavalry Corps, Army of the Potomac, risen so high.[28]

A quick resumption of active campaigning dampened the prevailing enthusiasm, but only slightly. The day following Lee's crossing, Meade's army trudged downstream to Harpers Ferry, near which various units crossed into Virginia aboard pontoons. On the seventeenth the cavalry obtained rations and forage from the local garrison, after which they continued downriver to prepared crossing sites. After passing through South Mountain and reaching the village of Berlin, most of Gregg's division crossed the bridge that had been thrown across the river there. On the Virginia shore, the command trotted toward one of its old haunts, Aldie, then on to Manassas Junction, where it resumed guard duty along the Orange & Alexandria Railroad.[29]

Already one-third of Gregg's command had seen action on Virginia soil. On the fifteenth, after crossing the river opposite Harpers Ferry, Irvin Gregg's brigade, theoretically supported by Huey's brigade but in reality left on its own, ranged upriver to Shepherdstown to investigate reports of Rebel cavalry in the area. Gregg found the place held in force, but by hard fighting—something he had avoided for more than a week—he took possession of the town and prepared to hold it.

His arrival drew the attention of J. E. B. Stuart, who had withdrawn his still-potent command to nearby Bunker Hill. Advancing on occupied Shepherdstown early on the sixteenth, Stuart deployed Ferguson's brigade to threaten Gregg's right and hold his attention while Fitz Lee and Chambliss struck him in front. When Ferguson failed to make his appearance on time, Gregg devoted his energy to repulsing the main effort. Although outnumbered, he charged Lee's brigade just as it readied a dismounted attack. Numerous Confederates were swept under by the energetic and unexpected assault, but the next brigade in line, Chambliss's—supported at last by Ferguson, as well as by horse artillery and a small body of infantry—parried the blow and delivered one of its own, propelling Gregg into headlong retreat. After fleeing two miles, the Federal leader halted, placed his men behind a stone fence atop a commanding ridge, and stanched the pursuit.[30]

At dark, with Huey finally on hand to cover his rear, Gregg cleared out. Stuart, still fuming over the day's miscues, let him go. A pursuit was not needed to drive home the point that the Yankees had received an old-fashioned whipping. Reflecting on the strategy that had sent a small force into unknown territory, and on Huey's failure to support it in a pinch, Lieutenant Brooke admitted that "on our part, the whole thing was badly managed."[31]

Gregg's travail notwithstanding, the crossing of the Potomac continued. On the eighteenth Buford's men, marching just behind the army headquarters' train, moved across the river at Berlin. Once on the other shore, the division turned southwestward to Lovettsville, close to the eastern rim of the Blue Ridge. Behind that mountain range, Lee's army was heading south at a rapid pace, planning to cross to the Culpeper Court House vicinity via one or more of the lower gaps. A new race was shaping up; the Rebels might yet be dealt the blow that an indecisive Meade had failed to land on the Maryland shore.[32]

Also heading for the Lovettsville vicinity on the eighteenth was Kilpatrick's division, which bivouacked that evening at Purcellville, fourteen miles from the river. One branch of the army was making good progress south, but Lee's retreat column had gotten such a head start as to be assured of reaching its destination in advance of Meade's infantry. Thus the cavalry must hasten to plug the gaps before the enemy could clear them, then hold on until the main army could join it.[33]

The opportunity to intercept Lee's army gleamed like a beacon in the night, but it faded away thanks to the same lack of coordination that had hamstrung the Federals at Falling Waters. This time the cavalry lacked the cooperation of Meade's infantry advance, the III Army Corps. This command, once Dan Sickles's, had been led since his July 2 wounding by a slow-moving old Regular, Maj. Gen. William H. French, a prewar artilleryman of some note but a mediocre infantry leader. Meade, who lacked an appreciation of French's limitations, had directed him to support the cavalry along the Blue Ridge quickly and precisely. French, however, seemed to have had other priorities, the first being the security of his command.[34]

By the twentieth John Buford, leading the cavalry's advance, had determined that Lee would attempt to cross the mountains via two defiles. That day he dispatched Merritt's brigade to Manassas Gap and sent Gamble's farther south to Chester Gap. The following morning, Merritt seized his pass just ahead of the enemy's arrival there, then pushed through to the valley beyond, capturing more than two dozen Rebels. The troopers were tempted to pursue others who fled from them; instead, as per orders, they fell back to the gorge, which they blocked with the assistance of Graham's battery.[35]

The Reserve Brigade held Manassas Gap throughout the twenty-second against a steadily arriving force of infantry, foiling several attempts to clear the gorge—some via indirect approaches, others by head-on assault. Merritt took a few casualties but gave better than he got. His only problem was the total absence of infantry support. Instead of marching to his side with a sense of urgency, French moved at a glacial pace, fearing that a trap had been laid for him. By July 20 the head of his column was only sixteen miles from the gap, but he failed to reach Merritt until early on the twenty-third.

Considering the stakes involved, French's dawdling bordered on the criminal. Had he appeared a day sooner, he might have cut off at least part of Lee's army; by the twenty-third, however, he was too late to achieve anything of tactical or strategic consequence. Pushing through Manassas Gap, French discovered that Ewell's corps, bringing up Lee's rear, had passed that point on its way toward another outlet farther south. French staged a half-hearted pursuit but failed to overtake his quarry.[36]

If French did little to help Merritt, he did nothing to aid Gamble. Since arriving opposite Chester Gap late on the twenty-first, the commander of Buford's 1st Brigade had been blocked and neutralized by what remained of Pickett's division, backed by a portion of Imboden's brigade and several artillery pieces, all of which occupied the gorge. Gamble drove some of his opponents to the crest of the gap but, because he lacked infantry support, progressed no farther. Late in the day, Pickett and his friends formed as if to counterattack, but failed to move against the outnumbered cavalry. Tomorrow was another matter: An uneasy George Chapman turned in for the night, "not liking our position."[37]

Morning validated the colonel's fears. When the Confederates finally sallied forth, they headed straight for his regiment. Sgt. James A. Bell of the 8th Illinois observed that "skirmishers broke from their cover, supported by two columns of Infantry. They first came on the 3rd Indiana, who held the left of our position. They [Chapman's men] lost quite a number in taken prisoners [and] we were obliged to fall back." In fact, Gamble decided to depart the vicinity with his entire brigade. "Lacking a sufficient force to drive the enemy from the Gap, [and] having no support nearer than 20 miles," he withdrew to Barbee's Crossroads, accompanied by about thirty prisoners and some 1,500 head of horses and cattle that his men had wrested from the despoilers of Pennsylvania.[38]

Thanks largely to French's tardiness, Lee's army was able to clear Chester Gap and other passes farther south. By the twenty-fourth the Confederate vanguard had returned to the country below the Rappahannock, where the invasion of the North had begun. Meade could only follow, massing above the river in and around Warrenton. Reviewing the debacle at Manassas Gap, the army commander criticized French's "very feeble effort" to halt Lee's retreat. Despite his failure, however, French kept his command until another execrable performance four months later finally took it from him.[39]

As for the cavalry, Meade had no complaints about its service at the gaps—by all indications, it had almost single-handedly cut off Lee's retreat, atoning for its failure at Falling Waters. And yet the horsemen's exertions had gone for naught: The Army of Northern Virginia had been permitted to slip the trap and resume fighting on its home ground. Untold numbers of soldiers on both sides would fall during the twenty-one months of life that had been awarded to the Army of Northern Virginia at Manassas Gap.

Chapter Seventeen

Regular Bull Dog Fighting

As Lee reoccupied the Rappahannock line, Meade's cavalry probed his front and flanks. The work mainly devolved upon Buford and Kilpatrick, who ranged well in front of their army. Since portions of Lee's command were in motion, not yet in position below the river, the job tended to be dangerous.

Custer was the first to appreciate the fact. By July 23 his brigade had moved from Ashby's Gap in the Blue Ridge, where it had supported French's tardy foray beyond the mountains, to Amissville, twelve miles north of Culpeper. The young brigadier's eyes lit up when his scouts reported a "considerable force" of Rebel infantry on the road to the courthouse. At once he jabbed southward, striking a detachment of A. P. Hill's corps, capturing a few of its members, and liberating additional spoils from Pennsylvania and Maryland, mainly herds of cattle and sheep.[1]

The next day, in response to Pleasonton's unnecessary order that he keep in contact with Hill, Custer trotted southwestward to Newby's Cross Roads. There his advance encountered Hill's rear guard, whose men appeared to be spoiling for a fight. Knowing no other course, Custer attacked with the 5th and 6th Michigan, stunning the enemy and for a time placing it on the defensive. When Hill recovered his composure and lashed out at his opponents, he was at first kept back from Custer's position by repeating-carbine fire and the accurate shelling of Pennington's battery. After failing to land a direct blow, the Rebel commander shifted about and extended his lines until able to press the 5th and 6th Michigan from three directions at once. The embattled regiments held on against mounting pressure until they could disengage, slipping away just before they were surrounded. After some long-range skirmishing, Custer rode off to rejoin Kilpatrick. As the boy general later observed, the "great courage [displayed] by both officers and men" had staved off disaster. So had the firepower of the brigade's Spencer rifles (the carbine version of which was just now coming into the army). That formidable combination had enabled the Wolverine Brigade to survive Custer's First Stand.[2]

As the Michiganders fell back, other horsemen advanced on Culpeper to scrutinize Lee's latest dispositions. John Buford did so under circumstances made difficult by his comrades in the infantry and the support arms. On the twenty-seventh Pleasonton ordered most of the 1st Division across the river via a pontoon bridge that, as it turned out, took days to erect. The delay so rankled Buford that he complained of it to cavalry headquarters. Pleasonton sympathized but told him to ford the river instead.[3]

A disgusted Buford did so on the thirty-first. His black mood did not pass until he reached the south bank, where the next day he drove two of Stuart's brigades to within a mile and a half of Culpeper. At that point his command was brought up short by the approach of 5,000 infantrymen and several batteries. Soon Buford's flanks came under much the same threat Custer had faced at Newby's Cross Roads. With greater ease than his colleague, Buford withdrew to safe and familiar ground at Brandy Station, within supporting range of Maj. Gen. John Newton's I Corps. By then, however, the 1st Division was smarting from wounds it had received outside Culpeper. Most of its members, Buford included, were also bone weary.[4]

His fatigue, his division's losses, and its precipitate retreat, combined with the lack of assistance he had experienced on the thirtieth, depressed Buford. His frame of mind did not improve when, a few days later, he read newspaper accounts of the fighting at Culpeper that credited Newton with saving Buford from total destruction. By now the Kentuckian doubted he could count on the infantry for basic support, let alone to rescue him in a crisis.

His less-than-cordial relations with foot soldiers resurfaced on August 3, when General Slocum appropriated Devin's brigade—without Buford's knowledge, to say nothing of his approval—to cover a movement along the Rappahannock by the XII Corps. Slocum's meddling left Buford, as he informed Pleasonton, "disgusted and worn out. . . . There is so much apathy and so little disposition to fight and co-operate that I wish to be relieved from the Army of the Potomac." A horrified Pleasonton rejected the petition. Buford accepted the ruling with good grace, satisfied that he had publicized an issue that deserved the attention of the high command.[5]

Possibly Buford's anger hearkened back to the pursuit through Maryland, where poor tactics and vacillation by the main army had served to cancel out the gains his division had made on July 1. Whatever their origin, Buford's dissatisfaction and dismay were justified. Unless the various combat arms cooperated with each other precisely and thoroughly, the fruits of Gettysburg would be wasted, and Lee's army would remain intact indefinitely.

➤━◆➤━○━◆━┥━◄

August saw few changes in the opposing armies' positions, as though the war had suddenly reached a stalemate. Through most of the month, the armies glowered at each other across the Rappahannock, maneuvering to little effect. Even the cavalry, which had become used to a daily diet of skirmishing, saw

only intermittent action. Among other factors, the late-summer weather discouraged strenuous activity. On the tenth Colonel Chapman described the
afternoon as "oppressingly hot." Temperatures remained high even after the
sun went down; by month's end, a growing number of troopers were sleeping in
the nude.[6]

The relative inactivity permitted each of Pleasonton's divisions to refit
behind the lines and, in the case of one brigade, far to the rear. Pleasonton regularly inspected the weapons and equipment of his 12,945 officers and men,
and he worked hard to rectify deficiencies. Combat-scarred horse batteries
were also overhauled; in mid-August John Tidball's brigade was exchanged
for fresher units formerly part of the Artillery Reserve. A corps-wide shortage
of horses, which predated Gettysburg, was remedied at this time by a wholesale remounting. None of these solutions, however, succeeded in revitalizing a
few badly deteriorated units, including the Reserve Brigade, which had not
undergone a large-scale refit for two years. As a result, on August 15 Merritt's
Regulars and Pennsylvanians were ordered to Washington, where they were
recruited back to fighting strength through the issuance of everything a
mounted brigade wore and used.[7]

Merritt's refit was conducted under the supervision of a newly created
branch of the War Department that had been months in the planning. This was
the Cavalry Bureau, the only government organization empowered to care for
a particular arm of the service. From his headquarters in the Chain Building on
H Street in Washington, the bureau's first chief, George Stoneman (at last free
of his health problems, at least temporarily), oversaw a vast bureaucracy dedicated to the mounting, equipping, arming, and promotion of cavalrymen
throughout the Union. The bureau's most visible mission was to inspect, purchase, corral, train, and distribute to the field mature, able-bodied mounts, broken for field service. Its principal depot was at Giesboro Point, a commodious
plantation along the south bank of the Anacostia River near its confluence with
the Potomac. The eighteenth-century estate had been converted to accommodate 625 acres of corrals, stables, blacksmith's shops, and veterinary facilities,
staffed by 1,500 full-time employees.[8]

The depot, which the government leased for $6,000 per year, accommo-
dated upward of 30,000 horses and provided hospital space for 2,650. The preeminent supplier of horseflesh to the Army of the Potomac, Giesboro Point
was a self-contained community: It grew its own vegetables, slaughtered its
own beef, and milled its own wheat, while loading and unloading boatloads of
animals at its extensive wharfage on the Anacostia. Giesboro also boasted the
means to sustain, at any one time, hundreds of troopers sent to "Camp Stoneman," the dismounted rendezvous, in search of remounts.[9]

In addition to Giesboro Point, the Cavalry Bureau operated remount
depots at St. Louis; Nashville; Harrisburg, Pennsylvania; Wilmington,
Delaware; and Greensville, in occupied Louisiana. In addition to Washington
and St. Louis, agents of the bureau maintained inspection facilities at

Pittsburgh; Buffalo, Syracuse, Albany, and Rochester, New York; Boston; Chicago; Detroit; Indianapolis; Columbus, Ohio; Madison, Wisconsin; Augusta, Maine; and Clarksburg, in the new state of West Virginia. These resources enabled the bureau, by the fall of 1863, to assemble and distribute more than 37,500 horses, 80 percent of them purchased through contract at the prevailing price of up to $145 per head, the remainder bought at more fluctuating prices on the open market. Horses purchased in 1864–65 dwarfed these figures, making the Cavalry Bureau the most powerful War Department entity to emerge during the war. The bureau flourished despite the administrative failings of Stoneman and his successor, Brig. Gen. Kenner Garrard. Only under Garrard's replacement, the able and no-nonsense Brig. Gen. James H. Wilson, who took over in January 1864, did the bureau become a monument to efficiency as well as a major source of support to Union troopers throughout the war zone.[10]

>-◄►-○-◄►-I-◄

Toward the close of August, sustained action returned to the Rappahannock River basin, where both armies had lain quiescent for nearly a month. By the twentieth Pleasonton was warning his subordinates of a rumored advance by a large number of Confederates supposedly intent on smashing Kilpatrick's right flank, outside Warrenton. Although Kill-cavalry's pickets redoubled their vigilance, the fact that only small bands of cavalry appeared north of the river eased everyone's mind.[11]

While Kilpatrick kept his eyes peeled for Stuart's cavalry and their infantry comrades, elements of his division clashed with the partisan rangers of John Mosby, who raided almost daily in Meade's rear. Two expeditions out of Warrenton, both made up of Custer's men, scoured the haunts of the Gray Ghost well to the north and east of the river. Each mission fell short of the general's expectations—Custer believed that if Mosby was flushed out of his hiding places in the Loudoun Valley, he could be annihilated. Even so, one operation, assigned to Mann's 7th Michigan and which scoured the Gum Springs-Broad Run vicinity, resulted in the seizure of a dozen rangers, eighty horses, and much equipage. Though rather meager, the captures dwarfed those of forces that, in previous months, had gone in search of the elusive Mosby and returned empty-handed.[12]

By month's end Kilpatrick grew weary of chasing Stuart and Mosby and turned his attention to fighting—of all things—warships. The previous winter, under orders from his superiors, he had scuttled four captured gunboats near Port Conway on the Rappahannock below Fredericksburg. In later months, resourceful Confederates had dredged up two of the vessels and had made them seaworthy. Now they were serving as transports, hauling large quantities of foodstuffs and forage that commissary officers had gathered along the north bank of the river, around Meade's left flank, to Lee's headquarters. On the twenty-seventh Kilpatrick offered to seize and sink the boats a second time; three days later he received permission to do so.[13]

Early on September 1 Kill-cavalry led part of his command, including Pennington's and Elder's batteries, downriver, supported at a distance by Buford's horsemen as well as by a small fleet of gunboats and ironclads in the river. Although it would seem that the size of the expedition would have hampered its ability to surprise the foe, it appears that when Kilpatrick reached his objective the next day, word of his coming had not preceded him. After chasing some cavalry out of King George Court House, north of the river, the brigadier went into position, training his cannons on the river. At 5:40 A.M. on September 2 the guns opened on their target at a range of 700 yards. The transports made the easiest of targets. As one of Buford's men observed, "it was excellent practice. . . . We plunked shot into the old carcasses at our leisure." Riddled with shells, the vessels quickly sank. Another member of Buford's division summed up the operation: "Found it, Captured it, and sent it to the bottom of the river."[14]

The gunboats had furnished a novel diversion, but within days of returning to Warrenton, Kilpatrick was accompanying Buford and Gregg against more conventional targets. The lull in active campaigning was now a memory, thanks largely to a Confederate troop transfer to the western theater. That transfer, and Meade's reaction to it, kept the troopers of both armies on the jump for a month, and longer.

On September 9, implementing a decision reached at a high-level conference at Richmond, Lee detached the corps of James Longstreet—approximately one-third of his army—and placed it aboard trains bound for Georgia. In the northern reaches of that state, Gen. Braxton Bragg's Army of Tennessee was seeking refuge from its opponent, the Army of the Cumberland, commanded by the able but overconfident and incautious Maj. Gen. William S. Rosecrans, who had recently evicted Bragg from the communications center of Chattanooga, then out of Tennessee altogether. To rescue the command that ranked just below Lee's in strategic importance, and to enable it to return to battle against Rosecrans on equal terms, Lee's political and military advisors had directed the detaching of Longstreet's troops.[15]

When, on the eleventh, Meade got wind of Longstreet's departure, he determined to exploit his enemy's weakness. The next day he sent horsemen over the river on reconnaissance, with infantry units right behind. David Gregg, relieved at last of his railroad guard duty, joined Buford in crossing at Rappahannock Station, while Kilpatrick's men splashed across at Kelly's Ford. Once on the far shore, the divisions bivouacked for the night near their crossing sites. When the sun came up on the thirteenth, Gregg and Buford headed cross-country, while Kilpatrick moved slowly down the line of the Orange & Alexandria. From the south bank of the river, Meade's recently appointed aide-de-camp, Lt. Col. Theodore Lyman, observed the cavalry's advance in the early-morning light:

In a few minutes, quite as if by magic, the open country was alive with horsemen; first came columns of skirmishers who immediately deployed and went forward, at a brisk trot, or canter, making a

connected line, as far as the eye could reach, right and left. Then followed the supports, in close order, and with and behind them came the
field batteries, all trooping along as fast as they could scramble. . . . The
whole spectacle was, to a greenhorn, like me, one of the most pic-
turesque possible.[16]

Encountering Stuart's pickets just below the river, all three divisions
pressed forward, driving the enemy through sheer force of numbers to the outskirts of Culpeper Court House. As they came on, Stuart deployed to meet
them north of the town. Farther south, Lee, certain that infantry would soon be
moving in rear of the mounted men, withdrew his foot soldiers and artillerymen below the Rapidan River.[17]

To buy his commander time, Stuart made a strong defense, holding back
the first troops to reach him, Buford's and Gregg's. Captain Newhall of the 3rd
Pennsylvania recalled how the fighting escalated on Gregg's front: "It wasn't
long before we went from skirmishing to Battery firing and then to break neck
charging & regular bull dog fighting." Stuart's defense line was anchored by
his horse artillery, whose constant shelling kept his left flank and center intact,
felling attackers by the droves and at one point nearly decapitating Buford.

At a critical stage in the fight, Kilpatrick made a belated appearance along
the Rebel right, whose attention was directed elsewhere. Sizing up the situation, the bewhiskered Irishman realized he was in position to relieve the pressure on his colleagues. Pointing westward, he ordered a charge by Brig. Gen.
Henry E. Davies, a dapper little New Yorker who had recently succeeded to
command of Farnsworth's brigade—one of the very few officers without prewar military experience to win a star in this army's cavalry.[18]

Davies hoped to prove himself worthy of the appointment. At the head of
the 2nd New York, a regiment in which both Kilpatrick and he had served in
1861, he slammed into Stuart's distracted right, the horsemen of Brig. Gen. L.
L. Lomax. The unexpected blow staggered Lomax, cost him two cannons, and
sent the whole line to wobbling. The embattled flank came completely
unhinged when Custer charged in with a regiment recently added to his command, the 1st Vermont. Having recovered from their bloodletting on July 3, the
Vermonters rode down several Rebels and seized a third artillery piece. To
secure the gun, their general exposed himself to enemy fire so recklessly that
shell fragments gouged his foot and killed his horse.

While Gregg and Buford pressed the Confederate left and center and Kilpatrick the right, other elements of Custer's and Davies's brigades struck
toward Stuart's rear, southeast of Culpeper. Fearing encirclement, the Beau
Sabreur sent his riders galloping south. Below the town, he rallied them
briefly. By now, however, his opponents were closing in on all sides, and
he resumed his retreat, heading for the north bank of the Rapidan. More than
100 of his men failed to accompany him; they had been killed, disabled, or
taken prisoner.[19]

Stuart's adversaries pursued all the way to the river, where, opposite several fords, they encountered Confederates of all arms, in force. The defenders' numbers suggested that, rather than falling back on his capital, as reports had it, Lee was staying put where he was. At length, the troopers disengaged and pulled back out of artillery range. For the next few days they skirmished with the Rebels and scouted along the riverbank. Then they turned back toward the Rappahannock, which the rest of the army had crossed on the sixteenth. Four days later Meade led the main body toward his enemy's new position, cavalry leading the way, guarding the rear, and hovering protectively on the flanks.[20]

On the twenty-first Pleasonton directed the 2nd Division under Gregg to cover the army's front by itself. Gregg complied, stretching his line to fill vacant spaces; as he did, the men of Buford and Kilpatrick, Buford in overall command, headed west to study the location and composition of Lee's left flank, near Liberty Mills. To get there, they forded Robertson's River and proceeded to Madison Court House. Near that point they split up, Buford taking an easterly route toward Gordonsville, Kilpatrick moving south on the direct road to Liberty Mills.[21]

As Buford rode east, Stuart's main body came up to challenge him. The two forces squared off in dismounted fighting, a tactic at which the more experienced Federals had an advantage. As the fight continued, Stuart's men slowly but surely gave way under the pounding of their enemy's breechloaders. Suddenly, the sounds of fighting erupted in the Confederate rear. Kilpatrick, pursuing his route to Liberty Mills, had come in on Stuart's rear at an opportune moment.

In contrast to the success he had achieved on September 13, Kilpatrick's timely arrival this day brought him grief. Before his division could form line of battle, Stuart pounced on it and pummeled it mercilessly, causing much of Davies's brigade—only days after its triumph at Culpeper—to break for the rear. Custer's brigade, led in the wounded general's absence by Col. George Gray, eventually came up to assist; it thrust the Rebels against Buford, who was pounding away at what was now Stuart's rear. Though still minus the Reserve Brigade, the 1st Division packed a punch. Stuart, who suffered more from Buford's opposition than from Gray's, regrouped and concentrated on shoving the latter aside. Through desperate fighting, he broke free at last, escaping along a road that Gray was late to block.[22]

For his part, Buford was pleased that both Stuart and Kilpatrick had had a bad day. The pair shared qualities he found distasteful, including a flamboyant personality and sometimes outrageous behavior. Buford may have liked Kilpatrick less than he did their common enemy, for he considered the Irishman a braggart and a bully with too little regard for the well-being of his men and their horses. Then, too, while Kilpatrick courted newspaper publicity (he had permanently attached to his headquarters Edward A. Paul of the *New York Times*), Buford detested all reporters, whom he considered gossips and meddlers. Recently, he had taken the unheard-of step of arresting two correspondents who had attached themselves to his command against his wishes.[23]

Given Buford's attitude toward the man, it is not surprising that he gloated over Kilpatrick's thrashing at Liberty Mills. What is surprising is that he publicized his feelings. On October 3, when submitting a return covering his division's activities during the previous month, Buford claimed that on the twenty-first he had arrived just "in time the save the 3d Division of Cavalry from being annihilated."[24]

The remark drew a sharp reprimand from Pleasonton, who criticized it as incorrect as well as "highly improper." The cavalry leader considered such a statement bad for the morale of the corps as a whole. Even so, he shared Buford's opinion that Kilpatrick was less than a model soldier. Only recently, he had blasted Kilpatrick for a lack of military decorum throughout his division, which the cavalry chieftain considered "highly detrimental to good discipline."[25]

Apparently, Kilpatrick failed to clean up his act. Months later Pleasonton decided that "a very great want of discipline" still existed in the 3rd Division, even at Kilpatrick's headquarters, a situation the major general found "reprehensible." Later still, Pleasonton upbraided Kilpatrick for those newspaper connections that Buford abhorred—especially after Mr. Paul published captured enemy correspondence that Pleasonton had neither seen nor authorized for dissemination.[26]

>━┥━◄►━○━◄►┥━◄

While Meade's army lumbered toward the Rapidan, the Northern public paid greater heed to more active operations in Georgia and Tennessee. Ten days after being ordered to Bragg's army, James Longstreet helped the Army of Tennessee overwhelm General Rosecrans at Chickamauga Creek, near Rossville, Georgia. The bloodied, demoralized Federals recrossed the border to seek refuge in Chattanooga. Bragg followed, albeit at a leisurely pace, and lay siege to the city, whose supply lines he severed. Within a week of the defeat, Rosecrans's troops appeared doomed to surrender or starvation.

Who else should go to the rescue but the Union's preeminent general? Before September ended, Grant was en route to Chattanooga in advance of thousands of troops awaiting transportation from Mississippi to Tennessee. Fearing that these would prove insufficient for the job at hand, the War Department emulated the Richmond authorities by sending thousands of soldiers from Virginia to the West. Between September 25 and October 2 Meade was stripped of the XI and XII Corps, dispatched to Chattanooga under overall command of the once-disgraced, since-rehabilitated Joseph Hooker.[27]

Like Lee's troop movement, the transfer of Grant's and Hooker's soldiers exerted a powerful impact on the war in the West. It formed the basis of Grant's latest and most dramatic triumph of arms. The Illinois general used the reinforcements from Mississippi and Virginia to lift Bragg's siege and then, in late November, to destroy the Army of Tennessee in battle outside Chattanooga. Having captured or dispersed his third Rebel army of the war, Grant would ride his victory at Chattanooga to the summit of military frame.[28]

Just as Meade had reacted boldly to news of Longstreet's detaching, by October 9 Lee had gotten wind of Meade's depletion and was preparing to take advantage. That morning increased activity below the Rapidan suggested a Confederate movement. Infantry maneuvered in such a way as to threaten a crossing in force, while a part of Hampton's brigade forded Robertson's River, attacking cavalry outposts and driving troopers along Meade's right toward James City. Meade was afraid he knew the reason for this activity, but to be certain, he sent his horsemen to investigate.[29]

On the afternoon of the ninth all three divisions advanced south: Gregg on the right, moving from near Sulphur Springs; Kilpatrick in the center, starting from below Culpeper; and Buford on the left, advancing from the Stevensburg area. In the troopers' rear, the main army poised to advance or withdraw, as appropriate. Alone among the infantry units, the I Corps knew where it was going.

While Kilpatrick and Gregg demonstrated north of the river, drawing enemy fire and counting the heads that rose above Lee's shoreline earthworks, on the morning of the tenth Buford's men approached the Rapidan at Germanna Ford, followed for a time by Newton's foot soldiers, who then moved upriver to Morton's Ford. At about 1:00 P.M. Buford's 1st Brigade—formerly William Gamble's and now, with Gamble on medical reassignment to Washington, led by George Chapman—plunged into the stream and fought its way across against Fitz Lee's skirmishers, who gave the Federals what Buford called "a very warm reception." Once Chapman was over, Devin's brigade crossed. (Merritt's remained at Giesboro Point.) With Devin went the batteries that had replaced Calef's and Graham's: B/L, 2nd United States Artillery, under Lt. Albert O. Vincent, and Lt. Edward B. Williston's Battery D, also of the 2nd Artillery.[30]

As soon as he formed a marching column, Buford pressed on to Morton's Ford, where Newton's infantry was supposed to join him. The only soldiers he found there, however, turned out to be more of Lee's troopers, ensconced behind earthworks. At once Buford suspected that Newton had pulled north in the face of a general advance by Lee. Lodging another black mark against the infantry's name (in fact, Gregg and Kilpatrick had pulled north along with Newton), Buford hunkered down, engaging the Rebels at Morton's, until the next morning. Only then did he receive an overdue message from army headquarters warning him that the enemy was on the move.

Feeling abandoned and ill used, Buford put the full weight of his command into wresting the breastworks at Morton's Ford from their occupants. That done, he crossed Devin and the batteries to the north bank, Chapman covering the rear against new assailants, both cavalry and infantry. When above the river, Buford headed for home—in this case, Stevensburg and points nearby. En route, he picked up followers—Fitz Lee's pesky troopers—but the Federals managed to stay far enough ahead that the Confederates could hardly be called pursuers. Robert E. Lee's main army remained well to the west and south; Buford was beyond its reach as well.[31]

Upon arriving at Stevensburg, where apologetic infantrymen greeted him, Buford met a supply train earmarked for his care; he escorted it to Kelly's

Ford, en route passing the hallowed ground near Brandy Station. Afterward, he waited his turn to cross the river in rear of Meade's foot soldiers. While he queued up, however, he learned that Kilpatrick's division was moving to the Rappahannock from Culpeper, trailed by a force of troopers larger than the one Buford had to contend with, and so he decided to remain on the south bank until the newcomers arrived. Just before nightfall, as Kilpatrick drew near, Fitz Lee abandoned Buford and turned westward against the 3rd Division, striking its right flank, while comrades to the south—the brigades of Hampton and Brig. Gen. Thomas L. Rosser, accompanied by Stuart—dosed the Federals' rear with cartridges and shells.

For the second time in three weeks, Buford was obliged to rescue an associate he neither liked nor admired. At his order, Tom Devin charged Lee, slowly prying him apart from his new target. Meanwhile, Kilpatrick fought in two directions at the same time. Davies took on Rosser and Stuart, while the impatient Custer—just back from convalescent leave—formed an assault column, pointed it northward, and shouted to its members: "Boys of Michigan, there are some people between us and home. I'm going home! Who else goes?"[32]

Right on cue, his brigade band blared out the inspiring strains of "Yankee Doodle," and Custer's troopers broke into wild cheering. At his signal, they surged forward, saber arms raised and adrenaline pumping. It took three or four attempts, the last couple made in darkness, but at last the Wolverines broke through, joining Buford along the south bank. After some further difficulty, both divisions succeeded in fording the river to safety. A dispirited Stuart collected his riders and led them south, aware that an opportunity to crase a large percentage of his enemy had been lost.

The next day Buford was again south of the stream, this time as part of a reconnaissance in force that also included elements of the II, V, and VI Corps. Meade had dispatched them all to gain definite word of Lee's positions and intentions. Pushing ahead of its comrades, the 1st Cavalry Division returned to Brandy Station, where a portion of Rosser's brigade lingered. Heavily outnumbered and susceptible to being flanked and cut off, the Confederates steadily retired. As Buford pursued, Rosser's men were joined near Culpeper by more of Stuart's people, along with five cannons.

Now it was Buford's turn to withdraw; before evening he was back with the infantry near Brandy Station. There he took pains to recover the bodies of the troopers—his and Kilpatrick's—who had fallen the previous day and been left behind when the bluecoats retreated. The division leader was outraged, if not shocked, to find that many of the dead had been stripped not only of weapons and equipment but also of coats, caps, and boots.[33]

The reconnaissance brought Meade the intelligence he was seeking: Lee was making, or about to make, a move toward the right flank of the Army of the Potomac. That operation was, in fact, already under way. Lee had started one of his two remaining corps, Hill's, on a northwestward arc toward Sperryville and Amissville, while Ewell's corps moved directly on Meade via Jefferson and Sulphur Springs. The two forces were to join in their enemy's midst, near Warrenton. The information should have come from General Gregg, whose division had been patrolling along Meade's right. Uncharacteristically, Gregg had permitted Confederate cavalry to thrust his troopers so far from the Rapidan that he could not bring Meade timely word of the Rebels' crossing. The lapse prompted Meade's chief of staff, Maj. Gen. Andrew A. Humphreys, to declare that the cavalry commander ought to be brought up on charges and, if found guilty of gross negligence, to be shot.

Even when made aware of the movement, at first Meade did not know how to react. He considered advancing to battle, but the longer he mulled over his options, the better a retreat sounded. But a retreat where? The best possible position in which to withstand assault, one abounding in long, high ground, lay thirty miles to the north, near the Bull Run battlefields. After further deliberation, Meade decided to head there with everyone in his command.[34]

The army moved out in two columns. Covered by Gregg's division, the I, V, and VI Corps marched up the Orange & Alexandria, while the II and III Corps, preceded by Kilpatrick, trekked east of the rail line, via Auburn and Greenwich. Buford, whose division had seen enervating service during the past two weeks, was chosen for a chore that Meade appears to have considered easy, but that Buford regarded as a vexing burden: escorting the army's long, slow supply train across Bull Run to Centreville.

With a sigh of resignation, Buford met the train at Catlett's Station on the fourteenth and led it north. Once again he had been prescient: The pace of the train was slow enough, the roads were rough enough, and enough wagons broke down and went astray that even Job would have bellowed with frustration. As it happened, Buford was soon heaping invective on each mule and teamster that came under his eye.

The trip proved physically as well as mentally exhausting. By the sixteenth, when the train crawled into Centreville, Buford was clearly unwell. Three days later Colonel Lyman found him "cold and tired and wet," though he bore up well: "The General takes his hardships good-naturedly."[35]

Buford was not the only cavalryman having a hard time of it recently. During the withdrawal to Centreville, Gregg's division several times tangled with Rebels intent on halting the army short of a safe haven, inflicting and taking casualties. On at least two occasions, on the fifteenth along the O & A and two days later at Wolf Run Shoals, a Bull Run tributary, the division fended off infantry closing in on Meade's rear. One of Gregg's troopers complained of the frequent and stressful activity, even as he assured his family that although falling back the army was conceding nothing to the enemy: "The Army of the Potomac is still alive and able to walk about right smart."[36]

Lee's pursuit lost much of its momentum on the afternoon of the fourteenth, when A. P. Hill came up to the rail depot of Bristoe Station and found Meade's rear echelon, the II Corps of Maj. Gen. G. K. Warren, dug in behind the railroad embankment and nearby earthworks. Hill made the mistake of challenging the Yankees, and they made him pay, knocking his attack column to bits before it could properly form. By sundown, having taken nearly 2,000 casualties (Warren had suffered fewer than 500), an ashen-faced Hill drew off, and when Warren resumed his journey to Centreville, an equally chastened Lee headed north at a slower, less confident pace. On the seventeenth, after examining the equally well-constructed works Meade's main body had thrown up on the heights of Centreville, Lee gave up his pursuit as a lost cause and returned to the Rappahannock, where he dug in as if intent on staying.[37]

When Lee withdrew, Meade launched a cautious pursuit. As always, the cavalry led the way—not so cautiously. Kilpatrick was especially impetuous, hustling southward with the intention of locating Stuart and repaying him for the drubbing he had administered at Liberty Mills and Brandy Station. Instead, Stuart found Kilpatrick and gave him another licking. At midday on October 19 the 3rd Division, Davies's brigade in front, Custer's behind, advanced south of Gainesville, the Confederate cavalry's most recent port of call.

Unknown to Kilpatrick's point riders, Stuart's men lingered in the vicinity, preparing to welcome them. Kill-cavalry remained ignorant of his enemy's plans until Stuart suddenly interposed between the two widely separated brigades and stunned both with dismounted and mounted attacks. With Davies's right flank caving in under pressure from Fitz Lee, Custer hastened over Broad Run to escape a similar fate, but too slowly to prevent more than fifty officers and men from being cut off and captured.[38]

While Custer broke contact, part of Lee's brigade staged a limited pursuit; the rest moved south to confront Davies, already under siege by Stuart, Hampton, and Rosser near Buckland Mills, on the Warrenton Turnpike. Denied Custer's support, Davies faced a dire situation. By late afternoon, at Kilpatrick's order and after fighting a losing battle on all sides, more than 200 of his men being killed, wounded, or captured, the New Yorker led those who remained in a wild ride through the Southern lines. For the second time in less than a month, Davies's brigade had skedaddled in panic to escape a further beating from Stuart.

Enough riders made it to safety to maintain the brigade as a going concern, but it had been a near thing. As if their flight were not enough of a transgression, the troopers abandoned to the enemy the divisional supply train they had been escorting. By any standard, what Stuart's men called "the Buckland Races" constituted one of the most lopsided defeats ever suffered by a component of the Cavalry Corps, Army of the Potomac. The outcome was wholly attributable to Judson Kilpatrick's penchant for sending his command into territory teeming with enemy troops for the sake of professional advancement—a reprise of Farnsworth's Charge on a larger, more disastrous scale.[39]

>─┼─◆>─○─<◆─┼─<

Buckland Mills was the last major cavalry confrontation until close to the end of the year. By that time the Cavalry Corps had suffered an irrecoverable loss, though not on any battlefield. Two weeks after Colonel Lyman commented on John Buford's physical condition, the general's health began a steady decline. He refused, however, to take medical leave in Washington until mid-November, and by then it was too late. Worn down by weeks of near-constant campaigning, often in wretched weather, Buford was laid low by typhoid fever, a bacterial infection he may have contracted by drinking from a contaminated stream. In Washington, he was put to bed at the home of his old commander, George Stoneman. There he went rapidly downhill; by early December he was slipping in and out of consciousness.

Distressed by Buford's illness and wishing to recognize the services he had rendered his country on so many fields, Lincoln sent him a commission as a major general of volunteers. This was an honor Buford had long coveted, but it was also a deathbed promotion. He died on December 16, a soldier to the last, in his delirium calling on subordinates to patrol the roads and corral fugitives from the front. He would be missed.[40]

Chapter Eighteen

War for Extermination

While Buford lay dying, Meade made a final attempt to bring Lee to battle before the weather forced them both into winter quarters. By now, the Army of Northern Virginia had returned to its old lines below the Rapidan. On November 7, just before Buford took sick leave in Washington, Meade had attacked two crossing points on the Rappahannock that Lee had fortified, Rappahannock Bridge and Kelly's Ford. The main effort was made against the burned railroad bridge by the V and VI Corps, both under Sedgwick, while French's III Corps forced a crossing downstream at Kelly's. Although French moved too slowly to accomplish much on his front, Sedgwick's effort upstream resulted in the capture of 1,500 Rebels and every artillery piece that had guarded the bridge. His success forced Lee, who had planned to isolate and attack French, to withdraw in defeat; by the tenth his army was on familiar ground south of the Rapidan.[1]

Cavalry participation in the fighting on November 7 was light. The 3rd Division, led by Custer while Kilpatrick was on leave, skirmished with Hampton's troopers near Grove Church, east of Kelly's Ford. The balance of Pleasonton's corps did not see action until the following day, when some units crossed the Rappahannock and engaged Lee's rear guard. While the horsemen hit hard at their counterparts in gray, Hampton's brigade suffering especially heavily, they were unable to slow, let alone halt, Lee's retreat.[2]

Meade's main force did not head south to confront its foe until the nineteenth. It moved only after its engineers had repaired the O & A—the army's lifeline, much of which the Confederates had destroyed—as far as Brandy Station. By then Meade had formed a plan to cross the Rapidan at three points, stealing a march on Lee, then to curl around the Rebel right, which was anchored on the east side of a Rapidan tributary known as Mine Run.

Meade's idea won quick approval in Washington, where Lincoln, Stanton, and Halleck were anxious to see the Army of the Potomac on the offensive while favorable weather continued. It is doubtful, however, that Meade's veterans looked forward to returning to the treacherous woods south of the

Rapidan. For too many of them, the Wilderness conjured up memories of a disastrous defeat under Hooker. They feared a repeat performance under Fighting Joe's successor.

Meade issued marching orders on the evening of November 23, but heavy rains forced him to postpone his advance until the twenty-sixth. In the meantime, Gregg's division, which had been patrolling the far left at Ely's Ford, clashed on the twenty-fifth with the troopers of Thomas Rosser. News of this action, combined with scouting reports of enemy preparations for a march, persuaded Lee that the Army of the Potomac was about to bestir itself. At first he believed that the Federals intended to break his link to his capital, the Richmond, Fredericksburg & Potomac Railroad. By the twenty-sixth, however, Lee realized that his army was Meade's target.[3]

On that foggy morning—the dawn of America's first Thanksgiving Day— the Army of the Potomac moved out. French's corps crossed the Rapidan at Jacob's Ford, followed by Sedgwick and the VI Corps. Earlier, the II Corps, under Warren, had crossed downstream at Germanna Mills Ford, while the easternmost column—the V Corps, followed by the I Corps—had plunged across at Culpeper Mine Ford. The columns planned to converge in the vicinity of Locust Grove, southwest of the Rebel right.

Meade's plan had promise; it would succeed if carried out speedily enough. It had, however, a major flaw. Instead of putting an aggressive commander at the head of his right wing—that closest to the enemy, charged with making the initial assault—Meade had appointed French, who had been tardy at Kelly's Ford on the seventh just as he had at Manassas Gap the previous July. As his superior should have expected, French moved slowly and erratically again today. For much of the day, in fact, he appeared to be under the influence of alcohol. His deliberate pace not only permitted Warren's corps to forge ahead and stumble into a fight with a Rebel force of unknown size, it also gave Lee the time he needed to shore up his exposed flank. By the time Meade was ready to strike across Mine Run at daylight on the twenty-eighth, the Rebel position had been heavily fortified, its every approach covered by artillery, and extended farther south.[4]

That day saw inconclusive action, but on the twenty-ninth Warren attempted to circumvent the new line and attack from a different direction. Lee, however, shifted position to counter him. Seeing no opportunity for a breakthrough, Warren called off his attack, which had been set for 9:00 A.M. on the thirtieth, and a frustrated Meade was forced to withdraw. He led his cold, mud-covered army north early on the morning of December 1. The following day, it was back in the camps it had vacated five days before. Although a sense of dejection permeated the camps, the rank and file appeared thankful that Warren had spared it from another bloodletting in the Wilderness.[5]

Throughout the abortive campaign, the cavalry had not been used to maximum effect—in fact, only a third of it had seen any action of consequence. While the infantry maneuvered south of the Rapidan, Buford's division, under

Wesley Merritt, guarded its trains near Richardsville and covered its rear between Culpeper and Brandy Station. On December 1 Merritt helped secure Meade's retreat across Germanna Ford and other points. Meanwhile, Kilpatrick's division, still in Custer's hands, feinted as if to cross the river at several places. Despite Custer's energetic efforts, the maneuver failed either to distract Lee from Meade's advance or to hold his army in its original positions.[6]

Only Gregg's division saw action south of the river, and it achieved mixed results. The command had begun the campaign with a false start, crossing the river on the afternoon of the twenty-fourth, then recrossing once the offensive was postponed. On the twenty-sixth Gregg forded the Rapidan a second time, now in company with the main army, whose left flank he protected. The next morning the division took the advance as far as Parker's Store on the Orange Plank Road southeast of Locust Grove. Soon afterward, it ran into Stuart—and trouble.

From Parker's Store, at about 9:30 A.M. on the twenty-seventh, Gregg started west toward New Hope Church, clearing the way for Maj. Gen. George Sykes's V Corps. The three-mile march should have taken little more than an hour, but the resistance that Stuart's people put up so slowed the Federals that the trip lasted almost six hours. The trees were so dense in this area that the commander of Gregg's leading brigade, John P. Taylor, dismounted portions of the 1st Massachusetts and 3rd Pennsylvania and sent them forward afoot. Slowly, gradually, the dragoons drove Stuart's men back.[7]

By 3:00 P.M., still short of New Hope Church, Gregg reported that the cavalry in his front had "disappeared behind a line of infantry." Thereafter, his men faced massed musketry. To his dismounted regiments, Taylor added the 1st Pennsylvania and the 1st New Jersey, advancing both outfits under a barrage from Martin's 6th New York Battery, which had been reconstituted following its decimation at Brandy Station. As Gregg observed, "This strong line of dismounted cavalry rushed upon the enemy, firing volleys from their carbines, and drove the infantry line to the cover of a dense woods and there held it at bay." Thirty-four prisoners fell into the attackers' hands before Sykes arrived to take over the fighting. Once relieved, the cavalry withdrew to Parker's Store.[8]

The 2nd Division saw no further action until the afternoon of the twenty-ninth, when Hampton's cavalry suddenly attacked its bivouac at the store, driving in Taylor's pickets. Surprised while in the act of distributing rations, two of Gregg's regiments broke and rushed north toward Wilderness Tavern, allowing the Rebels to capture and loot their camp. Taylor's retreat was covered by Irvin Gregg's brigade, today commanded by Pennock Huey. Two of Huey's regiments, the 2nd and 16th Pennsylvania, then rushed up to stem the rout with the aid of Battery A, 4th Artillery, Lt. Rufus King, Jr. After repulsing Hampton, the Pennsylvanians reoccupied the camp and recovered all but one of Taylor's baggage wagons. Thereafter, the division served on the fringes of Sykes's advance. On December 1 it covered Meade's rear, in cooperation with Devin's brigade of Merritt's division, as the infantry recrossed the Rapidan in defeat.[9]

Where was Alfred Pleasonton while his cavalry was scouting above the river and fighting below it? He remained on the north bank throughout the campaign, laid low by an attack of neuralgia. From a position far apart from most of his units, he tried, when well enough, to direct their activities through relays of couriers. When not otherwise engaged, he bombarded anyone within earshot with criticism of Meade's logistics. Pleasonton was especially upset that Meade had rejected his advice as to the best route for Warren and Sedgwick to take below the Rapidan. He did not seem to notice that the army maneuvered south of the river well enough without him.

When the campaign ended in failure, Pleasonton considered his criticism valid and redoubled it. For some reason, Meade appears not to have learned of Pleasonton's strictures through the usual channels, but early in the new year the cavalry commander repeated them—along with a scathing critique of Meade's generalship at Gettysburg— before the Joint Committee on the Conduct of the War. The committee's Radical Republican majority hoped to use the criticism to replace conservative Democrat Meade with a commander more in tune with its political philosophy. When he read newspaper accounts of Pleasonton's testimony, the army leader was livid. The result was that Pleasonton's days in the Army of the Potomac were numbered.[10]

>─+─+>─•─O─•─<+─+─<

As December wore on, the soldiers stockaded their tents and built log huts to ward off the winds and snows of what a *New York Times* reporter called a "frightfully cold" month. As they settled into winter quarters, members of all arms of the service tried to forget the miscues and disappointments of the past six months. Since Gettysburg, the army had made mistakes that had cost it one chance after another to end this long and terrible conflict. Yet the troops could not afford to dwell on unpleasant experiences; they had to force themselves to look forward to the opportunities, the possibilities, of the future.[11]

Cavalrymen may have found it easier than their comrades to keep their minds off the past. As always, while the infantry, the artillery, and the support units remained snug in their cabins, leaving them only to answer roll call and walk guard duty, the mounted arm was kept in motion every day, picketing the camps that sprawled between Warrenton and the Rapidan, reconnoitering enemy positions, and crossing the river to take prisoners who could be interrogated for clues to Lee's movements and intentions. The near-constant moving about had predictable results. "We are all starved or sick," wrote William Rawle Brooke on December 4, "and have had a very hard time of it." Two weeks later the recent graduate of the University of Pennsylvania noted in his diary: "Everything muddy and gloomy in camp. The suffering is very great in the regiment, many of the men ill clothed and ill shod, owing to the Parker's Store affair."[12]

The gloom that pervaded the 3rd Pennsylvania increased dramatically when the regiment learned not only of Buford's death, but also of the tragic drowning of its own Walter Newhall. The captain's horse had pulled him under while foundering in the Rappahannock on the first leg of a Christmas furlough that Newhall had planned to spend with his family in Philadelphia. "He was a brave and popular officer," Joseph Galloway commented, "and [his loss] will be much regretted."[13]

The cavalry may have been burdened with guard and scouting duty, but it saw little action in the weeks preceding year's end. Only two missions, both involving units of David Gregg's division, broke the monotony of the winter solstice. On Christmas Day, members of Taylor's brigade rode north, then swept down on the village of Salem, where Mosby and some of his officers were rumored to be enjoying a Christmas "frolic." The mission showed initiative, but Taylor encountered neither the Gray Ghost nor any of his men and returned to base empty-handed.[14]

The other mission, which preceded Taylor's by a few days, achieved greater success. On the twenty-first, having learned that Rosser's cavalry had gone west to bolster Confederate forces in the Shenandoah Valley, Meade countered by having Pleasonton dispatch the 1st Maine and the 2nd, 8th, and 16th Pennsylvania to the vicinity of Luray. The troopers, culled from Irvin Gregg's brigade and in his continued absence led by Col. Charles H. Smith, moved rapidly from Bealton Station to Sperryville, then forced their way through Thornton's Gap in the Blue Ridge. Just inside the valley, they put a band of Confederate horsemen to flight.

From Thornton's Gap, Smith turned south, passing through a gorge in Masanutten Mountain and heading for Luray. Near the town, he attacked the camp of a guerrilla leader nearly as famous as Mosby, Capt. Harry Gilmor. After scattering Gilmor's irregulars and burning their camp, Smith advanced on nearby factories, storehouses, and tanneries that supplied the Confederate forces. The raiders thoroughly destroyed this industrial complex. Smith was about to resume his pursuit of Rosser when he learned that the Texan had left the Valley to rejoin Stuart forty-eight hours earlier. Realizing that any pursuit was futile, the disappointed colonel turned eastward and, by hard riding, reentered his army's lines on Christmas Day.[15]

As the new year dawned, the cavalry, Army of the Potomac (which on paper consisted of 494 officers and 12,889 enlisted men, supported by thirty artillery pieces), continued to patrol the Rapidan, while reconnoitering in various directions. Soon, however, the weather began to limit the range of mounted operations. In the first week of January, a large detachment of Gregg's division marched from Bealton to Warrenton, then scouted westward in the general direction of Smith's expedition. Cold winds and intermittent snow played hob with the mission and ended it prematurely. Captain Randol, who accompanied the expedition at the head of Battery H, 1st Artillery, recalled that "this march . . . was one of the coldest I ever experienced. . . . It seemed impossible for us to keep warm by either walking, riding, or running." Eventually the weather became a greater menace than the Army of Northern Virginia, and long-range scouting missions ceased.[16]

The weather may have played a part in an incident early in January that prompted Pleasonton to rebuke the acting commander of the 1st Cavalry Division for disobedience of orders. That day, Wesley Merritt had summarily suspended Pleasonton's directive that he place 100 of his men on the windswept summit of Cedar Mountain, an observation post on the west side of the O & A south of Culpeper. If Pleasonton suspected that Merritt had acted to protect his men's health, he was no less angry at his subordinate.[17]

This was not the first time he had seen fit to scold Merritt. Despite the young general's reputation as a strict disciplinarian, two months prior Pleasonton had called him on the carpet after "marauding parties" of the Reserve Brigade had burned farms, looted homes, and committed "the most unheard of outrages on women and children." Merritt had taken steps to curb these abuses, allowing no member of the brigade to leave camp unless under specific orders. The depredations suggested that the Regulars who constituted the majority of the command were no longer the highly disciplined professionals they had been at the war's start. Haphazard recruiting was at least partially to blame; over the past two years the Regulars had acquired numerous enlistees who were criminals rather than soldiers.[18]

>-+4>-•-O-+<>-+-<

The weather was not so severe as to prevent soldiers from amusing themselves in winter camp. When snow fell in January and February, officers as well as enlisted men held snowball fights, took toboggan rides, and devised other forms of recreation. A captain in the 1st Massachusetts informed a back-home friend that "the boys here coast down the hills on sleds just as we do in Boston, and they skate too in the old-fashioned way. Some of the officers have been trying to hunt up a sleigh." Recreation did not stop at sundown, when the men retired to their cabins. Messmates in the 3rd Pennsylvania played the flute and violin, others sang, and all shared hot rum punch. "Between it [the liquor] and the music," observed Joseph Galloway, his outfit enjoyed "the jolliest times we ever had in the army."[19]

While some officers partied, others ruminated, theorized, and planned. One of these was Judson Kilpatrick, recently returned to the army. The new year found the commander of the 3rd Cavalry Division in a contemplative mood, for both his life and his career appeared to be at a crossroads. In late November his wife, Alice, had died in childbirth at their home in New Jersey, and in January the infant son she had delivered died as well. Despite his scrawny build and lantern jaw, Kilpatrick had a reputation as a ladies' man. Even so, he and his wife had been close, and the loss of her and their child had staggered and dazed him.[20]

The double tragedy failed to change Kilpatrick in essential ways. He was, as he had always been, highly ambitious. His ambitions ranged beyond the army to a postwar career in politics. He coveted the governorship of his state, a post he would use as a springboard to the White House, and he believed that a dramatically successful career in arms would help him reach his goal. As of January 1864, he lacked a career of that caliber, but as the weeks passed, he perceived a way to gain one. In striving for such a prize, Kilpatrick risked his career and possibly his life. And yet, in a sense, he had nothing more to lose.

In November the War Department had created the Department of Virginia and North Carolina, headquartered at Fort Monroe under Benjamin F. Butler. This military fiefdom in Hampton Roads later spawned a second Union army in Virginia, the Army of the James, which cooperated with the Army of the Potomac during the spring 1864 campaign. Like Kilpatrick, politician-general Butler looked forward to a postwar political career; like Kilpatrick, too, he believed that a triumph of arms would gain it for him.

Early in February the opportunistic Butler placed his commander at York-town, Brig. Gen. Isaac J. Wistar, at the head of a hefty infantry-cavalry force and sent him to attack Richmond, destroying its military facilities and liberating the inmates of Libby and Belle Isle Prisons. To distract Lee's attention from this operation and to prevent him from reinforcing the city, elements of Meade's army, including Kilpatrick's command, staged a series of feints near Morton's Ford on the Rapidan.

In the end, Wistar's mission came to naught, thwarted by the treachery of a deserter who carried word of its coming to the Richmond authorities. Thus forewarned, the local commander unplanked bridges the raiders had to cross and massed troops across their path. When he studied the results of the raid, however, Kilpatrick was impressed less by its failure than by its near-success. He began to believe that a better-organized expedition, one launched in secrecy, could take the lightly defended capital. Even if a raiding force failed to hold Richmond for more than a few hours, its commander would have achieved enough to become a hero throughout the North.[21]

Kilpatrick quietly publicized his plan for a second strike at Richmond. He brought it to the attention of General Meade and was undeterred by the army commander's coolness toward the idea. In time, word of the plan reached Washington. It made its way to the White House, whose occupant was desperately seeking a way to halt the bloodshed in Virginia and elsewhere in the fractured Union. Less than a week after Wistar's failure, Lincoln called Kilpatrick to the capital, and on February 14 the general conferred with him and Secretary Stanton. In laying out his plan before his civilian superiors, which called for a two-pronged advance and simultaneous attacks on Richmond, Kilpatrick may have quoted recent escapees from Libby Prison, which they had described as an absolute hell-hole. In addition to freeing POWs, Kilpatrick promoted his expedition as a vehicle for distributing copies of Lincoln's recently announced offer of conditional amnesty for war-weary Virginians who wished to return to the Union.[22]

A few days after Kilpatrick returned to his snow-covered camps near Stevensburg, he received word that Lincoln and Stanton had persuaded Meade to accept and support the project. A jubilant Kill-cavalry set about to select and staff the expeditionary force. As he did, Pleasonton, who had no great expectations for the mission, devised a diversionary movement west of Kilpatrick's projected route, to be conducted by units of the III and VI Corps as well as by a mounted contingent under Custer.[23]

Even before he chose the units he would lead to Richmond, Kilpatrick took on a new subordinate. Ulric Dahlgren—eagles newly perched on his shoulders, a mustache and goatee framing his thin face—had hobbled back to Virginia after recuperating aboard one of his father's warships from his post-Gettysburg wound. Though he walked with the aid of a wooden leg and a gutta-percha cane, the admiral's son wished to prove to the army he was far from a helpless cripple. To Kilpatrick's chagrin, Dahlgren had learned of the upcoming raid in Washington, a hotbed of military rumor. The venture promised all the adventure the youngster could ever hope for, and he wanted in on it.

Aware that Dahlgren's social credentials would lend the raid extra prestige, Kilpatrick granted his wish. Although the colonel was not his ranking subordinate, Kilpatrick assigned him a major role in the expedition. While Kill-cavalry led the main force—consisting of about 3,500 men and one battery—against Richmond from the north, Dahlgren would command the 400-man contingent that would strike from the south side of the James. The two columns, which would communicate with each other via signal rockets, would launch their attacks at 10:00 A.M. on March 1. After freeing prisoners and destroying factories and foundries, including the Tredegar Iron Works, the principal source of heavy ordnance for the Confederate armies, the columns would depart by the way they had come or would descend the Peninsula to seek safety within Butler's lines.[24]

A week was given over to shaping the plan and forming the raiding force. At an early stage in the preparations, an officer from Kilpatrick's headquarters went to Washington to confer with General Wilson at the Cavalry Bureau and to select a suitable number of horses at Giesboro Point. Meanwhile, Kilpatrick culled out of the cavalry corps the greater part of Davies's brigade, a portion of Custer's, and picked units from the 1st and 2nd Divisions. Dahlgren's force took shape with the selection of detachments from five regiments in Kilpatrick's division.[25]

On the twenty-sixth the leader of the raiding column received confidential orders from Pleasonton's headquarters. As Kilpatrick hoped, they were sketchy and open-ended, giving him *carte blanche* to act as he chose. He was directed to cross the Rapidan the next evening "with the utmost expedition possible on the shortest route past the enemy's right flank to Richmond," there to free Union prisoners. No other objective was mentioned. Dahlgren, meanwhile, was expected "to render valuable assistance from his knowledge of the country and his well-known gallantry, intelligence and energy."[26]

As the raiders poised to break camp, the diversionary movements were put in motion. On the twenty-seventh much of Sedgwick's corps trudged southwestward to Madison Court House, while a division of the III Corps marched in the same general direction, but only as far as James City. The primary diversion was made by Custer, who on the twenty-seventh led 1,500 troopers—members of seven Regular and volunteer outfits assigned him for the mission—in rear of Sedgwick's men, before passing the infantry and proceeding southward. Custer's expedition returned to base on March 2, reporting its failure to achieve its stated objectives, the destruction of a railroad bridge and enemy stores near Charlottesville. Even so, the mission so alarmed J. E. B. Stuart that he sent a brigade to shadow Custer—cavalry that might otherwise have picked up Kilpatrick's and Dahlgren's trail.[27]

The preliminaries having been attended to, Kilpatrick's raid got off to a promising start. Dahlgren led his command out of Stevensburg at 6:00 P.M. on the twenty-eighth; Kilpatrick's column rode forth an hour later. Under cover of darkness, Dahlgren's advance guard slipped across the river downstream from Ely's Ford and captured a picket post before any of its men could sound an alarm. Secrecy having been preserved, Dahlgren crossed and moved southeastward to Spotsylvania Court House, then southwestward to Frederick's Hall Station on the Virginia Central Railroad. When he, too, reached Spotsylvania, Kilpatrick headed south at a characteristically rapid pace to another depot on the Virginia Central, Beaver Dam Station. When the columns hit the rail line, they were eight miles apart. They would remain apart for the next forty hours.[28]

As per Kilpatrick's orders, Dahlgren burned a stretch of track near Frederick's Hall, while destroying support facilities and taking several prisoners. He failed, however, to strike the nearby winter quarters of the artillery of the II Corps, Army of Northern Virginia, which was so lightly guarded that it would have been his for the taking. Nor did the colonel notice a train approaching Frederick's Hall from the west. A more vigilant officer would have captured the train and its few passengers; they included Robert E. Lee.[29]

Dahlgren, fearing to dally along the Virginia Central, pushed on toward the James. Thus far all had gone well for his column, which not only had destroyed track and taken captives, but had also struck a blow against the local economy by luring dozens of slaves away from their masters. Dahlgren's men even found the time to distribute hundreds of leaflets publicizing Lincoln's amnesty policy.

Good times continued on the twenty-ninth, when the column stopped for a rest near Goochland Court House. Learning that Mrs. James Seddon, wife of the Confederate secretary of war, lived nearby, the well-mannered Dahlgren called on the lady to assure her that her property would not be harmed. The impromptu visit turned into a cordial affair. After hostess and guest exchanged pleasantries, Mrs. Seddon confided that thirty years before, the colonel's father had been one of her beaux. In a moment apart from the war, the couple toasted that memory and each other's health from goblets filled with blackberry wine.[30]

Dahlgren was in a bright mood as he led his men out of Goochland Court House, but soon his spirits began to plummet. Reaching the James late that afternoon, he found the rain-swollen river too high to cross. Unless a shallow ford could be found, he would be unable to cooperate with Kilpatrick against

Richmond. In desperation he located a guide, an African-American youth named Martin Robinson, who assured the colonel that he knew where to cross the stream. But when Robinson led Dahlgren to Jude's Ferry, that point was also unfordable. His plans ruined, Dahlgren lost his temper and accused the guide of deliberately leading the command astray. At his intemperate order, troopers laid hands on the youth, while comrades fashioned a noose from a bridle strap. Within minutes, Robinson's lifeless body was dangling from a shoreline tree.[31]

Realizing he could no longer act in accord with the plan of operations, Dahlgren pushed on through the night along the north bank of the James, snow drifting down on him and his men. The snow combined with fog and a lack of prominent observation points to prevent Dahlgren's signal officer from communicating with Kilpatrick's column. The colonel sent couriers to inform Kilpatrick that he would reach Richmond later than expected. The messengers, however, never got through; Confederate pursuers captured them soon after they left Dahlgren's side.

The couriers' loss was one bit of bad news that never came to the colonel's attention, but the next morning, while his column was still several miles from Richmond, he heard the distant sounds of cannon fire, indicating that Kilpatrick had launched his attack. The racket eventually tapered off, suggesting that the raiders had been repulsed—an outcome for which Dahlgren blamed himself and his shattered timetable. With painful clarity, he saw that the expedition had failed; all he could do now was to save his command. After meeting resistance on the outskirts of the capital and suffering several casualties to sharpshooter fire, the heartsick colonel turned his column about and headed northeastward toward the Pamunkey River.[32]

The return march was made miserable by rain, snow, and snipers. The weather not only slowed Dahlgren's retreat, but also caused his column to split in two. Losing contact with the colonel, 300 men under Capt. John F. Mitchell of the 2nd New York struck out in a different direction. Through good luck the band made it to an emergency rendezvous, Tunstall's Station on the Richmond & York River Railroad, where the following day they made contact with Kilpatrick's column.[33]

At the head of some eighty followers, Dahlgren forged on through a raging storm, trailed by a growing force of home guards and veterans of Lee's army on local furlough. Near King and Queen Court House, north of the Pamunkey, several dozen Confederates surrounded what remained of the column in the dark hours of March 2. When the colonel drew his pistol and challenged his adversaries, he was shot dead, along with several of his men. Most of the others were rounded up and started off for Richmond prisons, along with the slaves that had followed them in hopes of being escorted to freedom.[34]

The disaster that befell Dahlgren need not have doomed Kilpatrick's plans—instead, Kilpatrick's vacillation and indecision did. As a result, the main column achieved no more success than had the one surrounded near King and Queen Court House. After leaving Beaver Dam Station on the morning of the twenty-ninth, Kilpatrick's troopers trotted south, their path lit by the glow of depot buildings they had set ablaze. Late that day the column reached Ashland Station on the Richmond, Fredericksburg & Potomac, seventeen miles northwest of the enemy capital. Near that point, Kilpatrick left behind a 450-man detachment in response to erroneous reports of Rebel infantry hovering along his right rear. Even with this detaching, Kilpatrick retained enough troops to mount a successful assault on Richmond. He remained confident he would do this.[35]

But when he neared the city the following morning, Kilpatrick met unexpectedly stiff resistance from the Richmond garrison, which had been augmented by battalions of government workers and home guards—boys too young and men too old for regular service. The defenders had been alerted to the raid the previous day by scouts from Wade Hampton's brigade, a few of whom, disguised as Yankees, had infiltrated Kilpatrick's column. When isolated opposition expanded into a full-scale defense, including salvos of artillery, the Federals began to take casualties. A shaken Kilpatrick realized that with all the noise, he would be unable to hear Dahlgren's attack from the south.[36]

Unable to use his own artillery for lack of good cover, and finding a mounted assault impossible on the slick, snowy ground in front of the nearest works, Kilpatrick attempted a dismounted attack. The tactics failed when his carbineers took fire from so many directions that they could not mount a sustained offensive. When his ranking subordinate, General Davies, suggested a concerted strike at a key sector of the works, Kilpatrick at first agreed to it, but then called it off at the last minute. For a time, the fighting continued along the northern approaches of the city, raiders toppling from their saddles dead or wounded, Kilpatrick unwilling to attack or retreat.

He was finally moved to act when captured defenders reported Lee's army filing into the city's defenses, relieving the citizen-soldiers. The reports were fabrications, but they sounded all too accurate to the raiding leader. His resolve shaken, his confidence in tatters, Kilpatrick ordered everyone to disengage and pass northward around the capital. The movement, made over the protests of some of his subordinates, led the raiders to Mechanicsville, a battlefield of the Peninsula Campaign. There the column was restored to its original size upon the arrival of the 450 men left to counter phantom opponents near Ashland.[37]

In the hastily prepared bivouac at Mechanicsville, the same officers who had protested the retreat from Richmond clamored for a second assault on a city that remained within striking distance. Their argument carried weight, for although the gravity of their situation had served to magnify the enemy's numbers, the raiders had been repulsed by fewer than 500 defenders, most of them amateurs at warfare, supported by a few cannons. Prone to second-guessing himself, Kilpatrick finally acceded to his subordinates' wishes. About midnight on March 1–2, he formed two assault forces, each 500 strong, and ordered them to return to the defenses of Richmond. With the balance of the command, Kilpatrick would remain at Mechanicsville, guarding the attackers' rear. His officers might be anxious to see action, but Kill-cavalry had exposed himself to enemy fire long enough.

As the attack parties prepared to move out, pickets who had been placed along the road to Hanover Court House came galloping through Kilpatrick's bivouac, pursued by yelling, shooting horsemen. Kilpatrick's camp became a scene of bedlam as Hampton's troopers charged through it from several directions, pistols flaming against the night sky. Kilpatrick tried to form a defense, but when hidden batteries lobbed shells his way, he lost his last vestige of nerve and called retreat. In the darkness, the general was indistinguishable to most of his men, but a member of the 17th Pennsylvania heard him shout, "Forward." The man asked himself, "But just which way was the query, as it was utterly impossible to distinguish roads, points of compass or anything else." Only by following the pounding hooves of comrades' horses was he able to accompany Kilpatrick out the road to Old Church and safety.[38]

By the time the raiders had cleared the scene of Hampton's attack, it was close to daylight. Confederate riders continued to pursue, but by 8:00 A.M. the Federals had reached defensible ground around Old Church, where Hampton could not harm them. Now, however, they were miles from their objective, and the countryside was swarming with defenders of the sort who had ambushed Dahlgren. Kilpatrick, fearful that the whole of Stuart's cavalry would soon be on his heels, saw no alternative to joining Butler on the Peninsula. He could not know that the Rebels who had routed him at Mechanicsville had been so few that only under cover of night could they have hoped to scare their opponents away. And those troopers were the only element of Lee's army within fifty miles of Kilpatrick's column.

Kilpatrick remained near Old Church until early afternoon, hoping for word of Dahlgren's whereabouts. Captain Mitchell's prodigal detachment could not fill in the gaps, for when it had lost touch with Dahlgren, the colonel was hours away from his ultimate destination. At length, a frustrated and dejected Kilpatrick took up the march to Yorktown, where he had found safe haven, under happier circumstances, at the conclusion of Stoneman's Raid. This day he made the journey minus numerous dead or captured men and broken-down horses. All told, the raiding columns had suffered more than 300 casualties, while losing nearly 600 animals. Hundreds of other mounts that completed the journey had been ridden so hard they would be of no further service to the Cavalry Corps, Army of the Potomac.

All that Judson Kilpatrick had to show for these losses was the destruction of a few miles of railroad track and some depot facilities. Dahlgren had accomplished a little more, not only wrecking trackage, but also demolishing canal boats and granaries along the banks of the James. Both columns had also papered courthouses, country stores, and homes with copies of a presidential proclamation that would lure few if any Virginians into the Union fold.[39]

Only after he entered Butler's lines did rumors of Dahlgren's demise reach Kilpatrick's ear. Several more days passed before definitive word of the colonel's fate reached Yorktown. At that time, Kilpatrick discovered that though his raid may have ended days before, its aftereffects had only begun to be felt.

Reports out of Richmond, which in less than a week's time were circulating throughout the country, portrayed the raid as an exercise in terror tactics. Minutes after Dahlgren had been felled by his assailants, a home guardsman had found on the dead man's body a packet of papers that included the text of an order, thought to have been composed by Dahlgren himself. The handwritten document imputed more than military objectives to the mission. Apparently intended for dissemination among the officers and men of the expeditionary force, the order announced that "we will cross the James River into Richmond, destroying the bridges after us and exhorting the released prisoners to destroy and burn the hateful city, and do not allow the Rebel leader Davis and his traitorous crew to escape." Another passage left no doubt as to the meaning of the foregoing: "Jeff. Davis and Government must be killed on the spot."[40]

The incriminating papers were turned over to the Confederate government for study, and excerpts were leaked to local newspapers, which gave the story wide coverage. Reactions ran along predictable lines. The *Richmond Examiner,* among other journals, called for retaliation against those who had turned the conflict into "a war for extermination." High officials added their voices to the clamor. The Confederate chief of ordnance, Josiah Gorgas, suggested hanging every captured raider. Even Secretary of War Seddon, whose wife had entertained young Dahlgren in her parlor, urged that at least some of the captives be executed. Meanwhile, Confederate diplomats circulated copies of the so-called Dahlgren Papers abroad in an eleventh-hour attempt to gain support in England and France.[41]

Only when more reasonable officials, including Jefferson Davis, argued publicly against retribution did cooler heads prevail. One of the more influential spokesmen for moderation was Robert E. Lee, whose son Rooney had been in a Union prison since being captured while convalescing at home from his Brandy Station wound. Lee did, however, send a letter of inquiry about the affair through the lines, one that George Meade answered after Kilpatrick rejoined the army on the Rapidan. Meade quoted Kilpatrick's vehement denial that he had prepared any such order as the Confederates claimed to have found. While absolving himself and other subordinates of blame, however, the raiding leader failed to address Dahlgren's possible role in preparing the order, thus giving the impression—either inadvertently or deliberately—that if anyone was responsible for the inflammatory document, it was the dead colonel.[42]

Although Confederate officials strove mightily to authenticate the Dahlgren Papers, it took twentieth-century historians, employing detective methods, to prove that the colonel had either penned or dictated them. Even so, the idea behind the burn-and-kill directive may well have come from Judson Kilpatrick, whose trademark purple prose oozes from the document. The order also reflected Kill-cavalry's gloves-off approach to warfare. While Dahlgren had been a romantic, a throwback to earlier wars, Kilpatrick was a hard-edged realist who believed the Union could be saved only by piling up as many enemy bodies as possible, as quickly as possible. He did not seem to care whether they came clothed in uniforms or civilian attire.

For his part, Meade gave the impression that he did not believe Kilpatrick's assertion of innocence. In private, the army leader alluded to the existence of "collateral evidence" that incriminated the Irishman as the author of the Dahlgren Papers. Meade had supported his subordinate in the controversy out of concern that a political firestorm would follow any hint of Kilpatrick's complicity.[43]

Along with his failure on the doorstep to Richmond, the strained relations that developed between Meade and Kilpatrick in the aftermath of the raid made inevitable Kill-cavalry's exit from the Army of the Potomac. On April 15, one month after Kilpatrick's return from Yorktown to Stevensburg, he was sent west to command a cavalry division in Maj. Gen. William T. Sherman's Military Department of the Mississippi. He left Virginia carrying baggage that would have threatened the career of many a soldier, but his new superior did not seem to mind. "I know that Kilpatrick is a hell of a damned fool," Sherman later confided, "but I want just that sort of man to command my cavalry."[44]

Significantly, the twisted compliment came from the officer who stands as the embodiment of total war—war waged against not only an enemy's military establishment, but also his government, his economic base, and his civilian population. Viewed in such a light, Kilpatrick's transfer to Sherman marked a merger of kindred spirits.

Chapter Nineteen

Whip Them so They Will Stay Whipped

On the day Ulric Dahlgren fell victim to a shotgun blast, the U.S. Senate confirmed Lincoln's nomination of Ulysses Grant as lieutenant general in command of all the armies of the United States. The victor at Fort Donelson, Shiloh, Vicksburg, and Chattanooga had been rewarded with a rank higher than any worn since Washington's time. Two days later, Grant was summoned to the capital, where on March 9 he received his commission at a White House reception hosted by the president and attended by congressmen, cabinet members, and the city's political and social elite.[1]

Republican onlookers hoped that Grant would remain in the East, either to relieve Meade in command of the Army of the Potomac or to replace him with a hand-picked subordinate. In fact, editors and pundits were already announcing Meade's demise. Yet it did not happen. On the tenth, following a series of conferences with Lincoln, Stanton, Halleck (now the army chief of staff), and other officials, Grant traveled to Virginia for his first meeting with the slow-moving, temper-prone army leader whom he had indeed given thought to replacing. From the first, however, Grant was struck by the military and social qualities of his host. Meade prefaced their discussion by offering to step down should Grant so desire and to serve in whatever capacity the lieutenant general considered him qualified to fill. Grant was so taken by Meade's graciousness, amiability, and lack of ego that he decided to keep him on.

Aware that the war would be won or lost in the East, Grant planned to make his headquarters with the Army of the Potomac and to steer its strategic course. Meade would continue to make the tactical decisions, supervise logistics, and guide the army in battle. Such a division of responsibilities might be difficult to maintain—tactical and strategic decisions have a habit of overlapping—but Grant counted on Meade's spirit of cooperation to make the relationship work.[2]

On this first trip to Virginia, Grant inspected the camps of the army and studied Meade's preparations for the coming campaign. He was impressed by the fighting trim of the soldiers he encountered and the enthusiasm of those he

Gen. George H. Thomas
LIBRARY OF CONGRESS

Gen. Innis N. Palmer
PHOTOGRAPHIC HISTORY OF THE CIVIL WAR

Gen. Irvin McDowell
NATIONAL ARCHIVES

Gen. Philip St. G. Cooke
NATIONAL ARCHIVES

Gen. George B. McClellan
LIBRARY OF CONGRESS

Gen. William H. Emory
LIBRARY OF CONGRESS

Gen. George Stoneman
LIBRARY OF CONGRESS

Gen. William W. Averell
LIBRARY OF CONGRESS

Gen. David McM. Gregg
HISTORY OF THE THIRD PENNSYLVANIA CAVALRY

Gen. Alfred Pleasonton
LIBRARY OF CONGRESS

Gen. George D. Bayard
LIBRARY OF CONGRESS

Gen. Ambrose E. Burnside
PHOTOGRAPHIC HISTORY OF THE CIVIL WAR

Gen. August V. Kautz
LIBRARY OF CONGRESS

Gen. John B. McIntosh
LIBRARY OF CONGRESS

Col. Sir Percy Wyndham
LIBRARY OF CONGRESS

Gen. H. Judson Kilpatrick
LIBRARY OF CONGRESS

Gen. Henry E. Davies
LIBRARY OF CONGRESS

Gen. Thomas C. Devin
LIBRARY OF CONGRESS

Gen. Wesley Merritt
LIBRARY OF CONGRESS

Gen. George A. Custer
LIBRARY OF CONGRESS

Capt. Alanson M. Randol
LIBRARY OF CONGRESS

Gen. Philip H. Sheridan
LIBRARY OF CONGRESS

Gen. Alfred T. A. Torbert
LIBRARY OF CONGRESS

Gen. James H. Wilson
LIBRARY OF CONGRESS

Gen. Wade Hampton, C. S. A.

Gen. George Crook

General J. E. B. Stuart, C. S. A. Photographic History of the Civil War

Gen. John Buford (seated) and Staff LIBRARY OF CONGRESS

The First Massachusetts Cavalry PHOTOGRAPHIC HISTORY OF THE CIVIL WAR

Stoneman's Raiders LIBRARY OF CONGRESS

Gen. George G. Meade (third from left) and His Subordinates LIBRARY OF CONGRESS

Gen. George H. Chapman (seated) and Staff LIBRARY OF CONGRESS

>━◆>━○━<◆━<

The Third Indiana Cavalry PHOTOGRAPHIC HISTORY OF THE CIVIL WAR

Officers of the 5th United States Cavalry PHOTOGRAPHIC HISTORY OF THE CIVIL WAR

Capt. John C. Tidball (second from left) and Lt. Alexander C. McW. Pennington, Jr. (far right) LIBRARY OF CONGRESS

Return of Sheridan's Richmond Raiders LIBRARY OF CONGRESS

The First United States Cavalry PHOTOGRAPHIC HISTORY OF THE CIVIL WAR

Drawing of Kilpatrick-Dahlgren Raiders LIBRARY OF CONGRESS

>–‹◆›–◦–‹◆›–‹

Drawing of Wilson-Kautz Raiders LIBRARY OF CONGRESS

interviewed. When serving in the West, he had heard rumors that the Army of the Potomac was defeat-weary and demoralized. From personal observation, he knew this was not the case.

The army's spirit might be strong, but Grant considered its organization in need of change. The I and III Corps had been so decimated at Gettysburg and on other fields that they had shrunk to division size. By early 1864 their regiments, along with those of the other corps, were being rebuilt by a steady stream of new soldiers—recruits, substitutes, and conscripts. Even so, consolidation appeared imperative. Meade agreed, and on March 23 the I Corps was disbanded and its troops were assigned to the V Corps, now commanded by General Warren. One day later, the III Corps was abolished and its manpower distributed between Hancock's II Corps and Sedgwick's VI. Three major generals were displaced by the reorganization; two of them, Newton and Sykes, were transferred to field commands in the western theater and the Trans-Mississippi Department, respectively. William French, whose tippling and erratic generalship had cost him not only Meade's confidence, but also that of the War Department, was reduced to garrison and staff service in Maryland.[3]

The conventional wisdom in Washington was that when Grant came to Virginia, he would appoint numerous subordinates from the West, not only to Meade's job, but also to other high positions in the Army of the Potomac. In reality, only two generals came east with Grant, one being his chief of staff, Maj. Gen. John A. Rawlins. The other was William Farrar Smith, the former division commander who had worked tirelessly to undermine Ambrose Burnside. After his transfer west in September 1863, Smith had helped Grant lift the siege of Chattanooga. Grant had considered putting the brilliant but difficult Smith in Meade's place. Once he decided to keep Meade in power—and when he learned that Smith was *persona non grata* in the Army of the Potomac—Grant assigned him to the Army of the James as Butler's senior subordinate.[4]

Another western general joined Meade's army two weeks after Grant's first visit. This was Maj. Gen. Philip Henry Sheridan, an infantry division commander who had distinguished himself at Perryville, Stones River, Chickamauga, and Chattanooga. Sheridan also had experience in mounted operations, having entered field service in May 1862 as colonel of one of the most celebrated cavalry regiments in the West, the 2nd Michigan.[5]

Sheridan came to fill a recent vacancy. On March 24 Alfred Pleasonton had been relieved from command of the Cavalry Corps and ordered to the Department of Missouri. Years later, Grant denied that Pleasonton's transfer had been his doing, "for I did not know but that he had been as efficient as any other cavalry commander." Grant, however, was being disingenuous. Even before leaving the West, he had formed an opinion of Pleasonton's ability, and it was not a high one.[6]

That opinion probably mirrored an editorial in the March 26 edition of the *New York Times,* which observed that "although the service now possesses a considerable number of more than respectable leaders of horse, we have no one of such preeminent distinction . . . [as to be] the fit head of all the cavalry of so great an army as that of the Potomac." The editorialist believed that "John Buford came the nearest to it, if he did not actually snatch the laurels." Pleasonton, however, lacked "the qualities, mental and physical, that go [in]to the composition of a first-class cavalry leader." Grant had used similar language when, during his initial interview with Lincoln, he expressed his "dissatisfaction with the little that had been accomplished by cavalry so far in the war." His criticism applied to every theater of operations, but it was also a specific allusion to the Army of the Potomac. Then, too, when conferring with Halleck, Grant had made known his desire that Meade take on a new cavalry leader. Supposedly Halleck, not Grant, had suggested Sheridan for the post, with Grant replying that the bandy-legged Irishman was "the very man I want."[7]

His preference for Sheridan gained an enthusiastic response from Meade, even though the army leader knew little about the man personally. Grant learned that Meade considered Pleasonton not only a backstabber, but a rival for his job. As recently as December, Washington had been buzzing with rumors that Pleasonton was about to replace Meade, a prospect that left many cavalry officers, as one of them put it, "in a great stew." This man, a captain in the 6th Pennsylvania, called the idea "absurd" and declared Pleasonton "not fit to command a regt in active service," much less an army. Whether or not Grant shared this view, he was pleased that his desire that Sheridan take over meshed with Meade's wish to get rid of a subordinate he no longer trusted. It is possible that Grant helped Meade gain Secretary Stanton's permission to jettison Pleasonton and replace him with "Little Phil."[8]

Considering the fame he was to win in Virginia, Sheridan was curiously reluctant to accept his new assignment. He claimed to prefer infantry command—that was where he had made his record—and he must have wondered if, having served apart from the arm for almost two years, he could make himself into an aggressive, energetic cavalryman. By March 27, when relieved of command in Tennessee, Sheridan looked almost frail, standing five feet, five inches tall and weighing no more than 115 pounds following a debilitating campaign outside Chattanooga. In time, however, he embraced the challenge that awaited him in Virginia.[9]

Arriving in Washington on April 4, Sheridan secured an audience with Halleck—Grant was out of town—as well as with Stanton. Both men scrutinized their guest and asked provocative questions as if trying to uncover his strengths and weaknesses. Both found Sheridan confident of his abilities, committed to making a new start in the cavalry, and basically apolitical. At some point Stanton escorted Sheridan to the White House, where the president greeted him warmly and wished him well. Even Lincoln commented that the cavalry of the Army of the Potomac had not lived up to its potential—he hoped it would under Sheridan. He liked what he saw in his guest, telling Sheridan that he looked short and wiry enough to make a good cavalryman. Then the chief executive made the mistake of repeating an old canard: the virtual impossibility of finding a dead trooper. Sheridan found the remark insulting, but he did not make a caustic reply. Perhaps he was more of a political animal than he let on.[10]

The following day, Sheridan took the train to army headquarters, where he met with Grant and Meade and studied the dispositions of the units he had inherited. He impressed several of those he met at Brandy Station. "Sheridan makes everywhere a favorable impression," Lieutenant Colonel Lyman noted approvingly. Because nearly all of those Sheridan met in Virginia lacked a prior connection with him, few knew the man beneath the star-encrusted shoulder straps. In time, however, many came to know him well. More than a few saw him as brash, blunt, and impatient to the point of rudeness. Without necessarily intending to offend, he could be short and disrespectful even to long-time members of his staff.[11]

Sheridan's behavior stemmed from an exaggerated sense of self. He was devoted to success—his own and, by extension, his command's—and he let no one stand in the way of his ambition. He pursued his goal with almost mechanized efficiency. An acquaintance described him as the "incarnation of business, and business only." A subordinate observed that he "works like a mill-owner or an iron-master, not like a soldier." But Sheridan possessed a ruthlessness not found in every captain of industry. Those who tried to thwart him, he crushed without a second thought. He had no pity for the weak, and he feared only those whose power and authority exceeded his own. To one nineteenth-century historian Sheridan's most visible trait was "the recklessness with which he pursued his own personal aggrandizement at the expense of . . . the forfeiture of claim to fair dealing."[12]

Grant was one of the few superiors Sheridan respected and trusted, but he neither shared nor appreciated Grant's humanity and sensitivity. Grant understood the frailties of human nature and, when possible, made allowances for them; Sheridan sneered at weakness and rid himself of those who displayed it. Still, Grant had decided that this was the man he wanted to manage Meade's consistently underachieving horsemen. Therefore, he upheld Sheridan in his disputes with other generals, Meade included. He gave the Irishman latitude not only to defeat, but to trample, the enemy. He put up with Sheridan's sometimes tactless, often curt behavior because he admired the man's all-out approach to warfare, his determination to triumph against all odds. No one before him had approached Sheridan's level of intensity or shared his wholehearted commitment to victory. If he could communicate these values to the officers and troopers of the army's cavalry, Grant would be vastly pleased.

The lieutenant general was not Sheridan's only admirer in the army. General Patrick, the provost marshal, found him "a very quiet determined little man." After serving under Sheridan for only a few weeks, Col. Charles Russell Lowell of the 2nd Massachusetts described him as "the first General I have seen who puts as much heart and time and thought into his work as if he were

doing it for his own exclusive profit." Other observers, who concentrated on
the man's unprepossessing appearance, were not so well disposed toward him.
Colonel Wainwright of the artillery, an upstate New York patrician, decided
that Sheridan "certainly would not impress one by his looks any more than
Grant does. He is short, thickset, and common Irish-looking . . . and his dress is
in perfect keeping with that character."[13]

Whether or not Sheridan cut an imposing figure, the army would give him
the chance to prove himself worthy of his uncommon promotion. Under the
circumstances, that might not prove a Herculean task. "If he is an able officer,"
Lyman observed, "he will find no difficulty in pushing along [his] arm, several
degrees."[14]

>─┤◄►─○─◄►┼─◄

While he harbored no doubts that he could serve Grant faithfully and well,
Sheridan was uncertain whether he could do the same for Meade. During his
early inspection tour of the cavalry's camps, the new general decided that his
command was built of promising material—well-armed, well-equipped veterans who had assimilated the nuances as well as the basics of mounted service.
Despite the uneven record they had gained under Stoneman and Pleasonton,
their morale appeared high, and they looked to be in good physical health.
Many of their mounts, however, "were thin and very much worn down with
excessive and, it seemed to me, unnecessary picket duty, for the cavalry picket-
line almost completely encircled the infantry and artillery camps of the army,
covering a distance, on a continuous line, of nearly sixty miles, with hardly a
mounted Confederate confronting it at any point."[15]

One of his first acts was to ask Meade to reduce the cavalry's picket
duties, while approving a cutback in outpost and escort service. While Meade
agreed to relieve as many of the cavalry's burdens as he felt able to, he gave
Sheridan cause for worry. The cavalryman received the impression that his
superior considered horsemen appendages to the main army, useful at reconnaissance and, under certain conditions, in battle, but truly valuable only when
providing close support to infantry and artillery. Sheridan vowed to change
Meade's attitude. If he failed to do so, he doubted he would be able to function
smoothly as Meade's subordinate.

Meade made good on his word. In later days, Sheridan found that 100 or
fewer men from each of his brigades were assigned each day to picket duty—
about half the previous number. He spent the month of April inspecting these
lines to ensure that the mounted guards were alert and vigilant and that, when
not on duty, they received proper rest and regular rations and their mounts
were kept in forage. At other times, he held reviews to evaluate the physical
condition and readiness of his command. On the first of these occasions, he
had the entire corps, more than 10,000 effectives, parade past an inspection
committee that included Meade, Hancock, and Sedgwick. The infantry leaders
gave Sheridan's command polite but unenthusiastic reviews. However, as the

spring wore on, as the troopers assimilated new arms and accoutrements, and as carload after carload of remounts arrived at Brandy Station, the riders made increasingly an impressive showing on the parade ground. Before April was out, Sheridan was convinced that he had inherited a command with which he could make history.[16]

When not inspecting or reviewing his troopers, Little Phil acquainted himself with their officers, few of whom he had known in the prewar army. He developed an early cordiality toward several of his subordinates, especially the younger ones like Merritt and Custer. At first he was not as close to the older, more reserved David Gregg, but he came to respect the division leader's generalship and tactical acumen. As a group, Sheridan's lieutenants were capable and reliable; he considered himself lucky to have them.

Two of his ranking subordinates were new either to him or to the cavalry service. On April 10 he welcomed to the corps Brig. Gen. Alfred T. A. Torbert, recently a brigade commander in the VI Corps. Torbert's long friendship with Sheridan—they had been West Point classmates—had recommended him for this transfer from one combat arm to another, which he had been seeking for some time. Torbert thus became the only general officer without experience in mounted service ever to gain a command in the cavalry of the Army of the Potomac. Upon reporting, Torbert became permanent successor to John Buford by displacing Buford's temporary replacement, Merritt, in command of the 1st Cavalry Division.[17]

Torbert seemed to possess the right qualifications for his new post: He was an expert horseman; at thirty, was relatively young; and sported a powerful physique. He also had the cavalryman's eye for flashy attire. Something of a dude (at West Point, his nickname had been "Daisy"), he created a more dapper version of Custer's Gettysburg-campaign uniform, complete with the same sailor's neck cloth. Yet appearances seem to have been deceiving, for many of those who served under Torbert found him wanting. Typical was the comment of Lt. Frederick Whittaker of the 6th New York, who considered Torbert "an infantry general if anything . . . utterly unfit to have control of cavalry, and [he] soon proved it." The 6th Michigan's James Kidd also regarded Torbert as "an infantry officer whose qualifications as a commander of Cavalry were not remarkable."[18]

As of April 1864 the jury was still out on Torbert, the cavalryman, but had Sheridan talked to his former superiors, he would have heard that the man lacked maturity, served capably only when closely supervised, and appeared to take his responsibilities too lightly. For one thing, Torbert took leave more often than most other general officers; moreover, he made a habit of extending his time away from the army to attend social functions in his home state of Delaware and in nearby Philadelphia. Reportedly, General Sedgwick had reacted to one especially ill-timed leave by remarking that "Gen. Torbert ought to be old enough now to be over this sort of thing."[19]

The second newcomer, a stranger to Sheridan, reported for duty a week after Torbert. Successor to Judson Kilpatrick as commander of the 3rd

Division, twenty-seven-year-old Brig. Gen. James Harrison Wilson was embarking on his first field command. While Torbert owed his appointment to Sheridan's friendship, Wilson had become a division leader through the patronage of Ulysses Grant, on whose staff he had served from November 1862 to January 1864. Grant had considered Wilson his most versatile aide, an all-purpose troubleshooter whose ingenuity, tactical skill, and infectious energy solved problems great and small. Grant called him a "member of the get-there gang."[20]

Like Sheridan, Wilson was a young man on the move—ambitious, impatient, outspoken, a stranger to humility and self-doubt. He had made a success of his recent stint in the Cavalry Bureau; up to the day he handed the post to his principal assistant, Brig. Gen. August Kautz, Wilson had tirelessly supplied Sheridan for the campaign ahead. He had showered the Cavalry Corps with remounts (35,000 of them just since the start of March), as well as with equipment, ammunition, and hundreds of Spencer carbines, the seven-shot repeater Wilson believed would revolutionize mounted warfare. He expected to achieve similar if not greater success in the field, leading thousands of Spencer-wielding troopers.[21]

Through the remainder of April, Torbert and Wilson held their own reviews, inspections, and get-acquainted sessions with superiors, subordinates, and colleagues. Early on, both tackled the task of organizing (or reorganizing) their commands. The work was completed by the first of May, close to the jumping-off point of the spring campaign.

By that time, the Cavalry Corps consisted of seven brigades. Torbert's command included three, led by Custer, Devin, and Merritt. Custer's presence in the 1st Division instead of the 3rd owed to his dislike of Wilson, which dated to their years together at the Military Academy. Moreover, Custer was incensed that Wilson, his junior, should be placed above him through Grant's favoritism. Thus he had successfully importuned Sheridan to transfer him to Torbert's division.[22]

Custer's Wolverines—the 1st, 5th, 6th, and 7th Michigan—had followed him to his new assignment. Devin's brigade consisted of the 4th New York (which was on detached duty when the spring campaign began), the 6th and 9th New York, and the 17th Pennsylvania. Merritt's Reserve Brigade continued to comprise the 6th Pennsylvania as well as the 1st, 2nd, and 5th United States Cavalry. The 6th United States had left the brigade to serve as Sheridan's escort; its loss had been made good by the addition of Col. Alfred Gibbs's 1st New York Dragoons and later the 2nd Massachusetts.[23]

As of early May 1864, the 2nd Cavalry Division consisted of two brigades instead of its original three. The first was led by Davies, who, like Custer, had lost his place in the 3rd Division when Wilson, his junior, took it over. Unlike Custer, Davies appears to have been willing to waive seniority in order to remain with his old command, but Wilson had insisted that he go. Davies's new brigade was made up of the 1st Massachusetts (all but one squadron of it), as well as the 1st New Jersey, the 6th Ohio, the 1st Pennsylvania, and the 4th Pennsylvania (one battalion strong). Irvin Gregg's 2nd Brigade, 2nd Division, consisted of the 1st Maine, the 10th New York (which later transferred to Davies's command), and the 2nd, 8th, 13th, 16th, and the balance of the 4th Pennsylvania. The 3rd Pennsylvania was serving, along with the detached squadron of the 1st Massachusetts, with Patrick's provost guard.[24]

The inclusion in Gregg's brigade of the 8th Pennsylvania indicated that its colonel, Pennock Huey, no longer had a brigade of his own. Ostensibly because its battle-thinned ranks called for consolidation, no doubt also due to Huey's less-than-expert leadership, his old command had been broken up six weeks after Gettysburg, its units distributed between the remaining brigades. Huey ended up as second-in-command to Irvin Gregg. He was permitted to lead Gregg's brigade, as he had at Parker's Store in November, only when its permanent leader was on leave or detached duty. When, late in 1864, the 2nd Division expanded to regain a third brigade, Huey was not tendered command of it.[25]

When the army retook the field, Wilson's division also mounted two brigades. The first was commanded by an old Regular, Colonel Timothy M. Bryan, Jr., of the 18th Pennsylvania, although one day after the campaign began, Bryan was superseded by John B. McIntosh. The brigade consisted of Bryan's own regiment plus the 1st Connecticut and the 2nd and 5th New York. Wilson's second brigade, George Chapman's, was initially made up of the six-company 3rd Indiana, the 8th New York, the 1st Vermont, and a detachment of the 8th Illinois. Companies A and C of the 1st Ohio served as Wilson's escort, as they had for his predecessor, Kilpatrick.[26]

During the 1864–65 campaign, the Cavalry Corps underwent considerable change. By war's end, eight regiments or parts of regiments were no longer serving as cavalry in the main theater of operations: the 2nd, 13th, and 18th Pennsylvania, the 4th and 5th New York, the 1st and 2nd Massachusetts, and the detachment of the 3rd Indiana. In their place, the corps gained nine new regiments, seven of them transferred from infantry corps.

The two regiments that did not come over from the infantry were the first to arrive, in June 1864; each, however, was only eight companies strong. The 1st New Hampshire, which became a member of Chapman's brigade, was made up of raw recruits, having been organized only five months earlier. The other unit wore a familiar face: the 1st Rhode Island, which had been recruited nearly back to standard strength following its mauling at Middleburg the previous June. The regiment returned to the army—originally as a member of the Reserve Brigade, later as Torbert's escort—after five months' service in the defenses of Washington, where enlistees and draftees had helped make good its combat loss.[27]

Of the regiments that came over from the infantry, some had been serving mounted, others on foot, for the past several months. When it took the field under Grant, Meade's army comprised not only the II, V, and VI Corps but also the IX Army Corps, which, after leaving the Army of the Potomac early in 1863, had served in Kentucky, Mississippi, and Tennessee. Now the corps was back in familiar surroundings under an equally familiar leader—Burnside, who had survived being deposed from army command in the wake of the Mud March. Since Burnside was senior to Meade, for the first three weeks of the spring campaign he reported directly to Grant. As of May 24, however, Grant subordinated Burnside to the commander of the Army of the Potomac.[28]

When it came east in April 1864, the IX Corps consisted not only of four divisions of infantry but six regiments of cavalry. As soon as the corps came under Meade's command, Sheridan gained authority over three of those regiments. He assigned all three to the 3rd Division. Wilson distributed the 3rd New Jersey and the 2nd Ohio to McIntosh and the 22nd New York to Chapman. Months later, three other mounted outfits left the IX Corps for Sheridan's command. In October the 24th New York joined Davies's brigade of Gregg's division; in November, the 2nd New York Mounted Rifles became part of the new 3rd Brigade, 2nd Division, which had been assigned to Colonel Smith; and in December, the 13th Ohio also joined Smith's brigade. In May 1864, yet another cavalry regiment, the 21st Pennsylvania, was detached from the infantry (in this case, the V Corps) to join Irvin Gregg's brigade.[29]

The Cavalry Corps continued to include two brigades of horse artillery. Batteries and sections were doled out to Sheridan's brigades as conditions dictated. The 1st Brigade, commanded by James Robertson, consisted of Martin's 6th New York Battery; Lieutenant Edward Heaton's Combined Batteries B/L, 2nd United States Artillery; Williston's D, 2nd Artillery; Pennington's M, 2nd Artillery; King's A, 4th Artillery; and Lieutenant Charles L. Fitzhugh's C/E, 4th Artillery. Captain Dunbar Ransom's 2nd Brigade was composed of E/G, 1st Artillery, commanded by Lt. F. S. French; H/I, 1st Artillery, under Alanson Randol; K, 1st Artillery, Lt. John Egan; A, 2nd Artillery, once John Calef's, now Lt. Robert Clarke's; G, 2nd Artillery, Lt. William N. Dennison; and C/F/K, 3rd Artillery, Lt. James R. Kelly.

At least three battery commanders displayed enough versatility and leadership to win promotion and high station in the cavalry. Before the year ended, now-Colonel Fitzhugh was commanding the 2nd Brigade, 1st Division; Colonel Pennington headed the 1st Brigade, 3rd Division; and Colonel Randol led the 2nd New York, of Pennington's brigade.[30]

>·!·+>·0·<>·!·<

In the past, when the Army of the Potomac took the field for active service, it had operated without reference to the other armies of the Union. Grant's strategic vision ensured that from now on, things would be different. He projected simultaneous advances on several fronts by armies working in close cooperation with each other. His theory was that the resource-poor Confederacy could not hope to defend more than one or two positions at the same time. Pressed hard everywhere, the South could not duplicate the troop transfer that had sent Longstreet to Georgia in time to turn the tide at Chickamauga.

Thus it was that as the 120,000-man Army of the Potomac poised to cross the Rapidan on the evening of May 3, 1864, five other Union forces were likewise preparing to move out against their enemy. Two shared the Virginia theater with the Army of the Potomac. While Grant and Meade confronted the Army of Northern Virginia with the intention of driving it back upon its capital, the Army of the James was to strike Richmond via its namesake river. If Butler's 36,000-man army proved unable to take its objective by storm, it would help Meade besiege the city once Lee's 65,000 troops were driven inside it. And while Meade and Butler advanced on Richmond from opposite directions, Franz Sigel would lead 6,500 troops up the Shenandoah to curtail Confederate operations in that fertile valley, the primary source of foodstuffs and forage for Lee's army.[31]

Beyond the Shenandoah, two campaigns prepared to get under way, while a third, already in progress, neared its climax. In the new state of West Virginia, Brig. Gen. George Crook (Sheridan's West Point roommate) would lead the troops of his Kanawha District from the mouth of the Gauley River to strike the railroad that linked Virginia and Tennessee. From southern Tennessee, Sherman, Grant's successor as the head of the Military Division of the Mississippi, would throw no fewer than three armies against Joseph E. Johnston's Confederates on the road to Atlanta, the manufacturing and communications hub of the Deep South. Finally, a large force under Nathaniel P. Banks (who had been stationed in Louisiana since December 1862) was well into a campaign to capture and occupy Texas via the Red River.

Not every offensive ended as Grant hoped. Ultimately, the forces under Butler, Banks, and Sigel were defeated in battle and failed to accomplish their assigned missions. Crook achieved only partial success but did well enough that in August he won command of the Department of West Virginia. Sherman bested his enemy and took Atlanta, but only after desperate fighting—and after Jefferson Davis replaced the defensive-minded Johnston with the risk-taking John Bell Hood. Despite its mixed results, however, Grant's strategy of putting pressure on a wide stretch of his enemy's homeland achieved ultimate success, validating the faith the government had shown in naming him to overall command.[32]

The Army of the Potomac played a key role in Grant's grand strategy. This knowledge was a burden to many officers as they prepared to move out against the enemy. Everyone in the ranks hoped for a successful effort on the road to Richmond, but none felt a greater sense of urgency than did the newcomers from Tennessee. Grant was taking a risk in this, his first advance, and he prayed that the gamble would not backfire. Rather than strike Lee head-on, fearing the heavy casualties that would result, he had determined to flank his opponent out of his position west of Mine Run. Given the choice of sectors to strike, Grant had rejected the long, circuitous route he would have to take to reach Lee's left in favor of heading directly south of the Rapidan and curling around the Rebel right. In so deciding, Grant was gambling that Lee would not rush up to oppose him until Meade's people cleared the trees below the river.

If Lee gave battle in the vision-obscuring, movement-restricting Wilderness, he might neutralize the Army of the Potomac's numerical advantage. In that event, any outcome was possible.[33]

For his part, Sheridan had much to prove. He had received a bit of advice from General Sedgwick, and he may have continued to mull it over. The VI Corps commander, a veteran of the 1st and 2nd Cavalry, had warned Sheridan (and perhaps Torbert as well) that only by achieving success in the field would he overcome "the traditional prejudices that cavalrymen were supposed to hold against being commanded by an infantry commander."[34]

To succeed, Sheridan had to beat the great J. E. B. Stuart—something that politicians, newsmen, and his own officers had reminded him ever since he reached Virginia. The idea gave Sheridan nagging discomfort. Like John Buford, he looked down on Stuart's foppish, flamboyant style and bridled at the Beau Sabreur's near-legendary reputation, which Sheridan considered greatly exaggerated. Although not himself a newshound, Sheridan may also have resented the publicity that the Virginian commanded, not only in the South, but in the northern press as well. Little Phil had no doubt that he would best Stuart in an open fight, and the more he dwelled on this thought, the more enjoyment it gave him.

The campaign represented a moment of truth as much for Sheridan's officers and men as it did for their leader. In answer to Lincoln's quizzical jest, the Cavalry Corps of the Army of the Potomac had had its share of dead cavalrymen; it lacked only sustained success in the field. Having achieved an uneven record under Stoneman and Pleasonton, it seemed imperative that the corps gain victories for its new leader. With a critical national election coming up in the fall, Union troops everywhere, especially in the East, had to win often enough to persuade the electorate to sustain the war effort. Therefore, the 1864 campaign had a sense of criticality, of finality, to it. The prevailing mood was summed up by one of Custer's sergeants: "This is the last campaign of the war. Either we are going to whip them so they will stay whipped or else they are going to whip us and if they do . . . we will never be able to raise another army to fight them. This is the final struggle and we will know before next fall whether there will be a [permanent] Southern Confederacy or not."[35]

>—+◆>—O—<◆+—<

The do-or-die campaign began in the dark, early hours of May 4 with horsemen taking the road in advance of Meade's infantry. First to march were the men of Wilson's division, who left Stevensburg for the eight-mile march to Germanna Ford. After brushing aside the pickets opposite the ford, the division crossed there, screening the advance of the V and VI Corps. On the south bank, the troopers resumed the march toward their initial objective, a crossroads hostelry known as Wilderness Tavern. The division's position gave it the role of protecting the front and right flank of Meade's infantry as it crossed the Rapidan on pontoons. Well to the east, in the meantime, Gregg's division crossed at Ely's Ford in advance of the II Corps—Meade's left wing—and headed for another crossroads, this with the familiar name of Chancellorsville.[36]

The order of march, which had been devised by Meade, was not to Sheridan's tastes. He disliked placing troops under an inexperienced commander such as Wilson well forward of the rest of the army, nearest the presumed location of the enemy. The veteran Gregg would have been a more appropriate choice to cover such an exposed position. Then, too, Sheridan grumbled over Meade's decision to keep Torbert's men well in the rear, guarding the army's supply wagons and ambulances. That assignment—one Sheridan considered more suited to infantry—would prevent Torbert from crossing the river until evening. Sheridan regarded the 1st Division's positioning as proof of Meade's ignorance in handling cavalry.[37]

Late on the fourth, as Gregg marched southeastward to the Orange Plank Road and Torbert moved over the Rapidan, Wilson bivouacked near Parker's Store. Already the young brigadier had sent detachments of Chapman's brigade to reconnoiter toward Lee's last-known positions. He did so again after reaching Parker's Store, sending the 5th New York of Bryan's brigade out the Orange Plank Road toward Mine Run. The regiment encountered a band of Stuart's men, whom, after sharp fighting, it chased toward New Verdiersville.[38]

Attaching no great importance to the brief encounter, Wilson and his men turned in for the night. By 5:00 A.M. on May 5 they were heading southwestward toward Craig's Meeting House. Because his scouts had done an imperfect job, Wilson's advance had run its course. Shortly after he departed Parker's Store, the 5th New York, which he had left on the plank road until relieved by Warren's or Sedgwick's infantry, came under attack by the advance of a massive column of infantry, which proved to be Longstreet's corps, coming up from the west. At the same time, Ewell's corps was rushing eastward along the Orange Turnpike, north of and roughly parallel to the plank road. Lee had not waited for his enemy to clear the trees before taking him on. Grant's hopes had been dashed, his fears realized.[39]

Despite facing forty-to-one odds, the 5th New York, now under the supervision of the newly arrived McIntosh, held its position on the Orange Plank Road for almost six hours. The regiment had the same advantage that Buford's troopers had enjoyed on the first day at Gettysburg: Its Spencer repeaters convinced Longstreet that he was facing a large body of infantry. Also as on July 1, Union foot soldiers—today, the advance guard of Sedgwick's corps—were pounding up in the New Yorkers' rear. The regiment eventually fell back, taking position on the foot soldiers' flanks. There it remained, cut off from its command, until late in the day.[40]

Not long after the 5th New York was attacked, Rosser's brigade of Stuart's cavalry struck the head of Wilson's division above Craig's Meeting House. At about 8:00 Rosser drove in Chapman's flank guard, the 1st Vermont, before thudding into Bryan's brigade, its men dismounted behind the trees that surrounded the meetinghouse. Bryan absorbed a series of limited assaults before remounting his command and making what Wilson called "several handsome charges." Bryan's final effort drove Rosser's men a couple of miles in the direction from which they had come, temporarily easing the pressure on Wilson's position.[41]

At first the novice division commander determined to hold his ground until reinforced. But Warren and Sedgwick were too far off to aid him, and then he discovered that it was his enemy who was being augmented. Some time after 1:00 P.M., Rosser's enlarged force launched a dismounted attack (something of a rarity for Southern troopers, most of whom preferred fighting in the saddle) that struck the exposed flank of Chapman's brigade. Chapman's line broke at first touch; his men fled to the rear and failed to rally until a frustrated and angry Wilson blunted Rosser's assault with well-directed salvos from Pennington's and Fitzhugh's batteries.

Then, however, Wilson learned that the enemy not only was in his front near Craig's Meeting House, but also had gathered in his rear at Parker's Store. Fighting down panic, he decided to clear out in the direction of Todd's Tavern, at the junction of three woodland roads, about fifteen miles to the northeast. There, near the old Chancellorsville battlefield, Wilson might find refuge among Hancock's foot soldiers and Gregg's horsemen.

Wilson had barely begun his dash to safety when he discovered infantry as well as cavalry moving to cut him off. He responded by accelerating his withdrawal, sending Chapman's men, followed by Bryan's, racing across Corbin's Bridge over the Po River. While most of the Federals avoided being intercepted short of Todd's Tavern, Stuart pressed Wilson's rear so heavily that the escape was a near thing.[42]

When the head of Wilson's column reached its destination, it found help waiting for it. Although Sheridan had lost touch with Wilson, Meade had learned of the 3rd Division's plight and, despite being in a fight with two Rebel corps, had taken steps to aid it. Meade's action embarrassed Sheridan, for it made him appear unable to solve his own problems. But the rescue call was a godsend for Wilson, for Meade sent Gregg's division to Todd's Tavern late that morning and had it form a line of defense. The sight of Gregg's men must have relieved Wilson greatly, for only fresh units could have checked the enemy's pursuit—Wilson's men were too demoralized to save themselves.

Once at the tavern, Wilson's fugitives re-formed in Gregg's rear. As soon as their pursuers appeared, Gregg's men lashed them with carbine and artillery fire, then charged them with pistols and sabers. The Rebels turned and fled; Gregg pursued them for four miles before returning his men to the tavern. There they joined a thankful Wilson in holding the area for future use. With daylight fading, the crisis on Meade's forward flank had ended.[43]

>─┼─◆➤─O─◄◆─┼─◄

Late in the day, Sheridan joined Wilson and Gregg at the tavern. To that place he also summoned Torbert's division, which Meade had released from its rear-guard duties. Fighting was still raging to the north and west, but mainly on the infantry's front; the cavalry's initial participation in what would become known as the Wilderness Campaign was over. It had been a bad day for almost everyone involved, Sheridan included. Even he would have admitted that the opening gambit in his violent chess match with Stuart had gone to the man in the ostrich-plumed hat.

Sheridan thought Todd's Tavern worth holding, and Grant agreed. Situated only a mile from the outer edge of the Wilderness, it anchored a corridor through which Meade's army might exit the forest and make another attempt at flanking Lee. For that reason May 6 was a frustrating day for Sheridan. That afternoon Lee struck many sectors of Meade's line, held by all three of his corps as well as by Burnside's. Just shy of noon, Lee launched an especially vigorous drive against the Union left, northwest of Sheridan's position. The attackers drove some of Hancock's troops from the Brock Road, one of the avenues that met near Todd's Tavern. The retreat spawned an erroneous report—one Meade believed—that Lee had interposed between the II Corps and Sheridan. At 1:00 P.M., Meade—again fearing for the safety of his horsemen—ordered Sheridan to withdraw from the tavern and take position in rear of the infantry.

Sheridan agreed reluctantly, foreseeing the necessity of reoccupying the vacated ground. Muttering that Meade did not know his business, he evacuated the fortified clearing, thereby breaking contact with Stuart. By late afternoon Gregg and Wilson had withdrawn to Chancellorsville, where they reunited with Torbert. The Cavalry Corps was intact for the first time since it had crossed the Rapidan.[44]

By evening the heavy fighting that had swirled through the Wilderness for the past eighteen hours began to peter out. Meade's path to Lee's right flank had been effectively blocked at the cost of 25,000 casualties on both sides. In similar situations, Grant's predecessors had retreated to salve their wounds and plan anew, but the lieutenant general was not made in that mold. As he informed his cavalry protégé on the morning of the seventh, "It's all right, Wilson, the army is moving toward Richmond!" Yet it was moving west as well as south, in the direction of Spotsylvania Court House. Because the Brock Road was the most direct route to that point, Todd's Tavern, which Stuart had occupied after his enemy's departure, had to be retaken, as Sheridan had predicted.[45]

The upshot was a spirited fight at and near the tavern on the seventh—the largest dismounted cavalry battle of the war. Only the 1st and 2nd Divisions were engaged; Wilson's battle-weary troopers remained at Chancellorsville, resting, refitting, and scouting along the Union left. That placed the fighting in the hands of Gregg and Merritt, who had reassumed command of the 1st Division that morning. Torbert, pained by what he described as a "spinal abscess," had left the army for Washington, where he would undergo surgery. Although he liked and trusted Merritt, Sheridan could not have been pleased by Torbert's leave-taking. Surely the man's condition predated the start of the campaign; why had he had not attended to it sooner?[46]

Sheridan had no cause for alarm, for Merritt opened the fight with a decisive flourish. Custer's brigade, supported by a part of Devin's as well as by

Heaton's battery, charged down the Brock Road above Todd's Tavern, driving Rebel pickets almost a mile beyond the intersection with the road to Catherine Furnace. With the northern approaches to the tavern now clear, both of David Gregg's brigades prepared to confront the Rebels who had occupied the tavern vicinity—portions of Lee's and Hampton's brigades. By hard fighting, Irvin Gregg's dismounted troopers, covered by a section of King's battery, pried Hampton's men from the tavern and flung them into the surrounding woods. Combat afoot continued for perhaps two hours, at which time Hampton mustered enough energy for a counterattack. From its close-up position, however, King's rifles drove back charging Rebels. Gregg's men halted, rallied, and pursued, chasing Hampton across the Po River, where he posed no further threat.[47]

While Gregg's troopers fought, Davies's brigade, most of its men also afoot, advanced on their left. They targeted Fitz Lee's position on the Piney Branch Church Road, northeast of Todd's. Unwilling to await attack, Lee rushed north and struck his opponents' front and flanks. Thanks to their rapid-fire carbines, however, Davies's dragoons withstood the onslaught, then pressed their antagonists rearward. When the Federals occupied farm buildings that commanded Lee's flank and rear, his men retreated all the way to the tavern. One of Davies's chaplains, who had witnessed the fighting from up close, remarked that "it is almost impossible to conceive of anything finer than the style in which these troopers first received the enemy's charge and then advanced against them, sweeping them back before the fierceness of their fire."[48]

In midafternoon, while Lee clung to his old position at Todd's, Sheridan committed his last available force, the Regulars and volunteers of the Reserve Brigade, this day led by Alfred Gibbs. The Reserves performed ably enough to wipe from their escutcheon at least a part of the stain placed there by their assaults on Virginia civilians. After probing Fitz Lee's line with the 6th Pennsylvania, Gibbs dismounted his other regiments and led all four of them south under cover of a barrage by Williston's battery.

Thanks in large part to their artillery support, the Reserves drove Lee's men from one fallen-log and fence-rail barricade to another. Then resistance stiffened; over the next couple of hours, Gibbs's command lost the majority of the 154 casualties it suffered this day. Most occurred in the ranks of Gibbs's own 1st New York Dragoons, which ran up the longest casualty list of any mounted regiment in a single engagement. Even so, Fitz Lee appears to have suffered even more, proportionate to his numbers engaged.[49]

Evening, not enemy opposition, halted Gibbs's advance. By then Lee's troopers had been shoved so far south of the tavern that the Brock Road was available for Grant's and Meade's immediate use. Day's end found Sheridan's weary but pleased troopers in possession not only of the weather-beaten hostelry, but also of their first victory of the campaign. It was, perhaps, an inconclusive triumph—Stuart had been whipped, but would he stay whipped? Even so, it was a start.

Chapter Twenty

To Richmond and Beyond

Given the importance of reaching and securing Spotsylvania, Sheridan was curiously late in directing his troops to that place. Not until 1:00 A.M. on May 8 did he issue orders to two of his division commanders, and by then it was too late. About an hour earlier, as the main army tried to clear the Wilderness, Meade reached Todd's Tavern, where he found Merritt and Gregg awaiting orders from Sheridan, who was beyond their immediate reach. Cursing his cavalry leader's inefficiency, Meade took it upon himself to order the 1st and 2nd Divisions into action. The result was a foul-up that may have cost Grant a critical advantage over his opponent.[1]

Sheridan had already ordered Wilson to move the next morning to Spotsylvania, which he was to hold until relieved by the infantry. To prevent interference, Sheridan intended that Merritt and Gregg guard the south bank of the Po River, which Lee had to cross to reach Spotsylvania. Gregg was to lead the way, crossing the river at Corbin's Bridge and marching south to Shady Grove Church. Merritt would follow as far as Shady Grove Church, before heading southeastward to a landmark known as the Block House, near which he would make contact with Wilson. Meade's orders changed all that. He assigned Gregg the task of guarding the Po River, but only at and near Corbin's Bridge. Merritt he sent to Spotsylvania in advance of Warren's infantry. Wilson, who received no instructions from Meade, did not know that cavalry, rather than infantry, would establish contact with him at Spotsylvania.

Meade's orders had far-reaching effects. One result was that Gregg was not in a position to stop the movement across the Po of Lee's advance, under Maj. Gen. Richard H. Anderson, successor to the recently wounded James Longstreet. Nor could Gregg prevent a portion of Stuart's cavalry—the brigade of Brig. Gen. Williams C. Wickham—from reaching Spotsylvania in advance of Wilson. The most visible effect of Meade's orders, however, was a cavalry-infantry traffic snarl on the road to Spotsylvania, which effectively killed Grant's hope of reaching the courthouse in advance of Lee.[2]

The trouble began at about 5:00 A.M. on the eighth, when the head of Merritt's column met Anderson's infantry and Fitzhugh Lee's horsemen a few miles short of Spotsylvania. Not surprisingly, Merritt's troopers were brought to a halt in the narrow, tree-lined road. Detachments went forward on foot to clear the roadblock, but that barrier was still intact when the head of the V Corps came up about an hour later. Unable to advance with Merritt in his front, Warren complained to Meade about the road jam. In turn, Meade complained by courier to Sheridan. Sheridan rode to the scene, listened tensely to Warren's complaints, and ordered Merritt's men out of the road. Though Sheridan did so without comment, staff officers had never seen him in a blacker mood.[3]

Merritt's men were every bit as unhappy. They resented having to give way to foot soldiers who did not understand what was happening up the road. Lt. Charles Veil of the 1st United States Cavalry recalled that the commander of Warren's lead division, Brig. Gen. John C. Robinson, angrily pushed to the head of the line: "As he rode by where I was I heard him say to someone 'Oh, get your double-damned cavalry out of the way, there is nothing ahead but a little cavalry, we will soon clean them out. . . .' I thought to myself, old man, you will find something more than a little cavalry on ahead; but he went on and in less than fifteen minutes afterwards I saw them carry my General Robinson back on a stretcher with a leg shot off."[4]

Effectively blocked by Anderson and Stuart, Warren failed to reach Spotsylvania in time to aid Wilson, whose troopers had entered the village at about 8:00. Wilson's crossing of the Ny had been opposed by pickets of Wickham's brigade, but the Federals had driven their opponents to Spotsylvania. There Wilson was greeted by Wickham's main body, which at first offered stout resistance. The opposition ceased, however, when Wilson held the Rebels in place with Chapman's brigade, then struck their flank with McIntosh's. When McIntosh hit home, Wickham's brigade, as Wilson wrote, "scattered in all directions."[5]

The troopers held the town for nearly two hours, until Anderson and Stuart came up to challenge them. Committed to maintaining his position until relieved—the IX Corps was supposedly moving up in his rear—Wilson again maneuvered to strike the enemy's flank and rear with McIntosh's brigade. McIntosh was getting into position when a staff officer brought Wilson Sheridan's imperative order that he withdraw at once from Spotsylvania. The aide informed Wilson of the fighting on the road from Todd's Tavern, which meant that Warren, Merritt, and Burnside would not be within supporting range of him any time soon. Finally aware of the danger facing him, Wilson regrouped his command and led it northward to safety. His departure ensured that the Confederates gained a foothold around Spotsylvania, foiling Grant's latest attempt to circumvent Lee's right.[6]

The traffic jam north of Spotsylvania and its effect on Meade's inability to hold Spotsylvania provoked angry words and much finger-pointing. At about noon on the eighth, Sheridan caught up with Meade and the pair had an expletive-filled confrontation. Still mindful of Wilson's travail on the sixth, for which he blamed Sheridan, and incensed that the cavalry had prevented Warren from reaching Spotsylvania, Meade loudly implied that his cavalry chief was incompetent. For his part, Sheridan was infuriated by Meade's meddling, which not only prevented the occupation of Spotsylvania, but also endangered Wilson.

Sheridan's anger appears understandable under the circumstances, but he allowed it to override his sense of fairness. In lashing out at Meade, he stretched the truth beyond recognition. Although he told Meade that he had not been informed of Meade's midnight orders to Merritt and Gregg, he did learn of Meade's action through the regular channels, although some time after the fact. Sheridan also declared that had his own orders to Merritt and Gregg been carried out, there would have been no congestion on the road to Spotsylvania. This assertion lacks credibility, for Sheridan had intended that the 1st and 2nd Divisions start for the Po River bridges at 5:00 A.M. By that time, Warren's column—which had begun its march to Spotsylvania eight hours earlier— would have been in the cavalry's way, ensuring the same crowding and confusion that had occurred that morning.[7]

The Sheridan-Meade encounter ended as acrimoniously as it had begun. By Sheridan's own account, "Finally, I told him that I could whip Stuart if he (Meade) would only let me, but since he insisted on giving the cavalry directions without consulting or even notifying me, he could henceforth command the Cavalry Corps himself—that I would not give it another order." With that, the horseman stalked off, leaving Meade fuming in his wake. The latter promptly sought out Grant, hoping the lieutenant general would take his side in the argument and rebuke Sheridan for conduct unbecoming an officer. Instead, as Sheridan told it, when Meade recounted the Irishman's wish that he be allowed to challenge and destroy Stuart, Grant replied: "Did he say so? Then let him go out and do it."[8]

Grant may well have spoken as Sheridan quoted him, for by 1:00 A.M. the general in chief was issuing orders that called on Sheridan to concentrate his divisions for the first time since the campaign began and to "proceed against the enemy's cavalry" in the direction of Richmond. After besting Stuart, Little Phil was to lead his command to Haxall's Landing, Ben Butler's supply base on the James River, where he would refit in prelude to rejoining the army.[9]

Like Kilpatrick on the eve of his Richmond expedition, Sheridan had been given wide latitude to carry out a mission dear to his heart. He responded immediately, grouping his scattered ranks at a country crossroads known as Aldrich's, north of the Ny River. There his commissary and quartermaster's officers issued the command three days' rations and one day's forage. Other officers culled out those men and mounts who were in such poor physical condition that their ability to complete the journey was doubtful. Small detachments of virtually every regiment in the corps were left behind, along with the entire 4th New York. That polyglot outfit had been dismounted and demoted to guard duty by order of General Torbert. Some of its men attributed the treatment to the fact that the 4th was the only unit in its division whose men had not agreed to reenlist as a body when their service term expired in August. Other observers blamed the army's anti-immigrant bias, which had long worked to the detriment of the regiment.[10]

Sheridan was determined that his first independent mission in the eastern theater would be a rousing triumph. He planned to head for the Confederate capital, not to capture it, as Kilpatrick had intended, but to draw Stuart after him and into a fight. Once he confronted them on open ground, he would thrash the overrated Confederates. As he informed Merritt, Gregg, and Wilson only hours before they left Aldrich's, they were going to engage Stuart as a result of his own suggestion, "and in view of my recent representations to General Meade I shall expect nothing but success."[11]

The raiders took to the road on the warm, sunny morning of the ninth, angling toward Lee's right. The column wound southeastward to Hamilton's Crossing, below Fredericksburg, and from there down the historic Telegraph Road toward the Virginia Central Railroad. Every man in the column was glad to be in uninterrupted motion following four days of marching and counter-marching in the movement-clogging and vision-obstructing Wilderness. At first, however, visibility seemed no better on the road to Richmond. The column kicked up dust "so thick," as one trooper recalled, "that we could not see our file leader." The heat of the day did not help matters. Within an hour of starting out, "our shirts were stiff as boards with the perspiration and dust."[12]

Beyond the discomforts of the march, the men remarked about two unusual occurrences. In contrast to the killing pace they had maintained under leaders such as Kilpatrick, the march from Aldrich's was slow and deliberate, suggesting that Sheridan did not fear being overtaken by the enemy. Then, too, unlike previous raids, on most of which two or more columns had moved on parallel roads, this day a single column of riders and supply vehicles, fully thirteen miles long, was proceeding along one road. The formation gave Stuart a single target, but a formidable one.[13]

As Sheridan and Grant had foreseen, within two hours of the raiders' departure, Stuart set out in pursuit of a force about which he knew only one thing—it was heading in the direction of Richmond. Perhaps, however, its target was not the capital but the railroads that served it. Uncertain not only of Sheridan's intentions but of the size of his command, and unwilling to leave Robert E. Lee without cavalry support, the Beau Sabreur rode out of Spotsylvania at less than full strength. Over the winter Lee had permitted Stuart to reorganize his cavalry into a corps consisting of seven brigades. Stuart left four of these, under Hampton, with the main army, while starting on Sheridan's trail with the Stuart Horse Artillery, two brigades under Fitz Lee, and the brigade of Brig. Gen. James B. Gordon—part of the division of Rooney Lee, who had recently been freed from captivity. By leaving such a large force behind, Stuart was hoping to halt more than 10,000 Federals with fewer than 5,000 of his own men. He took another gamble by dividing this force, sending Wickham to harass the enemy's rear while, by furious riding, he and Fitz Lee sought to interpose between Sheridan and Richmond with Gordon's men and the brigade of Lunsford Lomax.[14]

The opening clash of the expedition occurred late that afternoon, when Wickham's advance reached Jerrald's Mills, about twenty miles from Aldrich's, and caught up with the rear of Sheridan's column, Davies's brigade. According to one of his officers, Davies was incapable of mounting a successful operation on his own but served competently enough under the close supervision of his superiors. On this occasion, he did well under the watchful eye of David Gregg. Although Wickham's advance struck unexpectedly, inflicting several casualties, Davies fought back with both physical strength and guile. His rear regiments, the 1st New Jersey and the 1st Pennsylvania, counterattacked, rocking the enemy back on their heels. Then, at a signal, members of both regiments broke contact and raced around a bend in the road as if in panicky retreat. The Confederates regrouped and pursued at top speed; as they rounded the curve, dozens of saddles were emptied by the carbine fire of dismounted skirmishers whom Davies had posted in roadside woods. Those not killed or wounded in the ambush cleared harm's way with the same desperation their opponents had feigned.[15]

Wickham having been repulsed, the march continued without further interruption. Sheridan's vanguard, Custer's brigade, led the column across the North Anna River and onto a road that paralleled the Virginia Central. Passing along the tracks, a detachment of the 1st Michigan made for Kilpatrick's old port of call, Beaver Dam Station, where railcars stocked with supplies and rations for Lee's army sat virtually unguarded. Just short of the depot, other spoils fell into the raiders' hands: a few dozen Rebels escorting to Richmond-bound trains nearly 400 Union soldiers captured in the Wilderness. The POWs were quickly liberated; many of them joined Sheridan's column, accompanying it aboard ambulances and supply wagons. At Beaver Dam, the Wolverines pried up track and torched depot facilities, while also emptying boxcars carrying everything from oats and hay to beef and crackers. Minutes later, two locomotives and more than 100 cars went up in flames.[16]

Shortly before dawn on May 10, after bivouacking for the night between the North Anna and the burning depot, Sheridan prepared to resume his march toward the enemy capital. For Gregg's division, which had camped on the north bank of the river, "reveille was sounded by the enemy with artillery and carbines, instead of the friendly trumpet or bugle." By hard riding, Stuart's advance had overtaken its quarry, but in strength sufficient to inflict only a few casualties. An unfazed Sheridan started Merritt's division south; he would not fight until Stuart challenged him in front, in which case his raiders could maneuver more freely. As Merritt moved out, Wilson covered Gregg's crossing of the North Anna. As soon as the 2nd Division was across the stream, Wilson's men moved in front of it and resumed the march.[17]

Thus far Stuart had failed to slow his enemy, but he was readying a decisive blow. The safety of Richmond and its communications rested in his hands;

he would protect them with his own life and the lives of every man under him. By now he had made new dispositions that would continue in effect until the enemy had been brought to bay. The three North Carolina regiments of Gordon's brigade tailed Sheridan, while Stuart, Lee, Wickham, and Lomax raced along the Virginia Central to get in front of the Yankees before they could do greater damage.[18]

Sheridan's people saw little action during the balance of the day, which closed with them in bivouac along the South Anna. The next morning, they pressed on to Allen's Station on the Richmond, Fredericksburg & Potomac. At that depot they joined Davies's brigade, which had been sent to destroy track near Ashland. Resistance to the raiding force remained light until 11:00 A.M., when the head of the column drew within sight of Yellow Tavern, a landmark on the Brook Turnpike six miles from Richmond. Along wooded ridges and astride fields north and northwest of the tavern, Stuart had deployed to offer battle, Wickham's brigade on his right, Lomax's to his left. The confrontation Sheridan desired had come at last.[19]

Little Phil seized the opportunity offered him. While keeping Gregg to the rear, confronting Gordon, he deployed the rest of his force to the front, Wilson's division facing Wickham and, farther south, Merritt's opposing Lomax. Fighting broke out in two sectors at about the same time. Merritt advanced under heavy fire toward the Rebel left, gaining a position between Stuart and Richmond. As he did, Gordon's Rebels sprayed the Union rear with carbine and pistol fire. Some of Irvin Gregg's men broke and fled under pressure, but other units of the brigade launched a mounted attack whose power surprised the North Carolinians. The counterstroke stabilized Gregg's line and restored order in a critical sector.[20]

His rear secure, Sheridan concentrated on pressing Stuart's flanks. The effort was largely unsuccessful against the Rebel right, where Wickham's Virginians, seeking revenge upon the Federals who had chased them from Spotsylvania, charged on foot against Wilson's upper flank and bent a part of it backward. As Wilson rushed up reinforcements, Sheridan concentrated on exploiting the foothold Merritt had gained along the other end of Stuart's line. While Devin's brigade, assisted by Gibbs's, held the Brook Turnpike, Sheridan had Merritt advance Custer toward a pivotal point on Lomax's left flank, where a well-positioned battery was threatening the Union right center. The Michiganders would be supported on their left by Chapman's brigade of Wilson's division. Before leading his men forward, Custer personally reconnoitered the ground leading to Lomax's position and decided that "a successful charge might be made upon the enemy battery by keeping well to the right."[21]

Charging artillery was a risky proposition, but Custer proved the accuracy of his prediction. Carefully he dismounted his 5th and 6th Michigan and positioned both regiments, along with Lieutenant Heaton's battery, to support a mounted charge. Then he sent his most seasoned outfit, Lt. Col. Peter Stagg's 1st Michigan, across 200 yards of open ground toward the guns.

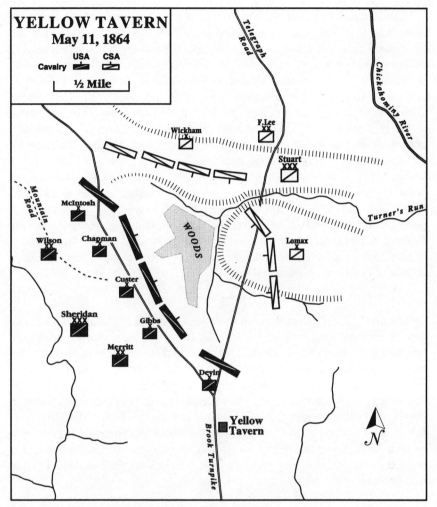

Map of the Battle of Yellow Tavern, May 11, 1864

Heedless of the carbine and cannon fire directed at them, the Wolverines covered the distance with what Custer called "a yell which spread terror before them." Stagg's troopers reached their objective so quickly that the gunners could not depress the barrels of their cannons far enough to offer resistance. The 1st Michigan swarmed over the battery, the men flailing about with their sabers. Artillerymen who eluded the slashing blades raced to the rear, followed by their cavalry comrades. Just before the Wolverines charged, Wickham had begun to withdraw to a position about a quarter of a mile farther east. Under the prodding of Stagg's swordsmen, Lomax fell back as well, forming at a right angle to Wickham's new line.[22]

Aware that Stagg's regiment had fought itself out, Custer ordered up others in the hope of turning retreat into full-scale rout. A mounted charge by the 7th Michigan against the Confederate left went awry, costing the attackers several casualties, but simultaneous advances by dismounted elements of the 5th and 6th Michigan paid dividends. A pistol-wielding member of the 5th—formerly a member of Berdan's Sharpshooters—advanced near enough to Lomax's front to single out a mounted officer wearing a plumed hat, whom he shot in the abdomen. Days would pass before the officer's assailant learned that the victim—who died of his wound the following morning—was J. E. B. Stuart.[23]

Stuart had been urging on some of Wickham's units who were mounting a counterattack against the 1st Michigan. The effort, however, lost momentum at about the time that litter bearers carried their wounded general to the rear. Within an hour of Stuart's fall, Wickham's men, followed by Lomax's, moved beyond range of Sheridan's carbines and cannons. Many headed north toward Ashland, others south, planning to make a last-ditch stand outside their capital. But how they expected to prevail against the juggernaut that had flattened them at Yellow Tavern no one could say.[24]

>─┼─◆>─O─<◆─┼─<

By defeating Stuart's horsemen on three sectors of the battlefield at the same time, in the process killing their leader, Sheridan had accomplished more in a few hours than his predecessors had achieved in three years. It was true that he had outnumbered Stuart, but perhaps only two-thirds of his troopers had been engaged; moreover, they had succeeded on the offensive, a more difficult task than defending against an attack. The Federals realized the importance of their victory, and many vocalized their reaction. The historian of the 10th New York noted that even before the battlefield was clear of the enemy, his comrades began to shout for joy: "The cheers . . . were taken up by other regiments of the brigade on either flank, and . . . made an impression on the mind that was not readily effaced."[25]

Sheridan held the field he had won for several hours after the fighting ceased. Some time past midnight—after burying his dead, tending to his wounded, and corralling his several dozen prisoners—he ordered everyone into the saddle and led them down the Brook Pike toward the outer defenses of Richmond. Cloudy skies and intermittent rain kept the moon from lighting their way, and men and horses were almost exhausted. Consequently, the column—now led by Wilson's division—experienced hours of start-and-stop progress. An officer of the 4th United States Artillery recalled that the halts "were frequent and exasperating. It was so dark that we could only follow the cavalry by putting a bugler on a white horse directly in rear of the regiment in front of us, with orders to move on as soon as they did."[26]

Although only Gordon's plucky Tar Heels were in close pursuit, the raiders experienced numerous dangers this night. The road to Richmond—like the road from Yorktown in May 1862—had been mined with subterranean torpedoes. When the horses of Wilson's advance guard tripped their wires, the land mines detonated, killing a few mounts and at least one rider. An enraged Sheridan dismounted several of the prisoners and forced them to search for the infernal weapons and disarm them before they caused further casualties. At his order, the Confederates placed the unearthed torpedoes in the homes of local citizens. At lease one raider expressed the hope that the torpedoes would explode under the tread of passing horses. Other troopers recalled the outrage Virginians had expressed over the supposed objectives of Kilpatrick and Dahlgren. Apparently, Yankees had no monopoly on terrorism.[27]

Another danger—one that threatened the entire raiding column—was the proximity of the Richmond garrison, which was protected by banks of artillery. Sheridan had a healthy respect for those works and weapons; if he had his way, his men would bypass them by detouring eastward around the city in the direction of Mechanicsville. The raiding commander had already accomplished his primary mission, and even if he fought his way inside the city, he could not stay there for long. Unlike Kilpatrick, whose primary goal had been to enter Richmond and free its POWs, Sheridan was realistic enough—and sufficiently hard-hearted—to dismiss that idea. His ultimate destination was Haxall's Landing; he wanted to get there without further delay and additional casualties.

He was nearly forced to enter the city against his will. In the darkness, Wilson's command missed the road that led to Mechanicsville via Meadow Bridge over the Chickahominy. Ignorant of its mistake, the 3rd Division forged south while the rest of the column—which in the sodden darkness had become separated from Wilson—located the proper path and veered eastward. Only when the head of Wilson's column drew a fusillade did Sheridan realize that something had gone awry. Later he learned that a local guide, whom Wilson had suspected of being a spy, had led the division to the nearest works, where defenders blasted it from several directions. As soon as he was assailed, Wilson dismounted most of McIntosh's brigade, placed its men behind whatever cover was available, and returned fire. Meanwhile, in a scene reminiscent of Dahlgren's confrontation with Martin Robinson, McIntosh summarily executed the guide.[28]

Sheridan sent a courier to tell Wilson to hold his position until the road to Mechanicsville could be cleared. "He *can* hold it," Sheridan told the messenger, "and he *must* hold it!" Wilson, who liked to give the impression of coolness under stress, replied by quoting a popular humorist: "Our hair is badly entangled in his fingers and our nose firmly inserted in his mouth, and we shall, therefore, hold on here till something breaks!"[29]

By then, Wilson was not the only commander in trouble. Merritt had discovered that Meadow Bridge had been partially unplanked and that its approach was commanded not only by Richmond defenders on the south side, but by hundreds of Fitz Lee's troopers on the north bank. As if the raiders' predicament were not dire enough, Gordon's men attacked Gregg's rear with renewed vigor, making it appear that Sheridan and his men were trapped.

Especially for those officers and men who had been in a similar predicament, on the same ground, under Kilpatrick, the parallels with March 1 were a bit unnerving. Maj. John W. Phillips of the 18th Pennsylvania remarked that their precarious position "and the pelting rain and howling thunder all conspired to make things look gloomy." Lieutenant Veil heard fellow officers of the 1st Cavalry wonder aloud if they would escape from "the hole we were in." Most, however, expressed confidence that they would.[30]

In this moment of crisis, every raider went to work with a common goal—deliverance—in mind. Despite mounting pressure—defenders were rushing up from other sectors to oppose him—Wilson held his ground. Gregg's men rose up and deflected Gordon's latest blow, killing Gordon himself. And under Sheridan's watchful eye, Merritt's troopers stripped lumber from nearby houses and used it to repair the bridge.[31]

Completed as it was under fire and in a downpour, the bridge restoration was quite a feat. To protect the repair crews from enemy missiles, Custer's men charged across a railroad trestle parallel to the footbridge, while members of Gibbs's brigade gingerly crossed Meadow Bridge upon the few remaining beams, "creeping, crawling—any way to get across," as Captain Sanford described it. Once across, Custer and Gibbs put the nearest defenders to flight. As soon as the gray troopers raced off, the bridge replacement proceeded at full speed.[32]

The work was completed by dawn, when the bulk of Merritt's division crossed to Mechanicsville. As it did, Wilson disengaged from his standoff with Richmond's protectors, his withdrawal covered by Gregg. Both divisions followed Merritt across the bridge and then down along the meandering Chickahominy. Their enemy let them go grudgingly. A final blow fell when Gordon's more determined pursuers crossed the bridge in the raiders' wake and struck their rear. The effort resulted only in additional Confederate casualties. Wilson's division, now at the rear of the column, turned about, counterattacked, and hustled the assailants back the way they had come.[33]

Although home free on the road to the James River, Sheridan marched only a short distance from Meadow Bridge before bivouacking near Walnut Grove. The gesture was calculated to show the men that although still within range of Confederate cavalry, they were too numerous, too strong, and too confident to fear anything the enemy might throw at them. After everyone had rested and eaten, Sheridan resumed the ride at 9:00 A.M. on the thirteenth, crossing to the south side of the Chickahominy at Bottom's Bridge and proceeding, virtually unmolested, to Haxall's Landing. The next day, after crossing White Oak Swamp and passing Malvern Hill, the column encamped within sight of Butler's army and under cover of gunboats in the James.[34]

>-+-+>-•-O-•-+-+-<

The raiders remained on the river for three days, resting, remounting, and taking on rations and forage. The refit was sorely needed; by now they had suffered almost 600 casualties and the loss of 300 horses. As Bugler Walter Jackson of the 1st New York Dragoons reported, during the greater part of their stay at Haxall's, "there was nothing going on of any notice." Butler's army, however, was busy advancing to attack the southern approaches of Richmond, and once he learned of the operation, Sheridan offered to assist. On the morning of the fifteenth, he sent a portion of his command to demonstrate up the New Market Road toward the southeastern outskirts of the capital. Although energetically made, the effort failed to stave off Butler's defeat when his army was attacked the following day by a smaller but more energetic enemy at Drewry's Bluff, seven miles from the city. By late afternoon the Army of the James was in retreat to its fortified base at Bermuda Hundred, a peninsula formed by loops in the James and Appomattox Rivers.[35]

Sheridan had visited the headquarters of the Army of the James early on the fifteenth. During the meeting, Butler, who feared his own cavalry force (led by Wilson's colleague, now Brig. Gen. August Kautz) was too small to support his main army, suggested that Sheridan's horsemen help Kautz guard his flanks at Drewry's Bluff. Sheridan received the impression that Butler wished to add the raiders to his army for an indefinite period—permanently, if he could get away with it. Little Phil wished no part of any troop transfer, and so on the evening of the seventeenth—earlier than he had originally intended—he led his horsemen north from Haxall's Landing to rejoin the Army of the Potomac.[36]

The troopers who had demonstrated toward Richmond had informed Sheridan that what remained of Stuart's cavalry had rejoined the Army of Northern Virginia. Thus the week-long return march—which began with another crossing of the Chickahominy, this time at Jones's Bridge—was devoid of all but isolated, spasmodic opposition. The only obstacle was the terrain, which included, as Bugler Jackson wrote, "thick woods and swamps" crossed by the "worst road I have traveled in a long time."[37]

The difficulties of this march did not prevent the Federals from conducting side operations—some authorized, some not. On the nineteenth Custer's brigade made an unsuccessful attempt to destroy railroad bridges over the South Anna near Hanover Court House. Gregg and Wilson covered the movement by feinting again toward Richmond from a crossroads settlement known as Cold Harbor, ten miles northeast of the city. The remainder of Merritt's division, its men now skilled at bridge repair, replanked the burned railroad bridge at White House, permitting the reassembled column to cross the Pamunkey. Afterward the raiders camped at Aylett's on the Mattaponi, where Sheridan learned from citizens and prisoners that Meade's army lay along the upper bank of the North Anna near Chesterfield Station on the Richmond, Fredericksburg & Potomac Railroad. Soon the raiders were heading in that direction.[38]

On the last leg of the return trip, dozens of foragers left the column, invaded civilians' homes, and helped themselves to food, forage, and personal property. In a retrospective on the raid, Sheridan called such behavior "disgraceful" and condemned "the system of marauding and wanton destruction of household furniture, clothing &c through the country just passed over by this command." Thievery was bad enough, but when civilians attempted to defend their possessions, many were assaulted and a few killed. Major Phillips recorded in his diary "many instances of cruel treatment to citizens," adding, "I did all I could to stop it." It is doubtful that he achieved much success: looting had been a way of life for many troopers since war's outset, and by mid-1864 it had become a cherished tradition. Many considered stealing one of the fringe benefits of a cavalryman's life. Others believed it their patriotic duty to destroy the enemy's economy, one household at a time.[39]

Good soldiers and vandals alike rejoined their army at Chesterfield Station on May 24, two weeks after cutting loose to challenge J. E. B. Stuart. They learned that during their absence, Grant and Meade had fought a series of battles outside Spotsylvania that featured some of the most horrific carnage ever seen on North American soil. By the twenty-first, having gained no ground in the direction of Richmond, the Army of the Potomac had shifted eastward and southward; Lee countered by falling back to the line of the North Anna. The Federals were battling him across that stream when Sheridan returned.

The horsemen saw little action during the balance of the North Anna Campaign, which on the twenty-sixth ended just as inconclusively, although less bloodily, than the fighting at Spotsylvania. That same day, Sheridan covered the front of the army as it moved south and east in response to Grant's latest attempt to outflank his opponent. This time the march carried Meade's people across the Pamunkey River—one of the last natural barriers to Richmond—at and near Hanovertown.[40]

Sheridan advanced south of the river at two-thirds strength. Early that day Grant had sent Wilson's horsemen to cover the far right of the army. The 3rd Division reconnoitered to a point three miles below the North Anna. The rest of the Cavalry Corps—including the 1st Division, again under Torbert, who had returned from Washington on the seventeenth, his health restored—took the advance. After an all-night march, Torbert's men reached the Pamunkey at Hanovertown Ferry to find the opposite bank defended by a handful of pickets—evidence that Wilson's maneuvering opposite the Rebel left had confused Lee as to Grant's next move.

The cavalry strove to make the most of this opportunity. Custer's brigade, whose performance at Yellow Tavern had made it the "go-to" element of the 1st Division, spearheaded the crossing, men and horses swimming the river under fire. Once on dry ground, the Wolverines chased off those pickets they did not capture. Meade's engineers then laid a pontoon bridge upon which the remainder of the cavalry crossed the stream.[41]

The next day, the army's infantry and artillery followed Sheridan's people across the water. Meade kept some rear-guard elements on the north side for a few days, and it was not till the last day of May that Wilson ended his feint against the Rebel left and crossed the river. Despite the progress they made southward, however, the Federals failed to prevent Lee from getting ahead of them. Although as yet unaware that the enemy had crossed the Pamunkey, the Army of Northern Virginia headed down the R, F & P, halting between the Chickahominy River and the headwaters of Totopotomoy Creek.

Here Lee was in position to thwart Grant's latest movement—if he could determine from what direction it was coming. By the twenty-seventh, he was uncertain whether Grant planned to cross the Pamunkey at Hanovertown or somewhere else. Thus he assembled his mounted arm for its first large-scale mission under Stuart's permanent successor, Wade Hampton. Lee told his new cavalry leader to drive Sheridan away from his army, uncover Meade's infantry, and discern Grant's intentions.[42]

As Hampton started off to find his enemy on the sunny morning of May 28, Sheridan was attempting to do the same. Hoping to determine Lee's reaction to Grant's latest maneuvers, Little Phil was demonstrating in the direction of Mechanicsville, at the head of Gregg's division. Torbert was to follow as soon as his men were relieved along the Pamunkey by Meade's infantry.

At about 10:00 A.M. Gregg's advance pulled rein near a nondescript group of dwellings known as Haw's Shop, where it planned to secure a road junction that connected the Hanovertown area with Richmond. As the Federals dug in, videttes from the 10th New York of Davies's brigade moved out the Mechanicsville Road. About half a mile beyond Haw's Shop they spied Hampton's troopers heading their way. Lacking the time to form a defensive line, the videttes turned and raced back to their main body, Confederates baying at their heels.

Alerted by the commotion, the 1st Pennsylvania, which had been picketing in the New Yorkers' rear, galloped up to take on the Rebels. As usual, momentum decided the outcome, counterattack defeating attack. Struck in front along a narrow, fence-lined road, the hemmed-in Rebels turned and fled. They took refuge with Hampton's vanguard, which threw up a line of breastworks astride the Mechanicsville Road near Enon Church. Soon this line was held in strength by dismounted troopers. Here was an indication that Hampton did not share Stuart's supposed aversion to fighting on foot. Henceforth, cavalry clashes reflected the tactics of mounted infantry, although saber charges were resorted to whenever conditions favored them.[43]

By about 11:00 Sheridan and Gregg had come up to oppose the Rebels behind a parallel line of works held by Davies's troopers and guns. The 10th New York held the right flank, facing Rosser's brigade, which was supported by two brigades under Fitz Lee. Farther south, the 1st Pennsylvania and the 1st New Jersey confronted the Virginians of Williams Wickham. The Union left was held by the 6th Ohio, which opposed Hampton's old brigade, including two regiments of raw recruits from South Carolina armed with long-range Enfield rifles. Hampton had emplaced a couple of batteries along his left flank, but these were opposed by the six 3-inch ordnance rifles of the 6th New York Battery. It was the 6th's last fight at full strength. Three days later, along with every other artillery unit in the army, the battery was reduced, at Grant's order, to four guns. The commanding general feared that the heavily wooded terrain that Meade's army had encountered since entering the Wilderness limited the number of cannons that could be used profitably. Ironically, despite this situation—which had formed the basis of early-war arguments against the raising of a large force of cavalry—Grant showed no disposition to cut back on the mounted arm.[44]

The fighting near Haw's Shop, which lasted until sundown, seesawed back and forth in typical fashion. The heavier Confederate forces made their numbers felt early in the contest, forcing Davies's men to give ground. Then David Gregg sent forward two regiments from his cousin's brigade, the 13th and 16th Pennsylvania. Going into position on Davies's right, the newcomers halted the enemy drive. In turn, a part of Hampton's force appeared to give way, but then the line stiffened, its defenders leveling a heavy fire at all sectors of Gregg's position. The firing was especially intense on the Rebel right, where the rookies from South Carolina performed like veterans, the long-distance accuracy of their Enfields threatening to unhinge Davies's lower flank. Concerned that the 6th Ohio might go under, Sheridan sent a courier to see how the regiment was faring. Colonel Stedman shouted above the din, "You tell the general that we are licking the bile out of them!"[45]

Stedman had his hands full merely holding his position, but late in the afternoon Davies attempted to advance his center. A portion of the 1st New Jersey left its works and rushed on foot through a woodlot, uprooting a line of Confederates and chasing them across an undulating field. When the cheering Jerseymen reached the top of a rise, they were stunned by a volley from riflemen just beyond. The regiment lost thirteen officers and dozens of enlisted men killed or wounded before withdrawing to bind up its wounds. In his after-action report, the outfit's commander described the day as "the severest cavalry fighting of the war." Many participants on both sides endorsed his opinion.[46]

The savage contest was finally decided late in the afternoon, when a part of Torbert's division reached Haw's Shop and Custer's Wolverines entered the fray. All four of his regiments attacked on foot up the Mechanicsville Road, their Spencers ablaze. Unknown to Custer, the Confederates had begun to withdraw, Hampton having learned from prisoners what he had been sent to find out—that Union infantry had crossed the Pamunkey in Sheridan's rear. The Rebel center fell back just as the Michigan men came on, inflicting on Hampton his heaviest casualties of the fight. "In a minute," wrote James Kidd, of the 6th Michigan, "the fight was hand to hand. The rebels fought with desperation, but were routed." Fighting their way to the now-abandoned Rebel defenses, Torbert's men found them filled with bodies. "Their dead were piled up in heaps," wrote Trooper Jackson, who admitted that for the remainder of the fight, "our boys used them for breastworks."[47]

After Hampton retired, and once his dead, dying, and wounded had been tended to, Sheridan withdrew four miles to the rear. He had lost 340 men this day, Hampton just as many, if not more. Casualties, however, told only part of the day's story. Although Haw's Shop never took a place beside Spotsylvania or the Wilderness in the annals of American carnage, few of those who survived it ever forgot the desperate ferocity with which both sides had grappled throughout that bright spring day.[48]

Chapter Twenty-one

Heated Clashes

Despite its recent exertions, Sheridan's people got little rest. The day after Haw's Shop, they returned to Hanovertown, then scouted the lower bank of the Pamunkey toward New Castle Ferry. From there the horsemen ranged southeastward, in the direction of a landmark of the Peninsula Campaign and Kilpatrick's raid on Richmond, Old Church. On the thirtieth, Devin's and Custer's brigades drove Rebel cavalry out of Old Church and chased them toward Cold Harbor.

The next morning Cold Harbor—a misnamed hamlet, shimmering in the heat of late spring—became Meade's next destination. Only by holding Cold Harbor would the army secure a route to White House, its future base of supply. Grant also hoped to use the place as a stepping-stone for another attempt to outflank Lee on the road to Richmond. He feared that if Lee reached Cold Harbor before Meade, the army would lack the room it needed to cut between its enemy and the fast-approaching James River. Grant was acutely aware that he was running out of two equally valuable commodities, time and land.[1]

The cavalry did its part to ease his mind. Early on the thirty-first Torbert's division, supported by Gregg's, advanced on Cold Harbor, which turned out to be held in force by all arms. Merritt's brigade, trooping down the road from Old Church, met Rebel pickets a mile and a quarter from Cold Harbor and pushed them inside unfinished breastworks just north of the village. Coming up to his division's new position, Torbert placed Custer on Merritt's left, Devin farther to the east. Early in the afternoon, as Sheridan looked on approvingly, Torbert led all three brigades in an assault that, despite stubborn resistance, pried the enemy out of their position. The key to victory was a turning movement by Merritt against the Rebel left, which, as Sheridan wrote, "stampeded" the enemy.[2]

Once the former occupants had been driven nearly a mile to the south, Sheridan's divisions regrouped in the hamlet, which they held until after dark. But when, just shy of midnight, scouts reported a division of Confederate infantry coming his way, Little Phil decided it was time to go. As yet, he had not been fully apprised of Grant's intentions for Cold Harbor. These he learned soon enough: Shortly after he left the place, about 1:00 A.M. on June 1, he received Meade's imperative order to retake Cold Harbor and hold it until relieved by infantry. No doubt with a string of oaths—orders that risked the health of his command brought out the color in his vocabulary—Sheridan reoccupied the Cold Harbor breastworks minutes before the Southerners arrived. Even as Torbert's division and part of Gregg's exchanged shots with the newcomers, fatigue parties improved the works until, by daybreak, they could be held against mounting pressure.[3]

After two poorly coordinated assaults on the strengthened position, the Rebels drew off in defeat. By 10:00 A.M. Meade's advance, the VI Corps (now commanded by Maj. Gen. Horatio G. Wright, Sedgwick having been killed by sniper fire at Spotsylvania), arrived to relieve the tired cavalry. To help his men regain their energy, Sheridan put them in bivouac on familiar ground, the north bank of the Chickahominy River near Bottom's Bridge. There, as the troops under Meade and Lee converged on Cold Harbor, Torbert and Gregg remained during the next five days, resting and resupplying in anticipation of renewed operations. As they lolled about, Wilson's division continued to cover the far right flank, picketing, reconnoitering, and battling various combinations of infantry and cavalry. It skirmished on the thirty-first near Hanover Court House; along the South Anna the following day, where its men wrecked bridges and ripped up track on the R, F & P; and on June 3 on the battle-scarred terrain of Haw's Shop.[4]

Wilson's detached position left him out of the planning that provided Sheridan, Torbert, and Gregg with a new mission. By June 6 Grant had exhausted Meade's resources in a series of costly and fruitless offensives at Cold Harbor. These ill-coordinated frontal assaults against well-entrenched positions were symptoms of Grant's frustration at being blocked, once again, by an enemy able to maneuver on interior lines. The attack of June 3 alone cost the Army of the Potomac 7,000 casualties, many of them veterans whose experience was needed to offset the greenness of the many recruits and draftees in the ranks.[5]

Grant, sobered by the carnage, felt constrained to return to his flanking strategy. Now, however, he lacked the room to maneuver around Lee and reach Richmond. After consultation with Meade, he adopted a strategy born of desperation but that held great promise. He decided to cross the Chickahominy east of the capital and then the broad, swift-moving James. His new objective was Petersburg, twenty-two miles south of Richmond, via which the capital and Lee's army received rations, forage, and supplies from the Deep South. To take Petersburg was to break Richmond's link with the Confederate interior; with the "Cockade City" in Union hands, Richmond must wither and die in a matter of months, perhaps weeks.

Grant's plan demanded secrecy. He hoped to slip away from Cold Harbor so stealthily that Lee would not realize he was gone until Meade's men were pounding on the gates of Petersburg. To a large extent, success rested on Sheridan's ability to keep the Confederate cavalry from blocking the army's route south. Grant developed a plan that would take the divisions of Torbert and Gregg toward Charlottesville. Surely Hampton would follow Sheridan just as Stuart had followed him to Yellow Tavern.

This time Sheridan might do more than draw his enemy after him and into a fight. Grant hoped he would also destroy a long stretch of the Virginia Central Railroad and, farther south, portions of the James River Canal. That would stanch the flow of foodstuffs from the "Breadbasket of the Confederacy," the Shenandoah Valley, into Richmond. Furthermore, there was an outside chance that Sheridan could make contact with a small army operating in the Valley under a Virginia-born Yankee, Maj. Gen. David Hunter, and cooperate with it to damage additional communication lines.[6]

Sheridan shared Grant's enthusiasm for the project, though he doubted his ability to locate the erratic Hunter. To ensure his ability to realize his other objectives, Little Phil planned to start his demolition twenty-five miles northeast of Charlottesville, at Trevilian Station, a loading point and water stop on the Virginia Central. Grant gave his approval, whereupon Sheridan transferred Torbert and Gregg to the lower bank of the Pamunkey at New Castle Ferry. There everyone was outfitted for the expedition.

While Torbert and Gregg resupplied, Wilson remained with the army. His mission was to guide Meade to Petersburg and, by elaborate feinting north of the Chickahominy, convince Lee that his opponents remained at Cold Harbor. The 3rd Division's role was essential to the success of Grant's strategy, for while Hampton pursued Sheridan with his old division and Fitz Lee's, Rooney Lee remained at his father's side. If Wilson did not hold his attention, Lee might detect the Army of the Potomac's pullout, ruining Grant's strategy before it could unfold.[7]

Early on the seventh, Sheridan guided officers and men, troopers and horse artillerymen, and a long column of supply wagons and ambulances across the Pamunkey to the south bank of the Mattaponi River, then turned west toward the railroad. Six thousand members of Torbert's and Gregg's divisions followed him, no fewer than 2,000 others having been dropped from the raiding force as physically unfit. Here was a graphic illustration of how used-up the Cavalry Corps had become since the start of the campaign under Grant. But Sheridan could count on the stamina of the three-quarters that had made the cut.

As was the case during the trip to and beyond Richmond, the marching pace this time out was slow to the point of leisurely—the better to permit Hampton to keep up with the column. In fact, the Confederate leader did much better. Thanks to hard riding and interior lines—he rode along the Virginia Central while Sheridan took a more circuitous northerly route—Hampton was able to reach the Yankees' destination before they did. While Sheridan's men were still on the march, Hampton deployed the three brigades of his division around Trevilian, while stationing two brigades under Fitz Lee to guard the rear at Louisa Court House, three miles southeast of the depot.[8]

At their unhurried pace, Sheridan's men had ample time to strike enemy communications before Hampton intervened. Although its route lay north of the Virginia Central, the raiding column crossed the Richmond, Fredericksburg & Potomac on the second day out; sections of track quickly fell prey to levers and crowbars. Thereafter, whenever the road dipped down toward the Virginia Central, parties were detached to pry up track and put the torch to stacks of ties. More than military targets went up in smoke. As on the homeward leg of the Richmond Raid, a number of troopers left the column, by one stratagem or another, to loot houses, barns, chicken coops, springhouses, and corncribs. Following the mission, one of Sheridan's officers declared that raids were no longer instruments of strategy, having become "not much more than stealing expeditions."[9]

The ride to Trevilian took place under a torrid sun; the heat seemed to grow more oppressive as the march went on. Despite Sheridan's efforts to field only the best-conditioned animals, dozens of horses, made ill by heat as well as by the dust kicked up thousands of hooves, staggered to the roadside, where many collapsed and died. Every day, dozens of disabled animals were shot by members of the rear guard. To some extent, the loss was made good by authorized foraging from private stables; still, a shortage of horseflesh plagued the column throughout the mission.

Surviving mounts struggled on, hauling their riders through Chilesburg and New Market on the ninth. The following day, horses and riders turned south toward Trevilian, fording two branches of the seemingly omnipresent North Anna River and bivouacking four miles from their objective. Thus far the only opposition had come from guerrillas, some of whom visited justice on the looters in the column. Now, however, signs indicated that Confederate cavalry and horse artillery were just ahead. The free and easy march had ended.[10]

Hampton had grown tired of waiting for Sheridan to appear. When the Yankees advanced on the depot at about 5:00 on the morning of June 11, he rushed to engage them on the Clayton's Store Road, northeast of the depot. According to a carefully devised plan, he was to hit the enemy head-on while Lee struck Sheridan's left flank via the road from Louisa Court House. When both forces joined the fray, the Confederates would pit perhaps 5,000 men against Sheridan, making the contest close to an even match. As it happened, however, Lee was late in leaving the courthouse, ensuring that for an indefinite period Hampton battled two-to-one odds.[11]

Numbers alone would not carry the day. When Hampton slammed into Sheridan about two miles north of the depot, the blue line recoiled as if in horror. Within minutes, however, Torbert's division recovered its composure. While horsemen slashed at the Rebels with their sabers, dismounted skirmishers took position among the heavy timber that lined both sides of the Clayton's Store Road. George Sanford described the battleground as "one of the thickest tangles of brush that I have ever seen. We were so close to the enemy that we

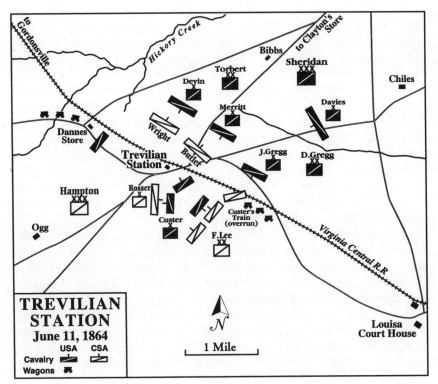

Map of the Battle of Trevilian Station, June 11, 1864

could hear [their] every word of command as distinctly as those of our own people, but the woods were so dense that we could see no one. Many men and officers on either side were captured by accidentally getting into each others' lines."[12]

Merritt's brigade, at first supported on the right by Devin's and later on the left by Irvin Gregg's, opposed Hampton's men north of the depot for several hours under a blazing sun. The fighting, though fierce and at times desperate, threatened to end indecisively, in part because neither Sheridan nor Hampton was at full strength. Lee had not appeared, and at first Sheridan kept Davies's brigade north and east of the fighting to guard the trains of the column. Not until late in the afternoon, when Sheridan committed the better part of Davies's brigade and the batteries of Williston, Dennison, and Heaton found closer positions, did the Federals have the strength for a decisive push. When that push came, however, its success endangered the missing one-fifth of Sheridan's command, Custer's brigade.[13]

Before the fighting erupted, Sheridan had positioned the boy general northeast of the station to meet the anticipated arrival of Fitz Lee. Just short of dawn, Custer's rear guard had begun to spar with Lee's skirmishers at long range, but when the Rebels backed off and sounds of battle drifted in from the west, the brigadier headed there via a woodcutter's trail that met the Clayton's Store Road southeast of Trevilian. The impulsive movement took Custer to a point behind the Confederate line facing Torbert. There he captured hundreds of Hampton's mounts, along with their horse holders.

While the position offered Custer the opportunity to strike the enemy in rear while also opposed in front, it was he who became caught in a trap. Soon after the Wolverines reached the Rebel rear, Torbert, with Davies's help, launched an assault that stunned Hampton's troopers and sent hundreds of them speeding south. The armed and dangerous fugitives rallied short of Custer's position and swarmed over it, recapturing their horses and blasting the Michiganders from many angles. Hoping to extricate himself, Custer started to retrace his path up the woodcutter's trail, only to find it blocked by Fitz Lee, making a belated appearance on the field.

Having fought his way out of encirclement at Newby's Cross Roads and again at Culpeper Court House, Custer now made his third stand of the war. He dismounted the three regiments on hand (the fourth had raced westward before Hampton arrived, chasing a lightly guarded wagon train), and he spread them out until their men faced north, west, and southeast. For an hour or more, they fought in all three directions at the same time, taking almost 400 casualties and seeing their supply train fall into enemy hands. Yet, thanks to their repeaters and the support of Pennington's battery, the trapped men gave as good as they got. They held their oval-shaped line so determinedly that Custer was even able to free one of Pennington's cannons from the hands of would-be captors.[14]

The Wolverines' travail finally ended when, late in the afternoon, Torbert broke through from the north and Davies from the northeast, forcing back what remained of the enemy line. By early evening, Hampton and Lee had retreated, the former westward, the latter back to Louisa Court House. Neither could be said to have been whipped. Casualties had run high on both sides—at least 600 for Sheridan, somewhat more for his enemy. An objective observer would have called the fight a draw.[15]

As was his custom, Sheridan held the field throughout the night, patching his serried ranks and burying the dead, which included Colonel Sackett of the 9th New York, who had so ably commanded Devin's skirmish line on the first day at Gettysburg. The general also spent time questioning some of his nearly 400 prisoners. Among other information, they relayed a rumor that General Hunter, rather than advancing on Charlottesville, was idling in the far reaches of the Shenandoah Valley. Sheridan believed his informants—one feels that he wanted to believe them. He likewise accepted their false assertions that Confederates had occupied Gordonsville, the western terminus of the Virginia Central.

Sheridan already knew that Hampton had taken position about three miles west of Trevilian. When, during the night, he learned that Lee had made a roundabout march to join Hampton, he doubted his ability to make headway in that direction. For these and other reasons, he decided to turn about and rejoin his army "by leisurely marches, which would keep Hampton's cavalry away from Lee while Grant was crossing the James River."[16]

The next morning, Sheridan returned Gregg's men to the task of destroying rails and ties; the work of destruction, which extended for several miles on either side of Trevilian Station, was the last the raiders would inflict on the rail line. At about 3:00 P.M., while the demolition teams labored under the burning sun, Sheridan remounted Torbert's division and, despite the proximity of his antagonists, trotted westward in the hope of securing a certain ford on the North Anna. After crossing the river, he planned to head east—via Spotsylvania Court House, Bowling Green, and Dunkirk—to the supply base at White House, and from there to rejoin Meade.

Sheridan's decision to head west before turning for home proved to be a bad idea. Two and a half miles beyond the depot, his advance ran aground in front of a well-entrenched line of dismounted skirmishers. When the Federals deployed, they found Hampton's men facing their left and front and Lee's their right, blocking the ford road. With some misgivings, Sheridan attacked both on foot and in the saddle. When a series of frontal assaults failed, he sent Merritt's Regulars and volunteers to skirt the Rebel left along the railroad. Hampton deftly strengthened that sector, and again his opponents were repulsed. For a time, his counterattack threatened to roll up Sheridan's right. Hastily summoned reinforcements, including Williston's battery, stabilized the flank just in time to avert disaster.[17]

Unwilling to curtail the destruction of the Virginia Central by bringing Gregg to the front, Sheridan faced the fact that he would not reach his ford of choice. He determined, instead, to backtrack to the less commodious Carpenter's Ford. Unable to break free of his enemy's embrace, he engaged Hampton and Lee throughout the afternoon. After dark he carefully disengaged and ordered the column to clear the vicinity by the way it had come. Thus ended the last long-range expedition Sheridan would conduct in middle Virginia.[18]

>-+-+>-O-<+-+-<

During the return march, Sheridan gave little thought to damaging additional track and no thought at all to attacking the river canal. His attitude later earned him the criticism of infantry officers as well as colleagues such as Wilson, who believed the raiders had done an inadequate job of breaking communications. Another target of criticism was Sheridan's return route, well north of the path he had taken to Trevilian. When Hampton failed to pursue him, Little Phil ought to have realized that somewhere to the south his enemy was racing to get ahead of him before he could rejoin Grant and Meade.[19]

Despite leaving himself open to second-guessing, the Irishman was more popular than ever among his troops. Having observed him in action and under stress from the Wilderness to Trevilian Station, the majority of his officers and men had formed a high opinion of his leadership. As an officer in the 1st Maine put it, "He had secured our confidence thoroughly." He and his comrades would follow this man into the unknown "without hesitation."[20]

Due to the hundreds of casualties that burdened the column, the homeward journey was not only slower than the trip to Trevilian, but also a greater ordeal. After cantering past dozens of ambulances full of shattered men in all stages of suffering, Colonel Stedman announced that "no consideration would tempt me to go over that course again and see the sights and hear the groans that I have this day seen and heard." The dead as well as the wounded attracted attention. On the fifteenth the column crossed the killing fields of Spotsylvania, a vast graveyard from which more than a few bones protruded. A member of the 4th Pennsylvania attempted to make light of the scene; with his saber he lifted a bullet-dented skull above his head for his comrades to see. The joke turned on its perpetrator when decomposing brain matter ran down the blade and into his coat sleeve, leaving him "prostrated with a deathly sickness."[21]

From Spotsylvania, the march proceeded across the Mattaponi River to Guiney's Station and Bowling Green. On the seventeenth the column passed on to Newton and Clarksburg, and the following day to Walkerton and King and Queen Court House, near the spot where Dahlgren had been ambushed. Soon after recrossing the Mattaponi on the nineteenth, Sheridan shed his wounded, his prisoners, and his dismounted men. These men, along with hundreds of slaves who had fallen in with the raiding column, were sent to West Point, where transports would carry them down the York River to Yorktown. With his remaining troops, Sheridan turned back to the north, hugging the Pamunkey until he arrived opposite White House. There he expected to find enough rations and forage to satisfy his command; instead, he found a battle in progress.[22]

When he left the army for Trevilian Station, Sheridan realized that Grant was poised to cross the James, a move that would end White House's value to the Army of the Potomac. The crossing, via pontoons, had taken place on the fourteenth and fifteenth. Soon afterward, the evacuation of White House had begun; supplies that could not be transported by wagon had been transferred by ship to Grant's new headquarters at City Point, northeast of Petersburg. By the time Sheridan arrived, the base on the Pamunkey was in the hands of an elderly rear-echelon commander, Brig. Gen. John J. Abercrombie.

The troops at Abercrombie's disposal, which included a contingent of United States Colored Troops (USCT) from the IX Corps, were relatively few and had little experience in combat. They proved to be an easy target when, shortly after dawn on the twentieth, many of the troopers Sheridan had opposed at Trevilian Station, under Hampton and Fitz Lee, appeared on the river bluffs west of the base and opened fire with small arms and artillery. Their objective was to destroy or capture the 900-wagon supply train of the Cavalry Corps, which remained in park at White House.

Abercrombie's people protected the train with the aid of shells from gunboats in the York River, but they were hard-pressed throughout the day. When, at about 5:00 P.M., he learned of Sheridan's approach on the north shore, the sixty-six-year-old brigadier appealed to Little Phil for help. Abercrombie need not have panicked, for by the time the raiders halted above White House, the enemy was falling back. The head of the column crossed the river and briefly pursued the attackers, then recrossed to join Sheridan. The supply train was moved to within protective range of the cavalry.[23]

Sheridan remained near White House for forty-eight hours, but the stopover was not a respite from hard work. Like any energetic horseman, Little Phil was upset to learn that he must escort the slow-moving train to City Point, a chore he believed the White House garrison should have handled on its own. It would be a frustrating mission, as well as a dangerous one, since the train would attract every Confederate between the Pamunkey and the James.

While at White House, Sheridan heard another troubling piece of news. Just as planned, Grant's furtive advance from Cold Harbor to Petersburg had taken the Army of Northern Virginia by surprise. By the fifteenth, with Lee still unsure of his enemy's location, Grant's advance was poised to take the lightly defended Cockade City by storm. But through a series of poor decisions and questionable acts, the strategic opportunity had slipped through the attackers' hands.[24]

The primary culprit was Baldy Smith, commander of the XVIII Corps, Army of the James, who had been chosen to lead the advance. Grant's protégé, the officer he considered worthy of the top command in Virginia, dithered and deliberated outside Petersburg and withheld until too late the attack that might have taken the city in a matter of hours. Over the next three days, poorly coordinated assaults by Smith and Meade's subordinates failed to crack the city's hastily strengthened defenses, Finally, late on the eighteenth, Lee—deceived no longer about his enemy's intentions—occupied the Petersburg works, ensuring that the city would remain in Confederate hands. By the time Sheridan reached White House, Grant was considering laying siege to the city. The war that might have ended on June 15 would continue indefinitely.[25]

Although he was as disappointed as anyone else over the current situation, Sheridan had a job to do. Before escorting Meade's wagons south, he must clear a path through an enemy who, after their repulse at White House, had massed south of the Pamunkey. On the twenty-first he dismounted Gregg's division and had its men lead their horses across the railroad bridge that the 1st Division had repaired a month ago. Almost immediately, Gregg engaged cavalry on the road to Tunstall's Station. He informed Sheridan that the enemy appeared determined to retake the position it had relinquished the previous day. Little Phil responded by sending Torbert over the trestle and into position southeast of Tunstall's, near Saint Peter's Church, where it covered Gregg's left flank and rear. The Confederates turned on Torbert, for a time pinning down Devin's brigade on difficult terrain. When Devin mustered the strength for a counterattack, however, the Rebels withdrew.[26]

His grip on the south bank now secure, the following day Sheridan dispatched the 9th New York of Devin's brigade to secure Jones's Bridge, where men and wagons would cross the Chickahominy. After the New Yorkers chased off troopers who had been attempting to destroy the span, Devin and Custer crossed it to cover the passage of Merritt, Gregg, and the supply train. Hampton and Lee made little effort to interfere with the crossing, but on the morning of the twenty-third, when Torbert's advance reached the James River east of McClellan's old stamping ground at Harrison's Landing, they attacked

Devin's pickets along the Long Bridge Road. Although the Confederates inflicted more than a dozen casualties, they failed to rattle "Old Tommy" or loosen his grip on the north side of the James. As Torbert reported, Devin "held his ground with his usual stubbornness." Devin ascribed his men's "desperate tenacity" to their awareness that the route to the James must be kept open. In the face of such resolve, the Confederates "retired with precipitation."[27]

The blows Hampton and Lee had landed at Saint Peter's Church and on the Long Bridge Road formed a prelude to the major attack they made on the twenty-fourth, when Torbert's division escorted to the north bank of the James the supply train and the escort troops that used to be Abercrombie's and now were assigned to Brig. Gen. George W. Getty, a VI Corps division leader detached from his command because of wounds. Seven miles northwest of Charles City Court House, near an Episcopal chapel known as Saint Mary's Church, Sheridan stationed Gregg's troopers to guard the rear. Taking up his blocking position at about 8:00 A.M., Gregg chased a party of Southerners away from the chapel. After posting videttes on the roads north, southwest, and southeast of town, he grouped his main body and two batteries—Martin's 6th New York and King's A, 4th United States—around the church itself. As he did, the wagon train trundled southward, heading for Douthat's Landing, opposite Windmill Point on the south bank of the James.[28]

From midmorning until midafternoon, Gregg's outriders skirmished with small but unassertive groups of horsemen. The clashes did not worry Gregg, but two facts did. By 3:00 P.M. he was so far from Torbert's rear as to be beyond quick assistance. Then, too, a large force of cavalry was known to have passed through the vicinity the previous night—perhaps it would return, in a fighting mood.

This prospect became reality shortly after 3:00 on that sultry afternoon, when a long line of gray riders appeared in front of Irvin Gregg's position on the right flank of the divisional line. The Rebels quickly spread out until facing Davies's brigade on the left. There seemed no end to the Rebel column—clearly, it consisted of Hampton's entire command. A Pennsylvania trooper posted beside the church saw General Gregg "looking anxious and riding to and fro in different directions; then I knew there was something interesting on hand." It became even more interesting when the enemy attacked the length of the Federal line.[29]

Gregg saw that the attackers outnumbered his command by a wide margin. Hoping that Torbert would arrive in time to assist him, he sent couriers galloping toward Charles City Court House—couriers who were overtaken and captured well short of their destination. For two hours the 2nd Division fought alone against increasing pressure, trying to stave off encirclement. At the height of the combat, Gregg ran his batteries to within a few hundred yards of the enemy. Hampton's men rushed forward to seize the guns and took a blast at point-blank range. "It was one grand sheet of flame along the whole line," exclaimed an onlooker; the nearest Confederates "were shot down within 30 feet of the guns." Survivors raced for cover, from behind which they popped away at the battery horses, dropping several in their traces. Gregg had to yank the guns to the rear to avoid abandoning them.[30]

In the end, he had no recourse but to retreat. Minutes before the road to Charles City could be blocked, Gregg ordered his regiments to disengage and leapfrog to the rear. As they broke contact, he cobbled together a rear guard and erected fieldworks along the road south. A trooper heard Gregg refer to the position as "the end of the line," insisting, "We must hold this point till after dark!" Somehow, against all odds, they did. Protected by the works, the rear guard enabled Davies and Irvin Gregg to retire in tolerable order toward the security of Torbert's lines. By nightfall the division had absorbed 357 casualties, including the mortal wounding of Col. George H. Covode of the 4th Pennsylvania, son of Congressman John Covode. But they had held their lines at the chapel long enough to ensure the safe passage of Sheridan's train, without whose cargo— everything from crackers to cartridges—the horsemen of the Army of the Potomac could not have remained at Petersburg for more than a week.[31]

>─┤─◆⟩──○──⟨◆─┤─◄

After ferrying the wagons over the James aboard steamboats, Sheridan's divisions remained on the north bank for three days, catching their breath, salving their wounds, and trying to avoid sunstroke. On the twenty-seventh and twenty-eighth they too boarded transports for the trip to Windmill Point. Reaching shore, they went into camp not far from the river. Rumor had it that they would remain there, fifteen miles from the trench lines east and south of Petersburg, for additional days of rest and resupply. But the grapevine got it wrong. Within a day of crossing the river, most of them were ordered out on a rescue mission that would carry them well south of the Cockade City. The object of their effort was the 3rd Cavalry Division.[32]

Wilson's men had been kept busy throughout Torbert's and Gregg's absence from the army. Soon after those divisions started for Trevilian Station, Wilson divided his command to guard both of Meade's flanks, McIntosh's brigade on the right, Chapman's on the far left. Both forces saw action almost immediately, as the cavalry of Rooney Lee, sometimes backed by infantry, tried to lift Wilson's counterreconnaissance screen so they might study Meade's dispositions.

While the army remained at Cold Harbor, Wilson guarded not only its flanks, but also several fords on the Chickahominy; his men pulled forty-eight-hour shifts of picket duty. At times the division found itself hard pressed and severely handled; on June 10, for instance, Rooney Lee attacked a picket post near Old Church, killing one officer and capturing a half dozen men of the 1st Connecticut and 18th Pennsylvania. Even so, when Grant began his withdrawal to the James the division was, in the words of Wilson's aide, Maj. Eugene Beaumont, "in good order & spirits."[33]

The division paved Meade's path to the river. On the evening of the twelfth, while McIntosh covered the army's rear, Wilson led Chapman's men to the ruins of Long Bridge on the Chickahominy, a dozen miles southeast of Cold Harbor. Pontoons were to be laid there, but a small body of riflemen on the south bank kept the bridge-builders idle. By great effort, the 3rd Indiana and the 22nd New York crossed the stream on logs and limbs and chased the Rebels away, permitting the pontoons to be laid. The balance of the brigade then crossed, followed by the V Corps, which had been assigned to cooperate with Wilson in shielding the army's right flank as it moved to the James.[34]

As the II Corps followed the V across the Chickahominy (Hancock's rear and wagon train were now covered by McIntosh), Wilson and Chapman, backed by Warren's infantry, ranged westward. Their path led toward White Oak Swamp and, beyond, Richmond. As Grant had hoped, Lee sent down troops to fend off what he feared was the third raid on the city since February. Early on the thirteenth, horsemen under the Confederate commander's son struck Chapman near White Oak Swamp; the two forces skirmished over a three-mile course until the V Corps came up to push the Rebels beyond the swamp. After they withdrew, Chapman moved a few miles to the south to picket a web of roads that converged in the direction of the enemy capital.

About 6:00 P.M. Chapman's advance—now moving in the direction of Malvern Hill—encountered the enemy at Riddell's Shop on the Long Bridge Road. The new arrivals were not Rooney Lee's horsemen, but the advance of A. P. Hill's infantry corps, supported by artillery. Chapman sparred with the infantry at long distance, hoping to keep out of rifle range. By dusk his brigade had been driven two miles, at which point a portion of Warren's command again came up to cover the cavalry. This time, Hill shoved both foot soldiers and troopers almost a mile before breaking contact and departing. Wilson then withdrew Chapman's brigade to the future site of David Gregg's near disaster, Saint Mary's Church.[35]

At daylight on the fourteenth, Wilson ordered Chapman down to the river near Westover Church, where his soldiers drew rations and oats from a temporary supply depot. That afternoon pickets Chapman had left behind at Saint Mary's Church came under attack, but their assailants were repulsed by a rear guard the colonel had established nearby. In the evening Chapman moved toward Charles City Court House, where McIntosh's brigade had arrived hours earlier; there the 3rd Division united for the first time in ten days.

On June 15 and 16 Chapman and McIntosh demonstrated westward along a line between Saint Mary's Church and Malvern Hill. At the latter point, Confederate cavalry and infantry lurked, their scouts still striving to discover where Meade's army was heading. By now, however, it was too late to stop the Army of the Potomac short of Petersburg; the II Corps had begun crossing the James on transports early on the fourteenth. Smith's troops had already reached Petersburg by boat and overland march to make the initial attack on the unguarded city. Grant's carefully orchestrated deception had proven its worth.[36]

In rear of the II Corps, the VI and IX Corps crossed the James on the fifteenth and sixteenth via a 155-pontoon bridge near Douthat's Landing. Their job of screening Meade's march well and faithfully done, Wilson's troopers followed the V Corps over the floating bridge at 5:00 A.M. on June 17. Once on the south side of the river, they bivouacked near Prince George Court House, six miles east of Petersburg. From there, on the eighteenth, the division moved south to Mount Sinai Church, along the Blackwater River.[37]

On the twentieth Meade ordered Wilson to prepare his men for a raid below Petersburg. While always an exciting prospect, a long-range expedition was not something that many of Wilson's weary troopers could look forward to. They had been on the go every day since Sheridan left the army; they had not unsaddled since crossing the Chickahominy. Grant realized, of course, that the 3rd Division had had a hard time of it lately, but he needed its services. Not yet committed to a siege, he wondered if he could achieve by breaking Petersburg's rail connections with North Carolina and Tennessee the same goal that had prompted him to cross the James: to stop the flow of edibles and hard goods from the Deep South to Lee's army. Only a mounted force could find out.

Four Petersburg-area railroads were in Union hands, but two others continued to supply the Army of Northern Virginia: the Petersburg & Weldon, which ran into North Carolina, and the Petersburg & Lynchburg (also known as the Southside Railroad), which led southwestward toward the Tennessee border. At Burkeville Junction, fifty miles west of Petersburg, the Southside crossed the Richmond & Danville, another supply conduit to the Petersburg-Richmond front. Grant wished Wilson to tear up as much track as possible on all three lines. Widespread destruction might force Lee out of his rifle pits in search of rations and ammunition. Once on open ground, his army would be at the mercy of the combined forces of Meade and Butler.[38]

The 3rd Division would not make the journey alone; Grant considered it too small to conduct safely a mission that was bound to attract a great deal of opposition, especially since Wilson would leave 800 men behind to scout and picket for Meade. Ever since Meade's troops joined the XVIII Corps outside Petersburg, Grant controlled the movements of the Army of the James, a large portion of which continued to man the Bermuda Hundred defenses, across the Appomattox River from Petersburg. Thus Grant was able to augment Wilson with Kautz's small division.[39]

While the assignment reunited him with his Cavalry Bureau subordinate, Wilson was not impressed by Kautz's four-regiment command, which he described as "about 2000 of the wildest rag-tag and bob-tail cavalry I ever saw." Kautz did bring one strength to the mission: unlike Wilson, he knew the territory to be covered, having raided along all three railroads at the outset of Butler's abortive drive on Richmond.[40]

As befit Wilson's perfectionist bent, many details were attended to in a short time to ready his command for its assignment. A trooper of the 2nd Ohio recalled that throughout June 21 "every body seemed in a hurry. The surgeon was examining the men & all not fit for duty were being sent back to City Point; there were . . . rations to be drawn, also requisitions to be made out for

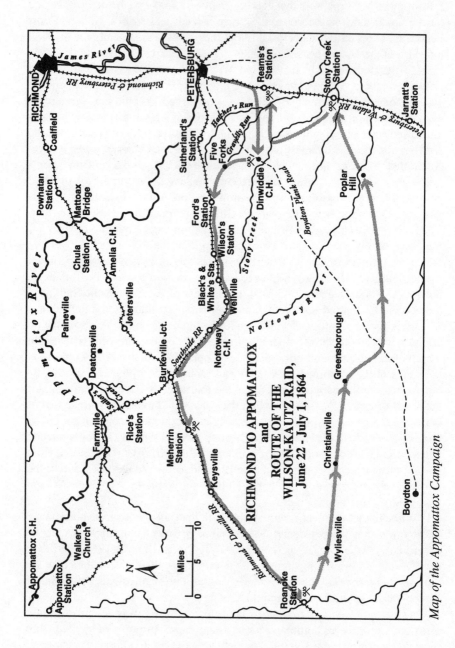

Map of the Appomattox Campaign

clothing, then drawn & issued. The butchers were killing beeves, the Q. M. [quartermasters] were running around wildly . . . broken down horses [were] being condemned & turned over to the Q. M. and it was plain to be seen some move was to take place . . . I found orders had been issued, saying we would break camp at 2 A.M. next morning."[41]

The man was off by only an hour; the combined force of 3,300 troopers and two batteries (each mounting six guns in spite of Grant's decree) left Mount Sinai Church at 3 A.M. on the twenty-second. It was about the only event that did not go like clockwork during the first leg of the raid. By seven o'clock, the head of the column had halted at Reams's Station, seven miles south of Petersburg, to destroy the depot, several freight cars, and a few hundred feet of track on the Weldon Railroad. While Wilson's men labored under a burning sun, Kautz's took the advance, moving westward to Ford's Station on the Southside, where his men demolished four miles of track, two locomotives, and thirty cars. It was an auspicious start to a mission that meant career advancement to the success-obsessed Wilson.

At first the raiders' only problem was the division of Rooney Lee, which had bivouacked along the Southside but which Kautz, on his westward jaunt, had managed to avoid. Wilson was not so lucky; late that afternoon the Rebels stuck the rear of his column, compelling Chapman to turn about and fend him off, enabling the rest of the expeditionary force to move on, unimpeded. By 3 A.M. on the twenty-third Kautz was at Burkeville Junction, where his soldiers were levering up track in four directions. They moved on to the Richmond & Danville line before doing a complete job, but Wilson's men added finishing touches later in the day. The column's progress thus far kept Wilson's spirits high, although he noted that Rooney Lee continued to strike his rear with infuriatingly regularity. Then, too, although no one in any of the trackside villages he had visited had attempted to offer resistance, signs indicated that the countryside was beginning to fill up, as it had during Dahlgren's return march from Richmond, with home guards, veterans on furlough, and embattled farmers.[42]

Over the next two days, Wilson and Kautz laid systematic waste to the third railroad on their itinerary. This was not a Herculean task, for the rails of the R & D were fastened to wooden stringers that proved so combustible the raiders could destroy track without having to pry it up. Not until the afternoon of June 25, when the column reached the Staunton River bridge over the Roanoke River, seventy-five miles southwest of Petersburg, did the easy part of the expedition come to an end. The railroad bridge at Roanoke was defended on both sides of the stream by nearly 1,000 Confederates, including the militia of eight counties, supported by enough cannons to give the force staying-power.

Hoping for the best, Wilson sent Kautz's men forward as dismounted skirmishers. A sharp fight broke out in the heat of afternoon. Though Kautz suffered few men killed or wounded—more fell victim to the sun than to enemy missiles—the attackers were stopped well short of the span, which Wilson had hoped to destroy as a means of capping his railroad demolition. After a half-dozen assaults failed, Kautz pulled back and Wilson ordered a retreat—although he would have called it a tactical repositioning. He had come as far into the Confederate interior as he would get.[43]

While Kautz held back the foe, Wilson's men turned about and rode eastward, Kautz disengaging and following as soon as possible. A two-and-a-half-day ride took both divisions past villages and across farms, over streams, and through woods, some of which hid bushwhackers who peppered the Yankees' rear, then fled before they could be captured. Wilson dismissed the few losses that resulted, aware that the expedition had been almost casualty-free thus far. He concentrated on bringing his command home in that same condition.

He decided to return to the Weldon railroad below Reams's Station. Before starting on the expedition, he had received assurances from Meade's chief of staff, General Humphreys, that within hours of Wilson's departure the Army of the Potomac would have possession of the railroad as far south as Reams's, and probably farther. Humphreys had promised more than he could deliver, however, for troops under A. P. Hill had repulsed Meade's effort to gain a foothold on the Weldon the day Wilson left Mount Sinai Church. The raiding leader had not heard the news; thus he expected to be among friends by the time he reached the railroad, if not sooner. Some of his men appear to have been more skeptical. "We are on the back track," a diarist in the 8th New York observed on the twenty-sixth, ". . . but expect that we shall have some fighting before we get back."[44]

When he neared Stony Creek Station on the Weldon, ten miles south of Reams's, on the afternoon of the twenty-eighth, Wilson was shocked at being challenged by hundreds of cavalry and infantry. Pugnacious Rebels surged out of woods and from behind ridges, threatening to surround his column. As Wilson's men hurriedly deployed, a desperate struggle ensued, each side gaining and losing the advantage. The fighting, which took numerous casualties among the raiding column, continued into the evening.[45]

In the darkness, Wilson sent Kautz, along with at least one regiment from his own division, by a back road to Reams's Station, which he hoped lay within Meade's lines. Instead, Kautz, and later Wilson, found themselves in the fight of their lives. Reams's Station was held in force not by the Army of the Potomac but by Rooney Lee's horsemen, along with the rest of the mounted wing of the Army of Northern Virginia. Behind well-constructed works surrounding the depot were the troopers of Hampton and Fitz Lee. They had slipped away from Sheridan north of the James as soon as they leaned of Wilson's and Kautz's expedition. Meade's headquarters had made more than one promise it could not keep, having persuaded Wilson that Sheridan would keep Hampton and Fitz Lee occupied well north of him for the duration of the raid. Another startling revelation was the presence, in rear of the cavalry, of two brigades of infantry under Maj. Gen. William Mahone.[46]

Wilson had already lost a substantial number of men, including virtually the entire 22nd New York, when breaking free at Stony Creek. Now he lost many more—hundreds, in fact—to death or capture, as Hampton and the Lee cousins muscled their way forward on three sides. Only nightfall—assuming the raiders held out that long—would save them from obliteration. By late afternoon the diarist in the 8th New York reported, "I don't think that thare is 200 men fit for duty in the Regmt. They have got us surrounded and we are to cut our way out at dark tonight."[47]

Before his command was forced to break and run, every man for himself, Wilson sent a staff officer, escorted by forty of Kautz's riders, to Meade's headquarters at City Point, with an urgent request for help. The gesture must have seemed like a forlorn hope, even to Wilson. To his astonishment, the officer slipped through the lines and, by hard riding, completed his errand. Wilson would have been overjoyed by the man's success but infuriated by the result.

As soon as they learned of Wilson's plight, Grant as well as Meade expressed concern for the safety of the 3rd Division. Meade sent a message to General Wright, whose VI Corps was gaining a reputation as the most reliable component of the army, ordering the entire command to Reams's Station. Then, realizing that the foot soldiers would take hours to cover so much ground, the army leader called on Sheridan to join the rescue effort.[48]

Little Phil appeared less concerned about his colleague's predicament than Grant, Meade, or for that matter, Wright. Certainly he did not consider himself responsible for it; he rejected Wilson's subsequent charge that he was to have kept Hampton and Lee off the raiders' tail—no such mission had been assigned him, Sheridan insisted. Even so, Wilson forever claimed a prior understanding that "Sheridan will look after Hampton" until the strike at Petersburg's railroads was over. Almost fifty years later, the division leader was still complaining that his raid had failed through the "great neglect" of Meade, Humphreys, and Sheridan. He remained especially resentful toward Little Phil, whom he also blamed for abandoning the 3rd Division on the first day of the fighting in the Wilderness. The failure to tie up Hampton was "one of two great stains on the escutcheon of Sheridan."[49]

Wilson was also incensed by Sheridan's reluctance to help rescue the raiders. Although he later asserted that he rode off to save Wilson and Kautz "the moment [I] received orders from General Meade," Sheridan appears to have been guilty of foot-dragging—perhaps for good cause. Torbert and Gregg had just returned from a two-week stint of hard riding and hard fighting; Captain Sanford called the result "worn out horses and exhausted men." Of course, the 1st and 2nd Divisions had no monopoly on fatigue. One of Wilson's surgeons noted that by the time the raiders reached Reams's Station, they had gone four days and nights "without one hours sleep & had but one meal . . . in each 24 hours."[50]

One indication that Sheridan could not or would not rush to the rescue was that by the time he reached Reams's Station via Prince George Court House and Lee's Mills, well after 7:00 that evening, Wright's troops were already there, having chased away the few Rebels they had found on arriving.

The combined force lingered about the depot until the evening of the thirtieth, making fruitless inquiries for the 3rd Cavalry Division, before returning to the siege lines.[51]

Later, the would-be rescuers learned that, lacking other options, Wilson had ordered his own and Kautz's men to fight their way to safety as best they could. One escapee described the upshot as "a wild skedaddle through heavy timber, shells from rebel batteries knocking the branches about our ears." During the stampede, the raiders abandoned their artillery, supply wagons, wounded, prisoners, and dozens of runaway slaves. Hundreds of troopers and horse artillerymen were felled by saber, carbine, and cannons; hundreds more were cut off, herded together, and started off for the lock-ups of Richmond.[52]

Unlike Wilson's men, most of Kautz's made it to safety, many by clinging to him like leeches. Their leader, after all, knew every thicket, every back road, every blind ford in the area. At about the time Sheridan reached the abandoned battlefield, the German-born brigadier was leading a substantial remnant of his command inside Ben Butler's lines at Petersburg. Reporting to Grant, he gave the commanding general and, later, the visiting assistant secretary of war, Charles Dana, a highly excited account of raid and rout, complete with his belief that Wilson and most of his men had been gobbled up. The interview over, Kautz joined his weary men and their jaded mounts in camp. Later, someone at army headquarters asked him to help rescue Wilson, but Kautz, unlike Sheridan, was permitted to beg off.[53]

For a time, Wilson and most of his people were given up for lost. Not everyone in the army, however, was heartsick over that prospect. George Custer exulted in a letter to his bride that "the upstart and imbecile" Wilson had sacrificed his troopers to "his total ignorance and inexperience of cavalry." Custer hoped Wilson's performance would cost him his command, creating a vacancy at the divisional level.[54]

Meade was trying to figure out how to replace an entire cavalry division when word reached City Point, early on the first of July, that the raiding leader had entered Union lines with a good portion of his command, following a roundabout ride east and north of Reams's Station and a crossing of the Blackwater River on a half-ruined bridge. For days afterward, fugitives of the 3rd Division, many without hats or caps, their uniforms torn by branches and briars, their horses foam-flecked and heaving, staggered back to the Army of the Potomac. A laconic member of the 1st Connecticut spoke for his comrades when he termed the operation just ended "as severe a raid as was ever made." Major Beaumont of Wilson's staff described the expedition as "many an anxious hour . . . I would not endure the same again, for untold gold."[55]

In later weeks the frustrated Wilson sought not only to shift the blame for a mission gone wrong, but also to promote it as a strategic success. The sixty miles of track he and Kautz had mangled on three important railroads compensated, he claimed, for their losses, which initially amounted to 1,300 officers and men killed, wounded, and missing—although many in the latter category later rejoined their commands—plus thirty wagons and a dozen artillery pieces.

In public, Grant and Meade agreed with their young subordinate. In private, they questioned the long-range value of the undertaking. Then, too, they winced at the storm of protest the raid generated in enemy circles. Southern editors and Confederate officials branded Wilson's and Kautz's men a pack of godless thieves. Evidence supported their strident claims. Among the contents of the wagons abandoned at Reams's Station were not only edibles but also table silver, plush curtains, men's and women's clothing, even a communion service from a church in Lunenburg County.[56]

Allegations of looting were nothing new, and eventually the controversy blew over. A more lasting concern was the fact that it took repair crews out of Richmond and Petersburg less than a week to fix the damage the raiders had inflicted on the enemy's communications. In the interim, wagon trains substituted for locomotives in transporting the goods that kept the Army of Northern Virginia alive.[57]

At the heart of the Wilson-Kautz raid was a lesson worth heeding. The damage that Sheridan had inflicted on the Virginia Central had also been fixed within days of the end of the Trevilian Raid. The difference between his expedition and Wilson's was that rail wrecking had been Sheridan's secondary objective. By timing his raid with the movements of Meade's army, he had achieved his primary goal: preventing Hampton from detecting Meade's pullout from Cold Harbor and striking his flanks and rear as his army moved to the James. The Wilson-Kautz Raid, on the other hand, had railroad busting as its first order of business. To have enduring value, such a mission had to be closely coordinated with the operations of the main army. Because such coordination proved lacking, Wilson's expedition had achieved fleeting, short-term gains. The outcome validated Grant's reluctant description of the expedition as a "disaster."[58]

Chapter Twenty-two

Emptying the Breadbasket

Observing Wilson's escapees as they straggled into camp at Light House Point, twenty-some miles in rear of the siege lines, a *Philadelphia Inquirer* correspondent noted that they presented a "sorry picture." Dozens had made the trip on foot, their horses dead or stuck in a swamp somewhere. In later days, whole companies of Wilson's command were sent by steamer to Giesboro Point for remounting. Many of those whose horses had carried them through were also lost to active duty for a period, banished to the quartermaster depots at City Point. There they were issued new blouses, pants, caps, boots, arms, accouterments, and tack—replacements for the myriad items the raiders had lost on the frantic ride from Reams's Station.[1]

Wilson's was not the only cavalry in need of remounting and refitting. Many of the troopers under Torbert and Gregg were nearly as ragged as the fugitives of the 3rd Division, and dozens lacked able-bodied mounts. George Sanford observed that even before they made that "dreadful march through the heat and dust" to rescue Wilson and Kautz, the 1st and 2nd Divisions had been in terrible condition: "The horses were actually reduced to skin and bone, and were greatly in need of shoeing. The men's clothing was in rags, and they were worn out and nervous from the constant strain of marching by night and fighting by day, with little sleep and less food, and incessant guard and picket duty." The commander of the Army of the Potomac agreed: On July 2, after his inspectors reported on the condition of all three divisions, Meade pronounced the entire corps "unserviceable." Sheridan predicted that at least twelve to fifteen days of rest and refurbishment were needed to return everyone to fighting trim.[2]

As it turned out, they did better than that. For three and a half weeks, officers and men recruited their strength far from the sound of guns. While the "good resting spell" lasted, everyday chores such as picket and scouting duty were assigned to less put-upon troopers, such as the 800 Wilson had left behind on June 22. The respite not only allowed the average trooper to recover from his recent exertions, it helped expand his regiment. As now-Colonel James Kidd noted, between July 2 and 26, "many hundred convalescent wounded and sick men returned from hospital to duty; many also who had been dismounted by the exigencies of the campaign returned from dismounted camps."[3]

Everyone knew the idyll could not last. On the thirteenth William Wells of the 1st Vermont, whose regiment had lost more than 100 men on Wilson's raid, informed his sister that despite the lull in campaigning, he kept "at work most of the time," since he did "not know how long before we may have to spring into the Saddle at a moments notice." Presumably, comrades in the 1st and 2nd Divisions prepared themselves as well, for when active campaigning resumed, they, not Wilson's people, were called on to handle it.[4]

On July 9 Meade had formally imposed a siege on Petersburg, but there remained an outside chance that a breakthrough could be achieved, and quickly. Since June 25 a team of prewar coal miners, members of an infantry regiment in Burnside's corps, had been digging a mine shaft under the defenses opposite them, northeast of Petersburg. By late July hard work had created a tunnel more than 500 feet long and twenty feet deep, which extended beneath a Rebel position known as Elliott's Salient. With Grant's hopeful endorsement and Meade's grudging approval, the miners filled the end of the shaft with 320 kegs of blasting powder, enough to blow the salient sky-high and carve a path into Petersburg. Accordingly, Burnside drilled a division of USCT (later replaced, for political reasons, with a division of untrained white soldiers) to exploit the breakthrough with a bayonet charge. Banks of cannons were positioned to pave their way, and other infantry commanders were assigned to support the attack, although kept in ignorance of the mine.[5]

If the project succeeded, Grant wanted Lee to lack the strength to counterattack in the wake of the blast. As a result, on the twenty-sixth Meade told off Hancock's infantry and Sheridan's cavalry for an expedition across the Appomattox and the James that, by threatening Richmond, would shift out of position thousands of potential opponents of Burnside's assault. Other benefits might accrue from the movement. Grant hoped that the cavalry would find an opening to head west and wreak havoc anew on the Virginia Central Railroad—an implied criticism, perhaps, of the Trevilian Raid. Sheridan might also return to the bridges on the North and South Anna and destroy them.[6]

By the twenty-sixth Sheridan admitted that the strength of the cavalry corps had been "pretty well restored." Even so, when starting out on his latest mission, he left Wilson's division behind to relieve Torbert's and Gregg's pickets. The clear implication was that the 3rd Division was still too worn down to retake the field. To compensate for Wilson's absence, Butler made Kautz's division available for the operation, during which it served under Sheridan's command. Apparently, only half of those who had been ambushed at Reams's Station suffered from its lingering effects.[7]

Late on the twenty-seventh Hancock and Sheridan—most of whose men knew nothing of the impending mine explosion except, perhaps, for a rumor or two—moved north of Petersburg, crossing the Appomattox on pontoons, then the rear of Butler's lines at Bermuda Hundred. After some difficulty in locating the newly laid bridge, the expeditionary force crossed on it in early-morning darkness, landing opposite a marshy creek mouth called Deep Bottom. In that area, Kautz, who had been awaiting his comrades for several hours, fell in with the column. The cavalry remained in position as Hancock's foot soldiers forged northward and then westward toward New Market Heights, a high plateau directly south of Richmond.[8]

Presently, the II Corps happened upon a lightly held line of breastworks along the east side of Bailey's Creek. This position the foot soldiers carried after brief resistance, taking several prisoners and, what was more valuable, four 20-pounder Parrott rifles. As daylight broke, Sheridan moved his men and Kautz's across Strawberry Plains, a grassy expanse east of Deep Bottom, until they connected with the right of Hancock's line.

Forging north, the horsemen uncovered a second, stronger line of defenses on the other side of Bailey's Creek at a point where the New Market Road crossed the stream. The works stretched northward across the Central (or Darbytown) Road. Cavalry videttes in advance of the enemy's position galloped over a ridge to the safety of the Rebel rear. As they did, Merritt, whose brigade led Sheridan's column, sent the 2nd United States Cavalry, supported by the 5th Cavalry, charging after them.

The Federals did not get far before a counterattack by a brigade from Maj. Gen. Joseph B. Kershaw's command drove them, with heavy loss, back over the ridge and into a fence-lined, ditch-filled field. Not content to scatter a few Regulars, the Confederates advanced on Sheridan's main body in line of battle, skirmishers deployed in front as if intent on dispersing every trooper in their path. They did not halt until within range of Merritt's horse herds and horse holders, just beyond the rise. Then, seconds before the Rebels could seize those prizes, the balance of Merritt's brigade—the 1st United States, the 6th Pennsylvania, and the 1st New York Dragoons—bobbed up from behind another rise and sprayed the head of the skirmish line with carbine fire.

At the same time, Devin's brigade advanced dismounted through a woods that flanked the enemy and, upon emerging from the trees, attacked "with a yell & a volley," according to a member of the 9th New York. Their opponents promptly broke, and "close behind the fleeing Rebels was our thin line of skirmishers, dealing well aimed shots into them." While the Rebels "ran like good fellows for the woods," George Sanford, his regiment, and the rest of Merritt's men, got to their feet. "As our trumpets sounded the charge," the captain recalled, "the men sprang forward in pursuit and drove them clear across the valley."[9]

The New York diarist surveyed the position the enemy had relinquished: "The dead on this field exceeded anything of the kind I ever saw . . . 240 lay in front of our Brigade [alone]." About as many prisoners fell into Merritt's hands, along with three regimental colors. Here was proof that even a strong line of infantry could not withstand the fire of dismounted cavalry, properly directed and timed.[10]

At last free to go forward, Sheridan's scouts studied the works beyond the second ridge and reported them held by at least two divisions of infantry. Sheridan and Hancock were surprised that the Rebels had detected the movement from the Southside, which had been shrouded in secrecy, and had gotten into position so quickly to block it. Grant, who came up from Petersburg to survey the field, was positively astounded. He decided that little could be accomplished in that quarter except to divert enemy attention from the mine. It appeared unlikely that Sheridan would gain any ground toward Richmond, much less break away to strike the Virginia Central and the North and South Anna. That evening Grant determined to withdraw from the Northside and to detonate the mine early on the thirtieth.[11]

In so deciding, he ensured that Sheridan's people had no further opportunity to test the Confederate line, which was soon reinforced by Maj. Gen. Henry Heth's infantry division and the cavalry of Rooney Lee. With nearly half of his army north of the James and his lines at Petersburg considerably thinned, Robert E. Lee had reacted (or overreacted) to Hancock's and Sheridan's advance in such a way as to ensure that an attack in the aftermath of the mine blast would be lightly opposed.

The primary purpose of the operation having been achieved, on the afternoon of the twenty-eighth Hancock withdrew his troops to a defensive line near the pontoon bridge they had crossed the day before. Meanwhile, Sheridan and Kautz retired to a position on the infantry's right. A minor skirmish was the only activity along the line the next day, and it involved only Kautz. That night, Hancock recrossed the river on the pontoons, and Sheridan followed. The last man reached the south shore before sunup on the thirtieth, ending an abortive offensive on the doorstep to Richmond.[12]

For Sheridan's men, the operation was not over. According to plan, they were to help exploit the detonation of the mine by moving in the early hours of the thirtieth to Lee's Mill, where they would advance against Rebel forces opposite Meade's left. Everything changed, however, when the mine exploded before the cavalry could get into position to support it. At 4:45 A.M. a deafening roar went up northeast of Petersburg. An artillery colonel likened the blast to the cacophony of cannons at the height of Pickett's Charge. When the noise faded away, observers found that a crater, 170 feet long and 40 feet deep, had been blown in Elliott's Salient. Dozens of Rebels had been killed or wounded in the explosion; few remained on their feet to oppose the attack Burnside had readied.

The path to downtown Petersburg—and perhaps to the war's finale—lay open, but the white soldiers who had taken the places of the trained USCT botched an assault that would have exploited the mine's success. After recovering from the initial shock, Confederates rushed up from other sectors to plug the gap and shoot down the attackers—many of whom had descended into the still-smoking pit—like fish in a barrel.[13]

The Army of the Potomac had squandered another shining opportunity to end the killing once and for all. How many more could it expect to come its way?

>-+-•>-•-O-•<•-+-<

After the failure of the attack of July 30, Sheridan returned Torbert's and Gregg's commands to their camps on the James, where Wilson's troopers joined them. The reunited force remained static for less than a week, when two-thirds of it left middle Virginia on an extended visit to the Shenandoah Valley. The horsemen would not return to the Petersburg front for nearly seven months.[14]

Even a trooper with a low-level awareness of events elsewhere in the country could have seen the transfer coming. It had originated with a flawed campaign in the Shenandoah Valley by David Hunter. Less than a week after he failed to link with the Trevilian raiders, the new commander of the Department of West Virginia moved against strategic Lynchburg with two infantry divisions, one of them under George Crook, and cavalry led by a trio of exiles from the Army of the Potomac: William Averell, Julius Stahel, and Alfred Duffié. Perhaps inevitably, Hunter's 18,000 troops were halted outside their objective on June 18 by troops under Maj. Gen. John C. Breckinridge and Lt. Gen. Jubal A. Early, the latter recently transferred from Petersburg at the head of the II Corps, Army of Northern Virginia. Finding no opening for an attack, and worried by Early's arrival, Hunter began a roundabout retreat that took him not only away from Lynchburg, but out of the Valley. By the end of the month he had holed up in the mountains of West Virginia, across the Kanawha River from Parkersburg.[15]

By quitting the Valley, Hunter was offering it to his opponents to do with as they pleased. It pleased the feisty Early to move his 16,000 soldiers to Staunton on the twenty-seventh. From there he made for Winchester, near the bottom (the northern part) of the Valley, which he reached on July 2. A week later he made one of the war's boldest moves by crossing the Potomac and heading for Washington, D.C., thereby stoking the worst fears of Lincoln and Stanton. Reacting to the crisis, Grant had Meade detach Wright's corps, which was sent by transport up the James and the Potomac to man the capital defenses before Early could strike.[16]

Accompanying the VI Corps were no fewer than 3,000 cavalrymen in search of fresh horses at Giesboro Point—another graphic indication of the played-out condition of Sheridan's command. Many of the newcomers joined Wright's soldiers and the forces of the Department of Washington—which included the 13th and 16th New York Cavalry and detachments of other mounted units—in opposing Early. When they reached the capital, the dismounted men, members of forty regiments in the Army of the Potomac, were organized into units corresponding to their divisional affiliation in Virginia. The entire force was placed under William Gamble, commander of the dismounted camp at Giesboro Point. The oft-wounded colonel, who considered himself no longer fit for field duty, had secured that position in January as an alternative to being forced into the Invalid Corps. His clout was such that he brought with him to Washington the reenlisting veterans of his old 8th Illinois. A small detachment of recruits remained with the army at Petersburg.[17]

On the tenth, after defeating a heterogeneous force sent to stop him short of Baltimore, Early advanced on Washington. The next day the bulk of the VI Corps reached the capital, followed by the advance contingent of the XIX Corps, two divisions of which had recently been transferred from Louisiana to Petersburg. That same day, about half of Gamble's command took its place in the Washington defenses. The reinforcements persuaded Early to defer an all-out assault, although during skirmishing around Fort Stevens, troops and spectators including Abraham Lincoln came under sharpshooter fire. On the evening of the twelfth Early left the Washington suburbs; two days later he recrossed the Potomac to Leesburg, Virginia. On the sixteenth he headed back to the Valley, encamping at Berryville. "Old Jube" had not captured the Union's seat of government, but he had brought to life one of the most vivid nightmares of the present administration.[18]

Lincoln's and Stanton's panic over the raid drove Grant to make a major decision. After visiting the president at Fort Monroe on July 31, the commanding general went to Frederick, Maryland, to confer with David Hunter. He came away from the meetings convinced that a more enterprising and energetic officer than Hunter should command the Army of West Virginia and other troops as well. Grant envisioned the new man as leading not only Hunter's troops (now known as the VIII Corps), but also Wright's corps, that part of the XIX Corps in Virginia (under the direct command of an old cavalryman, William Emory), and at least one and possibly two divisions of horsemen to be transferred from Meade's army. Over the initial objections of Lincoln and Stanton, who considered him too young for independent command, on August 1 Grant named Sheridan to head the Middle Military Division—a consolidation of four previously separate geographical commands— and instructed him to rid the Valley of the enemy and deny its resources to Lee. Little Phil recalled that Grant wished him to follow wherever Early went. Should Old Jube again cross the Potomac, "I was to put myself south of him and try to compass his destruction."[19]

By the first week of August, most of the forces earmarked for Sheridan were moving toward the Shenandoah. Originally, Torbert's was the only unit of the Cavalry Corps destined for the new army, but Wilson's men were released to Sheridan a week after the 1st Division left Petersburg. Although David Gregg proposed that his command, rather than Wilson's, go to the Valley, the 2nd Cavalry Division stayed at Meade's side while the rest of the corps went west. For the next seven months Gregg's division, working in close cooperation with Kautz, picketed the flanks and rear of the Army of the Potomac, supported it during every offensive it undertook, and served in every major engagement it fought. Gregg's was a thankless task, a mission that did not attract the attention given the forces in the Valley. Nevertheless, throughout the fall and winter of 1864, the officers and men of the 2nd Division performed their myriad duties tirelessly, conscientiously, and effectively.[20]

With Sheridan now an army leader, Torbert, as his ranking lieutenant in the field, rose to command all the cavalry in the Middle Military Division. This included not only the 1st and 3rd Divisions (which retained their numerical designations within Sheridan's Army of the Shenandoah), but also the greater part of the cavalry that had served Hunter. Its leader, Averell, who had forged a commendable record since his transfer to western Virginia in mid-1863, was senior to Torbert. To lead his horsemen, however, Sheridan wanted a man who had served under him. While Torbert remained relatively new to the cavalry and showed no evidence of being a latter-day Murat, Sheridan believed he could rely on the man. He could not say as much about Averell, whose 2nd Cavalry Division, Army of the Shenandoah, lacked the high reputation of the transferees from Petersburg. Further, Torbert's promotion permitted a deserving subordinate, Merritt, to gain permanent command of the 1st Division.[21]

The road to the Valley led through Giesboro Point, where the 1st Division headed by steamboat on July 31. By August 6 the division had undergone a thorough refit and had assimilated those troopers sent to the city to oppose Early's raid. That evening the riders trotted through Georgetown, then out into the Maryland countryside, their shiny new accoutrements on conspicuous display.[22]

Two days later—one day after Sheridan's arrival—the division reached Harpers Ferry, Virginia, the army's staging area. There, on the ninth, Torbert was announced as chief of cavalry, and Merritt assumed the post thus vacated. At first Torbert commanded only the 1st Division, for the seven regiments that comprised Averell's division— all of which had seen hard service in western Virginia—were undergoing a refit beyond Torbert's immediate reach. His command was not materially enlarged until Wilson joined him at Winchester, twenty-two miles southwest of Harpers Ferry, on the seventeenth. The 3rd Division had not reached Giesboro Point until the tenth and had not left it—each of its men now armed with his commander's favorite, the Spencer—until the twelfth.[23]

The order of battle of the 1st and 3rd Divisions was much as it had been at the outset of Grant's Overland Campaign. The only changes were the addition of the 25th New York to Custer's brigade and the transfer of the 1st New York Dragoons from the Reserve to Devin's brigade. The Dragoons' loss was made good on September 9, when the 2nd Massachusetts, formerly a part of the Washington garrison, joined the Reserve Brigade. By virtue of seniority, the 2nd's colonel, Charles Russell Lowell, a highly regarded professional soldier and a scion of one of New England's most distinguished families, assumed command of the brigade.[24]

When Sheridan's army, originally 26,000 strong, massed at Harpers Ferry and nearby Halltown, most of Early's four infantry brigades and one cavalry division were camped fifteen miles to the west, just below Martinsburg. At first the Confederates were too few to meet Sheridan on equal terms, but by mid-August Lee sent Early a force under Richard Anderson, consisting of

Kershaw's infantrymen and Fitz Lee's troopers. The additions gave Old Jube about 23,000 officers and men. Rumors that heavier reinforcements had reached him from Petersburg made Sheridan believe for a time that he was outnumbered. Not until early September, when the balance of the XIX Corps reached him, giving him some 45,000 officers and men, did he quit worrying.[25]

For the first six weeks of his campaign in the Valley, Sheridan engaged in, as he explained, "offensive and defensive maneuvering for certain advantages, the enemy confining himself meanwhile to measures intended to counteract my designs." A strategy of caution had been urged upon him by Washington and endorsed by Grant. As Merritt later observed, Grant "saw that the Valley was not useful to the Government for aggressive operations." If Early's command was indeed larger than the Army of the Shenandoah, Sheridan had best move carefully, taking the offensive only if certain he could win.[26]

In meetings with Sheridan before he left for Harpers Ferry, Stanton and Halleck had impressed on him that any blunder might be viewed in some circles as evidence that the war was being lost and that the administration was to blame for it. Early's raid on Washington, coupled with the stagnant situation at Petersburg and Sherman's failure to take Atlanta, had frustrated and depressed the Northern public. The price of gold was soaring, suggesting that the financial community was losing faith in the wartime dollar. Lincoln, who had accepted his party's renomination, secretly believed that his reelection was unlikely. The Democratic Party was on the verge of nominating General McClellan for president and placing an antiwar platform under him. New reverses in the field might sweep Little Mac into the White House and impose a negotiated peace with the Confederacy, a peace that would vitiate the sacrifice of thousands of Union lives.[27]

At first Sheridan sought an opening to strike his enemy a blow. On the tenth he moved south from the Harpers Ferry-Halltown area to Berryville, threatening Early's communications and hoping to force him to fight. The first cavalry action of the campaign took place on the eleventh, when Lowell's and Devin's brigades of Merritt's division, leading Sheridan's advance, encountered Wickham's Confederates at the point where the Millwood-Winchester Turnpike crossed Opequon Creek. In an effort to determine Early's movements, Merritt drove the cavalry back on its army. That same day Custer's brigade, while reconnoitering across the Opequon toward Winchester, encountered gray infantry in force. The sharp fight that ensued told Custer that Early was retreating up (southward through) the Valley. A limited attack by the Southerners was repulsed by a saber charge by a battalion of Kidd's 6th Michigan. Later, Merritt observed that this fight gave his division "increased confidence" in its ability to stand up to foot soldiers as well as to cavalry, even when the odds were with the enemy.[28]

On the sixteenth, Sheridan halted his pursuit of the now-reinforced enemy. That afternoon Custer's and Devin's brigades were attacked along the Winchester Turnpike near Cedarville by the newly arrived troops under Anderson. Custer counterattacked both mounted and afoot, losing about fifty men but inflicting three times as many casualties. By day's end a stray bullet had shorn one of the brigadier's golden locks, but the Wolverine Brigade had prevailed.[29]

Tom Devin—who on the eleventh had suffered several casualties in a confrontation with Early's infantry near Newtown—was also credited with success on the sixteenth. In a series of charges, his brigade took prisoners and captured banners. The key to victory on his front was an attack by the 4th New York, which this day made amends for past mistakes, including its shameful abandonment of Colonel diCesnola at Aldie. The men of the immigrant-rich outfit put spurs to their horses, charged furiously, and routed two Rebel regiments, capturing 150 men and horses. Ironically, after the engagement, diCesnola announced his intention to resign, explaining that "I cannot depend upon them; they have covered me with glory to-day, they may disgrace me to-morrow."[30]

Then began Sheridan's retrograde. As the army headed north, it began to accomplish one of the missions assigned it, destroying the crops and natural resources that gave the Breadbasket of the Confederacy its title. The scorched-earth policy invited retaliation by regular Confederates, bushwhackers, and the partisan rangers of John Mosby. The Federals struck back, burning the homes and property of Valley residents suspected of aiding the enemy. Atrocities were committed on both sides. Soldiers and civilians alike were gunned down in cold blood, sometimes after surrendering, and prisoners were forced to draw lots to learn which of them would be hanged by their captors.[31]

Early, who had moved south to Front Royal, discovered his opponent's withdrawal early on the seventeenth and turned around. That afternoon he struck Sheridan's rear guard at Winchester; the attackers' numerical advantage allowed Anderson to thrust Torbert's command—which now included the 3rd Cavalry Division, today supported by a VI Corps brigade—out of the town; in his first fight in the Valley, Wilson suffered fifty casualties. Afterward, Sheridan resumed his retreat (he had "not yet found himself," Wilson decided), abandoning Winchester, and Early continued his pursuit. On the twenty-first he again struck the Union rear near Berryville. Sheridan's infantry, especially the VI Corps, took heavy casualties, but things might have been worse: Torbert slowed the advance of Anderson's command so much that it never added its weight to the attack on the infantry. Afterward, Sheridan, still heeding the caution that Washington had imposed on him, retired all the way to Halltown.[32]

For three days Early demonstrated against the Union lines, but, finding Sheridan too strongly entrenched, turned away and gave thought to another raid into Maryland. On the twenty-fifth he left Anderson to occupy Sheridan and marched east to Leetown with four divisions of foot soldiers and Lee's horsemen. From there the cavalry went to Williamsport, on the Potomac, while the infantry moved downstream to Shepherdstown via Kearneysville, halting there as if intending to cross the river. Torbert's cavalry, dispatched to run the Confederates to earth, overtook them before they could cross. Outside Kearneysville, Merritt and Wilson struck Breckinridge's corps just below the local stretch of the Baltimore & Ohio and shoved it back toward Leetown with decisive force. At first Torbert believed he had run into cavalry; when he learned from prisoners that he had taken on a sizable force of infantry, he swallowed hard. "Of course," George Sanford observed, "Torbert was not out there for the purpose of fighting the whole of Early's army, and accordingly after this exceedingly creditable success, he directed a retreat." As the main body pulled out, Custer stayed behind to secure its withdrawal. The Rebels turned on the rear guard, trapping the Michigan Brigade against the riverbank and forcing Custer to cross the Potomac at Shepherdstown Ford. While his comrades in the 1st and 3rd Divisions guarded other crossings to prevent a belated passage by the Rebels, the boy general rejoined Torbert the next day, by a circuitous route, at Halltown.[33]

By the twenty-eighth Grant had assured Sheridan that most of Early's reinforcements would soon be returned to Petersburg to counter new offensives by Meade and Butler. Gingerly, Little Phil began a new offensive, moving southwestward to Charles Town. Desultory clashes between Torbert's troopers, leading the advance, and Early's infantry and cavalry took place over the next few days. Then the pace of operations accelerated, for when September came in, a heavy burden was removed from Sheridan's shoulders. On the second, Sherman battered his way past the gates of Atlanta; his triumph revived war enthusiasm across the North. The following day, Confederates of all arms demonstrated at Bunker Hill, near Martinsburg, to cover the withdrawal of Kershaw's division from the Valley. Lee's horsemen, however, remained with Early.[34]

Kershaw's leave-taking changed the complexion of the Valley campaign. By the twelfth Early's depleted army was west of Opequon Creek and east of Winchester. It was not arrayed in a particularly strong position, for its leader did not fear his opponent, whom he considered timid and indecisive.

The news that Kershaw was about to quit the Valley came to Sheridan from a company of scouts and spies, about sixty in number, which he had formed early in September under Maj. Henry H. Young. The timing of Kershaw's departure was confirmed by a civilian informant, Rebecca Wright, a twenty-six-year-old schoolteacher living in Winchester. The news helped persuade Little Phil to take the offensive, as did a hastily arranged conference with Grant at Charles Town on the sixteenth. Grant urged Sheridan to "go in" and drive Early from the fertile region he occupied, and then lay waste to its crops. Sheridan agreed, promising to advance by the nineteenth.[35]

Sheridan's cavalry was quite ready to stop marching and countermarching. William Wells complained that "we have been up the Valley and down the Valley" too many times. As James Kidd informed his parents, "backwards and forwards and forward and backward again, has been the programme. You undoubtedly are surprised that Sheridan doesn't fight Early." The cavalry made aggressive moves whenever permitted to. On the thirteenth now–Brigadier General McIntosh's brigade of Wilson's division crossed the Opequon to reconnoiter Early's dispositions outside Winchester. It met a column of infantry and cavalry trooping along the Berryville-Winchester Pike. McIntosh promptly flanked the Rebels with the 2nd Ohio, then charged them with the "Butterflies" of the 3rd New Jersey, driving the enemy into a woods. Surrounding their hiding place, McIntosh received the surrender of the entire 8th South Carolina Infantry and portions of six mounted units.[36]

The little coup below the Opequon told Sheridan that his army was ready for a fight, even if Early was not. McIntosh's reconnaissance, coupled with the results of other scouting missions toward Winchester, revealed that Early had deployed his command helter-skelter, as if daring Sheridan to hurt him. He had split his force, sending two of his infantry divisions and a mounted brigade toward Martinsburg, leaving only half his original strength outside Winchester. Neither of his flanks was secure, and in an act of almost criminal negligence, he had failed to secure the long, wooded gorge that gave access to his right, known as the Berryville Canyon. A thankful Sheridan revamped his strategy on the seventeenth and eighteenth. Originally intent on outflanking Early and cutting his communications, now he planned to overwhelm the troops that remained at Winchester before Early could redeploy.

Sheridan moved against his foe at 2:00 A.M. on September 19. It took him almost seven hours to go into position opposite Early's discontinuous line and mass for the attack. From the start, his cavalry played a prominent role in the proceedings. Wilson's division, led by McIntosh's brigade, splashed across the Opequon at about 8:30 and charged through the gorge toward Early's lightly fortified right. At the western end of the defile, the troopers of the 3rd Division wrested a line of breastworks from a small body of defenders. By 9:00 Wilson's people had cleared the way for the infantry in their rear: the VI Corps, followed by the two divisions of the XIX Corps, then by the VIII Corps. Meanwhile, Torbert, with Merritt's cavalry, was advancing against the Confederate left via Ridgway's Ford on the Opequon and the Charles Town Road. Northeast of Winchester, the 1st Division was to join with Averell's division, which was coming down the turnpike from Martinsburg. The linkup enabled Sheridan to put pressure on both ends of Early's overextended line.[37]

The infantry in Wilson's rear should have overwhelmed the Confederate right, anchored as it was by only a few infantry brigades under one of Wilson's West Point classmates, Maj. Gen. Stephen Dodson Ramseur. At a critical time, however, supply wagons were mistakenly directed through Berryville Canyon, slowing the VI Corps' advance to a shuffle. While the bottleneck was unforeseeable, Sheridan should not have opted to send three corps and a cavalry division through such a narrow ravine. It was, perhaps, his only blunder of the day.

Slowly advancing beyond Wilson's troopers, Wright's corps drove Ramseur from his initial position, then waited for the XIX Corps to clear the traffic jam. When Emory's divisions finally appeared, just before noon, Sheridan sent both corps northward to smash Early's left. Meanwhile, Wilson's troopers shifted south, taking position on the Senseny Road, where they mixed with Lomax's cavalry. Wilson enjoyed the upper hand throughout the afternoon,

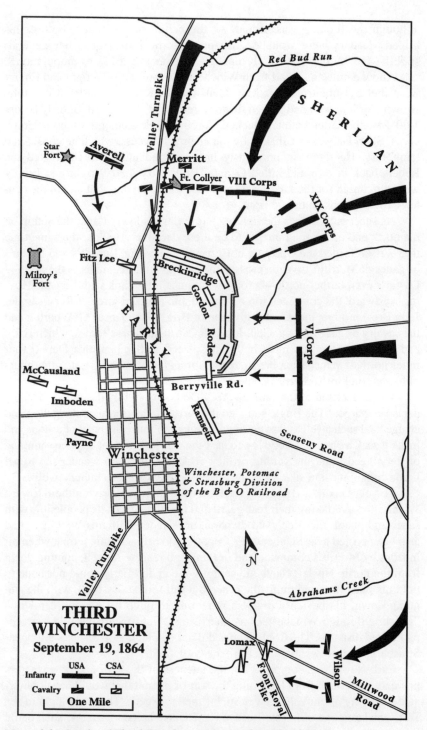

Map of the Battle of Third Winchester, September 19, 1864

although the fighting was heated. At the height of the action, both of his brigade leaders were wounded, Chapman (now also a brigadier general) slightly and McIntosh severely enough that he lost a leg to amputation.[38]

About a mile and a half from Winchester, the troops of Wright and Emory were met by infantry under Maj. Gen. Robert Rodes and Maj. Gen. John Brown Gordon, who had rushed down to reinforce Early's left. Shortly before 1:00 P.M. the latter counterattacked, forcing back elements of both Union corps. Sheridan was not shaken by the enemy's success, which he considered temporary. He threw in previously uncommitted units, which shoved the Rebels back in turn and killed General Rodes. By 4:30 Wright and Emory were moving in for the kill, the VI and XIX Corps on the right and in the center, Crook's corps on the far right.

As successful as was the fighting along Early's lower flank, the action on the north end of the field proved to be more decisive. At about the same time that Wilson forded the Opequon at Berryville Crossing, Lowell's and Devin's brigades of Merritt's division crossed the river about three miles to the north—Custer's even farther north—before swinging south to link with Lowell. Moving westward, the combined force rammed into a mixed force of Rebels under John Breckinridge: the infantry division of Brig. Gen. Gabriel C. Wharton and the cavalry brigade of Brig. Gen. John McCausland. These forces, which Early had detached from his main body and placed at Stephenson's Depot, four miles north of Winchester, began to give ground at about 5:00 P.M., after hours of hammering by Torbert's people.

Walter Jackson of the 1st New York Dragoons vividly described Merritt's decisive charge: "The Bugle sounded the forward, the trot, then the gallop and charge, and such a yell as was given was enough to shake the heart of a stone and make it seek a place of safety. . . . To hear the clashing of steel, and the stamping of fiery steeds, and the yelling of their reckless riders, no wonder the Rebel horde broke and ran like so many sheep before so many hungry wolves."[39]

Lowell, Devin, and Custer raced after the fugitives, driving them toward Winchester, overtaking their rear guard and laying many of its people low with saber and pistol. Fitz Lee's old division, now under Williams Wickham, had also been posted near Stephenson's Depot; it too beat a frantic retreat when hit in front by Merritt's command and in flank and rear by Averell, coming down from the north. His left flank and center gone under, Early could not hope to hold his position; grudgingly, he ordered a full retreat. By 6:00, with the sun going down, his beaten army was retreating through the streets of town—"whirling through Winchester," as Sheridan's chief of staff put it in a much-publicized dispatch. The Confederates did not halt until atop Fisher's Hill, near Strasburg, almost twenty miles from the battlefield.[40]

Early's rout was complete, but the lateness of the hour and other factors prevented Sheridan from launching the sort of pursuit that would have obliterated the Army of the Valley. Even so, his men rejoiced. "This is the fight of the War," declared one of his staff officers. "To have helped fight one such battle and win one such victory," an enlisted man said, "was to prove that we have not lived in vain."[41]

Enthusiasm over the triumph on the Opequon soon swept the North. In Washington and other cities, minute guns saluted the victory. Gushing like many other journals, the *New York Times* lauded the "carefully conceived plans . . . the matured purpose, the resolute action, and the matchless valor" displayed by Sheridan and his troops. The *New York Tribune,* which had been fence-sitting before the battle, immediately endorsed Lincoln's reelection. Within days of the fighting, the price of gold declined sharply.[42]

The president got into the spirit of things, telegraphing the general he had feared to be too young for such an important command: "God bless you all, officers and men." Lincoln had reason to be thankful: Combined with the fall of Atlanta, Sheridan's victory had long-term political ramifications. As Maj. Gen. James A. Garfield, himself a future president, put it, "Phil Sheridan has made a speech in the Shenandoah Valley more powerful and valuable to the Union cause than all the stumps[peakers] in the Republic can make—our prospects are everywhere heightening."[43]

>━┥◄❭━O━❬►┝━◄

Sheridan was not content with beating Early a single time. The darkness of evening and the speed with which the panic-stricken Confederates had fled prevented Sheridan from cutting off their retreat. He planned to do so as soon as possible. At daylight on the twentieth he started after Early with his infantry, plus Averell's and Devin's horsemen. The rest of Merritt's division and the whole of Wilson's he sent, under Torbert, to get south of Early's new position and block his escape. Below Strasburg, the Valley is divided vertically by Massanutten Mountain, a forty-mile-long chain that can be crossed by several passes. Torbert's mission was to ford the Shenandoah River, pass down the Luray Valley on the east side of the mountain, and clear away cavalry guarding Early's right flank. He was then to recross the Shenandoah and move through a pass to New Market, where he would be astride Early's line of retreat.[44]

Torbert started out in good order, giving Sheridan every reason to anticipate success. On the twentieth Little Phil moved into position opposite Early's line, and he spent the following day maneuvering for an assault. At dawn on the twenty-second, he attacked frontally with the troops of Wright, Emory, Averell, and Devin, holding Early in place. Infantry and cavalry avoided the Rebel right, which, in addition to being well guarded, was anchored on forbidding terrain. Then, as he had at Winchester, Sheridan enveloped Early's left with a well-conducted turning movement, this time using Crook's VIII Corps instead of Merritt's horsemen. By late in the afternoon Early was again in full flight up the Valley, having lost more than 1,200 men to add to the nearly 4,000 casualties he had suffered three days before.[45]

Sheridan took greater satisfaction in his second overthrow of Early than in the first. At Fisher's Hill, the enemy had been beaten by superior planning and generalship rather than by brute strength and Early's lax dispositions. For this reason, Sheridan was bitterly disappointed to learn, early on the twenty-third, that Torbert had failed to cut off Early at New Market.

Torbert had tried hard to reach New Market—or had he? At 11:00 A.M. on September 22, after advancing up Luray Valley, he had come upon a line of horsemen—Wickham's division—posted along the south bank of Milford Creek. The Rebels' presence should not have come as a surprise, but the strength of their position did. Wickham's left flank rested on the Shenandoah River, which, as Torbert later reported, "runs so close under the mountain it was impossible to turn it." The Rebel right was also inaccessible, resting as it was on the mountain itself. Moreover, the banks of Milford Creek were "so precipitous it was impossible for the men to get across in order to make a direct attack." Torbert had not heard that Sheridan had evicted Early from Fisher's Hill; unwilling to commit his command without that knowledge, he demonstrated rather feebly against Wickham's position, then retreated down Luray. Not till 4:00 P.M. the following day, by which time Torbert had withdrawn to Front Royal, at the north end of the Massanutten, did he learn of Sheridan's great victory; at that hour he received orders from army headquarters to retrace his path up Luray Valley.[46]

Sheridan fumed over Torbert's failure to gain Early's rear, and his anger grew with the years. In his after-action report, he confined his criticism to what might have been: "Had General Torbert driven this cavalry or turned the defile and reached New Market, I have no doubt but that we would have captured the entire rebel army." Years later, when he wrote his memoirs, Sheridan criticized Torbert more directly, declaring that "my disappointment was extreme" over the incident and adding: "To this day, I have been unable to account satisfactorily for Torbert's failure. No doubt, Wickham's position near Milford was a strong one, but Torbert ought to have made a fight. . . . His impotent attempt not only chagrined me very much, but occasioned much unfavorable comment throughout the army."[47]

In time, Torbert would pay for his inability to carry out his superior's orders. In the short term, however, Sheridan took out his frustration on Averell. Having reached Woodstock, seven miles south of Fisher's Hill, early on the twenty-third, the army pushed on to Edinburg. Its vanguard, Devin's brigade, trailed at a distance by Averell, strove to overtake Early's column. In midmorning, when the Confederate rear guard rose up and lashed out at Devin, the New Yorker looked about for help. But Averell did not appear until noon; by then, Early had moved on and, as Sheridan saw it, a grand opportunity had been lost.

When Little Phil reached the headquarters of the 2nd Cavalry Division, he exchanged "hot words" with Averell, whom Sheridan believed was nursing a grievance over his failure to gain Torbert's position. When, late in the day, Devin again engaged Early's rear, Averell held back and then, without orders, put his men in bivouac. A furious Sheridan promptly relieved him of command; ordered him to Wheeling, West Virginia, to await further orders; and replaced him with an energetic subordinate, Col. William H. Powell. Averell took his fall from grace—his second in a year and a half—quite hard. As on the first occasion, he could not hide his misery. "I saw Gen. Averell sitting in front of a tent," recalled Captain Sanford, who rode past division headquarters in company with a group of staff officers. " . . . He was dreadfully depressed and broken. I believe he started for the rear within a few moments after we left him, and never was employed again during the war."[48]

Averell's replacement did not translate into a faster, more effective pursuit. Sheridan sent Powell to cut around Early's left and Devin to continue pressing the Confederates' rear, but Early moved up the Valley as though the fires of hell were licking at his heels. On the twenty-fourth his men passed New Market, ending, as Sheridan admitted, "all hope of Torbert's appearing in rear of the Confederates." That day Torbert engaged some of Early's cavalry near Luray, Custer driving them for about eight miles and taking seventy prisoners. Already, however, Early was home free on the road to Brown's Gap in the Blue Ridge. By the next morning, as Sheridan, wrote "the enemy had disappeared entirely from my front."[49]

>⊶⊷⊙⊶⊷⊰

For a week, Sheridan lingered in the upper Valley, encamped at Harrisonburg. While the main army probed toward Early's new position, Torbert's men partially demolished the railroad bridge at Waynesboro, while destroying farm fields and burning granaries. On a reconnaissance to Port Republic on the twenty-sixth, Merritt's division ran into Kershaw's infantry, which was returning to Early from the Petersburg front; outgunned and outpositioned, the cavalry fell back to Cross Keys. When he learned of the engagement, Sheridan entertained hopes of again luring Early into the open, to be pummeled by the entire Army of the Shenandoah, but Old Jube refused his offer. Finally, on October 6, Sheridan began his return march to the bottom of the Valley. Four days later he settled into position on the north side of Cedar Creek, fourteen miles below Winchester.[50]

Throughout the return trip, Sheridan's rear guard fell prey to Early's cavalry, now led by Thomas Rosser (Fitz Lee had been seriously wounded at Winchester). Rosser landed blows with infuriating persistence, as if daring the Yankees to stop and fight. On the eighth his punches were especially painful. Major Phillips of the 18th Pennsylvania, commanding in the rear, saw his regiment "pitched into furiously. I held them and fell back and held them again for 3 miles when the 2nd N. Y. came to my assistance. . . . I lost 8 men killed and wounded [and] 15 missing."[51]

Sheridan put up with the growing annoyance for three days, but by the evening of the eighth he had had enough. Calling Torbert to his tent, he spoke plainly of his irritation. "I can testify quite freely," wrote Captain Sanford, who had heard a portion of their conversation, "that Sheridan was 'mad clear through,' and was quite willing that everybody should know it. Among other things that he said to Torbert was: 'I want you to go out there in the morning and whip that Rebel cavalry or get whipped yourself.'"[52]

Sanford found Torbert to be nearly as angry as his superior, "but he had a different way of showing temper." He showed it by accepting Sheridan's challenge on behalf of the two divisions in his immediate charge. (Powell's was on a detached assignment.) Calling together his ranking subordinates, he told them what Sheridan expected of them all on the morrow. His lieutenants responded enthusiastically, especially George Custer, who stood on the threshold of his first fight in permanent division command.[53]

On October 1, while it scouted Early's position at Brown's Gap, the Cavalry Corps had lost the services of James Wilson, who had been called to the western theater to command Sherman's cavalry, minus those who, under Kilpatrick, were to take part in the upcoming march from Atlanta to the sea. The transfer meant a brevet major generalship for Wilson, as well as an opportunity to make a record in semi-independent command. His departure was also a boon for his rival, Custer, as well as for the men of the 3rd Cavalry Division. Most of them had long disliked Wilson's heavy-handed approach to discipline and his tendency to berate officers and men for offenses real and imagined. Custer they considered their savior as well as an officer who would lead them to glory. In this belief they were correct. After the war, a member of the 22nd New York remarked, with pardonable hyperbole, that Custer took the division, which under Wilson "had only held its reputation with respectability, and transformed it into the most brilliant one of the whole Army (east or west) and so much impressed [it] with his individuality that every officer in the command was soon copying his eccentricities of dress and ready to adore his every motion and word."[54]

Custer began to fulfill his men's expectations on the morning of the ninth, when, at Torbert's directive, he placed his new command on the Back Road south of Fisher's Hill. As he went into position, Merritt's division assembled astride the Valley Pike, two to three miles east of Custer. Both columns moved south—Custer at daylight, Merritt at about 7:00 A.M.—angling toward Rosser's latest position, just south of Tom's Brook. The divisions attacked as soon as they made contact with the enemy. What followed was a two-hour, all-cavalry fight. Sheridan deliberately held his infantry well to the north, while Early's main army lay more than twenty miles south of Tom's Brook, too far from Rosser to give him any support.[55]

Custer's men, moving at a trot, then a gallop, charged into Rosser's "Laurel Brigade" along the Back Road, while Merritt's brigades attacked Lomax's division, which was dug in along both sides of the turnpike, outside Woodstock. The 3rd Division pressed Rosser's pickets back on his main body, before being halted by stone fences and breastworks manned by cavalry and horse artillery. Custer dismounted his men in turn and sent them forward as skirmishers, while his batteries returned the enemy's fire, salvo for salvo.

As on many past occasions, Custer's subordinate, Alexander Pennington, was at the general's side in the heat of combat. This day, however, the exartilleryman wore eagles on his shoulders instead of silver bars, having been Custer's choice to replace the wounded McIntosh in command of the 1st Brigade. Most of Pennington's regiments attacked Rosser's position in front, while two others, the 8th and the 22nd New York, crept into position off Rosser's left flank. When Custer's bugles blew, the entire line surged forward, crumpling first the flank and then the center, and putting the defenders to flight. The Confederates raced to their mounts, swung aboard, and pounded southward; those of Custer's men still in the saddle pursued at high speed for more than two miles. Fear communicated itself from horse to horse, rider to rider, and Rosser could rally no one. As a result, the attackers captured six of his artillery pieces and all of his wagons, making the day a humiliating experience for his entire command.[56]

Merritt's success on the Valley Pike equaled, if not surpassed, Custer's. Even before reaching Lomax's position, the 1st Division seized the advantage by maneuvering the Rebels out of hilly, easily defensible terrain and onto naked ground, where they were vulnerable to overthrow. Before Lomax could fully deploy on the new ground, he was struck in the center as well as on the right by Lowell's brigade, and on the left by the troopers and cannoneers of Tom Devin. Like Rosser's position, the line facing Merritt cracked and then shattered, pieces flying in all directions. Rebels who could reach their horses galloped south, all semblance of formation gone, each man trying to save himself.

Merritt's pursuit was just as furious as Custer's. He chased Lomax's fugitives for mile after mile, although at intervals he was forced to halt and take on small groups of defenders who dared rally and offer resistance. In every case, the Confederates were surrounded and overwhelmed, more than fifty being rounded up as prisoners. "Each time our troopers came in view," Merritt testified, "they would rush on the discomfited rebels with their sabers, and send them howling in every direction."[57]

The pursuit up the Valley Pike, like that on the Back Road, ended only after the last grayback was chased inside Early's lines near Rude's Hill, twenty-six miles from the scene of the initial fighting. In addition to a retreat of unprecedented proportions, the Confederates had suffered several dozen men killed and wounded, although no casualty count was ever tabulated. In addition to these losses, Rosser and Lomax had transferred to their enemy's possession seventy horses and mules, more than forty wagons, three ambulances, four caissons, a sizable cache of Enfield rifles, and at least one battle flag.

Tom's Brook had been what Sheridan had hoped it would be: a defining moment, a landmark battle, "the most decisive the country had ever witnessed," as Torbert described it. In Union circles, the fight became known as the "Woodstock Races," a reply to the Buckland Races of October 1863, when the Union troopers had done the running. It looked as if those Yankees would never run again.[58]

Chapter Twenty-three

God Bless You, Boys!

Long before Sheridan fell back from the Blue Ridge to Cedar Creek, his enemy had been defeated, demoralized, and humiliated. Certainly he was in no condition to take the offensive. So, at any rate, thought Sheridan, who on October 1 wired Grant that he ought to leave the Shenandoah and return to the Army of the Potomac, burning, destroying, and confiscating as he went. Sheridan's suggestion led to his being called to Washington for a confab with Stanton and Halleck. Certain that he could safely absent himself for a few days, he entrained for the capital on the fifteenth. After conferring with his superiors, who feared that Washington would not be safe until the last Rebel was driven from the Valley, he reached Winchester, a long ride from Cedar Creek, on the evening of the eighteenth. He expected to be back at his headquarters the following afternoon.[1]

The opinions Sheridan had expressed with regard to devastating the Valley carried considerable weight in Washington, because he had already done much in that line. He and his men had worked hard to "peel the land," denying rations and forage to the troops of Lee and Early. The systematic destruction of farms and homes—many of which fell victim to torches and sulfur matches—would be known forever after as "The Burning." Looting and destroying came naturally to some of Sheridan's men, but most engaged in the work without enthusiasm. James Kidd, for one, doubted the necessity behind it, and the grief and sorrow it caused troubled him deeply. He recalled a typical barn and farmhouse burning and the effect it had on the family who lived there: "The anguish pictured in their faces would have melted any heart not seared by the horrors and 'necessities' of war. It was too much for me and . . . I hurried away from the scene."[2]

The thoroughness with which the Burning was carried out worried Early and prompted him, soon after Sheridan left his front, to gamble. Should the enemy further devastate the Valley, Early's army would be unable to subsist, in its present position, through the coming winter. Therefore he followed Sheridan north at a respectful distance; by October 13 he was back at Fisher's Hill, only ten miles south of the Federal camps. Thus far he had acted in such a way that Sheridan was not threatened by his presence. But over the next five days, Early and his subordinates mapped a multipronged attack, one that depended on the element of surprise to neutralize the two-to-one numerical edge of the Army of the Shenandoah—commanded, in Sheridan's absence, by Horatio Wright.[3]

The surprise element was enhanced by a fog that cloaked Early's approach to Cedar Creek in the early-morning hours of October 19. Another advantage was the unsuspecting complacency of the Federals, which stemmed from Wright's belief that the Army of the Valley had gone south in a desperate search for food and forage. Thus, most of his soldiers were taken unawares when the Rebels came calling shortly before dawn. A skillfully choreographed attack by three divisions succeeded in hitting the exposed flank and rear of Crook's corps, on the far left of Wright's line. After minimal resistance, the troops of the Army of West Virginia—many of whom had been asleep when the shooting started—fled westward through the lines of the XIX Corps, breaking that command's formation. By perhaps 7:30 most of the XIX Corps was also in retreat, heading northeast across Middle Marsh.

Crook's and Emory's flight left the fate of the Army of the Shenandoah in the hands of Wright's own VI Corps. To their lasting credit, his men did not panic, but stood their ground. Pushed back from their initial position, they rallied just west of the village of Middletown; there, over a period of hours, they repulsed a succession of attacks on their front and left. Beaten elements of Crook's and Emory's corps huddled in their rear; a few returned to the firing lines to fight beside the VI Corps.[4]

Wright's infantry was covered, first on one flank, then on the other, by Torbert's troopers. When the fighting began, most of the cavalry was stationed on the right, Merritt's division along Middle Marsh Brook, Custer's about a mile and a half farther west. Both had almost missed this opportunity to defend their army, for Sheridan had intended that Torbert lead them on another raid along the Virginia Central in response to a suggestion from Grant. Just before going to Washington, however, Little Phil had deferred the operation until his return.[5]

Now Merritt and Custer were on hand to cover the infantry's retreat and engage the approaching enemy. Custer rendered especially good service by intercepting Rosser's horsemen at Cupp's Ford and preventing them from reaching the Federal rear. Later in the morning, however, Wright moved Custer to the far left, the sector most in need of quick support. The 3rd Division left a single horse artillery unit, Lt. F. E. Taylor's Battery K/L, 1st United States, to guard the right. Taylor and his gunners won Sheridan's praise for their "admirable service" throughout the day and, especially, for being "the last artillery to leave that front."[6]

By early afternoon, Sheridan's army was teetering on collapse. Almost all of it had been driven back, two-thirds of it well to the rear. Some fugitives had fled as far as Sheridan's temporary quarters in Winchester. Only the strung-out condition of Early's troops, which required them to halt and reorganize, and

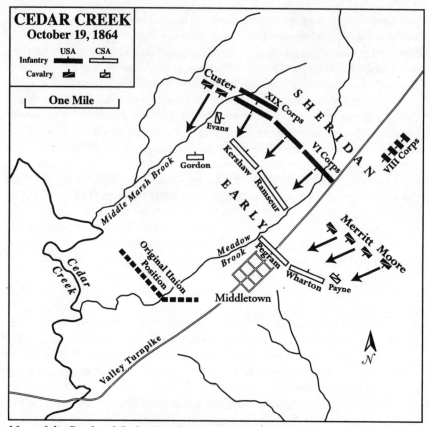

Map of the Battle of Cedar Creek, October 19, 1864

the fact that many of the famished soldiers could not be lured away from loot-ing Crook's and Emory's camps, prevented Early from sweeping everything before him. A lull settled over the field while Old Jube planned a renewed assault and as the VI Corps shored up its line.[7]

By 4:00, before Early could resume his advance, he had lost the decisive advantage. Having heard the booming of cannons in Winchester, Sheridan had left the private home in which he had been staying (and, according to at least one historian, the bed of a female resident) and galloped back to Cedar Creek on his coal black charger, Rienzi, his 300-man escort straining to keep up with him. On the way, he shouted orders and encouragement to the stragglers he passed, enjoining them to turn about and help him lick the Rebels, assuring them they would be back in their old camps before evening.

Arriving at about 11:30 on the scene of Wright's near-disaster, Sheridan was cheered and mobbed by officers and men alike, each of whom appeared to be revitalized by the sight of him. Custer was so happy to see him that he picked up his diminutive superior and planted a kiss on his cheek.[8]

Little Phil went to work at once, directing everyone to rally on the strong line held by Getty's division of the VI Corps. He rallied many of Emory's soldiers and built a new position for them on Getty's right. In rear of the VI Corps, Sheridan placed as many of Crook's troops as he could gather up. By early afternoon, with Early's men at last ready to deliver a blow, Sheridan was determined to meet them, halt them, and hurl them back. So were the tired but energized troops behind him.

At about 3:45 Early's troops launched a poorly executed assault on Wright's front, as well as against the far right of the line near the point to which Sheridan had returned Custer's division. When the feeble effort spent itself, Little Phil hurled his troops forward in a massive counterattack. Executing a half wheel to the left, the infantry thudded into the divisions of Gordon, Kershaw, Ramseur, and Brig. Gen. John Pegram. At the same time, Custer struck Early's left flank, and Merritt, in conjunction with one of Powell's brigades, his right. Custer helped Emory break Gordon's line to pieces, while Merritt pried Wharton's division from its position on Early's far right. The counterattack split the Confederate line in two, led to Ramseur's mortal wounding, and forced Early's left, then his center and right, to give way.[9]

By 5:00 P.M. the Army of the Valley was running for its life. At the behest of Sheridan, who had no mercy for a beaten foe, Torbert's 6,000 riders pursued with wild abandon, driving before them herds of panic-stricken Confederates. "I never saw an Army so demoralized as was the rebs," marveled Colonel Wells, now leading Custer's 2nd Brigade. He and his comrades rode down the enemy's rear guard, capturing guns, wagons, and caissons, as well as dozens of soldiers—a reprise of Tom's Brook, but on a larger scale. Once again, pockets of resistance failed to slow the pursuers, even when cannons were turned on them. "I have never been exposed to such murderous discharges," James Kidd wrote of the guns, "but nothing could demoralize the men who constitute the superb cavalry force of the Middle Military Division."[10]

The pursuit did not cease until what remained of the Rebel force—pitiful fragments of a once-proud army—had been driven beyond Strasburg. Even then, two regiments, Custer's 1st Vermont and 5th New York, continued to press the dwindling number of fugitives in their front, not rejoining their division till well after sunup the next day.[11]

As indicated by the fury of the pursuit, Early had been routed as thoroughly as any commander in this war. He had lost almost 3,000 men—more than one-third of them as prisoners—along with twenty-five guns, every ambulance and ammunition wagon, and most of his supply vehicles. He had also been forced to abandon the abundant spoils taken from the camps his men had overrun. Sheridan had suffered even heavier casualties, most of them during the overthrow of the VIII Corps and the retreat of the XIX; victory always came at a price. Perhaps the highest was the mortal wounding of Charley Lowell, who had been shot through the body while leading his Reserves in an attack that fulfilled his last request: "I want to lead in the final charge." His long-overdue appointment as brigadier general had been made out in Washington the day before he died.[12]

>-+-<>-·-O-·-<>-+-<

Toward the close of the pursuit to Strasburg, Major Phillips of the 18th Pennsylvania expressed a doubt that many of his comrades shared: "I do not think that Genl Early will try us on again in the valley." The prediction hit the mark, for the totality of Old Jube's defeat, which sent his broken ranks to Fisher's Hill and later as far south as Staunton and Waynesboro, ended active operations in the Shenandoah for 1864.[13]

In succeeding weeks, the opposing forces skirmished at long range, especially when cavalry on reconnaissance encountered the enemy they had been seeking. Fighting occurred when Mosby's partisans and local bushwhackers struck at Yankee units who burned and confiscated. Still, no large-scale fighting developed; Early's men, unless substantially reinforced, were incapable of sustained resistance to Sheridan's depredations. Several times, bodies of Rebels—infantry as well as horsemen—fled upon the approach of Torbert's men. On November 1 Wells questioned some prisoners and concluded that "they are more afraid of our Cav[alry] than Infantry. Sheridan & Custer are to[o]much for them, whenever they show themselves."[14]

On a couple of occasions, when Early placed his paper-thin ranks in a particularly vulnerable position, Sheridan regretted that he failed to seize the opportunity to crush out the last embers of opposition. Still, he did not feel compelled by time or events to rush into battle yet again; Early was not going anywhere with winter coming on. When the snow stopped and the roads dried, he would still be in Sheridan's front, ready for another whipping. Little Phil felt so confident of his invulnerability that, beginning in late December, he sent excess troops to Petersburg. Two divisions of the VIII Corps were the first to go, followed by the VI Corps in its entirety.[15]

Operations effectively shut down when Sheridan turned his back, one last time, on Early. On November 10—two days after Lincoln won reelection, stamping out the Confederacy's only hope for long-term survival—Little Phil led his army from Cedar Creek to Winchester, where he placed it in winter quarters. By year's end everyone seemed to be constructing a log hut, its walls chinked with mud, its chimney fashioned from hollowed-out barrels, its interior warmed by heat from portable stoves. Rude stables sheltered the army's horses from cold, wind, and snow.[16]

Not everyone could remain by a comfortable fire, however. Men and mounts spent considerable time outdoors, reconnoitering, picketing, and occasionally raiding. Most of the few expeditions that went forth this winter covered short distances, but one, which took place from December 19 to 26, led all three cavalry divisions, under Torbert's supervision, from Winchester to Gordonsville and back.

Via this expedition, Sheridan hoped to address Grant's continuing concern over the Virginia Central, but little came of the effort. One reason was that throughout the mission, the raiders battled weather so severe that 200 of them were frostbitten and at least two horse artillerymen froze to death. Then, too, food and forage were scarce throughout the journey. "The command was obliged to live off the country for six days," recalled a member of the 17th Pennsylvania, "and mighty scant living it was. . . . All in all, it was an extremely hard trip on man and beast."[17]

The elements were bad enough, but the raiders had to battle Confederates who should have been too demoralized to resist but were not. As a result, neither wing of the expeditionary force accomplished its purpose. Merritt and Powell, marching through Chester Gap in the Blue Ridge, were stopped short of Charlottesville by one of the infantry divisions that had been beaten but not destroyed at Cedar Creek. Meanwhile, Custer's diversionary force was attacked unexpectedly near Lacey Springs, north of Harrisonburg, by what remained of the cavalry under Rosser. As a disappointed Sheridan noted, Custer was forced to retreat after suffering "the loss of a number of prisoners, a few horses, and a good many horse equipments."[18]

It was Custer's withdrawal that freed the infantry to block Torbert farther south. Torbert made an effort to remove a human roadblock above Gordonsville, failed, and quickly "concluded it was useless to make a further attempt to break the Central railroad." At bottom, it was a poor performance all around—the perhaps inevitable result of an ill-timed and hazardous assignment. Sheridan, however, saw it differently. Once again a force under Torbert's overall command had "utterly failed," as the army leader put it, and although Little Phil had not expected much of the mission, he appears to have held its outcome against his cavalry leader.[19]

Early in the new year, Torbert paid for his inability to please his boss. In February, having secured a twenty-day leave, he departed the army on the eve of its return to Grant and Meade. Sheridan's decision not to recall him in time to take part may seem unjust, but Torbert ought not to have gone home—where he was feted by Philadelphia's Union League—so close to the end of winter. His poor timing appears to have combined with Sheridan's desire to punish him for sins of omission and commission. This combination hurt Torbert's career: By failing to see action in the climactic phase of the war in the East, he lost some of the leverage he needed to gain rank and recognition in the postwar service.[20]

On the gray, frosty morning of February 27, 1865, the majority of the horsemen in the Army of the Shenandoah broke camp at Winchester and, despite the snow that clung to the earth and tinged the air, started on the march that would return them to Petersburg. Sheridan rode at the head of the column beside his new chief of horse, Wesley Merritt. Behind them trotted the 1st Cavalry Division, under now-Brigadier General Devin; then came Custer's 3rd Division, three brigades strong, having assimilated four of the regiments that had fought under Averell and Powell, now parts of a brigade led by Col. Henry Capehart of the 1st West Virginia Cavalry. A fifth regiment of Powell's had been added to Devin's division.

In rear of these 10,000 troopers and horse artillerymen, another 3,000 officers and men were bidding them farewell. Sheridan had originally intended to take with him a portion of this force, composed of members of the Army of West Virginia and the dismounted troopers of Devin and Custer. He had been dissuaded by Lincoln and Grant, who had urged him to leave behind a larger contingent, one that might guard the mountainous corridor that Early had taken to Washington. Initially commanded by Chapman, this force was assigned to Torbert upon his return from leave.[21]

Instead of heading home via the bottom of the Valley, where he had entered it in August, Sheridan moved south to Strasburg, passing familiar terrain. From there his column marched to Edinburg and Mount Jackson, then across the North Fork of the Shenandoah to Harrisonburg and Mount Crawford. On the evening of March 1 the command bivouacked on ice-coated ground near Staunton. From that town, the site of Torbert's recent failure, the troopers turned east toward Charlottesville, via Waynesboro.[22]

It was no accident that Sheridan's route led him to the place where the vestiges of Early's army had taken refuge. On the morning of the second, the Federals attacked Old Jube for the fourth time, and for the fourth time they defeated him badly. This time, when the smoke cleared, Early was left with debris—spiked guns, shattered caissons, demolished wagons, regiments the size of platoons, and divisions the size of regiments.

Custer had done most of the damage. Three regiments from his division had enveloped the left of the Rebel line, which sat on a ridge west of town, while the rest attacked frontally. After deflecting token resistance, Custer carried the line and everything else before him. In addition to killing and wounding hundreds, he captured 1,600 prisoners, the last of Early's artillery, and every supply wagon not taken at Cedar Creek. By day's end, the Army of the Valley had effectively ceased to exist—nothing remained to threaten Abraham Lincoln's city.[23]

➤─┤◄►─○─◄►┤─◄

From the scene of his latest and most complete triumph, Little Phil sent his captives to Winchester, in company of 1,200 of his men. The rest of his command followed him through the Blue Ridge toward Charlottesville. On March 3 the column slogged through what a member of the 7th Michigan called "the rain-soaked roads of red Virginia clay, churned into thin mortar by the hoofs of many thousands of horses." The men spent the balance of that day and all of the next in the university town. Lucky troopers kept their feet dry in commandeered dormitories and faculty quarters, while less fortunate comrades braved the cold to attack the Virginia Central for the first time since the Trevilian raid. On March 6 everyone climbed back into the saddle and followed Sheridan to the James River Canal, which they finally damaged nine months after Grant first sought its destruction.[24]

After the main column wrecked canal boats and locks, and detachments demolished local bridges, Sheridan discovered that the bridge on which he had planned to cross the James at Columbia had also been burned, by local

Confederates. The act prevented him from carrying out Grant's request that he again strike the railroads at and near Lynchburg. There is some question as to whether Sheridan would have carried out this mission even had the bridge remained intact. Extensive railroad demolition would have prevented him from reaching Petersburg in time to take part in the offensive Grant and Meade were planning to launch as soon as the weather cleared. That was one campaign Sheridan did not wish to miss.[25]

Continuing east by north, Sheridan's soldiers spent two weeks damaging communications along their route, including additional stretches of the Virginia Central and the James River Canal. The command also torched mills, factories, warehouses, and bridges, while liberating thousands of slaves and capturing a growing number of Confederates who saw the end fast approaching. By the twenty-sixth, when Little Phil at last crossed the James and reported to Grant's headquarters at City Point, his people had captured—in addition to their prisoners—2,154 horses and mules, seventeen cannons, 2,010 stands of small arms, and sixteen battle flags. They had also inflicted immense damage to public and private property, from which the local economy would take months, if not years, to recover. The list of resources destroyed, rendered inoperable, or carried off by the Federals takes up nearly seventy lines of text in the *Official Records*.[26]

>─┤─◆┼◆─○─◆┼◆─┤─◄

When they reported for duty outside Petersburg, Sheridan's troopers and horse artillerists were still considered members of the Army of the Shenandoah. But many, perhaps most, thought of themselves as part of the Cavalry Corps, Army of the Potomac. Technically, only David Gregg's division had a claim to this title, for over the past eight months, it alone had remained physically a part of Meade's command. Those months of service had provided the 2nd Division with much activity, many burdens, and several opportunities to win distinction.

The division's role as the only cavalry directly supporting Meade's army had begun with a return to the meadows above the James. On August 13, only a few days after Merritt left for the Valley and with Wilson at Giesboro Point, Grant sent the 2nd Division, along with Hancock's infantry and the X Corps of Butler's army, by steamboat and overland march to the bridgehead opposite Deep Bottom. Once on the Northside, the combined force spent the next week trying to verify reports that Lee had depleted his Bailey's Creek line to reinforce Early. If the intelligence proved accurate, Gregg was to move up the Charles City Road and either attack Richmond or damage the railroads running into it from north and east.[27]

The reports on which the expedition was based were accurate, but it turned out that Kershaw's division alone had been sent west. Two other infantry divisions still held the Deep Bottom-Chaffin's Bluff line, and during the operation, more foot troops under Mahone, plus cavalry under Hampton, joined them in opposing the Federals. These troops held back the II and X

Corps, although Gregg did make progress up the Charles City Road. On the sixteenth the cavalry, followed by Miles's brigade of Hancock's corps, moved as far north as White's Tavern, seven miles from Richmond, driving the riders of Rooney Lee before them. Then, however, the reinforcements shoved Gregg and Miles across Deep Creek; in the fierce fighting, the 2nd Division suffered many casualties, including the wounding of Irvin Gregg. The invaders made no further progress toward Richmond. The operation was effectively over well before everyone recrossed the James to Bemuda Hundred on the evening of the twentieth.[28]

Having failed to make inroads along Lee's upper flank, Grant determined to strike the lower end of his line by destroying hitherto-untouched sections of the Weldon Railroad. On the eighteenth, the V Corps had moved to the railroad, which it had destroyed to a point below Globe Tavern, two miles from Petersburg, before turning north toward Lee's defenses. It was halted short of the city by A. P. Hill, who attacked in the unlikely prospect of regaining the railroad. Fighting went on for three days, with neither Hill nor Warren gaining as much ground as he desired.

During the confrontation, Hancock and Gregg, along with one of Kautz's brigades, moved to the Weldon line. Grant wished them to extend Warren's demolition to Reams's Station, four miles south of Globe Tavern. By the morning of the twenty-fifth, infantry and cavalry had ripped up track to a point three miles below Reams's. That, however, was the extent of their accomplishments. At about 8:00 A.M. Hampton's cavalry—the lead element of a mighty force sent to drive the Federals from the railroad—chased Kautz's brigade from its position south of the depot. A few hours later two of Hill's divisions attacked the horseshoe-shaped breastworks that Hancock's men occupied near Reams's.

The first few efforts failed to carry the position, but at about 2:00 P.M. some recruit- and draftee-laden regiments suddenly broke for the rear, allowing the Rebels to pour through the breach. Although Gregg's and Kautz's troopers did their best to safeguard Hancock's flanks and rear, the II Corps was forced to withdraw—the first time in its proud history that it had relinquished a prepared position to a force of approximately equal size. Disaster was averted only through the cavalry's ability to cover the northward retreat. In some circles, Gregg and Kautz were credited with saving the once-invincible II Corps from extinction.[29]

Back inside its lines southeast of Petersburg, the 2nd Division returned to picketing the rear and flanks of the army. The work was arduous, unexciting, and never-ending. As one veteran remarked, the division "moved from right to left and from left to right of the line in front of Petersburg without any regard for rest or comfort." One compensation was a several-week respite from battle, broken only by an energetic but fruitless pursuit of 4,000 horsemen under Hampton and Rosser, who in mid-September raided around Meade's rear and attacked the combined armies' cattle herd at Coggins's Point on the James. A portion of Irvin Gregg's 13th Pennsylvania, which had been guarding the herd, was dispersed, and many of its men were taken captive. The raiders escaped, driving 2,500 head of cattle and 300 prisoners inside Lee's lines.[30]

While stolen beef might sustain the Army of Northern Virginia for a few weeks, its lines north and south of Petersburg continued to lengthen and to grow thin. Late in September Grant launched major offensives against both of Lee's flanks simultaneously. The drives were designed to stretch those lines to the breaking point and gain ground toward both Richmond and Petersburg. Butler's army carried out the attack on the Northside; to the south, Gregg's regiments guarded the left and rear of an expeditionary force comprising the V and IX Corps. The infantry gained ground near Peebles's Farm and Poplar Springs Church, extending the Army of the Potomac's lines across the Vaughan Road, three miles west of the Weldon Railroad. Gregg's men saw action throughout the offensive. Although roughly handled near Wyatt's house, east of the Vaughan Road, late on the twenty-ninth, the next day they gave a strong account of themselves near the Armstrong house, and on October 1 they held their position beside the Wyatt Road-Vaughan Road intersection despite a strong counterattack by Hampton's cavalry. In the fight, Gregg's troops suffered ninety casualties but inflicted nearly half again as many.[31]

As always, the cavalry guarded the flanks and rear of the army in its new position beyond the Vaughan Road. It advanced once again on the twenty-seventh, when Grant directed Meade to gain possession of the next major byway to Petersburg, the Boydton Plank Road, which ran just east of the Southside Railroad, Lee's last functional supply line. Hancock's corps made the principal effort, crossing Hatcher's Run and turning toward Petersburg. By noon the advance had reached the Boydton Plank Road, with Gregg on the infantry's right.

When the V and IX Corps proved unable to cover Hancock's advance, A. P. Hill hurled three divisions at him, while Hampton attacked Gregg's division in strength sufficient to overwhelm him. Instead, to the Rebels' surprise, Davies's brigade repulsed attack after attack on the plank road, finally counterattacking and driving Hampton from the field. When, after the fight, a Confederate officer was informed that Davies alone had provided the opposition, the captive exclaimed: "Impossible! why, we had three brigades against you!"[32]

Despite the cavalry's heroics, Hancock was forced to give up his forward position as untenable. Gregg accompanied his consequent withdrawal, deflecting blows aimed at the infantry's rear. Again back in its camps astride the Vaughan Road, in late November and early December Gregg's men stockaded their tents and erected log cabins to keep them warm in winter. They left the snug confines of their makeshift homes to picket and reconnoiter, but only twice did they brave the weather for extended periods.

The first occasion was a raid against the lower reaches of the Petersburg & Weldon, which remained in the enemy's possession. At 4:00 A.M. on the first of December, the division moved down the tracks, crossing Rowanty Creek. Along the stream, Gregg stationed his newly formed 3rd Brigade, under Charles Smith. A few miles farther south, Davies's brigade was left behind to guard an important crossing, while the brigade of Irvin Gregg (who had fully recovered from his August wounding) proceeded to the division's primary objective, Stony Creek Station. At the depot where the Wilson-Kautz raiders had encountered so much trouble, the Gregg cousins discovered an earthwork held by 200 Confederates and two cannons. By judicious maneuvering, the 2nd Brigade surrounded the position and forced its surrender. En route north with their prisoners and a large cache of spoils, Gregg reached Davies's position in time to assist him in repulsing a Rebel assault. The two brigades capped off the expedition by destroying miles of Weldon track.[33]

A week later the 2nd Division returned to the far end of the Weldon line, this time in company with the V Corps. For four days, Gregg's riders covered the flanks of Warren's troops as the infantry mangled that section of the right-of-way between the Nottoway and Meherrin Rivers. On December 10, when Gregg's scouts found an enemy force dug in below the Meherrin, the demolition ceased, and the combined force headed back north. On the return, the 2nd Division fought off some of the many guerrilla bands that infested the region.

The second December operation was memorable, less for the damage inflicted on the railroad than for two tragic incidents that illustrated the brutality and recklessness of the war. On its return march, the division found some of its members, who had fallen out of the column for one reason or another, lying dead beside the road, their throats cut and their bodies dismembered by bushwhackers. The other tragedy occurred on the tenth, after Gregg found the Rebels in strength below the Meherrin. While Warren's infantry prepared to return to Petersburg, Gregg sent Davies's brigade across the stream to study a line of earthworks the Rebels had thrown up on the south bank.[34]

Without David Gregg on hand to dissuade him, Davies ordered an assault on the position despite the nine cannons and the slashing of timber that protected it. While the 1st New Jersey and the 1st Pennsylvania advanced afoot, Davies ordered Maj. Lucius M. Sargent, Jr., to lead a saber charge at the head of his 1st Massachusetts. Against his better judgment, Sargent obeyed and fell mortally wounded from a shell fragment. His regiment was quickly dispersed. As he was carried past Davies on a litter, the dying officer cursed the brigadier for his rashness. A New Jersey officer complained that the artillery should have made a mounted assault unthinkable.[35]

A third tragedy, of a sort, was played out shortly before the 2nd Division entered upon its next field assignment. In early February 1865 a second attempt by Meade's army to gain the Boydton Plank Road succeeded gloriously. This was to be expected, for the flanks of the Army of Northern Virginia were now almost forty miles apart, and Lee could hold the line in between with only 35,000 effectives. The division reaped accolades for its part in the operation, but none went to David Gregg. The general's cousin, not he, commanded on the mission. This was because as early as the previous November, the division leader had made up his mind to resign his commission.

Gregg submitted his resignation neither because he wanted to go home to "a pretty wife," as army gossip had it, nor because he resented being passed over for honors in favor of younger officers such as Sheridan, as some historians have suggested. Gregg could have returned to his wife and family years earlier, and he had gained honors aplenty, including, on the eve of his resignation, the brevet (or honorary rank) of major general of volunteers, to date from August 1.[36]

His stated reason came as a surprise to those few he shared it with, and it retains the power to surprise today. "The fact of it is," he told Colonel Smith during a conversation overheard by the surgeon of the 6th Ohio, "I am a good deal of a coward. Every engagement tells upon my nervous system to the last degree, and it is only by the exercise of all my will power that I can appear natural and unafraid."[37]

The surgeon's version of Gregg's statement was reconstructed from memory, and it is not a verbatim quote. It may not be accurate in all details. Yet it cannot be dismissed out of hand. It is entirely possible that Gregg's famous imperturbability under fire was a pose, one maintained by sheer force of will. This is not to say that Gregg was not brave. To play the part of a brave man in battle requires a certain amount of courage, no matter what the man thinks of himself. It is also true that even a brave man can be worn down psychologically to the point that he cannot face another day under fire without fear of disgracing himself.

Gregg postponed his intended action for two months, submitting his resignation on January 26, 1865. He gave as his written reason the need to attend to personal matters at home in Berks County, Pennsylvania. It was accepted on February 8, three days after the Boydton Road mission that he did not accompany, and on the tenth Gregg left the Army of the Potomac. Irvin Gregg took over the division for a time, then gave it up to Davies. A permanent successor was not named until March 26, when George Crook, now a major general of volunteers, unexpectedly took it.[38]

Crook had stayed behind when Sheridan left the Valley, for he had been captured by partisan rangers a week earlier. After a brief stint in Libby Prison, he was exchanged and brought to Petersburg. It was said that Secretary Stanton attributed the general's capture not simply to carelessness, but to stupidity, and that he would not have cared had Crook rotted in prison. It may be that Sheridan rescued his old classmate and perhaps promoted him as Gregg's successor.[39]

When Crook assumed command on the eve of the Appomattox Campaign, his reputation followed him. The men of the 2nd Cavalry Division heard that he was a good leader and a fair man. Not surprisingly, however, many regarded him warily. Crook might be "the best cavalry commander in the world," one trooper observed, "but we know little about him. He had not been tried by our fire," unlike the respected and trustworthy officer he had replaced. Still, most of the division was philosophical about the situation. Those who would serve under or beside Crook "did not know what was in store for [them], nor did [they] really care, providing Sheridan was at the head."[40]

>─┤─◆▷─◦─◁◆─┤─◄

As a rainy dawn broke on March 29, Sheridan led Merritt, Devin, Crook, Custer, and their 13,000 officers and men from their bivouacs near Hancock Station, on the military railroad southeast of Petersburg, along the familiar length of the Weldon Railroad. The column veered westward at Reams's Station, crossed Rowanty Creek, and headed for Dinwiddie Court House, on the Boydton Plank Road twelve miles southwest of Petersburg and five miles southeast of a strategic crossroads known as Five Forks. There, along the extreme right flank of Lee's defense line, Sheridan had been directed—in conjunction with a movement farther north by the V and II Corps—to sweep around the Rebel flank and into Lee's rear.[41]

Sheridan was to advance in such a fashion as to cause the defenders—infantry as well as horsemen—to leave their entrenchments and battle him on open ground. Should the Rebels sally forth, Grant told him, "move in with your entire force in your own way, and with the full reliance that the army will engage or follow the enemy, as circumstances will dictate." Grant also hoped that Sheridan would range far enough west to strike and if possible destroy Lee's last supply lines, the Southside and the Richmond & Danville Railroads.[42]

Grant's orders both pleased and concerned Sheridan. He enjoyed the prospect of turning Lee's extended flank and gaining his rear, and he appreciated the fact that he had been granted the authority of an independent commander, answerable to Grant alone. But Sheridan had no desire to strike the railroads Grant had in mind, for the mission smacked of an earlier directive that Sheridan believed he had talked his superior into rescinding. Two days earlier Sheridan had joined Grant and two distinguished visitors—Abraham Lincoln and William T. Sherman—aboard a steamboat off City Point. During the conference, Sherman, just up from Goldsborough, North Carolina, had promoted a plan that Grant appeared to favor, under which the cavalry of the Army of the Shenandoah and Army of the Potomac would wreck the railroads south and west of Petersburg, then head south to join Sherman on the last leg of his march to Petersburg.[43]

The plan held no allure for Sheridan. The last thing he wanted was to leave the front for service in a secondary theater such as North Carolina, thereby missing the final confrontation with Lee. Like the majority of his troopers, Sheridan realized that Lee's flanks were so thin they would soon be shredded. Their loss would doubtless force the Confederates to abandon Petersburg and Richmond. Where they headed in that event was anyone's guess, but it did not take a genius to see that when the Army of the Potomac and the Army of the James (now under Maj. Gen. Edward O. C. Ord) overtook Lee's army on open ground, its life could be measured in hours.

Lee's army destroyed, the war would be over. The fighting in the western theater had effectively been quelled by Sherman's March to the Sea and his subsequent campaign in the Carolinas, as well as by a series of Union victories in Tennessee, in which Wilson's Cavalry Corps, Military Division of the Mississippi, had played a major role. Now, as Sheridan closed up on Dinwiddie, Wilson was one week into a month-long raid through Alabama and Georgia, stamping out pockets of resistance in the Deep South. The struggle to save the Union was nearly won. There would be a final kill, and Sheridan was determined to be in on it.

Therefore, he was frustrated by the rain that fell throughout the twenty-ninth and continued next day, making active operations difficult and buying the enemy precious time. By the time the rain ceased, Lee had countered Sheridan's move by shifting a 19,000-man force of all arms under the Gettysburg hero, George Pickett, to Five Forks. Though large, this command was also mobile enough to counter an attempt by Sheridan to gain Lee's rear or slip across the North Carolina border to join Sherman.[44]

Sheridan was so impatient to land a blow against the new folks in his front that he moved north on the thirtieth in a downpour. Despite the weather, he was in an ebullient mood, for Grant had canceled the raid on the railroads. The good humor vanished, however, when another message from Grant suspended Sheridan's move toward Lee's rear and advised him to return to Petersburg, where he might procure forage for his hungry steeds. Little Phil was so upset over the cessation of active operations that he galloped to Grant's headquarters along Gravelly Run and gave him a piece of his mind. After some further discussion, Grant adopted Sheridan's view, vowing, "We will go on."[45]

The only part of Sheridan's command that saw action on the thirtieth was Devin's division, which, supported by Davies's brigade, advanced from Dinwiddie Court House to Five Forks. Sheridan had directed Devin to gain possession of the crossroads, but he got no closer than a mile away before he was forced to return by Pickett's foot and horse units. Devin did scout the Rebel position, but at a cost: At one point, the 5th and 6th United States Cavalry of Gibbs's brigade found themselves surrounded and had to cut their way out with heavy loss.[46]

About 9:00 on the relatively dry morning of the thirty-first, Sheridan again advanced on Five Forks, this time with a much larger force. Two miles short of the objective, Devin's division was set upon by Pickett's approaching troops and again roughly handled. Farther to the left, Crook, with the balance of the 2nd Division, was challenged by Pickett's cavalry—the divisions of Rosser, Rooney Lee, and Col. Thomas T. Munford, the whole under Fitz Lee—along Chamberlain's Creek, northwest of Dinwiddie Court House. Custer's division, which the previous day had guarded supply wagons in the rear, remained detached, this time corduroying roads.

Sheridan could have used the 3rd Division's support his day. About 11:00 A.M. Rebel infantry and cavalry trooped down Scott's Road, one of the thoroughfares that comprised Five Forks, and slipped around the Union left. The attackers took a heavy toll of Devin's and Crook's divisions, both of which were steadily forced back. Most of Crook's men and those under Gibbs withdrew to Dinwiddie, but the remainder of the 2nd Division and Devin's troopers had to retire eastward before they were able to circle back to Sheridan's new line at the courthouse.[47]

When the last of the fugitives reached Dinwiddie, it was late afternoon, and darkness was coming on. They joined their comrades inside a semicircular cordon of earthworks three-quarters of a mile above the courthouse, which was under attack by Pickett. By now Custer's division had come up; it held the center of the line, with Crook's division to its left and Devin's on its right. At first, fearing themselves in dire straits, the troopers fought desperately to hold back the Confederates. The combined effect of thousands of repeating carbines blazing away made the difference, keeping Pickett's troops at bay. A staff officer marveled at the volume of firepower that came from "the carbines of five brigades . . . blazing in the twilight, the repeating Spensers [sic] puffing out their cartridges like Roman candles."[48]

Rather than worried about being routed, Sheridan was exultant that Pickett had left his defenses at Five Forks to take on the cavalry. Little Phil had no doubt that his carbineers and artillerymen would retain possession of the courthouse. The longer they kept Pickett engaged, the greater his chance of being taken in flank by a larger force of Union infantry such as the V Corps, which earlier in the day had fought on the White Oak Road, northeast of Dinwiddie.

Early that evening, with fighting still raging at the courthouse, Sheridan petitioned Grant for an infantry force—preferably the VI Corps, which had served him so well in the Valley. With the VI by his side, he had no doubt he would "turn the enemy's left or break though his lines," either of which would doom the Army of Northern Virginia. As it happened, however, Wright's corps was too far off to reach Sheridan by morning; instead Grant ordered the V Corps to his assistance, assuring him that it would arrive by midnight.[49]

Given the soggy roads and overflowing streams in that region, Grant's timetable was unrealistic. Warren made what he always insisted was a good-faith effort to reach Dinwiddie Court House by early morning, but the head of his column did not meet Sheridan until an hour before daybreak on April 1. Little Phil was angered by the delay, for it had permitted Pickett—at last appreciative of his vulnerability—to return to his fortified crossroads. Over the months, including last May 8 outside Spotsylvania, Sheridan had had several run-ins with Warren, whom he considered a slow mover, a complainer, and perhaps also a defeatist. As the V Corps was now under Sheridan's control, Little Phil had the authority to relieve its commander if circumstances warranted—a point that Grant had recently brought to Sheridan's attention.[50]

His plan to take Pickett in flank gone up in smoke, Sheridan devised an attack by the cavalry against the right and center of Pickett's position on the White Oak Road. At the same time, Warren would strike at Pickett's refused left flank, which had been made vulnerable by the three-mile gap that separated it from the rest of the Petersburg defenses. This gap, and Warren's right flank, would be covered by the cavalry of the Army of the James, under Brig. Gen. Ranald S. Mackenzie, Kautz's recent successor.

Unwilling to wait for the remainder of Warren's people to reach him, Sheridan led Merritt's two divisions and Crook's command toward Five Forks just after sunrise. En route, the cavalry flanked and drove some infantrymen from the swampy bottoms of Chamberlain's Creek. Moving into position on the left of Merritt's two-and-a-half-mile-long line, Custer's division began, at about 2:00 P.M., to demonstrate afoot in order to deflect Pickett's attention from Warren's assault. Farther to the east, Devin's troopers, most of them also dismounted, did the same; beside them, ordnance rifles pounded away at defenses and defenders. Well to the south, on the other side of Chamberlain's Creek, Crook's division, still recovering from its battering of the previous day, protected the rear.[51]

The cavalry had been skirmishing for nearly two hours, raising the possibility that they would soon run out of ammunition, when Warren's vanguard finally appeared on the right and formed for an attack. Sheridan already was greatly displeased with the infantry's, and especially Warren's, conduct. Soon after the V Corps' attack began, he grew livid. Warren's men went forward in two lines, neither of which struck the angle where the front of Pickett's defenses met its refused flank, as Sheridan had intended. One of Warren's three divisions attacked too far to the east and struck nothing but open air. Meanwhile, the second line struck too far in the other direction. Other units saw the mistake, corrected the angle of attack, and hit Pickett's flank head-on. But when Sheridan sought out Warren to learn what had gone wrong, the corps leader was not where Little Phil expected him to be. In a fit of rage, he relieved Warren from command and ordered him back to Petersburg, refusing Warren's subsequent request that he rethink his action, exclaiming, "Reconsider, hell. I don't reconsider my decisions."[52]

While the infantry attack righted itself, Custer and Devin stopped feinting and struck along the length of Pickett's line. Many troopers went forward afoot; others jumped their horses over the parapets, shooting and sabering as they rode. Still other men grappled hand-to-hand with the defenders, physically taking the defenses apart. "Hardly halting to reform," Sheridan recalled, "the intermingling infantry and dismounted cavalry swept down inside the intrenchments, rushing to and beyond Five Forks, capturing thousands of prisoners."[53]

As men in blue continued to pour over and through the works, Pickett's men were forced out by the crush of bodies. Dozens dropped their weapons and fled, some evading one would-be captor only to run into the arms of another. Slowly, gradually, resistance melted away, one sector after another falling to the attackers. Pickett himself, who had spent most of the afternoon in the rear, eating shad and perhaps also drinking whiskey, rushed to the scene, but only in time to behold a disaster greater than the charge that had been named for him.

By nightfall, almost one-third of Pickett's command had surrendered to Sheridan and his subordinates. A few thousand others had escaped across Hatcher's Run, north of the battlefield. The rest lay dead or wounded inside Pickett's works. Lee's far right flank had ceased to exist, threatening the continued existence of Petersburg, Richmond, and Lee's army. Victory had many authors, but none more eloquent than Sheridan's troopers and cannoneers.[54]

>─┼─◆>─○─<◆─┼─<

What followed the breakthrough at Five Forks was anticlimatic. Although the war in Virginia went on for another week, its outcome was a foregone conclusion. It should have been clear to anyone who observed the lines of fugitives leaving Petersburg and Richmond that the Confederacy was a shadow quickly dissipating. The flow of retreating troops increased immeasurably after April 2, when the VI and IX Corps, backed by some of Ord's troops, attacked all along the line. The Federals not only took Petersburg's outer works, but swept the Rebels from Hatcher's Run, killing A. P. Hill and reaching the Southside Railroad. Richmond was evacuated that night; the next morning, the city was occupied by white and USCT units.

At first, no fewer than five retreat columns—two from Richmond, three out of Petersburg—started west. They converged at Amelia Court House on the Richmond & Danville. When they started off in pursuit, Meade's and Ord's armies kept well south of these lines, uncertain if the enemy was heading for Lynchburg or for the railroad to North Carolina, there to link with Sherman's principal opponent, Joseph E. Johnston. In fact, Lee's initial plan was to march down the tracks to Danville via Burkeville Junction; further movements would be governed by circumstances.[55]

Their mobility made the troopers under Sheridan the point men of the pursuit. The troopers of Merritt and Crook (to whom was attached, for much of the pursuit, Mackenzie's division) started out late on April 2, after hearing what Bugler Jackson called the "glorious news" of Petersburg's fall. Having crossed Hatcher's Run to the Southside Railroad following Pickett's overthrow, the cavalry, in response to Grant's order, moved toward the Appomattox River as if to strike another blow at Petersburg, this from the rear. Sheridan, however, talked Grant into letting him head west on the south side of the river. This, as it turned out, was the right course. Crossing the Appomattox would have meant abandoning the most direct route to the place where Lee was heading.[56]

The pursuit began in earnest early on the third. Soon it was proceeding in two roughly parallel columns, Merritt, with Devin's and Custer's divisions, taking the direct road to Amelia Court House, and Crook's division moving farther south toward Jetersville Station. Sheridan came to see Jetersville as such a strategic location that late on the fourth he ordered Merritt there as well. That same day, he persuaded Meade to send the II, V, and VI Corps to the same point. The move effectively prevented Lee from reaching Burkeville, Danville, and, perhaps, the Carolinas.

The way south blocked, Lee left the railroad and headed west toward Deatonsville and, beyond, Farmville on the Appomattox. As he did so, Sheridan had Crook send Davies's brigade on a reconnaissance to Paineville, seven miles north of Jetersville. En route to Paineville, Davies discovered a major prize: the wagon train of what remained of Lee's army, trundling northwestward toward Farmville. Impulsive as always, Davies raced to get ahead of the train, which his men halted by shooting down the teams that hauled the wagons. The brigade captured more than 300 guards, 400 horses and mules, and five guns, while burning 200 wagons—a serious loss to the fugitives from Petersburg. Many wagons escaped being burned, however, and on his return to Jetersville, Davies was set upon by larger bodies of horsemen—the troopers of Rosser and Munford—who threatened to smash his brigade and recover its spoils. Only the timely intervention of Crook's main force allowed Davies to return to Jetersville with his trophies intact.[57]

The location of Lee's train so far to the north and west told Sheridan that the Rebels were heading for Lynchburg. Meade, however, was not so sure; when the advance of his main body located the Rebels at Amelia Court House on the fifth, he got the impression that Lee was concentrating, perhaps preparing to move south; even if he was not, he presented a tempting target. Despite Grant's concerns and over Sheridan's protests, Meade won permission to advance north to Amelia early on the sixth. Too late, he saw he had been wrong. He found the courthouse village empty; in the night, Lee had left for points west. Meade was now in his rear instead of parallel to his march. It was problematical whether the Army of the Potomac, in its new position, could overtake the still-mobile Rebels.[58]

Sheridan had acted on his own better judgment by continuing west toward Deatonsville and Rice's Station. His strategy succeeded in bringing his troopers within range of that part of Lee's train that Davies had failed to overtake. They found it parked just west of Farmville, along Little Sailor's Creek.

Sheridan attacked at once with Crook's division, which made minimal gains, and then with the Michigan Brigade, which, under Peter Stagg, he had detached from Devin's division for "special service." Stagg's attack was truly special: It bagged 300 prisoners. Soon afterward, Custer's division happened on the scene. The long-haired brigadier, today garbed in an olive-colored uniform of corduroy, attacked other sections of the immense train. By day's end, more than 300 wagons had been captured, along with three batteries that had been trying to guard the train. Custer's success was only slightly tarnished when a body of infantry from the retreat column, including what remained of Kershaw's division, came up to thrash the wagon burners. Custer put out another call for help; Devin, with two of his brigades, came up to help him disengage with slight loss.[59]

The attack on Lee's trains was but one facet of the fighting at Sailor's Creek. Through human error, a gap had developed in the retreat column. One result was that approximately half of what remained of the Army of Northern

Virginia was cut off and captured along the creek. While Meade's hard-marching infantry, notably the VI and II Corps, received much of the credit, many of the attacks on the surrounded Rebels had been delivered by the regiments under Merritt and Crook, notably those of Custer's division.[60]

After sending some of its men back to Petersburg in charge of the thousands of prisoners taken at Sailor's Creek, the cavalry resumed its westward jaunt, with Meade's and Ord's infantry to the rear. Crook pushed on to Farmville, where Lee had crossed the Appomattox hours before. According to plan, every bridge across the river was to have been burned to stymie or at least slow the pursuit. Because High Bridge was fired too late, the vanguard of the II Corps reached it in time to douse the flames and save the bridge. The corps crossed the span, and on the other side it pressed forward, Crook's troopers in the advance. The road west seemed clear. Rushing ahead precipitately, Gregg's brigade fell into a trap prepared by Rosser and Munford; Gregg, along with several officers and men, was captured. He would remain prisoner for only two days.[61]

Now certain that Lee's remnants would continue west, Sheridan determined to get ahead of them short of Lynchburg. Early on April 8, while at Prospect Station on the Southside, he learned from a member of the scouting company he had organized in the Shenandoah that four boxcars filled with rations for Lee's army were waiting twenty miles away at Appomattox Station. Clothed in Confederate gray, the scout had impersonated a commissary officer so convincingly that railroad officials had sent the cars to a place where Sheridan would find them but Lee would not.

A cheerful Sheridan led the way to the depot, which Custer's men captured with an old-fashioned cavalry charge—the last they would conduct in this war. Cowed by the sight of flashing steel, the train guards fled, whereupon Custer ran off three cars and burned the fourth, denying their abundant contents to Confederates who had not had a square meal in days. Its work well done, that evening the 3rd Division joined its comrades under Crook and Devin in marching north to Appomattox Court House. There the cavalry took up a position across Lee's path; the head of the retreat column lay only a short distance to the east.[62]

Lee's army was still capable of shows of strength; the previous night its advance guard had struck and bloodied a part of Custer's division near Appomattox Station. Still, by dawn on Palm Sunday, April 9, everyone under Sheridan realized that the end was near. A few men had heard that Grant and Lee were exchanging messages relating to the surrender of the Army of Northern Virginia. Grant seemed to think that Lee would come around to that idea if prodded a bit. Sheridan agreed to do the prodding, but he knew he could stop Lee's retreat only if the foot soldiers in his rear—of whom Ord's XXIV Corps was closest to him—could come up to support him.[63]

Hoping that help would reach him in time, Sheridan dismounted many of his men and faced them eastward before sunup that morning. He built a line astride the Richmond-Lynchburg Stage Road, Lee's avenue of retreat, and on either side of it. Part of Devin's division held the right flank, Crook's the center—Smith's brigade blocking the road itself—and Mackenzie's small body of horsemen, which had been reorganized into a brigade, the left. Custer's men and many of Devin's covered the far rear. Most of the troopers knew nothing of Ord's presence only a few miles to the south; they feared they would have to hold this line, alone and indefinitely. They would have to fight and fall back, as they had done on so many fields, delaying the enemy's advance as much as possible, playing for time. Some men wondered if they were on a suicide mission, but no one left his place in line.

For hours that must have seemed like weeks, morning darkness shrouded the Confederates up the road, but as sunlight began to streak the sky, the slowly advancing enemy came into view. A trooper of the 1st Maine stared at the ragged but dangerous Rebels: "More than an army, they resembled an armed mob of mad men, determined, desperate. When they came within range we opened on them with our carbines, but our fire produced no perceptible effect on them."[64]

When the Confederates opened in turn with their longer-range arms, Sheridan's line shook from flank to flank, as if trembling, but the men held their places. Suddenly Merritt rode past, shouting orders and advice. At one point, he barked out: "Hold on as long as possible, and if our infantry does not come up, withdraw by the right flank!"[65]

Then the infantry came closer, rifles spitting, and cavalrymen began to fall. At first a few troopers, then a growing number, followed Merritt's command, passing to the flanks, where they joined their comrades in popping away at the advancing troops. Eventually, some time after 9:00 A.M., the road was open to the Rebels. Only a few men held on there, willing to die where they stood or kneeled rather than let the enemy pass. But how long any sector of Sheridan's line could hold, with the road beginning to overflow with Confederates, not even the commanders could say. Merritt later admitted that it was "like opposing the force of a cyclone with a wall of straw." Then, just before ten o'clock, movement was perceptible toward the west. Lieutenant Veil of the 1st Cavalry wrote that he "looked to the rear and saw the whole hillside covered with a line of Yankee infantry. As soon as the enemy saw them they stopped firing."[66]

As the rattle of musketry slowly died out, the Rebels pulled back a short distance, then milled about as if uncertain of their course. Troopers stared at each other in wonder, not daring to believe that the fighting was over. Then the gray troops began to stack arms, and from out of their ranks rode an officer bearing a white flag. At that moment, recalled one trooper, an eerie silence settled over the field.

The silence lasted only a few minutes. Then the realization set in: Not only the day's fighting, but the war itself, was over. The troopers began to cheer. The cheering grew ever louder, spilling out over the ridges and hills, echoing in the valley beyond, and blending with the shouts of Ord's infantry-men in the rear. It reached its crescendo when Little Phil came riding down the line on a gray charger, waving his hat in salute to officers and men and shouting a benediction that might have been intended for every trooper who ever served in the Army of the Potomac:

"God bless you, boys! God bless you, boys!"[67]

AFTERWORD

Historians consistently portray the cavalry of the Army of the Potomac as struggling against adversity born of chronic ineptitude, and rising to competence only after a long and painful period of trial and error. Many who make pronouncements on the subject have stated or implied that the Union troopers prevailed only because their enemy went downhill during the last year and a half of the war. Emasculated by attrition, between late 1863 and the spring of 1865 the Confederacy lacked the mounts, weapons, equipment, and ammunition to keep the horsemen of J. E. B. Stuart and Wade Hampton at peak efficiency. In other words, the Federals won, but it was not a fair fight.

A more accurate assessment is that the Union cavalrymen triumphed because, as early as late or even mid-1862, they were clearly superior to their celebrated opponents not only in arms, equipment, and horseflesh, but also in tactics, training, and the caliber of their manpower. On the Virginia Peninsula, the Federals first displayed the ability to outride and outfight their adversaries. They ably guarded the front, flanks, and rear of their army; struck enemy communications with a precision and thoroughness that the Confederate horsemen never matched; and more than held their own at Williamsburg, Slash Church, and in numerous skirmishes and engagements. Only when gathering intelligence on their enemy, charging massed infantry at Gaines's Mill, and trying to stop Stuart's Chickahominy Raid did the Federals come up short, and these failures were mainly due to the incapacity of their commanders, especially Stoneman and Cooke.

A lack of imagination on the part of McClellan and Burnside meant that neither at Antietam nor at Fredericksburg did the cavalry contribute to the fortunes of its army in combat. Pleasonton proved a burden to his cavalry, failing to gain intelligence of strategic value and shying from contact with Stuart's Chambersburg raiders. An indication of the high command's inability to use its mounted arm to advantage was Burnside's neglect of his horsemen once the army crossed the Rappahannock. Not surprisingly, one-third of the cavalry spent the entire day of December 13, 1862, on the north bank of the river.

During the Chancellorsville campaign, some things changed for the better. Though unable to tap its full potential, Hooker upgraded his cavalry, which had fallen into decline through overwork and inadequate support. Of greater importance, he enhanced the cavalry's might and morale by grouping its regiments into a corps commanded by one of the army's most experienced—though least able—officers, Stoneman. Almost immediately, the rejuvenated troopers made their strength felt by besting Stuart and Fitz Lee at Kelly's Ford, avenging the humiliation Lee had inflicted on them weeks earlier at Hartwood Church. Though Averell—who was not long for the army—behaved tentatively and timidly throughout the battle, and while only a portion of the corps took part, the entire command received a psychological boost from the unprecedented success of March 17, 1863.

Pleasonton's inadequacies as a field commander and intelligence manager combined with Duffié's slowness and inflexible tactics to make Brandy Station something less than the great moral victory that most historians pronounce it. Not only on that field, but also during the fighting in the Loudoun Valley, at Hanover and at Hunterstown, the cavalry's high command, especially Judson Kilpatrick, failed to gather critical intelligence, employed faulty tactics, and fought in piecemeal fashion. By the campaign's end, however, aggressive new generals such as Custer and Merritt had begun to assert themselves, with far-reaching effects on their corps. Moreover, commanders of the horse artillery units attached to the cavalry of Meade's army—men such as John C. Tidball, James M. Robertson, John Calef, Alexander C. M. Pennington, Alanson Randol, and William C. Fuller—had begun to make a name for themselves. The close and timely support they gave their cavalry comrades on many fields made the horse batteries one of the true success stories of the Army of the Potomac.

Nowhere was the ability of the cavalry of the army better displayed than during the epic struggle at Gettysburg. That ability was highlighted by Buford's against-all-odds stand on the first day of the battle and Gregg's decisive repulse of Lee's infantry on the second and Stuart's horsemen on the third. The cavalry capped the campaign with an energetic and harassing, if inconclusive, pursuit of Lee's defeated army into Virginia.

The heavy slate of fighting throughout the autumn of 1863 and the few engagements the following winter signified a tangible shift in cavalry power, as the Federals consistently outpointed their foe in the Rappahannock-Rapidan River basin. The major exceptions to this run of success were Kilpatrick's miscues at Buckland Mills and on the threshhold of Richmond, failures that presaged both his and Pleasonton's departure from the eastern theater.

Their exodus coincided with the passing of the underappreciated Buford, as well as with the appearance of new faces such as Torbert, Wilson, and Davies, whose flaws and failings sometimes overshadowed their talents and achievements. The concomitant rise of Phil Sheridan meant that no longer would the Union cavalry in the East lack a driving force at the top. A better soldier than a man, Little Phil exhibited qualities long missing from the cavalry's hierarchy, including a relentless energy, a disregard of the popular and the politic, and a growing contempt for the Confederate horsemen.

Supported by Grant, Lincoln, and the Cavalry Bureau, during the last year of the war Sheridan persuaded his troopers to settle for nothing less than victory. With ruthless proficiency, he pursued success from Todd's Tavern to Haw's Shop, Cold Harbor, and Petersburg, then through the Shenandoah Valley. On expeditions to Richmond and Trevilian Station, he demonstrated that a large, vigilant, and well-led raiding column might occasionally be fought to a draw but could never be halted short of its objectives. The ability of Sheridan's troopers to fight mounted and afoot with equal success paid special dividends from Five Forks to Appomattox, a campaign that saw the zenith of Union cavalry proficiency.

This is a record of quick and consistent achievement, but it comes with a caveat. The Union horsemen successfully opposed their enemy far earlier than most historians would have us believe, but the key to sustaining that success proved elusive. In fact, more than two years passed before the ingredients of lasting victory—proper organization, tactical versatility, and effective leadership—combined to make Lincoln's cavalrymen unbeatable.

NOTES

ABBREVIATIONS USED IN NOTES

ACPF	Appointments, Commissions, and Personal Branch File
B&L	*Battles and Leaders of the Civil War*
CWTI	*Civil War Times Illustrated*
GRSWR	Generals' Reports of Service, War of the Rebellion
HSP	Historical Society of Pennsylvania
JCCW	*Report of the Joint Committee on the Conduct of the War*
JMSIUS	*Journal of the Military Service Institution of the United States*
JUSCA	*Journal of the United States Cavalry Association* (also known as *Cavalry Journal*)
LC	Library of Congress
MB	*Maine Bugle*
MOLLUS	Military Order of the Loyal Legion of the United States
MSS	Correspondence/Papers
NA	National Archives
OR	*The War of the Rebellion: A Compilation of the Official Records of the Union and Confederate Armies*
PMHSM	*Papers of the Military Historical Society of Massachusetts*
RG-, E-	Record Group, Entry
USAMHI	United States Army Military History Institute
USMAL	United States Military Academy Library

CHAPTER 1

1. Carl Schurz, *The Reminiscences of Carl Schurz,* 3 vols. (Garden City, N.Y., 1917), 2: 230; Hans L. Trefousse, *Carl Schurz: A Biography* (Knoxville, Tenn., 1982), 104–05, 316n.; James H. Stevenson, *"Boots and Saddles": A History of . . . the First New York (Lincoln) Cavalry . . .* (Harrisburg, Pa., 1879), 13–24.

2. Schurz, *Reminiscences,* 2: 230–31; Trefousse, *Carl Schurz,* 104–5; Walter Kempster, "The Early Days of Our Cavalry, in the Army of the Potomac," *War Papers: Wisconsin MOLLUS* 3 (1903): 65.

3. Trefousse, *Carl Schurz,* 105, 316n.; Stevenson, *"Boots and Saddles,"* 13–24; William H. Beach, *The First New York (Lincoln) Cavalry, from April 19, 1861, to July 7, 1865* (Milwaukee, 1902), 20, 25; Charles D. Rhodes, "The Federal Cavalry: Its Organization and Equipment," in *The Photographic History of the Civil War,* 10 vols. (New York, 1911), 4: 52.

4. Mary Lee Stubbs, "Cavalry in the Civil War," 56–57, Office of the Chief of Military History, Washington, D.C.; *Army and Navy Journal,* Nov. 10, 1866.

5. Theophilus F. Rodenbough, comp., *From Everglade to Cañon with the Second [United States] Dragoons . . .* (New York, 1875), 60–69.

6. Randy Steffen, *The Horse Soldier, 1776–1943: The United States Cavalryman—His Uniforms, Arms, Accoutrements, and Equipments,* 4 vols. (Norman, Okla., 1977–80), 1: 128-36; Laurence D. Schiller, "A Taste of Northern Steel: The Evolution of Federal Cavalry Tactics, 1861–1865," *North & South* 2 (Jan. 1999): 32-33.

7. R. P. P. Wainwright, "The First Regiment of Cavalry," in Theophilus F. Rodenbough and William L. Haskin, eds., *The Army of the United States: Historical Sketches of Staff and Line . . .* (New York, 1896), 153–57; Alfred E. Bates, "The Second Regiment of Cavalry (1836–65)," in *ibid.,* 173–76; Theophilus F. Rodenbough, "Cavalry of the Civil War: Its Evolution and Influence," in *Photographic History of the Civil War,* 4: 22–23.

8. Wainwright, "First Regiment of Cavalry," 158–59; Bates, "Second Regiment of Cavalry (1836–65)," 177–78; Charles Morton, "The Third Regiment of Cavalry," all in Rodenbough and Haskin, eds., *Army of the United States,* 193–98.

9. "The Fourth Regiment of Cavalry," in *ibid.,* 211; Eben Swift, "The Fifth Regiment of Cavalry," in *ibid.,* 221; Stephen Z. Starr, *The Union Cavalry in the Civil War,* 3 vols. (Baton Rouge, La., 1979–84), 1: 54.

10. Robert M. Utley, *Frontiersmen in Blue: The United States Army and the Indian, 1848–1865* (New York, 1967), 23; Edward S. Wallace, *General William Jenkins Worth, Monterey's Forgotten Hero* (Dallas, 1953), 68.

11. Starr, *Union Cavalry in the Civil War,* 1: 53–54.

12. Grady McWhiney and Perry D. Jamieson, *Attack and Die: Civil War Military Tactics and the Southern Heritage* (University, Ala., 1982), 126–27.

13. Don Russell, "Jeb Stuart's Other Indian Fight," *CWTI* 13 (Apr. 1974): 11; Rodenbough, *From Everglade to Cañon,* 180–84; Edward G. Longacre, *General John Buford: A Military Biography* (Conshohocken, Pa., 1995), 42–50; Lawrence Kip, *Army Life on the Pacific* (New York, 1859), 64–65.

14. Rodenbough, *From Everglade to Cañon,* 105–11.

15. K. Jack Bauer, *The Mexican War, 1846–1848* (New York, 1974), 60, 62.

16. Henry R. Pyne, *The History of the First New Jersey Cavalry* (Trenton, N.J., 1871), 55–56.

17. McWhiney and Jamieson, *Attack and Die,* 126–27, 130.

18. Antoine Henri Jomini, *Summary of the Art of War* (New York, 1854), 307–16; D. H. Mahan, *An Elementary Treastise on Advanced-Guard, Outpost, and Detached Service of Troops . . .* (New York, 1853), 57.

19. McWhiney and Jamieson, *Attack and Die,* 62–63, 130.

20. *Ibid.,* 63–64.

21. *Ibid.,* 63.

22. Philip St. George Cooke, "The Charge of Cooke's Cavalry at Gaines's Mill," *B&L*, 2: 344–46; Stephen W. Sears, *To the Gates of Richmond: The Peninsula Campaign* (New York, 1992), 245–46.

23. Stubbs, "Cavalry in the Civil War," 69; McWhiney and Jamieson, *Attack and Die*, 62–64.

24. *Ibid.*, 53–64.

25. *Ibid.*, 67; Rhodes, "Federal Cavalry: Its Organization and Equipment," 62.

26. *Army and Navy Journal*, Feb. 6, 1869, June 27, 1874.

27. James H. Kidd, *Personal Recollections of a Cavalryman with Custer's Michigan Cavalry Brigade in the Civil War* (Ionia, Mich., 1908), 232–33.

28. McWhiney and Jamieson, *Attack and Die*, 67.

CHAPTER 2

1. Stubbs, "Cavalry in the Civil War," 56; Caroline Baldwin Darrow, "Recollections of the Twiggs Surrender," *B&L*, 1: 33–39; *OR*, I, 51, pt. 1: 343n.

2. *Ibid.*, 1: 667; William W. Averell, *Ten Years in the Saddle: The Memoir of William Woods Averell, 1851–1862,* ed. by Edward K. Eckert and Nicholas J. Amato (San Rafael, Calif., 1978), 247–73.

3. Starr, *Union Cavalry in the Civil War,* 1: 58; Stubbs, "Cavalry in the Civil War," 57.

4. Rodenbough, *From Everglade to Cañon,* 231.

5. *Ibid.*, 232, 235, 242.

6. *OR*, I, 2: 578–83, 587-88; 51, pt. 1: 345–56.

7. *Ibid.*, 346, 356.

8. *Ibid.*, 355–58; I, 2: 699.

9. Averell, *Ten Years in the Saddle,* 276.

10. *Thirty-sixth Anniversary and Reunion of the Tenth New York Cavalry Veterans . . .* (Homer, N. Y., 1897), 42, 46–47.

11. *Ibid.*, 45.

12. *OR*, I, 2: 792–94.

13. Stevenson, *"Boots and Saddles,"* 14; Beach, *First New York (Lincoln) Cavalry,* 12; Charles D. Rhodes, *History of the Cavalry of the Army of the Potomac* (Kansas City, Mo., 1900), 175.

14. Stubbs, "Cavalry in the Civil War," 58; William H. Carter, "The Sixth Regiment of Cavalry," in Rodenbough and Haskin, eds., *Army of the United States,* 232; *Statutes, 1859–63* (Washington, D.C., 1864), 12: 279–80.

15. Stubbs, "Cavalry in the Civil War," 59–60.

16. Carter, "Sixth Regiment of Cavalry," 232.

17. Averell, *Ten Years in the Saddle,* 330, 332; Richard W. Johnson, *A Soldier's Reminiscences in Peace and War* (Philadelphia, 1886), 171.

18. *OR*, I, 2: 37–44; Kempster, "Early Days of Our Cavalry," 63; *Thirty-sixth Reunion of Tenth New York Cavalry,* 42; George F. Price, comp., *Across the Continent with the Fifth [United States] Cavalry* (New York, 1883), 13.

19. E. B. Long, *The Civil War Day by Day: An Almanac, 1861–1865* (Garden City, N.Y., 1971), 77–78; William C. Davis, *Battle at Bull Run: A History of the First Major Campaign of the Civil War* (Garden City, N.Y., 1977), 9.
20. *Ibid.,* 22–32.
21. *OR,* I, 2: 60; Price, *Fifth [United States] Cavalry,* 493.
22. *OR,* I, 2: 59, 62; Percy G. Hamlin, *"Old Bald Head" (General R. S. Ewell): The Portrait of a Soldier* (Strasburg, Va., 1940), 61–62.
23. *OR,* I, 2: 60, 63–64.
24. *Ibid.,* 61; *Philadelphia Inquirer,* June 3, 1861; Judith W. McGuire, *Diary of a Southern Refugee during the War, by a Lady of Virginia* (New York, 1867), 23.
25. *OR,* I, 2: 63; Hamlin, *"Old Bald Head,"* 64.
26. *OR,* I, 2: 61.
27. Mark M. Boatner, III, *The Civil War Dictionary* (New York, 1959), 841; James B. Fry, "McDowell's Advance to Bull Run," *B&L* 1: 174.
28. *OR,* I, 2: 63–64; William Couper, *One Hundred Years at V.M.I.,* 4 vols. (Richmond, 1939–40), 2: 117; Hamlin, *"Old Bald Head,"* 62–64.
29. *OR,* I, 2: 44–50, 64–65, 194–211, 288; Davis, *Battle at Bull Run,* 85–86, 89.
30. *OR,* I, 2: 52–54, 77–82; Joseph B. Carr, "Operations of 1861 about Fort Monroe," *B&L* 2: 144–52.
31. *New York Times,* June 1, 1861.
32. *OR,* I, 2: 664–65; Fry, "McDowell's Advance," 171–75; William Howard Russell, *My Diary North and South* (Boston, 1863), 396, 403.
33. *OR,* I, 2: 315 and n.; Ezra J. Warner, *Generals in Blue: Lives of the Union Commanders* (Baton Rouge, La., 1964), 357–58, 377–78.
34. *Ibid.,* 297–98; Davis, *Battle at Bull Run,* 9–12.
35. Patricia L. Faust, ed., *Historical Times Illustrated Encyclopedia of the Civil War* (New York, 1986), 561–62; *OR,* I, 2: 160, 181–82, 184, 622, 658, 669, 697, 703.
36. Davis, *Battle at Bull Run,* 42–48, 70, 78–79, 86.
37. *Ibid.,* 77.
38. *OR,* I, 2: 124–30.
39. *Ibid.,* 179–80; Davis, *Battle at Bull Run,* 86–87.
40. *Ibid.,* 87–89.
41. *OR,* I, 2: 472-73.
42. Davis, *Battle at Bull Run,* 85–86.
43. *OR,* I, 2: 303-05, 309; *New York Times,* July 3, 1861.
44. *OR,* I, 2: 310–14, 441–44, 461–63; Davis, *Battle at Bull Run,* 111–31.
45. *Ibid.,* 159–97.
46. *OR,* I, 2: 393, 403; Charles C. Gray memoirs, 3–7, Univ. of North Carolina Lib.
47. *Ibid.,* 7; George A. Custer, "War Memoirs," *Galaxy* 21 (1876): 629.
48. *OR,* I, 2: 393; Davis, *Battle at Bull Run,* 198–236.

49. *OR,* I, 2: 532–35; Robert F. O'Neill, Jr., "'What Men We Have Got Are Good Soldiers & Brave Ones Too': Federal Cavalry Operations in the Peninsula Campaign," in William J. Miller, ed., *The Peninsula Campaign: Yorktown to the Seven Days,* 3 vols. (Campbell, Calif., 1997), 3: 79–80.

50. *OR,* I, 2: 393; Davis, *Battle at Bull Run,* 237–52; *Statutes, 1859–63,* 12: 268.

CHAPTER 3

1. Eben Swift, "The Tactical Use of Cavalry," *JMSIUS* 44 (1909): 359–69; John K. Mahon, "Civil War Infantry Assault Tactics," *Military Affairs* 25 (1961): 67–68; Averell, *Three Years in the Saddle,* 328–29.

2. *Philadelphia Sunday Dispatch,* Oct. 27, 1861; Henry Norton, comp., *Deeds of Daring; Or, History of the Eighth N.Y. Volunteer Cavalry* . . . (Norwich, N. Y., 1889), 107; Smith H. Hastings, "The Cavalry Service, and Recollections of the Late War," *Magazine of Western History* 9 (1890): 261.

3. Rhodes, "Federal Cavalry: Its Organization and Equipment," 60.

4. Charles F. Adams, Jr., *Charles Francis Adams, 1835–1915: An Autobiography* (Boston, 1916), 166; *Philadelphia Sunday Dispatch,* Oct. 27, 1861; Edward P. Tobie, *History of the First Maine Cavalry, 1861–1865* (Boston, 1887), 3; Stubbs, "Cavalry in the Civil War," 57.

5. D. M. Gilmore, "Cavalry: Its Use and Value as Illustrated by Reference to the Engagements of Kelly's Ford and Gettysburg," *Glimpses of the Nation's Struggle: Minnesota MOLLUS* 2 (1890): 39.

6. Custer, "War Memoirs," *Galaxy* 21 (1876), 630; James Albert Clark, *The Making of a Volunteer Cavalryman* . . . (Washington, D.C., 1907), 27.

7. William Harding Carter, *The Life of Lieutenant General Chaffee* (Chicago, 1917), 12.

8. Adams, *Autobiography,* 128–31; Edward Chase Kirkland, *Charles Francis Adams, Jr., 1835–1915: The Patrician at Bay* (Cambridge, Mass., 1965), 23; Hampton S. Thomas, *Some Personal Reminiscences of Service in the Cavalry of the Army of the Potomac* (Philadelphia, 1889), 1.

9. Noble D. Preston memoirs, 13, New York Pub. Lib.

10. Suzanne C. Wilson, comp., *Column South: With the Fifteenth Pennsylvania Cavalry from Antietam to the Capture of Jefferson Davis* (Flagstaff, Ariz., 1960), 1–3.

11. Edward G. Longacre, *Custer and His Wolverines: The Michigan Cavalry Brigade, 1861–1865* (Conshohocken, Pa., 1997), 86, 94; Jesse E. Peyton, *Reminiscences of the Past* (Philadelphia, 1895), 44–45.

12. Starr, *Union Cavalry in the Civil War,* 1: 78–93; Kidd, *Personal Recollections,* 31–43; F. W. Kellogg to James H. Kidd, Aug. 28, 1862, Kidd MSS, Univ. of Michigan Lib.

13. Warner, *Generals in Blue,* 149–50, 520–21; Luigi P. diCesnola to Erastus Corning, Nov. 10, 1862, HSP; Fred A. Shannon, *The Organization and Administration of the Union Army, 1861–1865,* 2 vols. (Cleveland, 1928), 1: 161.

14. Bert D. Wood, *Franklin's Yesteryear* (Ann Arbor, Mich., 1958), 92; Joseph D. Galloway diary, Aug. 18, 1861, New York Pub. Lib.; Elliott Wheelock Hoffman, "Vermont General: The Military Development of William Wells, 1861–1865," 25, M.A. thesis, Univ. of Vermont.
15. Horace Greenwood to his sister, Jan. 21, 1862, Greenwood MSS, Chicago Hist. Soc.; *OR,* I, 5: 82.
16. *Ibid.;* Thomas T. Ellis, *Leaves from the Diary of an Army Surgeon . . .* (New York, 1863), 17.
17. Horace B. Sargent to John A. Andrew, Oct. 22, 1861, Sargent MSS, Massachusetts Hist. Soc.; *OR,* I, 5: 82.
18. Joseph D. Galloway diary, Oct. 9, 22, 1861.
19. William H. Mallory to "Dear Nellie," Jan. 14, 1862, Mallory MSS, Connecticut Hist. Soc.; Adams, *Autobiography,* 147.
20. William Wells to his parents, Aug. 9, 1862, Wells MSS, Univ. of Vermont Lib.; Lucien P. Waters to his parents, Aug. 20, 1862, Waters MSS, New-York Hist. Soc.
21. Edward P. McKinney, *Life in Tent and Field, 1861–1865* (Boston, 1922), 29; Hillman A. Hall, W. B. Besley, and Gilbert G. Wood, comps., *History of the Sixth New York Cavalry . . .* (Worcester, Mass., 1908), 31.
22. Benjamin W. Crowninshield and D. H. L. Gleason, *A History of the First Regiment of Massachusetts Cavalry Volunteers* (Boston, 1891), 296–97.
23. George N. Bliss to David Gerald, Oct. 6, 1862, Bliss MSS, Rhode Island Hist. Soc.; Tobie, *First Maine Cavalry,* 118.
24. Robert Cummings to his sister, Dec. 23, 1861, Cummings MSS, Rutgers Univ. Lib.
25. Joseph D. Galloway diary, Dec. 24–25, 1861.
26. *Ibid.,* Mar. 18, 21, 1862; William Band to his wife, Mar. 23, 1862, Band MSS, USAMHI.
27. Thomas W. Smith to Joseph W. Smith, Jan. 26, 1862, Smith MSS, HSP; George N. Bliss to David Gerald, Mar. 15, 23, 1862, Bliss MSS.
28. Benjamin W. Crowninshield to his father, Mar. 20, 1862, Crowninshield MSS, Essex Inst.; *Philadelphia Sunday Dispatch,* Feb. 2, 1862; Charles H. Greenleaf to his parents, Dec. 21, 1861, Greenleaf MSS, Connecticut Hist. Soc.
29. Francis A. Lord, *They Fought for the Union: A Complete Reference Work on the Federal Fighting Man* (Harrisburg, Pa., 1960), 75; Starr, *Union Cavalry in the Civil War,* 1: 119.
30. George S. Fobes, *Leaves from a Trooper's Diary* (Philadelphia, 1869), 9; A. J. Speese, *Constitution and By-Laws of Company H, Third Pennsylvania Cavalry, With a Brief History . . .* (Shippensburg, Pa., 1878), 15.
31. Walter S. Newhall to "My Dear Bob," Feb. 14, 1863, Newhall MSS, HSP.
32. Aurora Hunt, *The Army of the Pacific: Its Operations . . . 1860–1866* (Glendale, Calif., 1951), 281–84; John H. Morison, *Dying for Our Country: A Sermon on the Death of Capt. J. Sewall Reed and Rev. Thomas Starr King . . .* (Boston, 1864), 28.

33. Asa B. Isham, Henry M. Davidson, and Henry B. Furness, *Prisoners of War and Military Prisons: Personal Narratives* . . . (Cincinnati, 1890), 13–14.

34. Stephen Z. Starr, "The Inner Life of the First Vermont Volunteer Cavalry, 1861–1865," *Vermont History* 46 (1978): 165.

35. Michael Barton, ed., "'Constantly on the Lark': The Civil War Letters of a New Jersey Man," *Manuscripts* 30 (1978): 16; *Army and Navy Journal*, Feb. 20, 1864.

36. Charles F. Adams, Jr., et al., *A Cycle of Adams Letters, 1861–1865*, ed. by Worthington Chauncey Ford, 2 vols. (Boston, 1920), 2: 70.

CHAPTER 4

1. Stephen Z. Starr, "Cold Steel: The Saber and the Union Cavalry," *CWH* 11 (1965): 144; Elias W. H. Beck, "Letters of a Civil War Surgeon," *Indiana Magazine of History* 27 (1931): 139; *Rochester Daily Union and Advertiser*, May 26, 30, June 2, 6, 1862; Hoffman, "Vermont General," 26.

2. Joseph G. Bilby, *Civil War Firearms: Their Historical Background, Tactical Use and Modern Collecting and Shooting* (Conshohocken, Pa., 1996), 146.

3. *Ibid.*, 187–89; Carl L. Davis, *Arming the Union: Small Arms in the Civil War* (Port Washington, N.Y., 1973), 156–57; Longacre, *Custer and His Wolverines*, 86, 198.

4. Davis, *Arming the Union*, 88–94; Shannon, *Organization and Administration of the Union Army*, 1: 131–33; Robert V. Bruce, *Lincoln and the Tools of War* (Indianapolis, 1956), 113–16, 261–64, 287; James Harrison Wilson, "The Cavalry of the Army of the Potomac," in *PMHSM* 13 (1913): 85.

5. Bruce, *Lincoln and the Tools of War*, 116; Davis, *Arming the Union*, 88, 122–25.

6. *Ibid.*, 77, 83–86, 120–21.

7. *Ibid.*, 77–86; Bilby, *Civil War Firearms*, 124.

8. Davis, *Arming the Union*, 83–84.

9. *Ibid.*, 156; *Rochester Daily Union and Advertiser*, May 26, June 6, 1862; Stubbs, "Cavalry in the Civil War," 63; *Volunteer Cavalry—The Lessons of a Decade, by a Volunteer Cavalryman* (New York, 1871), 12; Rhodes, "Federal Cavalry: Its Organization and Equipment," 56, 58.

10. Hoffman, "Vermont General," 26; George Stoneman to anon., Sept. 10, 1861, RG-393, E-1469, NA.

11. Bilby, *Civil War Firearms*, 158, 161, 165; Richard Wormser, *The Yellowlegs: The Story of the United States Cavalry* (Garden City, N.Y., 1966), 148; W. N. Pickerill, *History of the Third Indiana Cavalry* (Indianapolis, 1906), 12.

12. Hoffman, "Vermont General," 26; Stubbs, "Cavalry in the Civil War," 63–64.

13. Starr, "Cold Steel," 142–59; *Army and Navy Journal*, Oct. 17, 1863; Schiller, "A Taste of Northern Steel," 33.

14. Starr, "Cold Steel," 147; *Pennsylvania at Gettysburg*, 2 vols. (Harrisburg, Pa., 1893), 2: 779; *History of the Third Pennsylvania Cavalry, Sixtieth*

Regiment Pennsylvania Volunteers, in the American Civil War, 1861–1865 (Philadelphia, 1905), 210.

15. *Volunteer Cavalry—Lessons of a Decade,* 7; William W. Averell, "With the Cavalry on the Peninsula," *B&L* 2: 429; George N. Bliss to David Gerald, Apr. 3, 1862, Bliss MSS.

16. *Volunteer Cavalry—Lessons of a Decade,* 6.

17. S. L. Gracey, *Annals of the Sixth Pennsylvania Cavalry* (Philadelphia, 1868), 26; Thomas F. Thiele, "Some Notes on the Lance and Lancers in the United States Cavalry," *Military Collector & Historian* 7 (1955): 34–37; Rodney Hilton Brown, *American Polearms, 1526–1865* . . . (New Milford, Conn., 1967), 104–110; Richard H. Rush to George B. McClellan, July 24, 1861, McClellan MSS, LC.

18. *Army and Navy Journal,* Nov. 14, 1863; David H. Morgan to his mother, July 17, 1862, Morgan MSS, War Lib., MOLLUS Natl. Cmdry.

19. O'Neill, "Federal Cavalry in the Peninsula Campaign," 114; Thomas W. Smith to Joseph W. Smith, n.d. [ca. May 1862], Smith MSS; Eric J. Wittenberg, "Learning the Hard Lessons of Logistics: Arming and Maintaining the Federal Cavalry," *North & South* 2 (Jan. 1999): 64; Rhodes, "Federal Cavalry: Its Organization and Equipment," 56.

20. *Ibid.,* 58; Stubbs, "Cavalry in the Civil War," 64; *Army and Navy Journal,* Feb. 20, 1864; McKinney, *Life in Tent and Field,* 35–36; *History of the Eleventh Pennsylvania Volunteer Cavalry* . . . (Philadelphia, 1902), 14, 22; Benjamin W. Crowninshield and D. H. L. Gleason, *A History of the First Regiment of Massachusetts Cavalry Volunteers* (Boston, 1891), 11.

21. James M. Merrill, *Spurs to Glory: The Story of the United States Cavalry* (Chicago, 1966), 128; Rhodes, "Federal Cavalry: Its Organization and Equipment," 62, 64; David J. Gerleman, "War Horse! Union Cavalry Mounts, 1861–1865," *North & South* 2 (Jan. 1999): 58.

22. *Ibid.,* 57; Charles Dana Gibson, "Hay: The Linchpin of Mobility," *ibid.,* 51–53.

23. Moses Harris, "The Union Cavalry," in *War Papers: Wisconsin MOLLUS* 1 (1891): 350–51; Gerleman, "War Horse!", 49–50; John V. Barton, "The Procurement of Horses," *CWTI* 6 (Dec. 1967): 16–24.

24. Stubbs, "Cavalry in the Civil War," 67; Shannon, *Organization and Administration of the Union Army,* 1: 64; Russell F. Weigley, *Quartermaster General of the Union Army: A Biography of M. C. Meigs* (New York, 1959), 256–57.

25. *Ibid.,* 186; Francis Colburn Adams, *The Story of a Trooper* . . . (New York, 1865), 27–28.

26. William Harding Carter, *Horses, Saddles and Bridles* (Baltimore, 1902), 15; Rhodes, *Cavalry of the Army of the Potomac,* 80; *Volunteer Cavalry— Lessons of a Decade,* 37; Gerleman, "War Horse!", 60.

27. Sidney Morris Davis, *Common Soldier, Uncommon War: Life as a Cavalryman in the Civil War,* ed. by Charles F. Cooney (Bethesda, Md., 1994),

63; Abner Hard, *History of the Eighth Cavalry Regiment, Illinois Volunteers, during the Great Rebellion* (Aurora, Ill., 1868), 47.

28. Frank W. Hess, "The First Cavalry Battle at Kelly's Ford, Va.," *MB* 3 (July 1893): 5; William P. Lloyd, comp., *History of the First Reg't Pennsylvania Reserve Cavalry . . .* (Philadelphia, 1864), 12.

29. Willard Glazier, *Three Years in the Federal Cavalry* (New York, 1870), 35.

30. William C. Archibald, *Home-Making and Its Philosophy . . .* (Boston, 1910), 255–56.

31. Adams et al., *Cycle of Adams Letters,* 2: 3; *Philadelphia Sunday Dispatch,* Jan. 26, 1862; Pickerill, *Third Indiana Cavalry,* 157; Walter R. Robbins, *War Record and Personal Experiences of Walter Raleigh Robbins from April 22, 1861, to August 4, 1865,* ed. by Lilian Rea (Chicago, 1923), 17–18.

32. David J. Gerleman, ed., "'My Companion in All Places': A Massachusetts Cavalryman's Apeal to Lincoln," *North & South* 2 (Jan. 1999): 54–55.

33. Adams et al., *Cycle of Adams Letters,* 3: 4–5.

34. Lucien P. Waters to his parents, Apr. 3, 1862, Waters MSS; Hastings, "Cavalry Service," 261.

35. *Eleventh Pennsylvania Cavalry,* 14.

36. *Ibid.;* Silas D. Wesson diary, Dec. 1, 1861, USAMHI.

37. Asa B. Isham, *An Historical Sketch of the Seventh Regiment Michigan Volunteer Cavalry, from Its Organization, in 1862, to Its Muster Out, in 1865* (New York, 1893), 9–10; William O. Lee, comp., *Personal and Historical Sketches and Facial History of . . . the Seventh Regiment Michigan Volunteer Cavalry, 1862–65* (Detroit, 1903), 26; *Address by P. O'Meare Delivered at the Second Annual Meeting of the First Vermont Cavalry Reunion Society, at Montpelier . . .* (Burlington, Vt., 1874), 27–29; William Wells to his parents, Apr. 5, 1862, Wells MSS.

38. Wood, *Franklin's Yesteryear,* 93; Charles B. Coxe to John Cadwalader, Jr., Jan. 11, 1863, Coxe MSS, HSP.

39. *Third Pennsylvania Cavalry,* 23.

40. Charles B. Coxe to John Cadwalader, Jr., Dec. 22, 1862, Coxe MSS.

41. *Ibid.,* Dec. 2, 1862; Tobie, *First Maine Cavalry,* 16; N. D. Preston, *History of the Tenth Regiment of Cavalry, New York State Volunteers, August, 1861, to August, 1865* (New York, 1892), 13.

42. George N. Bliss to David Gerald, Mar. 18, 1862, Bliss MSS.

43. Charles H. Greenleaf to his parents, Feb. 24, 1862, Greenleaf MSS.

44. Charles E. Lewis, *With the First [New York] Dragoons in Virginia* (London, 1897), 63–64.

CHAPTER 5

1. Stephen W. Sears, *To the Gates of Richmond: The Peninsula Campaign* (New York, 1992), 9–23.

2. *Ibid.,* 4–5.

3. Ellis, *Diary of an Army Surgeon,* 26; David C. Ashley to his family, Jan. 21, Mar. 3, 1862, Ashley MSS, USAMHI; Preston, *Tenth New York*

Cavalry, 15, 20; Burton B. Porter, *One of the People: His Own Story* (Colton, Calif., 1907), 112–13; George A. Rummel, III, *72 Days at Gettysburg: Organization of the Tenth Regiment, New York Volunteer Cavalry & Assignment to the Town of Gettysburg Pennsylvania (December 1861 to March 1862)* (Shippensburg, Pa., 1997), 123–25.

4. George Stoneman to William H. Young, Sept. 11, 1861, RG-393, E-1469, NA; *OR,* I, 51, pt. 1: 477; *Third Pennsylvania Cavalry,* 9; Samuel P. Bates, *History of Pennsylvania Volunteers, 1861–5,* 5 vols. (Harrisburg, Pa., 1869–71), 2: 360; Stevenson, *"Boots and Saddles,"* 39, 56.

5. *OR,* I, 5: 113-14; Beach, *First New York (Lincoln) Cavalry,* 36–37; Stevenson, *"Boots and Saddles,"* 41; James H. Stevenson, "The First Cavalry," in *Annals of the War, Written by Leading Participants, North and South* (Philadelphia, 1879), 637; *Third Pennsylvania Cavalry,* 11.

6. George B. McClellan, *The Civil War Papers of George B. McClellan: Selected Correspondence, 1860–1865,* ed. by Stephen W. Sears (New York, 1989), 71–75; O'Neill, "Federal Cavalry in the Peninsula Campaign," 85.

7. Averell, "With the Cavalry on the Peninsula," 429; William E. Miller, *War History: Operations of the Union Cavalry on the Peninsula . . .* (Carlisle, Pa., 1908), 2–3.

8. Warner, *Generals in Blue,* 481; Starr, *Union Cavalry in the Civil War,* 1: 236–37.

9. Hiram Wells to his wife, Nov. 17, 1861, Wells MSS, Chicago Hist. Soc.; Adams ct al., *Cycle of Adams Letters,* 2: 8.

10. Surgeon's Certificate, May 20, 1863, General's Papers of George Stoneman, RG-94, E-159, NA; Surgeon's Certificate, June 8, 1863, ACPF of George Stoneman, RG-94, *ibid.;* Charles Devens to Rutherford B. Hayes, Jan. 28, 1881, *ibid.; OR,* I, 11, pt. 3: 40.

11. *Ibid.,* 5: 15; George Stoneman to A. V. Colburn, Sept. 4, 1861, RG-393, E-1469, NA.

12. *OR,* I, 5: 15–18; 51, pt. 1: 491, 552; GRSWR, 1: 841–42, RG-94, E-160, NA.

13. George Stoneman to Simon Mix, Sept. 5, 1861, RG-393, E-1469, *ibid.*; George Stoneman to Seth Williams, Sept. 3, 1861, HSP.

14. George Stoneman to R. B. Marcy, Oct. 6, 1861, RG-393, E-1469, NA.

15. Geoge Stoneman to R. B. Marcy, Oct. 18, 1861, *ibid.*

16. Innis N. Palmer to George Stoneman, Oct. 19, Nov. 2, 1861, RG-393, E-1471, *ibid.*; George Stoneman to David Campbell, Oct. 28, 1861, RG-393, E-1469, *ibid.*

17. David C. Ashley to anon., May 31, 1862, Ashley MSS.

18. *House [of Representatives] Report No. 2, 37th Congress, 2nd Session, December 17, 1861* (Washington, D.C., 1862), Testimony Section, 171–88, 460–61; Report Section, 40-52; G. Wayne King, "The Civil War Career of Hugh Judson Kilpatrick," 62–64, Ph.D. diss., Univ. of South Carolina, 1969; *Thirty-sixth Reunion of Tenth New York Cavalry,* 18.

19. Sears, *To the Gates of Richmond,* 6–10.

20. *Ibid.,* 7, 11.

21. *Ibid.,* 3–9; *OR,* I, 5: 18.

22. "E. J. Allen" [Allan Pinkerton] to George B. McClellan, Nov. 15, 1861, McClellan MSS; Sears, *To the Gates of Richmond,* 8–9, 12, 24, 26.

23. *OR,* I, 7: 124-30, 159–61, 170–82, 236–40; 9: 74–81, 197–207, 270–76.

24. James Moore, *Kilpatrick and Our Cavalry* (New York, 1865), 39.

25. *Ibid.*; Sarah Butler Wister, *Walter S. Newhall: A Memoir . . .* (Philadelphia, 1864), 54–55.

26. *OR,* I, 5: 548–49, 740–42; *Third Pennsylvania Cavalry,* 38-39; William W. Averell to his father, Mar. 13, 1862, Averell MSS, New York State Lib.; George B. Sanford, *Fighting Rebels and Redskins: Experiences in Army Life of Colonel George B. Sanford, 1861–1892,* ed. by E. R. Hagemann (Norman, Okla., 1969), 149–51.

27. Wister, *Walter S. Newhall,* 56.

28. Davis, *Common Soldier, Uncommon War,* 93–96.

29. *OR,* I, 5: 550–51; Frank Moore, ed., *The Rebellion Record: A Diary of American Events,* 12 vols. (New York, 1861–68), 4: 296; George A. Custer to his parents, Mar. 17, 1862, Custer MSS, USMAL.

30. *Ibid.;* Moore, *Rebellion Record,* 4: 296–97.

31. Davis, *Common Soldier, Uncommon War,* 97.

32. *OR,* I, 5: 550.

33. Sears, *To the Gates of Richmond,* 14–16.

34. *Ibid.,* 17–20; *OR,* I, 5: 54.

35. *Ibid.,* 55–57; Davis, *Common Soldier, Uncommon War,* 101; Sears, *To the Gates of Richmond,* 21–24.

36. McClellan, *Civil War Papers,* 213.

CHAPTER 6

1. *OR,* I, 11, pt. 3: 36–37, 46; 51, pt. 1: 558–59, 562; William Band to his wife, Mar. 23, 1862, Band MSS; Thomas W. Smith to his father, Apr. 8, 1862, Smith MSS; David C. Ashley to his family, Apr. 12, 1862, Ashley MSS; McKinney, *Life in Tent and Field,* 42; Warner, *Generals in Blue,* 216–17.

2. *OR,* I, 11, pt. 3: 36–37; 51, pt. 1: 558–59.

3. *Ibid.*

4. *Ibid.*

5. *Ibid.,* 5: 21

6. *Ibid.*

7. *Ibid.,* 22, 559; 51, pt. 1: 562; Pickerill, *Third Indiana Cavalry,* 157.

8. Frederick H. Dyer, comp., *A Compendium of the War of the Rebellion,* 3 vols. (New York, 1959), 3: 1104–5, 1372, 1374–78, 1557–59; Bates, *History of Pennsylvania Volunteers,* 2: 320, 523; Newel Cheney, *History of the Ninth Regiment, New York Volunteer Cavalry, War of 1861 to 1865 . . .* (Jamestown, N.Y., 1901), 42–43.

9. Sears, *To the Gates of Richmond*, 8, 32; Robert G. Tanner, *Stonewall in the Valley: Thomas J. "Stonewall" Jackson's Shenandoah Valley Campaign, Spring 1862* (Garden City, N.Y., 1976), 117–30.

10. *Ibid.*, 130–31; *OR*, I, 11, pt. 3: 60–62, 66; Beach, *First New York (Lincoln) Cavalry*, 98; Bates, *History of Pennsylvania Volunteers*, 2: 523; Dyer, *Compendium of the War of the Rebellion*, 3: 1373; Sears, *To the Gates of Richmond*, 32–34.

11. Dyer, *Compendium of the War of the Rebellion*, 3: 1563; Bates, *History of Pennsylvania Volunteers*, 3: 902.

12. Sears, *To the Gates of Richmond*, 28-32; Calvin D. Cowles, comp., *Atlas to Accompany the Official Records of the Union and Confederate Armies* (Washington, D.C., 1891–95), Plate XIV, Map 1; Plate XV, Maps 1–4.

13. Long, *Civil War Day by Day*, 106; Thomas W. Smith to his sister, Apr. 8, 1862, Smith MSS; William W. Averell to his sister, Mar. 28, 1862, Averell MSS; *OR*, I, 11, pt. 3: 42; 51, pt. 1: 564–65.

14. *Third Pennsylvania Cavalry*, 44; Miller, *Union Cavalry on the Peninsula*, 3; *OR*, I, 11, pt. 1: 8; Cowles, *Atlas to Accompany the Official Records*, Plate XVIII, Maps 1–2.

15. William W. Averell to his sister, Mar. 28, 1862, Averell MSS; *OR*, I, 11, pt. 1: 285, 292–95, 297–98.

16. *Ibid.*, 300, 358.

17. *Ibid.*, 285; pt. 3: 66–68.

18. *Ibid.*, pt. 1: 14–18, 286–300; Wister, *Walter S. Newhall*, 57–58.

19. *OR*, I, 11, pt. 1: 358–59; pt. 3: 70–71.

20. Sears, *To the Gates of Richmond*, 37–38.

21. *OR*, I, 11, pt. 1: 308–10, 359; pt. 3: 74–75.

22. *Ibid.*, pt. 1: 316–58; Cowles, *Atlas to Accompany the Official Records*, Plate XIV, Map 1.

23. Samuel A. Duncan to his mother, Oct. 18, 1863, Duncan MSS, New Hampshire Hist. Soc.

24. Abraham Lincoln, *The Collected Works of Abraham Lincoln*, ed. by Roy P. Basler et al., 8 vols. (New Brunswick, N. J., 1953), 5: 182.

25. William W. Averell to his brother, Apr. 27, 1862, Averell MSS; William Band to his wife, Apr. 16, 1862, Band MSS; David C. Ashley to his parents, Apr. 19, May 4, 1862, Ashley MSS.

26. *JCCW*, 1868-pt. 2: 5; Charles E. Bates to his parents, Apr. 13, 1862, Bates MSS, Virginia Hist. Soc.; *OR*, I, 11, pt. 1: 363–80, 413–22.

27. William Band to his wife, Apr. 16, 1862, Band MSS.

28. *OR*, I, 11, pt. 2: 247; 51, pt. 1: 665, 690; Cheney, *Ninth New York Cavalry*, 42–47; Wilber G. Bentley, *Address Delivered at the Dedication of a Monument of the Ninth New York Cavalry . . .* (Chicago, 1883), 6–7; O'Neill, "Federal Cavalry in the Peninsula Campaign," 95–96.

29. David C. Ashley to his parents, May 4, 1862, Ashley MSS.

30. Sears, *To the Gates of Richmond*, 61–67; *OR*, I, 11, pt. 1: 19, 423–24.

31. *Third Pennsylvania Cavalry,* 47; Wister, *Walter S. Newhall,* 58–59; Charles B. Haydon, *For Country, Cause & Leader: The Civil War Journal of Charles B. Haydon* (New York, 1993), 231; *JCCW,* 1868-pt. 2: 5.

32. David C. Ashley to his parents, May 4, 1862, Ashley MSS.

33. *OR,* I, 11, pt. 1: 424–41; pt. 3: 135.

34. L. Van Loan Naisawald, *Grape and Canister: The Story of the Field Artillery of the Army of the Potomac* (New York, 1960), 38, 43–44; James C. Hazlett, "The 3-Inch Ordnance Rifle," *CWTI* 7 (Dec. 1968): 30–36; Warren Ripley, *Artillery and Ammunition of the Civil War* (New York, 1970), 22; Charles H. Greenleaf to his parents, Aug. 14, 1862, Greenleaf MSS.

35. GRSWR, 1: 949; 6: 301–2, RG-94, E-160, NA.

36. *OR,* I, 11, pt. 1: 440–41, 444–45.

37. *Ibid.,* 19, 424, 426, 427, 429, 433–35; pt. 2: 246; pt. 3: 134–35; Miller, *Union Cavalry on the Peninsula,* 3-4; *Third Pennsylvania Cavalry,* 47–49; Alexander S. Webb, *The Peninsula: McClellan's Campaign of 1862* (New York, 1881), 70.

38. *OR,* I, 11, pt. 1: 19, 424, 426, 427–28, 430–32, 436–43, 445–46; Sears, *To the Gates of Richmond,* 68–70; O'Neill, "Federal Cavalry in the Peninsula Campaign," 101–4; *New York Times,* May 6, 1862; Price, *Fifth [United States] Cavalry,* 216.

39. *OR,* I, 11, pt. 1: 425, 428.

40. *Ibid.,* 425, 429–30; Averell, "With the Cavalry on the Peninsula," 429.

41. *OR,* I, 11, pt. 1: 425, 429.

CHAPTER 7

1. *OR,* I, 11, pt. 1: 448–613; Sears, *To the Gates of Richmond,* 70–82; Elisha Hunt Rhodes, *All for the Union: The Civil War Diary and Letters of Elisha Hunt Rhodes,* ed. by Robert Hunt Rhodes (New York, 1991), 64–65.

2. *OR,* I, 11, pt. 1: 20–22, 425, 433–36; Wister, *Walter S. Newhall,* 59; GRSWR, 1: 951, RG-94, E-160, NA; Comte de Paris, *History of the Civil War in America,* 4 vols. (Philadelphia, 1876–88), 2: 18.

3. *OR,* I, 11, pt. 1: 22, 614–15.

4. Christian Geisel to his sister, May 12, 1862, Geisel MSS, Pennsylvania State Archives; David C. Ashley to his parents, May 17, 1862, Ashley MSS.

5. Bates, *History of Pennsylvania Volunteers,* 2: 569; O'Neill, "Federal Cavalry in the Peninsula Campaign," 110–11.

6. Christian Geisel to his sister, May 12, 1862, Geisel MSS; *OR,* I, 18: 11–13, 203–09, 262–66, 390–91, 595–98; *Vital Facts: A Chronology of the College of William and Mary* (Williamsburg, Va., 1970), 15.

7. *OR,* I, 11, pt. 1: 614–33; Beach, *First New York (Lincoln) Cavalry,* 106–8.

8. Sears, *To the Gates of Richmond,* 86–97.

9. *OR,* I, 11, pt. 2: 247; Comte de Paris, *Civil War in America,* 2: 28; Webb, *The Peninsula,* 83; Averell, "With the Cavalry on the Peninsula," 429.

10. *OR,* I, 11, pt. 3: 152–53.

11. Adams, *Story of a Trooper,* 452; George W. Flack diary, May 20, 1862, Rutgers Univ. Lib.; *Philadelphia Inquirer,* May 31, 1862.

12. Sears, *To the Gates of Richmond,* 103–4; *OR,* I, 11, pt. 2: 242; Robert Milligan to "My Dear Levi," May 18, 1862, Milligan MSS, State Hist. Soc. of Wisconsin.

13. *Philadelphia Inquirer,* May 24, 1862; Hard, *Eighth Illinois Cavalry,* 122–23.

14. Price, *Fifth [United States] Cavalry,* 217; *Philadelphia Inquirer,* May 24, 1862.

15. *Ibid.,* May 31, 1862; *OR,* I, 11, pt. 1: 656–57; O'Neill, "Federal Cavalry in the Peninsula Campaign," 112–13.

16. *OR,* I, 11, pt. 1: 652–53; Jeffry Wert, *Custer: The Controversial Life of George Armstrong Custer* (New York, 1996), 53.

17. *OR,* I, 11, pt. 1: 26–32.

18. *Ibid.,* 667–68; O'Neill, "Federal Cavalry in the Peninsula Campaign," 114; Thomas W. Smith to Joseph W. Smith, May 27, 1862, Smith MSS; Thomas W. Smith to his sister, n.d. [ca. June 1862], *ibid.*

19. *OR,* I, 11, pt. 1: 33, 677–78, 681–82, 685–86, 693; Miller, *Union Cavalry on the Peninsula,* 5–6; Webb, *The Peninsula,* 94–95; Fitz John Porter, "Hanover Court House and Gaines's Mill," *B&L* 2: 320; Davis, *Common Soldier, Uncommon War,* 146–49.

20. *OR,* I, 11, pt. 1: 682–83, 694–98; Gracey, *Sixth Pennsylvania Cavalry,* 45; GRSWR, 1: 951, RG-94, E-160, NA; Averell, "With the Cavalry on the Peninsula," 430; Porter, "Hanover Court House and Gaines's Mill," 321–22.

21. *OR,* I, 11, pt. 1: 686–90, 693, 695; pt. 2: 247–48; pt. 3: 194; GRSWR, 1: 953, RG-94, E-160, NA; Averell, "With the Cavalry on the Peninsula," 430; Porter, "Hanover Court House and Gaines's Mill," 322; Angus J. Johnston, II, *Virginia Railroads in the Civil War* (Chapel Hill, N.C., 1961), 58; O'Neill, "Federal Cavalry in the Peninsula Campaign," 116–18.

22. *OR,* I, 11, pt. 1: 25–31, 35; Boatner, *Civil War Dictionary,* 190–91.

23. *OR,* I, 11, pt. 1: 749–994; Sears, *To the Gates of Richmond,* 117–51.

24. *OR,* I, 11, pt. 1: 1009–10, 1020; 51, pt. 1: 671; Robert Cummings to his sister, June 14, 1862, Cummings MSS; Davis, *Common Soldier, Uncommon War,* 151–52; David C. Ashley to his family, June —, 1862, Ashley MSS; Averell, "With the Cavalry on the Peninsula," 430; O'Neill, "Federal Cavalry in the Peninsula Campaign," 118–20; *Philadelphia Inquirer,* June 17, 1862.

25. *OR,* I, 11, pt. 1: 1036; Emory M. Thomas, *Bold Dragoon: The Life of J. E. B. Stuart* (New York, 1986), 111–16.

26. *OR,* I, 11, pt. 1: 47, 1020–24, 1026; R. B. Marcy to Fitz John Porter, June 13, 1862 [two MSS], McClellan MSS; John B. McIntosh to his wife, June 14, 1862, McIntosh MSS, Brown Univ. Lib.; Miller, *Union Cavalry on the Peninsula,* 6; Price, *Fifth [United States] Cavalry,* 295; *Philadelphia Inquirer,* June 17, 1862; Averell, "With the Cavalry on the Peninsula," 430.

27. *OR,* I, 11, pt. 1: 1008, 1010, 1013, 1015–16, 1019, 1025, 1027; Fitz John Porter to R. B. Marcy, June 13, 1862 [three MSS], McClellan MSS; Rufus Ingalls to George B. McClellan, June 14, 1862, *ibid.*; George B. McClellan to Edwin M. Stanton, June 14, 1862, *ibid.*; Robert Morris, Jr., to William H. Emory, June 14, 1862, *ibid.*; William Averell to his brother, June 15, 1862, Averell MSS; Christian Geisel to his sister, June 19, 1862, Geisel MSS; Adams, *Story of a Trooper,* 543.

28. *OR,* I, 11, pt. 1: 1008, 1010–11, 1015, 1030, 1037–38; Fitz John Porter to R. B. Marcy, June 14, 1862 [two MSS], McClellan MSS; Henry Lyle to his mother, June 16, 1862, Lyle MSS, USAMHI.

29. *OR,* I, 11, pt. 1: 1012, 1014, 1016–19, 1028–29, 1033–34, 1039; John F. Reynolds to R. B. Marcy, June 14, 1862, McClellan MSS; Fitz John Porter to R. B. Marcy, June 16, 1862, *ibid.*; Thomas W. Smith to Jane Smith, June 17, 1862, Smith MSS; Christian Geisel to his sister, June 19, 1862, Geisel MSS; Gracey, *Sixth Pennsylvania Cavalry,* 52; *Philadelphia Inquirer,* June 17, 1862; Thomas, *Bold Dragoon,* 122–23.

30. George Stoneman to Fitz John Porter, June 17, 1862, McClellan MSS; John B. McIntosh to his wife, June 14, 1862, McIntosh MSS.

31. *OR,* I, 11, pt. 1: 1009, 1012–13, 1014; R. B. Marcy to Fitz John Porter, June 15, 1862, McClellan MSS.

32. *OR,* I, 11, pt. 3: 232; Robert Cummings to J. M. Kenderdine, June 17, 1862, Cummings MSS.

33. *OR,* I, 11, pt. 3: 233; Fitz John Porter to George B. McClellan, June 22, 1862, McClellan MSS.

34. *OR,* I, 11, pt. 1: 49–50; O'Neill, "Federal Cavalry in the Peninsula Campaign," 123; Sears, *To the Gates of Richmond,* 181–83; Porter, "Hanover Court House and Gaines's Mill," 329 and n.

35. Sears, *To the Gates of Richmond,* 197–209.

36. *OR,* I, 11, pt. 1: 51–55; pt. 2: 406; 51, pt. 1: 701; *Philadelphia Inquirer,* July 3, 1862; Sanford, *Fighting Rebels and Redskins,* 155.

37. *OR,* I, 11, pt. 2: 223, 330–31; pt. 3: 273, 276; 51, pt. 1: 700; Porter, "Hanover Court House and Gaines's Mill," 329n., 335; Averell, "With the Cavalry on the Peninsula," 430; Gracey, *Sixth Pennsylvania Cavalry,* 60; *Philadelphia Inquirer,* July 3, 1862.

38. Sears, *To the Gates of Richmond,* 210–48.

39. *OR,* I, 11, pt. 2: , 225, 233–34, 244, 249–50, 406; Fitz John Porter to Seth Williams, July 4, 1862, ACPF of Philip St. George Cooke, RG-94, NA; Porter, "Hanover Court House and Gaines's Mill," 333, 335; James A. Morgan, III, *Always Ready, Always Willing: A History of Battery M, Second United States Artillery from Its Organization through the Civil War* (Gaithersburg, Md., n.d.), 7, 9; A. K. Arnold, "The Cavalry at Gaines' Mill," *JUSCA* 2 (1889): 356.

40. *OR,* I, 11, pt. 2: 41, 226; Philip St. George Cooke to Brevet Promotions Board, St. Louis, Mo., Mar. 6, 1866, ACPF of Philip St. George Cooke, RG 94, NA.

41. *Ibid.*; Philip St. George Cooke, "The Charge of Cooke's Cavalry at Gaines's Mill," *B&L* 2: 344–46.
42. *OR,* I, 11, pt. 2: 41–42, 44–46; Comte de Paris to Philip St. George Cooke, Feb. 2, 1877, Cooke MSS, Virginia Hist. Soc.; Fitz John Porter to Seth Williams, July 4, 1862, ACPF of Philip St. George Cooke, RG-94, NA; Arnold, "Cavalry at Gaines' Mill," 358-59; Swift, "Fifth Regiment of Cavalry," 225; Comte de Paris, *Civil War in America,* 2: 102.
43. *OR,* I, 11, pt. 2: 226; pt. 3: 297-98; Fitz John Porter to A. V. Colburn, June 27, 1862, McClellan MSS; Philip St. George Cooke to Edwin M. Stanton, Aug. 16, 1865, ACPF of Philip St. George Cooke, RG-94, NA.
44. *OR,* I, 11, pt. 2: 43; 51, pt. 1: 715; Charles E. Bates to his parents, July 10, 1862, Bates MSS; John B. McIntosh to his wife, July 5, 1862, McIntosh MSS; Warner, *Generals in Blue,* 90; Edward Bates to Philip St. George Cooke, Feb. 28, 1863, Cooke MSS; Philip St. George Cooke to Adjutant General's Office, Nov. 31, 1864, ACPF of Philip St. George Cooke, RG-94, NA.

CHAPTER 8

1. *OR,* I, 11, pt. 1: 60–71; Sears, *To the Gates of Richmond,* 249–348.
2. Price, *Fifth [United States] Cavalry,* 217; *Philadelphia Inquirer,* July 1, 1862; *OR,* I, 11, pt. 2: 330–31; GRSWR, 1: 955, 957, RG-94, E-160, NA; Miller, *Union Cavalry on the Peninsula,* 11.
3. Sanford, *Fighting Rebels and Redskins,* 157–58.
4. *OR,* I, 11, pt. 2: 234–35; Averell, "With the Cavalry on the Peninsula," 431; Speese, *Company H, Third Pennsylvania Cavalry,* 23–24; Miller, *Union Cavalry on the Peninsula,* 8–9.
5. *OR,* I, 11, pt. 2: 235, 238–39, 243, 250; Davis, *Common Soldier, Uncommon War,* 194–99; Silas D. Wesson diary, July 2, 1863.
6. Averell, "With the Cavalry on the Peninsula," 432.
7. Silas D. Wesson diary, July 1, 1862; John B. McIntosh to his wife, July 5, 1862, McIntosh MSS.
8. William Hyndman, *History of a Cavalry Company: A Complete Record of Company "A," 4th Penn'a Cavalry* (Philadelphia, 1870), 60.
9. *Third Pennsylvania Cavalry,* 95–96; Averell, *Ten Years in the Saddle,* 365–66; Averell, "With the Cavalry on the Peninsula," 430, 433; *OR,* I, 51, pt. 1: 715–17; Walter S. Newhall to "My Dear Gil," July 5, 1862, Newhall MSS; Walter S. Newhall to his father, Aug. 10, 1862, *ibid.*
10. *OR,* I, 51, pt. 1: 716–17.
11. *Ibid.; Third Pennsylvania Cavalry,* 96–97.
12. *OR,* I, 11, pt. 3: 307–8; 51, pt. 1: 716–17; Rhodes, *Cavalry of the Army of the Potomac,* 16.
13. *OR,* I, 51, pt. 1: 717; GRSWR, 6: 319–20, RG-94, E-160, NA; Price, *Fifth [United States] Cavalry,* 217; Warner, *Generals in Blue,* 143.
14. *Ibid.,* 13, 150, 188, 373.

15. *OR,* I, 11, pt. 2: 47–48.
16. Edward G. Longacre, "Alfred Pleasonton: 'The Knight of Romance,'" *CWTI* 13 (Dec. 1974): 11, 13.
17. *OR,* I, 11, pt. 3: 314–15, 337–38.
18. Long, *Civil War Day by Day,* 236; *OR,* I, 12, pt. 3: 435, 568; John Codman Ropes, *The Army under Pope* (New York, 1882), 15.
19. O'Neill, "Federal Cavalry in the Peninsula Campaign," 135.
20. Robert Cummings to his sister, Aug. 1, 1862, Cummings MSS; Christian Geisel to his sister, Aug. 5, 1862, Geisel MSS.
21. Thomas W. Smith to Joseph W. Smith, Aug. 7, 1862, Smith MSS.
22. *OR,* I, 11, pt. 2: 948; Averell, "With the Cavalry on the Peninsula," 433; John B. McIntosh to his wife, Aug. 4, 1862, McIntosh MSS; Miller, *Union Cavalry on the Peninsula,* 11–12; Walter S. Newhall to "My Dear Gil," Aug. 6, 1862, Newhall MSS; George A. Custer and Elizabeth Bacon Custer, *The Custer Story: The Life and Intimate Letters of General George A. Custer and His Wife Elizabeth,* ed. by Marguerite Merington (New York, 1950), 32–33.
23. Janet Hewett et al., comps., *Supplement to the Official Records of the Union and Confederate Armies,* 80 vols. to date (Wilmington, N.C., 1994–), 2: 481–82; *JCCW,* 1868–pt. 2: 5; Miller, *Union Cavalry on the Peninsula,* 12; Frank L. Byrne and Andrew T. Weaver, eds., *Haskell of Gettysburg: His Life and Civil War Papers* (Madison, Wis., 1970), 133–34.
24. *OR,* I, 11, pt. 2: 964–67; O'Neill, "Federal Cavalry in the Peninsula Campaign," 138; John J. Hennessy, *Return to Bull Run: The Campaign and Battle of Second Manassas* (New York, 1993), 27–28.
25. *OR,* I, 11, pt. 2: 965; pt. 3: 376–78.
26. Warner, *Generals in Blue,* 26; Samuel J. Bayard, *The Life of George Dashiell Bayard . . .* (New York, 1874), 171; George Stoneman to George D. Bayard, Sept. 14, 1861, RG-393, E-1469, NA; George D. Bayard to his mother, Apr. 22, 1861, Bayard MSS, USMAL; George D. Bayard to "My Dear Ettie," May 9, 1862, *ibid.;* Edward G. Longacre, *Jersey Cavaliers: A History of the First New Jersey Volunteer Cavalry, 1861–1865* (Hightstown, N.J., 1992), 41–42.
27. Longacre, *General John Buford,* 33–86.
28. Hennessy, *Return to Bull Run,* 200–452, 464–65.
29. Stephen W. Sears, *Landscape Turned Red: The Battle of Antietam* (New Haven, Conn., 1983), 69–73.
30. *Ibid.,* 17, 77–79.
31. *Ibid.,* 102; *OR,* I, 12, pt. 3: 811, 813; 19, pt. 1: 169–80.
32. *Ibid.,* pt. 2: 242; 51, pt. 1: 797, 830; Rhodes, *Cavalry of the Army of the Potomac,* 26.
33. Longacre, *General John Buford,* 87–115.
34. *Ibid.,* 112–14; *OR,* I, 51, pt. 1: 787; George D. Bayard to R. B. Marcy, Sept. 5, 1862, McClellan MSS; Virgil Brodrick to his mother, Sept. 5, 1862, Brodrick MSS, in possession of Mr. Blair Graybill, Portland, Ore.

35. *OR,* I, 19, pt. 1: 180.
36. William W. Averell to his brother, Sept. 15, 1862, Averell MSS; *OR,* I, 19, pt. 2: 305; Winthrop S. G. Allen, *Civil War Letters of Winthrop S. G. Allen,* ed. by Harry E. Pratt (Springfield, Ill., 1932), 14–15; Ashley H. Alexander to "Frien[d] Akerly & family," Sept. 30, 1862, Alexander MSS, Illinois State Hist. Lib.; James V. Murfin, *The Gleam of Bayonets: The Battle of Antietam and the Maryland Campaign of 1862* (New York, 1965), 147–54; Thomas Bell, *At Harper's Ferry, Va., September 14, 1862: How the Cavalry Escaped . . .* (Brooklyn, N.Y., 1900), 11–12; *In Memoriam: Hasbrouck Davis . . .* (n. p., 1871), 11; John F. McCormack, "The Harpers Ferry Skedaddlers," *CWTI* 14 (Dec. 1975): 32–39.
37. *OR,* I, 19, pt. 1: 169–80.
38. *Ibid.,* 12, pt. 3: 789, 797, 803–4; 51, pt. 1: 786–87, 789; Thomas W. Smith to Joseph W. Smith, Sept. 11, 1862, Smith MSS; Sears, *Landscape Turned Red,* 72–73.
39. Alfred Pleasonton to R. B. Marcy, Sept. 5–6, 9, 1862, McClellan MSS; *OR,* I, 19, pt. 2: 185–86, 192–95.
40. *Ibid.,* 219; Alfred Pleasonton to R. B. Marcy, Sept. 13, 1862, McClellan MSS; Jennings Cropper Wise, *The Long Arm of Lee: The History of the Artillery of the Army of Northern Virginia,* 2 vols. (Lynchburg, Va., 1915), 2: 594.
41. Alfred Pleasonton to R. B. Marcy, Sept. 5–7, 10, 1862, McClellan MSS; *OR,* I, 19, pt. 2: 186.
42. Alfred Pleasonton to R. B. Marcy, Sept. 6–14, 1862; *OR,* I, 19, pt. 2: 192–95, 199–201; 51, pt. 1: 803.
43. *Ibid.,* 802–3, 807–9, 817; Alfred Pleasonton to R. B. Marcy, Sept. 10–11, 1862, McClellan MSS; GRSWR, 1: 112, RG-94, E-160, NA; Murfin, *Gleam of Bayonets,* 329.
44. *Ibid.,* 162, 167, 171–72; *OR,* I, 51, pt. 1: 827, 829–30; George B. Davis, "The Antietam Campaign," *PMHSM* 3 (1903): 47; Jacob D. Cox, "Forcing Fox's Gap and Turner's Gap," *B&L* 2: 585; John W. Schildt, *September Echoes: The Maryland Campaign of 1862 . . .* (Middletown, Md., 1960), 18.
45. *OR,* I, 19, pt. 2: 290; I, 51, pt. 1: 833; Murfin, *Gleam of Bayonets,* 173, 189; Davis, "Antietam Campaign," 47–48; Sanford, *Fighting Rebels and Redskins,* 174–75; Beck, "Letters of a Civil War Surgeon," 144; Cox, "Forcing Turner's Gap," 585–86; Sears, *Landscape Turned Red,* 129–30; Adams et al., *Cycle of Adams Letters,* 1: 188–89.
46. *OR,* I, 19, pt. 1: 210.
47. *Ibid.,* 211.
48. *Ibid.,* 211–13, 339; GRSWR, 1: 114–15, RG-94, E-160, NA; *JCCW,* 1868–pt. 2: 6; Adams et al., *Cycle of Adams Letters,* 1: 189; James Abraham to "Dear Friends," Sept. 20, 1862, Abraham MSS, USAMHI; John B. McIntosh to his wife, Sept. 19, 22, 1862, McIntosh MSS; Lloyd G. Pendergast to his brother, Sept. 25, 1862, Pendergast MSS, Minnesota Hist.

Soc.; David H. Morgan to his mother, Sept. 18, 1862, Morgan MSS; Crowninshield and Gleason, *First Massachusetts Cavalry,* 14–15; Gracey, *Sixth Pennsylvania Cavalry,* 100; Beck, "Letters of a Civil War Surgeon," 148–49; Rhodes, *Cavalry of the Army of the Potomac,* 24; William L. Haskin, comp., *The History of the First Regiment of Artillery from Its Organization in 1821, to January 1st, 1876* (Portland, Me., 1879), 516; Morgan, *Always Ready, Always Willing,* 13.

49. Robert Milligan to "Dear Levi," Oct. 7, 1862, Milligan MSS; Alfred Pleasonton to R. B. Marcy, Sept. 17, 1862, McClellan MSS.

CHAPTER 9

1. *OR,* I, 19, pt. 1: 199–200; Edward W. Emerson, *Life and Letters of Charles Russell Lowell . . .* (Boston, 1907), 226.

2. *OR,* I, 51, pt. 1: 848–53; *JCCW,* 1868–pt. 2: 6; *Philadelphia Inquirer,* Sept. 22, 1862; Daniel W. Pulis to his brother, Sept. 21, 1862, Pulis MSS, Rochester Pub. Lib.

3. James Abraham to "Dear Friends," Sept. 23, 1862, Abraham MSS.

4. *JCCW,* 1868–pt. 2: 6.

5. *Ibid.; OR,* I, 19, pt. 1: 66–87; Sears, *Landscape Turned Red,* 323–38.

6. *OR,* I, 19, pt. 1: 212, 339; 51, pt. 1: 852–54; Beck, "Letters of a Civil War Surgeon," 149; Charles H. Greenleaf to his parents, Sept. 20, 1862, Greenleaf MSS; Sanford, *Fighting Rebels and Redskins,* 182.

7. *Ibid.,* 183; *OR,* I, 19, pt. 1: 340.

8. *Ibid.,* 51, pt. 1: 856, 858, 860, 862.

9. *Ibid.,* 19, pt. 2: 355, 366–67; 51, pt. 1: 870, 873, 913; Charles M. Smith to his parents, Oct. 22, 1862, Smith MSS, USAMHI.

10. Moore, *Rebellion Record,* 5: 622.

11. *Ibid.,* 622–23.

12. Beck, "Letters of a Civil War Surgeon," 144, 150.

13. Sears, *Landscape Turned Red,* 323–29; *OR,* I, 19, pt. 2: 52; Thomas, *Bold Dragoon,* 173.

14. *OR,* I, 19, pt. 1: 72; pt. 2: 38, 41, 52; 51, pt. 1: 881; Charles E. Cadwalader to Richard Rush, Oct. 14, 1862, Cadwalader MSS, HSP; Charles M. Smith to his parents, Oct. 22, 1862, Smith MSS; Davis, *Common Soldier, Uncommon War,* 239.

15. *OR,* I, 19, pt. 1: 72; pt. 2: 40–41, 59; *Third Pennsylvania Cavalry,* 135–37; Wilbur S. Nye, ed., "Stuart's Chambersburg Raid: An Eyewitness Account," *CWTI* 4 (Jan. 1966): 43.

16. Alfred Pleasonton to R. B. Marcy, Oct. 11, 12, 1862, McClellan MSS; *OR,* I, 19, pt. 2: 38; 51, pt. 1: 878; *Philadelphia Inquirer,* Oct. 13, 1862; Moore, *Rebellion Record,* 6: 16.

17. *OR,* I, 19, pt. 2: 38–39; Nye, "Stuart's Chambersburg Raid," 43.

18. *OR,* I, 19, pt. 1: 73; pt. 2: 39, 42–44; Nye, "Stuart's Chambersburg Raid," 43–44, 47–48.

19. *Ibid.,* 44; Alfred Pleasonton to R. B. Marcy, Oct. 12, 1862, McClellan MSS; OR, I, 19, pt. 2: 39–40, 53; Morgan, *Always Ready, Always Willing,* 14; Moore, *Rebellion Record,* 6: 18; Edward G. Longacre, *Mounted Raids of the Civil War* (South Brunswick, N. J., 1975), 42–44.

20. *OR,* I, 19, pt. 1: 73–74; pt. 2: 39–40, 44–45; Moore, *Rebellion Record,* 6: 17–18.

21. *OR,* I, 19, pt. 2: 52-56; Longacre, *Mounted Raids of the Civil War,* 35, 44–45.

22. *OR,* I, 19, pt. 2: 40, 44, 417; 51, pt. 1: 881–82.

23. Charles S. Wainwright, *A Diary of Battle: The Personal Journals of Colonel Charles S. Wainwright, 1861–1865,* ed. by Allan Nevins (New York, 1962), 115; Marsena Rudolph Patrick, *Inside Lincoln's Army: The Diary of Marsena Rudolph Patrick, Provost Marshal General, Army of the Potomac,* ed. by David S. Sparks (New York, 1964), 115.

24. *OR,* I, 19, pt. 2: 460.

25. *Ibid.,* 416, 422–23, 485.

26. Walter S. Newhall diary, Oct. 23, 1862, HSP.

27. *OR,* I, 19, pt. 2: 104, 125, 494; 51, pt. 1: 894; GRSWR, 1: 117, RG-94, E-160, NA; *Third Pennsylvania Cavalry,* 143.

28. *OR,* I, 19, pt. 2: 104–112, 125, 136, 514, 518–19, 524–25; 51, pt. 1: 896, 898, 907, 913; George N. Bliss to David Gerald, Nov. 6, 1862, Bliss MSS; W. S. McClure to his sister, Nov. 10, 1862, Indiana State Lib.; George D. Bayard to "My Dear Esther," Oct. 27, 1862, Bayard MSS; Adams et al., *Cycle of Adams Letters,* 1: 198–203.

29. *OR,* I, 19, pt. 2: 112–14, 125–26, 129–30, 136–37; 51, pt. 1: 903–4, 907, 910–12, 916, 921–22; GRSWR, 1: 118, RG-94, E-160, NA; Moore, *Rebellion Record,* 6: 56–57; Allen L. Bevan to his sister, Nov. 4, 1862, Bevan MSS, USAMHI; Comte de Paris, *Civil War in America,* 2: 551–52.

30. *OR,* I, 19, pt. 2: 685–87, 689, 692–98; Sears, *Landscape Turned Red,* 337–38.

31. *Ibid.,* 338–45; Warner, *Generals in Blue,* 57–58; Rodenbough, *From Everglade to Cañon,* 284.

32. *OR,* I, 19, pt. 2: 552–54; 21: 83–85, 103–04.

33. *Ibid.,* 19, pt. 2: 583–84.

34. *Ibid.,* 21: 49, 53, 57, 61, 785–86.

35. *Ibid.,* 6–7, 759–60, 765–66; Sanford, *Fighting Rebels and Redskins,* 189; Edward J. Stackpole, *Drama on the Rappahannock: The Fredericksburg Campaign* (Harrisburg, Pa., 1957), 79–80.

36. *OR,* I, 21: 776; George H. Chapman diary, Nov. 25, 1862, Indiana Hist. Soc.; Pickerill, *Third Indiana Cavalry,* 37.

37. Davis, *Common Soldier, Uncommon War,* 271.

38. Adams et al., *Cycle of Adams Letters,* 1: 203; George H. Chapman diary, Nov. 30, 1862.

39. *OR,* I, 21: 61–65, 86–87, 812–13.

40. *Ibid.*, 814; Patrick, *Inside Lincoln's Army,* 183.

41. *Official Records of the Union and Confederate Navies in the War of the Rebellion,* 30 vols. (Washington, D.C., 1894–1922), I, 5: 186; George H. Chapman diary, Dec. 3–4, 1862; *OR,* I, 21: 842.

42. *Ibid.,* 21: 63–65, 88–95.

43. *Ibid.,* 142, 218–21, 449–51; GRSWR, 1: 120, RG-94, E-160, NA; Hall, Besley, and Wood, *Sixth New York Cavalry,* 87; David H. Morgan to his mother, Dec. 14, 1862, Morgan MSS; Stackpole, *Drama on the Rappahannock,* 236; Davis, *Common Soldier, Uncommon War,* 318–22.

44. Stackpole, *Drama on the Rappahannock,* 159, 198, 235–36; Thomas, *Personal Reminiscences of Service,* 8; Lloyd, *First Pennsylvania Cavalry,* 38–40; Pyne, *First New Jersey Cavalry,* 134–35.

45. Thomas, *Personal Reminiscences of Service,* 8; *New York Times,* Dec. 15, 16, 1862; Robbins, *War Record and Personal Experiences,* 49; Bayard, *Life of George Dashiell Bayard,* 273–74; George D. Bayard to "My Dear Esther," Oct. 27, 1862, Bayard MSS.

46. Stackpole, *Drama on the Rappahannock,* 237; Joseph D. Galloway diary, Dec. 13, 14, 1862; John B. McIntosh to his wife, Dec. 14, 1862, McIntosh MSS; Adams et al., *Cycle of Adams Letters,* 1: 211.

CHAPTER 10

1. *OR,* I, 21: 65–66, 95; Ashley H. Alexander to his sister, Jan. 17, 1863, Alexander MSS; Thomas M. Covert to his wife, Dec. 19, 1862, Covert MSS, in possession of Mr. William G. Burnett, Rocky River, Ohio; Adams et al., *Cycle of Adams Letters,* 1: 213.

2. John B. McIntosh to his wife, May 16, 1862, McIntosh MSS.

3. Davis, *Common Soldier, Uncommon War,* 317.

4. Adams et al., *Cycle of Adams Letters,* 1: 212; *OR,* I, 21: 867, 870, 873; 51, pt. 1: 958–61; Douglas Southall Freeman, *Lee's Lieutenants: A Study in Command,* 3 vols. (New York, 1942–44), 2: 398–99.

5. *OR,* I, 21: 697–701, 873.

6. Silas D. Wesson diary, Dec. 25, 1862; Joseph D. Galloway diary, Dec. 25, 1862.

7. *OR,* I, 21: 706–42, 893–94, 919–24; 51, pt. 1: 965–66; Freeman, *Lee's Lieutenants,* 2: 399–408; Adams et al., *Cycle of Adams Letters,* 1: 225–29; Peter Boyer to his father, Dec. 29, 1862, Boyer MSS, USAMHI; Charles H. Greenleaf to his parents, Jan. 8, 1863, Greenleaf MSS.

8. Bliss Perry, *Life and Letters of Henry Lee Higginson* (Boston, 1921), 176.

9. *JCCW,* 1863–pt. 1: 747–50; Rhodes, *Cavalry of the Army of the Potomac,* 30; Patrick, *Inside Lincoln's Army,* 197.

10. *JCCW,* 1863–pt. 1: 748; *OR,* I, 21: 894–96, 900–01.

11. *Ibid.,* 895–96.

12. *JCCW,* 1863–pt. 1: 750–51.

13. *Ibid.,* 751; *OR,* I, 21: 900–02.

14. *Ibid.*, 941, 944–45, 953–54.

15. *Ibid.*, 945, 976–79, 984–86; Adams et al., *Cycle of Adams Letters,* 1: 246.

16. Allen L. Bevan to his sister, Jan. 23, 1863, Bevan MSS.; Charles E. Bates to his parents, Jan. 21, 1863, Bates MSS.

17. *OR,* I, 21: 990–91, 994–95; Allen L. Bevan to his sister, Jan. 23, 1863, Bevan MSS; William Band to his wife, Jan. 24, 1863, Band MSS.

18. George N. Bliss to David Gerald, Jan. 23, 1863, Bliss MSS; Davis, *Common Soldier, Uncommon War,* 349.

19. George N. Bliss to David Gerald, Jan. 23, 1863, Bliss MSS.

20. *OR,* I, 21: 998–99.

21. *Ibid.*, 1004–5; 25, pt. 2: 4.

22. *Ibid.*, 21: 983.

23. *Ibid.*, 19, pt. 2: 484–85; Charles H. Smith to his parents, Oct. 22, 1862, Smith MSS; Tobie, *First Maine Cavalry,* 102–03; Crowninshield and Gleason, *First Massachusetts Cavalry,* 16, 33; Wainwright, *Diary of Battle,* 121.

24. *OR,* I, 19, pt. 2: 485.

25. Daniel W. Pulis to his family, Nov. 12, 1862, Pulis MSS; John W. Johnson, "A Sheldon Soldier in the Civil War," *Historic Wyoming [County, New York]* 15 (1961–62): 42; *OR,* I, 19, pt. 2: 484–85.

26. Pyne, *First New Jersey Cavalry,* 137–38; Davis, *Common Soldier, Uncommon War,* 349; Starr, *Union Cavalry in the Civil War,* 1: 337–42.

27. William H. Medill to his sister, Mar. 15, 1863, Medill MS, LC; James H. Kidd to his mother, Mar. 6, 1863, Kidd MSS.

28. *OR,* I, 25, pt. 2: 51.

29. Glazier, *Three Years in the Federal Cavalry,* 125; *OR,* I, 21: 815.

30. *Ibid.*, 25, pt. 2: 51, 59, 211–12; 51, pt. 1: 983.

31. *Ibid.*, 25, pt. 2: 71–72, 584–85.

32. *Ibid.*, 72; Longacre, *General John Buford,* 124–25, 140–42.

33. *Ibid.*, 125; Charles E. Bates to his parents, n.d. [ca. Nov. 1862], Bates MSS; "The Fourth Regiment of Cavalry," in Rodenbough and Haskin, *Army of the United States,* 214.

CHAPTER 11

1. *OR,* I, 25, pt. 2: 111; Edward J. Stackpole, *Chancellorsville: Lee's Greatest Battle* (Harrisburg, Pa., 1958), 38.

2. *Ibid.*, 42–45; *OR,* I, 25, pt. 1: 21–25; *New York Times,* Feb. 27, 28, 1863; Starr, *Union Cavalry in the Civil War,* 1: 343–44.

3. George N. Bliss to David Gerald, Feb. 28, 1863, Bliss MSS.

4. Adams et al., *Cycle of Adams Letters,* 1: 255–58.

5. Stackpole, *Chancellorsville,* 46–48; *Third Pennsylvania Cavalry,* 203; Wiley Sword, "Cavalry on Trial at Kelly's Ford," *CWTI* 13 (Apr. 1974): 33.

6. *OR,* I, 25, pt. 2: 100–07; Norman Ball diary, Feb. 25–28, 1863, Connecticut Hist. Soc.

7. *OR,* I, 25, pt. 2: 108.

8. *Ibid.*, pt. 1: 24.

9. *Ibid.*, 23–24.

10. Walter H. Hebert, *Fighting Joe Hooker* (Indianapolis, 1944), 186.

11. *OR,* I, 25, pt. 2: 116–17; Patrick, *Inside Lincoln's Army,* 219; *Third Pennsylvania Cavalry,* 203; William Band to his wife, Mar. 16, 1863, Band MSS; *New York Times,* Mar. 22, 1863; Adams et al., *Cycle of Adams Letters,* 1: 263; Silas D. Wesson diary, Feb. 28, 1863.

12. Kidd, *Personal Recollections,* 87-96; *OR,* I, 25, pt. 1: 38–40; pt. 2: 116, 120, 183 and n., 856; William Wells to his parents, Mar. 17, 1863, Wells MSS.

13. *OR,* I, 25, pt. 2: 136.

14. *Ibid.*, 139.

15. *Ibid.*, pt. 1: 47–48, 1073; Crowninshield and Gleason, *First Massachusetts Cavalry,* 115; John Bigelow, Jr., *The Campaign of Chancellorsville: A Strategic and Tactical Study* (New Haven, Conn., 1910), 89–90; Wister, *Walter S. Newhall,* 92; Moore, *Rebellion Record,* 6: 459; *Third Pennsylvania Cavalry,* 204; William Band to his wife, Mar. 16, 20, 1863, Band MSS; Jacob B. Cooke, *The Battle of Kelly's Ford, March 17, 1863* (Providence, R.I., 1887), 13.

16. *OR,* I, 25, pt. 1: 48, 61; Bigelow, *Campaign of Chancellorsville,* 92–93; Frederic Denison, *Sabres and Spurs: The First Regiment Rhode Island Cavalry in the Civil War, 1861–1865* (Central Falls, R.I., 1876), 208; *Third Pennsylvania Cavalry,* 204–07; Hyndman, *History of a Cavalry Company,* 87; Cooke, *Battle of Kelly's Ford,* 14–15; William E. Meyer, *The Sailor on Horseback* (Providence, R.I., 1912), 28.

17. *OR,* I, 25, pt. 1: 48; Bigelow, *Campaign of Chancellorsville,* 93; Denison, *First Rhode Island Cavalry,* 209; Wister, *Walter S. Newhall,* 92; *Third Pennsylvania Cavalry,* 205–07; George B. Davis, "The Cavalry Combat at Kelly's Ford in 1863," *JUSCA* 25 (1915): 395–96; Cooke, *Battle of Kelly's Ford,* 16–20.

18. *OR,* I, 25, pt. 1: 48–49; *Third Pennsylvania Cavalry,* 208.

19. *OR,* I, 25, pt. 1: 58–59, 61.

20. *Ibid.*, 49, 54–58, 61; pt. 2: 147; *Philadelphia Inquirer,* Mar. 19, 20, 1863; Meyer, *Sailor on Horseback,* 32; Norman Ball diary, Mar. 17, 1863.

21. *OR,* I, 25, pt. 1: 49; Bigelow, *Campaign of Chancellorsville,* 97–98; Wister, *Walter S. Newhall,* 93; Henry I. Bowditch, *Memorial [of Lieutenant Nathaniel Bowditch]* (Boston, 1865), 29, 36, 44; Denison, *First Rhode Island Cavalry,* 210–11; *Third Pennsylvania Cavalry,* 209–10.

22. *OR,* I, 25, pt. 1: 56–58; Walter S. Newhall to his father, Mar. 18, 1863, Newhall MSS; Wister, *Walter S. Newhall,* 93; *Third Pennsylvania Cavalry,* 210; Norman Ball diary, Mar. 17, 1863; Stephen W. Sears, *Chancellorsville* (Boston, 1996), 89–90.

23. *OR,* I, 25, pt. 1: 49; *Third Pennsylvania Cavalry,* 210–11; Norman Ball diary, Mar. 17, 1863.

24. *OR,* I, 25, pt. 1: 49–50; Wister, *Walter S. Newhall,* 93; *Third Pennsylvania Cavalry,* 211–13; Denison, *First Rhode Island Cavalry,* 211–12; Norman Ball diary, Mar. 17, 1863.

25. *OR,* I, 25, pt. 1: 50, 52–53, 1073; Bigelow, *Campaign of Chancellorsville,* 102–03; *Third Pennsylvania Cavalry,* 213–14; Comte de Paris, *Civil War in America,* 3: 16–17; Guy S. Norvell, "The Equipment and Tactics of Our Cavalry, 1861–65, Compared With the Present," *JMSIUS* 49 (1911): 371.

26. *OR,* I, 25, pt. 1: 59–60; pt. 2: 148; *Third Pennsylvania Cavalry,* 214–15; Bigelow, *Campaign of Chancellorsville,* 101.

27. *New York Times,* Mar. 20, 1863; Crowninshield and Gleason, *First Massachusetts Cavalry,* 115; Walter S. Newhall to his father, Mar. 18, 1863, Newhall MSS; William E. Doster, *Lincoln and Episodes of the Civil War* (New York, 1915), 190.

28. Starr, *Union Cavalry in the Civil War,* 1: 350.

29. Daniel W. Pulis to his parents, Apr. 8, 1863, Pulis MSS.

30. Johnson, "Sheldon Soldier in the Civil War," 44; *Rochester Daily Union and Advertiser,* Apr. 13, 1863.

31. Doster, *Lincoln and Episodes of the Civil War,* 190; *OR,* I, 25, pt. 2: 574.

32. *Ibid.,* pt. 1: 1066; pt. 2: 199–201.

33. *Ibid.,* 204–05.

34. Thomas W. Smith to Joseph W. Smith, Apr. 16, 1863, Smith MSS; Daniel W. Pulis to his parents, May 1, 1863, Pulis MSS.

35. *OR,* I, 25, pt. 1: 1088.

36. *Ibid.,* pt. 2: 213–14.

37. Crowninshield and Gleason, *First Massachusetts Cavalry,* 120.

38. *OR,* I, 25, pt. 1: 1065; pt. 2: 228–29, 244–45; Sears, *Chancellorsville,* 131–32, 166; Longacre, *Mounted Raids of the Civil War,* 156–57.

39. *OR,* I, 25, pt. 1: 1058; Sears, *Chancellorsville,* 166.

40. *OR,* I, 25, pt. 1: 1058, 1074; Doster, *Lincoln and Episodes of the Civil War,* 192; Adams et al., *Cycle of Adams Letters,* 1: 286–87.

41. *OR,* I, 25, pt. 1: 1075–76, 1098; Walter S. Newhall to his father, May 3, 1863, Newhall MSS.

42. *OR,* I, 25, pt. 2: 1072–73, 1076.

43. Doster, *Lincoln and Episodes of the Civil War,* 200–01.

44. *OR,* I, 25, pt. 1: 1059; Longacre, *Mounted Raids of the Civil War,* 157.

45. *OR,* I, 25, pt. 1: 1060, 1082, 1096, 1098.

46. *Ibid.,* 1060; pt. 2: 244–45.

47. *Ibid.,* pt. 1: 1085, 1097–98; Pyne, *First New Jersey Cavalry,* 144–45; Samuel H. Merrill, *The Campaigns of the First Maine and First District of Columbia Cavalry* (Portland, Me., 1866), 98; Robbins, *War Record and Personal Experiences,* 55–56; Moore, *Rebellion Record,* 6: 607–08.

48. *OR,* I, 25, pt. 1: 1083–84; pt. 2: 441, 452–53; Glazier, *Three Years in the Federal Cavalry,* 181; Moore, *Kilpatrick and Our Cavalry,* 49–50; Moore, *Rebellion Record,* 6: 604.

49. *Ibid,* 604–05; *OR,* I, 25, pt. 1: 1085–87; William H. Redman to his mother, May 9, 1863, Redman MSS, Univ. of Virginia Lib.; *In Memoriam: Hasbrouck Davis,* 13–14.

50. *OR,* I, 25, pt. 1: 1071–72, 1082–83; Moore, *Rebellion Record,* 6: 608.

51. *OR,* I, 25, pt. 1: 1089, 1091–95, 1097–98; Sanford, *Fighting Rebels and Redskins,* 200; Moore, *Rebellion Record,* 6: 608.

52. *OR,* I, 25, pt. 1: 1062–65; George H. Chapman diary, May 7, 1863; Adams et al., *Cycle of Adams Letters,* 1: 293; Sears, *Chancellorsville,* 206, 221–23, 230, 232, 257–58, 298–99.

53. *OR,* I, 25, pt. 2: 463, 468, 513, 533, 543; Surgeon's Certificate, May 20, 1863, Generals' Papers of George Stoneman, RG-94, E-159, NA.

CHAPTER 12

1. William H. Redman to his mother, May 9, 1863, Redman MSS; Allen L. Bevan to his sister, May 12, 1863, Bevan MSS; George A. Custer to Isaac P. Christiancy, May 31, 1863, Custer MSS, USMAL.

2. Henry C. Frost to his sister, May 8, 1863, USAMHI; Charles B. Coxe to John Cadwalader, Jr., May 12, 1863, Coxe MSS.

3. Pyne, *First New Jersey Cavalry,* 146–47; Kenneth P. Williams, *Lincoln Finds a General: A Military Study of the Civil War,* 5 vols. (New York, 1949–59), 2: 603–04.

4. *JCCW,* 1868–pt. 2: 7.

5. *OR,* I, 25, pt. 2: 533.

6. *Ibid.,* pt. 1: 777–79; Charles M. Munroe diary, Apr. 30, 1863, American Antiquarian Soc.; Hall, Besley, and Wood, *Sixth New York Cavalry,* 101–07; *New York Times,* May 4, 1863; W. L. Heermance, "The Cavalry at Chancellorsville," *Personal Recollections of the War of the Rebellion: New York MOLLUS* 2 (1897): 225–28; Alfred Pleasonton, "The Successes and Failures of Chancellorsville," *B&L* 3: 175; Sears, *Chancellorsville,* 177, 190–91.

7. *OR,* I, 25, pt. 1: 781, 784; Charles C. Kelsey, *To the Knife: The Biography of Major Peter Keenan, 8th Pennsylvania Cavalry* (Ann Arbor, Mich., 1964), 35–38; Theodore A. Dodge, *The Campaign of Chancellorsville* (Boston, 1881), 110–11.

8. *OR,* I, 25, pt. 1: 781, 784; Kelsey, *To the Knife,* 38–39; Charles I. Wickersham, "Personal Recollections of the Cavalry at Chancellorsville," *War Papers: Wisconsin MOLLUS* 3 (1903): 460–61; Pennock Huey, J. Edward Carpenter, and Andrew B. Wells, "The Charge of the Eighth Pennsylvania Cavalry [at Chancellorsville]," *B&L* 3: 186–88; G. W. Hodge, *A Sermon Preached . . . on the Occasion of the Unveiling of a Mural Tablet in Memory of Major James Edward Carpenter* (Lancaster, Pa., 1902), 6–7.

9. Augustus C. Hamlin, *The Battle of Chancellorsville . . .* (Bangor, Me., 1896), 93–95; Sears, *Chancellorsville,* 287–90.

10. *JCCW,* 1868–pt. 2: 7–9; *OR,* I, 25, pt. 1: 772–76, 786–88; GRSWR, 1: 121–24, RG-94, E-160, NA; Pleasonton, "Successes and Failures of

Chancellorsville," 179–82; McKinney, *Life in Tent and Field,* 92–93; Hamlin, *Battle of Chancellorsville,* 51, 82, 90–96; Alfred Pleasonton to Clarence C. Buel, Aug. 27, 1884, May 21, Oct. 5, 1886, NYPL; Alfred Pleasonton to "The Editor of the *Century,*" June 22, July 3, 1886, *ibid.*; Kelsey, *To the Knife,* 43–47.

11. *OR,* I, 51, pt. 1: 1036–37, 1040; Pennock Huey to "Editor of the *Century Magazine,*" Mar. 23 [1886], NYPL; J. F. Huntington to "Editor of the *Century,*" Sept. 3, 9, 1886, *ibid.*; J. F. Huntington to Clarence C. Buel, Oct. 8, 1886, *ibid.*; James F. Huntington, "The Artillery at Hazel Grove," *B&L* 3: 188; Pleasonton, "Successes and Failures of Chancellorsville," 180n. See also: Pennock Huey, *A True History of the Charge of the Eighth Pennsylvania Cavalry at Chancellorsville* (Philadelphia, 1883).

12. Adams et al., *Cycle of Adams Letters,* 1: 293.

13. Charles Gardner memoirs, 37, USAMHI; Thomas W. Smith to Joseph W. Smith, May 8, 1863, Smith MSS.

14. Doster, *Lincoln and Episodes of the Civil War,* 200–01; John B. McIntosh to his wife, May 13, 1863, McIntosh MSS.

15. Walter S. Newhall to his father, May 14, 1863, Newhall MSS; Beck, "Letters of a Civil War Surgeon," 152.

16. Alfred Pleasonton to John F. Farnsworth, June 23, 1863, Pleasonton MSS, LC.

17. John B. McIntosh to his wife, May 13, 1863, McIntosh MSS.

18. *OR,* I, 25, pt. 2: 480, 515–16, 521, 524.

19. *Ibid.,* 515–16.

20. *Ibid.,* 524–25.

21. *Ibid.,* 533–34.

22. *Ibid.,* 529–30, 538; 27, pt. 3: 32–33.

23. *Ibid.,* 25, pt. 2: 522, 536–37.

24. *Ibid.,* 516, 538.

25. *Ibid.,* pt. 1: 1119; pt. 2: 571–72, 593, 595; 27, pt. 1: 29, 32; pt. 3: 8, 12.

26. Edwin B. Coddington, *The Gettysburg Campaign: A Study in Command* (New York, 1968), 47–55; *OR,* I, 25, pt. 2: 529; 27, pt. 1: 29, 32–33; Thomas W. Smith to Joseph W. Smith, June 8, 1863, Smith MSS.

27. *OR,* I, 27, pt. 1: 32; pt. 3: 27–28; Coddington, *Gettysburg Campaign,* 54.

28. *OR,* I, 27, pt. 3: 34, 37; Coddington, *Gettysburg Campaign,* 55.

29. Edward G. Longacre, *The Cavalry at Gettysburg: A Tactical Study of Mounted Operations during the Civil War's Pivotal Campaign, 9 June–14 July 1863* (Rutherford, N.J., 1986), 41–42, 63.

30. *Ibid.,* 29–31, 39–40; Coddington, *Gettysburg Campaign,* 53–55.

31. Jasper Cheney diary, June 9, 1863, USAMHI; Hewett et al., *Supplement to the Official Records,* 5: 227–28; James A. Bell to Augusta Hallock, June 10, 1863, Bell MSS, Henry E. Huntington Lib.; Ulric Dahlgren diary, June 9, 1863, LC; *Rochester Daily Union and Advertiser,* June 18, 1863; Alfred Pleasonton, "The Campaign of Gettysburg," in *Annals of the War, Written*

by Leading Participants, North and South (Philadelphia, 1879), 448–49; Fairfax Downey, *Clash of Cavalry: The Battle of Brandy Station, June 9, 1863* (New York, 1959), 94.

32. *Rochester Daily Union and Advertiser,* June 18, 1863; Jasper Cheney diary, June 9, 1863; Albert Huntington, *8th New York Cavalry: Historical Paper* (Palmyra, N.Y., 1902), 9; Hard, *Eighth Illinois Cavalry,* 65, 243; Pickerill, *Third Indiana Cavalry,* 73–74; Clark B. Hall, "Buford at Brandy Station," *Civil War* 8 (July–Aug. 1990): 12–17, 66-67; George M. Neese, *Three Years in the Confederate Horse Artillery* (New York, 1911), 172.

33. Hewett et al., *Supplement to the Official Records,* 228; Custer and Custer, *Custer Story,* 58–59.

34. Davis, *Common Soldier, Uncommon War,* 391–92; Longacre, *Cavalry at Gettysburg,* 70–73.

35. Henry C. Whelan to his sister, June 11, 1863, HSP; Hewett et al., *Supplement to the Official Records,* 5: 228–29, 238–39, 245; Gracey, *Sixth Pennsylvania Cavalry,* 164; David H. Morgan to his mother, June 10, 1863, Morgan MSS; Charles Coxe to John Cadwalader, Jr., June 12, 1863, Coxe MSS.

36. Longacre, *Cavalry at Gettysburg,* 73, 75–77; Thomas, *Bold Dragoon,* 222–24.

37. Henry C. Whelan to his sister, June 11, 1863; Hewett et al., *Supplement to the Official Records,* 5: 229, 239–40, 245–46; Rodenbough, *From Everglade to Cañon,* 288–89.

38. *OR,* I, 27, pt. 1: 903–04, 1045; Hewett et al., *Supplement to the Official Records,* 5: 230.

39. *OR,* I, 27, pt. 1: 961; Adams et al., *Cycle of Adams Letters,* 2: 31; Charles F. Adams, Jr., diary, June 9, 1863, Massachusetts Hist. Soc.; William Rawle Brooke to his mother, June 12, 1863, Brooke MSS, War Lib., MOLLUS Natl. Cmdry.

40. *OR,* I, 27, pt. 1: 961; Hewett et al., *Supplement to the Official Records,* 5: 282, 290–91.

41. *OR,* I, 27, pt. 1: 961; pt. 2: 729–30; Adams et al., *Cycle of Adams Letters,* 2: 32; Hewett et al., *Supplement to the Official Records,* 5: 282, 291; Charles M. Smith to his parents, June 14, 1863, Smith MSS; Crowninshield and Gleason, *First Massachusetts Cavalry,* 129–30.

42. *OR,* I, 27, pt. 2: 683, 743–45; Morgan, *Always Ready, Always Willing,* 19; William Rawle Brooke to his mother, June 12, 1863, Brooke MSS.

43. *OR,* I, 27, pt. 1: 950, 962; pt. 2: 730–31; Hewett et al., *Supplement to the Official Records,* 5: 282–83; Crowninshield and Gleason, *First Massachusetts Cavalry,* 131; Doster, *Lincoln and Episodes of the Civil War,* 208; Denison, *First Rhode Island Cavalry,* 230.

44. *OR,* I, 27, pt. 1: 950, 965, 1024, 1053; Walter S. Newhall to his father, June 12, 1863, Newhall MSS; Henry C. Meyer, *Civil War Experiences under Bayard, Gregg, Kilpatrick, Custer, Raulston, and Newberry, 1862, 1863, 1864* (New York, 1911), 27; Lloyd, *First Pennsylvania Cavalry,* 53.

45. *OR,* I, 27, pt. 2: 681–82, 721–22, 726–29, 732–33, 755, 768–69, 772; Freeman, *Lee's Lieutenants,* 3: 9.

46. *OR,* I, 27, pt. 1: 950, 965; Hewett et al., *Supplement to the Official Records,* 5: 276–77; Meyer, *Civil War Experiences,* 28.

47. *OR,* I, 27, pt. 1: 950–51, 965–66, 1053; pt. 2: 681, 684, 755, 769; Lloyd, *First Pennsylvania Cavalry,* 54–56; Pyne, *First New Jersey Cavalry,* 148–54; Aaron E. Bachman memoirs, 15-16, USAMHI.

48. *OR,* I, 27, pt. 1: 1024–25; pt. 2: 769; Hewett et al., *Supplement to the Official Records,* 5: 280–81; Moses P. Clark to James W. Martin, June 21, 1863, in possession of Mr. Allan Melia, Rahway, N.J.

49. Theophilus Gaines to Edwin M. Stanton, Jan. 13, 1863, ACPF of H. Judson Kilpatrick, RG-94, NA; *Camden* [N.J.] *Democrat,* Feb. 21, 1863.

50. *OR,* I, 27, pt. 1: 985, 996–97, 1027; pt. 2: 755; Thomas, *Personal Reminiscences of Service,* 11; Glazier, *Three Years in the Federal Cavalry,* 218–19; Preston, *Tenth New York Cavalry,* 83; Moore, *Kilpatrick and Our Cavalry,* 59; Merrill, *First Maine and First District of Columbia Cavalry,* 109; John P. Sheahan to his father, June 10, 1863, Sheahan MSS, Maine Hist. Soc.; Charles W. Ford, "Charge of the First Maine Cavalry at Brandy Station," *War Papers: Maine MOLLUS* 2 (1902): 278–84.

51. *OR,* I, 27, pt. 1: 951, 962, 985–86; pt. 2: 722, 732, 763.

52. *Ibid.,* pt. 1: 951, 962; Hewett et al., *Supplement to the Official Records,* 5: 278.

CHAPTER 13

1. *OR,* I, 27, pt. 1: 168–70, 904; pt. 2: 718–20; Longacre, *Cavalry at Gettysburg,* 87–89.

2. *OR,* I, 27, pt. 3: 45–48, 59, 71–72, 83, 89.

3. *Ibid.,* pt. 1: 1044–46; pt. 3: 57, 64.

4. Crowninshield and Gleason, *First Massachusetts Cavalry,* 307–08; Pyne, *First New Jersey Cavalry,* 153; John B. McIntosh to his wife, May 16, 1863, McIntosh MSS.

5. *OR,* I, 27, pt. 1: 932; pt. 3: 57, 64, 90, 177, 373, 376; "Colonel Samuel H. Starr," 1–2, Starr MSS, Missouri Hist. Soc.

6. *OR,* I, 27, pt. 3: 80–84, 87–89; Benjamin W. Crowninshield diary, June 13, 1863; Hebert, *Fighting Joe Hooker,* 237.

7. *OR,* I, 27, pt. 3: 87–89.

8. *Ibid.,* 106, 116–17; 51, pt. 1: 1054–55; Charles F. Adams, Jr., diary, June 15, 1863; Norman Ball diary, June 14–15, 1863; Gracey, *Sixth Pennsylvania Cavalry,* 176; Jasper Cheney diary, June 13–15, 1863; Daniel Townsend memoirs, 3–4, in possession of Mr. Christopher Densmore, Getzville, N.Y.; Charles M. Smith to his parents, June 14, 1863, Smith MSS.

9. *OR,* I, 27, pt. 1: 952; pt. 3: 71–72; Hebert, *Fighting Joe Hooker,* 238–39.

10. *OR,* I, 27, pt. 1: 962.

11. *Ibid.,* 906–07, 952–53; pt. 3: 105, 171–73; Moore, *Kilpatrick and Our Cavalry,* 66.

12. *OR,* I, 27, pt. 1: 906, 953; pt. 2: 739, 747; Hewett et al., *Supplement to the Official Records,* 5: 298; GRSWR, 3: 320, RG-94, E-160, NA.

13. Daniel Townsend memoirs, 5.

14. *OR,* I, 27, pt. 1: 1052; pt. 2: 745; Crowninshield and Gleason, *First Massachusetts Cavalry,* 144; Adams, *Autobiography,* 131; Perry, *Henry Lee Higginson,* 194–95; Adams et al., *Cycle of Adams Letters,* 2: 36–37.

15. *OR,* I, 27, pt. 1: 171, 972–73, 1052; pt. 2: 740, 742; Hewett et al., *Supplement to the Official Records,* 5: 253; Moore, *Kilpatrick and Our Cavalry,* 66–67; Crowninshield and Gleason, *First Massachusetts Cavalry,* 148–49; Charles F. Adams Jr., diary, June 17, 1863; *New York Times,* June 22, 1863.

16. Moore, *Kilpatrick and Our Cavalry,* 67–70; Luigi P. diCesnola, *Ten Months in Libby Prison* (n.p., 1865), 1–2.

17. *OR,* I, 27, pt. 1: 171, 907, 953, 979–80, 1052; pt. 2: 741–43, 746; Hewett et al., *Supplement to the Official Records,* 5: 253; Custer and Custer, *Custer Story,* 55–56; Jay Monaghan, *Custer: The Life of General George Armstrong Custer* (Boston, 1959), 130; William O. Howe to anon., n.d. [June 1863], Maine State Archives.

18. *Ibid.*

19. *OR,* I, 27, pt. 1: 906; Robert F. O'Neill, Jr., *The Cavalry Battles of Aldie, Middleburg and Upperville: "Small but Important Riots,"* June 10–27, 1863 (Lynchburg, Va., 1993), 63–64.

20. *OR,* I, 27, pt. 1: 963.

21. *Ibid.,* 962–63, 1055; Albert Porter Tasker, "A Yankee Cavalryman Gets 'Gobbled Up': A First Person Account," *CWTI* 6 (Jan. 1968): 42; Denison, *First Rhode Island Cavalry,* 233; George N. Bliss, "A Review of Aldie," *MB* n.s. 1 (1894): 124–26.

22. *OR,* I, 27, pt. 1: 963, 1056; Tasker, "Yankee Cavalryman Gets 'Gobbled Up'," 42; George N. Bliss, *The First Rhode Island Cavalry at Middleburg, Va., June 17, 1863* (Providence, R.I., 1911), 11–15; Bliss, "Review of Aldie," 130.

23. *OR,* I, 27, pt. 1: 963–65; pt. 2: 688; pt. 3: 193, 210–11, 482; Coddington, *Gettysburg Campaign,* 77–78; Charles O. Green, *An Incident in the Battle of Middleburg, Va., June 17, 1863* (Providence, R.I., 1911), 22; Tasker, "Yankee Cavalryman Gets 'Gobbled Up'," 43; Denison, *First Rhode Island Cavalry,* 234–36, 271–72; *New York Times,* June 22, 1863; Alfred Pleasonton to Adj. Gen., Army of the Potomac, June 29, 1863, RG-393, E-1439, NA; Alfred N. Duffié to Edwin M. Stanton, July 4, 1863, Duffié MSS, HSP.

24. *OR,* I, 27, pt. 1: 908–09, 969, 1029; pt. 3: 193, 227; Lloyd, *First Pennsylvania Cavalry,* 57; *Third Pennsylvania Cavalry,* 254; Hall, Besley, and Wood, *Sixth New York Cavalry,* 129-30; Norman Ball diary, June 18, 1863; John D. Follmer diary, June 18, 1863, Univ. of Michigan Lib.

25. *OR,* I, 27, pt. 1: 32, 575, 910; pt. 3: 117, 175–77, 191, 195, 208; William Wells to his mother, June 21, 1863, Wells MSS; Luther S. Trowbridge, *The Operations of the Cavalry in the Gettysburg Campaign* (Detroit, 1888), 78.

26. *OR,* I, 27, pt. 1: 909, 953, 975; pt. 2: 690; pt. 3: 195; Alfred Pleasonton to David M. Gregg, June 18, 1863, Gregg MSS, LC.

27. *OR,* I, 27, pt. 1: 953; Roy P. Stonesifer, Jr., "The Union Cavalry Comes of Age," *Civil War History* 11 (1965): 280–81; Meyer, *Civil War Experiences,* 36.

28. *OR,* I, 27, pt. 1: 953, 972, 975–76, 1034; Hewett et al., *Supplement to the Official Records,* 5: 254, 299; Meyer, *Civil War Experiences,* 38; John P. Sheahan to his father, June 20, 23, 1863, Sheahan MSS; Norman Ball diary, June 19, 1863; Tobie, *First Maine Cavalry,* 165–68; *Pennsylvania at Gettysburg,* 2: 846.

29. *OR,* I, 27, pt. 1: 911; pt. 3: 213, 227–30.

30. *Ibid.,* pt. 1: 911–13, 920–21; pt. 2: 750–51, 766; Hewett et al., *Supplement to the Official Records,* 5: 236–37.

31. *OR,* I, 27, pt. 1: 614, 616, 945–47, 954, 972–73, 984–85, 1035; pt. 2: 690–91; Hewett et al., *Supplement to the Official Records,* 5: 254–56; Doster, *Lincoln and Episodes of the Civil War,* 212; David McMurtrie Gregg, Jr., "Brevet Major General David McMurtrie Gregg," 196, Gregg MSS, LC; Meyer, *Civil War Experiences,* 39–40; *Philadelphia Inquirer,* June 24, 1863; Daniel Townsend memoirs, 11.

32. *OR,* I, 27, pt. 1: 921, 947–48; Benjamin Engle to Samuel H. Starr, Aug. 7, 1891, Starr MSS; James W. Milgram, ed., "The Libby Prison Correspondence of Tattnall Paulding," *American Philatelist* 89 (1975): 1113–14; Davis, *Common Soldier, Uncommon War,* 414–19.

33. Hewett et al., *Supplement to the Official Records,* 5: 255–56.

34. *OR,* I, 27, pt. 1: 920–21, 932–33, 1029; pt. 2: 750–51, 756, 759, 766; Memo on Battle of Upperville, Oct. 1864, ACPF of William Gamble, RG-94, NA; Hard, *Eighth Illinois Cavalry,* 251.

35. *OR,* I, 27, pt. 1: 913; pt. 2: 442–43; pt. 3: 255; Daniel W. Pulis to his parents, June 23, 1863, Pulis MSS; Coddington, *Gettysburg Campaign,* 121–22.

36. *OR,* I, 27, pt. 1: 171–72, 193; pt. 2: 713, 719, 741.

37. Alfred Pleasonton to John F. Farnsworth, June 23, 1863, Pleasonton MSS, LC.

38. Elon J. Farnsworth to John F. Farnsworth, June 23, 1863, *ibid.*

39. *OR,* I, 27, pt. 3: 305–08, 312-13, 315, 322, 334–36, 349–50, 353, 370, 377; Kidd, *Personal Recollections,* 121; William Wells to his mother, June 28, 1863, Wells MSS; George W. Barbour diary, June 26, 1863, Univ. of Michigan Lib.; Frank L. Klement, ed., "Edwin B. Bigelow: A Michigan Sergeant in the Civil War," *Michigan History* 38 (1954): 219; *History of the Eighteenth Regiment of Cavalry, Pennsylvania Volunteers, 1862–1865* (New York, 1909), 38; Louis N. Boudrye, *Historic Records of the Fifth New York Cavalry . . .* (Albany, N.Y., 1865), 63; Joseph Hooker to E. D. Townsend, Sept. 28, 1875, Hooker MSS, Gettysburg Coll. Lib.; Joseph Hooker to David McConaughy, Oct. 17, 1875, *ibid.*; *JCCW,* 1868–pt. 2: 9; George L. Harrington diary, June 28, 1863, Western Michigan Univ. Lib.;

Samuel Harris, *The Michigan Brigade of Cavalry at Gettysburg, July 3, 1863* (Chicago, 1894), 5–6.

40. *OR,* I, 27, pt. 3: 333–35, 338, 350–52, 370, 377; Walter Kempster, "The Cavalry at Gettysburg," *War Papers: Wisconsin MOLLUS* 4 (1914): 399–400; James H. Kidd, "Address of Gen. James H. Kidd at the Dedication of Michigan Monuments upon the Battlefield of Gettysburg, June 12th, 1889," *JUSCA* 4 (1891): 41–46.

41. *OR,* I, 27, pt. 1: 143; pt. 3: 285–86, 305–06, 314; Coddington, *Gettysburg Campaign,* 122–27; William E. Miller, "The Cavalry Battle Near Gettysburg," *B&L* 3: 397; Meyer, *Civil War Experiences,* 42; Glazier, *Three Years in the Federal Cavalry,* 237.

42. *OR,* I, 27, pt. 3: 314, 319, 321–22, 333; Charles Gardner memoirs, 38; John L. Beveridge, "The First Gun at Gettysburg," *Military Essays and Recollections: Illinois MOLLUS* 2 (1894): 87; Miller, "Cavalry Battle Near Gettysburg," 397.

43. *OR,* I, 27, pt. 3: 369, 373–74; Hebert, *Fighting Joe Hooker,* 244–45; Coddington, *Gettysburg Campaign,* 128–33; George Gordon Meade to Margaret S. Meade, June 29, 1863, Meade MSS, HSP.

44. *OR,* I, 27, pt. 3: 373, 376, 813.

45. *Ibid.,* 376, 813; J. Irvin Gregg, "Private & Confidential Memo," n.d., Gregg MSS, HSP.

46. *OR,* I, 27, pt. 3: 373, 376, 813; Harris, *Michigan Brigade of Cavalry,* 3–4; Pleasonton, "Campaign of Gettysburg," 452; Joseph T. Copeland to HQ, Army of the Potomac, July 9, 1863, HSP; Joseph T. Copeland to Adj. Gen., Army of the Potomac, Aug. 31, Nov. 30, 1863, General's Papers of Joseph T. Copeland, RG-94, E-159, NA.

47. *OR,* I, 27, pt. 1: 1020–21; pt. 3: 373, 376.

48. *Ibid.,* pt. 1: 66–68, 143–44, 488; Cheney, *Ninth New York Cavalry,* 100–101; Favius J. Bellamy to his parents, July 3, 1863, Bellamy MSS, Indiana State Lib.; George H. Chapman diary, June 29, 1863; Coddington, *Gettysburg Campaign,* 131–32; D. M. Gilmore, "With General Gregg at Gettysburg," *Glimpses of the Nation's Struggle: Minnesota MOLLUS* 4 (1898): 97.

CHAPTER 14

1. *OR,* I, 27, pt. 2: 692, 696, 708–09; pt. 3: 913, 915, 923; Freeman, *Lee's Lieutenants,* 3: 41 and n., 48; Coddington, *Gettysburg Campaign,* 107–08; Williams, *Lincoln Finds a General,* 2: 663–64.

2. *OR,* I, 27, pt. 2: 693; pt. 3: 376–77, 397, 469–70; Miller, "Cavalry Battle near Gettysburg," 397–98; *Third Pennsylvania Cavalry,* 257, 263; Meyer, *Civil War Experiences,* 42; Gilmore, "With General Gregg at Gettysburg," 99; Norman Ball diary, June 29, 1863.

3. *OR,* I, 27, pt. 2: 694; pt. 3: 378, 717; Benjamin W. Crowninshield diary, June 30, 1863; Benjamin Franklin Cooling, *Symbol, Sword, and Shield:*

Defending Washington during the Civil War (Hamden, Conn., 1975), 162–64; Emerson, *Charles Russell Lowell,* 268–70; Robbins, *War Record and Personal Experiences,* 61.

4. Daniel Townsend memoirs, 19–20, 41; Miller, "Cavalry Battle near Gettysburg," 398; William E. Miller to William Brooke Rawle, Jan. 16, 1886, Rawle MSS, HSP; Hampton S. Thomas to William Brooke Rawle, Jan. 28, 1884, *ibid.*; Walter S. Newhall diary, June 29, 1863; Meyer, *Civil War Experiences,* 43; *Third Pennsylvania Cavalry,* 266.

5. *OR,* I, 27, pt. 2: 202, 695; James Harrison Wilson, *Captain Charles Corbit's Charge at Westminster . . . An Episode of the Gettysburg Campaign* (Wilmington, Del., 1913), 16–28; Walter S. Newhall diary, June 30, 1863; J. C. Hunterson to William Brooke Rawle, Feb. 1, 1884, Rawle MSS; Miller, "Cavalry Battle near Gettysburg," 398; *Third Pennsylvania Cavalry,* 264.

6. Daniel Townsend memoirs, 31–32.

7. Isaac R. Pennypacker, *General Meade* (New York, 1901), 141; Longacre, *Cavalry at Gettysburg,* 168.

8. *OR,* I, 27, pt. 3: 425–26.

9. *Ibid.,* pt. 1: 144, 991, 999; pt. 3: 400; William Anthony, *History of the Battle of Hanover . . . Tuesday, June 30, 1863* (Hanover, Pa., 1945), 1–2, 60; Kidd, *Personal Recollections,* 124–25; Moore, *Rebellion Record,* 7: 184; Samuel L. Gillespie, *A History of Company A, First Ohio Cavalry, 1861–1865 . . .* (Washington Court House, Ohio, 1898), 148; Charles Blinn diary, June 30, 1863, Gettysburg Natl. Mil. Park Lib.

10. Henry C. Potter memoirs, 2, *ibid.*; *OR,* I, 27, pt. 1: 986, 1011; *Eighteenth Pennsylvania Cavalry,* 87–89.

11. *Ibid.,* 78; *OR,* I, 27, pt. 1: 1008–09, 1018; pt. 2: 695–96; Henry C. Potter memoirs, 2; Anthony, *Battle of Hanover,* 2–5; Charles Blinn diary, June 30, 1863; George W. Barbour diary, June 30, 1863; Kidd, *Personal Recollections,* 127–29.

12. *Ibid.,* 128; *OR,* I, 27, pt. 1: 987–88, 997; Anthony, *Battle of Hanover,* 5–9, 60.

13. *Ibid.;* Edwin R. Havens to his family, July 9, 1863, Havens MSS, Michigan State Univ. Lib.; Kidd, *Personal Recollections,* 128–30; Longacre, *Custer and His Wolverines,* 137; Moore, *Kilpatrick and Our Cavalry,* 85–86; John Robertson, comp., *Michigan in the War* (Lansing, Mich., 1882), 580.

14. *OR,* I, 27, pt. 2: 696; Anthony, *Battle of Hanover,* 9–10.

15. *OR,* I, 27, pt. 1: 193, 924, 987–88, 992; pt. 2: 713–14.

16. John F. Reynolds to John Buford [with endorsement by Buford], June 30, 1863, RG-94, E-289, NA.

17. *OR,* I, 27, pt. 1: 914, 926; George H. Chapman diary, June 30, 1863; Daniel W. Pulis to his parents, July 6, 1863, Pulis MSS; Longacre, *General John Buford,* 180.

18. *Ibid.,* 180–81; *OR,* I, 27, pt. 1: 923–24; Coddington, *Gettysburg Campaign,* 232–33.

19. *OR,* I, 27, pt. 1: 923; Beveridge, "First Gun at Gettysburg," 89; William Gamble to William L. Church, Mar. 10, 1864, Chicago Hist. Soc.; Daniel

W. Pulis to his parents, July 6, 1863, Pulis MSS; Charles M. Munroe diary, June 30, 1863; Jasper Cheney diary, June 30, 1863; Hall, Besley, and Wood, *Sixth New York Cavalry,* 133; Cheney, *Ninth New York Cavalry,* 102; *Rochester Daily Union and Advertiser,* July 9, 1863.

20. *OR,* I, 27, pt. 1: 922–24; pt. 2: 443, 491, 607, 637; Gillespie, *Company A, First Ohio Cavalry,* 147.
21. *OR,* I, 27, pt. 1: 926–27; Longacre, *General John Buford,* 183–84.
22. *OR,* I, 27, pt. 1: 927, 934, 938; Hall, Besley, and Wood, *Sixth New York Cavalry,* 137–38; David G. Martin, *Gettysburg, July 1* (Conshohocken, Pa., 1995), 43–46.
23. Samuel P. Bates, *The Battle of Gettysburg* (Philadelphia, 1875), 55.
24. James L. McLean, Jr., "The First Union Shot at Gettysburg," *Lincoln Herald* 82 (1980): 318–23; Beveridge, "First Gun at Gettysburg," 91–92; William Gamble to William L. Church, Mar. 10, 1864, Chicago Hist. Soc.
25. *OR,* I, 27, pt. 1: 927, 934, 939, 1030–31; pt. 2: 637, 642–43, 646, 648–49; John H. Calef, "Gettysburg Notes: The Opening Gun," *JMSIUS* 40 (1907): 48; Jasper Cheney diary, July 1, 1863.
26. George H. Chapman diary, July 1, 1863; Coddington, *Gettysburg Campaign,* 266, 272–73; Hall, Besley, and Wood, *Sixth New York Cavalry,* 138–39; Cheney, *Ninth New York Cavalry,* 108–09; Flavius J. Bellamy to his parents, July 3, 1863, Bellamy MSS; Gary Kross, "'Fight like the Devil to Hold Your Own': General John Buford's Cavalry at Gettysburg on July 1, 1863," *Blue and Gray* 12 (Feb. 1995), 15; Charles H Veil to D. McConaughy, Apr. 7, 1864, Veil MSS, Gettysburg Coll. Lib.; David L. Ladd and Audrey J. Ladd, eds., *The Bachelder Papers: Gettysburg in Their Own Words . . .* (Dayton, Ohio, 1994), 62; Bates, *Battle of Gettysburg,* 59–60; *Proceedings of the Buford Memorial Association . . .* (New York, 1895), 18.
27. William Gamble to William L. Church, Mar. 10, 1864, Chicago Hist. Soc.; Huntington, *8th New York Cavalry,* 14.
28. George Meade, *The Life and Letters of George Gordon Meade,* 2 vols. (New York, 1913), 2: 35–36; Charles H. Veil to D. McConaughy, Apr. 7, 1864, Veil MSS.
29. Coddington, *Gettysburg Campaign,* 267–80; Martin, *Gettysburg, July 1,* 89–202.
30. *Ibid.,* 187, 426.
31. *Ibid.,* 170, 205; *OR,* I, 27, pt. 1: 938; pt. 2: 552.
32. *Ibid.,* pt. 1: 701–2, 939; Cheney, *Ninth New York Cavalry,* 109; Kross, "'Fight like the Devil to Hold Your Own'," 17–19; H. P. Moyer, comp., *History of the Seventeenth Regiment Pennsylvania Volunteer Cavalry* (Lebanon, Pa., 1911), 63; Josiah Bloss diary, July 1, 1863, Pennsylvania State Archives.
33. *OR,* I, 27, pt. 1: 702, 939; Martin, *Gettysburg, July 1,* 259–84.
34. *OR,* I, 27, pt. 1: 939; Hall, Besley, and Wood, *Sixth New York Cavalry,* 140; Cheney, *Ninth New York Cavalry,* 109–11; Moyer, *Seventeenth Pennsylvania Cavalry,* 63.

35. *OR*, I, 27, pt. 2: 468–69, 554, 639; Martin, *Gettysburg, July 1*, 277–306, 342–89, 394–400.

36. *Ibid.*, 419–28; Daniel W. Pulis to his parents, July 6, 1863, Pulis MSS.

37. *OR*, I, 27, pt. 2: 661–62, 665; Martin, *Gettysburg, July 1*, 422–29; Flavius J. Bellamy to his parents, July 3, 1863, Bellamy MSS; James A. Bell to Augusta Hallock, July 23, 1863, Bell MSS; Hard, *Eighth Illinois Cavalry*, 258.

38. Coddington, *Gettysburg Campaign*, 294–305; Martin, *Gettysburg, July 1*, 429–47.

39. E. P. Halsted, "Incidents of the First Day at Gettysburg," *B&L* 3: 285; Flavius J. Bellamy to his parents, July 3, 1863, Bellamy MSS; Martin, *Gettysburg, July 1*, 492.

40. Francis A. Walker, *History of the Second Army Corps in the Army of the Potomac* (New York, 1886), 266 and n.; Coddington, *Gettysburg Campaign*, 310–15, 324–30.

41. *OR*, I, 27, pt. 1: 145, 185, 914, 927–28, 930, 939, 1032, 1086; Hall, Besley, and Wood, *Sixth New York Cavalry*, 142–43; Cheney, *Ninth New York Cavalry*, 114–15; Moyer, *Seventeenth Pennsylvania Cavalry*, 398; Calef, "Gettysburg Notes," 51; George H. Chapman diary, July 2, 1863.

42. *Ibid.*; William H. Redman to his sisters, July 3, 1863, Redman MSS; Flavius J. Bellamy diary, July 2, 1863, Bellamy MSS; James A. Bell to Augusta Hallock, July 8, 1863, Bell MSS; Charles M. Munroe diary, July 2, 1863; Jasper Cheney diary, July 2, 1863; Hall, Besley, and Wood, *Sixth New York Cavalry*, 142–43; Cheney, *Ninth New York Cavalry*, 115.

43. *OR*, I, 27, pt. 3: 490; Coddington, *Gettysburg Campaign*, 323–410.

44. *OR*, I, 27, pt. 1: 927.

45. *Ibid.*, 956, 970; pt. 3: 470–72, 489; Norman Ball diary, July 2, 1863; Meyer, *Civil War Experiences*, 47; Miller, "Cavalry Battle near Gettysburg," 399–400; *Third Pennsylvania Cavalry*, 266.

46. *OR*, I, 27, pt. 1: 956, 977; Miller, "Cavalry Battle near Gettysburg," 400–01; Preston, *Tenth New York Cavalry*, 106–07; William Brooke Rawle, *With Gregg in the Gettysburg Campaign* (Philadelphia, 1884), 14.

47. *Ibid.*, 4–5; *OR*, I, 27, pt. 3: 381, 398.

48. *Ibid.*, pt. 1: 956; pt. 2: 504, 518, 521; *Pennsylvania at Gettysburg*, 2: 817; Doster, *Lincoln and Episodes of the Civil War*, 217–18; Charles F. Adams, Jr., diary, July 2–3, 1863; Miller, "Cavalry Battle near Gettysburg," 400–01; *Third Pennsylvania Cavalry*, 267; Preston, *Tenth New York Cavalry*, 110; Rawle, *With Gregg in the Gettysburg Campaign*, 15; Kempster, "Cavalry at Gettysburg," 414.

49. *OR*, I, 27, pt. 1: 956; Miller, "Cavalry Battle near Gettysburg," 401; *Third Pennsylvania Cavalry*, 267–68; Daniel Townsend memoirs, 46–47.

50. *OR*, I, 27, pt. 2: 504, 518–19; Coddington, *Gettysburg Campaign*, 430, 432–33; *Pennsylvania at Gettysburg*, 2: 798; Kempster, "Cavalry at Gettysburg," 415–16.

51. *Ibid.,* 415; Rawle, *With Gregg in the Gettysburg Campaign,* 17; William Rawle Brooke diary, July 2, 1863, Brooke MSS; David McMutrtie Gregg to William Brooke Rawle, May 25, 1878, Rawle MSS.

CHAPTER 15

1. *OR,* I, 27, pt. 3: 502; Kempster, "Cavalry at Gettysburg," 425–26; David McMurtrie Gregg, *The Second Cavalry Division of the Army of the Potomac in the Gettysburg Campaign* (Philadelphia, 1907), 10; Gregg, Jr., "Brevet Major General David McMurtrie Gregg," 207.
2. *OR,* I, 27, pt.1: 992–93; Robertson, *Michigan in the War,* 582–83; Samuel Harris, *Major General George A. Custer: Stories Told Around the Camp Fire of the Michigan Brigade of Cavalry* (Chicago, 1898), 5.
3. *OR,* I, 27, pt. 1: 956, 1050; *Pennsylvania at Gettysburg,* 2: 847, 855.
4. *OR,* I, 27, pt. 1: 956, 1050; pt. 2: 697; Kempster, "Cavalry at Gettysburg," 426; Miller, "Cavalry Battle near Gettysburg," 401.
5. Wilbur S. Nye, "The Affair at Hunterstown," *CWTI* 9 (Feb. 1971): 29–31; H. C. Parsons, "Farnsworth's Charge and Death," *B&L* 3: 394.
6. *OR,* I, 27, pt. 1: 992, 999–1000; pt. 2: 724; Robertson, *Michigan in the War,* 580, 586–87; Kidd, *Personal Recollections,* 134–35; Nye, "Affair at Hunterstown," 23; James H. Kidd to his parents, July 9, 1863, Kidd MSS; George W. Barbour diary, July 2, 1863; John A. Clark to "My Dear Friend," June 30, 1863, Univ. of Michigan Lib.; Edwin R. Havens to his brother, July 6, 1863, Havens MSS; *New York Times,* July 21, 1863.
7. *OR,* I, 27, pt. 1: 992; Kidd, *Personal Recollections,* 135; Longacre, *Custer and His Wolverines,* 142–44.
8. *Ibid.,* 144–45; *OR,* I, 27, pt. 1: 956, 1050; John B. McIntosh to William Brooke Rawle, June 21, 1878, Rawle MSS; Longacre, *Cavalry at Gettysburg,* 222.
9. John B. McIntosh to William Brooke Rawle, June 21, 1878, Rawle MSS; Hampton S, Thomas, "Notes as to the Cavalry Fight on the Right Flank at Gettysburg," n.d., *ibid.*
10. *Ibid.; OR,* I, 27, pt. 1: 1050; Kidd, *Personal Recollections,* 140–41; Miller, "Cavalry Battle near Gettysburg," 400.
11. *OR,* I, 27, pt. 2: 697–98; Kidd, *Personal Recollections,* 143–44; A. C. M. Pennington to Carle A. Woodruff, Dec. 5, 1884, Rawle MSS.
12. Miller, "Cavalry Battle near Gettysburg," 402; Kidd, *Personal Recollections,* 147; V. A. Witcher to Russell A. Alger, Aug. 2, 1898, Alger MSS, Univ. of Michigan Lib.; *Third Pennsylvania Cavalry,* 274; Thomas, "Notes as to the Cavalry Fight," Rawle MSS; David M. Cooper, *Obituary Discourse on Occasion of the Death of Noah Henry Ferry* (New York, 1863), 20–22.
13. *OR,* I, 27, pt. 1: 1051; Miller, "Cavalry Battle near Gettysburg," 400–02; *Third Pennsylvania Cavalry,* 274.
14. *OR,* I, 27, pt. 2: 698; Hewett et al., *Supplement to the Official Records,* 5: 285; Miller, "Cavalry Battle near Gettysburg," 402; Daniel Townsend

memoirs, 46–48; Haskin, *First Regiment of Artillery,* 521; A. M. Randol to
John B. Bachelder, Mar. 2, 1886, Bachelder MSS, New Hampshire Hist. Soc.;
E. E. Bouldin to John B. Bachelder, July 29, 1886, *ibid.*; Kidd, *Personal Rec-
ollections,* 145–46; James Chester to William Brooke Rawle, Dec. 3, 1884,
Rawle MSS; David M. Gregg to E. D. Townsend, Mar. 12, 1878, *ibid.*

15. *OR,* I, 27, pt. 1: 956; pt. 2: 698; H. B. McClellan to John B. Bachelder,
Dec. 28, 1885, Jan. 12, 1886, Bachelder MSS; Kidd, *Personal Recollec-
tions,* 141; Gregg, *Second Cavalry Division,* 11; John B. McIntosh to
William Brooke Rawle, June 21, 1878, Rawle MSS.

16. *Third Pennsylvania Cavalry,* 275–76; Miller, "Cavalry Battle near Gettys-
burg," 403–04; Meyer, *Civil War Experiences,* 50; Edwin R. Havens to his
brother, July 6, 1863, Havens MSS; John A. Clark to "My Dear Friend,"
July 30, 1864, Univ. of Michigan Lib.; H. B. McClellan to John B.
Bachelder, Apr. 14, 1886, Bachelder MSS; Hampton S. Thomas to John B.
Bachelder, July 1, 1886, *ibid.*; H. B. McClellan to William Brooke Rawle,
June 21, 1878, Rawle MSS; William Brooke Rawle to J. W. Kirkley, Dec.
21, 1883, *ibid.*; James M. Deems to William Brooke Rawle, Dec. 11, 1884,
ibid.; Thomas, "Notes as to the Cavalry Fight," *ibid.*; Luther S. Trowbridge
to his wife, July 7, 1863, Trowbidge MSS, Univ. of Michigan Lib.; Kidd,
Personal Recollections, 148–52; Isham, *Seventh Michigan Cavalry,* 22–29;
Lee, *Seventh Michigan Cavalry,* 56–58, 155–56.

17. Meyer, *Civil War Experiences,* 51; Kidd, *Personal Recollections,* 151–52;
Luther S. Trowbridge to his wife, July 7, 1863, Trowbridge MSS; Trowbridge, *Cavalry in the Gettysburg Campaign,* 13; Edwin R. Havens to his
brother, July 6, 1863, Havens MSS.

18. *OR,* I, 27, pt. 2: 724–25; *Third Pennsylvania Cavalry,* 277.

19. Miller, "Cavalry Battle near Gettysburg," 404.

20. *Ibid.;* Kidd, *Personal Recollections,* 154–55; Hewett et al., *Supplement to
the Official Records,* 5: 272; William Brooke Rawle to John Bachelder,
May 22, 1878, Rawle MSS; Hampton S. Thomas to John B. Bachelder,
July 1, 1886, Bachelder MSS.

21. *Third Pennsylvania Cavalry,* 279–80, 307–12; Miller, "Cavalry Battle near
Gettysburg," 404–05; John B. McIntosh to his wife, July 17, 1863, McIn-
tosh MSS; Meyer, *Civil War Experiences,* 51–52; Wister, *Walter S. Newhall,*
11–13; Harrison S. Newhall to William Brooke Rawle, Dec. 3, 1877, Rawle
MSS; David M. Gregg to J. Edward Carpenter, Dec. 27, 1877, *ibid.*;
William E. Miller to William Brooke Rawle, June 5, 1878, *ibid.*; William E.
Miller to John B. McIntosh, June 8, 1878, *ibid.*; William Brooke Rawle to
William E. Miller, June 12, 1878, *ibid.*; William Brooke Rawle to Cecil Bat-
tine, Feb. 21, 1908, *ibid.*; Thomas, "Notes as to the Cavalry Fight," *ibid.*;
Gilmore, "With General Gregg at Gettysburg," 110–11.

22. *OR,* I, 27, pt. 1: 186, 193, 957–58; pt. 2: 699, 714–15; Miller, "Cavalry
Battle near Gettysburg," 406.

23. *OR,* I, 27, pt. 1: 943, 948; Milgram, "Correspondence of Tattnall Paulding," 1114–15; *Pennsylvania at Gettysburg,* 2: 850; William Harding

Carter, *From Yorktown to Santiago with the Sixth U.S. Cavalry* (Baltimore, 1900), 95; Gracey, *Sixth Pennsylvania Cavalry,* 179; Theophilus F. Rodenbough, "The Regular Cavalry in the Gettysburg Campaign," *JMSIUS* 44 (1909): 29; *New York Times,* July 8, 1863; Davis, *Common Soldier, Uncommon War,* 427.

24. *OR,* I, 27, pt. 2: 752, 756, 760; pt. 3: 923, 927–28, 947–48; Neese, *Confederate Horse Artillery,* 184–87; Coddington, *Gettysburg Campaign,* 184–86; Milgram, "Correspondence of Tattnall Paulding," 1115; Carter, *From Yorktown to Santiago,* 95–96.

25. *OR,* I, 27, pt. 1: 948; pt. 2: 752, 760; Davis, *Common Soldier, Uncommon War,* 427–31.

26. *OR,* I, 27, pt. 1: 943, 948; pt. 2: 756; "Colonel Samuel H. Starr," 2, Starr MSS; Milgram, "Correspondence of Tattnall Paulding," 1115; Davis, *Common Soldier, Uncommon War,* 432.

27. *OR,* I, 27, pt. 1: 916, 943, 993; *Pennsylvania at Gettysburg,* 2: 829; Kempster, "Cavalry at Gettysburg," 421.

28. *OR,* I, 27, pt. 1: 943; Gracey, *Sixth Pennsylvania Cavalry,* 179–81; Comte de Paris, *Civil War in America,* 2: 653; Rodenbough, *From Everglade to Cañon,* 295; Coddington, *Gettysburg Campaign,* 524–25; William L. Richter, "The Federal Cavalry in the Gettysburg Campaign: The Development of the Mounted Arm of the Army of the Potomac," 137, M.A. thesis, Arizona State Univ., 1965; Eric J. Wittenberg, *Gettysburg's Forgotten Cavalry Actions* (Gettysburg, Pa., 1998), 56.

29. E. M. Law, "The Struggle for 'Round Top,'" *B&L* 3: 127; E. M. Law to John B. Bachelder, June 11, 13, 1876, Bachelder MSS.

30. *Pennsylvania at Gettysburg,* 2: 852–53.

31. *Ibid.*; OR, I, 27, pt. 2: 402; Law, "Struggle for 'Round Top,'" 328; E. M. Law to John B. Bachelder, June 13, 1876, Apr. 22, 1886, Bachelder MSS.

32. *OR,* I, 27, pt. 1: 993.

33. *Ibid.;* Wittenberg, *Forgotten Cavalry Actions,* 60.

34. Parsons, "Farnsworth's Charge and Death," 394.

35. *Ibid.,* 393–94; *OR,* I, 27, pt. 1: 993–95, 1018–19; Henry C. Potter memoirs, 3–4; *New York Times,* July 21, 1863; *Eighteenth Pennsylvania Cavalry,* 40–41; Law, "Struggle for 'Round Top,'" 327.

36. Parsons, "Farnsworth's Charge and Death," 393.

37. *Ibid.,* 394; Wittenberg, *Forgotten Cavalry Actions,* 25–26; H. C. Parsons, Memoir of Farnsworth's Charge at Gettysburg, 1–2, 5, LC.

38. *Ibid.,* 5.

39. *Ibid.,* 5–6.

40. *OR,* I, 27, pt. 1: 993, 1011–12; *Eighteenth Pennsylvania Cavalry,* 40–41, 80–82; Henry C. Potter memoirs, 4; *Pennsylvania at Gettysburg,* 2: 852–53, 895–98.

41. Parsons, "Farnsworth's Charge and Death," 394–96.

42. *Ibid.,* 395–96; *OR,* I, 27, pt. 1: 993, 1005, 1009, 1011–14, 1018–19; pt. 2: 391–92, 396–97, 400, 402–03; Law, "Struggle for 'Round Top,'" 328–29;

William Wells to his parents, July 7, 1863, Wells MSS; Charles Blinn diary, July 3, 1863; E. M. Law to John Bachelder, June 13, 1876, Bachelder MSS; Edward A. Carpenter to "Editor of the *Century*," Jan. 3, 1887, New York Pub. Lib.; O. P. Edson to H. N. Jackson, June 13, 1914, "South Cavalry Field" File, Gettysburg Natl. Mil. Park Lib.; Francis F. McKinney, "The Death of Farnsworth," *Michigan Alumnus Quarterly Review* 66 (1959): 77–79.

43. John L. Black, *Crumbling Defenses; or, Memoirs and Reminiscences of John Logan Black, Colonel, C.S.A.,* ed. by Eleanor D. McSwain (Macon, Ga., 1960), 43; GRSWR, 3: 695, RG-94, E-160, NA; Alfred Pleasonton to John F. Farnsworth, July 15, 1863, Pleasonton MSS, LC.

CHAPTER 16

1. *OR*, I, 27, pt. 1: 916–17, 928, 939, 943, 958–59, 967, 970, 977, 993–94; Coddington, *Gettysburg Campaign*, 543–44.

2. *Ibid.*, 542; *OR*, I, 27, pt. 2: 299, 309, 311, 322, 669; pt. 3: 531; *New York Times*, July 6, 1863.

3. *OR*, I, 27, pt. 3: 345, 389, 594, 924, 947–48; John D. Imboden. "The Confederate Retreat from Gettysburg," *B&L* 3: 420–22.

4. *OR*, I, 27, pt. 1: 970, 993–94, 998; pt. 2: 326; *Third Pennsylvania Cavalry*, 283; *Pennsylvania at Gettysburg*, 2: 836.

5. *OR*, I, 27, pt. 1: 994, 998; pt 2: 752–53; Robertson, *Michigan in the War*, 576–77, 579; Russell A. Alger to S. L. Gillespie, Apr. 27, 1899, Alger MSS.

6. Russell A. Alger to L. G. Estes, Feb. 12, 1897, *ibid.*; L. G. Estes to Secretary of War, Feb. 11, 1897, ACPF of Russell A. Alger, RG-94, NA; *OR*, I, 27, pt. 1: 970, 994; pt. 2: 700–01; James H. Kidd to his parents, July 9, 1863, Kidd MSS; Gershom W. Mattoon to his sisters, July 16, 1863, Mattoon MSS, Michigan State Univ. Lib.; Gilbert W. Chapman to "Friend James," July 29, 1863, Chapman MSS, Detroit Pub. Lib.; John R. Morey diary, July 4–5, 1863, Univ. of Michigan Lib.; Charles Blinn diary, July 4–5, 1863; Kidd, *Personal Recollections*, 168–71; Glazier, *Three Years in the Federal Cavalry*, 267–69; Moore, *Kilpatrick and Our Cavalry*, 99–101; Gillespie, *Company A, First Ohio Cavalry*, 154–59.

7. Imboden, "Confederate Retreat from Gettysburg," 422–25; *OR*, I, 27, pt. 1: 679, 959, 967–68, 977, 981; pt. 3: 517; Doster, *Lincoln and Episodes of the Civil War*, 232–33; Meyer, *Civil War Experiences*, 56–57; Charles Gardner memoirs, 39–40; Norman Ball diary, July 4–6, 1863; John P. Sheahan to his father, July 5, 6, 1863, Sheahan MSS; John P. Sheahan to his sister, July 12, 1863, *ibid.*; John D. Follmer diary, July 4–5, 1863; Tobie, *First Maine Cavalry*, 180; *Third Pennsylvania Cavalry*, 285; Glazier, *Three Years in the Federal Cavalry*, 266.

8. *OR*, I, 27, pt. 1: 917, 977–78, 1059; pt. 3: 582, 584, 593, 602, 621; *Third Pennsylvania Cavalry*, 285; *Pennsylvania at Gettysburg*, 2: 818–19; Doster, *Lincoln and Episodes of the Civil War*, 233–34; Charles Gardner memoirs, 39–40; Norman Ball diary, July 7–14, 1863; John D. Follmer diary, July 6–14, 1863.

9. *OR*, I, 27, pt. 1: 80, 967; pt. 3: 559–62, 595–96; 51, pt. 1: 196–97; GRSWR, 6: 275, RG-94, E-160, NA; Coddington, *Gettysburg Campaign*, 550–51.

10. *OR*, I, 27, pt. 1: 679.

11. *Ibid.*, 971, 994, 998–1000, 1006; pt. 2: 311, 700.

12. *Ibid.*, pt. 1: 971, 994–95, 1006, 1014; pt. 2: 700; James H. Kidd to his parents, July 9, 1863, Kidd MSS; Louis Fortescue memoirs, 167–68, War Lib., MOLLUS Natl. Cmdry.; Edwin R. Havens to his brother, July 6, 1863, Havens MSS; John R. Morey diary, July 5, 1863; A. B. Throckmorton, "Major-General Kilpatrick," *Northern Monthly* 2 (1868): 596; William Ball to his parents, July 9, 1863, Ball MSS, Western Michigan Univ. Lib.; Moore, *Kilpatrick and Our Cavalry*, 101.

13. Imboden, "Confederate Retreat from Gettysburg," 425; *OR*, I, 27, pt. 2: 214, 280, 436–38, 498–99, 653, 655, 703; pt. 3: 547–49; Coddington, *Gettysburg Campaign*, 542–43, 552–54.

14. *OR*, I, 27, pt. 1: 916, 928, 935, 939–40, 943, 995; pt. 2: 436–38; pt. 3: 586; Hall, Besley, and Wood, *Sixth New York Cavalry*, 145–46; Cheney, *Ninth New York Cavalry*, 117-18; Gracey, *Sixth Pennsylvania Cavalry*, 189; Moyer, *Seventeenth Pennsylvania Cavalry*, 66–67; George B. Davis, "From Gettysburg to Williamsport," *PMHSM* 3 (1903): 457; Flavius J. Bellamy diary, July 4–6, 1863, Bellamy MSS; William H. Redman to his mother, July 6, 1863, Redman MSS; Jasper Cheney diary, July 6, 1863; James A. Bell to Augusta Hallock, July 8–10, 1863, Bell MSS; Charles M. Munroe diary, July 4–6, 1863; James Barnet, ed., *The Heroes and Martyrs of Illinois in the Great Rebellion: Biographical Sketches* (Chicago, 1865), 74–76; *New York Times*, July 21, 1863.

15. *OR*, I, 27, pt. 1: 928, 995, 999–1000.

16. *Ibid.*, 75–77, 85, 995, 1006; pt. 3: 266, 498, 506–08, 526, 549–50, 931–32; Louis Fortescue memoirs, 93–94; John A. Dahlgren, *Memoir of Ulric Dahlgren* (Philadelphia, 1872), 160–63, 168–69; Gracey, *Sixth Pennsylvania Cavalry*, 189–91; Charles E. Cadwalader to his mother, July 12, 1863, Cadwalader MSS; Moore, *Rebellion Record*, 7: 193; Kempster, "Cavalry at Gettysburg," 428; *Pennsylvania at Gettysburg*, 2: 827–28, 850; *New York Times*, July 8, 21, 1863.

17. *OR*, I, 27, pt. 1: 995, 1046; *Eighteenth Pennsylvania Cavalry*, 17–18, 41, 85, 94–95.

18. *Ibid.*, 18, 94–98; *OR*, I, 27, pt. 1: 928, 995, 999–1000, 1006, 1009–11, 1014–15; pt. 2: 322, 361, 370, 581, 701–03, 764–65; Imboden, "Confederate Retreat from Gettysburg," 427–28; Kidd, *Personal Recollections*, 173–76; Gillespie, *Company A, First Ohio Cavalry*, 161–62; Glazier, *Three Years in the Federal Cavalry*, 276; Moore, *Kilpatrick and Our Cavalry*, 102–03; Comte de Paris, *Civil War in America*, 3: 712–14; *New York Times*, July 21, 1863; William Wells to his parents, July 7, 1863, Wells MSS; Coddington, *Gettysburg Campaign*, 553.

19. *OR*, I, 27, pt. 1: 83, 146; pt. 3: 621.

20. *Ibid.,* pt. 1: 81, 489; pt. 2: 299–301, 322–23, 438, 493; pt. 3: 517–18, 524, 538, 1069; 51, pt. 1: 540; *New York Times,* July 6, 1863; Imboden, "Confederate Retreat from Gettysburg," 425–26; Wise, *Long Arm of Lee,* 2: 700; Christopher A. Newcomer, *Cole's Cavalry; or, Three Years in the Saddle in the Shenandoah Valley* (Baltimore, 1895), 55; Codington, *Gettysburg Campaign,* 565–66.

21. *OR,* I, 27, pt. 1: 928, 944, 948–49, 966; pt. 2: 754, 760–61; *New York Times,* July 12, 1863; Carter, *From Yorktown to Santiago,* 99–102.

22. *OR,* I, 27, pt. 1: 925, 928–29, 935, 940–41, 996, 999, 1007, 1010–11, 1015–16, 1020; pt. 2: 703; Hall, Besley, and Wood, *Sixth New York Cavalry,* 146–48; Cheney, *Ninth New York Cavalry,* 120; Gracey, *Sixth Pennsylvania Cavalry,* 186–87; *Eighteenth Pennsylvania Cavalry,* 41; Hard, *Eighth Illinois Cavalry,* 262–63; Robertson, *Michigan in the War,* 579, 581–82; Kidd, *Personal Recollections,* 178-81; William V. Stuart to "Dearest Friend," July 9, 1863, Stuart MSS, Detroit Pub. Lib.; William H. Rockwell to Polly Rockwell, July 9, 1863, Rockwell MSS, Western Michigan Univ. Lib.; *New York Times,* July 10, 1863.

23. *OR,* I, 27, pt. 1: 63–64, 925–26, 929, 936, 941–42, 1033; pt. 2: 398–99, 704; Hall, Besley, and Wood, *Sixth New York Cavalry,* 149; Cheney, *Ninth New York Cavalry,* 120; Neese, *Confederate Horse Artillery,* 197–98; James A. Bell to Augusta Hallock, July 10, 1863, Bell MSS; Flavius J. Bellamy to his brother, July 17, 1863, Bellamy MSS; Daniel W. Pulis to his parents, July 11, 1863, Pulis MSS; Charles M. Munroe diary, July 10, 1863.

24. *OR,* I, 27, pt. 1: 664, 929, 958, 971, 988–89, 999–1000, 1036; pt. 2: 704–05; pt. 3: 633, 649, 651, 657–58, 664; Hall, Besley, and Wood, *Sixth New York Cavalry,* 149–50; Cheney, *Ninth New York Cavalry,* 120; *Eighteenth Pennsylvania Cavalry,* 41; Comte de Paris, *Civil War in America,* 3: 723, 726; Flavius J. Bellamy diary, July 14, 1863, Bellamy MSS; Charles M. Munroe diary, July 11, 1863; Jasper Cheney diary, July 11, 1863; James A. Bell to Augusta Hallock, July 12, 1863, Bell MSS; Kidd, *Personal Recollections,* 181–83; John R. Morey diary, July 12, 1863; Robertson, *Michigan in the War,* 579; Moore, *Kilpatrick and Our Cavalry,* 107; Gillespie, *Company A, First Ohio Cavalry,* 163–64; Klement, "Edwin B. Bigelow," 223; *New York Times,* July 21, 1863.

25. *OR,* I, 27, pt. 1: 118; pt. 2: 301–02, 309–10; Coddington, *Gettysburg Campaign,* 567.

26. *OR,* I, 27, pt. 1: 929, 936–37, 942, 990–91, 998–1000; pt. 2: 640–41, 705; pt. 3: 685, 698; John R. Morey diary, July 14, 1863; Benjamin J. Clark to his brothers and sisters, July 17, 1863, Clark MSS, Central Michigan Univ. Lib.; James H. Kidd to his parents, July 16, 1863, Kidd MSS; Kidd, *Personal Recollections,* 185–89; Hall, Besley, and Wood, *Sixth New York Cavalry,* 150; Moyer, *Seventeenth Pennsylvania Cavalry,* 67–68; Glazier, *Three Years in the Federal Cavalry,* 294; Cheney, *Ninth New York Cavalry,* 122; Gillespie, *Company A, First Ohio Cavalry,* 169–70; Robertson,

Michigan in the War, 581; Comte de Paris, *Civil War in America*, 3: 732–33; *New York Times*, July 21, 1863.

27. William Rawle Brooke to "Dear Uncle," Aug. 9, 1863, Brooke MSS.

28. Andrew N. Buck to his brother and sister, July 9, 1863, Buck MSS, Univ. of Michigan Lib.; *Battle Creek Journal*, July 24, 1863; William H. Redman to his mother, July 10, 1863, Redman MSS.

29. *OR*, I, 27, pt. 3: 713, 718, 720–21; Charles M. Munroe diary, July 15, 1863.

30. *OR*, I, 27, pt. 2: 303, 310; pt. 3: 722, 728; William Rawle Brooke diary, June 16, 1863, Brooke MSS; William Rawle Brooke to "Dear Uncle," Aug. 9, 1863, *ibid.*; Comte de Paris, *Civil War in America*, 3: 735–37.

31. William Rawle Brooke diary, July 16, 1863, Brooke MSS.

32. *OR*, I, 27, pt. 1: 721; pt. 2: 302–03, 310, 362.

33. *Ibid.*, pt. 1: 1004; Hewett et al., *Supplement to the Official Records*, 5: 262; Moore, *Kilpatrick and Our Cavalry*, 113; George A. Custer to his sister, July 26, 1863, Custer MSS, USMAL.

34. Warner, *Generals in Blue*, 161–62; *OR*, I, 27, pt. 1: 489.

35. *Ibid.*, 495–96, 945; pt. 3: 729, 734–36, 740, 742, 756.

36. *Ibid.*, 489–90, 495-96, 945; Gracey, *Sixth Pennsylvania Cavalry*, 193; Glazier, *Three Years in the Federal Cavalry*, 301–02; Jasper Cheney diary, July 20–22, 1863.

37. *OR*, I, 27, pt. 1: 932-33, 937; pt. 3: 729, 735, 741–42; Hard, *Eighth Illinois Cavalry*, 267; Flavius J. Bellamy diary, July 21–22, 1863, Bellamy MSS; George H. Chapman diary, July 21–22, 1863.

38. James A. Bell to Augusta Hallock, July 24, 1863, Bell MSS; William Gamble to anon., n.d. [Oct. 1864], ACPF of William Gamble, Microcopy 1064, reel 9, NA.

39. *OR*, I, 27, pt. 1: 118.

CHAPTER 17

1. *OR*, I, 27, pt. 3: 753–54; Edwin R. Havens to "Dear Nell," July 24, 1863, Havens MSS; Morgan, *Always Ready, Always Willing*, 23.

2. *OR*, I, 27, pt. 1: 999, 1002–4; pt. 3: 765–66; Hewett et al., *Supplement to the Official Records*, 5: 263, 266; Dexter Macomber diary, July 23–24, 1863, Central Michigan Univ. Lib.; *Detroit Free Press*, July 30, Aug. 2, 1863.

3. *OR*, I, 27, pt. 3: 772, 787–88, 819–21; Hall, Besley, and Wood, *Sixth New York Cavalry*, 153; Flavius J. Bellamy diary, July 27–31, 1863, Bellamy MSS; Jasper Cheney diary, July 27–31, 1863; James A. Bell to Augusta Hallock, July 27, 1863, Bell MSS; George H. Chapman diary, July 27–28, 1863.

4. *Ibid.*, Aug. 1–2, 1863; *OR*, I, 27, pt. 1: 111, 952; pt. 3: 822, 825, 827; Charles M. Munroe diary, Aug. 1, 1863.

5. *OR*, I, 27, pt. 3: 827, 835, 839–40; John Buford to Ambrose E. Burnside, Aug. 12, 1863, George Hay Stuart MSS, LC.

6. George H. Chapman diary, Aug. 10, 1863; William H. Redman to his mother, Aug. 25, 1863, Redman MSS.

7. *OR,* I, 27, pt. 3: 840; 29, pt. 2: 25, 33, 51–52.
8. *Ibid.,* III, 3: 580–81, 884–85; *Army and Navy Journal,* Aug. 29, 1864; Carter, *Horses, Saddles and Bridles,* 96; Charles D. Rhodes, "The Mounting and Remounting of the Federal Cavalry," in *The Photographic History of the Civil War,* 4: 326, 328; Weigley, *Quartermaster General of the Union Army,* 267–68.
9. Carter, *Horses, Saddles and Bridles,* 97; Gershom W. Mattoon to his brother and sister, Mar. 5, 1864, Mattoon MSS; George E. Dennis to "Friend Gus," Feb. 9, 1864, Dennis MSS, Univ. of Michigan Lib.
10. *OR,* III, 3: 886, 1041–42; 4: 2, 47, 219, 229; *Army and Navy Journal,* Feb. 20, 1864; Rhodes, "Mounting and Remounting," 336; Weigley, *Quartermaster General of the Union Army,* 267–68; Keith Poulter, "The Cavalry Bureau," *North & South* 2 (Jan. 1999): 70–71.
11. *OR,* I, 29, pt. 2: 74–75, 84.
12. *Ibid.,* 27, pt. 3: 830; Longacre, *Custer and His Wolverines,* 182–83.
13. *OR,* I, 29, pt. 2: 111–12; *Official Records of the Union and Confederate Navies,* I, 5: 327.
14. *OR,* I, 29, pt. 1: 96–99; pt. 2: 147, 151; Beck, "Letters of a Civil War Surgeon," 155; George H. Chapman diary, Aug. 31–Sept. 2, 1863; *Rochester Daily Union and Advertiser,* Sept. 10, 1863; Glazier, *Three Years in the Federal Cavalry,* 307–10; Charles H. Greenleaf to his parents, Sept. 6, 1863, Greenleaf MSS; Charles E. Cadwalader to his mother, Sept. 6, 1863, Cadwalader MSS; Silas D. Wesson diary, Sept. 1, 1863.
15. *OR,* I, 29, pt. 2: 699, 706, 742, 746; Freeman, *Lee's Lieutenants,* 3: 221–33.
16. *OR,* I, 29, pt. 1: 111; pt. 2: 179–80; George Gordon Meade to Margaret S. Meade, Sept. 13, 1863, Meade MSS, HSP; John B. McIntosh to his wife, Sept. 16, 1863, McIntosh MSS; Comte de Paris, *Civil War in America,* 3: 751–52; Willard Glazier, *Battles for the Union* . . . (Hartford, Conn., 1878), 170–71; Theodore Lyman, *Meade's Headquarters, 1863–1865: Letters of Colonel Theodore Lyman from the Wilderness to Appomattox,* ed. by George R. Agassiz (Boston, 1922), 15.
17. *OR,* I, 29, pt. 1: 111; pt. 2: 175; Glazier, *Battles for the Union,* 172; George H. Chapman diary, Sept. 13, 1863; *New York Times,* Sept. 15, 1863; *Rochester Daily Union and Advertiser,* Sept. 28, 1863.
18. *OR,* I, 29, pt. 1: 118; John B. McIntosh to his wife, Sept. 16, 1863, McIntosh MSS; Josiah Bloss to his sister, Sept. 19, 1863, Bloss MSS; Moore, *Kilpatrick and Our Cavalry,* 125; Walter S. Newhall to his father, Sept. 15, 1863, Newhall MSS; Allen L. Bevan to his sister, Sept. 21, 1863, Bevan MSS; Warner, *Generals in Blue,* 113.
19. *OR,* I, 29, pt. 1: 118–21, 125–31; Comte de Paris, *Civil War in America,* 3: 752 and n.; William Wells to his parents, Sept. 15, 1863, Wells MSS; Thomas, *Personal Reminiscences of Service,* 15; Gillespie, *Company A, First Ohio Cavalry,* 174–75; Joseph D. Galloway diary, Sept. 13, 1863;

Glazier, *Three Years in the Federal Cavalry,* 312–13; Charles M. Munroe diary, Sept. 13, 1863; *Philadelphia Inquirer,* Sept. 15, 1863; Moore, *Rebellion Record,* 7: 502–05.

20. *OR,* I, 29, pt. 1: 111–12, 121–22; pt. 2: 177–81, 186–92, 195–98, 200–10, 213–14; George H. Chapman diary, Sept. 13–14, 1863; Charles M. Munroe diary, Sept. 14, 1863.

21. *OR,* I, 29, pt. 1: 140–41; George H. Chapman diary, Sept. 21, 1863; Charles M. Munroe diary, Sept. 21, 1863; Glazier, *Three Years in the Federal Cavalry,* 317–18; Gillespie, *Company A, First Ohio Cavalry,* 177–78.

22. *OR,* I, 29, pt. 1: 141–42; George H. Chapman diary, Sept. 21–22, 1863; Glazier, *Three Years in the Federal Cavalry,* 318–19; Gillespie, *Company A, First Ohio Cavalry,* 178.

23. *OR,* I, 29, pt. 1: 140; *New York Times,* Sept. 17, 1863.

24. Alfred Pleasonton to John Buford, Nov. 5, 1863, RG-393, E-1439, NA.

25. *Ibid.*; Circular, 3rd Cav. Div., Army of the Potomac, Sept. 5, 1863, RG-393, E-1538, *ibid.*

26. Alfred Pleasonton to H. Judson Kilpatrick, Nov. 20, 1863, Feb. 22, 26, 1864, RG-393, E-1439, *ibid.*; *OR,* I, 33: 584–85, 600–01.

27. *OR,* I, 29, pt. 1: 146-95; pt. 2: 220, 227.

28. *Ibid.,* pt. 1: 9–10; pt. 2: 268, 279–80; Hall, Besley, and Wood, *Sixth New York Cavalry,* 159; Cheney, *Ninth New York Cavalry,* 136.

29. *OR,* I, 29, pt. 1: 347–48; pt. 2: 268, 272–74; Hard, *Eighth Illinois Cavalry,* 277; Hall, Besley, and Wood, *Sixth New York Cavalry,* 159.

30. *Ibid.,* 160; *OR,* I, 29, pt. 1: 342, 347–48; Cheney, *Ninth New York Cavalry,* 136; Pickerill, *Third Indiana Cavalry,* 96–97; George H. Chapman diary, Oct. 11, 1863.

31. *OR,* I, 29, pt. 1: 346, 348–49, 381, 390, 394–95; pt. 2: 293; Hall, Besley, and Wood, *Sixth New York Cavalry,* 160–61; Cheney, *Ninth New York Cavalry,* 137–38; *New York Times,* Oct. 14, 1863; Charles M. Munroe diary, Oct. 10–11, 1863; Rhodes, *Cavalry of the Army of the Potomac,* 85–87; Comte de Paris, *Civil War in America,* 3: 757; Moore, *Kilpatrick and Our Cavalry,* 127.

32. *OR,* I, 29, pt. 1: 375, 381, 385–86, 390–91, 393–95; Hewett et al., *Supplement to the Official Records,* 5: 589–90; Hall, Besley, and Wood, *Sixth New York Cavalry,* 160–61; Alonzo Foster, *Reminiscences and Record of the 6th New York V. V. [Veteran Volunteer] Cavalry* (Brooklyn, N.Y., 1892), 22–23, 47–52; George H. Chapman diary, Oct. 11, 1863; Joseph W. Martin to J. H. Bells, Oct. 26, 1863, in possession of Mr. Allan Melia, Rahway, N.J.; Boudrye, *Fifth New York Cavalry,* 79–80; S. A. Clark, "Brandy Station, October, 1863," *MB* n.s. 3 (1896): 226–28; George B. Davis, "The Bristoe and Mine Run Campaigns," *PMHSM* 3 (1903): 476–77 and n.; Lee, *Seventh Michigan Cavalry,* 36–38; Kidd, *Personal Recollections,* 206–09; Gillespie, *Company A, First Ohio Cavalry,* 181–83; Moore, *Rebellion Record* 7: 559–60; Comte de Paris, *Civil War in America,* 3: 758–60;

Harris, *Major General George A. Custer,* 7; Custer and Custer, *Custer Story,* 66; *New York Times,* Oct. 21, 1863.

33. *OR,* I, 29, pt. 2: 296–97; 51, pt. 1: 1102; Custer and Custer, *Custer Story,* 66–67; Kidd, *Personal Recollections,* 108-09; William Wells to his parents, Oct. 12, 1863, Wells MSS; Moore, *Kilpatrick and Our Cavalry,* 127–32; William Watson, *Letters of a Civil War Surgeon,* ed. by Paul Fatout (Lafayette, Ind., 1961), 74.

34. *OR,* I, 29, pt. 1: 10, 354–62; pt. 2: 299–300, 302–07; *JCCW,* 1868–pt. 2: 11; Freeman Cleaves, *Meade of Gettysburg* (Norman, Okla., 1960), 197.

35. Gillespie, *Company A, First Ohio Cavalry,* 183; Clark, "Brandy Station, October, 1863," 228; Comte de Paris, *Civil War in America,* 3: 765–71; Norman Ball diary, Oct. 13–16, 1863; Charles M. Munroe diary, Oct. 13–15, 1863; Harrison Miller to Mary Sofield, Oct. 31, 1863, Miller MSS, in possession of Mr. Allan Melia, Rahway, N.J.; Lyman, *Meade's Headquarters, 1863–1865,* 35.

36. Joseph D. Galloway diary, Oct. 15, 1863; William Rawle Brooke to his mother, Oct. 21, 1863, Brooke MSS; *Third Pennsylvania Cavalry,* 348–49, 356; Charles M. Smith to his parents, Oct. 17, 1863, Smith MSS.

37. *OR,* I, 29, pt. 1: 235–50, 406–08, 426–28.

38. *Ibid.,* 382; pt. 2: 354; S. A. Clark, "Buckland Mills," *MB* n.s. 4 (1897): 108–09; James H. Kidd to his parents, Oct. 26, 1863, Kidd MSS; Kidd, *Personal Recollections,* 216–22; Gillespie, *Company A, First Ohio Cavalry,* 186–87; Meyer, *Civil War Experiences,* 63–64; Moore, *Rebellion Record,* 7: 561–63; Comte de Paris, *Civil War in America,* 3: 780–82.

39. *OR,* I, 29, pt. 1: 383, 387–89; Clark, "Buckland Mills," 109–10; Moore, *Kilpatrick and Our Cavalry,* 132–33; Meyer, *Civil War Experiences,* 65–68; Moore, *Rebellion Record,* 7: 564; Charles H. Greenleaf to his mother, Nov. 18, 1863, Greenleaf MSS.

40. *OR,* I, 29, pt. 2: 459–61; John Buford to C. Ross Smith, Nov. 13, 1863, Microcopy 504, reel 32, NA; John Buford to Alfred Pleasonton, ca. Nov. 14, 1863, *ibid.;* John Buford to C. Ross Smith, Nov. 20, 1863, General's Papers of John Buford, RG-94, E-159, NA; A. J. Alexander to C. Ross Smith, Dec. 13, 1863, *ibid.;* Lincoln, *Collected Works,* 7: 74; Frank B. Borries, Jr., "General John Buford, Civil War Union Cavalryman," 61–62, M.A. thesis, Univ. of Kentucky, 1960; Longacre, *General John Buford,* 240–46.

CHAPTER 18

1. *OR,* I, 29, pt. 1: 555–637; Martin T. McMahon, "From Gettysburg to the Coming of Grant," *B&L* 4: 85–88.

2. *OR,* I, 29, pt. 2: 426, 429–30, 432, 439; Gillespie, *Company A, First Ohio Cavalry,* 190; George H. Chapman diary, Nov. 8–9, 1863; Charles M. Munroe diary, Nov. 7–9, 1863; Charles H. Greenleaf to his parents, Nov. 18, 1863, Greenleaf MSS.

3. *OR,* I, 29, pt. 2: 477–82, 484–89, 846; Jay Luvaas and Wilbur S. Nye, "The Campaign That History Forgot," *CWTI* 8 (Dec. 1969): 12–17.

4. *Ibid.,* 18-31; *OR,* I, 29, pt. 1: 694–97, 735–39, 744–48; pt. 2: 480–81, 489.

5. *Ibid.,* pt. 1: 697–99, 739–41; Luvaas and Nye, "Campaign History Forgot," 31–35.

6. *OR,* I, 29, pt. 1: 804, 806, 811–13, 815–16; Isham, *Seventh Michigan Cavalry,* 55; Charles H. Greenleaf to his parents, Dec. 12, 1863, Greenleaf MSS.

7. *OR,* I, 29, pt. 1: 806–07, 809; William Rawle Brooke diary, Nov. 27, 1863, Brooke MSS; Walter S. Newhall to his mother, Dec. 5, 1863, Newhall MSS.

8. *OR,* I, 29, pt. 1: 807–08; *New York Times,* Nov. 30, 1863.

9. *OR,* I, 29, pt. 1: 807, 810–11; pt. 2: 526.

10. *Ibid.,* I, 29, pt. 1: 802–03; *JCCW,* 1868–pt. 2: 11; George Gordon Meade to Margaret S. Meade, Mar. 9, 1864, Meade MSS, HSP.

11. *New York Times,* Dec. 1, 1863; Charles B. Coxe to John Cadwalader, Jr., Dec. 6, 1863, Coxe MSS.

12. William Rawle Brooke diary, Dec. 4, 18, 1863, Brooke MSS.

13. *Ibid.,* Dec. 18, 1863; Hall, Besley, and Wood, *Sixth New York Cavalry,* 168; Hard, *Eighth Illinois Cavalry,* 285–87; Gracey, *Sixth Pennsylvania Cavalry,* 211–13; *New York Tribune,* Dec. 17, 1863; Joseph D. Galloway diary, Dec. 18, 1863.

14. *OR,* I, 29, pt. 2: 585.

15. *Ibid.,* pt. 1: 987–89; Comte de Paris, *Civil War in America,* 3: 814.

16. *OR,* I, 29, pt. 2: 598; Haskin, *First Regiment of Artillery,* 524.

17. Alfred Pleasonton to Wesley Merritt, Jan. 4, 1864, RG-393, E-1439, NA.

18. Circular, Reserve Brig., 1st Cav. Div., Army of the Potomac, Nov. 2, 1863, RG-393, E-1538, *ibid.*

19. Benjamin W. Crowninshield to "Dear Frank," Jan. 10, 1864, Crowninshield MSS; Joseph D. Galloway diary, Jan. 17, 1864.

20. Moore, *Kilpatrick and Our Cavalry,* 134–35; H. Judson Kilpatrick to HQ, Cav. Corps, Army of the Potomac, Nov. 23, 1863, Jan. 16, 1864, General's Papers of H. Judson Kilpatrick, RG-94, E-159, NA.

21. Edward G. Longacre, *Army of Amateurs: General Benjamin F. Butler and the Army of the James, 1863–1865* (Mechanicsburg, Pa., 1997), 9–12, 18–19; *OR,* I, 33: 143–50.

22. Lincoln, *Collected Works,* 7: 178; *OR,* I, 33: 172, 551–52; Lyman, *Meade's Headquarters, 1863–1865,* 77; Virgil Carrington Jones, *Eight Hours before Richmond* (New York, 1957), 25–26.

23. *OR,* I, 33: 171–72, 174, 599–600.

24. *Ibid.,* 172–73; Dahlgren, *Memoir of Ulric Dahlgren,* 209–10.

25. *Ibid.,* 211; *OR,* I, 33: 173–74, 598–600, 607; Albert H. Shatzel diary, Feb. 26–27, 1864, Nebraska State Hist. Soc.; Simon M. Dufur, *Over the Dead Line; or, Tracked by Blood-Hounds* (Burlington, Vt., 1902), 11; Hall, Besley, and Wood, *Sixth New York Cavalry,* 173; Moyer, *Seventeenth Pennsylvania Cavalry,* 233.

26. *OR*, I, 33: 183.
27. *Ibid.*, 161–68, 170–71, 175, 597–98, 615–16, 628, 783; Thomas W. Smith to Joseph W. Smith, Mar. 3, 1864, Smith MSS; Allen L. Bevan to his sister, Mar. 6, 11, 1864, Bevan MSS; James O. Moore, "Custer's Raid into Albemarle County: The Skirmish at Rio Hill, February 29, 1864," *Virginia Magazine of History and Biography* 79 (1971): 338–48.
28. *OR*, I, 33: 169, 181–84; Robert G. Athearn, ed., "The Civil War Diary of John Wilson Phillips," *Virginia Magazine of History and Biography* 62 (1954): 96–97; Samuel Harris, *A Story of the Civil War: Why I Was Not Hung* (Chicago, 1895), 8; Moore, *Kilpatrick and Our Cavalry*, 144–47.
29. *Ibid.*, 147; *OR*, I, 33: 194; Jones, *Eight Hours before Richmond*, 51–53.
30. *OR*, I, 33: 185, 194–95.
31. *Ibid.*, 171, 185, 187, 195, 221.
32. *Ibid.*, 189–90, 195-96, 200; Harris, *Why I Was Not Hung*, 9–12; Reuben Bartley, Memoir of the Kilpatrick-Dahlgren Raid, 3, LC.
33. *OR*, I, 33: 196; Harris, *Why I Was Not Hung*, 13–14; Bartley, Memoir of Kilpatrick-Dahlgren Raid, 9; Jones, *Eight Hours before Richmond*, 75–76.
34. *OR*, I, 33: 186, 208–10, 219; Boudrye, *Fifth New York Cavalry*, 109; Jones, *Eight Hours before Richmond*, 86–91; Moore, *Rebellion Record*, 8: 586–87; Bartley, Memoir of Kilpatrick-Dahlgren Raid, 15, 22.
35. *OR*, I, 33: 184, 191, 201; Moyer, *Seventeenth Pennsylvania Cavalry*, 174; Hall, Besley, and Wood, *Sixth New York Cavalry*, 149.
36. *OR*, I, 33: 184, 191–92, 212–17; Athearn, "Diary of John Wilson Phillips," 97; Jones, *Eight Hours before Richmond*, 46–48.
37. *OR*, I, 33: 185, 192–93.
38. *Ibid.*, 185, 193, 201–02; Athearn, "Diary of John Wilson Phillips," 97; Kidd, *Personal Recollections*, 254–55; Moyer, *Seventeenth Pennsylvania Cavalry*, 243.
39. *OR*, I, 33: 185–86, 193; Athearn, "Diary of John Wilson Phillips," 98; Jones, *Eight Hours before Richmond*, 68.
40. *OR*, I, 33: 219–21, 223–24; J. William Jones, comp., "Kilpatrick-Dahlgren Raid against Richmond," *Southern Historical Society Papers* 13 (1885): 546–58; Boudrye, *Fifth New York Cavalry*, 112.
41. *OR*, I, 33: 218; *Official Records of the Union and Confederate Navies*, II, 3: 1070–72, 1113, 1115, 1146; *Richmond Examiner*, Mar. 5, 11, 1864; Faust, *Historical Times Encyclopedia*, 203.
42. *OR*, I, 33: 175–76, 178–80, 222–23; Bartley, Memoir of Kilpatrick-Dahlgren Raid, 1.
43. Jones, *Eight Hours before Richmond*, 174; Virgil Carrington Jones, "The Story of the Kilpatrick-Dahlgren Raid," *CWTI* 4 (Apr. 1965): 21; Longacre, *Mounted Raids of the Civil War*, 254–55; Faust, *Historical Times Encyclopedia*, 203.
44. Special Orders No. 12, HQ, Army of the Potomac, Apr. 15, 1864, General's Papers of H. Judson Kilpatrick, RG-94, E-159, NA; Warner, *Generals in Blue*, 266–67.

CHAPTER 19

1. *OR,* I, 33: 663, 669; Gideon Welles, *Diary of Gideon Welles, Secretary of the Navy under Lincoln and Johnson,* ed. by Howard K. Beale, 3 vols. (New York, 1960), 1: 538–39.
2. *OR,* I, 33: 663–64; Bruce Catton, *A Stillness at Appomattox* (Garden City, N.Y., 1953), 36–37; Ulysses S. Grant, *Personal Memoirs of U. S. Grant,* 2 vols. (New York, 1885–86), 2: 116–17; Meade, *Life and Letters of Meade,* 2: 177–78.
3. *OR,* I, 33: 22–24; David W. Howard diary, Mar. 24–25, 1864, Pennsylvania State Archives; Sanford, *Fighting Rebels and Redskins,* 220 and n.
4. *OR,* I, 33: 861, 916; Longacre, *Army of Amateurs,* 33–35.
5. Warner, *Generals in Blue,* 437–39; Sanford, *Fighting Rebels and Redskins,* 223–24; Frank A. Burr and Richard J. Hinton, *"Little Phil" and His Troopers: The Life of Gen. Philip H. Sheridan . . .* (Providence, R.I., 1888), 240–49.
6. *OR,* I, 33: 721–22, 732–33, 741; 51, pt. 1: 1152–53; Lyman, *Meade's Headquarters, 1863–1865,* 80–81; Patrick, *Inside Lincoln's Army,* 352; Cleaves, *Meade of Gettysburg,* 232; Grant, *Personal Memoirs,* 2: 133–34.
7. *Ibid.; New York Times,* Mar. 29, 1864.
8. George Gordon Meade to Margaret S. Meade, Mar. 9, 24, 1864, Meade MSS, HSP; Lyman, *Meade's Headquarters, 1863–1865,* 60; Patrick, *Inside Lincoln's Army,* 320, 344; Cleaves, *Meade of Gettysburg,* 220, 228; Charles B. Coxe to John Cadwalader, Jr., Dec. 10, 1863, Coxe MSS.
9. Philip H. Sheridan, *Report of Operations of the Cavalry Corps, Army of the Potomac, from April 6, to August 4, 1864* (New Orleans, 1866), 1; Burr and Hinton, *"Little Phil" and His Troopers,* 146–47; Philip H. Sheridan, *Personal Memoirs of P. H. Sheridan,* 2 vols. (New York, 1888), 1: 338, 341–43.
10. *Ibid.,* 344–47; Horace Porter, *Campaigning with Grant,* ed. by Wayne C. Temple (Bloomington, Ind., 1961), 23–24.
11. Lyman, *Meade's Headquarters, 1863–1865,* 82; Sanford, *Fighting Rebels and Redskins,* 221.
12. Emerson, *Charles Russell Lowell,* 336; Thomas W. Hyde, *Following the Greek Cross; or, Memories of the Sixth Army Corps* (Boston, 1894), 208; Richard M. Bache, *Life of General George Gordon Meade, Commander of the Army of the Potomac* (Philadelphia, 1897), 420.
13. Patrick, *Inside Lincoln's Army,* 355; Emerson, *Charles Russell Lowell,* 336; Wainwright, *Diary of Battle,* 517.
14. Lyman, *Meade's Headquarters, 1863–1865,* 81.
15. Sheridan, *Personal Memoirs,* 1: 353.
16. *Ibid.,* 353–57; Sanford, *Fighting Rebels and Redskins,* 221; Cheney, *Ninth New York Cavalry,* 151–52; Charles B. Coxe to John Cadwalader, Jr., Apr. 21, 1864, Coxe MSS; *Eighteenth Pennsylvania Cavalry,* 20; Wilson, "Cavalry of the Army of the Potomac," 37–38; *OR,* I, 33: 829–30, 835, 909–10, 923–24; 51, pt. 1: 1155–56.

17. *Ibid.*, 33: 835; 36, pt. 1: 803.
18. Sanford, *Fighting Rebels and Redskins,* 224; *Army and Navy Journal,* Nov. 13, 1880; *Volunteer Cavalry—Lessons of a Decade,* 61; Kidd, *Personal Recollections,* 261.
19. *Army and Navy Journal,* Nov. 13, 1880.
20. Warner, *Generals in Blue,* 566–68; Edward G. Longacre, *From Union Stars to Top Hat: A Biography of the Extraordinary General James Harrison Wilson* (Harrisburg, Pa., 1972), 61–75.
21. *Ibid.*, 95–106; *OR,* I, 33: 816, 893; Wilson, "Cavalry of the Army of the Potomac," 38.
22. *OR,* I, 33: 893, 1033; James H. Kidd to his father, Apr. 16, 1864, Kidd MSS; James Harrison Wilson, *Under the Old Flag: Recollections of Military Operations in the War for the Union, the Spanish War, the Boxer Rebellion, etc.,* 2 vols. (New York, 1912), 1: 361–62; Longacre, *Custer and His Wolverines,* 200–01.
23. *OR,* I, 33: 1043 and n.; 51, pt. 1: 1083; Joseph Flint, *Regimental History of the First New York Dragoons . . .* (Washington, D.C., 1865), 7.
24. *OR,* I, 36, pt. 1: 198; James H. Wilson to P. H. Sheridan, Apr. 14, 1864, Sheridan MSS, Henry E. Huntington Lib.; Allen L. Bevan to his sister, Apr. 19, 1864, Bevan MSS.
25. *OR,* I, 29, pt. 2: 35.
26. *Ibid.,* I, 33: 1044.
27. *Ibid.,* 46, pt. 1: 575–76; Dyer, *Compendium of the War of the Rebellion,* 3: 1345–46, 1627.
28. Boatner, *Civil War Dictionary,* 192–93; *OR,* I, 33: 1037–46; 36, pt. 3: 169–70.
29. *Ibid.,* pt. 1: 114; Dyer, *Compendium of the War of the Rebellion,* 3: 1354, 1372, 1381–82, 1473, 1479–80, 1568.
30. *OR,* I, 33: 1044.
31. *Ibid.,* 36, pt. 1: 12–13; Grant, *Personal Memoirs,* 2: 124–32; Warner, *Generals in Blue,* 61, 317, 448.
32. *OR,* I, 36, pt. 1: 14–15, 17; Warner, *Generals in Blue,* 18, 103, 443.
33. *OR,* I, 36, pt. 1: 18; Catton, *A Stillness at Appomattox,* 56–59.
34. Sheridan, *Personal Memoirs,* 1: 353.
35. Gilbert W. Chapman to "Dear Friend Jennie," May 18, 1864, Chapman MSS.
36. *OR,* I, 36, pt. 1: 787, 853, 875; pt. 2: 370.
37. Sheridan, *Personal Memoirs,* 1: 359–60; Edward Steere, *The Wilderness Campaign* (Harrisburg, Pa., 1960), 38–39, 64, 67–68, 94, 267; Edward J. McClernand, "Cavalry Operations: The Wilderness to the James River," *JMSIUS* 30 (1902): 337–38.
38. *OR,* I, 36, pt. 1: 876–77, 886; Steere, *Wilderness Campaign,* 72; Longacre, *From Union Stars to Top Hat,* 113–14.
39. *Ibid.,* 115; *OR,* I, 36, pt. 1: 797, 876, 886, 896–97; pt. 2: 371, 389, 427–29; Wilson, "Cavalry of the Army of the Potomac," 40; Athearn, "Diary of John Wilson Phillips," 100.

40. *OR,* I, 36, pt. 1: 876, 885–86; Wilson, *Under the Old Flag,* 1: 380.
41. *Ibid.,* 380–81; *OR,* I, 36, pt. 1: 876–77; Athearn, "Diary of John Wilson Phillips," 100.
42. Sheridan, *Personal Memoirs,* 1: 360–61; *OR,* I, 36, pt. 1: 877, 896–97; Wilson, *Under the Old Flag,* 1: 382–83; Henry S. Parmelee to his father, May 15, 1864, Parmelee MSS, Yale Univ. Lib.
43. Sheridan, *Personal Memoirs,* 1: 361; *OR,* I, 36, pt. 1: 853, 877; pt. 2: 427–29; Steere, *Wilderness Campaign,* 269–74.
44. *OR,* I, 36, pt. 2: 467, 470; pt. 2: 427; Andrew A. Humphreys, *The Virginia Campaign of '64 and '65: The Army of the Potomac and the Army of the James* (New York, 1883), 42; McClernand, "Cavalry Operations," 337–38.
45. James H. Wilson to George A. Forsyth, Feb. 25, 1910, Wilson MSS, LC; Wilson, *Under the Old Flag,* 1: 392.
46. Sheridan, *Personal Memoirs,* 1: 364; *OR,* I, 36, pt. 1: 803, 811.
47. *Ibid.,* 816–17, 826–27, 853, 857, 860, 862, 867; pt. 2: 514–16; Humphreys, *Virginia Campaign of '64 and '65,* 52; Kidd, *Personal Recollections,* 278–84.
48. *OR,* I, 36, pt. 1: 857, 860; Tobie, *First Maine Cavalry,* 252–54; Pyne, *First New Jersey Cavalry,* 231–33.
49. Sheridan, *Personal Memoirs,* 1: 364; *OR,* I, 36, pt. 1: 778, 811, 846; 51, pt. 1: 248–49; Allen O. Abbott, *Prison Life in the South . . .* (New York, 1865), 15–17; Morris Schaff, *The Battle of the Wilderness* (Boston, 1912), 335; Sanford, *Fighting Rebels and Redskins,* 228; Walter H. Jackson diary, May 7, 1864, Univ. of Michigan Lib.; James R. Bowen, *Regimental History of the First New York Dragoons . . .* (Lyons, Mich., 1900), 143–45; Gracey, *Sixth Pennsylvania Cavalry,* 235–36.

CHAPTER 20
1. *OR,* I, 36, pt. 1: 811–12; pt. 2: 551–52; Sheridan, *Personal Memoirs,* 1: 366; Humphreys, *Virginia Campaign of '64 and '65,* 58–59; Burr and Hinton, *"Little Phil" and His Troopers,* 160; Cleaves, *Meade of Gettysburg,* 241–42; McClernand, "Cavalry Operations," 330.
2. *OR,* I, 36, pt. 2: 553; Humphreys, *Virginia Campaign of '64 and '65,* 59.
3. Sheridan, *Personal Memoirs,* 1: 367–68; *OR,* I, 36, pt. 1: 540, 812; Wainwright, *Diary of Battle,* 356; Sanford, *Fighting Rebels and Redskins,* 228–29.
4. Charles H. Veil memoirs, 54, War Lib., MOLLUS Natl. Cmdry.
5. *OR,* I, 36, pt. 1: 789, 871, 878, 886–87; pt. 2: 554; Wilson, *Under the Old Flag,* 1: 393–94.
6. Sheridan, *Personal Memoirs,* 1: 366; *OR,* I, 36, pt. 1: 878, 887, 897; Wilson, *Under the Old Flag,* 1: 394; William Wells to his sister, May 17, 1864, Wells MSS; Henry S. Parmelee to his father, May 15, 1864, Parmelee MSS; Athearn, "Diary of John Wilson Phillips," 101.
7. Sheridan, *Personal Memoirs,* 1: 366–67; *OR,* I, 36, pt. 1: 788–89; pt. 2: 553; Lyman, *Meade's Headquarters, 1863–1865,* 106n.; Carswell McClellan, *Notes on the Personal Memoirs of P. H. Sheridan* (St. Paul,

Minn., 1889), 14–16; Bache, *Life of General George Gordon Meade,* 421; Pennypacker, *General Meade,* 285; Cleaves, *Meade of Gettysburg,* 241–42; William D. Matter, *If It Takes All Summer: The Battle of Spotsylvania* (Chapel Hill, N. C., 1988), 367–72.

8. Sheridan, *Personal Memoirs,* 1: 368–69; Grant, *Personal Memoirs,* 2: 153–54; Porter, *Campaigning with Grant,* 84.

9. *OR,* I, 36, pt. 2: 529, 552; Sheridan, *Personal Memoirs,* 1: 369.

10. Alexander Newburger diary, Apr. 27, May 9, 1864, LC.

11. Sheridan, *Personal Memoirs,* 1: 370.

12. Samuel H. Bradley, *Recollections of Army Life* (Olean, N.Y., 1913), 9.

13. Sheridan, *Personal Memoirs,* 1: 372–73; Theophilus F. Rodenbough, "Sheridan's Richmond Raid," *B&L* 4: 189; Louis H. Carpenter, "Sheridan's Expedition around Richmond, May 9–25, 1864," *JUSCA* 1 (1888): 304; Asa B. Isham, "Through the Wilderness to Richmond," *Sketches of War History, 1861–1865: Ohio MOLLUS* 1 (1888): 207–08.

14. Sheridan, *Personal Memoirs,* 1: 373, 375–76; Samuel H. Miller, "Yellow Tavern," *Civil War History* 2 (1956): 59, 62.

15. *OR,* I, 36, pt. 1: 857; Sheridan, *Personal Memoirs,* 1: 374; *Philadelphia Inquirer,* May 17, 18, 1864; Moore, *Rebellion Record,* 11: 453; Rodenbough, "Sheridan's Richmond Raid," 189; Alphonso D. Rockwell, "With Sheridan's Cavalry," *Personal Recollections of the War of the Rebellion: New York MOLLUS* 3 (1907): 230–31.

16. *OR,* I, 36, pt. 1: 777, 812, 817; Sheridan, *Personal Memoirs,* 1: 374–75; William Wells to his parents, May 15, 1864, Wells MSS; *Philadelphia Inquirer,* May 18, 1864; Walter H. Jackson diary, May 10, 1864; Carpenter, "Sheridan's Expedition around Richmond," 305; Harris, "Union Cavalry," 208.

17. Crowninshield and Gleason, *First Massachusetts Cavalry,* 206; *OR,* I, 36, pt. 1: 812, 853, 878, 887, 897; Sheridan, *Personal Memoirs,* 1: 375; Athearn, "Diary of John Wilson Phillips," 101; Moore, *Rebellion Record,* 11: 453.

18. Sheridan, *Personal Memoirs,* 1: 377.

19. *OR,* I, 36, pt. 1: 777, 813, 857; pt. 2: 645, 983; Sheridan, *Personal Memoirs,* 1: 376; Miller, "Yellow Tavern," 71, 73; Athearn, "Diary of John Wilson Phillips," 102; Moore, *Rebellion Record,* 11: 453–54; Rodenbough, "Sheridan's Richmond Raid," 190.

20. *OR,* I, 36, p. 1: 813, 853, 862, 864, 867, 870; Preston, *Tenth New York Cavalry,* 177–79; Crowninshield and Gleason, *First Massachusetts Cavalry,* 208–11; McClernand, "Cavalry Operations," 333.

21. *OR,* I, 36, pt. 1: 813, 818, 846–47, 879, 898; Sheridan, *Personal Memoirs,* 1: 378; Cheney, *Ninth New York Cavalry,* 186–87; *Rochester Daily Union and Advertiser,* May 21, 1864.

22. *OR,* I, 36, pt. 1: 818, 826–27; Kidd, *Personal Recollections,* 305–06; Longacre, *Custer and His Wolverines,* 213–14.

23. *OR,* I, 36, pt. 1: 818–19, 828; pt. 3: 800; Miller, "Yellow Tavern," 77–78; Longacre, *Custer and His Wolverines,* 214–15.

24. *OR,* I, 36, pt. 1: 777, 819; Sheridan, *Personal Memoirs,* 1: 379.

25. Preston, *Tenth New York Cavalry,* 181.

26. Rodenbough, "Sheridan's Richmond Raid," 191.

27. *OR,* I, 36, pt. 1: 792; Sheridan, *Personal Memoirs,* 1: 380; Hall, Besley, and Wood, *Sixth New York Cavalry,* 187; Pyne, *First New Jersey Cavalry,* 242.

28. *OR,* I, 36, pt. 1: 777, 791; William Wells to his sister, May 17, 1864, Wells MSS; William Wells to his parents, May 25, 1864, *ibid.*; Rodenbough, "Sheridan's Richmond Raid," 191; Henry S. Parmelee to his father, May 15, 1864, Parmelee MSS; *Rochester Daily Union and Advertiser,* May 21, 1864.

29. Wilson, *Under the Old Flag,* 1: 418.

30. Athearn, "Diary of John Wilson Phillips," 102; Charles H. Veil memoirs, 57.

31. *OR,* I, 36, pt. 1: 791, 813–14, 847, 854; Sheridan, *Personal Memoirs,* 1: 382; Sanford, *Fighting Rebels and Redskins,* 236; Preston, *Tenth New York Cavalry,* 181–83.

32. *OR,* I, 36, pt. 1: 791, 814, 819, 828; Sheridan, *Personal Memoirs,* 1: 382; Rodenbough, "Sheridan's Richmond Raid," 191; Charles H. Coller diary, May 12, 1864, USAMHI; Sanford, *Fighting Rebels and Redskins,* 236.

33. *OR,* I, 36, pt. 1: 777; Sheridan, *Personal Memoirs,* 1: 383; William Wells to his parents, May 25, 1864, Wells MSS; Hall, Besley, and Wood, *Sixth New York Cavalry,* 188; *Eighteenth Pennsylvania Cavalry,* 127–28.

34. *OR,* I, 36, pt. 1: 777–78, 792; pt. 2: 683, 765; Sheridan, *Personal Memoirs,* 1: 383-84; Athearn, "Diary of John Wilson Phillips," 103; Charles H. Coller diary, May 14, 1864.

35. *OR,* I, 36, pt. 1: 779, 781, 792, 814; pt. 2: 765–66; pt. 3: 199–200; Walter H. Jackson diary, May 15, 1864; Longacre, *Army of Amateurs,* 96–100.

36. *OR,* I, 36, pt. 1: 779, 792; pt. 2: 766, 797–98, 858, 931–32; Sheridan, *Personal Memoirs,* 1: 388; Athearn, "Diary of John Wilson Phillips," 103.

37. *OR,* I, 36, pt. 1: 779–80; Sheridan, *Personal Memoirs,* 1: 388; Walter H. Jackson diary, May 17, 1864.

38. *OR,* I, 36, pt. 1: 780–81, 792, 814, 819–20, 854, pt. 3: 23, 98–99, 171; Sheridan, *Personal Memoirs,* 1: 388–90; Rodenbough, "Sheridan's Richmond Raid," 191–92.

39. *OR,* I, 36, pt. 3: 22; Beck, "Letters of a Civil War Surgeon," 158; Athearn, "Diary of John Wilson Phillips," 103.

40. *OR,* I, 36, pt. 1: 782, 792, 815, 854; pt. 3: 171, 199; Sheridan, *Personal Memoirs,* 1: 390, 394–95; Rodenbough, "Sheridan's Richmond Raid," 192.

41. *OR,* I, 36, pt. 1: 792–93, 803, 820, 829, 871–72; pt. 2: 151–52; pt. 3: 230–32, 258–59; Sheridan, *Personal Memoirs,* 1: 395–97; Grant, *Personal Memoirs,* 2: 256; Humphreys, *Virginia Campaign of '64 and '65,* 133.

42. *OR,* I, 36, pt. 1: 872–73; Sheridan, *Personal Memoirs,* 1: 398–99.

43. *OR,* I, 36, pt. 1: 793, 854, 861; Humphreys, *Virginia Campaign of '64 and '65,* 164; Robbins, *War Record and Personal Experiences,* 86–87; Robert

A. Williams, "Haw's Shop: A 'Storm of Shot and Shell,'" *CWTI* 9 (Jan. 1971): 14–15.

44. *OR,* I, 36, pt. 1: 854; Morgan, *Always Ready, Always Willing,* 27; Haskin, *First Regiment of Artillery,* 559.

45. *OR,* I, 36, pt. 1: 793, 854, 858, 863, 869–70; Alphonso D. Rockwell, *Rambling Recollections: An Autobiography* (New York, 1920), 149.

46. *OR,* I, 36, pt. 1: 861; Longacre, *Jersey Cavaliers,* 207–08; Lyman Tremain, *Memorial of Frederick Lyman Tremain, Late Lieut. Col. of the 10th N.Y. Cavalry.* . . (Albany, N.Y., 1865), 30; *Philadelphia Inquirer,* June 3, 1864.

47. *OR,* I, 36, pt. 1: 793, 821, 829, 854; Sheridan, *Personal Memoirs,* 1: 400; James H. Kidd to his parents, June 3, 1864, Kidd MSS; Sanford, *Fighting Rebels and Redskins,* 238–39; Thomas W. Hill diary, May 28, 1864, Western Michigan Univ. Lib.; Francis M. Wright to John Ball, July 4, 1864, Wright MSS, *ibid.*; Walter H. Jackson diary, May 28, 1864.

48. *OR,* I, 36, pt. 3: 273; Sheridan, *Personal Memoirs,* 1: 400–401.

CHAPTER 21

1. *OR,* I, 36, pt. 1: 782–83, 805, 822; pt. 3: 258–59, 311, 361, 363; Sheridan, *Personal Memoirs,* 1: 402–04; Luke Davis diary, May 30, 1864; Walter H. Jackson diary, May 30, 1864; James H. Kidd to his parents, June 3, 1864, Kidd MSS.

2. *OR,* I, 36, pt. 1: 783, 805–06, 822, 848–49, 854; pt. 3: 411–12; Sheridan, *Personal Memoirs,* 1: 405–06; Haskin, *First Regiment of Artillery,* 525–26; Thomas W. Hill diary, May 31, 1864.

3. *OR,* I, 36, pt. 1: 783–84, 806, 822; pt. 3: 469–71; Sheridan, *Personal Memoirs,* 1: 406–08; William G. Hills diary, June 1, 1864, LC; Thomas W. Hill diary, June 1, 1864; Sanford, *Fighting Rebels and Redskins,* 240.

4. *OR,* I, 36, pt. 1: 806, 849, 872–75, 880–82, 888, 899–901; pt. 3: 361, 413–14, 510, 546, 558–62; Sheridan, *Personal Memoirs,* 1: 409–12; Grant, *Personal Memoirs,* 2: 263; Athearn, "Diary of John Wilson Phillips," 104–05; Theophilus F. Rodenbough, "Sheridan's Trevilian Raid," *B&L* 4: 233; *Philadelphia Inquirer,* June 3, 1864; Philip Koempel, *Phil Koempel's Diary, 1861–65* (n.p., 1921), 39; Luman Harris Tenney, *War Diary of Luman Harris Tenney, 1861–1865,* ed. by Frances Andrews Tenney (Cleveland, 1914), 118; William Wells to his parents, June 9, 1864, Wells MSS; Charles H. Greenleaf to his parents, June 20, 1864, Greenleaf MSS; George Musson memoirs, 13, Indiana Hist. Soc.; Robert W. Hatton, ed., "Just a Little Bit of the Civil War, as Seen by W. J. Smith, Company M, 2nd Ohio Volunteer Cavalry," *Ohio History* 84 (1975): 115.

5. *OR,* I, 36, pt. 3: 599, 603, 628–29; Grant, *Personal Memoirs,* 2: 282.

6. Sheridan, *Personal Memoirs,* 1: 413–16; Kidd, *Personal Recollections,* 342; Joseph Mills Hanson, "A Stolen March: Cold Harbor to Petersburg," *Journal of the American Military History Foundation* 1 (1937–38): 149; Rhodes, *Cavalry of the Army of the Potomac,* 114.

7. *OR*, I, 36, pt. 1: 806, 823, 882–83, 888–89, 901; pt. 3: 660–61; Sheridan, *Personal Memoirs*, 1: 417–18; William G. Hills diary, June 6, 1864; Kidd, *Personal Recollections*, 344.

8. *OR*, I, 36, pt. 1: 784, 806; Sheridan, *Personal Memoirs*, 1: 418; Foster, *6th New York Cavalry*, 58.

9. *OR*, I, 36, pt. 1: 806; Hyndman, *Company A, Fourth Pennsylvania Cavalry*, 203; Charles B. Coxe to John Cadwalader, Jr., July 19, 1864, Coxe MSS.

10. *OR*, I, 36, pt. 1: 784, 806–07; pt. 3: 716, 735–36; Sheridan, *Personal Memoirs*, 1: 419; Rodenbough, "Sheridan's Trevilian Raid," 233; Rockwell, *Rambling Recollections*, 154.

11. Sheridan, *Personal Memoirs*, 1: 420.

12. *OR*, I, 36, pt. 1: 784, 807, 849; Sheridan, *Personal Memoirs*, 1: 420; Rodenbough, "Sheridan's Trevilian Raid," 233; Sanford, *Fighting Rebels and Redskins*, 242.

13. *OR*, I, 36, pt. 1: 784, 807, 841, 849–50, 855, 868; Charles H. Veil memoirs, 65.

14. *OR*, I, 36, pt. 1: 784–85, 808, 823–24, 850; Sheridan, *Personal Memoirs*, 1: 420–21; Rodenbough, "Sheridan's Trevilian Raid," 233; Lee, *Seventh Michigan Cavalry*, 53–54; Jay Monaghan, "Custer's 'Last Stand'—Trevilian Station, 1864," *Civil War History* 8 (1962): 249–55; James H. Kidd to his parents, June 21, 1864, Kidd MSS.

15. *OR*, I, 36, pt. 1: 808, 824, 841, 855, 858; Sheridan, *Personal Memoirs*, 1: 421–22; Moyer, *Seventeenth Pennsylvania Cavalry*, 85; Custer and Custer, *Custer Story*, 103–05.

16. Sheridan, *Personal Memoirs*, 1: 422–23; Rodenbough, "Sheridan's Trevilian Raid," 234–35, 235n.; William G. Hills diary, June 11, 1864.

17. *OR*, I, 36, pt. 1: 784, 808–09, 824, 845–46, 850–51; Sheridan, *Personal Memoirs*, 1: 423–25; Rodenbough, "Sheridan's Trevilian Raid," 234; William S. Keller to his sister, June 22, 1864, Keller MSS, USAMHI; Charles H. Veil memoirs, 66.

18. *OR*, I, 36, pt. 1: 785; Sheridan, *Personal Memoirs*, 1: 425.

19. *OR*, I, 36, pt. 1: 786; pt. 3: 778–80; Sheridan, *Personal Memoirs*, 1: 426; Carswell McClellan, *The Personal Memoirs and Military History of U. S. Grant versus the Record of the Army of the Potomac* (Boston, 1887), 229–30; James H. Wilson to Thomas Fraser, Mar. 3, 1911, Wilson MSS, LC; James H. Wilson to Ezra B. Fuller, June 2, 1911, *ibid.*; Wilson, *Under the Old Flag*, 1: 440–41; Rhodes, *Cavalry of the Army of the Potomac*, 116; Johnston, *Virginia Railroads in the Civil War*, 207.

20. Edward P. Tobie, *Personal Recollections of General Sheridan* (Providence, R.I., 1889), 17.

21. *OR*, I, 36, pt. 1: 785, 851; Rodenbough, "Sheridan's Trevilian Raid," 235; Rockwell, *Rambling Recollections*, 151; Hyndman, *Company A, Fourth Pennsylvania Cavalry*, 205–06.

22. *OR,* I, 36, pt. 1: 786, 809; pt. 3: 784; 40, pt. 3: 14; Sheridan, *Personal Memoirs,* 1: 426–29; Sanford, *Fighting Rebels and Redskins,* 246; William G. Hills diary, June 18, 1864; Luke Davis diary, June 19, 1864.

23. *OR,* I, 36, pt. 3: 173–74, 364, 512, 669, 785, 787, 789; 40, pt. 3: 14; Sheridan, *Personal Memoirs,* 1: 429; *Philadelphia Inquirer,* July 4, 1864.

24. Sheridan, *Personal Memoirs,* 1: 430–31; *OR,* I, 40, pt. 1: 12–13, 18–25, 167–68.

25. Longacre, *Army of Amateurs,* 143–62.

26. *OR,* I, 36, pt. 1: 809, 843, 855; pt. 3: 789; 40, pt. 3: 14; Sheridan, *Personal Memoirs,* 1: 431; *Philadelphia Inquirer,* July 4, 1864.

27. *OR,* I, 36, pt. 1: 809–10, 843–44; pt. 3: 790–91, 795; Sheridan, *Personal Memoirs,* 1: 431.

28. *OR,* I, 36, pt. 1: 810, 855, 859; pt. 3: 791; Sheridan, *Personal Memoirs,* 1: 432.

29. *OR,* I, 36, pt. 1: 855; William S. Keller to his sister, June 26, 1864, Keller MSS.

30. *Ibid.; OR,* I, 36, pt. 1: 855, 859, 863, 869; Sheridan, *Personal Memoirs,* 1: 434; Rodenbough, "Sheridan's Trevilian Raid," 235; Sanford, *Fighting Rebels and Redskins,* 247.

31. *OR,* I, 36, pt. 1: 856, 866; Sheridan, *Personal Memoirs,* 1: 435; Alexander Newburger diary, June 24, 1864; *A Brief History of the Fourth Pennsylvania Veteran Cavalry . . .* (Pittsburgh, 1891), 97; William S. Keller to his sister, June 26, 1864, Keller MSS.

32. *OR,* I, 36, pt. 1: 810; pt. 3: 792–95, 797–99; Sheridan, *Personal Memoirs,* 1: 436; William G. Hills diary, June 26–27, 1864.

33. *OR,* I, 36, pt. 1: 883, 889–90; Henry S. Parmelee to his father, June 11, 1864, Parmelee MSS; Eugene B. Beaumont to his wife, June 12, 1864, Beaumont MSS, USMAL.

34. *OR,* I, 36, pt. 1: 544, 883, 902; pt. 3: 767; William Wells to his parents, June 19, 1864, Wells MSS; Eugene B. Beaumont to his wife, June 14, 1864, Beaumont MSS; Hanson, "A Stolen March," 140–41; *Rochester Daily Union and Advertiser,* June 23, 1864.

35. *OR,* I, 36, pt. 1: 883–84, 902; 40, pt. 2: 3, 6, 8, 11–12, 34–35; Hanson, "A Stolen March," 141.

36. *OR,* I, 36, pt. 1: 884, 889; 40, pt. 1: 644–45; pt. 2: 31–32, 35, 70–72; Eugene B. Beaumont to his wife, June 17, 1864, Beaumont MSS; William Wells to his parents, June 19, 1864, Wells MSS; Charles H. Greenleaf to his parents, June 20, 1864, Greenleaf MSS; George Musson memoirs, 13; *Eighteenth Pennsylvania Cavalry,* 103–06; *Rochester Daily Union and Advertiser,* June 23, 1864.

37. *OR,* I, 40, pt. 1: 620; 2: 139, 196–97; Eugene B. Beaumont to his wife, June 17, 19, 1864, Beaumont MSS; James Nesbitt to his parents, June 19, 1864, Nesbitt MSS, USAMHI; Henry S. Parmelee to his father, June 19, 1864, Parmelee MSS; Henry S. Parmelee to his mother, July 7, 1864, *ibid.*

38. *OR,* I, 40, pt. 1: 620, 625; pt. 2: 232, 255–56.

39. *Ibid.,* pt. 1: 730; pt. 2: 257, 267.

40. Wilson, "Cavalry of the Army of the Potomac," 59; Longacre, *Army of Amateurs,* 69–71, 88-90.

41. *OR,* I, 40, pt. 1: 620–21; Stephen Z. Starr, ed., "The Wilson [and Kautz] Raid, June, 1864: A Trooper's Reminiscences," *Civil War History* 21 (1975): 219.

42. *OR,* I, 40, pt. 1: 621, 625–26, 634–35, 645–46, 730–31; Wilson, *Under the Old Flag,* 1: 460; August V. Kautz memoirs, 79, USAMHI; William Wells to his parents, July 3, 1864, Wells MSS; Starr, "Wilson [and Kautz] Raid," 220–25; *Rochester Daily Union and Advertiser,* July 20, 1864.

43. *OR,* I, 40 pt. 1: 621–22, 626–27, 635, 646, 731; August V. Kautz diary, June 24–25, 1864, LC; Archibald, *Home-Making and Its Philosophy,* 239; William Wells to his parents, July 3, 1864, Wells MSS; Hatton, "Just a Little Bit of the Civil War," 117; George Musson memoirs, 13–14.

44. *OR,* I, 40, pt. 1: 620, 622, 627, 635, 646, 731; pt. 2: 267, 285–86, 304, 309, 316, 372; Humphreys, *Virginia Campaign of '64 and '65,* 236–37 and n.; Henry C. Carr diary, June 26, 1864, USAMHI.

45. *OR,* I, 40, pt. 1: 622–23, 627, 635–36, 646; Hatton, "Just a Little Bit of the Civil War," 117–18.

46. *OR,* I, 40, pt. 1: 623, 628–29, 636–37, 646, 731–32; Wilson, "Cavalry of the Army of the Potomac," 65; August V. Kautz diary, June 28–29, 1864; Starr, "Wilson [and Kautz] Raid," 233–35; Hatton, "Just a Little Bit of the Civil War," 118; Moore, *Rebellion Record,* 11: 523.

47. *OR,* I, 40, pt. 1: 623, 646; DeWitt Crumb, *22d Regiment N.Y. Vol. Cav.: Historical Address . . .* (South Otselic, N.Y., 1887), 1–2; Daniel W. Pulis to his parents, July 3, 1864, Pulis MSS; Edmund M. Pope, "Personal Experiences—A Side Light on the Wilson [and Kautz] Raid, June, 1864," *Glimpses of the Nation's Struggle: Minnesota MOLLUS* 4 (1898): 589; Henry C. Carr diary, June 29, 1864; Theodore J. Holmes, comp., *A Memorial of John S. Jameson . . .* (n.p., ca. 1866), 21.

48. *OR,* I, 40, pt. 1: 623, 628, 732; pt. 2: 449, 492–93, 505–09, 511, 516–17.

49. *Ibid,* 267; Sheridan, *Personal Memoirs,* 1: 440–42; Wilson, *Under the Old Flag,* 1: 441; James H. Wilson to J. W. Bush, June 2, 1911, Wilson MSS, LC.

50. *OR,* I, 40, pt. 2: 512; Sheridan, *Personal Memoirs,* 1: 444; Sanford, *Fighting Rebels and Redskins,* 249; Beck, "Letters of a Civil War Surgeon," 160.

51. *OR,* I, 40, pt. 2: 517–19, 521, 527, 530–31, 573; Sheridan, *Personal Memoirs,* 1: 444; Hyde, *Following the Greek Cross,* 217–18; Haskin, *First Regiment of Artillery,* 529; Mason Whiting Tyler, *Recollections of the Civil War: With Many Original Diary Entries and Letters Written from the Seat of War . . .,* ed. by William S. Tyler (New York, 1912), 235–36; *Philadelphia Inquirer,* July 4, 1864.

52. *OR,* I, 40, pt. 1: 624, 629–30, 637, 646–47, 732; Wilson, *Under the Old Flag,* 1: 470; Wilson, "Cavalry of the Army of the Potomac," 70; William

Wells to his parents, July 3, 1864, Wells MSS; Pope, "Personal Experiences," 590–604; Starr, "Wilson [and Kautz] Raid," 236–40; Hatton, "Just a Little Bit of the Civil War," 118.

53. *OR,* I, 40, pt. 1: 629, 732; pt. 2: 512, 518, 531, 540–41; August V. Kautz diary, June 29–30, 1864; Archibald, *Home-Making and Its Philosophy,* 240–41.

54. Custer and Custer, *Custer Story,* 110–11.

55. *OR,* I, 40, pt. 1: 624, 630, 637, 647; pt. 2: 612; Wilson, *Under the Old Flag,* 1: 470; Moore, *Rebellion Record,* 11: 523–24; Rodenbough, "Sheridan's Trevilian Raid," 236; Henry S. Parmelee to his mother, July 3, 1864, Parmelee MSS; Eugene B. Beaumont to his wife, July 5, 1864, Beaumont MSS.

56. *OR,* I, 40, pt. 2: 560; Patrick, *Inside Lincoln's Army,* 392; Wilson, *Under the Old Flag,* 1: 528–30; Longacre, *From Union Stars to Top Hat,* 142–43.

57. Angus J. Johnston, "Lee's Last Lifeline: The Richmond & Danville," *Civil War History* 7 (1961): 295; Pennypacker, *General Meade,* 330.

58. *OR,* I, 40, pt. 2: 560.

CHAPTER 22

1. *Philadelphia Inquirer,* July 4, 1864; Crumb, *22d N.Y. Cav.,* 3; Rodenbough, "Sheridan's Trevilian Raid," 236.

2. Sanford, *Fighting Rebels and Redskins,* 249; *OR,* I, 40, pt. 2: 574–76, 582, 592, 612–13.

3. William G. Hills diary, July 10, 1864; Henry S. Parmelee to his mother, July 9, 14, 1864, Parmelee MSS; Francis M. Wright to John Ball, July 9, 1864, Wright MSS; Moses Harris, "With the Reserve [Cavalry] Brigade," *JUSCA* 3 (1890): 9–10; Sanford, *Fighting Rebels and Redskins,* 250–51; James H. Kidd to his father, July 12, 20, 1864, Kidd MSS; Kidd, *Personal Recollections,* 370.

4. William Wells to his sister, July 13, 1864, Wells MSS.

5. Catton, *A Stillness at Appomattox,* 218–26.

6. *OR,* I, 40, pt. 3: 424–25, 437–38, 443, 448–50, 458, 475–78, 482–83; Grant, *Personal Memoirs,* 2: 310; Humphreys, *Virginia Campaign of '64 and '65,* 247.

7. Sheridan, *Personal Memoirs,* 1: 446; *OR,* I, 40, pt. 3: 435, 500.

8. *Ibid.,* pt. 1: 612–13, 618; pt. 3: 531–32; Sheridan, *Personal Memoirs,* 1: 446–47; William G. Hills diary, July 26, 27, 1864; Moyer, *Seventeenth Pennsylvania Cavalry,* 88.

9. *OR,* I, 40, pt. 1: 613, 619; pt. 3: 568–69; 43, pt. 1: 470–71; Sheridan, *Personal Memoirs,* 1: 447–48; William G. Hills diary, July 28, 1864; Walter H. Jackson diary, July 27, 28, 1864; Foster, *6th New York Cavalry,* 83–86; Rhodes, *Cavalry of the Army of the Potomac,* 120; Humphreys, *Virginia Campaign of '64 and '65,* 248–49; Sanford, *Fighting Rebels and Redskins,* 253.

10. William G. Hills diary, July 28, 1864; Edwin B. Payne to "Friend Hattie," Aug. 5, 1864, Payne MSS, USAMHI.

11. *OR*, I, 40, pt. 3: 551, 553, 596, 600, 616; Sheridan, *Personal Memoirs*, 1: 448-49.

12. *OR*, I, 40, pt. 1: 613, 619–20; pt. 3: 592–93, 602, 613–14; 43, pt. 1: 471; Moyer, *Seventeenth Pennsylvania Cavalry*, 9.

13. *OR*, I, 40, pt. 3: 636–40, 646, 656–68; Catton, *A Stillness at Appomattox*, 235–53; Wainwright, *Diary of Battle*, 444–45; Eugene B. Beaumont to his wife, July 30, 1864, Beaumont MSS; Humphreys, *Virginia Campaign of '64 and '65*, 254; Sheridan, *Personal Memoirs*, 1: 450–51.

14. *OR*, I, 40, pt. 3: 668–73.

15. *Ibid.*, 37, pt. 1: 94–103, 160; Sheridan, *Personal Memoirs*, 1: 456–57.

16. *Ibid.*, 457–58; *OR*, I, 37, pt. 1: 346–48; pt. 2: 592, 595–96; 40, pt. 3: 106–07, 121, 123.

17. *Ibid.*, 122; 43, pt. 1: 978; William Gamble to "My Dear Louisa," July 19, 1864, Gamble MSS, HSP; Dyer, *Compendium of the War of the Rebellion*, 3: 1026; Crumb, *22d N.Y. Cav.*, 3; George E. Pond, *The Shenandoah Valley in 1864* (New York, 1883), 60–61; *Philadelphia Inquirer*, Aug. 16, 1864.

18. *OR*, I, 37, pt. 1: 191–200, 204; pt. 2: 552, 596–97; 40, pt. 3: 122–24; Pond, *Shenandoah Valley in 1864*, 60.

19. U. S. Grant to Henry W. Halleck, July 18, 1864, Sheridan MSS, LC; Copy of Special Orders 68, HQ Armies of the U.S., Aug. 2, 1864, *ibid.*; *OR*, I, 40, pt. 3: 640–41, 669; 43, pt. 1: 681, 719; Sheridan, *Personal Memoirs*, 1: 461–63.

20. *OR*, I, 42, pt. 2: 46; 43, pt. 1: 516.

21. *Ibid.*, 501, 719, 744; Sheridan, *Personal Memoirs*, 1: 472, 474.

22. *OR*, I, 42, pt. 2: 12; 43, pt. 1: 682, 695; Sanford, *Fighting Rebels and Redskins*, 256; Walter H. Jackson diary, July 31, 1864.

23. *OR*, I, 43, pt. 1: 493–98, 516, 708–09, 719, 779, 825; Sanford, *Fighting Rebels and Redskins*, 257; *Eighteenth Pennsylvania Cavalry*, 26.

24. *OR*, I, 43, pt. 1: 111, 490; E. E. Billings, ed., "Letters and Diaries [Diary of Sgt. George W. Buhrer, 2nd Massachusetts Cavalry, 1864]," *CWTI* 1 (Apr. 1962): 18; Osborn Ayer to "Friends at home," Sept. 12, 1864, Ayer MSS, Nebraska State Hist. Soc.; Warner, *Generals in Blue*, 284–85.

25. *OR*, I, 37, pt. 2: 582; 43, pt. 1: 775, 822.

26. Sheridan, *Personal Memoirs*, 1: 475; Wesley Merritt, "Sheridan in the Shenandoah Valley," *B&L* 4: 500.

27. Long, *Civil War Day by Day*, 559, 563; John W. De Forest, *A Volunteer's Adventures: A Union Captain's Record of the Civil War*, ed. by James H. Croushore (New Haven, Conn., 1946), 166; Benjamin W. Crowninshield, "Sheridan at Winchester," *Atlantic Monthly* 42 (1878): 684.

28. *OR*, I, 43, pt. 1: 17–18, 41–42, 422, 438–39; Sheridan, *Personal Memoirs*, 1: 475–80; Charles H. Coller diary, Aug. 11, 1864; Kidd, *Personal Recollections*, 374–76; Merritt, "Sheridan in the Shenandoah Valley," 501–03.

29. *OR,* I, 43, pt. 1: 19, 43–44, 423, 439–40; Sheridan, *Personal Memoirs,* 1: 483–84.

30. *OR,* I, 43, pt. 1: 471–73; George N. Bliss, *Reminiscences of Service in the First Rhode Island Cavalry* (Providence, R.I., 1878), 25–26.

31. *OR,* I, 43, pt. 1: 466, 783, 816, 833, 841; pt. 2: 470–71; Sheridan, *Personal Memoirs,* 1: 485–88; Kidd, *Personal Recollections,* 399; *New York Times,* Aug. 25, 1864; Catton, *A Stillness at Appomattox,* 285–86; Monaghan, *Custer,* 203, 221–22; Wert, *Custer,* 184–85; William Thompson to his wife, Aug. 14, 22, 1864, Pennsylvania State Univ. Lib.; Charles H. Veil memoirs, 69–71.

32. *OR,* I, 43, pt. 1: 423–24, 516, 816–17, 825, 827, 830; Wilson, *Under the Old Flag,* 1: 539; Crumb, *22d N.Y. Cav.,* 6; Samuel Clarke Farrar, comp., *The Twenty-Second Pennsylvania Cavalry and the Ringgold Battalion, 1861–1865* (Pittsburgh, 1911), 348; Sanford, *Fighting Rebels and Redskins,* 258; Athearn, "Diary of John Wilson Phillips," 107.

33. Sheridan, *Personal Memoirs,* 1: 494-95; *OR,* I, 43, pt. 1: 45, 424–25, 440, 473, 517; Wilson, *Under the Old Flag,* 1: 540–42; Eugene B. Beaumont to his wife, Aug. 26, 1864, Beaumont MSS; Kidd, *Personal Recollections,* 377–83; Sanford, *Fighting Rebels and Redskins,* 263–65; Athearn, "Diary of John Wilson Phillips," 107; Charles H. Coller diary, Aug. 25, 1864; Crumb, *22d N.Y. Cav.,* 7–8; Merritt, "Sheridan in the Shenandoah Valley," 504–05.

34. *OR,* I, 43, pt. 1: 23–24, 45–46, 425–27, 440–41, 517, 952–53, 956, 961–62, 966; pt. 2: 3, 8–10, 35–36, 57, 60, 65–66, 83, 89, 96, 102; Sheridan, *Personal Memoirs,* 1: 495–500; Merritt, "Sheridan in the Shenandoah Valley," 505–06.

35. Sheridan, *Personal Memoirs,* 2: 1–9; Porter, *Campaigning with Grant,* 297.

36. William Wells to his parents, Sept. 8, 1864, Wells MSS; James H. Kidd to his parents, Sept. 9, 1864, Kidd MSS; *OR,* I, 43, pt. 1: 517, 529–31, 540–42; pt. 2: 73–74, 78, 87; John B. McIntosh to his wife, Sept. 13, 1864, McIntosh MSS; Athearn, "Diary of John Wilson Phillips," 110.

37. *OR,* I, 43, pt. 1: 46–47, 427, 441, 443, 454, 481–82, 498, 518; Sheridan, *Personal Memoirs,* 2: 11–17; A. T. A. Torbert to William W. Averell ("Confidential"), Sept. 18, 1864, Torbert MSS, Univ. of Alaska Lib.; J. J. Sutton, *History of the Second Regiment, West Virginia Cavalry Volunteers, during the War of the Rebellion* (Portsmouth, Ohio, 1892), 159–60; Athearn, "Diary of John Wilson Phillips,"111–12; Joseph P. Cullen, "Sheridan Wins at Winchester," *CWTI* 6 (May 1967): 7–8.

38. *OR,* I, 43, pt. 1: 47, 428, 518; Sheridan, *Personal Memoirs,* 2: 18–22; William Wells to his parents, Sept. 25, 1864, Wells MSS; Crumb, *22d N.Y. Cav.,* 9–11; De Forest, *A Volunteer's Adventures,* 173.

39. *OR,* I, 43, pt. 1: 47, 427, 444–46, 455–58, 482–83; pt. 2: 113; Sheridan, *Personal Memoirs,* 2: 23–26; Farrar, *Twenty-Second Pennsylvania Cavalry,* 374; Kidd, *Personal Recollections,* 387–91; James H. Kidd to John Robertson, Dec. 17, 1864, Kidd MSS; Walter H. Jackson diary, Sept. 19, 1864.

40. *OR,* I, 43, pt. 1: 47, 427, 446, 457–58, 483; pt. 2: 110; Sheridan, *Personal Memoirs,* 2: 26–32.

41. William Thompson to his wife, Sept. 25, 1864, Thompson MSS; *Sheridan's Veterans: A Souvenir of Their Two Campaigns in the Shenandoah Valley . . .* (Boston, 1883), 33.

42. *New York Times,* Sept. 22, 1864; Cullen, "Sheridan Wins at Winchester," 43.

43. *Ibid.;* Abraham Lincoln to Philip H. Sheridan, Sept. 20, 1864, Sheridan MSS, LC.

44. *OR,* I, 43, pt. 1: 47–48; 428, 441; pt. 2: 110–11, 113–14, 148; Sheridan, *Personal Memoirs,* 2: 33–40.

45. *OR,* I, 43, pt. 1: 48; pt. 2: 142; Sheridan, *Personal Memoirs,* 2: 34–40.

46. *OR,* I, 43, pt. 1: 48, 428–29, 441; pt. 2: 121–22, 170; Sheridan, *Personal Memoirs,* 2: 41; Harris, "With the Reserve [Cavalry] Brigade," 236–37; Sanford, *Fighting Rebels and Redskins,* 271–74; *Eighteenth Pennsylvania Cavalry,* 27; Athearn, "Diary of John Wilson Phillips," 113–14.

47. *OR,* I, 43, pt. 1: 48; pt. 2: 156–57, 170; Sheridan, *Personal Memoirs,* 2: 42.

48. *OR,* I, 43, pt. 1: 49, 475–77, 498–501, 505; pt. 2: 158; Sheridan, *Personal Memoirs,* 2: 42–44; Sanford, *Fighting Rebels and Redskins,* 274–75.

49. *OR,* I, 43, pt. 1: 49–50, 429, 441–42; Sheridan, *Personal Memoirs,* 2: 45–48.

50. *Ibid.,* 49–56; *OR,* I, 43, pt. 1: 49–50, 429–30, 441–42, 519; pt. 2: 172–73, 182–83, 201–3, 209–10, 288–89, 292–93; Sanford, *Fighting Rebels and Redskins,* 278–81; Athearn, "Diary of John Wilson Phillips," 114–15; Hatton, "Just a Litle Bit of the Civil War," 122; Walter H. Jackson diary, Sept. 24–Oct. 6, 1864; Billings, "Letters and Diaries," 18.

51. Athearn, "Diary of John Wilson Phillips," 116.

52. Sheridan, *Personal Memoirs,* 2: 56; *OR,* I, 43, pt. 1: 50; De Forest, *A Volunteer's Adventures,* 198; Sanford, *Fighing Rebels and Redskins,* 282–83.

53. *Ibid.,* 283; *OR,* I, 43, pt. 2: 320–21.

54. *Ibid.,* pt. 1: 519; pt. 2: 220, 249; Wilson, *Under the Old Flag,* 1: 563–64; Crumb, *22d N.Y. Cav.,* 12.

55. Sheridan, *Personal Memoirs,* 2: 56–57; *OR,* I, 43, pt. 1: 50–51, 431; pt. 2: 327, 329.

56. *Ibid.,* pt. 1: 520–22; Custer and Custer, *Custer Story,* 122; William Wells to his sister, Oct. 10, 1864, Wells MSS; William Wells to his parents, Oct. 21, 1864, *ibid.;* Crumb, *22d N.Y. Cav.,* 12–13; *Eighteenth Pennsylvania Cavalry,* 28; Sanford, *Fighting Rebels and Redskins,* 284; Athearn, "Diary of John Wilson Phillips," 116; Henry C. Carr diary, Oct. 27, 1864.

57. *OR,* I, 43, pt. 1: 447–48, 460–61, 477–78; Sanford, *Fighting Rebels and Redskins,* 284; Charles H. Veil memoirs, 81; Merritt, "Sheridan in the Shenandoah Valley," 513; James H. Kidd to John Robertson, Dec. 17, 1864, Kidd MSS; Kidd, *Personal Recollections,* 401–2.

58. *OR,* I, 43, pt. 1: 31–32, 431; pt. 2: 327, 329; William Thompson to his wife, Oct. 11, 1864, Thompson MSS; *Philadelphia Inquirer,* Oct. 11, 13, 1864.

CHAPTER 23

1. Sheridan, *Personal Memoirs,* 2: 59–67; P. H. Sheridan to U. S. Grant, Oct. 1, 1864, Sheridan MSS, LC; *OR,* I, 43, pt. 1: 51; pt. 2: 249–50, 307–08, 335; Alfred Gibbs to Benjamin W. Brice, Oct. 1, 1864, Gibbs MSS, HSP.
2. William Thompson to his wife, Oct. 11, 1864, Thompson MSS; Kidd, *Personal Recollections,* 399.
3. Sheridan, *Personal Memoirs,* 2: 61–62; *OR,* I, 43, pt. 1: 561; pt. 2: 364–65; Joseph P. Cullen, "Cedar Creek," *CWTI* 8 (Dec. 1969): 7–12, 42; Benjamin W. Crowninshield, *The Battle of Cedar Creek, October 19, 1864* (Cambridge, Mass., 1879), 9; Merritt, "Sheridan in the Shenandoah Valley," 514–16.
4. *OR,* I, 43, pt. 1: 158–60, 561–62; pt. 2: 410; Crowninshield, *Battle of Cedar Creek,* 14–15; Cullen, "Cedar Creek," 43–45.
5. Sheridan, *Personal Memoirs,* 2: 62; Sanford, *Fighting Rebels and Redskins,* 285–86.
6. *OR,* I, 43, pt. 1: 433, 522–23; Crumb, *22d N.Y. Cav.,* 13–14; Crowninshield, *Battle of Cedar Creek,* 21.
7. *Ibid.,* 20; *OR,* I, 43, pt. 1: 562.
8. Sheridan, *Personal Memoirs,* 2: 68–84; *OR,* I, 43, pt. 1: 32–33, 52–53; William Thompson to his wife, Nov. 1, 1864, Thompson MSS; Charles A. Humphreys, *Field, Camp, Hospital and Prison in the Civil War, 1863–1865* (Boston, 1918), 177. The information about Sheridan's sleeping arrangements on the night of October 18–19 was supplied to the author in 1971 by the award-winning historian Thomas Robson Hay, who was researching a biography of the general.
9. *OR,* I, 43, pt. 1: 433–34, 450–51, 479–81, 523–27, 532–33; Sheridan, *Personal Memoirs,* 2: 84–92; Crowninshield, *Battle of Cedar Creek,* 24–28; James H. Kidd to John Robertson, Dec. 17, 1864, Kidd MSS.
10. William Wells to his parents, Oct. 21, 1864, Wells MSS; James H. Kidd to his father, Oct. 21, 1864, Kidd MSS.
11. Sheridan, *Personal Memoirs,* 2: 97–99; *OR,* I, 43, pt. 1: 533; Augustus C. Hamlin, "Who Recaptured the Guns at Cedar Creek, Ocober 19, 1864?" *PMHSM* 6 (1907): 190–93; George A. Forsyth, *Thrilling Days in Army Life* (New York, 1900), 167.
12. *OR,* I, 43, pt. 1: 131–37, 435; pt. 2: 424, 426; Sheridan, *Personal Memoirs,* 2: 89–92; Billings, "Letters and Diaries," 18; Emerson, *Charles Russell Lowell,* 357–58; Humphreys, *Field, Camp, Hospital and Prison,* 170, 179–82; Samuel W. Backus, *Californians in the Field: Historical Sketch of the . . . 2d Massachusetts Cavalry: California MOLLUS* (San Francisco, 1889), 15–18; Sanford, *Fighting Rebels and Redskins,* 297.
13. *OR,* I, 43, pt. 2: 427; Athearn, "Diary of John Wilson Phillips," 119.

14. *OR,* I, 43, pt. 1: 55–56; pt. 2: 671–72, 679–80, 687; Sheridan, *Personal Memoirs,* 2: 99–100, 105–07; William Wells to his brother, Nov. 1, 1864, Wells MSS.

15. *OR,* I, 43, pt. 2: 683–84, 708, 717–18, 750, 756, 765; Sheridan, *Personal Memoirs,* 2: 99; W. G. Cummings, "Six Months in the Third Cavalry Division under Custer," *War Sketches and Incidents: Iowa MOLLUS* 1 (1893): 302–03.

16. *OR,* I, 43, pt. 1: 35; pt. 2: 582; Walter H. Jackson diary, Jan. 3, 7–11, 1865; Hiram Rix, Jr., diary, Jan. 3, 1865, Central Michigan Univ. Lib.; Stephen Z. Starr, ed., "Winter Quarters near Winchester, 1864–1865: Reminiscences of Roger Hannaford, Second Ohio Volunteer Cavalry," *Virginia Magazine of History and Biography* 86 (1978): 325–28.

17. *OR,* I, 43, pt. 1: 56; Sheridan, *Personal Memoirs,* 2: 102; Pliny A. Jewett to "Dear Uncle," Dec. 28, 1864, Jewett MSS, Virginia Hist. Soc.; Moyer, *Seventeenth Pennsylvania Cavalry,* 111.

18. *OR,* I, 43, pt. 1: 38–39, 56; pt. 2: 825; Sheridan, *Personal Memoirs,* 2: 102; Chauncey S. Norton, comp., *"The Red Neck Ties"; or, History of the Fifteenth New York Volunteer Cavalry* . . . (Ithaca, N.Y., 1891), 59–60; Monaghan, *Custer,* 223–24; Wert, *Custer,* 202–03; Hatton, "Just a Little Bit of the Civil War," 125–26.

19. *OR,* I, 43, pt. 1: 56, 677–79; pt. 2: 829, 833; Sheridan, *Personal Memoirs,* 2: 102, 104; Humphreys, *Field, Camp, Hospital and Prison,* 194–203; Johnston, *Virginia Railroads in the Civil War,* 233; Walter H. Jackson diary, Dec. 23–24, 1864.

20. Sanford, *Fighting Rebels and Redskins,* 12; *Army and Navy Journal,* Nov. 13, 1880.

21. *OR,* I, 46, pt. 1: 475; Sheridan, *Personal Memoirs,* 2: 112–13; Lincoln, *Collected Works,* 8: 316, 317n., 320–21; Philip H. Sheridan to George H. Chapman, May 10, 1865, Sheridan MSS, LC; William Russell, Jr., to George H. Chapman, Mar. 5, 13, 15, 27, Apr. 9, 22, 1865, Torbert MSS.

22. Walter H. Jackson diary, Feb. 27–Mar. 1, 1865; James Bradley diary, Feb. 27–Mar. 1, 1865, Connecticut Hist. Soc.; Stephen W. Thompson diary, Feb. 27, 1865, Central Michigan Univ. Lib.; Hiram Rix, Jr., diary, Feb. 27–Mar. 1, 1865; Sanford, *Fighting Rebels and Redskins,* 311–14; Starr, "Winter Quarters near Winchester," 338.

23. Sheridan, *Personal Memoirs,* 2: 114–16; *OR,* I, 46, pt. 1: 75–76, 485–86, 489, 495, 502–03, 505; pt. 2: 792, 818; Walter H. Jackson diary, Mar. 2, 1865; James Bradley diary, Mar. 2, 1865; Hiram Rix, Jr., diary, Mar. 2, 1865; Sanford, *Fighting Rebels and Redskins,* 315–17; William Wells to his sister, Mar. 18, 1865, Wells MSS; Harlan Page Lloyd, "The Battle of Waynesboro," *Sketches of War History: Ohio MOLLUS* 4 (1896): 195–212; Humphreys, *Field, Camp, Hospital and Prison,* 206–07.

24. Sheridan, *Personal Memoirs,* 2: 116, 118; *OR,* I, 46, pt. 1: 477, 486; pt. 2: 793; Isham, *Seventh Michigan Cavalry,* 77–78.

25. Sheridan, *Personal Memoirs,* 2: 118–19.

26. *OR,* I, 46, pt. 1: 477–82, 486–88.

27. *Ibid.,* 42, pt. 2: 149–50, 157–58; Humphreys, *Virginia Campaign of '64 and '65,* 268–69.

28. *OR,* I, 42, pt. 1: 637, 639; pt. 2: 149–50, 157–58, 167, 173–74, 179, 198–99, 200, 204, 210, 215–16, 218, 220–21, 228–30, 269–70, 301–02, 321, 327, 332–34, 337–38, 349; Humphreys, *Virginia Campaign of '64 and '65,* 269–71; Norman Ball diary, Aug. 13–20, 1864.

29. *OR,* I, 42, pt. 2: 375, 390, 393, 399, 407–08, 426, 428–29, 436, 441–42, 444–46, 455–56, 471–72, 477, 482, 484–86, 491–92, 517, 524–25; Humphreys, *Virginia Campaign of '64 and '65,* 278–82; Russell F. Weigley, "The Twilight of Mounted Cavalry: Gregg's Division in the Petersburg Campaign," *Historical Review of Berks County* 27 (1962): 84; Edward G. Longacre, "The Battle of Reams' Station: 'The Blackest of All Days'," *CWTI* 25 (Mar. 1986): 12–19.

30. *OR,* I, 42, pt. 1: 614–15; pt. 2: 856, 861, 867–70, 873–80, 891; Edward P. Tobie, *Service of the Cavalry in the Army of the Potomac* (Providence, R.I., 1882), 36; Norman Ball diary, Sept. 16–17, 1864; Lewis C. Rappalyea diary, Sept. 16–17, 1864, New Jersey Hist. Soc.; William Rawle Brooke to his mother, Sept. 18, 1864, Brooke MSS.

31. *OR,* I, 42, pt. 1: 634–36; pt. 2: 1069, 1078–79, 1091, 1093–94, 1106–08, 1120, 1124, 1139–41; pt. 3: 5, 23, 27–29; Longacre, *Army of Amateurs,* 211–17; Lewis Rappalyea diary, Sept. 29–Oct. 2, 1864; Richard J. Sommers, "Grant's Fifth Offensive at Petersburg: A Study in Strategy, Tactics, and Generalship . . .", 628–31, 638–48, 1068, Ph.D. diss., Rice Univ., 1970; Humphreys, *Virginia Campaign of '64 and '65,* 282, 290n.; Merrill, *First Maine and First District of Columbia Cavalry,* 286–87; Steven R. Clark to "Dear Del," Oct. 6, 1864, Clark MSS, USAMHI.

32. *OR,* I, 42, pt. 1: 608–10, 629–30, 641, 646–48; pt. 3: 359, 366, 373, 380–85; Lewis Rappalyea diary, Oct. 27–28, 1864; Norman Ball diary, Oct. 27–28, 1864; Merrill, *First Maine and First District of Columbia Cavalry,* 288–90; Humphreys, *Virginia Campaign of '64 and '65,* 295, 302; Weigley, "Twilight of Mounted Cavalry," 86, 89; Thomas, *Personal Reminiscences of Service,* 20.

33. *OR,* I, 42, pt. 1: 610–11, 632; pt. 3: 774, 781, 790–91; Lewis Rappalyea diary, Nov. 24–26, Dec. 1, 1864; Norman Ball diary, Nov. 29, Dec. 1, 1864; Merrill, *First Maine and First District of Columbia Cavalry,* 293–94; Weigley, "Twilight of Mounted Cavalry," 91, 93.

34. *OR,* I, 42, pt. 2: 611–13, 630–34, 638, 649; pt. 3: 842, 856, 866, 877, 881, 885–86, 898–99, 907–08, 910–11, 915, 919–20, 930–31, 951, 953, 980; Lewis Rappalyea diary, Dec. 7–12, 1864; Norman Ball diary, Dec. 7–12, 1864; Thomas, *Personal Reminiscences of Service,* 22; Humphreys, *Virginia Campaign of '64 and '65,* 310; Johnston, *Virginia Railroads in the Civil War,* 232; Merrill, *First Maine and First District of Columbia Cavalry,* 294–301; Weigley, "Twilight of Mounted Cavalry," 93, 95.

35. Robbins, *War Record and Personal Experiences,* 100–01; Pyne, *First New Jersey Cavalry,* 300–02; *OR,* I, 42, pt. 1: 83–84, 86, 611–13, 625, 631–34.
36. *Ibid.,* 46, pt. 1: 365–67; Lyman, *Meade's Headquarters, 1863–1865,* 310; David M. Gregg, Oath of Office as Bvt. Maj. Gen. of Vols., Dec. 5, 1864, ACPF of David M. Gregg, RG-94, NA.
37. Rockwell, *Rambling Recollections,* 164.
38. David M. Gregg to Adj. Gen., USA, Jan. 26, 1865, ACPF of David M. Gregg, RG-94, NA; *OR,* I, 46, pt. 1: 113; George Crook to R. B. Hayes, Mar. 28, 1865, Crook MSS, Rutherford B. Hayes Pres. Cntr.; George Crook, *George Crook: His Autobiography,* ed. by Martin F. Schmitt (Norman, Okla., 1960), 136.
39. *Ibid.,* 135–36; M. J. Darley to Philip H. Sheridan, Mar. 1, 1865, Sheridan MSS, LC.
40. Tobie, "Personal Recollections of General Sheridan," 21; Archibald, *Home-Making and Its Philosophy,* 260.
41. Sheridan, *Personal Memoirs,* 2: 135–39; *OR,* I, 46, pt. 1: 1101; pt. 3: 234–35; Humphreys, *Virginia Campaign of '64 and '65,* 324–25; Henry E. Tremain, "The Last Days of Sheridan's Cavalry," *MB* 5 (1898): 69; Frederick C. Newhall, "With Sheridan in Lee's Last Campaign," *MB* 1 (1894): 299–304.
42. Sheridan, *Personal Memoirs,* 2: 134–35; Grant, *Personal Memoirs,* 2: 438–40.
43. *Ibid.,* 437; Sheridan, *Personal Memoirs,* 2: 126–31.
44. Longacre, *From Union Stars to Top Hat,* 184–216; *OR,* I, 46, pt. 1: 1298–99; Freeman, *Lee's Lieutenants,* 3: 656–59.
45. Sheridan, *Personal Memoirs,* 2: 141–45; *OR,* I, 46, pt. 2: 266, 325.
46. *Ibid.,* pt. 1: 1102, 1122, 1128; pt. 3: 266–67, 281, 283, 302, 323, 326; Sheridan, *Personal Memoirs,* 2: 141–42; Humphreys, *Field, Camp, Hospital and Prison,* 234–35.
47. *OR,* I, 46, pt. 1: 1102–03, 1116–17, 1122–23, 1128, 1141–42; pt. 3: 339–40, 365–67, 381–82; Sheridan, *Personal Memoirs,* 2: 149–52; Robbins, *War Record and Personal Experiences,* 112–16; Crook, *Autobiography,* 136–37; Newhall, "With Sheridan in Lee's Last Campaign," 306–11.
48. *Ibid.,* 312; *OR,* I, 46, pt. 1: 1103, 1129–30; Sheridan, *Personal Memoirs,* 2: 152–54; Stephen Z. Starr, ed., "Dinwiddie Court House and Five Forks: Reminiscences of Roger Hannaford, Second Ohio Volunteer Cavalry," *Virginia Magazine of History and Biography* 87 (1978): 423.
49. *OR,* I, 46, pt. 3: 380; Sheridan, *Personal Memoirs,* 2: 154–55.
50. *OR,* I, 46, pt. 1: 1103; Sheridan, *Personal Memoirs,* 2: 156–57.
51. *OR,* I, 46, pt. 1: 1004, 1117, 1123, 1130, 1135, 1144, 1244; pt. 3: 435–37; Sheridan, *Personal Memoirs,* 2: 157–58.
52. *OR,* I, 46, pt. 1: 1100, 1104–05; pt. 3: 392; Sheridan, *Personal Memoirs,* 2: 159–66.
53. *OR,* I, 46, pt. 1: 1104–05, 1117–18, 1123, 1128, 1130–31, 1135–36; pt. 3: 394, 435–37; Sheridan, *Personal Memoirs,* 2: 162–65; George Crook to

R. B. Hayes, Apr. 12, 1865, Crook MSS, Rutherford B. Hayes Pres. Cntr.; Tenney, *War Diary,* 149; James Bradley diary, Apr. 1, 1865; William Wells to his parents, Apr. 2, 1865, Wells MSS; Tremain, "Last Days of Sheridan's Cavalry," 253–57; Hatton, "Just a Little Bit of the Civil War," 225–26; Starr, "Dinwiddie Court House and Five Forks," 424–37.

54. Freeman, *Lee's Lieutenants,* 3: 666–74.
55. *Ibid.,* 676–88; *OR,* I, 46, pt. 1: 1106; Starr, *Union Cavalry in the Civil War,* 2: 454–55.
56. *OR,* I, 46, pt. 1: 1106; Sheridan, *Personal Memoirs,* 2: 172–73; Walter H. Jackson diary, Apr. 2, 1865.
57. *OR,* I, 46, pt. 1: 1106–07, 1119–20, 1125, 1128–29, 1131–32, 1136, 1142, 1144–45, 1155, 1157–58, 1245; pt. 3: 528–29, 531-32, 556–61, 577–78; Sheridan, *Personal Memoirs,* 2: 173–77; Robbins, *War Record and Personal Experiences,* 117–22; Tenney, *War Diary,* 155; Thomas, *Personal Reminiscences of Service,* 24–25; Henry E. Davies, *General Sheridan* (New York, 1899), 239–40; Philip H. Sheridan to Ranald S. Mackenzie, Apr. 4, 1865, Sheridan MSS, HSP.
58. *OR,* I, 46, pt. 3: 577–78, 582–83, 594; Sheridan, *Personal Memoirs,* 2: 177–79.
59. *OR,* I, 46, pt. 1: 1107–08; pt. 3: 599, 610; Sheridan, *Personal Memoirs,* 2: 179–80; Frances Reece, ed., "The Final Push to Appomattox," *Michigan History Magazine* 28 (1944): 462; Tenney, *War Diary,* 155; Tremain, "Last Days of Sheridan's Cavalry," 295–98; Walter H. Jackson diary, Apr. 6, 1865.
60. *OR,* I, 46, pt. 1: 1108; pt. 3: 610; Sheridan, *Personal Memoirs,* 2: 180–84, 186; Crook, *Autobiography,* 138–39; Tremain, "Last Days of Sheridan's Cavalry," 298–300.
61. *OR,* I, 46, pt. 1: 1009; Sheridan, *Personal Memoirs,* 2: 187–88; Crook, *Autobiography,* 139–40; Davies, *General Sheridan,* 245–46; Tremain, "Last Days of Sheridan's Cavalry," 305–11.
62. *OR,* I, 46, pt. 1: 1009; pt. 3: 621, 633–35, 653–54; Sheridan, *Personal Memoirs,* 2: 188–90; Philip H. Sheridan, "Last Days of the Rebellion," *Military Essays and Recollections: Illinois MOLLUS* 1 (1891): 428, 433; Alanson M. Randol, *Last Days of the Rebellion . . . April 8 and 9, 1865* (Alcatraz Island, Calif., 1886), 4–6; Davies, *General Sheridan,* 246–47; Forsyth, *Thrilling Days in Army Life,* 180–81; Walter H. Jackson diary, Apr. 8, 1865.
63. Randol, *Last Days of the Rebellion,* 6–7; *OR,* I, 46, pt. 1: 1109; pt. 3: 652; Sheridan, *Personal Memoirs,* 2: 190–91; Starr, *Union Cavalry in the Civil War,* 2: 480–81; Longacre, *Army of Amateurs,* 306–07.
64. *OR,* I, 46, pt. 1: 1109; Sheridan, *Personal Memoirs,* 2: 191–93; William Wells to his sister, Apr. 20, 1865, Wells MSS; Randol, *Last Days of the Rebellion,* 8; H. C. Hall, "Some Recollections of Appomattox," *MB* 1 (1894): 136.

65. Sheridan, *Personal Memoirs,* 2: 192–93; Wesley Merritt, "The Appomattox Campaign," *War Papers and Personal Reminiscences, 1861-1865:
Missouri MOLLUS* 1 (1892): 124–25.
66. *Ibid.,* 125; Crook, *Autobiography,* 140; Cummings, "Six Months in the
Third Cavalry Division," 311; Thomas C. Devin, "Didn't We Fight Splendid," *CWTI* 17 (Dec. 1978): 38; Thomas M. Covert to his wife, Apr. 12,
1865, Covert MSS, in possession of Mr. William G. Burnett, Rocky River,
Ohio; Charles H. Veil memoirs, 100.
67. *OR,* I, 46, pt. 1: 1110; James Bradley diary, Apr. 9, 1865; William Wells
to his sister, Apr. 11, 20, 1865, Wells MSS; Hall, "Some Recollections of
Appomattox," 140.

BIBLIOGRAPHY

MANUSCRIPTS
General Officers of Cavalry, Army of the Potomac
Averell, William W. Correspondence, Diaries, 1861–63, and Memoirs. New York State Library, Albany.
Bayard, George D. Correspondence. United States Military Academy Library, West Point, N.Y.
Chapman, George H. Correspondence. Elmer E. Rasmuson Library, University of Alaska, Fairbanks.
_____. Diaries, 1862–63. Indiana Historical Society, Indianapolis.
Cooke, Philip St. George. Correspondence. Virginia Historical Society, Richmond.
Copeland, Joseph T. Letter of July 9, 1863. Historical Society of Pennsylvania, Philadelphia.
Crook, George. Correspondence. Rutherford B. Hayes Presidential Center, Fremont, Ohio.
_____. Correspondence. U.S. Army Military History Institute, Carlisle Barracks, Pa.
Custer, George Armstrong. Correspondence. Monroe County Historical Museum, Monroe, Mich.
_____. Correspondence. New York Public Library, New York, N.Y.
_____. Correspondence. Rochester Public Library, Rochester, N.Y.
_____. Correspondence. United States Military Academy Library.
Devin, Thomas C. Correspondence. In possession of Miss M. Catherine Devin, Midland Park, N.J.
Duffié, Alfred N. Correspondence. Historical Society of Pennsylvania.
Gamble, William. Correspondence. Historical Society of Pennsylvania.
_____. Letter of March 10, 1864. Chicago Historical Society, Chicago, Ill.
Gibbs, Alfred. Correspondence. Elmer E. Rasmuson Library, University of Alaska.
_____. Correspondence. Historical Society of Pennsylvania.

403

Gregg, David McMurtrie. Correspondence. Historical Society of Berks County, Reading, Pa.
_____. Correspondence. Library of Congress, Washington, D.C.
_____. Letter of March 8, 1864. Historical Society of Pennsylvania.
Gregg, J. Irvin. Correspondence. Historical Society of Pennsylvania.
McIntosh, John B. Correspondence. John Hay Library, Brown University, Providence, R.I.
Merritt, Wesley. Correspondence. New York Public Library.
Pleasonton, Alfred. Correspondence. Chicago Historical Society.
_____. Correspondence. Historical Society of Pennsylvania.
_____. Correspondence. Library of Congress.
_____. Correspondence. New-York Historical Society, New York. N.Y.
_____. Correspondence. New York Public Library.
_____. Correspondence. Schmucker Library, Gettysburg College, Gettysburg, Pa.
_____. Letter of May 30, 1863. United States Military Academy Library.
Sheridan, Philip H. Correspondence. Henry E. Huntington Library, San Marino, Calif.
_____. Correspondence. Historical Society of Pennsylvania.
_____. Correspondence. Library of Congress.
_____. Correspondence. United States Military Academy Library.
Stoneman, George. Correspondence. Historical Society of Pennsylvania.
Torbert, Alfred T. A. Correspondence. Elmer E. Rasmuson Library, University of Alaska.
Wells, William. Correspondence. Guy W. Bailey Library, University of Vermont, Burlington.
Wilson, James H. Correspondence. Henry E. Huntington Library.
_____. Correspondence. Library of Congress.
_____. Diaries, 1864–65. Delaware State Historical Society, Wilmington.

Regimental and Staff Personnel, Cavalry and Horse Artillery Units, Army of the Potomac

Abraham, James (1st West Virginia). Correspondence. U.S. Army Military History Institute.
Adams, Charles F., Jr. (1st Massachusetts). Correspondence. Library of Congress.
_____. Diary, 1863. Massachusetts Historical Society, Boston.
Ainsworth, Jared L. (1st New York Dragoons). Correspondence. U.S. Army Military History Institute.
Alexander, Ashley H. (12th Illinois). Correspondence. Illinois State Historical Library, Springfield.
Alger, Russell A. (5th Michigan). Correspondence. Bentley Historical Library, University of Michigan, Ann Arbor.
_____. Letter of September 18, 1865. Historical Society of Pennsylvania.
Allen, R. Alfred (22nd New York). Diaries, 1864–65. William R. Perkins Library, Duke University.

Allen, Winthrop S. G. (12th Illinois). Correspondence. Illinois State Historical Library.

Anderson, John (2nd Pennsylvania). Correspondence. Pennsylvania State Archives, Harrisburg.

Arnold, Delevan (1st Michigan). Correspondence. Kalamazoo Public Museum, Kalamazoo, Mich.

Arnold, William S. (1st Michigan). Correspondence. Michigan State University Library, East Lansing.

Ashley, David C. (6th New York). Correspondence. U.S. Army Military History Institute.

Ashley, William (6th New York). Letter of January 21, 1865. U.S. Army Military History Institute.

Atwater, Dorence (2nd New York). Memoirs. Smith College Archives, Northampton, Mass.

Ayer, Osborn (2nd Massachusetts). Correspondence. Nebraska State Historical Society, Lincoln.

Ayres, Chauncey L. (9th New York). Correspondence. Alexander Library, Rutgers University, New Brunswick, N. J.

Bachman, Aaron E. (1st Pennsylvania). Memoirs. U.S. Army Military History Institute.

Baird, William (6th Michigan). Letter of July 4, 1863. U.S. Army Military History Institute.

————. Memoirs. Bentley Historical Library, University of Michigan.

Baker, Allen (1st Rhode Island). Diaries, 1861–65. U.S. Army Military History Institute.

Baker, William B. (1st Maine). Correspondence and Diary, 1864. Wilson Library, University of North Carolina, Chapel Hill.

Ball, Norman (16th Pennsylvania). Diaries, 1863–64. Connecticut Historical Society, Hartford.

Ball, William (5th Michigan). Correspondence. Waldo Library, Western Michigan University, Kalamazoo.

Band, William (3rd Pennsylvania). Correspondence. U.S. Army Military History Institute.

Barbour, George W. (6th Michigan). Diary, 1863. Bentley Historical Library, University of Michigan.

Barnitz, Albert (2nd Ohio). Correspondence. Western Reserve Historical Society, Cleveland, Ohio.

Barrow, Atwell J. (1st Michigan). Correspondence. U.S. Army Military History Institute.

Bartlett, Chauncey L. (6th Ohio). Correspondence. U.S. Army Military History Institute.

Bartlett, Henry T. (1st Massachusetts). Letter of February 9, 1863. U.S. Army Military History Institute.

Bartley, Reuben (Staff Officer). Memoir of the Kilpatrick-Dahlgren Raid. Library of Congress.

Bates, Charles E. (4th United States). Correspondence. Virginia Historical Society.

Beaumont, Eugene B. (Staff Officer). Diaries, 1863–65, and Papers. United States Military Academy Library.

Beck, Elias W. (3rd Indiana). Correspondence. Indiana State Library, Indianapolis.

Bell, James A. (8th Illinois). Correspondence. Henry E. Huntington Library.

Bellamy, Flavius J. (3rd Indiana). Correspondence and Diary, 1863. Indiana State Library.

Benner, Wilson P. (2nd Pennsylvania). Correspondence. U.S. Army Military History Institute.

Bevan, Allen L. (1st Pennsylvania). Correspondence. U.S. Army Military History Institute.

Bevan, Henry C. (2nd Pennsylvania). Correspondence. U.S. Army Military History Institute.

Bigelow, Eustace (1st Maine). Correspondence. U.S. Army Military History Institute.

Blake, George A. H. (1st United States). Correspondence. In possession of Col. Walter Blake, U.S.A. (Ret.), Philadelphia, Pa.

Blinn, Charles (1st Vermont). Diary, 1863. Gettysburg National Military Park Library, Gettysburg, Pa.

Bliss, George N. (1st Rhode Island). Correspondence. Rhode Island Historical Society, Providence.

Bloss, Josiah (17th Pennsylvania). Correspondence and Diary, 1863. Pennsylvania State Archives.

Boardman, Henry (1st Connecticut). Correspondence. Connecticut State Library, Hartford.

Bodnmer, John A. (24th New York). Correspondence. New York State Library.

Boyer, Peter (17th Pennsylvania). Correspondence. U.S. Army Military History Institute.

Boyce, Robert (1st Pennsylvania). Diary, 1864. Soldiers and Sailors Memorial Hall, Pittsburgh, Pa.

Brackett, Aloin N. (1st Maine). Correspondence. U.S. Army Military History Institute.

Bradley, James (1st Connecticut). Diary, 1865. Connecticut Historical Society.

Brodhead, Thornton F. (1st Michigan). Correspondence. Detroit Public Library, Detroit, Mich.

Brodrick, Virgil (1st New Jersey). Correspondence. In possession of Mr. Blair Graybill, Portland, Ore.

Bromley, John (1st Michigan). Correspondence. Detroit Public Library.

Brooke, William Rawle (3rd Pennsylvania). Correspondence. Historical Society of Pennsylvania [known as Rawle Papers].

_____. Correspondence and Diaries, 1863-65. War Library, National Commandery, Military Order of the Loyal Legion of the United States, Philadelphia, Pa.

Brooks, Enoch (3rd New Jersey). Correspondence. Alexander Library, Rutgers University.

Brown, Charles (9th New York). Correspondence. New York State Library.

Brown, Frank M. (5th Michigan). Correspondence. Bentley Historical Library, University of Michigan.

Brown, Morris (13th Ohio). Correspondence. U.S. Army Military History Institute.

Bryant, John (1st Connecticut). Letter of July 28, 1864. Connecticut State Library.

Buck, Andrew N. (7th Michigan). Correspondence. Bentley Historical Library, University of Michigan.

Bull, Carpenter (8th Illinois). Letter of March 3, 1864. Illinois State Historical Library.

Burrows, James B. (9th New York). Correspondence. U.S. Army Military History Institute.

Cadwalader, Charles E. (6th Pennsylvania). Correspondence. Historical Society of Pennsylvania.

Camp, Charles W. (1st New Jersey). Letter of December 6, 1862. Historical Society of Princeton, Princeton, N.J.

Carpenter, Edward A. (Staff Officer). Correspondence. New York Public Library.

Carpenter, Emlen N. (6th Pennsylvania). Correspondence. U.S. Army Military History Institute.

Carpenter, Louis H. (6th United States). Correspondence. Historical Society of Pennsylvania.

Carr, Henry C. (8th New York). Diaries, 1864–65. U.S. Army Military History Institute.

Cesnola, Luigi P. di (4th New York). Correspondence. Historical Society of Pennsylvania.

_____. Letter of March 10, 1863. U.S. Army Military History Institute.

Chapin, Charles B. (1st Vermont). Correspondence and Diary, 1864. U.S. Army Military History Institute.

Chapman, Gilbert W. (5th Michigan). Correspondence. Detroit Public Library.

Charles, Henry F. (21st Pennsylvania). Correspondence and Memoirs. U.S. Army Military History Institute.

Cheney, Jasper (8th New York). Diaries, 1863–64. U.S. Army Military History Institute.

Clapp, Albert A. (2nd Ohio). Diary, 1864. U.S. Army Military History Institute.

Clark, Benjamin J. (1st Michigan). Correspondence. Clarke Historical Library, Central Michigan University, Mount Pleasant.

Clark, John A. (7th Michigan). Letter of July 30, 1863. Bentley Historical Library, University of Michigan.

Clark, John E. (5th Michigan). Correspondence. Nebraska State Historical Society.

Clark, Moses P. (6th New York Battery). Letter of June 21, 1863. In possession of Mr. Allan Melia, Rahway, N.J.

Clark, Steven R. (13th Ohio). Correspondence. U.S. Army Military History Institute.

Coller, Charles H. (6th Pennsylvania). Diary, 1864. U.S. Army Military History Institute.

Comte, Victor E. (5th Michigan). Letter of July 7, 1863. Bentley Historical Library, University of Michigan.

Cornelius, Edward (1st Michigan). Correspondence. Bentley Historical Library, University of Michigan.

_____. Correspondence. U.S. Army Military History Institute.

Courson, Hamilton (5th Michigan). Letter of March 9, 1863. Clarke Historical Library, Central Michigan University.

Covert, Henry H. (1st New Jersey). Letter of April 13, 1864. Alexander Library, Rutgers University.

Covert, Thomas M. (6th Ohio). Correspondence. In possession of Mr. William G. Burnett, Rocky River, Ohio.

Coxe, Charles B. (6th Pennsylvania). Correspondence. Historical Society of Pennsylvania.

Crawford, J. Milton (21st Pennsylvania). Letter of May 18, 1865. U.S. Army Military History Institute.

Crowninshield, Benjamin W. (1st Massachusetts). Correspondence and Diary, 1863. Essex Institute, Salem, Mass.

Crowninshield, Caspar (1st Massachusetts). Correspondence. Massachusetts Historical Society.

Cummings, Robert (8th Pennsylvania). Correspondence. Alexander Library, Rutgers University.

Dahlgren, Ulric (Staff Officer). Diary, 1863. Library of Congress.

Dains, Arnold P. (5th New York). Correspondence. U.S. Army Military History Institute.

Daniels, Jabez J. (9th Michigan Battery). Correspondence. Hudson Museum, Hudson, Mich.

Darling, Charles B. (1st New York Dragoons). Correspondence. Robert W. Woodruff Library, Emory University, Atlanta, Ga.

Davis, Luke (16th Pennsylvania). Diary, 1864. Fred Lewis Pattee Library, Pennsylvania State University, University Park.

Davis, Thomas M. (8th Pennsylvania). Letter of December 4, 1861. U.S. Army Military History Institute.

Dennis, George E. (1st Michigan). Correspondence. Bentley Historical Library, University of Michigan.

Dickerson, Frank W. (5th United States). Correspondence. U.S. Army Military History Institute.

Doherty, William (5th Michigan). Letter of April 10, 1865. Clarke Historical Library, Central Michigan University.

Dollar, John (8th Pennsylvania). Diaries, 1862-64. U.S. Army Military History Institute.

Donlon, Michael (2nd United States). Correspondence. U.S. Army Military History Institute.

Dougherty, Michael (13th Pennsylvania). Diaries, 1863–64. U.S. Army Military History Institute.

Dunkleberger, Isaac R. (1st United States). Memoirs. U.S. Army Military History Institute.

Elder, Samuel S. (1st United States Artillery). Correspondence. New York Public Library.

Elliott, William R. (1st Michigan). Correspondence. Detroit Public Library.

Emery, B. L. (1st Pennsylvania). Letter of January 18, 1862. U.S. Army Military History Institute.

Emmons, William H. (1st New York Dragoons). Correspondence. U.S. Army Military History Institute.

Esher, Jacob T. (8th Illinois). Correspondence. Chicago Historical Society.

Estes, L. G. (Staff Officer). Correspondence. New York Public Library.

Farnill, John S. (6th Michigan). Correspondence. Bentley Historical Library, University of Michigan.

Farr, Charles R. (1st Vermont). Diary, 1864. United States Army Military History Institute.

Faxon, John H. (1st Michigan). Diary, 1863. Bentley Historical Libarry, University of Michigan.

Fay, John C. (1st New Jersey). Correspondence. U.S. Army Military History Institute.

Fell, Albinus (6th Ohio). Correspondence. U.S. Army Military History Institute.

Fenton, Alcinus W. (6th Ohio). Correspondence. Western Reserve Historical Society.

Ferris, Weston (1st Connecticut). Memoirs. U.S. Army Military History Institute.

Fiala, Anthony (1st New York). Memoirs. U.S. Army Military History Institute.

Field, Frederick N. (1st Michigan). Correspondence. Bentley Historical Library, University of Michigan.

Fisher, Albert H. (7th Michigan). Correspondence. Waldo Library, Western Michigan University.

Fisher, Byron (7th Michigan). Correspondence. Waldo Library, Western Michigan University.

Fitton, Walter H. (5th Pennsylvania). Correspondence. U.S. Army Military History Institute.

Flack, George W. (8th Pennsylvania). Diaries, 1861–64. Alexander Library, Rutgers University.

Follmer, John D. (16th Pennsylvania). Diaries, 1862–65. University of Michigan Library.

Ford, Thomas J. (6th Michigan). Letter of January 4, 1865. Waldo Library, Western Michigan University.

Frank, Abner B. (12th Illinois). Correspondence. U.S. Army Military History Institute.

Franklin, William (5th Michigan). Letter of January 18, 1865. Bentley Historical Library, University of Michigan.

Frost, Henry C. (8th New York). Letter of May 8, 1863. U.S. Army Military History Institute.

Galloway, Joseph D. (3rd Pennsylvania). Diaries, 1861–64. New York Public Library.

Gantz, Frederick (6th United States). Correspondence. U.S. Army Military History Institute.

Gardner, Charles (1st Maine). Memoirs. U.S. Army Military History Institute.

Gardner, Elijah N. (1st Maryland). Letter of October 29, 1862. U.S. Army Military History Institute.

Gay, Calvin (15th New York). Correspondence. U.S. Army Military History Institute.

Gay, James (15th New York). Correspondence. U.S. Army Military History Institute.

Geisel, Christian (6th Pennsylvania). Correspondence. Pennsylvania State Archives.

Gillet, Joseph H. (1st Michigan). Correspondence. Waldo Library, Western Michigan University.

Gittleman, John (17th Pennsylvania). Diaries, 1863–64. Gilder Lehrman Collection, New York, N.Y.

Glass, Samuel P. (21st Pennsylvania). Correspondence. Pennsylvania State Archives.

Gould, Ebenezer (5th Michigan). Correspondence. Clarke Historical Library, Central Michigan University.

Gray, Charles C. (2nd United States). Memoirs. Wilson Library, University of North Carolina.

Green, Augustus P. (5th New York). Correspondence and Memoirs. New- York Historical Society.

Greenleaf, Charles H. (5th New York). Correspondence. Connecticut Historical Society.

Greenwood, Horace (8th Illinois). Letter of January 21, 1862. Chicago Historical Society.

Grommon, Franklin P. (6th Michigan). Diaries, 1864–65. Bentley Historical Library, University of Michigan.

Gross, Frank (6th Michigan). Diaries, 1864–65. Bentley Historical Library, University of Michigan.

Guild, Emmons D. (1st Rhode Island). Correspondence. John Hay Library, Brown University.

Gustin, John C. (13th Ohio). Correspondence. U.S. Army Military History Institute.

Hagar, George E. (1st Massachusetts). Correspondence. U.S. Army Military History Institute.

Hall, Rowland M. (3rd New York). Correspondence. North Carolina State Department of Archives and History, Raleigh.

Hall, Wilmer C. (1st Pennsylvania). Correspondence. Pennsylvania State
    Archives.
Hamilton, James (4th Pennsylvania). Correspondence. U.S. Army Military
    History Institute.
Hamlin, John H. (7th Michigan). Correspondence. Clarke Historical Library,
    Central Michigan University.
Hanna, Stewart (18th Pennsylvania). Letter of March 21, 1865. U.S. Army
    Military History Institute.
Hannaford, Roger (2nd Ohio). Diaries, 1864–65, and Memoirs. Cincinnati
    Historical Society, Cincinnati, Ohio.
Harrington, George L. (6th Michigan). Diary, 1863. Waldo Library, Western
    Michigan University.
Harvey, Edward H. (7th Michigan). Correspondence. Waldo Library, Western
    Michigan University.
Hathaway, Thomas (6th New York). Correspondence. Waldo Library, Western
    Michigan University.
Havens, Edwin R. (7th Michigan). Correspondence and Diary, 1864. Michigan
    State University Library.
Hazeltine, Asa (1st Maine). Correspondence. U.S. Army Military History
    Institute.
Hazeltine, John B. (1st Maine). Correspondence. U.S. Army Military History
    Institute.
Hickey, Myron (5th Michigan). Correspondence. Library of Congress.
Higginson, James J. (1st Massachusetts). Correspondence. Massachusetts His-
    torical Society.
Hill, Thomas W. (6th Michigan). Diary, 1864. Waldo Library, Western Michi-
    gan University.
Hiller, John (9th New York). Correspondence. In possession of Mr. Peter
    Brown, Lake View, N.Y.
Hills, William G. (9th New York). Diary, 1864. Library of Congress.
Hinman, Daniel B. (5th Pennsylvania). Letter of April 3, 1862. U.S. Army
    Military History Institute.
Hinman, S. N. (1st Connecticut). Correspondence. Virginia Historical Society.
Hitchcock, W. H. (Staff Officer). Correspondence. New York Public Library.
Hoffman, Clement (6th Pennsylvania). Correspondence. U.S. Army Military
    History Institute.
Hoffman, John E. (3rd West Virginia). Diary, 1863. West Virginia University
    Library, Morgantown.
Holman, Freeland N. (1st Maine). Correspondence. U.S. Army Military His-
    tory Institute.
Holmes, Augustus B. (6th Michigan). Correspondence. Michigan Department
    of State, Lansing.
Howard, David W. (18th Pennsylvania). Correspondence and Diary, 1864.
    Pennsylvania State Archives.
Howe, William O. (1st Maine). Correspondence. Maine State Archives, Augusta.

Huey, Pennock (8th Pennsylvania). Correspondence. New York Public Library.

Huff, Lewis (12th Illinois). Letter of March 28, 1863. U.S. Army Military History Institute.

Hunt, Henry (1st Rhode Island). Letter of April 24, 1864. U.S. Army Military History Institute.

Hutchins, Benjamin T. (1st New Hampshire). Letter of December 31, 1861. In possession of Mrs. Tillie Clement, Haddonfield, N.J.

Jackson, Walter H. (1st New York Dragoons). Diaries, 1864–65. Bentley Historical Library, University of Michigan.

Jessup, Joseph (5th Michigan). Correspondence. Bentley Historical Library, University of Michigan.

Jewett, Pliny A. (1st Connecticut). Correspondence. Virginia Historical Society.

Johnson, Ebenezer S. (1st Maine). Correspondence. U.S. Army Military History Institute.

Johnson, Elbridge S. (1st Maine). Correspondence. U.S. Army Military History Institute.

Johnson, William L. (1st Maine). Correspondence. U.S. Army Military History Institute.

Jones, Owen (1st Pennsylvania). Correspondence. Historical Society of Pennsylvania.

Joy, Henry S. (3rd New York). Correspondence. U.S. Army Military History Institute.

Kay, John B. (6th Michigan). Diaries, 1863–64. Bentley Historical Library, University of Michigan.

Keller, William S. (4th Pennsylvania). Correspondence. U.S. Army Military History Institute.

Kepner, John P. (6th Pennsylvania). Correspondence and Diary, 1864. Virginia Historical Society.

Kerr, William (8th Pennsylvania). Correspondence. Alexander Library, Rutgers University.

Kidd, James H. (6th Michigan). Correspondence. Bentley Historical Library, University of Michigan.

Kilborn, George H. (1st Michigan). Correspondence. Bentley Historical Library, University of Michigan.

King, Matthew W. (6th Ohio). Correspondence. U.S. Army Military History Institute.

Kirbey, Joseph A. (2nd United States). Letter of December 26, 1862. U.S. Army Military History Institute.

Kitchen, Marcus L. W. (1st New Jersey). Correspondence. New Jersey Historical Society, Newark.

Lacey, George (15th New York). Correspondence. U.S. Army Military History Institute.

Lamb, G. W. (3rd Indiana). Correspondence. Indiana State Library.

Lamb, S. F. (3rd Indiana). Letter of March 11, 1862. U.S. Army Military History Institute.

Lambert, W. H. (1st New Jersey). Letter of June 8, 1865. New Jersey Historical Society.

Layton, Joseph E. (1st New Jersey). Correspondence and Memoirs. In possession of Mr. Jesse R. Phillips and Mrs. Sonya Hulbert, Branchville, N.J.

Leach, Morgan L. (1st Michigan). Correspondence. Bentley Historical Library, University of Michigan.

Legg, Charles A. (1st Massachusetts). Correspondence. U.S. Army Military History Institute.

_____. Correspondence. William R. Perkins Library, Duke University, Durham, N.C.

Legg, William H. (1st Massachusetts). Correspondence. William R. Perkins Library, Duke University.

Leggett, Percival S. (5th Michigan). Correspondence. Detroit Public Library.

Leslie, Joseph (18th Pennsylvania). Diaries, 1863–64. Gilder Lehrman Collection.

Lester, Jacob (1st New York). Correspondence. U.S. Army Military History Institute.

Lindsley, Morgan W. (1st New York Dragoons). Correspondence. U.S. Army Military History Institute.

Litzenberg, William (1st Pennsylvania). Letter of March 19, 1864. U.S. Army Military History Institute.

Lloyd, William P. (1st Pennsylvania). Diaries, 1861–64. Wilson Library, University of North Carolina.

_____. Letter of November 30, 1861. Pennsylvania State Archives.

Logan, William P. (4th Pennsylvania). Correspondence. U.S. Army Military History Institute.

Lorish, Andrew J. (1st New York Dragoons). Correspondence. U.S. Army Military History Institute.

Loveland, C. F. (6th Ohio). History of the Sixth Ohio Cavalry. Ohio State Library, Columbus.

Lyle, Henry (11th Pennsylvania). Correspondence. U.S. Army Military History Institute.

Lyman, Carlos P. (6th Ohio). Correspondence and Diaries, 1862–64. Western Reserve Historical Society.

McClellan, James C. (1st New Jersey). Correspondence. In possession of Mr. William J. Monaghan, Edison, N.J.

McClure, W. S. (3rd Indiana). Correspondence. Indiana State Library.

McConnell, James J. (3rd Indiana). Correspondence. Virginia Historical Society.

McCord, Dorastus (6th Pennsylvania). Correspondence. U.S. Army Military History Institute.

McCord, George (8th Pennsylvania). Correspondence. U.S. Army Military History Institute.

McHue, James (15th New York). Correspondence. New York State Library.

McIlhenny, William A. (1st Maryland). Diary, 1864. Adams County Historical Society, Gettysburg, Pa.

McIlwraith, Stewart W. (2nd Pennsylvania). Letter of March 24, 1865. U.S. Army Military History Institute.

McLaughlin, Edward (8th Pennsylvania). Diaries, 1861–64, and Memoirs. Historical Society of Pennsylvania.

_____. Letter of December 23, 1861. Clarke Historical Library, Central Michigan University.

McVicar, Duncan (6th New York). Letter of January 4, 1863. Historical Society of Pennsylvania.

Macomber, Dexter M. (1st Michigan). Diaries, 1861–64, and Memoirs. Clarke Historical Library, Central Michigan University.

_____. Letter of December 19, 1862. U.S. Army Military History Institute.

Maley, Thomas E. (5th United States). Correspondence. U.S. Army Military History Institute.

Mallory, William H. (2nd New York). Correspondence. Connecticut Historical Society.

Martin, Arthur (3rd Pennsylvania). Correspondence. U.S. Army Military History Institute.

Martin, Joseph P. (6th New York Battery). Letter of October 26, 1863. In possession of Mr. Allan Melia.

Martin, William H. (18th Pennsylvania). Correspondence. U.S. Army Military History Institute.

Mason, Silas (5th New York). Correspondence. New York State Library.

Mathews, Amasa E. (1st Michigan). Letter of September 16, 1862. Bentley Historical Library, University of Michigan.

Mattoon, Gershom W. (6th Michigan). Correspondence. Michigan State University Library.

Maynard, Darius G. (1st Michigan). Correspondence. Ablah Library, Wichita State University, Wichita, Kan.

Medill, William H. (8th Illinois). Correspondence. Library of Congress.

Messeimer, A. M. (8th Pennsylvania). Letter of May 21, 1862. U.S. Army Military History Institute.

Miller, Charles B. (1st Pennsylvania). Correspondence. U.S. Army Military History Institute.

Miller, George H. (1st Rhode Island). Diary, 1864. U.S. Army Military History Institute.

Miller, Harrison (6th New York Battery). Correspondence. In possession of Mr. Allan Melia.

Miller, J. Wright (16th Pennsylvania). Letter of February 18, 1865. U.S. Army Military History Institute.

Miller, M. Murray (1st Pennsyania). Correspondence. Gilder Lehrman Collection.

Milligan, Robert (6th Pennsylvania). Correspondence. State Historical Society of Wisconsin, Madison.

Minter, Joseph (2nd United States). Correspondence. U.S. Army Military History Institute.

Mitchell, David (2nd Massachusets). Memoirs. In possession of Mr. Walter S. Harper, Daytona Beach, Fla.

Monaghan, John W. (7th Michigan). Correspondence and Diaries, 1864–65. Bentley Historical Library, University of Michigan.

Morey, John R. (5th Michigan). Correspondence and Diaries, 1863–64. Bentley Historical Library, University of Michigan.

Morey, William C. (1st New York Dragoons). History of the First New York Dragoons. William R. Perkins Library, Duke University.

Morgan, David H. (6th Pennsylvania). Correspondence. War Library, National Commandery, Military Order of the Loyal Legion of the United States.

Morrow, Isaac (20th Pennsylvania). Correspondence. U.S. Army Military History Institute.

Morrow, Joseph H. (20th Pennsylvania). Correspondence. U.S. Army Military History Institute.

Morton, F. Knox (8th Pennsylvania). Correspondence. William R. Perkins Library, Duke University.

Mulligan, James W. (15th New York). Correspondence. U.S. Army Military History Institute.

Munroe, Charles M. (6th New York). Diaries, 1862–64. American Antiquarian Society, Worcester, Mass.

Musson, George (2nd Ohio). Memoirs. Indiana Historical Society.

Neher, Philip (2nd New York). Correspondence. Albany Institute of History and Art, Albany, N.Y.

Nesbitt, James (2nd Ohio). Correspondence. U.S. Army Military History Institute.

Newburger, Alexander (4th New York). Diary, 1864. Library of Congress.

Newhall, Walter S. (3rd Pennsylvania). Correspondence and Diary, 1863. Historical Society of Pennsylvania.

O'Brien, William H. (7th Michigan). Correspondence and Diary, 1864. Bentley Historical Library, University of Michigan.

Overy, Charles (7th Michigan). Correspondence. William R. Perkins Library, Duke University.

Parmelee, Henry S. (1st Connecticut). Correspondence and Diary, 1864. Sterling Library, Yale University, New Haven, Conn.

Parsons, H. C. (1st Vermont). Memoir of Farnsworth's Charge at Gettysburg. Library of Congress.

Paulding, Tattnall (6th United States). Diary, 1863. U.S. Army Military History Institute.

Payne, Edwin B. (4th New York). Correspondence. U.S. Army Military History Institute.

Pearsons, Kimball (10th New York). Letter of June 19, 1863. U.S. Army Military History Institute.

Pendergast, Lloyd G. (1st United States). Correspondence. Minnesota Historical Society, Saint Paul.

Phelps, Edward D. (1st Rhode Island). Correspondence. Virginia Historical Society.

Phillips, William W. L. (1st New Jersey). Letter of May 16, 1862. Firestone Library, Princeton University, Princeton, N.J.

Pierce, Charles L. (9th New York). Correspondence. U.S. Army Military History Institute.

Pistorius, Frederick (1st Michigan). Correspondence. Bentley Historical Library, University of Michigan.

Potter, Henry C. (18th Pennsylvania). Memoirs. Gettysburg National Military Park Library.

Powers, Daniel H. (6th Michigan). Correspondence and Diary, 1864. In possession of Mrs. Alva B. Van Dyke, Nappanee, Ind.

Pownall, Henry M. (18th Pennsylvania). Correspondence. U.S. Army Military History Institute.

Prentice, Reuben T. (8th Illinois). Correspondence. Illinois State Historical Library.

Prentiss, George H. (7th Michigan). Letter of February 26, 1865. U.S. Army Military History Institute.

Preston, Noble D. (10th New York). Memoirs. New York Public Library.

Price, William R. (1st Massachusetts). Correspondence. U.S. Army Military History Institute.

Prime, John (6th New York). Correspondence. U.S. Army Military History Institute.

Pringle, John D. (18th Pennsylvania). Letter of May 8, 1865. U.S. Army Military History Institute.

Provost, John H. (2nd New York). Correspondence. U.S. Army Military History Institute.

Pulis, Daniel W. (8th New York). Correspondence. Rochester Public Library.

Putnam, Thomas C. (15th New York). Correspondence. U.S. Army Military History Institute.

Quincy, John (6th Pennsylvania). Correspondence. U.S. Army Military History Institute.

Ralph, Oscar S. (7th Michigan). Letter of January 7, 1863. Bentley Historical Library, University of Michigan.

Ramsey, William (1st Pennsylvania). Correspondence. U.S. Army Military History Institute.

Rand, Arnold A. (1st Massachusetts). Correspondence. U.S. Army Military History Institute.

Rappalyea, Lewis C. (1st New Jersey). Diaries, 1864–65. New Jersey Historical Society.

Redman, William H. (12th Illinois). Correspondence. Alderman Library, University of Virginia, Charlottesville.

Ressler, Isaac H. (16th Pennsylvania). Diaries, 1862–65. U.S. Army Military History Institute.

Reynolds, Charles (2nd New York). Correspondence. New York State Library.

Rice, Marcus (2nd New York). Correspondence. U.S. Army Military History Institute.

Richwine, David (1st United States). Correspondence. U.S. Army Military History Institute.

Rix, Hiram, Jr. (6th Michigan). Diary, 1865. Clarke Historical Library, Central Michigan University.

Robeson, William P. (3rd New Jersey). Correspondence. Firestone Library, Princeton University.

Robinson, J. G. (4th Pennsylvania). Diaries, 1863–64. U.S. Army Military History Institute.

Robinson, James C. (16th Pennsylvania). Correspondence. U.S. Army Military History Institute.

Rockwell, William H. (5th Michigan). Correspondence. Waldo Library, Western Michigan University.

Roebling, W. A. (6th New York Artillery.) Correspondence. New York State Library.

Rowe, James D. (1st Michigan). Memoirs. Bentley Historical Library, University of Michigan.

Ryder, Alfred G. (1st Michigan). Correspondence and Diaries, 1861–62. Bentley Historical Library, University of Michigan.

Sage, Theodore (6th Pennsylvania). Correspondence. U.S. Army Military History Institute.

Sanders, William (2nd West Virginia). Correspondence. U.S. Army Military History Institute.

Sargent, G. Alfred (1st Rhode Island). Correspondence. Eugene C. Barker Library, University of Texas, Austin.

Sargent, Horace B. (1st Massachusetts). Correspondence. Massachusetts Historical Society.

Sawyer, Henry W. (1st New Jersey). Correspondence. In possession of Mr. Clark T. Donlin, Cape May Court House, N.J.

_____. Letter of October 12, 1863. Cape May County Historical and Genealogical Society, Cape May Court House, N.J.

Scherich, Isaac W. (18th Pennsylvania). Memoirs. Washington County Free Library, Boonsboro, Md.

Schmalzried, Frederic (1st Michigan). Correspondence. Bentley Historical Library, University of Michigan.

Searles, Alvey P. (8th Illinois). Correspondence. U.S. Army Military History Institute.

Secrist, Robert B. (1st United States). Correspondence. Virginia Polytechnic Institute and State University Library, Blacksburg.

Sexton, Hiram (2nd New York). Letter of January 30, 1865. U.S. Army Military History Institute.

Shatzel, Albert H. (1st Vermont). Diary, 1864. Nebraska State Historical Society.

Sheahan, John P. (1st Maine). Correspondence. Maine Historical Society, Portland.

Shelmire, John H. (1st New Jersey). Letter of April 8, 1863. Chicago Historical Society.

Shubert, Joseph (1st New Jersey). Memoirs. U.S. Army Military History Institute.

Simmons, Canning (2nd Pennsylvania). Letter of May 18, 1862. U.S. Army Military History Institute.

Simonds, George W. (6th Michigan). Letter of August 1, 1865. Bentley Historical Library, University of Michigan.

Skinner, Rhoads (1st New York Dragoons). Diary, 1862. Alexander Library, Rutgers University.

Smith, Charles M. (1st Massachusetts). Correspondence. U.S. Army Military History Institute.

Smith, Elzar H. (1st Maine). Correspondence. U.S. Army Military History Institute.

Smith, Howard M. (1st New York Dragoons). Correspondence. Library of Congress.

Smith, John (16th Pennsylvania). Correspondence. U.S. Army Military History Institute.

Smith, Thomas W. (6th Pennsylvania). Correspondence. Historical Society of Pennsylvania.

Smith, William (6th Ohio). Correspondence. U.S. Army Military History Institute.

Sparks, Henry B. (3rd Indiana). Diary, 1864. Indiana State Library.

Sperry, J. L. (1st Connecticut). Correspondence. William R. Perkins Library, Duke University.

Starr, Samuel H. (6th United States). Papers. Missouri Historical Society, Saint Louis.

St. Clair, Hugh (18th Pennsylvania). Diary, 1863. Soldiers and Sailors Memorial Hall.

Stevens, Atherton H. (1st Massachusetts). Correspondence. Massachusetts Historical Society.

Steward, John (8th New York). Correspondence. Gilder Lehrman Collection.

Stewart, Daniel (6th Michigan). Correspondence. Waldo Library, Western Michigan University.

Stewart, Frederick (6th Michigan). Correspondence. Waldo Library, Western Michigan University.

Stewart, Henry W. (6th Michigan). Correspondence. Waldo Library, Western Michigan University.

Stewart, James (6th Ohio). Correspondence. U.S. Army Military History Institute.

Stone, Addison R. (5th Michigan). Correspondence. Bentley Historical Library, University of Michigan.

Stuart, William V. (5th Michigan). Correspondence. Detroit Public Library.

Taylor, John P. (1st Pennsylvania). Correspondence. Historical Society of Pennsylvania.

Telling, George (6th Michigan). Correspondence. U.S. Army Military History Institute.

Thomas, H. B. (16th Pennsylvania). Correspondence. William R. Perkins Library, Duke University.

Thomas, William H. (16th Pennsylvania). Correspondence. William R. Perkins Library, Duke University.

Thompson, Henry E. (6th Michigan). Letter of September 30, 1863. Bentley Historical Library, University of Michigan.

Thompson, James L. (1st Rhode Island). Correspondence. Elmer E. Rasmuson Library, University of Alaska.

Thompson, Stephen W. (5th Michigan). Diary, 1864. William R. Perkins Library, Duke University.

_____. Diary, 1865. Clarke Historical Library, Central Michigan University.

Thompson, William (Staff Officer). Correspondence. Fred Lewis Pattee Library, Pennsylvania State University

Thomson, Clifford (1st New York). Correspondence. New-York Historical Society.

Tidball, John C. (2nd United States Artillery). Correspondence. United States Military Academy Library.

_____. Memoirs. Library of Congress.

Timmerman, John (3rd New York). Correspondence and Diary, 1861. U.S. Army Military History Institute.

Tompkins, Aaron B. (1st New Jersey). Correspondence. Library of Congress.

Townsend, Daniel (1st United States Artillery). Memoirs. In possession of Mr. Christopher Densmore, Getzville, N.Y.

Townsend, George (5th Michigan). Correspondence. Bentley Historical Library, University of Michigan.

Trego, David R. (6th Michigan). Correspondence. Bentley Historical Library, University of Michigan.

Trowbridge, Luther S. (5th Michigan). Correspondence. Bentley Historical Library, University of Michigan.

True, Frank W. (1st Maine). Correspondence. U.S. Army Military History Institute.

Turner, Henry P. (1st Massachusetts). Correspondence. U.S. Army Military History Institute.

Turner, James B. (4th Pennsylvania). Correspondence. Illinois State Historical Library.

Unidentified Enlisted Man (8th New York). Letter of June 1, 1865. Waldo Library, Western Michigan University.

Unidentified Enlisted Man (5th New York). Correspondence. U.S. Army Military History Institute.

Unidentified Enlisted Man (1st Michigan). Diary, 1862. U.S. Army Military History Institute.

Unidentified Enlisted Man (10th New York). Diary, 1863. U.S. Army Military History Institute.

Unidentified Enlisted Man (3rd Indiana). Correspondence. Indiana State Library.

Unidentified Enlisted Man (3rd Pennsylvania). Correspondence. U.S. Army Military History Institute.

Unidentified Officer (2nd New York). Diaries, 1864–65. New York Public Library.

Unidentified Officer (13th Pennsylvania). Correspondence. U.S. Army Military History Institute.

Van Gieson, Lewis K. (5th Michigan). Correspondence. Bentley Historical Library, University of Michigan.

Veil, Charles H. (1st United States). Correspondence. Schmucker Library, Gettysburg College.

_____. Memoirs. War Library, National Commandery, Military Order of the Loyal Legion of the United States.

Walters, Charles C. (2nd New York). Correspondence. Schmucker Library, Gettysburg College.

Warner, John W. (1st Rhode Island). Correspondence. U.S. Army Military History Institute.

Warren, E. Willard (3rd Pennsylvania). Correspondence. William R. Perkins Library, Duke University.

Warren, John E. (1st Rhode Island). Correspondence. U.S. Army Military History Institute.

Washburn, Warren (8th Illinois). Letter of December 8, 1861. U.S. Army Military History Institute.

Watson, Edward M. (1st Michigan). Correspondence. Bentley Historical Library, University of Michigan.

Weaver, Augustus C. (3rd Indiana). Memoirs. U.S. Army Military History Institute.

Weed, Theodore H. (10th New York). Correspondence. William R. Perkins Library, Duke University.

Wells, E. P. (6th New York). Diary, 1862. Virginia Historical Society.

Wells, Hiram (8th Illinois). Correspondence. Chicago Historical Society.

Wesson, Silas D. (8th Illinois). Diaries, 1861–64. U.S. Army Military History Institute.

West, J. Waldo (1st New York Dragoons). Correspondence. Virginia Polytechnic Institute and State University Library.

Westerman, Thomas (1st Pennsylvania). Correspondence. U.S. Army Military History Institute.

Whelan, Henry C. (6th Pennsylvania). Letter of June 11, 1863. Historical Society of Pennsylvania.

White, A. H. (5th New York). Letter of September 4, 1864. U.S. Army Military History Institute.

White, Frank E. (4th New York). Diary, 1864, and Memoirs. William R. Perkins Library, Duke University.

Whitman, George (2nd Pennsylvania). Correspondence. U.S. Army Military History Institute.

Wilkin, William (1st West Virginia). Correspondence. U.S. Army Military History Institute.

Wilson, P. Benner (2nd Pennsylvania). Letter of December 8, 1862. U.S. Army Military History Institute.

Woolston, Charles (3rd Pennsylvania). Correspondence. Gilder Lehrman Collection.

Wox, Lucius C. (17th Pennsylvania). Correspondence. U.S. Army Military History Institute.

Wright, Francis M. (5th Michigan). Letter of July 4, 1864. Waldo Library, Western Michigan University.

Wright, Marvin (5th New York). Letter of March 29, 1863. U.S. Army Military History Institute.

Yard, W. C. (4th Pennsylvania). Correspondence. William R. Perkins Library, Duke University.

Yoder, Jonah (16th Pennsylvania). Diary, 1863. U.S. Army Military History Institute.

Young, Robert (3rd Indiana). Letter of May 10, 1864. U.S. Army Military History Institute.

Young, Samuel M. B. (4th Pennsylvania). Correspondence. U.S. Army Military History Institute.

Other Sources

Bachelder, John B. Correspondence. New Hampshire Historical Society, Concord.

Duncan, Samuel A. Correspondence. New Hampshire Historical Society.

Fortescue, Louis. Memoirs. War Library, National Commandery, Military Order of the Loyal Legion of the United States.

Grant, Ulysses S. Correspondence. Library of Congress.

Hooker, Joseph. Correspondence. Henry E. Huntington Library.

_____. Correspondence. Schmucker Library, Gettysburg College.

Huntington, J. F. Correspondence. New York Public Library.

Jefferds, Charles L. Letter of July 10, 1863. U.S. Army Military History Institute.

Johnson, Jesse. Diaries, 1861-64. Historical Society of Pennsylvania.

Kautz, August V. Correspondence. Illinois State Historical Library.

_____. Correspondence and Diary, 1864. Library of Congress.

_____. Memoirs. U.S. Army Military History Institute.

Lewis, Herman T. Correspondence. U.S. Army Military History Institute.

McAteer, Simon. Diary, 1864. Historical Society of Pennsylvania.

McClellan, George B. Correspondence. Library of Congress.

Meade, George Gordon. Correspondence. Historical Society of Pennsylvania.
_____. Correspondence. Schmucker Library, Gettysburg College.
Patrick, Marsena R. Diaries, 1861–65. Library of Congress.
Reynolds, John F. Letter of June 30, 1863. National Archives, Washington, D.C.
Smith, Henry C. Correspondence. Virginia Historical Society.
Stuart, George Hay. Papers. Library of Congress.
Tibbits, William B. Correspondence. Elmer E. Rasmuson Library, University of Alaska.
_____. Correspondence. New York State Library.
Waters, Lucien P. Correspondence. New-York Historical Society.
Weirick, Charles. Correspondence. U.S. Army Military History Institute.
Weiser, John. Correspondence. Pennsylvania State Archives.
White, Harrison. Correspondence. Historical Society of Pennsylvania.
Widdifield, Charles Y. Diaries, 1863–65. Gilder Lehrman Collection.

UNPUBLISHED RECORDS

Appointments, Commissions, and Personal Branch Files. Record Group 94, National Archives.
General's Papers. Record Group 94, Entry 159, National Archives.
Generals' Reports of Service, War of the Rebellion (13 vols.). Record Group 94, Entry 160, National Archives.
Records of Chief, United States Cavalry Bureau. Letters Sent and Received, Reports of Inspectors, Ordnance Surveys, etc., 1863–65. Record Group 108, Entries 69–75, National Archives.
Records of Headquarters, Bayard's [later Gregg's] Cavalry Division, Army of the Potomac. Letters Sent and Reports of Officers, December 1862–December 1864. Record Group 393, Entry 1532, National Archives.
Records of Headquarters, Cavalry Brigade, Army of the Potomac. Letters Received, October 1861–February 1862. Record Group 393, Entry 1471, National Archives.
Records of Headquarters, Cavalry Brigade, Army of the Potomac. Letters Sent, August 1861–April 1862. Record Group 393, Entry 1469, National Archives.
Records of Headquarters, Cavalry Corps, Army of the Potomac. Letters Sent, February 1863–April 1865. Record Group 393, Entry 1439, National Archives.
Records of Headquarters, Cavalry Division, Army of the James. Letters Sent, April 1864–August 1865. Record Group 393, Entry 1753, National Archives.
Records of Headquarters, First Cavalry Division, Army of the Potomac. Letters and Telegrams Received, 1861–64. Record Group 393, Entry 1508, National Archives.
Records of Headquarters, First Cavalry Division, Army of the Potomac. Letters Sent, April–May 1863. Record Group 393, Entry 1502, National Archives.

Records of Headquarters, Second Cavalry Division, Army of the Potomac. Letters Sent, June 1863–May 1865. Record Group 393, Entry 1535, National Archives.

Records of Headquarters, Third Cavalry Division, Army of the Potomac. Letters Sent, August 1863–June 1865. Record Group 393, Entry 1543, National Archives.

DISSERTATIONS, THESES, TYPESCRIPTS

Abernethy, Robert S. "The Advance of Grant's Army Towards Spottsylvania [*sic*], May 7, and the Rencontre Battle of May 8, 1864." Army War College Study, 1912. U.S. Army Military History Institute.

Alberts, Don E. "General Wesley Merritt, Nineteenth Century Cavalryman." Ph.D. dissertation, University of New Mexico, 1975.

Anderson, E. D. "Cavalry Operations in the Gettysburg Campaign." Army War College Study, 1912. U.S. Army Military History Institute.

Berry, L. G. "The Battle of Gaines' Mill, June 27, 1862." Army War College Study, 1912. U.S. Army Military History Institute.

Borries, Frank B., Jr. "General John Buford, Civil War Union Cavalryman." M.A. thesis, University of Kentucky, 1960.

Butterfield, Daniel. "Reminiscenses of the Cavalry in the Army of [the] Potomac . . ." Typescript in Appointments, Commissions, and Personal Branch File of Wesley Merritt, Record Group 94, National Archives.

"Captain John H. Calef's Battery Position [at Gettysburg, July 1, 1863]" File, Gettysburg National Military Park Library.

Cruse, Thomas. "Operations of the Union Cavalry during the Chancellorsville Campaign." Army War College Study, 1916. U.S. Army Military History Institute.

"Elon J. Farnsworth" File. Gettysburg National Military Park Library.

Fair, John S. "The Operations of the Federal and Confederate Cavalry in the Chancellorsville Campaign." Army War College Study, 1912. U.S. Army Military History Institute.

Fleming, R. J. "Campaign and Battle of Spotsylvania." Army War College Study, 1912. U.S. Army Military History Institute.

Gregg, David McMurtrie, Jr. "Brevet Major General David McMurtrie Gregg." Library of Congress.

Harsh, Joseph L. "George Brinton McClellan and the Forgotten Alternative: An Introduction to the Conservative Strategy in the Civil War, April-August 1861." Ph.D. dissertation, Rice University, 1970.

Hedekin, C. A. "Cavalry Operations (Federal and Confederate) during the Campaign and Battle of Fredericksburg." Army War College Study, 1913. U.S. Army Military History Institute.

Hoffman, Elliott Wheelock. "Vermont General: The Military Development of William Wells, 1861–1865." M.A. thesis, University of Vermont, 1974.

King, G. Wayne. "The Civil War Career of Hugh Judson Kilpatrick." Ph.D. dissertation, University of South Carolina, 1969.

Langhorne, George T. "The Cavalry in the Gettysburg Campaign . . ." Army War College Study, 1913. U.S. Army Military History Institute.

McDonald, J. B. "Operations of the Federal and Confederate Cavalry in the Chancellorsville Campaign." Army War College Study, 1913. U.S. Army Military History Institute.

Macomb, A. C. "Cavalry in the Gettysburg Campaign." Army War College Study, 1915. U.S. Army Military History Institute.

Nolan, James D. "'A Bold and Fearless Rider': The Life of Major General John Buford." M.A. thesis, St. John's University, 1994.

Pehrson, Paul C. "James Harrison Wilson: A Partial Biography." M.A. thesis, Southern Illinois University, 1967.

Pierce. John E. "General Hugh Judson Kilpatrick in the American Civil War: A New Appraisal." Ph.D. dissertation, Pennsylvania State University, 1983.

Richter, William L. "The Federal Cavalry in the Gettysburg Campaign: The Development of the Mobile Army of the Army of the Potomac." M.A. thesis, Arizona State University, 1965.

Rockenbach, S. D. "Cavalry Operations during the Federicksburg Campaign and Battle." Army War College Study, 1912. U.S. Army Military History Institute.

_____. "The Gettysburg Campaign: The Cavalry Fight at Rummel's Farm." Army War College Study, 1912. U.S. Army Military History Institute.

Sommers, Richard J. "Grant's Fifth Offensive at Petersburg: A Study in Strategy, Tactics, and Generalship . . ." Ph.D. dissertation, Rice University, 1970.

"South Cavalry Field" File. Gettysburg National Military Park Library.

Stonesifer, Roy P., Jr. "The Long Hard Road: Union Cavalry in the Gettysburg Campaign." M.A. thesis, Pennsylvania State University, 1959.

Stubbs, Mary Lee. "Cavalry in the Civil War." Office of the Chief of Military History, Department of the Army, Washington, D.C.

Thiele, Thomas F. "The Evolution of Cavalry in the American Civil War, 1861–1863." Ph.D. dissertation, University of Michigan, 1952.

NEWSPAPERS

Army and Navy Journal
Battle Creek Journal
Camden [N.J.] *Democrat*
Detroit Advertiser & Tribune
Detroit Free Press
Gettysburg Times
Hudson [Mich.] *Gazette*
Illustrated London News
New York Herald
New York Times

New York Tribune
Philadelphia Daily Evening Bulletin
Philadelphia Inquirer
Philadelphia Sunday Dispatch
Richmond Examiner
Rochester Daily Union & Advertiser

ARTICLES AND ESSAYS

Adams, William G., Jr. "Spencers at Gettysburg: Fact or Fiction?" *Military Affairs* 39 (1965): 41–42, 56.

"Appomattox and the Last Man Killed." *Maine Bugle* n.s. 3 (1896): 35–36.

Arnold A. K. "The Cavalry at Gaines' Mill." *Journal of the United States Cavalry Association* 2 (1889): 355–63.

_____. "With General Sheridan on [a] Raid Towards Richmond, Va., in 1864." *Journal of the United States Cavalry Association* 2 (1889): 28–33.

Athearn, Robert G., ed. "The Civil War Diary of John Wilson Phillips." *Virginia Magazine of History and Biography* 62 (1954): 95–123.

Averell, William W. "With the Cavalry on the Peninsula." *Battles and Leaders of the Civil War* 2 (1887–88): 429–33.

Bakeless, John. "The Mystery of Appomattox." *Civil War Times Illustrated* 9 (June 1970): 18–32.

Barton, John V. "The Procurement of Horses." *Civil War Times Illustrated* 6 (December 1967): 16–24.

Barton, Michael, ed. "'Constantly on the Lark': The Civil War Letters of a New Jersey Man." *Manuscripts* 30 (1978): 13–20.

Bates, Alfred E., and McClernand, Edward J. "The Second Regiment of Cavalry." In Theophilus F. Rodenbough and William L. Haskin, eds., *The Army of the United States: Historical Sketches of Staff and Line* . . . (New York: Merrill & Co., 1896), 73–92.

Beck, Elias W. H. "Letters of a Civil War Surgeon." *Indiana Magazine of History* 27 (1931): 132–63.

Bell, Harry, trans. "Cavalry Raids and the Lessons They Teach Us." *Journal of the United States Cavalry Association* 19 (1908–09): 142–52.

Beveridge, John L. "The First Gun at Gettysburg." *Military Essays and Recollections: Papers Read before the Commandry of the State of Illinois, Military Order of the Loyal Legion of the United States* 2 (1894): 79–98.

Billings, E. E., ed. "Letters and Diaries [Diary of Sgt. George W. Buhrer, 2nd Massachuetts Cavalry, 1864]." *Civil War Times Illustrated* 1 (April 1962): 16–18.

Black, James B. "General Philip Henry Sheridan." *War Papers: Read before the Indiana Commandery, Military Order of the Loyal Legion of the United States* 1 (1898): 42–72.

Bliss, George N. "The Cavalry Affair at Waynesboro." *Southern Historical Society Papers* 13 (1885): 427–30.

_____. "A Review of Aldie." *Maine Bugle,* n.s. 1 (1894): 123–32.

Boehm, Robert B. "The Unfortunate Averell." *Civil War Times Illustrated* 5 (August 1966): 30–36.

Calef, John H. "Gettysburg Notes: The Opening Gun." *Journal of the Military Service Institution of the United States* 40 (1907): 40–58.

Carpenter, J. Edward. "Gregg's Cavalry at Gettysburg." In *Annals of the War, Written by Leading Participants, North and South* (Philadelphia: Times Publishing Co., 1879), 527–35.

Carpenter, Louis H. "Sheridan's Expedition around Richmond, May 9-25, 1864." *Journal of the United States Cavalry Association* 1 (1888): 300-24.

Carr, Joseph B. "Operations of 1861 about Fort Monroe." *Battles and Leaders of the Civil War* 2 (1887–88): 144–52.

Carter, William H. "The Sixth Regiment of Cavalry." *Maine Bugle,* n.s. 3 (1896): 295–306.

Chaffee, Adna R. "James Harrison Wilson, Cavalryman." *Journal of the United States Cavalry Association* 34 (1925): 271–89.

Cilley, Jonathan P. "The Dawn of the Morning at Appomattox." *War Papers: Read before the Commandery of the State of Maine, Military Order of the Loyal Legion of the United States* 34 (1896): 87–101.

Clark, S. A. "Brandy Station, October, 1863." *Maine Bugle,* n.s. 3 (1896): 226–29.

_____. "Buckland Mills." *Maine Bugle,* n.s. 4 (1897): 108–10.

Clarke, Almon. "In the Immediate Rear: Experience and Observations of a Field Surgeon." *War Papers: Read before the Commandery of the State of Wisconsin, Military Order of the Loyal Legion of the United States* 2 (1896): 87–101.

Clarke, Augustus P. "A Cavalry Surgeon's Experiences in the Battle of the Wilderness." *United Service,* n.s. 11 (1894): 138–46.

_____. "The Sixth New York Cavalry: Its Movements and Service at the Battle of Gettysburg." *United Service,* n.s. 16 (1896): 411–15.

Cooke, Philip St. George. "The Charge of Cooke's Cavalry at Gaines's Mill." *Battles and Leaders of the Civil War* (New York, 1887–88), 2: 344–46.

Cox, Jacob D. "Forcing Fox's Gap and Turner's Gap." *Battles and Leaders of the Civil War* (New York, 1887–88), 2: 583–90.

Crowninshield, Benjamin W. "Sheridan at Winchester." *Atlantic Monthly* 42 (1878): 683–91.

Cullen, Joseph P. "Cedar Creek." *Civil War Times Illustrated* 8 (December 1969): 4–9, 42–48.

_____. "Sheridan Wins at Winchester." *Civil War Times Illustrated* 6 (May 1967): 4–11, 40–44.

Cummings, W. G. "Six Months in the Third Cavalry Division under Custer." *War Sketches and Incidents: As Related by Companions of the Iowa Commandery, Military Order of the Loyal Legion of the United States* 1 (1893): 296–315.

Custer, George A. "War Memoirs." *Galaxy* 21 (1876): 319–24, 448–60, 624–32, 809–18; 22 (1876): 293–99, 447–55, 684–94.

Darrow, Caroline Baldwin. "Recollections of the Twiggs Surrender." *Battles and Leaders of the Civil War* 1 (1887–88): 33–39.

Davis, George B. "The Antietam Campaign." *Papers of the Military Historical Society of Massachusetts* 3 (1903): 27–72.

____. "The Bristoe and Mine Run Campaigns." *Papers of the Military Historical Society of Massachusetts* 3 (1903): 470–502.

____. "The Cavalry Combat at Brandy Station, Va., on June 9, 1863." *Journal of the United States Cavalry Association* 25 (1914): 190–98.

____. "The Cavalry Combat at Kelly's Ford in 1863." *Journal of the United States Cavalry Association* 25 (1915): 390–402.

____. "From Gettysburg to Williamsport." *Papers of the Military Historical Society of Massachusetts* 3 (1903): 449–69.

____. "The Operations of the Cavalry in the Gettysburg Campaign." *Journal of the United States Cavalry Association* 1 (1888): 325–48.

____. "The Richmond Raid of 1864." *Journal of the United States Cavalry Association* 24 (1914): 707–22.

____. "The Stoneman Raid." *Journal of the United States Cavalry Association* 24 (1914): 533–52.

Day, C. R. "Cavalry Raids: Their Value and How Made." *Journal of the United States Cavalry Association* 23 (1912–13): 227–38.

De Forest, J. W. "Sheridan's Battle of Winchester." *Harper's New Monthly Magazine* 30 (1865): 195–200.

____. "Sheridan's Victory of Middletown [Cedar Creek]." *Harper's New Monthly Magazine* 30 (1865): 353–60.

Devin, Thomas C. "Didn't We Fight Splendid." *Civil War Times Illustrated* 17 (December 1978): 38–40.

Ford, Charles W. "Charge of the First Maine Cavalry at Brandy Station." *War Papers: Read before the Commandery of the State of Maine, Military Order of the Loyal Legion of the United States* 2 (1902): 268–89.

"The Fourth Regiment of Cavalry." In Theophilus F. Rodenbough and William L. Haskin, eds., *The Army of the United States: Historical Sketches of Staff and Line . . .* (New York: Merrill & Co., 1896), 211–20.

Fry, James B. "McDowell's Advance to Bull Run." *Battles and Leaders of the Civil War* 1 (1887–88): 167–93.

Garavaglia, Louis A., and Charles G. Worman, "Many Were Broken by Very Slight Shocks, as in Mounting and Dismounting." *North & South* 2 (June 1999): 40–47, 52–55.

Gerleman, David J. "War Horse! Union Cavalry Mounts, 1861–1865." *North & South* 2 (January 1999): 47–50, 57–61.

____, ed. "My Companion in all Places." *North & South* 2 (January 1999): 54–55.

Gibson, Charles Dana. "Hay: The Linchpin of Mobility." *North & South* 2 (January 1999): 51–53.

Gilmore, D. M. "Cavalry: Its Use and Value as Illustrated by Reference to the Engagements of Kelly's Ford and Gettysburg." *Glimpses of the Nation's*

Struggle: A Series of Papers Read before the Minnesota Commandery of the Military Order of the Loyal Legion of the United States 2 (1890): 38–51.

_____. "With General Gregg at Gettysburg." *Glimpses of the Nation's Struggle: A Series of Papers Read before the Minnesota Commandery of the Military Order of the Loyal Legion of the United States* 4 (1898): 93–111.

Gregg, David McMurtrie. "The Union Cavalry at Gettysburg." In *Annals of the War, Written by Leading Participants, North and South* (Philadelphia: Times Publishing Co., 1879), 372–79.

Hall, Clark B. "Buford at Brandy Station." *Civil War* 8 (July–August 1990): 12–17, 66–67.

Hall, H. C. "Some Recollections of Appomattox." *Maine Bugle,* n.s. 1 (1894): 133–40.

Halstead, E. P. "Incidents of the First Day at Gettysburg." *Battles and Leaders of the Civil War* 3 (1887–88): 284–85.

Hamlin, Augustus C. "Who Recaptured the Guns at Cedar Creek, October 19, 1864?" *Papers of the Military Historical Society of Massachusetts* 6 (1907): 183–208.

Hanson, Joseph Mills. "The Civil War Custer." *The Cavalry Journal* 43 (1934): 24–31.

_____. "A Stolen March: Cold Harbor to Petersburg." *Journal of the American Military History Foundation* 1 (1937–38): 139–50.

Harris, Moses. "The Union Cavalry." *War Papers: Read before the Commandery of the State of Wisconsin, Military Order of the Loyal Legion of the United States* 1 (1891): 340–73.

_____. "With the Reserve [Cavalry] Brigade." *Journal of the United States Cavalry Association* 3 (1890): 9–20, 235–47, 363–70; 4 (1891): 1–26.

Hassler, William W. "Yellow Tavern." *Civil War Times Illustrated* 5 (November 1966): 5–11, 46–48.

Hastings, Smith H. "The Cavalry Service, and Recollections of the Late War." *Magazine of Western History* 9 (1890): 259–66.

Hatfield, C. A. P. "The Evolution of Cavalry." *Journal of the Military Service Institution of the United States* 15 (1894): 89–103.

Hatton, Robert W., ed. "Just a Little Bit of the Civil War, as Seen by W. J. Smith, Company M, 2nd Ohio Volunteer Cavalry." *Ohio History* 84 (1975): 101–26, 222–42.

Havens, Edwin R. "How Mosby Destroyed Our Train." *Michigan History Magazine* 14 (1930): 294–98.

Hay, W. H. "Cavalry Raids." *Journal of the United States Cavalry Association* 4 (1891): 362–76.

Hazlett, James C. "The 3-Inch Ordnance Rifle." *Civil War Times Illustrated* 7 (December 1968): 30–36.

Heermance, W. L. "The Cavalry at Chancellorsville." *Personal Recollections of the War of the Rebellion: Addresses Delivered before the Commandery of the State of New York, Military Order of the Loyal Legion of the United States* 2 (1897): 223–30.

_____. "The Cavalry at Gettysburg." *Personal Recollections of the War of the Rebellion: Addresses Delivered before the Commandery of the State of New York, Military Order of the Loyal Legion of the United States* 3 (1907): 196–206.

Hess, Frank W. "The First Cavalry Battle at Kelly's Ford, Va." *Maine Bugle* 3 (July 1893): 3–6; 4 (October 1893): 8–22.

Hitchcock, W. H. "Recollections of a Participant in the Charge [of the Fifth United States Cavalry at Gaines's Mill]." *Battles and Leaders of the Civil War* 2 (1887–88): 346.

Huey, Pennock, J. Edward Carpenter, and Andrew B. Wells. "The Charge Of the Eighth Pennsylvania Cavalry [at Chancellorsville]." *Battles and Leaders of the Civil War* 3 (1887–88): 186–88.

Huntington, James F. "The Artillery at Hazel Grove." *Battles and Leaders of the Civil War* (New York, 1887–88), 3: 188.

Imboden, John D. "The Confederate Retreat from Gettysburg." *Battles and Leaders of the Civil War* 3 (1887–88): 420–29.

Isham, Asa B. "The Cavalry of the Army of the Potomac." *Sketches of War History, 1861–1865: Papers Prepared for the Ohio Commandery of the Military Order of the Loyal Legion of the United States* 5 (1903): 301–27.

_____. "Through the Wilderness to Richmond." *Sketches of War History, 1861–1865: Papers Prepared for the Ohio Commandery of the Military Order of the Loyal Legion of the United States* 1 (1888): 189–217.

Johnson, John W. "A Sheldon Soldier in the Civil War." *Historic Wyoming [County, New York]* 15 (1962): 39–45, 51.

Johnston, Angus J. "Lee's Last Lifeline: The Richmond & Danville." *Civil War History* 7 (1961): 288–96.

Jones, J. William, comp. "Kilpatrick-Dahlgren Raid against Richmond." *Southern Historical Society Papers* 13 (1885): 515–60.

Jones, Virgil Carrington. "The Story of the Kilpatrick-Dahlgren Raid." *Civil War Times Illustrated* 4 (April 1965): 13–21.

Kempster, Walter. "The Cavalry at Gettysburg." *War Papers: Read before the Commandery of the State of Wisconsin, Military Order of the Loyal Legion of the United States* 4 (1914): 397–429.

_____. "The Early Days of Our Cavalry, in the Army of the Potomac." *War Papers: Read before the Commandery of the State of Wisconsin, Military Order of the Loyal Legion of the United States* 3 (1903): 60–89.

Kennedy, William V. "The Cavalry Battle at Brandy Station." *Armor* 65 (1956): 27–31.

Kidd, James H. "Address of Gen. James H. Kidd at the Dedication of Michigan Monuments upon the Battlefield of Gettysburg, June 12th, 1889." *Journal of the United States Cavalry Association* 4 (1891): 41–63.

"Kilpatrick's and Dahlgren's Raid to Richmond." *Battles and Leaders of the Civil War* 4 (1887–88): 95–96.

King, G. Wayne. "General Judson Kilpatrick." *New Jersey History* 91 (1973): 35–52.

Klement, Frank L., ed. "Edwin B. Bigelow: A Michigan Sergeant in the Civil War." *Michigan History* 38 (1954): 193–252.

Kross, Gary. "'Fight like the Devil to Hold Your Own': General John Buford's Cavalry at Gettysburg on July 1, 1863." *Blue & Gray* 12 (February 1995): 9–22.

Kurtz, Henry I. "Five Forks: The South's Waterloo." *Civil War Times Illustrated* 3 (October 1964): 5–11, 28-31.

Law, E. M. "The Struggle for 'Round Top.'" *Battles and Leaders of the Civil War* 3 (1887–88): 318–30.

Lloyd, Harlan Page. "The Battle of Waynesboro." *Sketches of War History, 1861–1865: Papers Prepared for the Ohio Commandery of the Military Order of the Loyal Legion of the United States* 4 (1896): 194–213.

Longacre, Edward G. "Alfred Pleasonton, 'The Knight of Romance.'" *Civil War Times Illustrated* 13 (December 1974): 10–23.

_____. "The Battle of Reams' Station: 'The Blackest of All Days'." *Civil War Times Illustrated* 25 (March 1986): 12–19.

_____. "Boots and Saddles: Part I, The Eastern Theater." *Civil War Times Illustrated* 31 (March-April 1992): 35–40.

_____. "The Battle of Brandy Station: 'A Shock That Made the Earth Tremble'." *Virginia Cavalcade* 25 (1976): 136–43.

_____. "Cavalry Clash at Todd's Tavern." *Civil War Times Illustrated* 16 (October 1977): 12–21.

_____. "General James Harrison Wilson." *Delaware History* 16 (1975): 298–322.

_____. "Judson Kilpatrick." *Civil War Times Illustrated* 10 (April 1971): 24–33.

_____. "The Long Run for Trevilian Station." *Civil War Times Illustrated* 18 (November 1979): 28–39.

_____. "Sir Percy Wyndham." *Civil War Times Illustrated* 7 (December 1968): 12–19.

_____. "Wilson-Kautz Raid." *Civil War Times Illustrated* 9 (May 1970): 32–42.

_____, ed. "'Chaos Still Reigns in This Camp': Letters of Lieutenant George N. Bliss, 1st New England Cavalry, March–September 1862." *Rhode Island History* 36 (1977): 14–24.

Lord, Francis A. "Union Cavalry Equipment." *Civil War Times Illustrated* 1 (February 1963): 36–37.

Luff, William M. "March of the Cavalry from Harper's Ferry, September 14, 1862." *Military Essays and Recollections: Papers Read before the Commandery of the State of Illinois, Military Order of the Loyal Legion of the United States* 2 (1894): 33–48.

Luvaas, Jay. "Cavalry Lessons of the Civil War." *Civil War Times Illustrated* 6 (January 1968): 20–31.

Luvaas, Jay, and Wilbur S. Nye. "The Campaign That History Forgot." *Civil War Times Illustrated* 8 (November 1969): 12–37.

McClellan, George B. "The Peninsular Campaign." *Battles and Leaders of the Civil War* 2 (1887–88): 160–87.

McClernand, Edward J. "Cavalry Operations: The Wilderness to the James River." *Journal of the Military Service Institution of the United States* 30 (1902): 321–43.

McConnell, Charles C. "Service with Sheridan." *War Papers: Read before the Commandery of the State of Wisconsin, Military Order of the Loyal Legion of the United States* 1 (1891): 285–93.

McCormack, John F. "The Harpers Ferry Skedaddlers." *Civil War Times Illustrated* 14 (December 1975): 32–39.

McKinney, Francis F. "The Death of Farnsworth." *Michigan Alumnus Quarterly Review* 66 (1959): 75–79.

_____. "Michigan Cavalry in the Civil War." *Michigan Alumnus Quarterly Review* 63 (1956): 136–46.

McLean, James L., Jr. "The First Union Shot at Gettysburg." *Lincoln Herald* 82 (1980): 318–23.

McMahon, Martin T. "From Gettysburg to the Coming of Grant." *Battles and Leaders of the Civil War* 4 (1887–88): 81-94.

Mahon, John K. "Civil War Infantry Assault Tactics." *Military Affairs* 25 (1961): 57–68.

Mayo, William H. "Wilson's [and Kautz's] Cavalry Raid." *Maine Bugle,* n.s. 5 (1898): 212–16.

Merritt, Wesley. "The Appomattox Campaign." *War Papers and Personal Reminiscences, 1861–1865: Read before the Commandery of the State of Missouri, Military Order of the Loyal Legion of the United States* 1 (1892): 108–31.

_____. "Cavalry: Its Organization and Armament." *Journal of the Military Service Institution of the United States* 1 (1879): 42–52.

_____. "Sheridan in the Shenandoah Valley." *Battles and Leaders of the Civil War* 4: 500–521.

Milgram, James W., ed. "The Libby Prison Correspondence of Tattnall Paulding." *American Philatelist* 89 (1975): 1114–21.

Miller, Samuel H. "Yellow Tavern." *Civil War History* 2 (1956): 57–81.

Miller, William E. "The Cavalry Battle Near Gettysburg." *Battles and Leaders of the Civil War* 3 (1887–88): 397-406.

Millis, Wade. "A Forgotten Hero." *Michigan History Magazine* 14 (1930): 286–93.

Monaghan, Jay. "Custer's 'Last Stand'—Trevilian Station, 1864." *Civil War History* 8 (1962): 245–58.

Moore, James O. "Custer's Raid into Albemarle County: The Skirmish at Rio Hill, February 29, 1864." *Virginia Magazine of History and Biography* 79 (1971): 338–48.

Morton, Charles. "The Third Regiment of Cavalry." In Theophilus F. Rodenbough and William L. Haskin, eds., *The Army of the United States:*

Historical Sketches of Staff and Line . . . (New York: Merrill & Co., 1896), 193–220.

Narol, Raoul S. "Sheridan and Cedar Creek—A Reappraisal." *Military Affairs* 16 (1952–53): 153–68.

Nettleton, A. Bayard. "How the Day Was Saved at the Battle of Cedar Creek." *Glimpses of the Nation's Struggle: A Series of Papers Read before the Minnesota Commandery of the Military Order of the Loyal Legion of the United States* 1 (1887): 258–75.

Newhall, Frederick C. "The Battle of Beverly Ford." In *Annals of the War, Written by Leading Participants, North and South* (Philadelphia: Times Publishing Co., 1879), 134–46.

———. "With Sheridan in Lee's Last Campaign." *Maine Bugle,* n.s. 1 (1894): 201–13, 297–317; 2 (1895): 1–7, 96–112, 236–56, 289–308; 3 (1896): 1–14.

Norvell, Guy S. "The Equipment and Tactics of Our Cavalry, 1861–65, Compared with the Present." *Journal of the Military Service Institution of the United States* 49 (1911): 360–76.

Nye, Wilbur S. "The Affair at Hunterstown." *Civil War Times Illustrated* 9 (February 1971): 22–34.

———, ed. "Stuart's Chambersburg Raid: An Eyewitness Account." *Civil War Times Illustrated* 4 (Jan. 1966): 8–15, 42–48.

O'Neill, Robert F., Jr. "'What Men We Have Got Are Good Soldiers & Brave Ones Too': Federal Cavalry Operations in the Peninsula Campaign." In William J. Miller, ed., *The Peninsula Campaign: Yorktown to the Seven Days* (3 vols. Campbell, Calif: Savas Publishing Co., 1997), 3: 79–142.

"Our Cavalry." *United Service,* n.s. 1 (1879): 329–46.

Parker, James. "Mounted and Dismounted Action of Cavalry." *Journal of the Military Service Institution of the United States* 39 (1906): 381–87.

Parsons, H. C. "Farnsworth's Charge and Death." *Battles and Leaders of the Civil War* 3 (1887–88): 393–96.

Phipps, Michael. "'They Too Fought Here': The Officer Corps of the Army of the Potomac's Cavalry during the Battle of Gettysburg." In *Mr. Lincoln's Army: The Army of the Potomac in the Gettysburg Campaign* (Gettysburg, Pa.: Gettysburg National Military Park, 1998), 92–135.

Pleasonton, Alfred. "The Campaign of Gettysburg." In *Annals of the War, Written by Leading Participants, North and South* (Philadelphia: Times Publishing Co., 1879), 447–59.

———. "The Successes and Failures of Chancellorsville." *Battles and Leaders of the Civil War* 3 (1887–88): 172–82.

Pope, Edmund M. "Personal Experiences—A Side Light on the Wilson [and Kautz] Raid, June, 1864." *Glimpses of the Nation's Struggle: Papers Read before the Minnesota Commandery of the Military Order of the Loyal Legion of the United States* 4 (1898): 585–604.

Pope, John. "The Second Battle of Bull Run." *Battles and Leaders of the Civil War* 2 (1887–88): 449–94.

Porter, Fitz John. "The Battle of Malvern Hill." *Battles and Leaders of the Civil War* 2 (1887–88): 406–27.

_____. "Hanover Court House and Gaines's Mill." *Battles and Leaders of the Civil War* 2 (1887–88): 319–43.

Porter, Horace. "Five Forks and the Pursuit of Lee." *Battles and Leaders of the Civil War* 4 (1887–88): 708–22.

_____. "The Surrender at Appomattox Court House." *Battles and Leaders of the Civil War* 4 (1887–88): 729–46.

Poulter, Keith. "The Cavalry Bureau." *North & South* 2 (January 1999): 70–71.

Rawle, William Brooke. "Further Remarks on the Cavalry Fight on the Right Flank at Gettysburg." *Joural of the United States Cavalry Association* 4 (1891): 157–60.

_____. "Gregg's Cavalry Fight at Gettysburg, July 3, 1863." *Journal of the United States Cavalry Association* 4 (1891): 257–75.

Reece, Frances R., ed. "The Final Push to Appomattox." *Michigan History Magazine* 28 (1944): 456–64.

Rhea, Gordon. "Union Cavalry in the Wilderness." In Gary A. Gallagher, ed., *The Wilderness Campaign* (Chapel Hill: University of North Carolina Press, 1997): 106–35.

Rhodes, Charles D. "Cavalry Battles and Charges." In Francis Trevelyan Miller, ed., *The Photographic History of the Civil War* (New York: Review of Reviews Co., 1911), 4: 220–58.

_____. "The Federal Cavalry: Its Organization and Equipment." In Francis Trevelyan Miller, ed., *The Photographic History of the Civil War* (New York: Review of Reviews Co., 1911), 4: 46–70.

_____. "The Mounting and Remounting of the Federal Cavalry." In Francis Trevelyan Miller, ed., *The Photographic History of the Civil War* (New York: Review of Reviews Co., 1911), 4: 322–36.

_____. "Outposts, Scouts and Couriers." In Francis Trevelyan Miller, ed., *The Photographic History of the Civil War* (New York: Review of Reviews Co., 1911), 4: 186–202.

Rockwell, Alphonso D. "With Sheridan's Cavalry." *Personal Recollections of the War of the Rebellion: Addresses Delivered before the Commandery of the State of New York, Military Order of the Loyal Legion of the United States* 3 (1907): 228–39.

Rodenbough, Theophilus F. "Cavalry of the Civil War: Its Evolution and Influence." In Francis Trevelyan Miller, ed., *The Photographic History of the Civil War* (New York: Review of Reviews Co., 1911), 4: 16–38.

_____. "Cavalry War Lessons." *Journal of the United States Cavalry Association* 2 (1889): 103–23.

_____. "The Regular Cavalry in the Gettysburg Campaign." *Journal of the Military Service Institution of the United States* 44 (1909): 29–31.

_____. "Sheridan's Richmond Raid." *Battles and Leaders of the Civil War* 4 (1887–88): 188–93.

_____. "Sheridan's Trevilian Raid." *Battles and Leaders of the Civil War* 4 (1887–88): 233–36.

Russell, Don. "Jeb Stuart on the Frontier." *Civil War Times Illustrated* 13 (April 1974): 13–17.

_____. "Jeb Stuart's Other Indian Fight." *Civil War Times Illustrated* 12 (January 1974): 11–17.

Schiller, Laurence D. "A Taste of Northern Steel: The Evolution of Federal Cavalry Tactics, 1861–1865." *North & South* 2 (January 1999): 30–36.

Shanks, W. F. G. "Recollections of Sheridan." *Harper's New Monthly Magazine* 31 (1865): 298–305.

Shepard, James C. "'Miracles' and Leadership in Civil War Cavalry." *Military Review* 55 (1975): 49–55.

Sheridan, Philip H. "Last Days of the Rebellion." *Military Essays and Recollections: Papers Read before the Commandery of the State of Illinois, Military Order of the Loyal Legion of the United States* 1 (1891): 427–39.

Smith, Charles H. "Incidents of Appomattox." *Maine Bugle* 3 (April 1893): 41–45.

_____. "A Reconnaissance with the First Maine Cavalry." *Journal of the United States Cavalry Association* 44 (1909): 253–62.

Starr, Stephen Z. "Cold Steel: The Saber and the Union Cavalry." *Civil War History* 11 (1965): 142–59.

_____. "The Inner Life of the First Vermont Volunteer Cavalry, 1861–1865." *Vermont History* 46 (1978): 157–74.

_____, ed. "Dinwiddie Court House and Five Forks: Reminiscences of Roger Hannaford, Second Ohio Volunteer Cavalry." *Virginia Magazine of History and Biography* 87 (1978): 417–37.

_____, ed. "The Wilson [and Kautz] Raid, June, 1864: A Trooper's Reminiscences." *Civil War History* 21 (1975): 218–41.

_____, ed. "Winter Quarters near Winchester, 1864–1865: Reminiscences of Roger Hannaford, Second Ohio Volunteer Cavalry." *Virginia Magazine of History and Biography* 86 (1978): 320–38.

Steffen, Randy. "The Blakeslee Quickloader." *Civil War Times Illustrated* 1 (October 1962): 35–37.

Stevenson, James H. "The First Cavalry." In *Annals of the War, Written by Leading Participants, North and South* (Philadelphia: Times Publishing Co., 1879), 634–41.

"Stoneman's Raid in the Chancellorsville Campaign." *Battles and Leaders of the Civil War* 3 (1887–88): 152–53.

Stonesifer, Roy P., Jr. "The Union Cavalry Comes of Age." *Civil War History* 11 (1965): 274–83.

Stuart, Meriwether. "Colonel Ulric Dahlgren and Richmond's Union Underground." *Virginia Magazine of History and Biography* 72 (1964): 152–204.

Swift, Eben. "The Fifth Regiment of Cavalry." In Theophilus F. Rodenbough and William L. Haskin, eds., *The Army of the United States: Historical Sketches of Staff and Line* . . . (New York: Merrill & Co., 1896), 221–31.

_____. "The Tactical Use of Cavalry." *Journal of the Military Service Institution of the United States* 44 (1909): 359–69.

Sword, Wiley. "Cavalry on Trial at Kelly's Ford." *Civil War Times Illustrated* 13 (April 1974): 32–40.

Tasker, Albert Porter. "A Yankee Cavalryman Gets 'Gobbled Up': A First-Person Account." *Civil War Times Illustrated* 6 (January 1968): 42–44.

Thaxter, Sidney W. "Reconnaissance near Warrenton." *Civil War Times Illustrated* 8 (August 1969): 26–32.

Thiele, Thomas F. "Some Notes on the Lance and Lancers in the United States Cavalry." *Military Collector & Historian* 7 (1955): 34–37.

Throckmorton, A. B "Major-General Kilpatrick." *Northern Monthly* 2 (1868): 590–605.

Tompkins, Charles H. "With the Vermont Cavalry, 1861–6: Some Reminiscences." *The Vermonter* 17 (1912): 505–07.

Tremain, Henry E. "The Last Days of Sheridan's Cavalry." *Maine Bugle* n.s. 5 (1898): 168–81, 245–75, 295–312.

Tripp, Stephen. "The Cavalry at Appomattox, April 9, 1865." *Maine Bugle* n.s. 5 (1898): 212–16.

Turner, Charles W. "The Richmond, Fredericksburg and Potomac, 1861–1865." *Civil War History* 7 (1961): 255–63.

Wainwright, R. P. P. "The First Regiment of Cavalry." In Theophilus F. Rodenbough and William L. Haskin, eds., *The Army of the United States: Historical Sketches of Staff and Line . . .* (New York: Merrill & Co., 1896), 153–72.

Weigley, Russell F. "David McMurtrie Gregg: A Personality Profile." *Civil War Times Illustrated* 1 (November 1962): 11–13, 28–30.

_____. "John Buford: A Personality Profile." *Civil War Times Illustrated* 5 (June 1966): 14–23.

_____. "Philip H. Sheridan: A Personality Profile." *Civil War Times Illustrated* 7 (July 1968): 4–9, 46–48.

_____. "The Twilight of Mounted Cavalry: Gregg's Division in the Petersburg Campaign." *Historical Review of Berks County* 27 (1962): 81–86.

Weinert, Richard P. "Maj. Henry Young: A Profile." *Civil War Times Illustrated* 3 (April 1964): 38–42.

Wickersham, Charles I. "Personal Recollections of the Cavalry at Chancellorsville." *War Papers: Read before the Commandery of the State of Wisconsin, Military Order of the Loyal Legion of the United States* 3 (1903): 453–69.

Wiles, C. W. "A Skirmish at Little Auburn, Va." *Maine Bugle* 2 (October 1892): 71–74.

Willcox, Orlando B. "Actions on the Weldon Railroad." *Battles and Leaders of the Civil War* 4 (1887–88): 568–73.

Williams, Robert A. "Haw's Shop: 'A Storm of Shot and Shell'." *Civil War Times Illustrated* 9 (January 1971): 12–19.

Wilson, James Harrison. "The Cavalry of the Army of the Potomac." *Papers of the Military Historical Society of Massachusetts* 13 (1913): 33–88.

____. "Major-General John Buford." *Journal of the United States Cavalry Association* 13 (1895): 171–83.

Wilson, Spencer. "How Soldiers Rated Carbines." *Civil War Times Illustrated* 5 (May 1966): 40–44.

Wittenberg, Eric J. "Learning the Hard Lessons of Logistics: Arming and Maintaining the Federal Cavalry." *North & South* 2 (January 1999): 62–75.

BOOKS AND PAMPHLETS

Abbott, Allen O. *Prison Life in the South* . . . New York: Harper & Brothers, 1865.

Abraham, James. *With the Army of West Virginia, 1861–1864: Reminiscences & Letters of Lt. James Abraham.* Compiled by Evelyn A. Benson. Lancaster, Pa.: privately issued, 1974.

Adams, Charles F., Jr. *Charles Francis Adams, 1835–1915: An Autobiography.* Boston: Massachusetts Historical Society, 1916.

____, et al. *A Cycle of Adams Letters, 1861–1865.* Edited by Worthington Chauncey Ford. 2 vols. Boston: Houghton Mifflin Co., 1920.

Adams, Francis Colburn. *The Story of a Trooper* . . . New York: Dick & Fitzgerald, 1865.

Address by P. O'Meare Delivered at the Second Annual Meeting of the First Vermont Cavalry Reunion Society, at Montpelier . . . Burlington, Vt.: privately issued, 1874.

Allen, Stanton P. *Down in Dixie: Life in a Cavlary Regiment* . . . *from the Wilderness to Appomattox.* Boston: D. Lothrop, 1888.

Allen, Winthrop S. G. *Civil War Letters of Winthrop S. G. Allen.* Edited by Harry E. Pratt. Springfield, Ill.: Phillips Brothers Printing Co., 1932.

Anniversary and Re-union of the Tenth New York Cavalry Veteran Association. Homer, N.Y.: Republican Power Press, 1891.

Anthony, William. *History of the Battle of Hanover* . . . *Tuesday, June 30, 1863.* Hanover, Pa.: Hanover Chamber of Commerce, 1945.

Archibald, William C. *Home-Making and Its Philosophy* . . . Boston: privately issued, 1910.

Aston, Howard. *History and Roster of the* . . . *Thirteenth Regiment Ohio Cavalry Volunteers: Their Battles and Skirmishes, Roster of the Dead, Etc.* Columbus, Ohio: Fred J. Heer, 1902.

Averell, William W. *Ten Years in the Saddle: The Memoir of William Woods Averell, 1851–1862.* Edited by Edward K. Eckert and Nicholas J. Amato. San Rafael, Calif.: Presidio Press, 1978.

Bache, Richard M. *Life of General George Gordon Meade, Commander of the Army of the Potomac.* Philadelphia: Henry T. Coates & Co., 1897.

Backus, Samuel W. *Californians in the Field: Historical Sketch of the* . . . *2d Massachusetts Cavalry: Paper Prepared and Read before the California Commandery of the Military Order of the Loyal Legion of the United States.* San Francisco: privately issued, 1889.

Barnet, James, ed. *The Martyrs and Heroes of Illinois in the Great Rebellion: Biographical Sketches.* Chicago: J. Barnet, 1865.

Bartol, C. A. *The Purchase by Blood: A Tribute to Brig.-Gen. Charles Russell Lowell, Jr. . . .* Boston: John Wilson & Son, 1864.

Bates, Samuel P. *The Battle of Gettysburg.* Philadelphia: T. H. Davis & Co., 1875.

_____. *History of Pennsylvania Volunteers, 1861–5.* 5 vols. Harrisburg, Pa.: B. Singerly, 1869–71.

Battles Fought by the Cavalry under the Command of Major General P. H. Sheridan, U.S. Army, from May 4, 1864, to April 9, 1865. n.p., 1865.

Bayard, Samuel J. *The Life of George Dashiell Bayard . . .* New York: G. P. Putnam's Sons, 1874.

Beach, William H. *The First New York (Lincoln) Cavalry from April 18, 1861 to July 7, 1865.* Milwaukee: Burdick & Allen, 1902.

Bean, Theodore W. *The Roll of Honor of the Seventeenth Pennsylvania Cavalry . . .* Philadelphia: James S. Claxton, 1865.

Bell, Thomas. *At Harper's Ferry, Va., September 14, 1862: How the Cavalry Escaped . . .* Brooklyn, N.Y.: privately issued, 1900.

Bentley, Wilber G. *Address Delivered at the Dedication of a Monument of the Ninth New York Cavalry . . .* Chicago: privately issued, 1883.

Bigelow, John, Jr. *The Campaign of Chancellorsville: A Strategic and Tactical Study.* New Haven, Conn.: Yale University Press, 1910.

Bilby, Joseph G. *Civil War Firearms: Their Historical Background, Tactical Use and Modern Collecting and Shooting.* Conshohocken, Pa.: Combined Books, 1996.

Black, John L. *Crumbling Defenses; or, Memoirs and Reminiscences of John Logan Black, Colonel, C.S.A.* Edited by Eleanor D. McSwain. Macon, Ga.: J. W. Burke Co., 1960.

Black, Robert C., III. *The Railroads of the Confederacy.* Chapel Hill: University of North Carolina Press, 1952.

Bliss, George N. *Duffié and the Monument to His Memory.* Providence, R.I.: Snow & Farnham, 1890.

_____. *The First Rhode Island Cavalry at Middleburg, Va., June 17 and 18, 1863.* Providence, R.I.: privately issued, 1889.

_____. *Reminiscences of Service in the First Rhode Island Cavalry.* Providence, R. I.: privately issued, 1878.

Boatner, Mark M., III. *The Civil War Dictionary.* New York: David McKay Co., Inc., 1959.

Boudrye, Louis N. *Historic Records of the Fifth New York Cavalry . . .* Albany, N.Y.: J. Munsell, 1865.

_____. *The Libby Chronicle.* Albany, N.Y.: C. F. Williams Printing Co., 1889.

_____. *War Journal of Louis N. Beaudry [Boudrye], Fifth New York Cavalry: The Diary of a Union Chaplain, Commencing February 16, 1863.* Edited by Richard E. Beaudry. Jefferson, N. C.: McFarland, 1996.

Bowditch, Henry I. *Memorial [of Lieutenant Nathaniel Bowditch].* Boston: John Wilson & Son, 1865.

Bowen, James R. *Regimental History of the First New York Dragoons* . . . Lyons, Mich.: privately issued, 1900.

Brackett, Albert G. *History of the United States Cavalry, from the Formation of the Federal Government to the 1st of June, 1863.* New York: Harper & Brothers, 1865.

Bradley, Samuel H. *Recollections of Army Life.* Olean, N.Y.: privately issued, 1913.

Bradshaw, William T. *The Ninth N.Y. Cavalry, A Forlorn Hope: June 11th, 1864, Trevillian* [sic] *Station, Va.* Washington, D.C.: privately issued, 1864.

A Brief History of the Fourth Pennsylvania Veteran Cavalry . . . Pittsburgh: Ewens & Eberle, 1891.

Brown, Rodney Hilton. *American Polearms, 1526–1865* . . . New Milford, Conn.: N. Flayderman & Co., Inc., 1967.

Bruce, Robert V. *Lincoln and the Tools of War.* Indianapolis: Bobbs-Merrill Co., 1956.

Bruckeridge, J. O. *Lincoln's Choice.* Harrisburg, Pa.: Stackpole Co., 1956.

Buford, Marcus Bainbridge. *A Genealogy of the Buford Family in America.* . . . San Francisco: privately issued, 1903.

Burr, Frank A., and Richard J. Hinton. *"Little Phil" and His Troopers: The Life of Gen. Philip H. Sheridan* . . . Providence, R. I.: J. A. & R. A. Reid, 1888.

Byrne, Frank L., and Andrew T. Weaver, eds. *Haskell of Gettysburg: His Life and Civil War Papers.* Madison: State Historical Society of Wisconsin, 1970.

The Campaign Life of Lt.-Col. Henry Harrison Young . . . Providence. R.I.: Sidney S. Rider, 1882.

Campbell, Archibald W. *An Interesting Talk with General W. H. Powell, the Famous West Virginia Cavalry Officer* . . . Chicago: M. Embdenstock, 1901.

Carpenter, J. Edward, comp. *A List of the Battles, Engagements, Actions and Important Skirmishes in Which the Eighth Pennsylvania Cavalry Participated* . . . Philadelphia: Allen, Lane & Scott's Printing House, 1886.

Carter, Samuel, III. *The Last Cavaliers: Confederate and Union Cavalry in the Civil War.* New York: St. Martin's Press, 1979.

Carter, William Harding. *From Yorktown to Santiago with the Sixth U.S. Cavalry.* Baltimore: Lord Baltimore Press, 1900.

_____. *Horses, Saddles and Bridles.* Baltimore: Lord Baltimore Press, 1902.

_____. *The Life of Lieutenant General Chaffee.* Chicago: University of Chicago Press, 1917.

Catton, Bruce. *Glory Road: The Bloody Route from Fredericksburg to Gettysburg.* Garden City, N.Y.: Doubleday & Co., Inc., 1952.

_____. *Grant Takes Command.* Boston: Little, Brown & Co., 1969.

_____. *Mr. Lincoln's Army.* Garden City, N.Y.: Doubleday & Co., Inc., 1951.

_____. *A Stillness at Appomattox*. Garden City, N.Y.: Doubleday & Co., Inc., 1953.

Cavalry Tactics. Philadelphia: J. B. Lippincott & Co., 1862.

Cesnola, Luigi P. di *Ten Months in Libby Prison*. N.p., 1865.

Cheney, Newel. *History of the Ninth Regiment, New York Volunteer Cavalry, War of 1861 to 1865 . . .* Jamestown, N.Y.: Martin Merz & Son, 1901.

Clark, James Albert. *The Making of a Volunteer Cavalryman . . .* Washington, D.C.: privately issued, 1907.

Cleaves, Freeman. *Meade of Gettysburg*. Norman: University of Oklahoma Press, 1960.

Coggins, Jack. *Arms and Equipment of the Civil War*. Garden City, N.Y.: Doubleday & Co., Inc., 1962.

Colton, Matthias B. *The Civil War Journal and Correspondence of Matthias Baldwin Colton*. Edited by Jessie Sellers Colton. Philadelphia: Macrae-Smith Co., 1931.

Cooke, Jacob B. *The Battle of Kelly's Ford, March 17, 1863*. Providence, R.I.: privately issued, 1887.

Cooke, Philip St. George. *Cavalry Tactics or Regulations for the Instruction, Formations, and Movements of the Cavalry of the Army and Volunteers of the United States*. Washington, D.C.: Government Printing Office, 1862.

Cooling, Benjamin F. *Symbol, Sword, and Shield: Defending Washington during the Civil War*. Hamden, Conn.: Archon Books, 1975.

Cooper, David M. *Obituary Discourse on Occasion of the Death of Noah Henry Ferry . . .* New York: John F. Trow, 1863.

Cormany, Samuel E., and Rachel B. Cormany. *The Cormany Diaries: A Northern Family in the Civil War*. Edited by James C. Mohr and Richard E. Winslow III. Pittsburgh: University of Pittsburgh Press, 1982.

Couper, William. *One Hundred Years at V.M.I.* 4 vols. Richmond, Va.: Garrett & Massie, 1939–40.

Cowles, Calvin D., comp. *Atlas to Accompany the Official Records of the Union and Confederate Armies*. Washington, D.C.: Government Printing Office, 1891-95.

Crook, George. *General George Crook: His Autobiography*. Edited by Martin F. Schmitt. Norman: University of Oklahoma Press, 1960.

Crowninshield, Benjamin W. *The Battle of Cedar Creek, October 19, 1864*. Cambridge, Mass.: Riverside Press, 1879.

Crowinshield, Benjamin W., and D. H. L. Gleason. *A History of the First Regiment of Massachusetts Cavalry Volunteers*. Boston: Houghton Mifflin & Co., 1891.

Cruikshank, George L. *Back in the Sixties: Reminiscences of the Service of Co. A, 11th Pennsylvania [Cavalry] Regiment*. Fort Dodge, Ia.: Times Printing House, 1893.

Crumb, DeWitt. *22d Regiment N.Y. Vol. Cav.: Historical Address . . .* South Otselic, N.Y.: W. M. Reynolds, 1887.

Custer, George A. *Custer in the Civil War: His Unfinished Memoirs.* Compiled by John M. Carroll. San Rafael, Calif.: Presidio Press, 1977.

Custer, George A., and Elizabeth Bacon Custer. *The Custer Story: The Life and Intimate Letters of General George A. Custer and His Wife Elizabeth.* Edited by Marguerite Merington. New York: Devin-Adair Co., 1950.

Dahlgren, John A. *Memoir of Ulric Dahlgren.* Philadelphia: J. B. Lippincott & Co., 1872.

Dana, Charles A. *Recollections of the Civil War: With the Leaders at Washington and in the Field in the Sixties.* New York: D. Appleton & Co., 1897.

Davies, Henry E. *General Sheridan.* New York: D. Appleton & Co., 1899.

Davis, Carl L. *Arming the Union: Small Arms in the Civil War.* Port Washington, N.Y.: Kennikat Press, 1973.

Davis, Sidney Morris. *Common Soldier, Uncommon War: Life as a Cavalryman in the Civil War.* Edited by Charles F. Cooney. Bethesda, Md.: J. H. Davis, Jr., 1994.

Davis, William C. *Battle at Bull Run: A History of the First Major Campaign of the Civil War.* Garden City, N.Y.: Doubleday & Co., Inc., 1977.

Dedication of Battle Monument and Annual Re-union of the Tenth New York Cavalry Veteran Ass'n (Porter Guard Cavalry) . . . Cortland, N.Y.: Democrat Power Presses, 1889.

Dedication of the Monument of the Sixth Penna. Cavalry "Lancers," on the Battlefield of Gettysburg . . . Philadelphia: James Beale, 1888.

De Forest, John W. *A Volunteer's Adventures: A Union Captain's Record of the Civil War.* Edited by James H. Croushore. New Haven, Conn.: Yale University Press, 1946.

Denison, Frederic. *Sabres and Spurs: The First Regiment Rhode Island Cavalry in the Civil War, 1861–1865.* Central Falls, R.I.: E. L. Freeman & Co., 1876.

Denison, George T. *A History of Cavalry from the Earliest Times . . .* London: Macmillan Co., 1913.

DePeyster, J. Watts. *La Royale . . . The Grand Hunt of the Army of the Potomac on the 3d-7th (A.M.) April [1865], Petersburg to High Bridge . . .* New York: Julius R. Huth, 1872.

———. *La Royal, Part VII: Cumberland Church . . . 7th April, 1865 . . .* New York: Julius R. Huth, 1874.

Dixon, David. *Hero of Beecher Island: The Life and Military Career of George A. Forsyth.* Lincoln: University of Nebraska Press, 1994.

Dodge, Theodore A. *The Campaign of Chancellorsville.* Boston: James R. Osgood & Co., 1881.

Doster, William E. *Lincoln and Episodes of the Civil War.* New York: G. P. Putnam's Sons, 1915.

Doubleday, Abner. *Chancellorsville and Gettysburg.* New York: Charles Scribner's Sons, 1882.

Downey, Fairfax. *Clash of Cavalry: The Battle of Brandy Station, June 9, 1863.* New York: David McKay Co., Inc., 1959.

Dufur, Simon M. *Over the Dead Line; or, Tracked by Blood-Hounds.* Burlington, Vt.: Free Press Association, 1902.

Duganne, A. J. H. *The Fighting Quakers: A True Story of the War for Our Union.* New York: J. P. Robens, 1866.

Dyer, Frederick H. *A Compendium of the War of the Rebellion . . .* 3 vols. New York: Thomas Yoseloff, 1959.

Edmonds, Howard O. *Owen-Edmonds Incidents of the American Civil War, 1861–1865, Prepared from Family Records.* Chicago: Lakeside Press, 1928.

Ellis, Thomas T. *Leaves from the Diary of an Army Surgeon . . .* New York: John Bradburn, 1863.

Emerson, Edward W. *Life and Letters of Charles Russell Lowell . . .* Boston: Houghton, Mifflin & Co., 1907.

Faller, Leo W. and John I. *Dear Folks at Home: The Civil War Letters of Leo W. and John I. Faller . . .* Edited by Milton E. Flower. Carisle, Pa.: Cumberland County Historical Society, 1963.

Farrar, Samuel Clarke, comp. *The Twenty-Second Pennsylvania Cavalry and the Ringgold Battalion, 1861–1865.* Pittsburgh: New Werner Co., 1911.

Faust, Patricia, ed. *Historical Times Illustrated Encyclopedia of the Civil War.* New York: Harper & Row, 1986.

First Maine Cavalry Association: Record of Proceedings at the First Annual Re-Union . . . Augusta, Me.: privately issued, 1872.

Flinn, Frank M. *Campaigning . . . with Sheridan in the Shenandoah Valley in '64 and '65.* Lynn, Mass.: Thomas P. Nichols, 1889.

Flint, Joseph. *Regimental History of the First New York Dragoons . . .* Washington, D.C.: Gibson Brothers, 1865.

Fobes, George S. *Leaves from a Trooper's Diary.* Philadelphia: Bell, 1869.

Fordney, Ben F. *Stoneman at Chancellorsville: The Coming of Age of Union Cavalry.* Shippensburg, Pa.: White Mane Books, 1998.

Forsyth, George A. *Thrilling Days in Army Life.* New York: Harper & Brothers, 1900.

Foster, Alonzo. *Reminiscences and Record of the 6th New York V. V. [Veteran Volunteer] Cavalry.* Brooklyn, N.Y.: privately issued, 1892.

Freeman, Douglas Southall. *Lee's Lieutenants: A Study in Command.* 3 vols. New York: Charles Scribner's Sons, 1942–44.

Gardiner, William. *Operations of the Cavalry Corps . . . from February 27 to March 8, 1865 . . .* Providence, R.I.: privately issued, 1896.

Garraty, John A., and Mark C. Carnes, eds., *American National Biography.* 24 vols. New York: Oxford University Press, 1999.

Gillespie, Samuel L. *A History of Company A, First Ohio Cavalry, 1861–1865 . . .* Washington Court House, Ohio: Ohio State Register, 1898.

Glazier, Willard. *Battles for the Union . . .* Hartford, Conn.: Gilman & Co., 1878.

_____. *The Capture, the Prison Pen, and the Escape . . .* Albany, N.Y.: J. Munsell, 1868.

_____. *Three Years in the Federal Cavalry.* New York: H. Ferguson & Co., 1870.

Godfrey, Carlos E. *Sketch of Major Henry Washington Sawyer, First Regiment, Cavalry, New Jersey Volunteers . . .* Trenton, N. J.: MacCrellish & Quigley, 1907.

Goodrich, J. E. *Captain Hiram Henry Hall of the First Vermont Cavalry . . .* Burlington, Vt.: Free Press, 1913.

Gracey, S. L. *Annals of the Sixth Pennsylvania Cavalry.* Philadelphia: E. H. Butler & Co., 1868.

Grant, Ulysses S. *Personal Memoirs of U. S. Grant.* 2 vols. New York: Charles L. Webster & Co., 1885-86.

_____. *Report of Lieutenant-General U. S. Grant, of the Armies of the United States 1864-'65.* Washington, D.C.: privately issued, 1865.

Green, Charles O. *An Incident in the Battle of Middleburg, Va., June 17, 1863.* Providence, R.I.: privately issued, 1911.

Greenleaf, William L. *From the Rapidan to Richmond . . .* n.p., 1892.

Gregg, David McMurtrie. *The Second Cavalry Division of the Army of the Potomac in the Gettysburg Campaign.* Philadelphia: privately issued, 1907.

Hall, Hillman A., W. B. Besley, and Gilbert G. Wood, comps. *History of the Sixth New York Cavalry . . .* Worcester, Mass.: Blanchard Press, 1908.

Hamlin, Augustus C. *The Battle of Chancellorsville . . .* Bangor, Me.: privately issued, 1896.

Hamlin, Percy G. *"Old Bald Head" (General R. S. Ewell): The Portrait of a Soldier.* Strasburg, Va.: Shenandoah Publishing House, 1940.

Hard, Abner. *History of the Eighth Cavalry Regiment, Illinois Volunteers, During the Great Rebellion.* Aurora, Ill.: privately issued, 1868.

Harris, Samuel. *A Curious Way of Getting Rid of a Cowardly Captain . . .* Chicago: Adolph Selz, n.d.

_____. *In a Raid with the 5th Michigan Cavalry.* Chicago: privately issued, n.d.

_____. *Major General George A. Custer: Stories Told Around the Camp Fire of the Michigan Brigade of Cavalry.* Chicago: privately issued, 1898.

_____. *Michigan Brigade of Cavalry at the Battle of Gettysburg . . .* Chicago: privately issued, 1894.

_____. *Personal Reminiscences of Samuel Harris.* Chicago: Rogerson Press, 1897.

_____. *A Story of the Civil War: Why I Was Not Hung.* Chicago: Henneberry Press, 1895.

Haskin, William L., comp. *The History of the First Regiment of Artillery from Its Organization in 1821, to January 1st, 1876.* Portland, Me.: B. Thurston & Co., 1879.

Haydon, Charles B. *For Country, Cause & Leader: The Civil War Journal of Charles B. Haydon.* Edited by Stephen W. Sears. New York: Ticknor & Fields, 1993.

Heathcote, Charles W. *The Cavalry Struggle in the Battle of Gettysburg on July 3, 1863.* West Chester, Pa.: Horace Temple, 1959.

Heatwole, John L. *The Burning: Sheridan in the Shenandoah Valley.* Berryville, Va.: Rockbridge Publishing Co., 1999.

Hebert, Walter H. *Fighting Joe Hooker.* Indianapolis: Bobbs-Merrill Co., 1944.

Hennessy, John J. *Return to Bull Run: The Campaign and Battle of Second Manassas.* New York: Simon & Schuster, 1993.

Herr, John K., and Edward S. Wallace. *The Story of the U.S. Cavalry, 1775–1942.* Boston: Little, Brown & Co., 1953.

Hewett, Janet, et al., comps. *Supplement to the Official Records of the Union and Confederate Armies.* 80 vols. to date. Wilmington, N.C.: Broadfoot Publishing Co., 1994– .

Hinds, Thomas. *Tales of War Times . . .* Watertown, N.Y.: Watertown Herald, 1904.

History of the Eighteenth Regiment of Cavalry, Pennsylvania Volunteers, 1862–1865. New York: Wynkoop-Hallenbeck-Crawford Co., 1909.

History of the Eleventh Pennsylvania Volunteer Cavalry . . . Philadelphia: Franklin Printing Co., 1902.

History of the Third Pennsylvania Cavalry, Sixtieth Regiment Pennsylvania Volunteers, in the American Civil War, 1861–1865. Philadelphia: Franklin Printing Co., 1905.

Hodge, G. W. *A Sermon Preached . . . on the Occasion of the Unveiling of a Mural Tablet in Memory of Major James Edward Carpenter.* Lancaster, Pa.: New Era Printing Co., 1902.

Holmes, Theodore J., comp. *A Memorial of John S. Jameson . . .* n.p., ca. 1866.

House [of Representatives] Report No. 2, 37th Congress, 2nd Session, December 17, 1861. Washington, D.C.: Government Printing Office, 1862.

Howard, Hamilton G. *Civil-War Echoes: Character Sketches and State Secrets . . .* Washington, D.C.: Howard Publishing Co., 1907.

Huey, Pennock. *A True History of the Charge of the Eighth Pennsylvania Cavalry at Chancellorsville.* Philadelphia: Porter & Coates, 1883.

Humphreys, Andrew A. *The Virginia Campaign of '64 and '65: The Army of the Potomac and the Army of the James.* New York: Charles Scribner's Sons, 1883.

Humphreys, Charles A. *Field, Camp, Hospital and Prison in the Civil War, 1863–1865.* Boston: George H. Ellis Co., 1918.

Hunt, Aurora. *The Army of the Pacific: Its Operations . . . 1860–1866.* Glendale, Calif.: Arthur H. Clarke Co., 1951.

Huntington, Albert. *8th New York Cavalry: Historical Paper.* Palmyra, N.Y.: privately issued, 1902.

Hyde, Thomas, W. *Following the Greek Cross; or, Memories of the Sixth Army Corps.* Boston: Houghton, Mifflin & Co., 1894.

Hyndman, William. *History of a Cavalry Company: A Complete Record of Company "A," 4th Penn'a Cavalry.* Philadelphia: James B. Rodgers Co., 1870.

Ingersoll, Chalmers. *The Unknown Friends: A Civil War Romance.* Compiled by Charlotte Ingersoll Morse. Chicago: A Kroch & Son, 1948.

In Memoriam: Hasbrouck Davis . . . n.p., 1871.

Isham, Asa B. *An Historical Sketch of the Seventh Regiment Michigan Volunteer Cavalry, from its Organization, in 1862, to its Muster Out, in 1865.* New York: Town Topics Publishing Co., 1893.

Isham, Asa B., Henry M. Davidson, and Henry B. Furness. *Prisoners of War and Military Prisons: Personal Narratives* . . . Cincinnati: Lyman & Cushing, 1890.

John Hammond: Died May 28, 1889 . . . Chicago: P. F. Pettibone & Co., 1890.

Johnson, Richard W. *A Soldier's Reminiscences in Peace and War.* Philadelphia: J. B. Lippincott Co., 1886.

Johnston, Angus J., II. *Virginia Railroads in the Civil War.* Chapel Hill: University of North Carolina Press, 1961.

Johnston, R. M. *Bull Run: Its Strategy and Tactics.* Boston: Houghton Mifflin Co., 1913.

Jomini, Antoine Henri. *Summary of the Art of War.* New York: privately issued, 1854.

Jones, Virgil Carrington. *Eight Hours before Richmond.* New York: Henry Holt & Co., 1957.

Kelsey, Charles C. *To the Knife: The Biography of Major Peter Keenan, 8th Pennsylvania Cavalry.* Ann Arbor, Mich.: privately issued, 1964.

Kester, Donald E. *Cavalryman in Blue: Colonel John Wood Kester of the First New Jersey Cavalry in the Civil War.* Hightstown, N.J.: Longstreet House, 1997.

Kidd, James H. *The Michigan Cavalry Brigade in the Wilderness.* Detroit: Winn & Hammond, 1893.

———. *Personal Recollections of a Cavalryman with Custer's Michigan Cavalry Brigade in the Civil War.* Ionia, Mich.: Sentinel Printing Co., 1908.

King, Matthew W. *To Horse: With the Cavalry of the Army of the Potomac, 1861–1865.* Cheboygan, Mich.: privately issued, 1926.

Kip, Lawrence. *Army Life on the Pacific.* New York: Redfield, 1859.

Kirkland, Edward Chase. *Charles Francis Adams, Jr., 1835–1915: The Patrician at Bay.* Cambridge, Mass.: Harvard University Press, 1965.

Koempel, Philip. *Phil Koempel's Diary, 1861–65.* n.p., 1921.

Ladd, David L., and Audrey J. Ladd, eds. *The Bachelder Papers: Gettysburg in Their Own Words* . . . Dayton, Ohio: Morningside, 1994.

Lang, Theodore F. *Loyal West Virginia from 1861 to 1865* . . . Baltimore: Deutsch Publishing Co., 1895.

Larke, Julian K. *The Life of Gen. P. H. Sheridan, the Hero of the Shenandoah.* New York: T. R. Dawley, 1864.

Lee, William O., comp. *Personal and Historical Sketches and Facial History of* . . . *the Seventh Regiment Michigan Volunteer Cavalry, 1862–65.* Detroit: Ralston-Stroup Printing Co., 1903.

Leeds, S. P. *Address at the Funeral of Capt. Lorenzo D. Gove* . . . Hanover, N.H.: Dartmouth Press, 1863.

Lewis, Charles E. *With the First [New York] Dragoons in Virginia.* London: Simmons & Botten, 1897.

Lincoln, Abraham. *The Collected Works of Abraham Lincoln.* Edited by Roy P. Basler, et al. 8 vols. New Brunswick, N. J.: Rutgers University Press, 1953.

Lloyd, William P., comp. *History of the First Reg't Pennsylvania Reserve Cavalry* . . . Philadelphia: King & Baird, 1864.

Long, E. B. *The Civil War Day by Day: An Almanac, 1861–1865.* Garden City, N.Y.: Doubleday & Co., Inc., 1971.

Longacre, Edward G. *Army of Amateurs: General Benjamin F. Butler and the Army of the James, 1863–1865.* Mechanicsburg, Pa.: Stackpole Books, 1997.

_____. *Custer and His Wolverines: The Michigan Cavalry Brigade, 1861–1865.* Conshohocken, Pa.: Combined Publishing, 1997.

_____. *From Union Stars to Top Hat: A Biography of the Extraordinary General James Harrison Wilson.* Harrisburg, Pa.: Stackpole Books, 1972.

_____. *General John Buford: A Military Biography.* Conshohocken, Pa.: Combined Books, 1995.

_____. *Jersey Cavaliers: A History of the First New Jersey Volunteer Cavalry, 1861–1865.* Hightstown, N. J.: Longstreet House, 1992.

_____. *Mounted Raids of the Civil War.* South Brunswick, N.J.: A. S. Barnes & Co., 1975.

Lord, Francis A. *They Fought for the Union: A Complete Reference Work on the Federal Fighting Man.* Harrisburg, Pa.: Stackpole Books, 1960.

Lyman, Theodore. *Meade's Headquarters, 1863–1865: Letters of Colonel Theodore Lyman from the Wilderness to Appomattox.* Edited by George R. Agassiz. Boston: Atlantic Monthly Press, 1922.

McClellan, Carswell. *Notes on the Personal Memoirs of P. H. Sheridan.* St. Paul, Minn.: William E. Banning, Jr., 1889.

_____. *The Personal Memoirs and Military History of U.S. Grant versus the Record of the Army of the Potomac.* Boston: Houghton, Mifflin Co., 1887.

McClellan, George B. *The Civil War Papers of George B. McClellan: Selected Correspondence, 1860–1865.* Edited by Stephen W. Sears. New York: Ticknor & Fields, 1989.

_____. *McClellan's Own Story.* New York: Charles L. Webster & Co., 1887.

McClure, A. K. *Abraham Lincoln and Men of War-Times: Some Personal Recollections of War and Politics during the Lincoln Administration.* Philadelphia: Times Publishing Co., 1892.

McGuire, Judith W. *Diary of a Southern Refugee during the War, by a Lady of Virginia.* New York: E. J. Hale & Son, 1867.

McKinney, Edward P. *Life in Tent and Field, 1861–1865.* Boston: Richard G. Badger, 1922.

McWhiney, Grady, and Perry D. Jamieson. *Attack and Die: Civil War Military Tactics and the Southern Heritage.* University, Ala.: University of Alabama Press, 1982.

Mahan, D. H. *An Elementary Treatise on Advanced-Guard, Out-post, and Detached Service of Troops . . .* New York: John Wiley, 1853.

Martin, David G. *Gettysburg, July 1.* Conshohocken, Pa.: Combined Books, 1995.

Martin, Samuel J. *Kill-Cavalry: The Life of Union General Hugh Judson Kilpatrick.* Mechanicsburg, Pa.: Stackpole Books, 2000.

Meade, George. *The Life and Letters of George Gordon Meade, Major-General United States Army.* 2 vols. New York: Charles Scribner's Sons, 1913.

A Memorial of Philip Henry Sheridan. Boston: Rockwell & Churchill, 1889.

Merrill, James M. *Spurs to Glory: The Story of the United States Cavalry.* Chicago: Rand-McNally Co., 1966.

Merrill, Samuel H. *The Campaigns of the First Maine and First District of Columbia Cavalry.* Portland, Me.: Bailey & Noyes, 1866.

Meyer, Henry C. *Civil War Experiences under Bayard, Gregg, Kilpatrick, Custer, Raulston, and Newberry, 1862, 1863, 1864.* New York: Knickerbocker Press, 1911.

Meyer, William E. *The Sailor on Horseback.* Providence, R.I.: privately issued, 1912.

Military Order of the Loyal Legion of the United States: In Memoriam . . . Philip H. Sheridan . . . n.p., 1888.

Miller, William E. *War History: Operations of the Union Cavalry on the Peninsula . . .* Carlisle, Pa.: Hamilton Library Association, 1908.

Monaghan, Jay. *Custer: The Life of General George Armstrong Custer.* Boston: Little, Brown & Co., 1959.

Moore, Frank, ed. *The Rebellion Record: A Diary of American Events.* 12 vols. New York: various publishers, 1861–68.

Moore, James. *Kilpatrick and Our Cavalry.* New York: W. J. Widdleton, 1865.

Moore, James B. *Two Years in the Service.* n.p., 1865.

Morgan, James A., III. *Always Ready, Always Willing: A History of Battery M, Second United States Artillery from Its Organization through the Civil War.* Gaithersburg, Md.: Olde Soldier Books, n.d.

Morison, John H. *Dying for Our Country: A Sermon on the Death of Capt. J. Sewall Reed and Rev. Thomas Starr King . . .* Boston: John Wilson & Son, 1864.

Morris, Roy O. *Sheridan: The Life and Wars of General Phil Sheridan.* New York: Crown Publishers, 1992.

Moyer, H. P., comp. *History of the Seventeenth Regiment Pennsylvania Volunteer Cavalry.* Lebanon, Pa.: Sowers Printing Co., 1911.

Murfin, James V. *The Gleam of Bayonets: The Battle of Antietam and the Maryland Campaign of 1862.* New York: A. S. Barnes & Co., 1965.

Naisawald, L. Van Loan. *Grape and Canister: The Story of the Field Artillery of the Army of the Potomac, 1861–1865*. New York: Oxford University Press, 1960.

Neese, George M. *Three Years in the Confederate Horse Artillery*. New York: Neale Publishing Co., 1911.

Newcomer, Christopher A. *Cole's Cavalry; or, Three Years in the Saddle in the Shenandoah Valley*. Baltimore: Cushing & Co., 1895.

Norris, L. David, James C. Milligan, and Odie B. Faulk. *William H. Emory, Soldier-Scientist*. Tucson: University of Arizona Press, 1998.

Norton, Chauncy S., comp. *"The Red Neck Ties"; or, History of the Fifteenth New York Volunteer Cavalry* . . . Ithaca, N.Y.: Journal Book & Job Printing House, 1891.

Norton, Henry, comp. *Deeds of Daring; or History of the Eighth N.Y. Volunteer Cavalry* . . . Norwich, N.Y.: Chenango Telegraph Printing House, 1889.

____. *A Sketch of the 8th N.Y. Cavalry: Unwritten History of the Rebellion*. Norwich, N.Y.: privately issued, 1888.

O'Connor, Richard. *Sheridan, the Inevitable*. Indianapolis: Bobbs-Merrill Co., 1953.

Official Records of the Union and Confederate Navies in the War of the Rebellion. 30 vols. Washington, D.C.: Government Printing Office, 1894–1922.

O'Neill, Robert F., Jr. *The Cavalry Battles of Aldie, Middleburg and Upperville: "Small But Important Riots," June 10–27, 1863*. Lynchburg, Va.: H. E. Howard, Inc., 1993.

Paris, Comte de. *History of the Civil War in America*. 4 vols. Philadelphia: Porter & Coates, 1876–88.

Patrick, Marsena Rudolph. *Inside Lincoln's Army: The Diary of Marsena Rudolph Patrick, Provost Marshal General, Army of the Potomac*. Edited by David S. Sparks. New York: Thomas Yoseloff, 1964.

Patrick, Rembert W. *The Fall of Richmond*. Baton Rouge: Louisiana State University Press, 1960.

Pennsylvania at Gettysburg. 2 vols. Harrisburg, Pa.: B. Singerly, 1893.

Pennypacker, Isaac. *General Meade*. New York: D. Appleton & Co., 1901.

Perry, Bliss. *Life and Letters of Henry Lee Higginson*. Boston: Atlantic Monthly Press, 1921.

Pettingill, S. B. *The College Cavaliers: A Sketch of the Service of a Company of College Students in the Union Army in 1862*. Chicago: H. McAllaster & Co., 1883.

Peyton, Jesse Enlows. *Reminiscences of the Past*. Philadelphia: J. B. Lippincott Co., 1895.

Pickerill, W. N. *History of the Third Indiana Cavalry*. Indianapolis: Aetna Printing Co., 1906.

Pond, George E. *The Shenandoah Valley in 1864*. New York: Charles Scribner's Sons, 1883.

Porter, Burton B. *One of the People: His Own Story.* Colton, Calif.: privately issued, 1907.

Porter, Horace. *Campaigning with Grant.* Edited by Wayne C. Temple. Bloomington: Indiana University Press, 1961.

Potter, Henry Clay. *Autobiography: The American Civil War Memoir . . . of Harry Clay Potter, Captain, 18th Pennsylvania Cavalry, 1841–1912.* Compiled by Woodburn W. Potter. Philadelphia: privately issued, 1913.

Pratt, Fletcher. *Eleven Generals: Studies in American Command.* New York: William Sloane Associates, 1949.

Preston, N. D. *History of the Tenth Regiment of Cavalry, New York State Volunteers, August, 1861, to August, 1865.* New York: D. Appleton & Co., 1892.

Price, George F., comp. *Across the Continent with the Fifth [United States] Cavalry.* New York: D. Van Nostrand, 1883.

Price, William H. *The Battle of Brandy Station.* Vienna, Va.: Civil War Research Associates, 1963.

Proceedings of the Buford Memorial Association . . . New York: Buford Memorial Association, 1895.

Putnam, Elizabeth Cabot. *Memoirs of the War of '61: Colonel Charles Russell Lowell . . .* Boston: George H. Ellis Co., 1920.

Putnam, George H. *An Address . . . at the Funeral of Brig.-Gen. Charles Russell Lowell . . .* Cambridge, Mass.: Welch, Bigelow & Co., 1864.

———. *Some Memories of the Civil War.* New York: G. P. Putnam's Sons, 1924.

Pyne, Henry R. *The History of the First New Jersey Cavalry.* Trenton, N.J.: J. A. Beecher, 1871.

Randol, Alanson M. *Last Days of the Rebellion . . . April 8 and 9, 1865.* Alcatraz Island, Calif.: privately issued, 1886.

Rawle, William Brooke. *The Right Flank at Gettysburg: An Account of the Operations of General Gregg's Cavalry Command . . .* Philadelphia: Allen, Lane & Scott's Printing House, 1878.

———. *With Gregg in the Gettysburg Campaign.* Philadelphia: McLaughlin Brothers Co., 1884.

Report of the Joint Committee on the Conduct of the War. 8 vols. Washington, D.C.: Government Printing Office, 1863–68.

Re-union and . . . Anniversary of the Muster into the United States Service of the Tenth New York Cavalry. Pittsburgh: privately issued, 1888.

Re-union & Celebration of the Fiftieth Anniversary of Enlistment of the Ninth Regiment New York Volunteer Cavalry . . . Dunkirk, N.Y.: Alex Williams, ca. 1911.

Reunion Sixth New York Cavalry, North Scituate Beach, Mass., August the Seventeenth, Nineteen Hundred and Four. Worcester, Mass.: privately issued, 1904.

Rhodes, Charles D. *History of the Cavalry of the Army of the Potomac . . .* Kansas City, Mo.: Hudson-Kimberly Publishing Co., 1900.

Rhodes, Elisha Hunt. *All for the Union . . . the Diary and Letters of Elisha Hunt Rhodes.* New York: Orion Books, 1991.

Riggs, David F. *East of Gettysburg: Stuart vs. Custer.* Bellevue, Neb.: Old Army Press, 1970.

Ripley, Warren. *Artillery and Ammunition of the Civil War.* New York: Promontory Press, 1970.

Robbins, Walter R. *War Record and Personal Experiences of Walter Raleigh Robbins from April 22, 1861, to August 4, 1865.* Edited by Lilian Rea. Chicago: privately issued, 1923.

Roberts, John N. *Reminiscences of the Civil War.* n.p., 1925.

Robertson, John, comp. *Michigan in the War.* Lansing, Mich.: W. S. George & Co., 1882.

Rockwell, Alphonso D. *Rambling Recollections: An Autobiography.* New York: Paul B. Hober, 1920.

Rodenbough, Theophilus F., comp. *From Everglade to Cañon with the Second [United States] Dragoons . . .* New York: D. Van Nostrand, 1875.

Ropes, John Codman. *The Army Under Pope.* New York: Charles Scribner's Sons, 1882.

Rummel, George A., III. *72 Days at Gettysburg: Organization of the Tenth Regiment, New York Volunteer Cavalry & Assignment to the Town of Gettysburg, Pennsylvania (December 1861 to March 1862).* Shippensburg, Pa.: White Mane Publishing Co., Inc., 1997.

Russell, William Howard. *The Civil War in America.* Boston: G. A. Fuller, 1861.

_____. *My Diary North and South.* Boston: T. O. Burnham, 1863.

Sanford, George B. *Fighting Rebels and Redskins: Experiences in Army Life of Colonel George B. Sanford, 1861–1892.* Edited by E. R. Hagemann. Norman: University of Oklahoma Press, 1969.

Schaff, Morris. *The Battle of the Wilderness.* Boston: Houghton, Mifflin Co., 1912.

Schildt, John W. *Roads from Gettysburg.* Shippensburg, Pa.: Burd Street Press, 1998.

_____. *September Echoes: The Maryland Campaign of 1862 . . .* Middletown, Md.: Valley Register, 1960.

Schultz, Duane. *The Dahlgren Affair: Terror and Conspiracy in the Civil War.* New York: W. W. Norton & Co., Inc., 1999.

Schurz, Carl. *The Reminiscences of Carl Schurz.* 3 vols. Garden City, N.Y.: McClure Co., 1917.

Sears, Stephen W. *Chancellorsville.* Boston: Houghton Mifflin Co., 1996.

_____. *George B. McClellan: The Young Napoleon.* New York: Ticknor & Fields, 1988.

_____. *Landscape Turned Red: The Battle of Antietam.* New Haven, Conn.: Ticknor & Fields, 1983.

_____. *To the Gates of Richmond: The Peninsula Campaign.* New York: Ticknor & Fields, 1992.

Shanks, F. G. *Personal Recollections of Distinguished Generals.* New York: Harper & Brothers, 1866.

Shannon, Fred A. *The Organization and Administration of the Union Army, 1861–1865.* 2 vols. Cleveland: Arthur H. Clark Co., 1928.

Sheridan, Philip H. *Personal Memoirs of P. H. Sheridan.* 2 vols. New York: Charles L. Webster & Co., 1888.

_____. *Report of Operations of the Cavalry Corps, Army of the Potomac, from April 6, to August 4, 1864.* New Orleans: privately issued, 1866.

_____. *Report of Operations of the Cavalry Corps, Army of the Potomac, from March 29, 1865, to April 9, 1865, including the Appomattox Campaign, and the Subsequent March from Petersburg to the Dan River, and the Return.* n.p., 1865.

Sheridan's Veterans: A Souvenir of Their Two Campaigns in the Shenandoah Valley . . . Boston: W. F. Brown & Co., 1883.

Slease, William D. *The Fourteenth Pennsylvania Cavalry in the Civil War* . . . Pittsburgh: Art Engraving & Printing Co., 1915.

Smith, Thomas W. *"We Have It Damn Hard Out Here": The Civil War Letters of Sergeant Thomas W. Smith, 6th Pennsylvania Cavalry.* Edited by Eric J. Wittenberg. Kent, Ohio: Kent State University Press, 1999.

Speese, A. J. *Constitution and By-Laws of Company H, Third Pennsylvania Cavalry, With a Brief History* . . . Shippensburg, Pa.: privately issued, 1878.

Stackpole, Edward J. *Chancellorsville: Lee's Greatest Battle.* Harrisburg, Pa.: Stackpole Co., 1958.

_____. *Drama on the Rappahannock: The Fredericksburg Campaign.* Harrisburg, Pa.: Military Service Publishing Co., 1957.

_____. *From Cedar Mountain to Antietam, August–September, 1862: Cedar Mountain—Second Manassas—Chantilly—Harpers Ferry—South Mountain—Antietam.* Harrisburg, Pa.: Stackpole Co., 1959.

_____. *Sheridan in the Shenandoah: Jubal Early's Nemesis.* Harrisburg, Pa.: Stackpole Co., 1961.

_____. *They Met at Gettysburg.* Harrisburg, Pa.: Eagle Books, 1956.

Stamatelos, James. *Notes on the Uniform and Equipments of the United States Cavalryman, 1861–1865.* Cambridge, Mass.: privately issued, n.d.

Stanley, James C. *The Union Cavalry in West Virginia for the Civil War: Brilliant, Thrilling and Dangerous Service of the Second Virginia Cavalry* . . . August, Ill.: privately issued, n.d.

Stanton, Edwin M. *Reports of the Secretary of War.* Washington, D.C.: Government Printing Office, 1862–66.

Starr, Stephen Z. *The Union Cavalry in the Civil War.* 3 vols. Baton Rouge: Louisiana State University Press, 1979–84.

Statutes, 1859–63. Washington, D.C.: Government Printing Office, 1864.

Steere, Edward. *The Wilderness Campaign.* Harrisburg, Pa.: Stackpole Co., 1960.

Steffen, Randy. *The Horse Soldier, 1776–1943: The United States Cavalry-man: His Uniforms, Arms, Accoutrements, and Equipments.* 4 vols. Norman: University of Oklahoma Press, 1977–80.

Stern, Philip Van Doren. *An End to Valor: The Last Days of the Civil War.* Boston: Houghton Mifflin Co., 1958.

Stevens, Leverett C. *A Forlorn Hope.* Providence, R.I.: privately issued, 1903.

Stevenson, James H. *"Boots and Saddles": A History of . . . the First New York (Lincoln) Cavalry . . .* Harrisburg, Pa.: Patriot Publishing Co., 1879.

Stine, J. H. *History of the Army of the Potomac.* Philadelphia: J. B. Rodgers Printing Co., 1892.

Stockton, R. F. *Memorial Address . . . in Memory of Brevet Maj. Gen. A. T. A. Torbert . . .* Trenton, N. J.: William S. Sharp, 1880.

Stribling, Robert M. *Gettysburg Campaign and the Campaigns of 1864 and 1865 in Virginia.* Petersburg, Va.: Franklin Press Co., 1905.

Sutton, J. J. *History of the Second Regiment, West Virginia Cavalry Volunteers during the War of the Rebellion.* Portsmouth, Ohio: privately issued, 1892.

Swing, David. *A Discourse in Memory of Col. Minor Millikin, Delivered . . . 1863.* Oxford, Ohio: Richard Butler, 1863.

Swinton, William. *Campaigns of the Army of the Potomac.* New York: Charles B. Richardson, 1866.

Sypher, J. R. *History of the Pennsylvania Reserve Corps . . .* Lancaster, Pa.: Elias Barr & Co., 1865.

Tanner, Robert G. *Stonewall in the Valley: Thomas J. "Stonewall" Jackson's Shenandoah Valley Campaign, Spring 1862.* Garden City, N.Y.: Doubleday & Co., Inc., 1976.

Taylor, Nelson. *Saddle and Saber: Civil War Letters of Corporal Nelson Taylor, Ninth New York State Volunteer Cavalry . . .* Edited by Gray Nelson Taylor. Bowie, Md.: Heritage Books, Inc., 1993.

Tenney, Luman Harris. *War Diary of Luman Harris Tenney, 1861–1865.* Edited by Frances Andrews Tenney. Cleveland: Evangelical Publishing House, 1914.

Thirty-Sixth Anniversary and Reunion of the Tenth New York Cavalry Veterans . . . Homer, N.Y.: privately issued, 1897.

Thomas, Benjamin P., and Harold M. Hyman. *Stanton: The Life and Times of Lincoln's Secretary of War.* New York: Alfred A. Knopf, 1962.

Thomas, Emory M. *Bold Dragoon: The Life of J. E. B. Stuart.* New York: Harper & Row, 1986.

Thomas, Hampton S. *Some Personal Reminiscences of Service in the Cavalry of the Army of the Potomac.* Philadelphia: L. R. Hammersly & Co., 1889.

Tobie, Edward P. *History of the First Maine Cavalry, 1861-1865.* Boston: Emery & Hughes, 1887.

——. *Personal Recollections of General Sheridan.* Providence, R.I.: privately issued, 1889.

——. *Service of the Cavalry in the Army of the Potomac.* Providence, R.I.: privately issued, 1882.

Trefousse, Hans. *Carl Schurz: A Biography.* Knoxville: University of Tennessee Press, 1982.

Tremain, Lyman. *Memorial of Frederick Lyman Tremain, Late Lieut. Col. of the 10th N.Y. Cavalry. . .* Albany, N.Y.: Van Benthuysen's Printing House, 1865.

Trowbridge, Luther S. *The Operations of the Cavalry in the Gettysburg Campaign.* Detroit: privately issued, 1888.

Trudeau, Noah Andre. *Bloody Roads South: The Wilderness to Cold Harbor, May-June 1864.* Boston: Little, Brown & Co., 1989.

———. *The Last Citadel.* Boston: Little, Brown & Co., 1991.

———. *Out of the Storm: The End of the Civil War, April–June 1865.* Boston: Little, Brown & Co., 1994.

Turnbull, Robert. *Well Done: A Funeral Discourse for Captain Albert H. Niles.* Hartford, Conn.: Case, Lockwood & Co., 1863.

Turner, George E. *Victory Rode the Rails: The Strategic Place of the Railroads in the Civil War.* Indianapolis: Bobbs-Merrill Co., 1953.

Tyler, Mason Whiting. *Recollections of the Civil War: With Many Original Diary Entries and Letters Written from the Seat of War . . .* Edited by William S. Tyler. New York: G. P. Putnam's Sons, 1912.

Utley, Robert M. *Frontiersmen in Blue: The United States Army and the Indian, 1848–1865.* New York: Macmillan Co., 1967.

Vandiver, Frank E. *Jubal's Raid: General Early's Famous Attack on Washington in 1864.* New York: McGraw-Hill Book Co., 1960.

Van Orden, W. H. *General Philip H. Sheridan: A Story of His Life and Military Services.* New York: Street & Smith, 1896.

Vinter, Thomas. *Memoirs . . .* Philadelphia: Walter H. Jenkins, 1926.

Vital Facts: A Chronology of the College of William and Mary. Williamsburg, Va.: Earl Gregg Swem Library, 1970.

Volunteer Cavalry—The Lessons of a Decade, by a Volunteer Cavalryman. New York: privately issued, 1871.

Wagner, Arthur L., comp. *Cavalry Studies from Two Great Wars.* Kansas City, Mo.: Hudson-Kimberly Publishing Co., 1896.

Wainwright, Charles S. *A Diary of Battle: The Personal Journals of Colonel Charles S. Wainwright, 1861–1865.* Edited by Allan Nevins. New York: Harcourt, Brace & World, 1962.

Walker, Francis A. *History of the Second Army Corps in the Army of the Potomac.* New York: Charles Scribner's Sons, 1886.

Wallace, Edward S. *General William Jenkins Worth, Monterey's Forgotten Hero.* Dallas: Southern Methodist University Press, 1953.

Wallace, Robert C. *A Few Memories of a Long Life.* Helena, Mont.: privately issued, 1916.

War of the Rebellion: A Compilation of the Official Records of the Union and Confederate Armies. 4 series, 70 vols. in 128. Washington, D.C.: Government Printing Office, 1880–1901.

Warner, Ezra J. *Generals in Blue: Lives of the Union Commanders.* Baton Rouge: Louisiana State University Press, 1964.

Watson, William. *Letters of a Civil War Surgeon.* Edited by Paul Fatout. Lafayette, Ind.: Purdue University Studies, 1961.

Webb, Alexander S. *The Peninsula: McClellan's Campaign of 1862.* New York: Charles Scribner's Sons, 1881.

Weigley, Russell F. *Quartermaster General of the Union Army: A Biography of M. C. Meigs.* New York: Columbia University Press, 1959.

Welles, Gideon. *Diary of Gideon Welles, Secretary of the Navy under Lincoln and Johnson.* Edited by Howard K. Beale. 3 vols. New York: W. W. Norton & Co., Inc., 1960.

Wert, Jeffry. *Custer: The Controversial Life of George Armstrong Custer.* New York: Simon & Schuster, 1996.

_____. *From Winchester to Cedar Creek: The Shenandoah Campaign of 1864.* Carlisle, Pa.: South Mountain Press, Inc., 1987.

_____. *Mosby's Rangers.* New York: Simon & Schuster, 1990.

Whitaker, Frederick. *A Complete Life of Gen. George A. Custer . . .* New York: Sheldon & Co., 1876.

Williams, Kenneth P. *Lincoln Finds a General: A Military Study of the Civil War.* 5 vols. New York: Macmillan Co., 1949–59.

Williams, T. Harry. *Lincoln and His Generals.* New York: Alfred A. Knopf, 1952.

Wilson, James Harrison. *Captain Charles Corbit's Charge at Westminster . . . An Episode in the Gettysburg Campaign.* Wilmington: Historical Society of Delaware, 1913.

_____. *Under the Old Flag: Recollections of Military Operations in the War for the Union, the Spanish War, the Boxer Rebellion, etc.* 2 vols. New York: D. Appleton & Co., 1912.

Wilson, Suzanne C., comp. *Column South: With the Fifteenth Pennsylvania Cavalry from Antietam to the Capture of Jefferson Davis.* Flagstaff, Ariz.: J. F. Colton & Co., 1960.

Wise, Jennings Cropper. *The Long Arm of Lee; or, The History of the Artillery of the Army of Northern Virginia . . .* 2 vols. Lynchburg, Va.: J. P. Bell, 1915.

Wister, Sarah Butler. *Walter S. Newhall: A Memoir . . .* Philadelphia: C. Sherman, Son & Co., 1864.

Wittenberg, Eric. *Gettysburg's Forgotten Cavalry Actions.* Gettysburg, Pa.: Thomas Publications, 1998.

Wood, Bert D. *Franklin's Yesteryear.* Ann Arbor, Mich.: privately issued, 1958.

Wormser, Richard. *The Yellowlegs: The Story of the United States Cavalry . . .* Garden City, N.Y.: Doubleday & Co., Inc., 1966.

INDEX